P9-DFD-032

The Crowell Special Education Series

Sandford Reichart, ADVISORY EDITOR

Educating the Emotionally Disturbed

A Book of Readings

edited by

Hardwick W. L Harshman

PROFESSOR OF SPECIAL EDUCATION
RHODE ISLAND COLLEGE

Thomas Y. Crowell Company

NEW YORK • ESTABLISHED 1834

L.C. Card 69-19302
ISBN 0-690-25590-X

DESIGNED BY BARBARA KOHN ISAAC

Manufactured in the United States of America

First Printing, June, 1969
Second Printing, December, 1970

Preface

This book of readings has been planned to meet the requirements of a wide variety of persons who may be concerned with the psychoeducational problems of the emotionally handicapped child. While such persons would include teachers of the emotionally handicapped, administrators, school psychologists, and college instructors, another audience is clearly those students, both undergraduate and graduate, who are preparing themselves for roles as teachers and administrators.

Those who will profit by these selections will, of course, be planning to serve in a wide variety of settings—residential treatment centers, day care centers, child guidance clinics, as well as the public schools. It seemed important, therefore, that a book of this nature should include within its scope a broad range of approaches being used in the psychoeducation of the emotionally handicapped child.

Since every book must have a focus, this book is committed to the psychoeducational approach in working with emotionally handicapped children. This approach seeks to understand the antecedent psychological problems of a child's behavior and is vitally concerned about ego development. Erik Erikson in his chapter on "The Eight Stages of Man," * has demonstrated the efficacy of building a basic sense of trust in the child as the first stage of his development. The ability to tolerate frustrations and to postpone satisfactions is related to the child's building a trusting relationship with the mother or mother figure which at a later time in his life is seen as a parallel relationship of trust between the child and his teacher. Satisfactory ego development in the preschool years is essential if the child is to be ready for training and academic learning in the school setting. The psychoeducational approach when related to the school suggests that every attempt must be made to understand why the child is behaving as he is.

Fritz Redl, William Morse, and others have emphasized the importance of the child's total environment in getting at some understanding

* In *Childhood and Society* (New York: Norton, 1950).

of his inability to handle the stresses and strains demanded of him in the learning experience in the school. Many children come to school unprepared emotionally and socially for the school's contribution in the development of their cognitive and adaptive skills. In order to prepare these children for meaningful learning experiences, the school must provide a mental health setting that will foster ego maturity.

A careful reading of the literature on the psychoeducational approach emphasizes the role of the teacher as she influences the direction of the child's growth. While concern is given the curriculum for emotionally handicapped children in this approach, one is impressed with the importance attached to the teacher-child interaction. The teacher must be able to establish a secure and meaningful relationship between herself and the child. William Morse * has proposed that the teacher make use of the skills and orientations of a number of disciplines in the helping professions. This "team effort" would be directed at the child's total environment in the hope of giving him competence to replace his feelings of failure in academic and social spheres. What this really means is that the teacher must be dedicated to her task as an educator and she must realize that success in the learning experience of the school is therapeutic in itself and every effort must be given to provide these success experiences.

There are certain problems of emotionally handicapped youngsters which are relevant in virtually every setting. In Part I selections are presented which deal with the general nature of the problem along with attempts at definition, identification, various classification systems, and characteristics of these children. Part II is devoted to a short review of basic types of educational programs along with specific efforts that appear to offer some promise in three settings: day classes in the public schools, the special school, and residential centers. One of the major concerns of students preparing to teach emotionally handicapped children is the management of these children in the classroom. To bring together some experiences of those who have taught disturbed children in this kind of educational framework has been the aim of the readings offered in Part III. These selections deal with classroom content, control, learning, and other specialized techniques. No book of readings devoted to the education of emotionally handicapped children would be complete without some attention given to the increasing concern about the teacher preparation programs. It is to this problem that Part IV is devoted.

* "Public Schools and the Disturbed Child," in P. Knoblock, ed., *Intervention Approaches in Educating Emotionally Disturbed Children* (Syracuse, N.Y.: Syracuse University Press, 1966).

Every effort has been made to present in this volume a useful set of materials for those who would deal with the problems of the emotionally handicapped child, whether in the classroom, the playground, or the principal's office. Needless to say it was necessary to be selective in choosing the articles and in the process the editor's biases will be discovered. It is hoped, however, that a large number of readers will find these selections of value as they seek to provide meaningful learning experiences for emotionally disturbed children.

Many persons have contributed to the preparation of this book of readings. The editor gratefully acknowledges his indebtedness to the authors and publishers who granted permission to reprint their articles in this volume. They are given credit in the footnotes at the beginning of each selection. Special thanks is expressed to Melvyn Reich, a colleague at Rhode Island College, for permission to publish his article for the first time. The editor is deeply indebted to Dr. Sandford Reichart for reviewing the book and offering helpful suggestions in the selection and organization of the readings. Acknowledgement must also be given to Stanley M. Rinehart III, Herman Makler, and Elena Rosti for their many excellent suggestions and splendid editorial work, and to Virginia J. Fortiner for handling the time-consuming task of securing permissions. And finally, to my wife, Gretchen, deep appreciation is expressed for her encouragement, patience, and understanding throughout the preparation of this book.

H.W.H.

Contents

Educating the Emotionally Disturbed

A Book of Readings

I

The Problems the Emotionally Disturbed Pose for the School

All human beings are confronted with frustrations and disappointments in life and they face these irritations with varying degrees of disturbance. Some of our frustrations are caused by barriers we encounter in moving toward our goals and are peculiar to the environment we live in. Perhaps most of the discomfiture in the early years of our lives results from factors in the environment. As upsetting as some of these experiences may be, we are likely to find that our greatest anxiety develops from our inability to attain the standards we set for ourselves. This type of frustration does not originate in the environment but within the individual who has developed certain "levels of aspiration." Failure in this context is determined by the person himself; many times he is the only one who feels he has not performed at his best.*

In the process of growing up boys and girls must develop coping skills to handle their feelings and urges when these frustrations arise. In the opening article, *Redl* and *Jacobson* (1) describe five children who have had difficulty developing tools to handle their emotions. They point out the difference between being disturbed and being disturbing and note that emotional disturbances defy generalization. While general prescriptions for the management of emotionally disturbed children in the classroom will be of limited value, the authors offer some guidance that should prove fruitful to teachers.

The next four articles present various attempts to classify emotional disturbance on the basis of behavioral characteristics. If one can operationally define children with emotional problems, then hopefully school personnel will be in a better position to identify them at an early stage and provide them with meaningful emotional experiences. In the *Bower* (2) article, a case is made for considering these children under the category of "emotionally handicapped," and a set of behavioral characteristics is presented. *Morse* (3) describes patterns of maladjustment for the teacher in the hope that psychological insight will provide some clues for educational strategies. If teachers are to be effective in designing appropriate educational experiences for disturbed children, then a differential diagnostic approach is necessary to individualize children's needs. *Quay* (4) continues

* The reader is encouraged to read the excellent discussion of frustration and the self-concept presented in Chapter 15 of Warren R. Baller and Don C. Charles, *The Psychology of Human Growth and Development*, 2d ed. (New York: Holt, Rinehart and Winston, 1968), pp. 395–434.

this differential treatment of problem children by noting that past attempts to educate children with emotional problems can be classified under three headings: holding operations, quasi-therapeutic programs, and educational achievement settings. He then presents some guidelines for program operation of two major syndromes: acting-out, or "conduct problem," children and the withdrawn, or "personality problem," children. At this point it is well to remind the reader that despite attempts to classify emotionally disturbed children according to type, only a few will actually exhibit behavior to the point where this kind of classification can be made. The *Quay-Morse-Cutler* (5) article describes behavioral characteristics of emotionally disturbed children and divides them into three groups: conduct problems or unsocialized aggression, personality problems, and inadequacy-immaturity problems. It is quite apparent that if we are to help these children in their behavioral and academic problems we will need to institute differential treatment programs for them.

Many attempts have been made to provide school personnel with an effective means for identifying emotionally disturbed children early in the school program. While one will want to collect as much data as possible on children in order to plan appropriate educational experiences, it would seem highly desirable to have available instrumentation that would screen out these children who are in need of psychotherapeutic assistance. The teacher will be interested to know that on the basis of *Maes'* (6) study the teacher rating scale and group intelligence test scores proved to be as effective in identifying emotionally disturbed children as earlier attempts employing six or more variables.

All too often the child's real feelings about school and his teacher are given little consideration. *Schorer* (7) explores the results of a study of fifty-two disturbed children in terms of their views of the school and the teacher. This study should be of interest if for no other reason than that teachers will gain some idea of how they are perceived by their emotionally disturbed pupils.

Success in the educational process depends on the formation of an educational relationship between the teacher and the child, and a relationship providing meaningful contact and gratification for the child as both child and teacher move through various task levels. The reader will be greatly interested in *Hewett's* (8) framework of seven educational task levels; a careful examination of how child and teacher move through these seven levels should prove instructive.

Levison (9) calls attention to the child who has a phobic reaction about going to school, or rather, the child who has a phobic reaction about leaving home and being separated from the mother. In the last few years the wide variety of disturbances that can cause the child to exhibit "school phobia" has been recognized. Although several investigators have shown that a variety of types of school phobia exist, general agreement seems to follow Kahn and Nursten's * classification of three types—the neurotic states, the character disorders, and the childhood psychoses.

The foregoing articles have indicated some of the problems emotionally disturbed children pose for school personnel. *Westman* and his associates (10) direct attention to mental health screening techniques for nursery and early elementary school children and present evidence of the need for mental health services during the early school years. This study clearly indicates that maladjusted children can be identified at the nursery school level and provided with mental health resources. Those maladjusted children who received mental health care in the early school years showed greater improvement at the high school level than those who were not given any special care. The study also disclosed that one third of those children who had been identified as maladjusted at the nursery school level but had not received mental health care manifested maladjustment in the first four grades of elementary school. The mental health specialists in the study made their judgments on the basis of recorded observations and reactions from nursery school personnel. Apparently, teachers at the nursery school level are now much more adept at identifying behavioral characteristics of disturbed children, which is most helpful to those in mental health facilities.

* Kahn, J. H., and Nursten, J. P. "School Refusal: A Comprehensive View of School Phobia and Other Failures of School Attendance," *Am. J. Orthopsychiatry*, XXXII (1962) 707.

1. The Emotionally Disturbed

FRITZ REDL AND STANLEY JACOBSON

It isn't easy to become *an emotionally disturbed child*. We don't mean that it isn't easy to have an emotional disturbance—that's the easiest and most natural thing in the world. All of us have to meet the frustrations and disappointments that are standard procedure in living, and all of us react with more or less disturbance.

We feel hurt or angry or anxious or depressed or some subtle variation of some unnamed emotion. We behave in ways we wouldn't approve of —hopefully not for long and with minimum damage to ourselves or others. Then we get over the disturbance, and maybe we even learn from it so that the next time we face the frustration we aren't thrown quite so fast or far.

For children, especially, this process is as regular as meals, only more frequent. And with good reason. Children are still busy learning to recognize feelings and urges that are an old story to us. To learn to cope with those emotions is one important job of the growing child, and to make it doubly hard, he can't do it alone. He has to depend on us to help him. We expect the process to be punctuated by an occasional "disturbance," just as we expect a healthy child to suffer an occasional cold.

Because school is a natural focus for so much of the growing, school is also bound to be the scene of some of the disturbances. We learn to recognize the symptoms—a sudden change from typical behavior, more fighting or more crying or more absence or less concentration. Six-year-old Johnny suddenly refuses to come to school. Twelve-year-old Bobby cries when he sees the "C" in math on his report card. Teen-age Sally, an "A" student, suddenly stops trying.

As we probe behind this behavior with parent, child, or school counselor, we find there is a reason:

"Ever since the baby came, Johnny hangs around me all the time."

"My father said he'd buy me a bike if I got an 'A,' and now he won't buy it."

SOURCE: *National Education Association Journal,* XLVII (December, 1958), 609–11. Reprinted by permission.

"If I can't go away to college, I'm not going to do anything."

Then we apply the first aid that is usually all that is required. Johnny and his mother get some counseling about the meaning of the new baby. Bobby's father begins to look at his son's ability realistically. Sally learns the economic facts of life, and her parents learn about adolescent independency striving. And all is fixed.

But to become *an emotionally disturbed child* is another matter. For one thing, transient disturbances like the ones we mentioned above must have been repeatedly ignored, misjudged, or badly handled earlier in the game, before the child reached school age as well as afterward, so that anger or distrust or despair, a feeling of badness or wrongness in himself or in the world, has already begun to look like a permanent fixture in the personality.

By then, no one-sided, one-step remedy will work. By then, it isn't *simply* the chemistry of the glands or the focus of the eyes or the level of the IQ or what Papa said just before Johnny left for school this morning. By then, warmth and caring are not enough.

What is an emotionally disturbed child like? First of all, the term itself is much too broad. It covers illnesses as simple as measles and as serious as cancer, as different as tonsillitis and a broken arm.

For example, if little Johnny's screaming and vomiting and refusal to come to school continue even after ample demonstration that he is loved and appreciated as fully as the newly arrived infant, chances are that the baby is not the source of the problem, but only the last straw.

Johnny and his mother may need guidance deeper in focus and longer in duration. Mother may need to take an unsettling new look at her child-rearing attitudes, and Johnny may have to let off considerable steam in the safety of a therapist's office before he can take the risk of growing up.

There may be another Johnny in the same first-grade class who comes to school obediently day after day and goes robot-like through his classroom paces; but his teacher notices a mask-like quality about him, a pseudo-understanding. He's in another world.

Now it *may* be that this Johnny is by inheritance an especially slow child, as yet unequipped for the rigors of first-grade life. Or perhaps he is one of those unfortunate children so badly hurt by early experiences that his thinking is twisted, and he really *cannot* understand the world as we do. Both are certainly disturbed, but they are as different from each other as they are from our first Johnny.

As a fourth variety of disturbance, take the kind of child we have been studying at the National Institute of Mental Health. In the first grade, this Johnny would probably have the teacher threatening to resign, for he's the boy whose hand is quicker than his head, who wants but cannot share, who acts as if yesterday never happened and tomorrow's an eternity away. He's the acting-out boy, long on aggression and short on self-control.

All these children, and many more varieties, are emotionally disturbed. We could have added at least a fifth child—the wonderfully cooperative one whose private life is an anxious striving to meet self-imposed, perfectionistic goals—but we are not trying to list all the kinds of disturbance. That would be impossible in any case. Our point is that the term *emotionally disturbed* is too broad to have any practical meaning.

To say a child is emotionally disturbed is like saying that he has a fever: Both statements merely point out that something is wrong without indicating the nature of the illness, how serious it is, or what remedies are indicated to effect a cure.

Notice too, that there is a difference between *disturbed* and *disturbing*. The child who causes us most trouble may happen to be the most deeply troubled child in the room; but sometimes he is a normal child engaged in a temporary campaign—perhaps to overcome immigrant status in a new community or to prove he's "somebody" to the girl across the room. The opposite child, the quiet oasis of calm in a too easily distracted group, often needs our attention more, even though he does nothing to force it.

It is no doubt clear by now that emotional disturbances defy generalization. On the face of it, symptoms know no logic. Every situation requires its own analysis, every illness its own cure.

This means that general prescriptions for handling disturbed children in the classroom will have limited relevance for individual cases. It does not mean, however, that there are no guides for thinking about what to do. These there are, and many of them are already familiar to you. Here are only a few we would like to suggest:

A Teacher Is to Teach

Children bring their emotional problems to the classroom, and the teacher has to find ways of helping them to cope with the problems while they are in school. When the emotional disturbances become entangled with classroom and learning situations, it is the teacher's job to try to disentangle them for the duration. It is not the classroom teacher's job to solve the child's difficulties for good and all.

Disturbances Are Real

It may be true that a particular child "could" do the work if he "wanted" to, but this doesn't mean he isn't really disturbed. It only means that the trouble lies in the motivational machinery instead of in the cognitive machinery. We may call him stubborn, negative, resistant, or withholding; but whatever we call him, chances are the condition is beyond his control and as real a disturbance in its way as faulty vision.

This is also true of the child who promises but can't deliver, the one who has to keep his eye on everything but his assignment, and many others who try our patience day after day.

It Isn't Personal

Not only are disturbances real; they also run deeper than the events of the day, as we have tried to indicate. The boy who continues his nasty disruptions in spite of your efforts to contain him probably has nothing against you personally, nor have you created the problem by failing to smile his way in the morning. You may symbolize all the adults who "do nothing but boss me around all the time," or you may be an innocent casualty in a battle to win prestige in the gang.

The Exceptional Child Is an Exception

Although many disturbed children can be helped in a regular classroom, the fact remains that the disturbed child is exceptional, and the techniques that provide stimulating learning experiences for most normal children may only stimulate the disturbed child's pathology.

If a promising activities program leads to chaos in the classroom, the trouble may lie in one or two children with faulty control systems and not in the technique itself. Even in a very small class, with more than one teacher, some children cannot manage a program which depends on inner controls and self-maintained task-centeredness. On the other hand, one can see the very same activities producing significant learning in large classes of relatively normal children.

Is the answer to assign disturbed children to separate groups? Perhaps, but not for all of them. Some disturbed children need special classes or special schools and some cannot manage school at all, but the majority need the presence of a normal group in order to develop an image of constructive social behavior.

For these children, the answer lies in the kind of flexible planning that many schools are finding easier to achieve than they had imagined. Children are going to school part time, moving to different rooms and grades as their needs require it, staying home on bad days—and the schools are seeing the programs bear fruit.

What is right for any disturbed child still depends on an analysis of that case alone, but there are plenty of alternatives if a school is willing to be imaginative.

You Can't Go It Alone

What we have just said is not meant to imply that a teacher has to find a way to teach every child on the class roster. In the first place, some *disturbing* children are unmanageable (and therefore unteachable) even if they are not seriously *disturbed*. Others who might be reached are all too frequently lost because of special school conditions.

When the teacher is hamstrung by a rigid curriculum, a dearth of special facilities, ragged equipment, and short supplies, he can only choose the path of sanity and admit his limitations. Too many teachers still stand like martyrs, alone and unprovided with necessary tools, struggling to accomplish a task which requires artistry even under the best of circumstances.

Refer It

Tell somebody. The guidance counselor, the principal, the pupil personnel worker, the school social worker, the school psychologist—tell whichever person in your school has the job of knowing the resources for the troubled child and how to get child and resource together. And if the child you refer is lucky enough to arrive at the source of help, remember, specialists in helping troubled people can't go it alone either.

To be a specialist means to have special knowledge and skill in a specific area. It also means having less knowledge and skill in other areas. Psychiatrists, psychologists, and social workers may know as little about the classroom as teachers may know about the clinic. The helping specialist will depend on information from you to help him understand the case and plan the treatment *outside* the school.

As for the classroom program, that remains your area of specialty, and it will be up to you to translate findings about the child's personality and needs into classroom action. Education has perhaps done too little to develop specific educational techniques for the emotionally disturbed child, but that gap is being filled by a growing catalogue of literature and course work on the subject, and we urge you to take advantage of it.

Speak Up

Disturbed children need special services, not only in the school but in the recreation, health, and welfare fields as well. For too many years, teachers have tried to provide services beyond their scope because those services were not available elsewhere in the community. It is time the teachers shoved back—not to get even, but because it is hard enough to be what classroom teachers are trained to be without also trying to be social workers, psychologists, and psychiatrists. Only if we speak up can the community understand the need and begin to meet it.

2. The Emotionally Handicapped Child and the School

ELI M. BOWER

One of the major accomplishments of American public education has been the development and implementation of educational services for all children. Yet to many educators and lay persons this accomplishment is regarded with mixed feelings and some surprise. On the one hand there is the race into space, the National Defense Education Act, programs in the sciences and mathematics; on the other there are severely retarded children, children severely disabled by cerebral palsy, polio, or accident, children in hospitals, children who are multiply handicapped, children who are being treated for narcotic addiction, children in juvenile halls and mental hospitals, and children who can only be instructed in their own home. The expectations of almost all communities in America today are that all children of school age in the community will

SOURCE: *Exceptional Children,* XXVI (September, 1959), 6–11. Reprinted by permission.

attend school. Diffused and interspersed with these expectations are values which tend to define education as a somewhat selective process in which only the able and willing can function. The money and effort spent in the education of the less able and often unwilling student is often regarded as necessary, but on a hierarchy of values, less necessary than other services.

The continuous and dynamic mixture of these values creates a major psychic split in policy makers, school administrators, and teachers. Is the school and community responsible for the education of children who come to school resistant and antagonistic to the values of the school? Like marriage, education is a process which can only be accomplished with the consent of the learner. If some children do not "choose" to give such consent, can the school reasonably be asked to educate them? To what extent do compulsory education laws penalize interested and conscientious learners by forcing recalcitrant learners on the teacher and school? To what extent does the school act as a social irritant for the nonsuccessful learner? On the more positive side, can the school identify problem children early enough to plan successful curriculum and counseling programs for them? Is intervention in the life of a child who is not yet a problem but is rapidly becoming one possible in a free society? Can schools be equipped with staff and the inclination to deal with the beginnings of problems, rather than with the results of the problems?

Prevention in a Complex Society

If early identification and intervention is to be effective, it needs to intervene in the child's life at a point in time which may be regarded as rank interference without proof or cause. Indeed the vast problem of prevention has many conflicting roots in a free society. As Bellak points out:

> At present the governing of men and the raising of children seem to be among the very few occupations in civilized society for which no training or certified ability are required—and for fairly sound reasons. Imposition of laws on either activity could constitute invasion of personal freedom.[1]

Parents, however, are forced to send their children to school. Drivers must obey traffic laws and parents must provide proper nutrition and sanitation for their children. As our society becomes more and more interdependent and as each of us needs to depend more and more on the

[1] Bellak, Leopold, (Ed.) *Schizophrenia*, New York: Logos Press, 1958, XVIII.

sane, rational behavior of the other, more rules and restrictions are sure to follow. A motor freeway provides ease of travel by restricting freedom of direction, access, and exit. Similarly a society, as it grows complex, tends to decrease freedom of personal choice for the benefit of the group. Yet it is understandable that in a highly complex society directed toward powerful automobiles, jet airliners, explosive weapons, and highly urbanized living the narrow margin for individual error is critical. Early identification and help for persons with antisocial or asocial behavior becomes mandatory. Rules and regulations which make such help more prophylactic and salubrious rather than *post facto* treatment or incarceration need to be anticipated. Prevention is economical and socially advantageous whether one is talking about infantile paralysis, crime, or emotional disturbances. Preventive action of any kind entails doing something at a point in time which affects most if not all members of a society and is basically protective for all. Prevention does not have the drama and urgency of treatment; yet our society with its core of rationality looks eventually toward preventive horizons in an effort to deal with any factor which causes disease or unhappiness to a majority of its population.

The School's Role

In actual practice the school may face the Scylla of keeping emotionally handicapped children in school and educating them in some type of adjusted program or the Charybdis of sending them out into the community with little supervision, control, or guidance. Schools which accept the responsibility of educating the emotionally handicapped child have a legal and professional right to ask, "How do we do it?" The legal mandate of compulsory education for all children placed on the school district is empty and futile unless the school district has the professional know-how and staff to implement the law and its intent.

Certainly one area of greatest impact and strategic action of a school lies in early detection of the more vulnerable child followed by appropriate remedial steps.

Who are the more vulnerable children? What group of children are encompassed by the term "emotionally handicapped children"? Can such children be regarded as other handicapped children? Can such children be screened out for help in some economical method by school personnel?

Defining the Emotionally Handicapped

Someone once said that nothing would ever be attempted if all possible objections had to first be overcome. The definition of the term "emotionally handicapped" has many of the qualifications necessary for this kind of immobility. Not only is a scientific, understandable definition of the term prerequisite for research action, but one needs to be mindful of legal, financial, legislative, operational, and parental perceptions of any definition. An auditor in a department of finance will want to know which children are legally entitled to consideration as an "emotionally handicapped" child and why there are differences in relative numbers of such children among districts. A school administrator will want to know how he may differentiate between the children who have problems and those who are "emotionally handicapped." A parent might well ask, "There have been times in my life when I could have been called 'emotionally disturbed.' Does this mean I would come under the definition of emotionally handicapped?"

In addition, the complexity and difficulty of defining is increased since what one is attempting to define is the beginning of a process and not the ending—the sniffles and sneezes—as it were, rather than the full fever. One can communicate with some success the pronounced symptoms of a condition since the characteristics are often sufficiently recognizable to be described. In trying to differentiate early symptoms one runs the risk of defining characteristics which are more or less true of almost everyone.

Our language, with its subject-predicate structure, tends to define as black or white qualities which are seldom either. The use of the term "emotionally handicapped," for example, in place of emotionally disturbed, socially maladjusted, or other similar terms is designed to clarify somewhat the semantic problems inherent in delineations of states of emotion. The term "handicap" has a more lasting and persistent quality; disturbances are seen as transitory or temporary. The use of "disturbance" is usually indicative of the acting out, overtly aggressive problem; therefore one tends to perceive emotional problems as resulting in one type of behavior. In addition, the term "emotionally disturbed" is often associated with a formal psychological or psychiatric appraisal; "emotionally handicapped" has less of the black or white connotation of children's problems and is more illustrative of emotional problems existing to a degree. Lastly the term "emotionally handicapped" is often more realistically descriptive of the disability and does not mask the problem under vague or misleading terms. Part of the problem, however, of any attempt at an adequate description or definition of the term lies in the difficulty in cognitively describing the complex affective state called "emotion." Indeed, one dictionary states: "Emotion is virtually impossible to define except in terms of conflicting theories." [2]

Feelings and emotions are synonymous to most persons. Both are regarded as vague, misty things, highly variable and situational. In part this may be a result of not having any measurement devices or techniques comparable to those employed in measuring intellect, sight, hearing acuity, or academic achievement. Unlike sensory, intellectual, or physical handicaps which exhibit themselves along a single dimension primarily as a deficit, emotional handicaps can only be inferred from behavior which may be overly aggressive, inappropriate, overly withdrawn, or combinations of these. One can, for example, be just as handicapped by an overabundance of emotion as by a lack of emotion. One can be said to be emotionally handicapped by demonstrating normal emotional behavior at inappropriate times as one can show apparently "normal" grief at the death of a loved one—for 20 years. One may consistently develop strong and compelling feelings in one relationship and be relatively self-contained in another. In addition, one can be economically successful because of an emotional handicap or in spite of such a handicap just as one can be a blatant failure without benefit of neurosis or emotional conflict.

Predicting Emotional Vulnerability

The definition which would be of greatest use to school personnel would be one which is operationally related to the possibility of early detection and intervention in the school. Specifically, therefore, one is trying to predict which children in the school population will be markedly handicapped by emotional problems as adults. In this sense perhaps the term "handicapped" can best be understood as a restriction of choice or alternatives of behavior. To live is to make choices; when one's choices are severely limited by emotional lacks or injunctions one's behavior can be regarded as handicapped. The reduction of possible behavioral alternatives serves to further reduce the individual's degrees of freedom in social and educational endeavors. In addition this reduced maneuverability or inflexibility in a changing world of mobile peers and events increases his susceptibility to behavior difficulties and interpersonal friction. The emotionally handicapped child is therefore circumscribed as one having a higher degree of vulnerability to behavior problems and one who, as an adult, will exhibit this vulnerability in general health

[2] English, H. B., and English, A. C., *A Comprehensive Dictionary of Psychological and Psychoanalytical Terms*, New York: Longmans, Green and Company, 1958.

problems, poor interpersonal relationships, inability to function sexually or economically, inability to profit from experience, or lead a happy life. In its more pervasive form this vulnerability may lead to psychosis, neurosis, suicide, repetitive automobile accidents, alcoholism, narcotic addiction, or criminal behavior. One can, therefore, describe the emotionally handicapped child as a child who is unable or will be unable to take the slings and arrows of life without caving in, becoming immobilized, or exploding.

Significant Behavioral Deviations

In terms of their visibility in school they can be perceived as children who demonstrate one or more of the following characteristics to *a marked extent* and *over a period of time:*

1. An inability to *learn* which cannot be explained by intellectual, sensory, or health factors.

   An inability to learn is perhaps the single most significant characteristic of emotionally handicapped children in school. Such non-learning may be manifested as an inability to profit from experience as well as inability to master skill subjects. The non-learner seldom escapes recognition. Achievement tests often confirm what the teacher has long suspected. If all other possibilities have been ruled out, emotional conflicts or resistances can be ruled in.

2. An inability to build or maintain satisfactory *interpersonal relationships* with peers and teachers.

   It isn't just getting along with others that is significant here. Satisfactory interpersonal relations refer to factors such as demonstrating sympathy and warmth toward others, ability to stand alone when necessary, ability to have close friends, ability to be aggressively constructive and to enjoy working and playing with others as well as enjoying working and playing by oneself. In most instances, children who are unable to build or maintain satisfactory interpersonal relationships are most visible to their peers. Teachers are also able to identify such children after a period of observation.

3. *Inappropriate* types of behavior or feelings under normal conditions.

   Inappropriateness of behavior or feeling can often be sensed by the teacher and peer groups. "She acts funny" the peer group may say. The teacher may find some children reacting disproportionately to a simple command such as "Please take your seat." What is appropriate or inappropriate is best judged by the teacher using her professional training, her daily observation of the child, and her experience working and interacting with the appropriate behavior of large numbers of normal children.

4. A general, pervasive mood of *unhappiness* or depression.

   Children who are unhappy most of the time may demonstrate such feelings in expressive play, art work, written composition, or in discussion periods. They seldom smile and usually lack a *joie de vivre* in their curriculum or social relationships. In the middle or upper grades a self-inventory is usually helpful in confirming suspicions.

5. A tendency to develop *illnesses,* pains, or fears associated with personal or school problems.

   This tendency is sometimes difficult to observe without the help of the school nurse and parent. Illness may be continually associated with school pressures or develop when a child's confidence in himself is under stress. In some cases, such illnesses or fears may be apparent to the teacher, nurse, or parent; peers, however, are often aware of children who are sick after tests or have headaches before recitations.

The significant characteristics indicating a need for closer scrutiny are inability to learn, unsatisfactory interpersonal relationships, inappropriate behavior, unhappiness, and illness.

These characteristics can, of course, be said to be true of all children to some degree at different times. There seems to be little likelihood of bypassing the "how much is too much" question in any descriptive attempt at separating the more vulnerable from the less vulnerable child. A more satisfactory analysis can be made by assessing classes by some standardized process in which perceptions by teacher, peers, and self can be combined. Such a procedure has been employed and is being used at present with generally satisfactory results.[3]

A major caution in the descriptive definition of children with emotional handicaps is the problem of differentiating incipient pathology from normal behavioral deviation. Marked differences in behavior are noted in children with emotional handicaps, but they are also noted in children who choose to behave somewhat idiosyncratically. Perhaps the key in differentiating the child whose behavioral deviation is caused by emotional problems and the child whose behavior is simply different is one of determining the source of the behavior. The behavior of the emotionally handicapped child is, to the extent of his handicap, not a matter of choice, but necessity. The degrees of behavioral freedom for the emotionally handicapped individual may be restricted by internal con-

[3] Bower, E. M., Tashnovian, P. J., and Larson, C. A., *A Process for Early Identification of Emotionally Disturbed Children,* Sacramento: California State Department of Education, 1959.

flicts or by lack of inner controls. In any case, strange, unconventional, or deviant behavior cannot in and of itself be regarded as a sign of an emotional handicap. The film *Shyness*[4] is an excellent illustration of the difficulty in inferring causes solely on the basis of observed behavior. Of the three children referred as being shy and withdrawn only one could be said to be emotionally handicapped. On the other hand, Clare, in *Feelings of Hostility,*[5] although a successful and competent business woman, had pervasive feelings of loneliness and hostility toward men. Her overt behavior would hardly suggest the depth or intensity of her problems.

Teachers, with the help of peer- and self-perceptions, are in the best position to act as "suspecticians." Without knowing the cause, they may note children whose behavioral temperature is rising.

Behavior and Personality

In the final analysis the diagnosis of emotional handicap rests on an inference of motivation of behavior based on personality dynamics. This may be done by guidance specialists with the help of the teacher. The source or derivative of the behavior is the basic sought-after ingredient. Yet personality, at best, is an inference of the dynamic organization of needs, motivations, and drives in the individual. Behavior can be regarded as an interaction of personality and environmental factors mediated or defined by personality processes commonly called the self or ego. The driving forces in personality are often well masked from the observer as well as from the organism. It is interesting to note that the root of the word personality, *persona,* has reference to a theatrical mask.[6] In any case, differentiations among children to distinguish behavioral differences from incipient emotional pathology must be based on inferences relating to an appraisal of personality dynamics and relationships.

What kinds of observations about personality would be most helpful in making inferences or professional guesses as to cause of deviant behavior? To the teacher or principal the behavior of the emotionally disturbed child will be "driven" behavior, i.e., the energy level of the child will seem to be inappropriate or disproportionate to the task. The child

[4] McGraw-Hill Book Company, 330 West 42nd Street, New York 36, New York, 16 mm., sound, 23 minutes.

[5] Ibid., 32 minutes.

[6] English, H. B., and English, A. C., *A Comprehensive Dictionary of Psychological and Psychoanalytical Terms,* New York: Longmans, Green and Company, 1958, p. 382.

may play with an intensity and frenzy which bodes ill to anyone or anything interfering. He may be unable to obey rules in school even after repeated and varied contacts with accepting or disciplining adults. The non-emotionally handicapped child has relative freedom to change his behavior as a result of rewarding or punishing relationships or situations. The emotionally handicapped child has relatively little freedom to adapt. He is often regarded as especially stubborn and recalcitrant since the usual influence techniques of reward, punishment, recognition, praise, and the like are relatively ineffective in influencing his behavior. Or he may be regarded as a "real pushover," i.e., influenced almost completely by the wishes and ideas of others. Here the self or ego may be regarded as undeveloped as compared to other emotionally handicapped children who are immobilized or driven by inner conflicts. In healthy emotional development the individual has sufficient ego strength to vary his *persona* appropriately in accordance with the situation and at the same time to maintain a sufficient core of self in all situations. For example, one is not expected to be the same at church as at a party, yet the differences cannot be so radical as to involve complete changes in personality.

The emotionally handicapped child seems not to profit from experience and appears to behave in an automatic, repetitive pattern. His ideas about the teacher or his peers may be somewhat distorted. For example, he may see the teacher as a punishing, threatening adult and classmates as competitive siblings constantly outdoing him in reading, drawing, or sports. One would infer that in the relatively less emotionally handicapped child, behavior is motivated by forces at relatively greater levels of awareness; conversely, behavior motivated primarily by unconscious forces would be characteristic of the emotionally handicapped child. Thus, as Kubie notes, ". . . the essence of normality is flexibility, in contrast to the freezing of behavior into patterns of unalterability which characterize every manifestation of the neurotic process whether in impulses, acts, thoughts, or feelings. Whether or not a behavioral event is free to change depends not on the quality of the act itself, but upon the nature of the constellation of forces that has produced it . . . Wherever unconscious forces play the preponderant role in this constellation. . . . then behavior . . . is subject to a tendency to automatic and obligatory repetition." [7]

While the emotionally handicapped child might be characterized as having a greater load of problems and conflicts, in some cases he may

[7] Kubie, Lawrence S., "Social Forces and the Neurotic Process," in *Explorations in Social Psychiatry,* Alex H. Leighton, ed., New York: Basic Books, 1959, p. 81.

appear to have little conflict, little concern with others, and little, if any, conscience. Such individuals deal with emotional tensions by rapid action rather than by internalizing the subsequent anxiety. Whereas some children develop substantial self-concepts or egos through which their problems are expressed, others lack an adult or relatively mature concept of self. This is manifest by a lack of tension and a pattern of behavior which is stereotyped, childish, and relatively uninhibited. A large number of these emotionally handicapped individuals are found among juvenile delinquents.

The Continuum of Degree

Emotional handicaps may be displayed in transient, temporary, pervasive, or intense types of behavior. To complete our definition, it would be necessary to establish a continuum upon which the degree of handicap can be perceived and perhaps estimated, especially as it relates to possible action by the school. One could begin such a continuum with (A) children who experience and demonstrate the normal problems of everyday living, growing, exploration, and reality testing. There are some, however, who can be observed as (B) children who develop a greater number and degree of symptoms of emotional problems as a result of a crisis or traumatic experience. Such a crisis or traumatic experience may be death of father, birth of sibling, divorce of parents, brain or body injury, school entrance, junior high school entrance, adolescence, etc. Some move beyond this point and may be described as (C) children in whom symptoms persist to some extent beyond normal expectations but who can manage an adequate school adjustment. The next group would include (D) children with fixed and recurring symptoms of emotional disturbance who can, with help, maintain some positive relationships in a school setting. Beyond this are (E) children with fixed and recurring symptoms of emotional difficulties who are best educated in a residential school setting or temporarily in a home setting. For public school purposes, groups C and D are those presently included in the definition "emotionally handicapped." Past studies [8] and present research [9] indicate that the last three groups include about 10 per cent of the school population.

[8] Gorman, Mike, *Every Other Bed.*, New York: World Publishing Co., 1956, p. 23.
[9] Bower, E. M., Tashnovian, P. J., and Larson, C. A., *A Process for Early Identification of Emotionally Disturbed Children,* Sacramento: California State Department of Education, 1958, p. 57, 58.

3. The Educational Implications of Differential Diagnosis

William C. Morse

Patterns of Maladjustment

It is a truism that effective education grows out of psychological understanding. Since all children who are socially and emotionally disturbed do not suffer the same psychological limitations, it becomes useful to study basic patterns of maladjustment in order to predicate educational design. Otherwise, a valuable educational process may be inappropriately applied, since what one child needs is apt to be contraindicated for the next.

To speak of a "pattern of maladjustment" is not to minimize the all-important fact that, within a general pattern, each individual is a unique self having a growth history like no other. The term *pattern* is used as a conceptual frame of reference: we recognize that the individualizing of this general pattern is the important condition for the teacher. Two pupils steal or two adolescent girls are sexually promiscuous, but this does not make them pairs of psychological twins. The nuances of individuality in each case become the educator's first concern.

It is known, too, that many normal children, as they go through growth stages, exhibit symptoms which characterize the maladjusted. For example, at some time or another most children take something not rightfully theirs, yet only a few become "delinquents." The child who is

SOURCE: William C. Morse, "The Education of Socially Maladjusted and Emotionally Disturbed Children," in William M. Cruickshank and G. Orville Johnson, eds., *Education of Exceptional Children and Youth,* 2d ed. (Englewood Cliffs, N.J.: Prentice-Hall, Inc., 1967), pp. 578–93.

at times moody, discouraged, or aggressive is not by that fact atypical. The frequency, persistence, and intensity of the behavior must be taken into account.

One must also be concerned with the meaning of a particular bit of behavior in relationship to the whole personality. A child telling a lie may signify a "pathological liar" where this is a cue to a way of life; or he may signify a child with high loyalty to his friends, caught in a difficult social situation. Thus, many normal children at times show symptoms of the disturbed. Conversely, most disturbed children have areas of normal function and periods of adequate control. Under the proper conditions they may function normally for extensive periods of time. The whole gist of helping them is in providing a more reasonable situation so that their problem behavior will be reduced to the level where help is feasible. Extended observation verifies that the intensity and pervasiveness of the symptoms in the disturbed child far exceed that in the normal child.

A child with social or emotional difficulties is a child with poor mental health, and restoring good mental health is the goal of our efforts in his behalf. This term "mental health" is in itself ambiguous and diffuse in meaning. As used here, good mental health implies adequate personal strength to meet the usual vicissitudes of life with responses in keeping with the social mores of the community at large. Further, the child should have an appreciation of his limitations balanced by a satisfying and productive use of his capacities. This includes school accomplishment. His social adjustment should not bring him into undue conflict with his peers or authority. There should be incorporated a sense of values satisfying to himself and appropriate to his culture. With children, these items are all prefaced with the phrase "appropriate to his age." Even with good mental health an individual may be overwhelmed by catastrophic events. For example, a child may be in acute conflict as his parents work up to a divorce. He may reintegrate adequately after it is "settled" and a new pattern established. Or he may be so damaged by the trauma that he cannot meet more normal life demands. The implication of these situational or, as they are sometimes called, transient disorders where the child makes his own recovery after a difficult siege are seldom recognized in evaluating educational and therapeutic programs.

The over-all point of interest here can be summed up as follows: socially and emotionally disturbed children live in a chronic state of poor mental health. Certainly they need more protection, more support, and more corrective help than the normal child. But knowing this does not provide clues as to the *nature* of the educational program needed and how one type of a child might be different in his requirements from another.

Determining the Differences between Children

To be more specific one must resort to differential diagnosis, the delineation of particular dynamic patterns showing how one differs from another. This cannot be done by assembling a constellation of discrete symptoms for each deviation, since the symptoms overlap from one category to another. By combining some of *what* a child does with *why* he does it, it is possible to make a more dynamic appraisal. How does this operate?

Suppose there are a series of cases all showing hostility to the teacher as a major symptom. Obviously, such behavior can stem from a variety of motivations with quite different meaning for the personalities involved. Johnny is hostile to teachers and police because this is the ideology of all boys in his neighborhood. He would be a peer misfit otherwise, and yet it makes for severe stress in the school community. Joan's hostility is a sample of her exaggerated adolescent desire to be independent, now far out of hand. While one might hope that she will grow out of it, the consequences of her present behavior are too risky to permit taking such a chance. George, living in an atmosphere of rejection at home, transfers his feeling of being unliked to the teacher, leading off with self-protective hostility in order to show others he hates them before they can show hate to him. Since his teacher "acts like she likes him," George has continued his hostile behavior to test how honest this concern of the teacher really is. Sam, nurtured by a longstanding but unconscious feeling of inadequacy, is out to prove he can be a "somebody." As master of his own destiny he cannot be pushed around by anyone, and this includes teachers. Roger wants what he wants when he wants it, in a state of extended infantile omnipotence unwittingly fostered by his parents. The teacher interferes with his narcissistic impulses when he wants to loaf in the boys' room to puff on a cigarette; thus she reaps his hostility. Finally, Mary, ridden by shame and unconscious guilt over the separation of her parents, seeks punishment. Her hostility to the teacher is from a deep need for retaliation, and it keeps increasing until the teacher reacts, and then it repeats.

In each case the symptomatic behavior—here, the example of hostility—was and is a clue, but only a clue, to the underlying disturbance pattern. To assist children, educators need to know both what youngsters do and their motivation for doing it. The significance is a matter of the relationship of the behavior to the self-concept of the individual child. To know only from a projective test that a child has a hostile nature would not be enough either. Teachers respond to the motivation but get to it through the symptomatic expression. In this way response is not to the behavior but to the child, and useful educational plans can be evolved.

As the teacher of disturbed children develops skill in diagnostic assessment, it is possible to select appropriate educational procedures. The educational program contains new and traditional school experiences blended to meet the deeper emotional needs of the pupil.

The Matter of Delinquency

One step remains before a conceptualization of the various syndromes is made: This is to clarify the relationship of delinquency to such patterns, for it is not uncommon to see delinquency listed as a personality constellation. Society provides penal type institutions for those classed as delinquents and mental hospital type institutions for those categorized as disturbed, as if these were distinct and meaningful separations. The truth is there are many types of pathologies found in both settings as will be pointed out subsequently. Legally, a delinquent is a minor who has been apprehended for violating the law; his acts may range from stealing and destructiveness to sexual promiscuity. Little is gained in trying to synthesize a personality pattern which incorporates all of these, since the delinquent act is a symptom and symptoms do not define psychodynamics as has already been noted. It is important for teachers to recognize delinquency as a psychological rather than legal entity. Psychological delinquency includes not only the legal but also those lesser violations of ethics involved in the use of threats and aggression to intimidate others and the lack of compliance to constituted authority. A variety of motivations produce these symptomatic acts of transgression. Thus they properly belong in the discussions of the various pathologies which follow where due attention will be given to delinquent behavior and its many meanings.

The task of organizing child pathology around certain central dynamic concepts is most difficult. To do it justice would require detailed discussions far beyond the scope of this selection. The field itself lacks agreement and coherence, and new proposals are continually being made. For example, while it is common to use many categories, Quay has found only three major divisions when symptoms are factored: the acting out delinquent, the neurotic or withdrawn, and the immature or psychotic complexes. Nevertheless, the educator must have a general scheme for sorting out syndromes and, further, relating educational handling to syndromes. In the following brief condensation it should be kept in mind that there are few children who fall in any pure type. To label a child suggests a uniformity about his make-up which is not actually found. In practice it is essential to retain flexibility and pay particular attention to the individual child's case history which overlaps the generalization about him. With these cautions, what are some of the generalized patterns?

Socially Defective Children

The first general pattern includes children with various shortcomings in concern for others. They grow up without incorporating a satisfactory set of values. They are defective in conscience or superego. This defect may range from almost complete inability to empathize with any other person to cases where the ability is present but is much restricted. The potential for feeling sorry or guilty, which serves as a check on impulse, is either not present in these children or it is inadequate or temporarily inoperative. Estimates of the percentage of all maladjusted children with this general syndrome vary from 15 per cent to over 50 per cent. Since this general category represents such a broad range, it will be useful to examine three common subgroupings.

THE SEMI-SOCIALIZED CHILD This category is sometimes called the primary behavior disorder or conduct disorder group. There are many children growing up in a diverse and loose environment who come to have a limited, though intact, code relating to social behavior. They have a set of skills to meet the problems of life and a capacity to relate to certain others. Frequently they can relate to peers with a close gang or ingroup loyalty. Some have learned to respond to their families in a socialized way, but they have no concern for outsiders. Even to their own gang members they may at times be very caustic and rough, giving a chaotic kind of acceptance. While they have solicitation for the ingroup, those of the outgroup, which includes all others, do not share in this socialization. Aggression and other delinquent behavior toward the outgroup, rather than being reprehensible, is a worthy achievement and done without guilt. They are able to emulate adults, but imitate those who demonstrate impulsive behavior which fits their own desires.

These then are the children who have assimilated feeling for others, but on a limited basis. They are loyal to their own group, be it family, clique, or cultural or racial entity. Here they are governed by strict codes which are the manifestation of an unfinished conscience. Frequently these children have some residual uneasiness about their value system, since they are so often in conflict with society. A case in point is a preadolescent boy who has been bailed out of every difficulty in school and neighborhood by a mother who takes a stand that the teachers, police, and other community people are always out to get her son. She can't understand what the trouble is because he gets along tolerably well with her, the father, and the siblings. He is a terror at school and in the neighborhood. Though she protects him all she can, he runs into situation after situation where he finds himself "wrong" in the eyes of power figures outside his family. Like the gang delinquent, this boy intensifies his protective family ties. Nevertheless, in therapeutic work with him it became clear that he was also worried. He could not figure out why he got into so much trouble. He was afraid the police would take him away from his parents. This minimal anxiety was used in therapy.

Most semi-socialized children hold to a circumscribed code for self-direction and develop a strong defense against accepting the broader code of society to which they have been exposed. Such a maladjusted child is engaged in a civil war with the culture at large and a skirmish conflict with his own feelings. The significant battles are conducted against the cultural agents. Police are not protectors but "cops" out to get you; teachers are not helpers but "drill sergeants" ordering the educational draft. They represent the enemy. Unfortunately, it has become the fashion to lump all deprived children into this category, considering them automatically school alienated. Of course some are. But certain facets of deprivation are found in any class. Model deprivation, for example, can be found in any family where there is no viable image. But deprivation, like delinquency, has become a catch-all term and does not connote particular educational responses. There are even deprived children to whom regular school is a life oasis: they hate to leave it at the end of the day. But the lower class child who has failed in school and who is bitter about his experience may well become defensively alienated. After a time the alienation becomes so set as to defy alteration. Nourished on defeat and failure, such a youngster is not about to bypass his mistrust. Mistrust has become his first nature.

Even from so brief a description, it becomes clear that these socially defective children are acute educational problems, perhaps the most vexing to the school. They are frequently truant. Cruel behavior to those not in their circle is not uncommon, and they are often given to stealing, defiance, and destructiveness. Their shrewd belligerence in verbal argument makes them impervious to the teacher's persuasion attempts. Since these children are deficient in guilt and operate from an egocentric value system, appeals are useless.

What to do with them therapeutically is a problem. Many find their way to detention homes or state correctional schools—and find their way out older, more cunning, but essentially unchanged. Reasonable handling can serve as psychological aspirin, alleviating the tension but not removing the infection. Since they have great difficulty in identifying with proper social models, they absorb very little from most teachers. Many teachers have found it useful to walk the fence between sympathy, which the boys would see as stupidity, and counter-hostility, which they would see as justification for retaliation. Some of the boys divide teachers into "teachers" and a few "good guys." The latter are those who have not tried to moralize, punish, or expect the impossible. The complications of therapy with these children are described in the Redl and Wineman volume. The teacher can expect continual testing with permissiveness equated with weakness. On the other hand, counterhostility toward them will evoke only more antagonism. In addition to these therapeutically oriented problems, the teacher must work with the particular defect in school motivation which these children have. Some have been judged by educators as low in intellectual ability because they develop learning difficulties. However, as a group their school achievement lags behind their intellectual capacity. These youngsters are quick to learn what they deem useful to them and take great pride in being able to "case a job," picking up all the needed information in a brief moment. On the other hand, school work, especially the routine and drill aspects, holds little allure for them. Many are motoric in contrast to verbal in orientation. And as adolescents their prime interest is in money and jobs, cars and excitement far from the mundane school world of always preparing for the future. Their time myopia is evident to those who try to help them. Their school failures add much frustration. If they do not drop out, they may find educational salvation through sports, manual activities, and later through work study programs where they earn money on a job and go to school part time. Work is sometimes classed as "work therapy" and with good reason. They need a great deal of counseling and support or they will fail on the job just as they do in school: the incentive pattern alone seldom is enough.

The teacher's ability to establish and hold limits without hostility is essential. Since youngsters of this nature are quick to associate with others like themselves as well as catalyze impulsive actions in others, the teacher is very often faced with a group problem. Talking with one is hard enough; talking with a group requires special skill. Yet a teacher can get closer to them through group living situations, where it is possible slowly to work in some influence. The skills which are being developed by the social group workers who live and help the children in the neighborhood setting will eventually produce techniques. The concept of "reaching the unreached" implies going to where they are and working with gang and neighborhood groups in contrast to waiting for them to come to a center for help. If a skillful teacher devises a program which causes one gang member to defect from his buddies, this constitutes a threat to the unreformed. The one who responds to the teacher finds himself seen as a traitor by his peers. It is no accident that successful teachers of these children are teachers who have ceased to moralize, lowered their expectations, pruned the curriculum, added realism, and ignored the niceties of language. These teachers also serve as nondefensive examples of acceptable social standards. Secure in their own beliefs, these teachers have learned to tolerate children with different values. They call limits only when absolutely necessary, and then without rancor. All of this is to the end of mobilizing the latent potentialities of a broadened supergo.

CHILDREN ARRESTED AT A PRIMITIVE LEVEL OF SOCIALIZATION Not infrequently children grow up lacking any consistent family or gang culture. They may not be rejected, but they are left on their own. They first came to attention in the large cities where they are sometimes called "latch key kids," children living by their wits, coming and going on their own volition. Some of the children labeled "deprived" fit into this category too. They may be called *neglected,* a term which does not say what their nature is but describes the lack of adult supervision or support. There are those from wealthy families who suffer such psychological neglect. The special difficulties of the egoless children coming from completely disorganized and deprived families require long-term, depth-oriented socialization as described by Riese. They often make their own meals because their parents work or just take very little interest in them. The resulting personality is frequently coarse, rough, primitive, and amoral. But there is a lack of hate, and often a friendliness and warmth combined with impulsivity. They may steal and participate in sexual activity, all with a generally hedonistic outlook. Money for a show may be forthcoming from a parent when no attention is given to the child's teeth or clothes. They frequently come unkempt, hungry, and dirty to school. The behavior vacillates and attention to organized school tasks is sporadic. Since they lack the discipline of patterning, their activity is diffuse and unorganized, following temporary whims. In general, they are responsive to a warm adult who does not punish but is patient and gives opportunity for recognition. The thing these children need is a defined patterning and the teaching of necessary social mores. Frequently they make rather pronounced progress, soon hitting a plateau. They can be taught, but they are not easy in class. In order to exist, they acquire cunning and winning ways. Since scholastic skills require sustained effort, they are very likely to fall behind. There is no parental interest or support for the school's efforts. These children may be falsely thought to be dull because they accomplish so little. In an organized classroom they become restless and wander around in class or become frustrated at tasks—often not understanding the directions because of low language comprehension. They absorb much teacher time. The more severe cases resemble feral children, scrounging for food, begging, and roaming the street. Their delinquency tends to be an extension of their foraging, and they appear in school with a surprising array of objects. The school format and the discipline of organized tasks in a social situation is what they need, but they cannot absorb it too rapidly. The long, hard civilizing of these children, along with the teaching of skills and school content, requires patience, time, and usually more intensive contact than the regular class can possibly provide.

CHILDREN LACKING CAPACITY TO SOCIALIZE Two classifications of dissocial children have thus far been discussed, the semi-socialized ones and those with a primitive level of socialization. In many respects they behave alike, but each has its own design. A third type is far more serious from the point of view of teaching, for they have a severe lack of capacity to learn social behavior. Some clinics list as high as 10 per cent of their cases in this category, but this represents children with other serious defects, as well as the so-called psychopath or affectionless child with virtually no capacity at all to relate to others. It is the considered opinion here that while there are very few true psychopaths, there are a significant number of children with appreciable stigmata. Failure to recognize this has caused confusion among teachers. Diagnosing these "empty" children is a difficult task requiring skilled clinicians, which may be why there is so much trouble in this regard. There is some controversy regarding the etiology but little disagreement concerning the unfavorable prognosis. When the infant is not socially stimulated by a maternal figure, or when he resides in an impersonal institutional environment, the emotional development is arrested. These children then grow up without the capacity to empathize with others. To put it bluntly, they do not feel for other people. They have no conscience and feel no guilt. Their lack of social response makes them narcissistic and ruthlessly impulsive. The setting and enforcing of reality limits by others is the only way to inhibit the expression of these impulses. Often these children use delinquent tactics to gratify their needs. While they may have superficial sociability, it will not stand the test of friendship which requires as well as gives.

Bowlby isolates the central psychological problem as this inability to make meaningful social contact which results in deceit and lying. For the teacher there are important additional factors to keep in mind. A great deal of school learning depends upon the capability of the child to identify with the goals of society as exemplified in the teacher. This identification is impossible for these children. They are unable to borrow motivation and purpose from others, for they do not empathize with the feelings of others. On the surface, their behavior may look much like the opposition of the semi-socialized child, but their dilemma is far more pathetic. The semi-socialized children have an active but tangential learning pattern, while the psychopaths lack the capacity to incorporate by learning from experience. With their shallow affect, they are great disturbers in the classroom and respond only to enforced, ever-present reality controls. They do not "learn by experience," because they have such a different experience from other children where anxiety and guilt are brought to bear. They "forget" because they have not felt. Thus, "future goals" have no motivational value.

Further, they have been found to be defective in time sense and are confused in orientation. Since they are deficient in capacity to conceptualize and think abstractly, they fall behind the others in school learning. It is important to formulate the lessons in concrete material whenever possible. These children are poor in memory, since memory is partly an emotional phenomenon depending upon one's involvement in recall. It is exasperating to have them forget yesterday's words even after they really put forth effort. Language, being a socialized response, is also deficient. Educational programs must have very limited goals for these children. The pace of learning is slow.

Relationships are weak. They make excessive demands for gratification of their impulses. When this is denied, they become antagonistic. A teacher can give them constant affection and they soak it up without being able to utilize it for self-substantiation. Resorting to punishment produces resentment rather than corrective changes. The reality setting must always be maintained without counter-hostility so that they cannot exploit other children, and so that the consequences of their acts become as apparent as possible to them. Restrictions must be applied.

Psychotherapy for these children is still a matter of debate. Some therapists feel them hopeless while others are working on new methods. A modified operant conditioning model is thought by some psychologists to be the coming procedure. It is known to be a difficult and long-term process. Educationally, they have been a baffling group of pupils, from the point of both classroom discipline and learning. The teacher can never forget that they are limited by their emotional handicap. While persons familiar with the children now know better than to use permissive methods in handling them, each teacher is in a sense still an experimenter, learning to plot the pressure and gratification potentials, and striving to extend their attention span. These children usually have one well-developed skill area—ability to manipulate adults and other pupils for their own ends. They know how to be polite when it pays and often present a disarming surface charm.

A word of caution is needed in closing. It is very difficult to separate children who feel guilt but who ward it off by saying they do not care from those who even upon deep probing really do not care. It has been found that many so-called alienated youngsters are far from uninterested and are capable of learning and adjusting when they are given hope. But hope is hard to supply for lives as circumscribed as many live. These two groups should not be treated the same way, and many times long after the therapist has given up, feelings of anxiety and guilt are evidenced which rekindles hope for improvement. For example, gang youth were paid to talk about themselves on tape. They did have emotional involvement of an intense nature once one got to it. This is a prime illustration of the teacher's need for consultative help in planning programs for particular children.

Children with Neurotic Conflicts

All of the children so far described suffer from inadequate socialization to greater or lesser degrees. They are lacking in conscience. They can do things they should not do without feeling guilty about their acts. The neurotic children about to be discussed often have patches of similar behavior; they may act out and do delinquent acts. They may put on a show of bravado and "devil may care." They may wish to hurt someone. But underneath they have the capacity to relate to others and, when the barriers are removed, show feeling for others so necessary to learning. In fact, they may have a heightened sensitivity in contrast to the psychopath. In most instances the neurotic formulation results from defective relationships with the parent figures. The maladjustment may stem from very early family experiences or more recent handling. What neurotics have in common is a personal problem, an internalized conflict, which they are trying to manage. Certain thoughts or actions have made them guilty and anxious. Somehow they must cope with this anxiety.

NEUROTIC BEHAVIOR Since the conflicts are unconscious for the most part, the fact that these children are troubled does not mean that they necessarily recognize it or want help. Many of them act out their hurts and unhappiness by aggression, stealing, and hostility to adults so that their symptoms look at first glance like the unsocialized child.

Central in the nature of these children is a low sense of self-worth or a feeling of inadequacy which is the distillate of their life experience. For example, a rejected child feels unwanted, which is converted into self-feelings of not worth being wanted. The overprotected child resents the supervision and yet is fearful of meeting life, and so also feels inadequate about himself. A close, though different, pattern is found in children who do something they feel is wrong, such as masturbate, listen to sexual discussions, or express hatred of a parent or a sibling. The net result is to feel they are bad. As guilt accumulates, they become more and more anxious. It is important to remember that anxiety may build up on the unconscious level as, for example, when the child consciously expresses love for a sibling when there is really deep resentment.

Another increasingly important group of neurotics are the children who, because of poor teaching or special difficulties in learning, fail to learn the basic skills. This is especially frequent in the case of reading which requires so much ability, ego integration, and perceptual capacity. Perhaps the pupil is passed along the grades, but there comes a day when he finds himself hopelessly behind his fellows in the classroom experiences. Try as he may, without the skills he cannot compete. He may cover up, build defenses, but under it all remains the awareness that most of the others learn and he does not. Many of these children develop an acute sense of inadequacy, of being different, though they may accumulate extensive compensations in other ways, frequently employing bullying tactics. It has been found that an "evil self-image" is a common denominator in learning problems regardless of the genesis of the learning difficulty.

Still another type of neurotic reaction results when the child, fearing failure or criticism for expressing normal impulses, gradually inhibits response as insurance against criticism and turns to self-generated satisfactions in dreaminess, withdrawal, and phantasy. Some have their conflict around sexual identity, when they respond in ways not in keeping with biological sexuality. Others develop psychosomatic reactions, when the body function becomes the channel for conflict "solution." Aches, headaches, and fatigue may be the evidence. Many persons may be queasy on examination day. Some children are "sick" when they have to give a report. School phobia is on the increase as school demands are intensified, and school resistance is a prime way for the child to upset parents as well. There are others who have an asthmatic attack which keeps them out of school. Why one child comes upon one solution and not another is still baffling, although studies of individual cases make it clear what the forces were. The drama within the family constellation usually provides the key. To the uninitiated, it is hard to remember the unconscious nature of the problem and the fact that the behavior represents a solution to some conflict and therefore cannot be given up without a long struggle. There are, of course, many varieties of neurotic style, and the fact that there may be no reality evidence that they should feel "put upon" is not the issue: the distortion is still there.

EDUCATIONAL IMPLICATIONS Since there is no single pattern to neurotic behavior and no single genesis, the educational ramifications cover a broad spectrum. It may be represented by a school phobia where the child panics at going to school. It may be school failure achieved to thwart parents. It may be the "I can't" reaction to forestall possible failure. Therapeutically, the objective is to help the child develop insight into his difficulty and assuage his guilt, and to provide hygienic emotional patterns with which he can identify. From the teacher the child will need profound understanding, tolerance for neurotic symptoms, an opportunity for mildly cathartic and relaxing experiences, plus a selection of gratifying and possible tasks to do. At the same time control is present in the classroom: unbridled release in a classroom setting leads to chaos. There is no substitute for patience and support as the child rebuilds a serviceable self-image.

The neurotic cannot manage frustration adequately. To provide certain levels of permissiveness for the overwithdrawn child at the same time as the teacher limits the acting-out one is no easy task. We recognize those who externalize their conflict by acting it out—fighting and rebelling then breaking down and crying. The negative ones who refuse to work and yet disturb others are present in most classrooms. Perhaps their jealousy of a sibling is brought to the classroom and acted out on classmates, or their hostility to an oppressive father is transferred to an unsuspecting teacher. They carry their outside conflict into the classroom. The underlying anxiety and guilt must be remembered. For some, the more they act out the more upset they get, until in a hysterical outburst they do things for which they are afterwards very truly sorry. Early curbing by the teacher is most supportive. Dissipating their energy in handling their conflict, they often have little energy left to apply to the school tasks. Since most of these children require therapy for regaining good mental health, the teacher works closely with the therapist while she, as a teacher, deals with the conscious aspects.

Skill therapy is one effective means of help. Especially when the neurosis developed around a learning failure, remedial tutoring which opens the door to academic progress is very rewarding. The children are so pleased with themselves that they often want to rush pell mell into schooling, anticipating great progress overnight. The teacher, with the withdrawn, fearful, and dreamy ones brings them back to the task, encourages self-expression and participation in the activities of the classroom. It must be apparent that understanding the neurotics is a vast, complicated task, barely introduced in this cursory review.

Children with Psychotic Processes

By far the most serious of the emotionally maladjusted children are those with psychotic conditions. Fortunately the number of cases is small. How many are in the population is not known and different clinics, due to the clientele they serve and the diagnostic differences, report percentages ranging from 25 to less than 1 per cent of their intake as psychotic. But for most persons not trained in working with them, even one is too many to understand.

In most cases the psychotic child has a long history of atypical behavior extending to the earliest years. In fact, a leading psychiatrist, Kanner, has termed the early stage "infantile autism," which he suggests is a consequence of inadequate affectional tie with the mother. Gerard and Siegel emphasize that the mothers of the disturbed children overprotected the offspring in a family environment which was different in certain ways from the ordinary, especially in the underlying domination and anxiety which were present. The contrasting view, most actively espoused by Bender, holds that the cause lies in deep strata of biological functioning. The disease is seen to originate in an all-pervasive lag in maturation, including motor, intellectual, and social functioning. Added to this are anxiety reactions coming out of the attempt to adjust. Consequently, treatment includes attempts to stimulate the biological processes, including drugs, shock treatments, and educational encouragement. Also combined with this is psychotherapy to reduce the anxiety and foster adequate defenses. The literature is extensive in this area of maladjustment. The purpose here is merely to point out the range of opinion as to cause and treatment.

PSYCHOTIC BEHAVIOR The neurotic child distorts reality; the psychotic child creates his own distorted reality and lives in the distortion. Of course, no two do this in the same way. To this child, phantasy is real. The modes of handling his problem present many types of symptoms. The primary pattern may be a detachment from the world with withdrawing from social contacts, narrowing of interests, and nonresponse even to the point of immobility and refusal to eat.

Frequently a loss of identity is shown by an inability to recognize the self as distinct from the environment. For example, they may draw or write without recognizing the end of the paper, continuing on the desk as if nothing had happened. Their sexual identity may be confused, and at times they even totally lack the recognition of what they are. Others show infantile behavior, temper tantrums, extreme irritability, and aggressiveness. Another style incorporates more of a paranoid flavor, with great suspiciousness of others doing them harm through looks or poisoned food. Speech is almost always affected in some way—bizarre expressions, distorted, primitive sounds, a private language, or the absence of intelligible speech entirely. Some get hysterical at times, screaming, squealing, banging their heads, and biting themselves. A few hear voices telling them what they must do. In general, these children are without much ego structure. They appear to be overwhelmed by the environment, lost, confused, and disoriented.

EDUCATIONAL IMPLICATIONS Children with such atypical behavior are usually found in institutions, although teachers may see some with similar behavior of a lesser intensity. Detached laughter and facial and motor movements may show in milder cases. Gesturing and repetitive motions which have a symbolic meaning only to the child may be present. Frequently they move out of the field in dreamy phantasy. Change makes them anxious, since they lack orientation in time and place. They need fixed points of reference and explanations for alterations which interfere with their rigidity. Sometimes they concentrate on one task at a time to the exclusion of all others. New school processes may create great anxiety as in one child who complained about the change of rules whenever a new arithmetic lesson was given. Preoccupation with the same act over and over is noted, sometimes in stereotyped drawings, language, or maps. Their idiosyncratic language reduces communication in the classroom. Other children frequently say that the sick child is "nuts." The teacher, in working with cases of such seriousness, must be guided by the therapist. School handling should follow the design set by the clinician. Often these children will be in a special school or nursery for a long time without any visible response to the teacher. Some show evidence of learning, such as reading or speech, only after they have made therapeutic gains and feel interested in communicating what they have gained. Others have been taught some communication through the use of teaching machines. The task is to make the child as comfortable as possible and to take advantage of any normal structuring which the child can utilize. Warm and sympathetic handling is necessary to give security to the child. Regardless of biological or psychological causation, most of these children have proven a terrible burden to their parents, who have in all probability tried permissiveness, punishment, restraint, and everything else they could imagine. This added confusion has to be reversed by the teacher's consistent acceptance and the correlated therapy. Transition, changes, and new orientations require the presence of a known person to give protection. The stimulation of motor activity and reinforcement of such normal responses as can be induced are necessary. One cannot hope to speed up the processes of maturation too quickly. Mild social stimulation from peers make the small class setting useful for they often respond first to the other children. Needless to say, the completely dissociated child, even in a one-to-one relationship, will spend hours before he accomplishes anything. The remoteness of the child and the strangeness of his responses predicate more of a therapeutic understanding on the part of a teacher as a co-worker with the psychiatrist. Some make no progress under any treatment.

Conclusion

Broad patterns of childhood maladjustment have been reviewed. In a very general way the type of educational design which these children require because of their special pathologies has been suggested. This orientation to the different behavior does not constitute in any sense a definitive examination of these problems. Primarily it serves to show the directions in which the teacher's psychological insight must grow in order to construct effective educational designs. The implication that teacher and therapist must work together is plain. The questions now remain of how teaching and therapy differ and what, more specifically, is the educational process employed with emotionally and socially disturbed pupils.

4. Some Basic Considerations in the Education of Emotionally Disturbed Children

HERBERT C. QUAY

Education for the emotionally disturbed parallels education for the mentally retarded in some significant ways. Johnson's (1962) recent review of research on the efficacy of special class placement for the

SOURCE: *Exceptional Children,* XXX (September, 1963), 27–31. Reprinted by permission.

mentally handicapped cannot be easily dismissed by anyone concerned with any area of exceptionality. The sobering conclusions of this review and, more importantly, the factors that lie behind the failure of special class placement to demonstrate its worth, should be food for thought for special educators in all areas of exceptionality.

Lack of Basic Knowledge

Let us look at the possible reasons why controlled research has failed to demonstrate the efficacy of the special class. One basic reason is clear: we do not really know what the needs of the mentally retarded child are in terms of either a method or a curriculum. We really do not know what he can learn nor how best to teach it to him. We have not fully explored whether the laws of learning are different for IQ 50 than for IQ 100 for all types of learning. We do not know whether the low IQ child fails in input, output, retention, any two of these factors, or all three. As a result of the lack of basic knowledge of learning processes in the retarded, special class programs are not and cannot be clearly defined and scientifically based.

While the foregoing is certainly the basic factor mitigating against special class effectiveness, there is the added problem of pupil selection. While the 120 distinct factors of intellect proposed by Guilford (1959) seem, at best, to lack parsimony, intellective ability is clearly not unidimensional. Yet special class placement is generally made on the basis of a score on a test which probably does not measure all of even the major facets of intellect. In short, it is likely that we are not measuring and describing mental retardation as adequately as we might.

Now let us look at the situation with the emotionally disturbed. In terms of ongoing programs, education for the disturbed is far less advanced than education for the mentally handicapped. However, educators are responding both to their own and to the community's needs and are setting up classes for maladjusted children. There is concern about the problems of definition, identification, curriculum, methods, teacher training, and administrative practices. But for the most part some basic questions are being ignored in the rush to get programs underway. As yet, we do not even have any systematic knowledge of what actually is happening in the creating of programs, but what appears to be taking place leads one to conclude that it is only a matter of time until someone writes an article parallel to Johnson's on the efficacy of special class placement for the emotionally disturbed.

Classification and Placement

Classification and placement are both based primarily on an impressionistic basis. Children who do not fall under the rubric of some other area of exceptionality and who are unable to adjust to the regular class are labeled emotionally disturbed and placement is made on that basis. How good a placement procedure is this likely to turn out to be? Are all "not-otherwise-classifiable" non-adjusters emotionally disturbed? Is apparent inability to adjust to a regular class an adequate criterion for classification as disturbed? Are all disturbed children alike, of one and the same kind, behaviorally and psychologically homogeneous? The problem, always a basic one, of description and classification is involved.

We have had enough experience with behaviorally abnormal children to know that the standard psychiatric nomenclature is most often inapplicable to children. A special class made up of children all diagnosed as obsessive-compulsive would be indistinguishable on most educationally relevant variables from a class made up of children all diagnosed as phobics.

There is one thing we do know about problem-behavior children and we know this from a number of empirical research studies. There are certain recurrent, observable symptoms of problem behavior in children and these symptoms tend to cluster into two major syndromes or symptom-clusters. These have been called the acting-out or the "conduct problem" and the withdrawn or "personality problem" (Himmelweit, 1952; Becker, Peterson, Hellmer, Shoemaker and Quay, 1959; Peterson, 1961). It also appears that children with behavior disturbances can be reliably classified as belonging primarily to one group or the other and in the case of the acting-out dimension to one of three subdimensions. An important feature of this simple classification scheme is that it has, even at this early stage of our knowledge, implications for the educational process.

Current Practices

What are current practices in regard to curriculum and method? Special class programs for the emotionally disturbed seem generally to be classifiable under three major headings:

1. "Holding actions" which try to exert a minimum of achievement and performance demands while waiting either for some form of therapy to deal with the emotional disturbance or for the coming of the age at

which the child can leave school. Methods here are too varied to be describable.

2. A quasi-therapeutic program in which the educative process is seen as primarily therapeutic in its aim. The methods here are likely to be dictated by the assumptions of some theory about psychotherapy rather than any theory of learning or education.
3. The focus is on education and academic achievement rather than on therapy. However, the method still tends to be dictated more by a theory of personality than by a theory of learning. There is generally the assumption that the educative process will also foster better emotional adjustment.

While this classification may not be exhaustive, it does appear to cover the vast majority of present programs. If the primary business of the school is to educate, what is needed is a special class program designed to meet the special learning characteristics of the kinds of emotionally disturbed children contained in it. While we need much more research into both the classification schemes themselves and the principles of learning for the two kinds of maladjustment, there are at present a few guidelines available.

Educating the "Personality Problem" Child

The withdrawn or personality problem child is most likely to be anxious, either overtly or covertly. Taylor and Spence (Taylor, 1951, 1956; Spence, 1958) have presented both theory and substantiating research bearing on the relation of anxiety to learning. Basically, their theory is that anxiety facilitates the acquisition of simple conditioned responses but interferes with complex learning. That is, the anxious person fixates a simple response, particularly if he has made it from time to time before, more rapidly than a non-anxious person. At the same time, complex responses (and this includes most academic skills unless they are made simple on purpose) are acquired with more difficulty by the anxious. There are a number of ramifications of this hypothesis.

First of all, the already anxious child is quick to learn (by simple conditioning) additional fear and anxiety responses. Stimuli contiguously associated with stimuli causing fear and unpleasant emotion quickly come to have the capacity to elicit the same fear. "Guilt by association" has real meaning in this situation. Since stimulus generalization seems to be facilitated by anxiety, the anxious child's fear and avoidance overgeneralize. All of this means that unpleasant and fear-producing experiences are apt to have results quite beyond the immediate setting and such experiences should be minimized for this type of child whenever possible. Unpleasant experiences with one type of academic material quickly generalize to other types. Fear and avoidance of one teacher soon becomes fear and avoidance of many. There is, however, a positive side. The rapid acquisition of conditioned responses applies to "positive" responses as well as negative ones and these positive responses can be appropriate responses to academic problems if they are presented in such a way as to qualify as simple or to fit a conditioning paradigm.

The foregoing has certain useful implications. The early stages of special class placement for these children might well be devoted to making the academic situation and some academic materials less unpleasant. One way to do this might be to do one's best to associate the classroom, the teacher, and the learning materials with pleasant stimuli. Interest can then turn to making appropriate academic responses simple. It appears that programmed instruction may be one approach to this; complex materials are broken down into simpler sequences so that a conditioning model is approximated. Programmed instruction also seems to minimize the opportunity for wrong answers to occur. This is important because one of the basic effects of anxiety seems to be to produce wrong answers as well as right ones when there is a multiplicity of possible responses—hence anxiety hinders complex learning. For the anxious child it seems better if the right answer is the first one with which he responds; allowing the anxious child to make mistakes seems to hinder the efficiency with which he will eventually fixate the correct response.

As a by-product it is also quite likely that the de-sensitization procedures plus the experiences of academic success may also serve to reduce the anxiety of the disturbed child although this "therapy" is not the primary purpose of the educational program. It seems worthwhile to point out, however, that the current behavior therapy approach to the treatment of emotional disorders emphasizes just such deconditioning procedures and tends not to concern itself with hypothetical underlying complexes and conflicts.

Educating the "Conduct Problem" Child

The child of the "conduct problem" variety requires a different approach. There is considerable evidence to indicate that personalities of acting-out children are of three major dimensions (Peterson, Quay, and

Cameron, 1959; Peterson, Quay and Tiffany, 1961; Quay, 1964), all of which may look alike to the untrained observer because they all manifest acting-out, if not frankly delinquent behavior. One major category of conduct problem child, and the group which tends to be perhaps the most persistently troublesome, is that group of children referred to as unsocialized aggressive or psychopathic. There are really few of these youngsters, even among the legally delinquent, but their behavior can be so disconcerting and annoying if not actually dangerous that one may seem like many. The British psychologist H. J. Eysenck (1957) has theorized that these individuals are persons who are highly "extroverted" (by constitutional predisposition) and as such they learn conditioned reactions very slowly and with difficulty. The failure of these children to acquire conditioned fear and avoidance reactions does seem to provide a meaningful explanation for their persistent failure to benefit from experience in learning to hold their impulses in check. This poor conditionability, which is hypothesized to be present from the very first, has many ramifications. Consider for a moment how the average child comes to learn to respond to verbal praise and punishment; it is certainly through the process of pairing these verbal stimuli with more primary rewards and punishments. We do have experimental evidence that this psychopathic or unsocialized person fails to respond to verbal reward in the same way that others do (Johns and Quay, 1962).

What can be done educationally about these children? First of all, it appears that learning some fear and avoidance so that impulses can be controlled may be a requisite for doing anything else with them. The first step with these children may be to establish some impulse inhibition and behavioral control in the school situation. This will no doubt be a painful process to both teacher and student but it can be best accomplished by a system of definite rules for behavior with immediate rewards and punishments administered time and time again. These positive and negative reinforcers may have to be rather rudimentary in the beginning (e.g., physical restraint and isolation) but at the same time a determined effort should be made to pair them with the more verbal social reinforcers to which the child must eventually learn to respond.

Academic material, once some behavioral control has been established, should also be presented in such a way that problems and their answers are presented more repetitiously than would be the case with the ordinary child. There are suggestions that these unsocialized children tend to be "novelty seekers" (Fairweather, 1953; Petrie, McCulloch, and Kazdin, 1962) so that novel and unexpected rewards may succeed where other things fail. I have entertained the notion of teaching these children via teaching machines which provide not only the correct answer as the reinforcer but at the same time light up, ring bells, and perhaps even shoot fireworks.

The second major category of acting-out child seems to be primarily a phenomenon of the urban socially deteriorated area. This child comes from a subculture in which aggressive behavior and "conning" ability are valued and in which academic achievement and middle class behavior standards are not highly esteemed. There is a special point to be made about these children. It is probably inappropriate to consider them emotionally disturbed since in a very real sense they are only behaving in a way which is appropriate to their own world. There are currently educational programs for these children which try to show them a little of what the world is like outside the slum and at the same time try to provide them with skills which they can see as enabling them to participate in the larger world.

The third category of conduct problem children encompasses those children whose acting-out behavior seems to reflect a more or less neurotic condition; that is to say, beneath it all these children are anxious, insecure, and unhappy and actually regretful of their overt transgressions. If their acting-out tendencies are not too strong, it might be best to treat them as similar to the withdrawn child in terms of educational method, as suggested previously.

Summary

The foregoing provides only the briefest outline for program operation. It does suggest, however, that all children now called emotionally disturbed are not alike for educational purposes and should not be so considered. While we have only a rudimentary knowledge of educational approaches for the different categories of disturbed children it seems certain that a hodgepodge approach to a mixed group of maladjusted youngsters is not likely to be successful.

A final point merits consideration. In view of our sketchy knowledge about emotionally disturbed children we should not be too eager to create makeshift special classes since the disproportionate cost of such classes cannot be justified on the basis of the results they are likely to produce. If at all possible we should proceed slowly, select children carefully, group at least according to the basic withdrawal and acting-out dichotomies, and structure the special class experience as primarily educational, taking advantage of what we do know about the learning characteristics of the particular kinds of emotional disturbance.

References

EYSENCK, H. J. *The Dynamics of Anxiety and Hysteria.* New York: Praeger, 1957.

FAIRWEATHER, G. W. Serial rote learning by psychopathic, neurotic and normal criminals under three incentive conditions. Unpublished doctoral thesis, University of Illinois, 1953.

GUILFORD, J. P. "Three Faces of Intellect." *American Psychologist,* 1959, *14,* 469–479.

JOHNS, J. H., and QUAY, H. C. "The Effect of Social Reward on Verbal Conditioning in Psychopathic and Neurotic Military Offenders." *Journal of Consulting Psychology,* 1962, *26,* 217–220.

JOHNSON, G. O. "Special Education for the Mentally Handicapped—a Paradox." *Exceptional Children,* 1962, *29,* 62–69.

PETERSON, D. R. "Behavior Problems of Middle Childhood." *Journal of Consulting Psychology,* 1961, *25,* 205–209.

PETERSON, D. R., QUAY, H. C., and CAMERON, G. R. "Personality and Background Factors in Juvenile Delinquency as Inferred from Questionnaire Responses." *Journal of Consulting Psychology,* 1959, *23,* 295–399.

PETERSON, D. R., QUAY, H. C., and TIFFANY, T. L. "Personality Factors Related to Juvenile Delinquency." *Child Development,* 1961, *32,* 355–372.

PETRIE, ASENATH, MC CULLOCH, R., and KAZDIN, PHOEBE. "The Perceptual Characteristics of Juvenile Delinquents." *Journal of Nervous and Mental Disease,* 1962, *134,* 415–421.

QUAY, H. C. "Dimensions of Personality in Delinquent Boys as Inferred from the Factor Analysis of Case History Data." *Child Development,* 1964, *35,* 479–484 (b).

SPENCE, K. W. "A theory of Emotionally Based Drive (D) and Its Relation to Performance in Simple Learning Situations." *American Psychologist,* 1958, *13,* 131–141.

TAYLOR, JANET A. "The Relationship of Anxiety to the Conditioned Eyelid Response." *Journal of Experimental Psychology,* 1951, *41,* 81–92.

TAYLOR, JANET A. "Drive Theory and Manifest Anxiety." *Psychological Bulletin,* 1956, 303–321.

5. Personality Patterns of Pupils in Special Classes for the Emotionally Disturbed

HERBERT C. QUAY, WILLIAM C. MORSE, AND RICHARD L. CUTLER

Although there has been considerable interest in the kinds of children who might be considered for special class placement and in the ways these children might best be grouped, there has been no systematic investigation of the behavioral characteristics of children in the schools already defined, by whatever process, as emotionally disturbed. This paper reports the analysis of teacher ratings of problem behavior in a large group of children in special classes for the emotionally disturbed in a variety of school systems. The purpose of the research was to investigate the basic dimensions which might underlie the observed interrelationships of a representative number of deviant behavior traits.

Procedure

In the context of a much larger research effort (Morse, Cutler, and Fink, 1964), ratings of problem behavior traits of 441 children were made by 60 different teachers. The sample of classes varied widely in geographic locus and represented many different philosophies of placement and program operation. The sample was composed of approximately 80 percent boys and 20 percent girls; the mean ages were 9.4 and 9.8 years, re-

SOURCE: *Exceptional Children,* XXXII (January, 1966), 297–301. Reprinted by permission.

spectively. More complete information about the classes is provided in the earlier publication.

The problem behavior rating scale employed was first developed by Peterson (1961) and represents the most common problem behaviors of children referred to a child guidance clinic. Since its publication, the items of the scale have been subjected to a series of factor analyses on a variety of populations (Quay, 1964a; Quay and Quay, 1965; Quay, 1964). These studies have almost uniformly shown that three factorially independent dimensions account for about two-thirds of the variance of the interrelationships among the problem behaviors.

The first dimension is composed of aggressive, hostile, and contentious behavior which has been labeled, at various times, conduct disorder, unsocialized aggression, or psychopathy. The second dimension represents anxious, withdrawn, introvertive behavior and has been labeled personality problem or neuroticism. The third dimension involves preoccupation, lack of interest, sluggishness, laziness, daydreaming, and passivity. This factor generally has accounted for much less of a variance than the first two dimensions, and its meaning is less easily decided upon. The labels of inadequacy-immaturity and autism have been suggested.

While the design of this study did not permit the assessment of two rater reliability, the results of prior research have suggested that the scale can be used reliably by parents and teachers alike.

For statistical analysis, those traits rated present in at least 10 percent of the cases were intercorrelated and subjected to a principal axis factor analysis using the squared multiple correlation as the communality estimate. Factors having at least one variable with a loading of .40 or greater were then rotated to Kaiser's (1958) Varimax criterion.

Results

Rotated factor loadings are presented in Table 1. The three factors rotated accounted for 76 percent of the variance.

TABLE 1

ROTATED FACTOR LOADINGS

	Factors			
Variable	*Conduct Problem*	*Inadequacy-Immaturity*	*Personality Problem*	h^2
Defiant, disobedient	69	10	−14	50
Impertinent	68	09	−05	47

Variable	Factors: *Conduct Problem*	*Inadequacy-Immaturity*	*Personality Problem*	h^2
Uncooperative in group	65	20	07	47
Irritable	64	07	14	43
Boisterous	63	06	04	41
Show off, attention-seeking	64	00	03	41
Bullies	60	−01	03	36
Temper tantrums	59	−04	15	37
Hyperactive	59	−12	12	39
Restless	58	−12	11	36
Negative	53	24	−08	35
Irresponsible	53	38	−05	44
Swears, profane language	52	04	06	28
Destructive	53	06	07	29
Jealous	52	04	21	31
Inattentive	42	46	00	38
Tense	37	−08	39	31
Hypersensitive	32	03	57	42
Short attention span	32	32	12	22
Dislikes school	32	46	02	32
Shy	−40	27	42	40
Withdrawn	−32	40	36	39
Sluggish	−09	59	15	39
Lack of interest	14	57	06	34
Lazy	19	52	−02	31
Preoccupied	−03	51	18	29
Daydreams	−03	46	20	25
Drowsy	00	45	08	21
Reticent	03	44	31	29
Passive, suggestible	−18	30	22	17
Inferiority	11	02	64	42
Self-conscious	−09	07	60	38
Lacks self-confidence	02	02	57	33
Easily flustered	25	20	52	37
Fearful, anxious	23	09	48	29
Depressed	11	21	34	17
Clumsy	−01	18	27	11
Inability to have fun	−15	22	23	12
Aloof	−13	25	25	14
Plays with younger children	08	10	24	07
Masturbates	12	16	14	06
Headaches	10	15	12	05
Stomachaches	14	24	15	10

Decimal points omitted.

The first factor is clearly that of the conduct problem or unsocialized aggressive dimension, with the largest loadings appearing on such behaviors as defiant, impertinent, uncooperative, irritable, boisterous, etc. As noted above, the rating scale has been used in other studies; it is thus possible to compare the factors found in this research with those previously identified. Table 2 presents the variables common to both the present research and a number of the earlier studies, along with their respective factor loadings. Inspection of the pattern of loadings suggests

TABLE 2

ROTATED FACTOR LOADINGS OF COMMON VARIABLES FROM PRESENT RESEARCH AND PRIOR STUDIES

	Factors											
	8th Grade Students (Quay and Quay 1965)			*Adolescent Delinquents (Quay, 1964)*			*Preadolescent Delinquents (Quay, 1966)*			*Present Study*		
Variable	*P*	*C*	*I*	*P*	*C*	*I*	*P*	*C*	*I*	*P*	*C*	*I*
Restless	−04	70	15	14	46	37	03	44	04	11	58	−12
Attention-seeking	−08	61	19	−07	70	20	01	49	−09	03	64	00
Inability to have fun	31	−15	03	60	23	22	39	−12	10	23	−15	22
Self-conscious	54	00	−11	48	−05	39	59	−08	00	60	−09	07
Disruptive	−12	70	21	−05	77	11	00	67	15			
Feelings of inferiority	57	−07	17	47	05	29	65	06	05	64	11	02
Boisterousness	−03	60	15	−14	71	18	00	69	08	04	63	06
Preoccupation	21	−04	62	60	14	28	18	−21	48	18	−03	51
Shyness	38	−42	00	54	−28	13	59	−27	08	42	−40	27
Withdrawal	15	−18	12	67	−06	04	41	−34	27	36	−32	40
Short attention span	11	44	56	11	59	28	19	37	55	12	32	32
Lack of confidence	63	−17	22	66	12	30	57	03	22	57	02	02
Inattentive	−08	46	58	24	64	18	22	50	52	00	42	46
Easily flustered	34	14	02	55	19	46	60	21	25	52	25	20
Lack of interest	−02	−02	48	49	49	−02	29	−03	47	06	14	57
Reticence	18	−23	08				14	−04	25	31	03	44
Laziness in school	−15	22	59	20	55	00	09	24	66	−02	19	52
Irresponsibility	00	29	51	34	75	00				−05	53	38
Daydreaming	20	13	57	70	08	26	−07	41	50	20	03	46
Disobedience	00	62	22	11	74	00	−03	64	06	−14	69	10
Uncooperativeness	−07	36	25	15	74	01	−04	59	13	07	65	20
Aloofness	22	−32	20	29	−01	02	20	−30	27	25	−13	25
Passive, suggestible	14	13	38	21	47	30	28	12	27	22	−18	30
Hyperactivity	08	54	−01	03	37	53	−05	60	09	12	59	−12
Distractibility	−11	59	36	30	34	62	03	46	53			
Impertinence	07	33	11	21	62	29	−16	57	02	−05	68	09
Lethargy	02	−17	27	62	22	−05	29	−16	58	08	00	45
Nervous, jittery	35	28	−14	42	22	43	40	39	17	39	37	−08

Decimal points omitted.

a high degree of comparability across all of the analyses for the conduct problem factor. This apparent comparability was assessed by the calculation of Tucker's coefficients of factor similarity (Quay and Quay, 1965) which are presented in Table 3. As can be seen, the values are uniformly high among those factors labeled as "conduct problem."

TABLE 3

COEFFICIENTS OF FACTOR SIMILARITY FOR STUDIES OF RATINGS OF PROBLEM BEHAVIOR

		Present Study			*Eighth Grade Students*			*Adolescent Delinquents*		
		P	*C*	*I*	*P*	*C*	*I*	*P*	*C*	*I*
Eighth Grade	Personality	*.94*	−.42	−.28						
	Conduct	−.58	*.93*	−.39						
	Immaturity	−.51	.04	*.70*						
Adolescent Delinquent	Personality	*.59*	−.72	.41	*.75*	.02	.60			
	Conduct	−.83	*.85*	−.04	.00	*.84*	.72			
	Immaturity	.48	.09	−*.59*	.58	.55	*.44*			
Pre-Adolescent Delinquent	Personality	*.85*	−.66	.00	*.72*	−.09	.27	*.86*	.23	.63
	Conduct	−.54	*.92*	−.44	−.06	*.93*	.45	.27	*.87*	.48
	Immaturity	−.22	−.29	*.81*	.26	.29	*.89*	.62	.62	*.49*

Factor two, loading such variables as sluggishness, laziness, lack of interest, preoccupation, dislike for school, and inattentiveness, seems a representation of the factor identified in earlier studies as inadequacy-immaturity. It has also been suggested (Himmelweit, 1953; Peterson, Becker, Shoemaker, Luria, and Hellmer, 1961) that this factor is perhaps associated with autism or a prepsychotic condition. Unfortunately, none of the samples studied to date have contained adequate numbers of clearly autistic or frankly psychotic children to test this hypothesis. At present it seems best to consider this dimension as representing behavioral immaturity. Whether the basis is developmental or regressive remains a question for further research. The pattern of coefficients in Table 3 indicates that, despite difficulties of interpretation, this factor is comparable to those identified earlier in terms of salient variables.

Factor three, composed primarily of such behaviors as inferiority feelings, self-consciousness, lack of self-confidence, fearfulness, and depression, is clearly the dimension of personality problem or neuroticism identified in the earlier research. In this study, however, this dimension accounts for less of the variance than does inadequacy-immaturity—a reversal of the usual state of affairs. Comparability with previous studies is again indicated by Table 3.

Discussion

The results of this study indicate clearly that the behavior problems of children in a wide sampling of special public school classes for the emotionally disturbed can be understood within the three dimensional framework identified in earlier studies of ratings of problem behavior in other kinds of children. Prior research had also demonstrated that these three dimensions can be found in the analysis of both life history data (Quay, 1964b; Quay, 1964) and responses to personality questionnaires (Peterson, Quay, and Tiffany, 1961). Certainly these behavior dimensions, objectively observable and reliably rated, provide a potentially more useful way of looking at problem behavior children than does the application of psychiatric nosological labels which are of doubtful reliability even when applied to adults (Schmidt and Fonda, 1956).

The fact that, in the present group of children, the inadequacy-immaturity dimension accounted for a relatively greater proportion of the variance than has usually been the case suggests that children displaying these behavioral characteristics are perhaps more likely to find their way into special classes than are children whose behavior is more anxious and withdrawn. Whether this is due to the Wickman effect (Wickman, 1928) or whether children with immaturity characteristics are perceived as "more disturbed" or even frankly autistic by school personnel is not clear. What does seem clear is that despite a lack of overt aggression, such children are less able to function in the regular classroom than are the more neurotic children. In a later publication it is planned to report on the relationship of the scores of the children on the three factors to many of the other variables reported in the earlier monograph (Morse et al., 1964).

In other research, in addition to the dimensions reported here, there has frequently appeared a constellation of behavior traits which has been labeled subcultural or socialized delinquency. The failure of this syndrome to emerge in this study is likely due both to the fact that few items in the rating scale tap this factor, and to the fact that children representative of this syndrome are not quite so likely to be found in classes for the emotionally disturbed. As one of us has indicated elsewhere (Quay, 1963), these children are not truly emotionally disturbed and represent a quite different educational problem.

Even at this juncture it seems clear that differential programs are likely to be required to remediate both the behavioral and academic difficulties of "emotionally disturbed" children. While we can expect to find few children who are so clearly representative of a given syndrome as to be clearly one "type" or another, we nevertheless can experiment with classifying children with the three dimensional framework for the study of the effects of differential treatment methods. One of us has commented at greater length elsewhere (Quay, 1965) to the effect that present theory, however rudimentary, does suggest different ways to approach different children.

References

Himmelweit, Hilde T. A "Factorial Study of 'Children's Behavior Problems'." Cited in H. J. Eysenck, *The Structure of Human Personality*. London: Methuen, 1953. P. 88.

Kaiser, H. F. "The Varimax Criterion for Analytic Rotation in Factor Analysis." *Psychometrika,* 1958, *23,* 187–200.

Morse, W. C., Cutler, R. L., and Fink, A. H. *Public School Classes for the Emotionally Handicapped: A Research Analysis.* Washington: The Council for Exceptional Children, 1964.

Peterson, D. R. "Behavior Problems of Middle Childhood." *Journal of Consulting Psychology,* 1961, *25,* 205–209.

Peterson, D. R., Becker, W. C., Shoemaker, D. J., Luria, Zella, and Hellmer, L. A. "Child Behavior Problems and Parental Attitudes." *Child Development,* 1961, *32,* 151–162.

Peterson, D. R., Quay, H. C., and Tiffany, T. L. "Personality Factors Related to Juvenile Delinquency." *Child Development,* 1961, *32,* 355–372.

Quay, H. C. "Some Basic Considerations in the Education of Emotionally Disturbed Children. "*Exceptional Children,* 1963, *30,* 27–31.

Quay, H. C. "Personality Dimensions in Delinquent Males as Inferred from the Factor Analysis of Behavior Ratings." *Journal of Research in Crime and Delinquency,* 1964, *1,* 33–37. (a)

Quay, H. C. "Dimensions of Personality in Delinquent Boys as Inferred from the Factor Analysis of Case History Data." *Child Development,* 1964, *35,* 479–484. (b)

Quay, H. C. "Dimensions of Problem Behavior in Children and their Interactions with Approaches to Behavior Modification." Paper read at a symposium, University of Kansas, Kansas City, March, 1965.

Quay, H. C. "Personality Patterns in Preadolescent Delinquent Boys." *Educational and Psychological Measurement,* 1966, No. 1, 99–110.

QUAY, H. C. and QUAY, LORENE C. "Behavior Problems in Early Adolescence." *Child Development*, 1965, *36*, 215–220.

SCHMIDT, H. O. and FONDA, C. P. "The Reliability of Psychiatric Diagnosis: A New Look." *Journal of Abnormal and Social Psychology*, 1956, *52*, 262–267.

WICKMAN, E. K. *Children's Behavior and Teachers' Attitudes*. New York: Commonwealth Fund, 1928.

6. The Identification of Emotionally Disturbed Elementary School Children

WAYNE R. MAES

Mental health specialists have devoted many hours to identifying emotionally disturbed children in elementary schools. It is clear that individual psychological analysis is both costly and inefficient. There are not sufficient psychologists available nor sufficient funds to employ them in large enough numbers to accomplish the task of identifying the children in elementary schools who are in need of preventive or remedial mental health experiences.

Numerous efforts have been made to develop group survey techniques which could effectively and efficiently identify elementary school children in need of psychotherapeutic assistance. One of the more recent and more comprehensive of these studies was conducted by Bower, Tashnovian, and Larson (1958) in selected elementary schools in California. They collected data on pupil behavior which past research had shown to be related to emotional disturbance and which teachers could readily gather with a minimum of assistance from trained clinicians. Data were collected on 192 emotionally disturbed children and 4,871

SOURCE: *Exceptional Children*, XXXII (May, 1966), 607–9. Reprinted by permission.

children not previously identified as emotionally disturbed, all of whom were in grades four, five, or six. (The criterion of emotional disturbance was that of having been previously identified by a school clinician as emotionally disturbed.) The sources of data collected by Bower and their effectiveness in differentiating between the emotionally disturbed and normal children appear in Table 1.

TABLE 1

SOURCES OF DATA IN BOWER'S STUDY

Reading achievement (California Achievement Test) *
Arithmetic achievement (California Achievement Test) *
Intelligence (California Test of Mental Maturity—short form) *
Sociometric status (a class play) *
Teacher rating—behavior *
Teacher rating—physical *
Self-concept (thinking about yourself)
Age-grade relationship
Absences from school
Socioeconomic status of the family

* Statistically significant difference between the emotionally disturbed and normal children.

The authors suggested that the significant variables in Table 1 could profitably be used to identify emotionally disturbed children in grades four through six. A system of weighting the above variables based on the sizes of the respective critical ratios was developed. Total scores for individual pupils were derived by summing the weighted scores for the variables.

The following limitations existed in the procedures which Bower employed in analyzing the data:

1. The weights were not cross validated, and therefore they capitalized on random error, thus causing the predictability of the variables to appear spuriously high.
2. Assigning weights based upon the sizes of the critical ratios (a) does not identify suppressor variables which do not correlate with the criterion variable but which do contribute to prediction, (b) may assign too much weight to variables which are highly intercorrelated, and (c) necessitates the inclusion of each of the significant variables when a fewer number may predict just as effectively.

Using the basic techniques developed by Bower, a two phase study was conducted to determine the effect of the following on identification of emotionally disturbed children in grades four, five, and six: (a) employing a different statistical treatment of the data and (b) making additions and modifications in the data collecting instruments.

The Sample

All pupils in grades four through six in the Lansing, Michigan, public schools who had been previously diagnosed as emotionally disturbed were identified. This group was comprised of pupils who had been identified by the local school district psychological services staff and those identified by the community child guidance clinic. Each of these pupils had been identified through an intensive individual diagnostic study. Only those pupils who were thought to be sufficiently disturbed to require individual psychotherapy were considered emotionally disturbed. In this manner, 91 emotionally disturbed children were identified in grades four through six. Because the limitations of time and money obviated the study of all of the children, a random sample of 44 was selected. Insufficient data were available on four of the emotionally disturbed children so that the final sample consisted of 40 emotionally disturbed children and their 548 normal classmates in 22 different classrooms.

Phase I

Data were collected on each of the pupils in the present sample on the variables which Bower found significantly differentiated between the emotionally disturbed and normal pupils. Using Bower's method of assigning weights, a total score was derived for each child on the combined variables. A point biserial correlation was computed between these weighted scores and the dichotomous variable, emotional disturbance-normality. The correlation was .27, significantly different from zero at the .01 level. This provided a cross validated index of the prediction of Bower's weights.

The emotionally disturbed and normal groups were randomly divided in half, creating two groups of emotionally disturbed children with 20 in each group, and two groups of normal children with 274 in each group. A multiple regression analysis was computed on the significant variables in Bower's study on one of the emotionally disturbed and one of the normal groups. The variables, in decreasing order of prediction, were: teacher rating—behavior, arithmetic achievement (California Achievement Test), intelligence (California Test of Mental Maturity—short form), a class play, teacher rating—physical, and reading achievement (California Achievement Test).

The last three variables contributed negligibly to prediction of the criterion variable. Consequently, the beta weights on only the first three variables were used to derive weighted scores for the remaining two groups of 20 emotionally disturbed and 274 normal children. A point biserial correlation was computed between the derived weighted scores and the criterion variable. The correlation was .21, significantly greater than zero at the .01 level.

The point biserial correlation of .27 computed with Bower's weights on six variables was not significantly different from the correlation of .21 derived from use of three variables identified through multiple regression analysis in the study. The use of the three variables (teacher rating, arithmetic achievement, and intelligence) is preferable, because much less time is required in the collection of data, while prediction is not significantly reduced.

Phase II

Two modifications were made in the instruments used for data collection prior to this analysis. (a) Chi squares were computed on each item on the teacher rating of behavior and physical status, and only those items were included in this analysis which significantly differentiated between the emotionally disturbed and normal children. (b) A self-concept inventory, Projective Self-Concept Scale, designed for the purposes of this study, was also included in the analysis.

The emotionally disturbed and normal groups were randomly divided in half, creating two groups of emotionally disturbed children with 20 in each group, and two groups of normal children with 274 in each group. A multiple regression analysis was computed on the first group of 20 emotionally disturbed and 274 normal pupils. The variables, in decreasing order of prediction, were: teacher rating, intelligence (California Test of Mental Maturity—short form), arithmetic (California Achievement Test), and self-concept.

The last two variables made a negligible contribution to predicting the criterion variable. Beta weights on the first two variables were used in deriving weighted scores for the remaining two groups of 20 emotionally disturbed and 274 normal children. A point biserial correlation was computed between the derived weighted scores and the criterion variable. The correlation was .32, significantly greater than zero at the .01 level.

The prediction achieved with two variables (teacher rating and intelligence) is as effective as Bower achieved through use of six variables which required a great deal more time in data collection. This prediction may appear to be inflated by the circularity of the criterion measure (diagnostic study of children referred by teachers and others) and the teacher rating scale. The effect of this circularity is considerably reduced by the following: (a) Some of the emotionally disturbed children were identified by the local child guidance clinic as a result of direct referrals from parents. (b) With few exceptions, the emotionally disturbed children no longer had the teacher who had initially referred them. (c) Many pupils identified by the teachers as having emotional problems were not considered by the psychologists to be sufficiently emotionally disturbed to warrant referral for treatment, so they appear in the normal rather than the emotionally disturbed group. (d) Some of the emotionally disturbed children were referred by teachers for other than emotional reasons (e.g., intellectual or reading diagnosis).

Table 2 indicates the extent to which these two variables can assist in

TABLE 2

WEIGHTED SCORES ON TEACHER RATINGS AND INTELLIGENCE AS PREDICTORS OF EMOTIONAL DISTURBANCE

	Emotionally Disturbed		Normal	
Weighted Score	*Number*	*Percent*	*Number*	*Percent*
.1000–.3070	15	75	56	21
.0500–.0999	4	20	54	20
.0014–.0499	1	5	164	59
Total	20	100	274	100

the identification of children who are sufficiently emotionally disturbed to require treatment. If all children with a weighted score of .1000 or higher were referred for diagnostic study, 15 would be identified as emotionally disturbed, while 56 would not. Approximately one of every five children referred would be identified as sufficiently emotionally disturbed to require psychotherapy.

Reference

BOWER, E., TASHNOVIAN, P., and LARSON, C. *A Process for Early Identification of Emotionally Disturbed Children*. Sacramento: California State Department of Education, 1958.

7. How Emotionally Disturbed Children View the School

C. E. SCHORER

The purpose of this paper is to show the picture of school and teacher as it is seen by emotionally disturbed children interviewed by a psychiatrist. The data came from one-hour diagnostic interviews with 52 children. They ranged in age from five to 14 years; they included all diagnostic categories applicable to child psychiatry; and, whether spontaneously or upon inquiry, *school* almost invariably was discussed and the comments recorded in my notes of the interview. Since 46 of these 52 children made such comments, school life appears to be a subject of easier verbalization than I sometimes find the subjects of friends or family. This idea is supported by the relatively large proportion of time they were able to devote to discussing their school life—on the average at least 10 minutes out of the hour.

One is struck, in this investigation, by the remarkable contrast between the child's view of the teacher as simply an impersonal censor, and the many functions which the teacher actually assumes in referring the child to the doctor, informing the doctor, and treating the child's disorder. This gives rise to the question of whether or not the child's account of his difficulties varies with the person to whom he is talking. It has been suggested that children may not give the psychiatrist *or* the teacher a true account of their real feelings or attitudes about school and teachers. As if to support this contention, teachers seem to misjudge how emotionally disturbed children depict their school life. In presenting these findings to a convention of teachers, I first took a poll of the audience in order to discover what results they would expect. The audience correctly estimated that emotionally disturbed children feel mixed pleasure and displeasure about school, but placed much too great an emphasis on the teacher as a topic such children discuss, and similarly anticipated too

SOURCE: *Exceptional Children,* XXVII (December, 1960), 191–95. Reprinted by permission.

strongly the attitude that teachers blame children for the faults of others. Perhaps the picture is, in fact, not a stable one, but varies with the person to whom these children are talking.

The Child Views the Teacher

It is most revealing to learn what these children said and how they said it. The content of their comments may be represented in tabular form by listing the topics in order of frequency, together with the number of times the topic was discussed.

TABLE 1

CONTENT OF COMMENTS ON SCHOOL IN ORDER OF FREQUENCY OF MENTION

Topic	Frequency
Behavior difficulty	47
Academic failure	35
Academic success	35
Family	28
Teacher	27
Feeling about school	18

Illustrations of these topics include the following. "I bother the others," illustrates the first topic. "I have trouble in handwriting," exemplifies academic failure; and "Last year I was doing fine studying the violin," shows success. "I got a whipping from my mother for my report card," introduces the family into the area of school. "The teacher puts hard work on the board," brings in the teacher. "I get nervous in school," is one boy's comment about his feelings.

While this list is only a crude attempt to classify and quantify, it shows at once that the teacher has a definite place in the child patient's picture of the school, but a less frequent place than one might expect. More detail about this topic will be given in the pages that follow. First, however, let us consider what feelings about school these children express, directly or indirectly, in their psychiatric examinations.

TABLE 2

FEELINGS ABOUT SCHOOL

Feeling	Frequency
Pleasure and displeasure	12
Dislike	10
Fearful dislike	9
Guilty failure	8
Neutral	4
Pleasure	3

These categories are loose and self-explanatory. The remarkable feature is that most commonly these children report some pleasure, some pride in achievement, and some enjoyment, mixed with displeasure. Yet all except one had a serious school problem. It is probably more to one's expectation that a large number, 39, expressed some dislike, but only 10 reported pure dislike without an admixture of pleasure, fear, or guilt.

Finally, we come to the feelings these patients have about their teachers.

TABLE 3

FEELINGS ABOUT TEACHERS

Teacher doesn't understand, it's *her* fault	12
Teacher does understand, and helps	5
The trouble is my fault, but teacher is no help	4
Teacher blames me for another student's fault	3
I like teacher	2
Neutral	2

In scanning these comments it is interesting to note how few children identified their teacher by name; seldom did they distinguish them as "he" or "she" but more commonly as "the teacher"; and only two described what might be considered sketchy personal characteristics of their teachers. One child said her teacher is pretty; the other, who liked his English teacher, said, "He's a funny guy; he's my counselor." Although these patients remarkably failed to see and report about their teachers as individuals, they occasionally did recognize teachers as helpers for studies or for behavior problems, and even as personal models for a future career. A shy, ten-year-old girl, who had no use for the idea of getting married someday and having children, suggested that her ambition was "to be a nurse or a teacher and take care of sick people or children."

The Teacher as Censor

Usually, however, these children picture the teacher merely as someone to define their wrong behavior, but not their success, and to follow this with reprimand, exclusion, or other punishment. The teacher is reduced, by this representation, to a censor of bad behavior, and is not depicted as someone who imparts skill in learning and living with others. Furthermore, these children seem to be blind to the importance of the relationship between themselves and the teacher; instead, they give stress to the relationship they have with other children, or to their work in an impersonal sense. It is as if the teacher irrationally imposes rules, as if the teacher intrudes with standards felt to be foreign while the child is busy with others, or with his own activity, and says, "You are misbehaving."

As one might suppose, children who are patients commonly color this picture with the resentful "It's not fair," or the falsifying "I didn't do it." But it is surprising to discover that they most commonly rationalize without guilt by explanatory maneuvers such as saying that they were angry, or reacting to what someone else did, or just letting themselves go. In short, they see school as a sequence of understandable acts by themselves eventually opposed by the forbidding and uncomprehending teacher. A paraphrase of this attitude might be: "The teacher doesn't understand; she just says I'm bad."

Two variants of this usual picture may be briefly mentioned. One is already familiar to the reader: the child appears overtly antagonistic to the teacher for moralizing and punishing but is basically antagonistic to a parent and displaces this antagonism on to the teacher. Or the child may present a picture of himself and the teacher mutually defeating each other. A ten-year-old boy, for example, was referred by the school when he spoke of killing himself, and explained: "I was absent, and didn't take the study words home, and when I didn't know how to do the words, the teacher hit me. Then when I walked out of the room, she tried to make me come back. I told her I'd kill myself . . . Why? 'Cause I didn't like her. I thought it would worry her."

From these comments, therefore, it is inferred that emotionally disturbed children portray teachers as opposing, limiting adults, and regard themselves as the victims of control without understanding why such control is imposed on them. They seem unable to verbalize the picture of a constructive, affectionate relationship with the teachers—a relationship where teachers affectionately help children with subjects and behavior, and where pupils respond with affection by mastering the subjects and their behavior. This deficiency (as it seems to me) certainly prompts speculation. Perhaps their own internal troubles prevent them from conceiving of, or even recognizing such a relationship when it exists. Or, one wonders, could it be that some teachers, the teachers of *these* children, do give most of their energy and attention to limit-setting? Or could this picture reflect the influence of mother and father on the day of the diagnostic interview? Perhaps the parents explained to the child, "We're taking you because the teacher said you are bad." Or, finally, could this be a product of my method of interviewing?

One more intriguing point. A large number of children are able to speak of academic success without the least reference to the teacher. Again, one is prompted to wonder if this results from some unusual emphasis by the teacher, or if the teacher fails to indicate to the pupil that they both contribute to his mastery of a subject. Perhaps such a teacher over-credits the pupil by conveying the attitude, "You alone mastered arithmetic. I had nothing to do with that. But when you are bad, I alone can tell." Another likelihood is that these children learn to compartmentalize success and failure: success in studies is their sole achievement, compensating for failure in behavior as defined by the teacher.

In summary, then, the child-patient commonly speaks of misbehavior in school, or of his academic work, and often refers to the teacher in a depersonalized way as merely someone who "blames" him.

The Teacher as Referral Source

The psychiatric procedure permits a different and direct view of the teacher to develop—as a referral source, as a source of information, and as a therapist. Twenty of these 52 patients were referred by a teacher—about 40 percent. In one of the clinics where these children are examined, the school usually refers about one-half the patients, and is the party most commonly interested in the child's getting help—commoner than the family doctor, the minister, or the unaided parents. As a source of information, the teacher has unsurpassed value, since he can give a more reliable and objective report of the child, without moral tones and distortions, than can the parents or even the social worker. The teacher sometimes continues the contact with the therapist after the initial examination; I receive calls from several teachers to discuss and inquire about children originally seen by me. And the teacher may have great supportive value for parents whose children are under treatment. The mother of a child I was treating came in beaming one day, and explained by saying that her son was getting along better in school. She knew this from the teacher. No, she hadn't talked with the teacher, but on leaving her son at school she saw the teacher from afar, who signaled with her hand that all was perfect. A very small sign of support from a teacher may produce an enormous effect in the course of treatment.

From the reports made by teachers on many of these emotionally disturbed children, one has the opportunity to gain an understanding of the degree to which the teacher fathoms the children and their situation. Some teachers, in their reports, stress primarily intellectual failure. Consider AC, a pretty, shy, eight-year-old girl with blonde curls to her shoulder, her eyes fearfully averted. In spite of her timidity, she was able to say these things about school (condensed, for typographical simplicity, as if they were made consecutively without digressions): "I'm here because I'm afraid in school. My teacher is pretty. I like spelling best, arithmetic least. At home I play house and play school. We have a blackboard and I hope to get a nun's costume. I'm afraid about failing—about staying in the same grade, because then everyone would be ahead of me. When I grow up I want to be a nun and teach girls. My sisters are getting along better in school than me. My trouble is I am not so smart as average." The teacher of AC sent me a report as follows: "AC's achievement in major subjects has been retarded. There seems to be a block between the knowledge in her mind and the actual putting it on paper. At times her work improved but on the whole it has been very poor. AC can tell me orally what she knows. But the same thing she can tell me orally she cannot put on paper. AC is a very good child. She is not in the least a behavior problem. However, she tends to daydream quite often. AC does her work but shows very little interest. As I stated before, orally AC can do the work. But she *cannot* put the same thing on paper." Here the teacher, like the child, gets stuck on one point, rather narrowly concentrating on the academic problem. True, she unwittingly supplied us with even more important data—about her "goodness," her daydreaming, and her apathy.

Another teacher may stress family problems rather than academic difficulties. Consider GM, a sober, squirming, ten-year-old Hindu boy whose 65-year-old father had just died, leaving him alone with his 33-year-old mother. Of the school, he said, "I stay out late and don't get homework done. I'm best in English, and get B's and A's. I'm very slow in arithmetic, and never get to copy. Maybe that's because the class is cluttered up—everybody around me is talking. But I work very fast when I'm at home." This boy's mother attributed much of the difficulty to the teacher. "Before, he had Hitler type of teacher, who struck the children. He couldn't get along with him. He is better if built up by a concerned teacher. He had a very concerned teacher for arithmetic and so was never a behavior problem because the teacher was so concerned." In a phone conversation, this boy's teacher said, "The mother makes more of a to-do over the loss of the father than he does. She's striving for the unusual and the exceptional. He's perfectly normal but given too much indulgence. He tries to shock the mother. He was tardy almost daily. The mother is overconcerned and needs help herself. He has her buffaloed. She has very high ambition herself for him." Now here it was a struggle to get more information from the teacher about the *child;* one can see how the teacher reports primarily on the mother and her way of handling her son. This illustrates how the teacher and the mother may, perhaps without knowing it, be engaged in a feud. Rather than a purely academic person, the teacher in this instance appears as a person very much alert to, if not actually involved in, the personal power struggle between the child and the parent.

Usually, however, the teacher in reporting shows an interest in *many* aspects of the child in addition to his academic defects, and his home handling. The teacher ordinarily gives attention to the child's personal feelings, his attitudes, his probable needs and motives. An illustration is MB, an 11-year-old Negro boy referred as "the most socially maladjusted child in the school." This boy fluently detailed his school life as follows: "In school I fool around. In gym, I'm playing and talking with a boy friend. I wrote down something not nice—a bad word to a girl. They almost suspended me. I did it just to get even with the girl. She'd said I liked her. I said, no, you like Ronnie Wells. I got back at her for hitting me by writing this note." At this point the boy painstakingly drew a human figure for me—a rather puny, several times revised boy, and made up this story about the boy: "He's a boy about 10, a good boy, on his way to school; he starts playing around, the teacher catches him and makes him sit in a corner. Later he squirts ink at the girl. The teacher sent him down to the office. He did it just for the fun of it; he just gets in trouble." Then MB drew a picture of a girl, and gave another narrative about this. "She might be on her way home or to the library. She goes in, sees her friends, makes noise, and the librarian tells her to be quiet. For a little while she is, then again starts. The librarian says, 'I'll give you one last warning.' She gets her books, and is ready to leave. Before she can check the books out, the librarian says, 'Get out.' She tells her mother, and she says, 'You go right back down and apologize.'" Now *this* patient's mother, when interviewed later, could not believe that there was any problem in school. The principal, on the other hand, sent an elaborate report, in which I found this interesting remark: "MB's only interest was in reading library books. He had an intense interest in this, to the exclusion of any other possible interests." In addition, the boy's conference teacher sent around a circular letter to all the teachers, amounting to six pages, from which a few comments will be revealing: "After talking to MB and receiving promise of good behavior and more work—he promptly was in a crayon fight and causing commotion." "Continually causing trouble. Finally was sent to conference teacher with a filthy note." "I feel he must be handled with an iron hand until he feels that he is a part of the group—not one who is overlooked. Most of his trouble, I feel, stems from a broken home—no father in the home." And from the librarian: "MB is average in library; interested in reading when unable to do otherwise because he sits where I have direct supervision over his activities. I don't let him stray out of watch since he is not capable of self-direction in the library." Here the teacher emerges as a person frustrated after many, many tries, eager to help inform me, and able to recognize this boy's innocent-looking asocial behavior. In summary, from my direct contact, I conclude that the teacher may prove to be nearly everything that the emotionally disturbed child omits from his picture—someone who tries to understand and to give help. Certainly I should like to emphasize that whether the teacher's report shows the teacher's interest in the academic progress, in the mother-child tussle, or in the child's intentions and reactions, it adds a great deal to the psychiatrist's understanding.

Assuming that these findings are valid, it is hard to know exactly how to use them because of lack of comparable data. A comparison with normals must depend on questionnaires, such as are described by Fleege, Jersild, and Zulliger, rather than on psychiatric interviews, and the method of questionnaires *per se* seems likely to produce different results. Those results which are reported for normals suggest that disturbed children differ by substituting behavior difficulty for academic achievement as their main concern, and correspond to the normals in their mixed feelings about school and in their attitude that teachers don't understand children.

A comparison with other groups of emotionally disturbed children is impossible because only individual cases, analyzed to show the transfer of feelings from home to school are reported. While such individual analyses might allow us to infer and generalize an explanation for the common attitude that teachers don't understand children, a larger number of emotionally disturbed children need to be surveyed in order to demonstrate whether these findings occur generally, with all examiners, or are more specifically related to one examiner, one school system, and one population center. Another study might explore the variations in the picture of the school given by different diagnostic groups and at different ages. The alterations of the picture during outpatient or residential treatment would be of interest. At the present time, the least one can do is to offer some feedback to teachers who, after all, are real individuals and who, if for no other reason than personal curiosity, wish to know how they are pictured by their emotionally disturbed pupils.

References

1. BARON, S. "Transference and Counter Transference in the Classroom," *Psychoanal. and Psychoanal. Rev.*, 1960, *47*, 76–96.
2. FLEEGE, U. H. *Self-revelations of the Adolescent Boy*. Milwaukee, Wis.: Bruce, 1944.
3. FREUND, ANNA. *Psychoanalysis for Teachers and Parents*. New York, 1947.
4. JERSILD, A. T. *When Teachers Face Themselves*, New York, 1955.
5. JERSILD, A. T., GOLDMAN, B., & LOFTUS, J. "A Comparative Study of

the Worries of Children in Two School Situations," *J. Exp. Ed.*, 1941, *9*, 323–326.

6. KLEIN, E. "Psychoanalytic Aspects of School Problems," *Psychoanal. Study of the Child*, 1949, *3–4*, 369–390.
7. LISS, E. "Psychiatric Implications of the Failing Student," *Am. J. Ortho.*, 1949, *19*, 501–505.
8. ORTON, S. T. *Reading, Writing and Speech Problems in Children.* New York, 1937.
9. PEARSON, G. "A Survey of Learning Difficulties in Children," *Psychoanal. Study of the Child*, 1952, 7, 327–386.
10. REDL, F., & WATTENBERG, W. *Mental Hygiene in Teaching.* New York, 1951.
11. ZULLIGER, H. "Psychoanalytic Experiences in Public School Practice," *Amer. J. Ortho.*, 1940, *10*, 370–385.

8. A Hierarchy of Educational Tasks for Children with Learning Disorders

FRANK M. HEWETT

The child who fails to learn in school is communicating vital information about himself. He may be revealing his general intellectual limitations or some specific sensory or perceptual-motor handicap. He may be apprising us of the inadequacy of his previous schooling due to poor teaching methods or sporadic attendance. He also may be communicating an inability to cope with social and emotional stress which is manifest through poor concentration, comprehension, and recall in the classroom.

SOURCE: *Exceptional Children,* XXXI (December, 1964), 207–16. Reprinted by permission.

Seldom is such a child's message clearly understood and seldom is the explanation for his learning problem a simple and specific one. Constitutional, environmental, and psychological factors usually overlap, making it difficult for the educator to properly program the child according to his most basic needs.

In the search for remedial and educational guidelines, teachers have looked to the clinical psychologist, the educational psychologist, and the child psychiatrist for assistance. While these child specialists offer relevant generalizations regarding learning and behavior, their contributions are not always practical in the classroom setting. The battle strategies laid down by the military advisors in the tactical planning room may need alteration and clarification before they are useful to the field general on the front lines.

It is this gap between theory and practice that the concept of a hierarchy of educational tasks for children with learning disorders attempts to narrow. The basic assumption underlying the hierarchy holds that an effective educational program for children with learning disorders depends on the establishment of a point of meaningful contact between the teacher and the child. Such a point of contact is only possible when the child is experiencing gratification in the learning situation and the teacher is in control.

There is a wide range of types of gratification which the child may experience while learning (from a candy reward for each correct response to recognition for academic efforts by a place on the honor roll), and there are many levels of teacher control (from permissiveness in structuring to careful setting of behavioral limits and academic expectations). It is establishing this point of contact while providing appropriate student gratification and teacher control that is a crucial consideration for the teacher of children with learning problems. The normal achiever may be motivated by grades, competition with other students, and a variety of other social and intellectual rewards, but the nonachiever may be deterred from entering into the learning situation by these same factors. While normal classroom procedures may dictate that all students be held for definite academic and behavior standards, the child with a learning problem may have to be viewed within a broader educational frame of reference.

The theoretical framework to be presented in this paper has grown out of three years' experience teaching hospitalized emotionally handicapped children and adolescents with learning problems at the Neuropsychiatric Institute School (NPI) at the University of California, Los Angeles. It is the result of a felt need on the part of the staff teachers for a set of working hypotheses with which to formulate realistic goals for their complex and highly variable students.

Meaningful contact and varying degrees of student gratification and teacher control are possible on seven educational task levels. These will be discussed following a brief historical review of the concept of a hierarchy of human development and behavior.

Review of Hierarchies

Hierarchies of developmental tasks and human motives are basic to the writings of Freud (Munroe, 1955), Erickson, Havighurst, and Maslow.

Freud's psychosexual stages of development form such a hierarchy and presuppose mastery and gratification at each earlier level before an individual is free to devote his energies to succeeding stages. Thus, an individual who experiences a faulty oral stage of development may have to divert a disproportionate amount of his energies toward oral gratification during later years. In Freud's own metaphor, an army general is less likely to win a war if he must leave a number of his troops to deal with unfinished battles along the way.

Erickson (1950) and Havighurst (1952) have described developmental tasks of early and middle childhood, adolescence, and adult life. Learning a sense of trust in others, learning social and physical realities, building a wholesome attitude toward one's self, and developing a clear sense of identity are a few of the tasks to be mastered for successful ascension up the ladder of life.

Maslow (1954) has suggested that human motives arrange themselves in a hierarchy from the most basic biological needs for self-actualization. Beginning with body needs such as hunger and thirst and moving step by step through safety needs for self-preservation, love needs for approval of others, esteem needs for self-enhancement, and finally, at the top of the scale, self-actualization needs for realization of one's utmost potential, Maslow has constructed a hierarchy within which he attempts to explain all human motivation. Maslow postulates that successful achievement and satisfaction of higher level needs is dependent upon reasonable fulfillment of needs at the lower levels.

The hierarchy of educational tasks which makes up the subject matter of this paper represents an attempt to organize and formulate psychological principles of development into practical terms for the educator. Each level is concerned with the reciprocal tasks of student and teacher in the formation of a working educational relationship. In an ascending order, the hierarchy of educational tasks consists of primary, acceptance, order, exploratory, relationship, mastery, and achievement task levels.

Primary Task Level

The most primitive level on which teacher and child may interact is the primary task level. Here, the teacher's task is to provide maximum gratification and to establish contact on the student's own terms, thus laying the groundwork for future interactions in which more control and direction may be exercised. This level is generally only applicable in cases of severe learning disability where the student is inaccessible to social controls or totally resistant to learning. The child's task is minimal at the primary level. The teacher may appeal to such basic needs as a desire for candy or money rather than to more complex social needs. It is at this level that operant conditioning work with severely regressed schizophrenics and autistic children is undertaken. Lindsley (1956), Ferster (1961), Isaacs (1960), and Weiland (1961) have demonstrated that such inaccessible individuals may take note of a teacher or therapist who has a piece of candy, gum or the like, pay attention and begin to learn or re-learn appropriate behaviors in order to obtain the desired reward.

Related work starting at the primary level has been done by Slack (in a lecture to NPI Staff, 1963), who has shown how a desire for money may be an effective motivator for getting a school drop-out with serious motivation and learning problems to learn to read. Slack approached such individuals and asked them to help him evaluate a teaching machine reading program. For their efforts these boys were given a penny for each frame of the reading program. In the course of acquiring $30 and exposure to a basic reading vocabulary, many of these boys actually learned to read. More important, many manifested a new interest in school and learning and continued their formal education. Similar methods have proven successful with inmates in state prisons.

In the NPI school, a two-year educational program was recently completed with a twelve-year-old autistic boy who had never developed speech (Hewett, 1964). The goal of the program was to teach this withdrawn and unsocialized boy to read and write and thus enable him to communicate more appropriately with the environment. Candy gumdrops established the first point of contact between teacher and student. The boy paid attention and engaged in simple reading activities such as picture-word matching in order to obtain an immediate candy reward. Once this contact was established, the boy was given higher level tasks. This is an important characteristic of the hierarchy; while the teacher may initiate contact with the child on the lowest appropriate level, the eventual goal is to engage him in higher level tasks.

Acceptance Task Level

The second task level consists of acceptance tasks for both teacher and child. At this level, the teacher communicates complete acceptance of the child and attempts to establish the beginning of a relationship with him, still primarily on the child's terms. While the child may have perceived the teacher as an undifferentiated means to immediate gratification at the primary level, he now has the task of relating to the teacher as a social object. The child acknowledges the teacher's presence and responds more attentively to verbal interaction. This is only the very early stage of a genuine interpersonal relationship between teacher and child which will be the focus of a later level. At the acceptance level the teacher sets few behavioral limits and usually works on a one-to-one basis with the child. The student competes only with his own record and no grades are given. In addition, academic demands are minimal and the teacher's main goal is to make the child secure and successful in the learning situation. Toward this end a variety of activities such as playing games and taking walks may be utilized.

The child who refuses to get out of his parents' car and come into the classroom may be joined in the back seat by the teacher who initiates contact through reassurance and gradual building of an accepting relationship. At the NPI school, teachers often go on the wards and into the bedrooms of frightened withdrawn children who refuse to get out of bed and come to school. The teacher may sit on the bed next to the child and use a small projector to show him colored slides on the ceiling, or read him stories, or play simple games with him. The teacher who hopes to be successful with children who have serious learning problems and who are threatened by the prospect of further failure should be prepared to settle for the minimal but significant tasks on the acceptance level.

Order Task Level

Once the child feels accepted and is secure enough to form a limited relationship with the teacher, he is ready to be held for order tasks on the next level of the hierarchy. The teacher's task at this level is to increase her control and gradually impose structure, routine, and definite limits in the learning situation. Although academic deficiencies are still completely accepted, the student is now held for more appropriate behavior. He no longer works on his own terms and must accept certain conditions for learning. The work of Cruickshank (1961), Haring and Phillips

(1962) suggests that well structured classroom environments facilitate learning among hyperactive and distractible students with learning problems. The concept of order and routine is basic to an effective learning situation for all children but particularly important for children with learning disorders whose erratic patterns of functioning in the classroom have contributed to their failure to learn. At the order level the teacher carefully judges the child's capacity for choice, presents him with small realistically attainable units of work, and removes extraneous stimuli which are distracting in an effort to promote maximum gratification and success in the classroom.

At the NPI school, a resistant, nonconforming child who has failed to learn is often brought into the classroom for periods of ten to fifteen minutes a day. During this short period, the child's task is to function at the order level as a "student"—sit at a desk, follow simple directions and routines, and control his behavior. Longer periods are introduced as the student is able to tolerate them. During this time the child may be given certain order tasks to do such as sorting objects on the basis of size and color, puzzle making, or map coloring and labeling.

Recently a seventeen-year-old boy with a severe physical disability who had never learned to read was provided with an elaborate experiential reading program based solely on his great interest in rockets. The teacher spared no amount of effort in providing the boy with stimulating and interesting material. The boy, however, came to school when he pleased, would only work as long as he wished, and in essence set his own limits in the learning situation. Despite the ingenuity and total dedication of the teacher, the reading program was a complete failure. It was only after a staff conference during which the lack of limits and teacher control in the program were examined that a change was made. The boy was later told that an instructional program in reading was available for him but only at certain specific times. If he wanted to learn to read, he had to participate exactly as the teacher directed, otherwise he did not have to come to school. The results were surprising. The boy showed up in class regularly and began to learn to read. He worked diligently and functioned on the teacher's terms. While for some students, an experiential or exploratory program, such as the one first tried with this boy, would be successful, it was necessary in this case to engage the student in tasks at the order level before learning could take place. Exploratory educational activities, to be discussed at the next level, are more likely to be successful once the student is functioning on the order-task level.

The task of maintaining order may be over learned by the rigid and obsessive-compulsive child with a learning problem. It will be the teacher's task to direct such a child's energies from, rather than toward, more order and routine. This is another characteristic within all levels of the hierarchy. It is the teacher's task to help students who display extreme behavior to achieve a healthier balance.

Exploratory Task Level

Exploratory tasks are found on the next level of the hierarchy. Once the teacher and child have formed a beginning working relationship, they may explore the environment together. Now it is the teacher's task to introduce learning by offering the child a rich variety of multisensory experiences. The child's task is to reach out and explore the real world around him with his eyes, ears, hands, nose, and even his taste buds. It is the appeal that exploratory activities have for the child, not their appropriateness for his chronological age or grade level, that is important.

The teacher assesses the sense modalities by which the child learns best. Where sensory and perceptual motor problems exist, particular attention is paid to making the child's learning experience as reinforcing as possible. The work of Kephart (1961) and others has stressed the importance of readying a child for more complex educational tasks by special emphasis on the basic perceptual motor components of learning; these are undertaken at the exploratory level. Concrete experiences are utilized as a basis for instruction. The stimulus value and impact of all materials is enhanced and immediate feedback is provided the child following each exploratory experience. Exploratory activities such as music, simple games, imaginative play, story telling, and arts and crafts are often useful in reaching a child who is not ready for academic instruction.

The Fernald (1948) method of kinesthetic word tracing and experiential story writing as a means of teaching remedial reading and spelling is an example of an educational program organized at the exploratory level. The child is given a highly reinforcing means of word learning which provides him with visual, auditory, and kinesthetic cues. In addition he writes a daily story in class about anything of interest to him. This combination approach which reinforces reading and spelling offers an opportunity for expression of personal interest through written expression and is a highly successful approach with children with learning disorders.

An eleven-year-old catatonic schizophrenic boy in the NPI school was carried to school in a rigidly immobilized state. After several weeks he interacted and cooperated with his teacher for the first time by pushing a lever which turned on a slide projector and exposed a series of colored pictures of prehistoric animal life in front of him. The boy was motivated by a strong personal interest in prehistoric animals. A teacher of sixth grade normal children observed this boy's daily lever pushing interaction with the teacher and remarked that it was "interesting" but expressed concern because no regular sixth grade science curriculum in her school included the study of prehistoric life. Needless to say, the concept of a hierarchy of educational tasks and the necessity for establishing a point of contact with such a severely handicapped child was alien to her.

Relationship Task Level

Relationship tasks are found on the next level of the hierarchy. The teacher has the task of increasing her value as a social reinforcer and forming a genuine interpersonal relationship with the child. This implies more than mutual acceptance which was the focus of the acceptance task level, for the interpersonal relationship now becomes an important source of motivation. The child is concerned with gaining the teacher's approval and recognition. The teacher expresses more personal interest in the child and uses social approval and disapproval more freely as a means of motivation and control. It is at this level that the child's peer relationships also are of greater concern to the teacher. Students with similar interests and needs may be paired and more group instruction may be utilized.

Since the child who has failed to learn in school has often been subjected to considerable social devaluation, the tasks at this level are of particular importance. The teacher who sets realistic academic goals for the nonachiever and who helps him achieve success resulting in deserved praise and recognition will be shaping positive academic and social attitudes which may have far-reaching implications. A relationship with an adult who objectively deals with one's shortcomings while communicating respect and acceptance may be highly significant to the child with a learning disorder who has had previous faulty relationships with rejecting parents and unreasonable teachers.

A bright thirteen-year-old boy in the NPI school who was deficient in all achievement areas, particularly long division, had adopted the position that he was far too intelligent to concern himself with mundane educational matters. He was going to design a computer that would solve all mathematical problems in order to prove his genius. This boy's fear of facing the reality of his educational needs was prompted by achievement-conscious parents who would not settle for anything but an all "A" report card. The teacher devoted almost an entire semester forming a relationship with this boy. The relationship was developed while working on science experiments at the exploratory level. The turning point occurred when the boy completed a simple electrical device with the teacher's help. He found he could diagram and explain its function mathematically. The boy explained to the teacher, "This is the first thing I ever made that worked and that I really understand." From this point on, the boy talked less and less of his grandiose and unrealistic aspirations and began to work on his existing school problems.

The five previously discussed levels are essentially readiness levels for formal academic work. They have been stressed more than will be the remaining two levels because their importance may be overlooked by the teacher who views the child with a learning disorder as primarily in need of remedial academic help. Not until the child has shown the capacity to handle the lower level tasks is he seen as really ready to undertake remedial work solely on the mastery level. While remedial work may be given on any level, the emphasis will not be on academic accomplishment but on more basic educational needs as implied by the hierarchy.

Mastery Task Level

When the child is ready to deal with his academic deficiencies and concentrate on basic curriculum, mastery tasks on the next level of the hierarchy are undertaken.

The teacher's task at the mastery level is to help the student acquire essential information and understanding about the environment and to develop the intellectual and vocational skills necessary for social survival. The students learn reading, writing, and arithmetic since these skills are basic for all learning. The emphasis is on practical application of these skills to daily living. Intelligence and achievement testing are important at the mastery level. The teacher carefully assesses a given child's learning potential as well as his specific academic deficits before formulating a program on the mastery level. In addition, the use of progress tests and grading may be introduced.

Since the emotionally handicapped child with a learning disorder may have a marginal if not faulty reality orientation and limited resources for communication and social interaction, mastery skills are vitally important to him. One of the characteristics of emotionally handicapped children is that they often complete tasks on the hierarchy out of sequence. The schizophrenic child may learn to read, spell, and master number concepts while relating to the teacher on the primary level. Despite these academic gains, such a child may make no progress on the acceptance, order, exploratory, and relationship level. In the broadest sense, despite academic progress, the child is still suffering from a serious learning disorder and the teacher's goals should be set accordingly.

Achievement Task Level

Not a great deal needs to be said about achievement tasks which constitute the highest level on the hierarchy. The child who is consistently self-motivated, achieving up to his intellectual potential, eager for new learning experiences, and socially well-integrated in the classroom is functioning on the achievement level. All teachers know the joy of working with such children. These are the children who have successfully completed all the tasks described on the lower levels and who are in a position to devote their energies to learning.

Discussion

The staff teachers of the NPI school have found it useful to describe and program all students within the framework of the educational task levels on the hierarchy. The student's observed functioning level is plotted for each task shortly after his enrollment and an educational program is formulated for him. In the charting of these plans, the following considerations are made:

1. The most significant goals will be set on the lowest task levels where the student is either deficient or given to extremes. The chances that a student will be successful at a given task level are greatly increased if he is adequately functioning at all lower levels.
2. The educational program may be best instituted on a task level where the student is functioning reasonably well. This initial level may be above or below the level viewed as most in need of emphasis. Therefore, the schizophrenic overachiever may be reached initially on a purely academic and intellectual level with the more important tasks of the relationship and exploratory levels emphasized as soon as possible.
3. Once contact has been established with a student on a particular level, the teacher attempts to deal with unmet tasks on lower levels, and then to move up the hierarchy as quickly as possible.
4. Several task levels may be worked on concurrently and seldom will a teacher restrict an educational program to only one level. However, lower, unmet task levels will receive greater emphasis.

5. From time to time, students may regress in their functioning at a particular task level necessitating a reassessment of goals and a possible alteration of the educational program.

Figure 1 provides an example of the description and program of Steven, an eleven-year-old boy who had refused to go to school for more than a year prior to hospitalization. The teacher's initial observations appear in the left column and her suggestions for the educational program in the right column. In the case of Steven, the basic task for teacher and student was set at the acceptance level. The teacher was most concerned with communicating an attitude of acceptance and helping this boy feel secure in the classroom at the expense of higher level tasks. While this was her major concern, the boy was held for some level of functioning with higher tasks.

FIGURE 1

HIERARCHY OF EDUCATIONAL TASKS—STUDENT PROGRAM

Student: Steven

HIERARCHY OF EDUCATIONAL TASKS	*Description*	*Program*
	ACHIEVEMENT Not functioning at this level	
	MASTERY —Underachieving in all subjects. —Claims can't do basic addition and subtraction which he has previously demonstrated. —Will do some silent reading at approximately third grade level but has poor comprehension.	—De-emphasize academic accomplishments particularly in arithmetic and give easy third grade reading.
	RELATIONSHIP —Becomes very anxious when singled out by the teacher for praise. —Relates with other students only through provoking them to test classroom limits.	—Maintain distance both physically and interpersonally. —Respect his preference to be dealt with as member of group.
	EXPLORATORY —Demonstrates few interests. —Holds back in all activities and claims no interest in anything.	—Arrange to have science teacher let him experiment with an old projector.

FIGURE 1 (*continued*)

HIERARCHY OF EDUCATIONAL TASKS—STUDENT PROGRAM

	Description	*Program*
	—Has shown some interest in movie projector and how it works.	—Start him on a simple electrical project when he seems ready.
HIERARCHY OF EDUCATIONAL TASKS	ORDER —Overcontrolled, rigid in his behavior —Refuses to have haircut or remove his red jacket in the classroom.	—Arrange seating so he will not be next to volatile class members. —Encourage some freedom of movement. —Avoid discussion of jacket or haircut at present.
	ACCEPTANCE —Suspicious, guarded in relation to teacher. —Withdraws when teacher approches. —Asks to work in study booth alone.	*Initiate Contact Here* —Permit independent study in booth. —Give small units of work and request he bring to teacher's desk. —Approach initially in business-like but friendly manner. —Attempt to find some simple classroom chore he might do for teacher while other students working.
	PRIMARY Not functioning at this level.	

Most children with learning problems are given tasks at all levels with the possible exception of the primary and achievement levels which are not applicable in the majority of cases. Once establishing contact at the acceptance level, the teacher carefully weighed the factors of student gratification and her own control and initiated the program as described. Her educational plan was not a static one; it changed from day to day. The teacher increased her control step by step until after a six month period, she had the student functioning effectively on the mastery level. He was able to tolerate interaction with teacher and peers, explore the classroom environment more freely, and display a consistent level of performance in his class work.

It is hoped that this concept of a hierarchy of educational tasks may make psychological principles of development more meaningful to teachers and provide them with a measure of educational economy in understanding and adequately programing for children with learning disorders.

References

CRUICKSHANK, W. *A Teaching Method for Brain Injured and Hyperactive Children.* New York: Syracuse University Press, 1961.

ERICKSON, E. *Childhood and Society.* New York: W. W. Norton Company, Inc., 1950.

FERNALD, G. *Basic Techniques in Remedial School Subjects.* New York: McGraw-Hill, Inc., 1948.

FERSTER, C., and DE MEYER, M. "The Development of Performances in Autistic Children in Automatically Controlled Environments." *Journal of Chronic Diseases,* 1961, *13,* 312–345.

HARING, N., and PHILLIPS, E. *Educating Emotionally Disturbed Children.* New York: McGraw-Hill, Inc., 1962.

HAVIGHURST, R. *Developmental Tasks and Education.* New York: Longmans-Green and Company, 1952.

HEWETT, F. "Teaching Reading to an Autistic Boy Through Operant Conditioning." *The Reading Teacher,* 1964, *17,* 613–618.

ISAACS, W., THOMAS, J., and GOLDIAMOND, I. "Application of Operant Conditioning to Reinstating Verbal Behavior in Psychotics." *Journal of Speech and Hearing Disorders,* 1960, 25, 8–12.

KEPHART, N. *The Slow Learner in the Classroom.* Columbus, Ohio: Charles E. Merrill Books, Inc., 1961.

LINDSLEY, O. "Operant Conditioning Methods Applied to Research in Chronic Schizophrenia." *Psychiatric Research Reports,* 1956, 5, 118–139.

MASLOW, A. *Motivation and Personality.* New York: Harper and Brothers, 1954.

MUNROE, R. *Schools of Psychoanalytic Thought.* New York: The Dryden Press, Inc., 1955.

WEILAND, H., and RUDNICK, R. "Considerations of the Development and Treatment of Autistic Children." In Ruth S. Eissler et al. (Editors), *The Psychoanalytic Study of the Child.* Vol. 16. New York: International Universities Press, 1961.

9. Understanding the Child with School Phobia

BEATRICE LEVISON

In recent years increasing attention has been directed towards a clinical condition in children called "school phobia." The term itself refers to a state of acute anxiety about going to school. The word "phobia" suggests that the anxiety is localized, its focal point being an irrational fear of attending school. As is characteristic of phobias, the acute panic about being in school is an assumed cloak which hides the real source of anxiety. The school situation is invested with symbolic meaning and the response is not to school but to the private, though consciously unknown, meaning with which it has been endowed by the child.

The anxiety is expressed in a variety of ways. A child in a state of acute panic might turn pale, start to tremble, be unable to move or feel impelled to flight. Psychosomatic symptoms usually are associated with school phobia, even in the less acute states. The most frequent complaint is abdominal pain which may be accompanied by dizziness and vomiting. Enuresis, diarrhea, dysmenorrhea and sleep disturbances are frequent manifestations of the child's disturbance. These symptoms may disappear on days when the child is not required to go to school.

Phobia was one of the first syndromes recognized and treated by Freud in his study of hysteria. Sullivan (1953) has said that "when there is anxiety, it tends to exclude the situation that provoked it from awareness." In all types of phobias there seems to be a substitution of a real and therefore avoidable danger, for an unconscious internal and consequently unavoidable one. The individual can therefore free himself from anxiety by channeling it toward an external object or situation. In phobia, the fear is allowed to penetrate the consciousness on condition that its true nature is not revealed. The person displaces or projects the

SOURCE: *Exceptional Children,* XXVIII (April, 1962), 393–97. Reprinted by permission.

fear of his impulse or its consequences onto an external situation which becomes the symbol of his more general fears.

Johnson, Szurek, Falstein and Svendsen (1941) demonstrated that, as a phobia of childhood, school phobia was primarily a problem of separation anxiety related to an ambivalent attitude toward one or both parents. Thus, attempts to understand this condition are doomed to failure if efforts to discover the origins of the phobia are confined to investigation of the school situation itself. As in most phobic conditions, the fear has internal origins and is not explained by various features of the avoided locale. School phobia appears suddenly and dramatically in youngsters who seem to have been making a good school and life adjustment.

Truancy and School Phobia

A school phobia is very serious in our culture since the school is so large and important an area of life. A necessary distinction should be made between truancy—the reluctance to attend school—and school phobia. A study done by Talbot (1957) suggests that "school phobia is basically not a fear of school but a fear of leaving home—primarily a problem of separation from the mother. It differs from truancy in that the child has terror about being in school. He may flee school in a panic but unlike the truant, he dashes straight home to "mother." Persistent truancy is generally not of a phobic nature though it frequently is an indication of serious environmental difficulties, emotional disturbance, a deviant subculture or severe deprivation.

Even in cases of obvious phobia, a child must feel external as well as internal dangers. The onset of the phobia is generally coincident with a reality situation—an attack by bullies, a harsh teacher, school failure or illness in the home. These environmental factors serve merely to canalize and fixate an intense and pre-existing anxiety state.

Not attending school reduces anxiety and provides secondary gains. Here, too, environmental factors may be the hook in reality on which the child hangs his fears. When conflict exists between parents, the child may imagine or fear physical assault on the mother by the father, which the child by his presence feels he could prevent. Lightly made threats of abandonment by the mother for misbehavior may intensify his fear of losing her during his absence from home. A pre-school age sibling in the home frequently arouses fear of displacement in the mother's affections. The greater the child's secondary gain from his illness, the more he will delay returning to school and resist therapy.

While these environmental factors may exist at home and be the child's expressed concern, they serve only as reinforcement for the underlying conflict. Strong ambivalent feelings toward parents are always present. Fear of separation from the mother, repressed hostility toward her, resulting in fear for her welfare in his absence, and the wish to separate the mother from the father, or to dominate and control her at all times, may be some of the unconscious reasons for staying home.

The school itself, in some cases, may have only accidentally become the object of the phobia. The child may have experienced a violent attack of fear in school and, remembering this attack in its sensory context and wishing to avoid its recurrence, will avoid the site where the crucial attack occurred.

Characteristic Family Patterns

There is wide agreement by investigators about the dynamic intrafamilial and intrapsychic patterns found in studies of the family of the child with a school phobia. The patterns uncovered by Talbot (1957) in her study of 24 middle class children from small families, all treated at the Queens Center of the Bureau of Child Guidance, are characteristic.

In most instances, the family constellation was deeply inbred and a high degree of interdependence characterized the relationships between the parents, child and grandparents. There was a marked lack of interest in things outside the immediate family. Parents, children and grandparents lived an insular existence in close physical proximity to each other. Mothers and fathers were neurotically involved with their own parents, frequently giving second place to the needs of their own families. Marital adjustments tended to be on an immature level, each partner feeling neglected and resentful of the attention paid to the child by the other. There was a high incidence of preoccupation and concern with death on the part of both parents and children, with a seeming inability to differentiate between fact and fantasy. "Death" and "going away" were equated in their minds and fears expressed that their evil thoughts and wishes might be carried out during their absence. Finally, there was an intensely neurotic involvement of mother and child, each clinging to the other both physically and psychologically.

Most mothers were ambivalent in their feelings towards their offspring, with separation as difficult for the mother as for the child. Lack of consistency in dealing with their children was a prevailing pattern and contradictory handling of their children was extreme. The mothers could run the gamut from kissing to slapping within a few seconds and the children were the victims of correspondingly inconsistent standards and expectations. Confused by the unpredictable and infantile behavior of his parents and deprived of much-needed parental strength and support, practically every child in the study felt rejected.

It is small wonder, then, that in the struggle to emancipate himself from his mother, the resentment and hostility growing out of, or causing, the struggle are projected by the child to the teacher and the school where its consequences are emotionally less painful.

Role of Therapy

In past years the syndrome of school phobia often proved very refractory, frequently persisting for months and even years after the onset of treatment. This resulted in serious disruption of the child's education, hampered his social adjustment, perpetuated the distorted family relationships and provided the groundwork for severe character disturbance in later life. As a result, interest was aroused in learning more about the treatment and management of school phobia in the hope that such knowledge could facilitate preventive intervention.

Investigations begun by Waldfogel, Tessman and Hahn (1959) produced results which added new dimensions to the thinking on school phobia. Not long after they began their investigations, Waldfogel and associates discovered a striking and unexpected relation between the remission of the acute symptom and the promptness with which the treatment was begun.

Twenty-six cases of school phobia were seen in the first two years of the study. In those cases where treatment was initiated shortly after the symptom appeared, school attendance was resumed after a few weeks in most cases. If, however, treatment had been postponed for a semester or more after the onset of the phobia, the symptom continued long after treatment had begun. Also noteworthy in this study was the fact that the most seriously disturbed children and families were found in the group that was already beyond fourth and fifth grade. Although signs of trouble often had appeared earlier in the school careers of these children, they had been ignored, only to erupt in a more virulent form later on.

On the basis of these observations, an exploratory program was undertaken to identify cases of incipient school phobia in order to provide preventive help *within the school* when this was feasible. Only children demonstrating signs of widespread personality disturbance would receive more extensive therapy in a clinic setting.

Attendance at School

Earlier investigations, such as the studies done by Talbot (1957) and Klein (1945), had demonstrated that the timing of the child's return to school was of prime importance in the treatment of a school phobia. The sooner the child is gotten back to school—even if only to step inside the building—the more favorable is the prognosis.

Once a good treatment relationship is established with the child, the goal should be to return him to school at the earliest moment possible —at any level of school participation the child can tolerate. This implies a lack of rigidity on the part of both the school and the parents. Real progress for such a child might mean just sitting in the principal's office for a short period each day, or having his mother in the classroom, or participating only in art or in music.

Waldfogel and his associates enlisted the cooperation of the Newton (Massachusetts) Public Schools for their study and a field unit of the Judge Baker Guidance Center was installed in their Division of Counseling Service. A total of 36 children with symptoms of school phobia were referred to the Judge Baker field unit during its two years of operation. Of these, 16 received therapy in school, four received therapy in the clinic, five had made a spontaneous recovery when contacted and 11 received no therapy.

Every effort was made with all these children to keep them in school during the course of their treatment despite the fact that this often caused considerable distress to both children and parents. The therapist operated directly within the school, offering support to the child in the feared situation. He also worked closely with the principal and teacher with a view toward altering whatever reality factors existed which tended to aggravate the child's fears.

A follow-up study conducted one year later revealed that 14 of the 16 children who had received therapy in school were symptom-free, as were all four of those who had received therapy in the clinic. Four out of the five who had appeared to make a spontaneous recovery were still symptom-free. Only where there had been no therapeutic intervention was there a difference. Of these, only three out of the 11 remained symptom-free at the time of follow-up.

The success of this effort, though admittedly based on a small sample of the population, has implications which give the school tremendous potential for early detection and prevention of emotional disorders.

Seriousness in Adolescence

Despite the impressive amount of agreement expressed by independent observers on the etiology, dynamics and clinical course of the school phobia syndrome, the *severity* of the disturbance may differ sharply in individual cases. As noted earlier, the most severely disturbed children were found in the group that was already beyond the fourth or fifth grade. These are pre-adolescent or adolescent children for whom there is a poor prognosis.

Eisenberg (1958) states that when a school phobia occurs in adolescence it represents "a much more serious intrinsic disturbance of general adjustment." Coolidge, Miller, Tessman and Waldfogel (1960) characterize the adolescent's school phobia as "the symptomatic manifestation of a severe character disorder." In their experience it is preceded by a long history of unmet dependency needs which has seriously interfered with the development of the ego. The outbreak of the acute symptom is in reality an expression of panic in the face of adolescent pressures, usually accompanied by massive regression. Treatment must involve the parents as well as the child and, in addition to individual psychotherapy, must usually include management of all aspects of the child's environment. As in all cases of school phobia, it is desirable for the child to return to school as quickly as possible, but with these children one must be prepared to accept a longer absence. Time is needed to help them mobilize their resources and establish a clearer sense of their separate identities. Since some degree of chronic incapacitation is already involved, there is not the same urgency for getting the child back in school. If outpatient psychotherapy is unsuccessful, then separation and treatment in a residential setting may become necessary.

Role of the School

Although school phobia appears in conjunction with widely varying degrees of emotional disturbances—ranging from transient anxiety to severe character disorders—and generally requires skilled psychiatric help, what must not be lost sight of in these situations is the positive and constructive role the school can play. Lippman (1956, p. 100), discussing cases treated at the Wilder Child Guidance Clinic, states that "without cooperation from the school, treatment of school phobia is extremely difficult." A sensitive and flexible teacher can contribute immeasurably to the readjustment the school-phobic child has to make. An understanding of the underlying dynamics in such a situation coupled with a sympathetic and intelligent approach to both parent and child can hasten recovery. Rarely does the child with a school phobia voluntarily return to school and the parents are often ill-equipped to manage his return without help from both the therapist and the school.

School phobia reflects a neurotic relationship between mother and child in which *both* suffer from separation anxiety. It is in large part the mother's clinging to the child which makes severing the dependency tie so difficult for the child. Consequently, she too will grasp at straws designed to keep the child at home. The fear of retardation as a result of lost time, fear of being the object of ridicule by his peers or of return to a strict teacher—can all be rationalized by the mother, as well as the child, into valid reasons for refusal to return to school. In such situations, cooperation from the school is essential. If assurance can be given that the school will take special measures to help the child overcome his fears, some of the mother's resistance may be dissolved in the process.

By regarding these parents and children as troubled human beings in need of understanding and help, administrators and teachers within the school can render a vital and constructive service in the efforts to treat cases of school phobia.

References

COOLIDGE, J. C., MILLER, M., TESSMAN, E. and WALDFOGEL, S. "School Phobia in Adolescence: A Manifestation of Severe Character Disturbance." *Amer. J. Orthopsychiat.*, 30:599–607, 1960.

EISENBERG, L. "School Phobia: Diagnosis, Genesis and Clinical Management." *Ped. Clin. North America*, 5:645–666, 1958.

JOHNSON, A. M., FALSTEIN, E. I., SZUREK, S. A. and SVENDSEN, M. "School Phobia." *Amer. J. Orthopsychiat.*, 11:702–711, 1941.

KLEIN, E. "The Reluctance to Go to School." Vol. 1. *Psychoanalytic Study of the Child.* New York: International Universities Press, Inc., p. 263, 1945.

LIPPMAN, H. S. *Treatment of the Child in Emotional Conflict.* New York: McGraw-Hill Book Co., Inc., 1956.

SULLIVAN, H. S. *Conceptions of Modern Psychiatry.* New York: W. W. Norton Co., 1953.

TALBOT, MIRA. "Panic in School Phobia." *Amer. J. Orthopsychiat.* 286–295, 1957.

WALDFOGEL, S., TESSMAN, E. and HAHN, PAULINE B. "A Program for Early Intervention in School Phobia." *Amer. J. Orthopsychiat.* 29:324–333, 1959.

10. School Career Adjustment Patterns of Children Using Mental Health Services

JACK C. WESTMAN, BARBARA B. FERGUSON, AND RICHARD N. WOLMAN

What is the evidence that mental health screening and intervention are justified, or even possible, for nursery and early elementary school children? Although clinical experience strongly suggests the need for service at these early ages, supporting evidence is needed to confirm or contradict these impressions.

This report draws upon a previously described (1) sample of nursery school children who were followed retrospectively for seventeen years from the standpoint of their nursery school and later school adjustments. The previous report compared the nursery school adjustment of those children who did receive mental health service in later years and those children who did not. The findings disclosed that children with a low nursery school adjustment rating were more likely to show later maladjustment and use mental health services than children with high nursery school adjustment ratings.

This paper will focus on the youngsters in that larger sample who ultimately received mental health service or showed definite signs of maladjustment.

Method

Each child who used mental health service at some point during his school career was evaluated during five segments of his school career.

SOURCE: *American Journal of Orthopsychiatry* XXXVIII (July, 1968), 659–65.

Mental health service was defined as psychological, social work, or remedial therapy in the schools and private or clinic psychiatric service in the community. Rating scales based on clinical criteria were devised to evaluate each child's adjustment during nursery school, kindergarten through third grade, fourth grade through ninth grade, and tenth grade through twelfth grade (Tables 1 and 2). Data from school and community mental health records were then evaluated blindly and indepen-

TABLE 1

NURSERY SCHOOL ADJUSTMENT RATING

1. Relationships with Peers in Nursery School

Isolate, rejected, combative		Frequent and appropriate play with peers, shares and takes turn, prefers same sex in play, accepted by peers			
1	2	3	4	5	
poor		fair		good	——

2. Relationships with Nursery School Teachers

Rebellious, clinging, excessive need for attention		Cooperative, responds to limits, shows affection			
1	2	3	4	5	
poor		fair		good	——

3. Creative Use of Individual Activities

Ability to freely use play and art materials with enjoyment and self-satisfaction

1	2	3	4	5	
poor		fair		good	——

4. Signs of Behavioral Immaturity

Excessive thumb-sucking, security objects in school, enuresis, infantile speech, shyness, impulsive, separation anxiety, crying, temper tantrums

1	2	3	4	5	
many		few		none	——

5. Signs of Behavioral Eccentricity

Daydreaming, withdrawal, sneakiness, preoccupied with tale-telling, indifferent to others, lacks self-confidence, moody, silly, pseudo-mature, phobic, hair twisting, stuttering, excessive masturbation, nail biting, eating problems, soiling, somatic complaints, unhappy, tics, obsessions, compulsions, hyperkinetic syndrome

1	2	3	4	5	
many		few		none	——

6. Deviance in Family Structure

Parental death, divorce, separation, working mother, unusual number or spacing of children, prolonged parent absence, others living in home, serious illness of parent

1	2	3	4	5	
gross		minor		none	——

7. Pathological Family Relations

Idiosyncratic withdrawal of child from nursery school, maternal overprotection, parental rejection, frequent absences from school, sibling problems, parent in psychiatric treatment, open parental conflict

1	2	3	4	5	
gross		minor		none	——
				TOTAL SCORE	——

SCALE:

High adjustment	23–34
High medium adjustment	19–22
Low medium adjustment	16–18
Low adjustment	10–15

TABLE 2

SCHOOL ADJUSTMENT SCALE

1. Academic Achievement

(Comparison of school grades and individual or group IQ score)

failing		Moderate under-achievement		Appropriate achievement	
1	2	3	4	5	——

2. Relationships with Authority Figures

Overtly rebellious, excessively dependent		Control problems in classroom		Cooperative, self-reliant	
1	2	3	4	5	——

3. Apparent Neurotic Symptoms

Signs of overt anxiety, low self-esteem, unhappiness, phobias, enuresis, fearfulness of injury, sexual identification deviation

1	2	3	4	5	——
many		few		none	

4. Relationships with Peers

Isolate, rejected		Accepted by peers, capacity for giving and taking			
1	2	3	4	5	——

TABLE 2 (*continued*)

SCHOOL ADJUSTMENT SCALE

5. Participation in Extracurricular Activities

Athletics, elective offices, clubs, dramatics, music

.5	1.0	1.5	2.0	2.5	——
none		some		active	

6. Problems in Family Relationships

Reported friction between school and parents, child and parents, child and siblings

1	2	3	4	5	——
gross		minor		none	
				TOTAL SCORE	——

SCALE:

High	18–24
High medium	14.5–17.5
Low medium	11.5–14
Low	6–11

dently by three raters—a social worker, psychologist, and psychiatrist—in order to assess each child's adjustment during each of these periods and the point at which mental health service was first used. Similar information was obtained from school records on children who were identified as showing maladjustment but who did not receive mental health service.

The Sample

Of the children attending a private nursery school between 1945 and 1950, 96 were selected because they could be followed through their high school careers in the local public and private school systems. The children were predominately from middle-class socioeconomic backgrounds representing a variety of racial and religious groups and weighted toward professional and university families. Ample mental health services were available within the school systems and community during the period of the study. Of the 96, 29 received mental health service at some point during their school career, 20 did not receive mental health service but showed evidence of significant maladjustment, and 47 were not identified at any point during their school career as showing maladjustment or as receiving mental health service. This paper is concerned with the 29 who received mental health service and the 20 who did not receive mental health service but were identified as showing maladjustment.

Results

1. CHILDREN RECEIVING MENTAL HEALTH SERVICE DURING THEIR SCHOOL CAREERS Determination of the point at which treatment began with the youngsters who received mental health service revealed that over half the children received service prior to the fourth grade. As indicated in Table 3, 2 youngsters first received service in nursery school, 14 during the kindergarten through third grade level, 9 from the fourth through ninth grades, and 4 from the tenth through twelfth grades.

TABLE 3

CHILDREN RECEIVING MENTAL HEALTH SERVICE DURING THEIR SCHOOL CAREERS

	Level at Which Mental Health Service Was Instituted				
	Nursery School	*Kindergarten Through Grade 3*	*Grades 4 Through 9*	*Grades 10 Through 12*	Total
Girls	0	6	4	1	11
Boys	2	8	5	3	18
TOTAL	2	14	9	4	29

In the previously reported analysis of the total sample including both children who received and did not receive mental health service, a strong statistical correlation was found between maladjustment at the nursery school level and the use of mental health service in later years. When the nursery school adjustment ratings of only those children receiving mental health service were reviewed, the following results were noted (Table 4). The 2 youngsters receiving mental health service at the nursery school level had poor adjustment ratings. Of the 14 youngsters receiving service from the kindergarten through the third grade level, 12 received low nursery school ratings. Of the 9 receiving service from the fourth through ninth grade, 8 had low nursery school ratings. Of the 4 receiving mental health service from the tenth through twelfth grade, 4 had low nursery school ratings.

In summary, then, of the 29 youngsters receiving mental health service at some point during their school careers, 26, or 90%, showed manifest maladjustment at the nursery school level. The size of the group is

TABLE 4

CHILDREN RECEIVING MENTAL HEALTH SERVICE DURING THEIR SCHOOL CAREERS

	Level at Which Mental Health Service Was Instituted				
	Nursery School	*Kindergarten Through Grade 3*	*Grades 4 Through 9*	*Grades 10 Through 12*	Total
Low Nursery School Rating (10–18)	2	12	8	4	26
High Nursery School Rating (19–34)	0	2	1	0	3
TOTAL	2	14	9	4	29

too small to accord statistical significance to this figure, but the tendency is impressive and in accord with the previous findings.

2. CHILDREN WITH MANIFEST MALADJUSTMENT BUT NOT RECEIVING MENTAL HEALTH SERVICE When the children identified as maladjusted by the raters of the school records were examined from the point of view of when the maladjustment first became manifest, the results in Table 5 were noted. Less than half of the 20 showed maladjustment before the fourth grade: 7 showed maladjustment during the kindergarten through third grade level, 9 showed maladjustment in the fourth through ninth grades, and 4 from the tenth through twelfth grades.

TABLE 5

CHILDREN SHOWING MALADJUSTMENT BUT NOT RECEIVING MENTAL HEALTH SERVICE

	Level at Which Maladjustment Became Manifest			
	Kindergarten Through Grade 3	*Grades 4 Through 9*	*Grades 10 Through 12*	*Total*
Girls	5	4	1	10
Boys	2	5	3	10
TOTAL	7	9	4	20

When these children were examined from the point of view of the correspondence between their nursery school ratings and later maladjustment, 6 of the 7 children identified from the kindergarten through third grade had low nursery school adjustment ratings (Table 6), 8 of the 9 youngsters manifesting maladjustment from the fourth through the ninth grade had low nursery school ratings, and 1 of the 4 showing maladjustment during the high school years had a low nursery school rating. In summary, two-thirds of this group showed maladjustment at the nursery school level.

TABLE 6

CHILDREN SHOWING MALADJUSTMENT BUT NOT RECEIVING MENTAL HEALTH SERVICE

	Level at Which Maladjustment Became Manifest			
	Kindergarten Through Grade 3	*Grades 4 Through 9*	*Grades 10 Through 12*	*Total*
Low Nursery School Rating (10–18)	6	8	1	15
High Nursery School Rating (19–34)	1	1	3	5
TOTAL	7	9	4	20

3. HIGH SCHOOL FOLLOW-UP OF MALADJUSTED CHILDREN WHO RECEIVED MENTAL HEALTH SERVICE AND CHILDREN WHO DID NOT When the adjustment ratings at the tenth through twelfth grades were compared with adjustment ratings at earlier levels, 17 of the 25 children receiving mental health service showed improvement as judged by a shift from a low to a high adjustment rating (Table 7). In contrast, 3 of the 16 children showing maladjustment but not receiving mental health service were judged as improved as reflected in an upward shift to a high adjustment rating.

This group is sufficiently large to permit chi-square statistical analysis with a .01 significance level for a greater rate of improvement in those children who did than those who did not receive mental health service.

TABLE 7

HIGH SCHOOL FOLLOW-UP OF CHILDREN SHOWING MALADJUSTMENT DURING THEIR SCHOOL CAREERS

	Improved Grades 10–12 (Rating 14.5–17.5)	*Unimproved Grades 10–12 (Rating 6–14)*	*Total*
Children Receiving Mental Health Services (Prior to Grade 10)	17	8	25
Children Not Receiving Mental Health Services (Prior to Grade 10)	3	13	16
TOTAL	20	21	41

Discussion

The overall finding that 29 of 96 nursery school youngsters received mental health services at some point during their school career is striking in itself. This unusual incidence may be attributable to several factors. At the time these youngsters attended nursery school, World War II was in progress or had recently ended, leading to more instability in their homes than might otherwise have been experienced. At that time, also, youngsters with behavior problems tended to be placed in nursery school. It is likely, therefore, that the sample was biased in the direction of maladjustment. The children's families, also, were inclined to seek out and pursue mental health service if needed without the economic and cultural barriers that might be encountered in lower socioeconomic levels. Under these circumstances this study discloses that mental health services often are utilized prior to the fourth grade level.

Our data on children receiving mental health service points to the possibility that vulnerable children can be identified at the nursery school level. Of the children who were identified as maladjusted but who did not receive mental health service, one-third showed maladjustment during the first four years of elementary school. Furthermore, two-thirds of the untreated group had low ratings at the nursery school level.

This suggests that the nursery school observations were more sensitive in predicting maladjustment than those made during the early elementary years.

The size of this sample is insufficient to warrant conclusions about differences between maladjusted children who did and did not receive mental health service. Two tendencies are suggested, however. Children who were maladjusted but did not receive mental health service were somewhat more likely to show a higher nursery school adjustment rating and manifest maladjustment later in their school careers than the children receiving mental health services. This suggests that children receiving early mental health service are more obviously maladjusted than those who do not.

An important finding is that more of those maladjusted children who receive mental health service show improvement at the high school level than those who do not. This finding is attenuated by the fact that information about students is less specific at the high school level.

Implicit in the outcome of this study is the fact that the judgments made by the professional raters were drawn from the recorded observation and reactions of nursery school and later school teachers. Although they may not have felt qualified to evaluate their own data, the teachers clearly were gathering significant and meaningful information. Our results should strengthen the predictive confidence of nursery school teachers in particular.

Conclusions

1. A middle-class, professionally oriented group of families with children enrolled in nursery school during the late 1940's in a community with relatively abundant mental health resources showed a high usage of mental health services.
2. In over half the cases mental health services were instituted prior to the fourth grade.
3. Most of the children utilizing mental health service or showing evidence of maladjustment in later school years had low nursery school ratings irrespective of the time at which treatment was instituted or maladjustment became evident during their school careers.
4. More of the children showing maladjustment and receiving mental health service showed improvement at the high school level than those who showed maladjustment and did not receive mental health service.
5. The need for, and practicality of, mental health services at the early

elementary school level is supported by the evidence drawn from this study.

Reference

1. WESTMAN, J., D. RICE, and E. BERMANN. "Relationships Between Nursery School Behavior and Later School Adjustment." *Amer. J. Orthopsychiat.* 37:725–731.

II

Approaches to the Education of the Emotionally Disturbed

The selections in this Part demonstrate the wide variety of approaches being used in the education of emotionally disturbed children. Three settings have been chosen to illustrate arrangements currently in vogue: day classes in regular schools, the special school, and residential centers. Before examining these kinds of operations, we will start with three articles which provide a general orientation to the psycho-educational approach in working with disturbed children.

Although interdisciplinary clinical participation must be considered in the management of emotionally disturbed children, too little attention has been devoted to the role of the teacher. In his article, *Fenichel* (11) explains how the teacher is to play the key role in working with these children and how the psycho-educational assessment is an ongoing process of observations by the clinical staff and teacher. Fenichel stresses that a highly individualized educational program can provide opportunities for the child to experience success in his academic work, an experience that is therapeutic in itself. *Redl* (12) also focuses on the teacher in a therapeutic classroom as he examines the basic ingredients of the milieu approach. The author sees the need for all professional personnel to be sensitive to these children as individuals and to shift in their management techniques as the situation demands. This article shows that the milieu approach relies on effective person-to-person interaction.

While the *Fenichel* and *Redl* articles have focused on the teacher in the management of emotionally disturbed children, other professionals in the field have sought to provide new models for improving the effectiveness of teacher-pupil relationships. Some have felt that consultative service was needed from the practitioners if teachers of the disturbed are to translate their university education into action. Morse * has advocated an "improved learning climate" in which the individual child is helped by trained personnel acting as consultants in the school. Unique to his program has been the "school rescue operation"; here the "crisis teacher," working with other members of the educational team, prepares a program to help the disturbed child on an individual or small-group basis until he is able to return to the conventional classroom. Rather than have the school draw upon the supportive roles of consultants, *Reich*

* William C. Morse, "Public Schools and the Disturbed Child," in Peter Knoblock, ed., *Intervention Approaches in Educating Emotionally Disturbed Children* (Syracuse, N.Y.: Syracuse University Division of Special Education and Rehabilitation, 1966), pp. 113–28.

(13) sees the need for a new type of professional, the clinical educator. Recognizing that past experience has often found both clinic and school working at cross-purposes, Reich calls for a professional liaison between these two agencies and outlines ten duties of the "clinical educator" who would fill this position. To demonstrate that such a position can be used to bring clinic and school closer together, he cites his own experiences as a "clinical educator," drawing on anecdotes and case materials to show how the position can benefit all concerned. Reich's suggestion that this kind of professional be added to the clinic staff has much to commend it, and it is to be hoped that many clinics will explore the possibility.

Many attempts have been made by the public schools to provide educational experiences for emotionally disturbed children. In the section Day Classes in Regular Schools, articles 14 through 21 represent a sample of the efforts to meet the demands for special services of one kind or another.

For some time mental-health specialists have been searching for an alternative to the large mental hospital. In response to this quest the modern trend in mental health has been toward community psychiatry in which small community-type programs could be developed to serve the mentally ill. This same trend is pervading the field of child psychiatry, and communities are encouraged to survey their mental-health and educational resources to establish special school programs. In the section The Special Schools, *LaVietes et al.* (22) describe the first two years of the Godmothers' League Day Treatment Center and School in New York City, and *Cohen* (23) reports on the progress of the same center over a seven-year period in which the teacher acts as a valuable member of the treatment team that involves the four disciplines of psychiatry, psychology, teaching, and social work. *Nichtern et al.* (24) and *Fenichel et al.* (25) explain the programs in Elmont, New York, and the League School in Brooklyn, New York. The last selection in this division, *Newman* (26), describes a program for six acting-out boys in a special school at the children's research branch of the National Institute of Mental Health, Bethesda, Maryland.

Some children are so deviant and bizarre in their behavior that they are problems to themselves, to their classmates, and to school personnel. These are children whose emotional problems are so severe that continuance in the school setting is out of the question. For some of them outpatient facilities in the community, such as child guidance clinics and other psychiatrically oriented settings, have been tried and exhausted. To complicate matters, research in guidance clinics and other community agencies has demonstrated that many children can be helped only when placed in a totally planned treatment program. Needless to say, this kind of therapeutic environment is not possible as long as the child remains at home. The residential treatment center came into being to provide a round-the-clock environment that can be adapted to the changing levels of functioning of disturbed children and can also give support, control, and protection.* In selections 27 through 32, Residential Centers, the reader is introduced to the role of the teacher in residential treatment facilities. *Hewett* (27) notes that when a disturbed school-age child is placed in a psychiatric hospital, the continuation of his schooling is "indispensable to a normal and healthy adjustment." While an educational program is highly desirable, one must recognize that a traditional teacher with little knowledge and understanding of treatment goals can interfere with the child's adjustment. In addition, the hospital staff members should understand the role of the school in the total treatment process. In many instances educational programs, if they exist at all, operate in isolation from the rest of the treatment team without effective interdisciplinary communication, leading to a breakdown in the total institutional treatment program. It is important, therefore, for the reader of this section on residential facilities to work through some of the problems faced by those drawing up educational programs in a psychiatric setting. *Toussieng* (28) emphasizes the importance of the teacher as a vital part of the therapeutic process and insists that the teacher maintain his role and identity as an educator. *Huber* (29) sees the teacher as a member of the milieu team offering an individual treatment plan for each patient. *Herbert Cohen* (30) describes an academic-activity program at Hawthorne Cedar Knolls School in which social studies, mathematics, science, English, and job information were introduced in an industrial arts–general shop setting to a group of boys aged thirteen to sixteen. *Hobbs* (31) describes a departure from existing institutional arrangements under the title "Project Re-ED." At the heart of this program is the teacher-counselor, a new kind of mental-health worker, who is committed to the process of reeducation as outlined in twelve points. The reader is certain to be impressed with this systems approach as one alternative to

* The reader will find a splendid expansion of these ideas in the *Toussieng* (28) article.

existing residential centers in coping with the problem of emotional disturbance in children. In the last article, *Rubin* (32) examines the special school's contribution to the total treatment of the emotionally disturbed child at the Lafayette Clinic in Detroit, Michigan. While the long-range results of the school program are still being studied, a majority of the seriously disturbed children are back in the community and living in a family-type setting. These findings are quite promising.

11. Psycho-Educational Approaches for Seriously Disturbed Children in the Classroom

CARL FENICHEL

It is only within the past few years that attention is being paid to the education of mentally ill children diagnosed as schizophrenic, autistic, psychotic or pre-psychotic. Up to recently it was generally believed that education could do little or nothing for these children and that the medical, specifically the psychiatric, profession must assume the major or total treatment responsibility.

Except for a few small, costly, psychiatrically-supervised residential treatment centers that accepted a handful of these children, the majority of severely disturbed children ended up in state institutions or in the private and total isolation of their own homes.

Few of these mentally ill children were getting any kind of help or therapy in the community. The public schools, believing them uneducable or uncontainable, gave them "legal exemptions" or medical discharges. Clinics rejected them as untreatable. Private psychiatric treatment was much too expensive for most families. Even when parents could afford such treatment, it was the opinion of the few psychiatrists and child therapists willing and able to work with the pathology of these children that psychotherapy without the support of a total treatment program met with little or no success.

The critical scarcity of qualified and interested child therapists, the

SOURCE: *Intervention Approaches in Educating Emotionally Disturbed Children,* Peter Knoblock, ed. (Syracuse, N.Y.: Syracuse University Division of Special Education and Rehabilitation, 1966), pp. 5–18.

high cost of individual psychotherapy, and the reluctance of most parents to place their child in state hospitals or residential centers made it imperative that new therapeutic facilities and techniques be found.

In 1953 the League School [Brooklyn, N.Y.] started a new kind of treatment facility—one that attempted to keep severely disturbed children within the community by substituting the day treatment school and the home for the mental hospital.

We began with the hypothesis that behavioral changes could be achieved by the use of special educational techniques in a therapeutic setting without individual psychotherapy. This hypothesis was based on the assumption that a properly planned and highly individualized educational program with interdisciplinary clinical participation could result in social and emotional growth as well as in educational achievements.

It must be admitted that when we started 13 years ago we were very high in motivation but very short in method, program and direction. We thought we knew the kind of children we were getting when we announced that we would take only those with a psychiatric diagnosis of childhood schizophrenia or with the related syndromes of infantile autism or childhood psychosis. We said that we would not accept children who were primarily retarded or who suffered from neurological impairment.

It gradually became more and more obvious to us that our children didn't fit into the neat clinical packages we had ordered for them in our criteria for admission. Instead we found vast differences in behavior, pathology, prognosis and potential among all these children with a common psychiatric diagnosis. They ranged from the most passive and lethargic to the most impulse-ridden and hyperactive, from those who were completely infantile and helpless to those who were self-managing and independent, from the most regressed and defective to some with relatively intact intellectual functioning.

We found that very many of our children, even after their emotional disturbances were removed or reduced, continued to function on a retarded or pseudo-retarded level. Some showed the paradox of precocity or unique skills in a particular area and serious retardation in others. Many behaved as if they were brain-injured. Often we saw in the same child the co-existence and overlapping of features of childhood schizophrenia, infantile autism, retardation and neurological damage. All too often the specific diagnostic label chosen seemed to depend on the particular orientation of the agency, clinic, psychiatrist or psychologist making the diagnosis.

Over the years we have rid ourselves of the idea that sticking labels on the wide assortment and complex combination of disturbed behavior and disorders found among all our children tells us what we need to know about them. The fact is that the clinical categories in which these children are placed neither describe a specific illness nor help us prescribe a specific treatment.

The vast majority of children who come to us have all kinds of language handicaps. Many are unable to speak or to understand what is being said. At varying times and places they have been diagnosed as autistic, schizophrenic, aphasic, psychotic, brain-injured or retarded. None of these terms has much educational effectiveness or program value until —with the help of the psychiatrist, neurologist, speech pathologist, pediatric audiologist—the teacher learns more about the particular language disability or disorder.

We discovered that some of these children were unable to understand language because they were deaf and just didn't hear what was being said. Some were able to hear but were so withdrawn, distractible or self-preoccupied that they had never learned how to listen. Some were able to listen but because of a partial hearing loss could get only part of the message. Others had no hearing loss but because of a suspected central nervous system disorder had difficulty in interpreting, understanding, organizing and using the sounds, symbols and concepts that give meaning to language.

We realized that what each child needs is his own personal prescription of training and education based on a psycho-educational assessment of his unique patterns of behavior and levels of functioning. This means going beyond the medical and clinical work-ups and attempting to identify, analyze and describe each child's specific skills and strengths, disabilities and deficits, lags and limitations in the many basic areas involved in the learning process, including sensory and perceptual intactness, neuro-motor development, spatial relations, body image, visual and auditory discrimination and retention, ability to use symbols, understand language and form concepts. The assessment also includes the many observable secondary symptoms of emotional and behavioral disturbances related to the primary disorders and defects. It then prescribes for the teacher specific remedial, training and educational techniques and activities that attempt to reduce, correct or remove these disabilities, if possible, or to work around them and compensate for them if the disabilities are irremedial.

In a program such as ours where the discipline of special education plays the primary role, the clinical skills and experiences of the psychiatrist, psychologist, pediatric neurologist, speech pathologist, pediatric audiologist and social worker have little value unless and until they can be incorporated into the daily program of the child. The major role of the clinical staff at the League School is not to engage in individual psychotherapy but rather to pool their findings, skills and understanding of each child and then, with the help of the special educational supervisor and curriculum resource specialist, to translate and make all of it available in functional and meaningful form for the daily program of the teacher.

A psycho-educational assessment is never complete. It keeps on evolving as continual observations by the clinical staff and teacher confirm, challenge or raise new questions on the validity of the original findings.

The teacher's role in this ongoing assessment is often the most significant one. Unlike the periodic re-evaluations of the psychiatrist or psychologist that are usually in a one-to-one test situation, the teacher has the advantage of working with and watching the child in a multitude of daily learning and living situations. From this constant teacher-child feedback circuit may arise new insights and understanding of the child's pathology, problems and potentials. Together with the current findings of the clinical staff this should result in a more precise assessment with appropriate program revisions to meet the child's ever-changing needs.

When the League School started the field was relatively unexplored and uncharted with no substantial body of tested and recorded educational experiences to guide us. With rare exception, the few who had been working with disturbed children in child guidance clinics, residential treatment centers or in private practice assumed that childhood mental illness was psychogenic in origin. Individual psychotherapy was the treatment favored and prescribed.

Nearly every professional worker accepted the prevailing theory that "disturbed children were made disturbed by the mishandling of disturbed or inadequate parents." In his book "Love Is Not Enough," Dr. Bettelheim interprets the frantic, purposeless activity of children at his Orthogenic School as their defense against parents who prematurely forced them into pseudo-adequacy. A child who is constantly on the run and who talks incessantly is doing so, Dr. Bettelheim believes, to hide his incestuous desire for his mother behind a smokescreen of words and to prevent his father from discovering how much he hates him. Another child's perpetual motion and inadequate coordination is attributed to her need to remain a baby and her mother's need to infantilize her.

While right from the start we had said that the teacher would play the key role in working with our children, we weren't sure what that role should be. The psychoanalytic literature that dominated the field consisted of variations on a theme: "disturbed children had been traumatized by parents who had denied them their rightful pleasures and privileges of infancy." At the beginning we believed that our teachers should play a permissive and relatively unstructured "therapeutic" role that permitted their children the freedom to ventilate hostilities, aggressions and primitive drives until basic intra-psychic conflicts were "worked through" and resolved. We assumed that this was what mentally ill children with weak, fragile egos and strong, overwhelming conflicts needed.

Our children taught us otherwise. We learned that disorganized children need someone to organize their world for them. We began to recognize that disturbed children fear their own loss of control and need protection against their own impulses; that what they needed were teachers who knew how to limit as well as accept them. We learned the need for a highly organized program of education and training that could bring order, stability and direction to minds that are disorganized, unstable and unpredictable.

(This is as good a time as any for me to remind myself and you that no generalization about disturbed children holds true for all of them. Even as I tell you of the urgent need to give these children a highly organized program of limits and controls I immediately began to think of all the children I know and have known for whom this principle would not apply. There are those disturbed children who come to us, fearful, submissive and inhibited with their own built-in defense system of controls, routines and rituals. Such children often need to be stimulated and encouraged by their teacher to loosen up their rigid controls, to ventilate and release feelings that are under tight internal censorship, and to develop enough spontaneity and freedom to venture into new, unfamiliar and unstructured situations.)

There are those who attribute all of our children's problems to weak, inadequate egos and who maintain that "learning deficits could not be eliminated until the child had developed sufficient ego strength."

Now I believe it is generally agreed that by the concept "ego" is meant that part of the self, the "I," or the mind which is conscious, which is most in touch with reality, and which handles the problems of daily living. Unless one wants to invest the ego with a spiritual or mystical quality that must be treated in a metaphysical way one must recognize the absurdity of this kind of circular thinking. How can you develop sufficient ego strength in a child unless you remedy the learning and behavioral deficits which contributed to the ego deficiency in the first place?

Many will insist that sufficient ego strength can come only after inner emotional conflicts have been resolved through psychiatric intervention and individual psychotherapy. They attribute the learning and behavioral disorders of most severely disturbed children to the crippling effects of these conflicts.

We have found far too many immediate reasons for the overwhelming problems and deviant behavior of our children without having to dig and search for them in deeply buried conflicts arising from the repression of the libido, an uncontrolled Oedipal drive or parental deprivation. I strongly believe that the pathology of our children—their disorganization, withdrawal, disorientation and confusion—is more closely related to serious learning disorders and language handicaps than to the repression of traumatic childhood memories or unresolved intrapsychic conflicts.

No one will deny that emotional conflicts can and do interfere with learning and functioning. But far too often, especially with severely disturbed children like ours, we lose sight of the fact that their emotional conflicts and disturbed behavior are usually not the cause but rather the result of specific learning disabilities and deficits which in turn may be caused by some constitutional, neurological or biochemical disorder.

Even if we believed that a child's learning or behavioral difficulties had their origin in early childhood conflict, e.g., maternal rejection, incestuous desires, hostility toward father, etc., the present difficulties and deviant behavior are not only far removed and disassociated from these original causes but are creating new problems which must be met NOW.

No matter what the primary cause of a child's disturbed behavior, we believe the teacher cannot afford to wait until first causes are dug up, "worked through" and resolved. Something must be done NOW to correct the confusion, impulsivity, anxiety and other secondary symptoms that disrupt and overwhelm him today.

Many of our children are inattentive. They cannot focus on what the teacher is saying or trying to get them to do. They seem to be easily distracted by competing stimuli and find it impossible to discard or inhibit responses to the stream of competing, irrelevant stimuli that assail them. The teacher may have to devote much of her time at first toward reducing the distractibility. She may have to protect the child from excessive stimuli by a program that is carefully regulated, simplified and sharply focused. She may be able to reduce the inattentiveness by training or conditioning the child in new ways to respond to certain stimuli or situations. She may have to change the classroom setting by modifying or reducing environmental stimuli. A drug program prescribed by the psychiatrist may improve the child's ability to concentrate on relevant stimuli or tasks.

Many may question the lasting value of alleviating or correcting symptoms since "it isn't getting to the heart of the problem." They assert that all we are doing is to suppress or repress the symptoms, and that unless we uncover and eliminate the primary conflict, other symptoms will arise to replace the repressed ones. All that we would accomplish therefore is to substitute one symptom for another.

We believe that quite the reverse is true: that the removal of one symptom is more likely to facilitate the removal of other symptoms by reducing the child's overall anxiety and confusion and improving his feelings of well-being and self-esteem.

A neurological impairment may be the primary cause of a child's language disorder. However, the many problems and difficulties that the child experiences every time he tries to communicate are likely to result in a wide range of emotional and behavioral disturbances: situational stress, frustrations, temper tantrums, anxiety, withdrawal—any one of which only serves to perpetuate and intensify the language disorder far beyond the original physiological impairment. While the teacher—with the help of the neurologist, pediatric audiologist and speech therapist—works to correct or reduce the language handicap, she simultaneously tries to alleviate or eliminate the many secondary symptoms that accompany it.

Improvement in one area is likely to result in improvement in other areas. Achievement can do for the disturbed child what it does for any other human being: make him feel more self-confident and motivate him toward further achievement. Get an enuretic to stop bedwetting or a child with a reading disability to begin to read and you have achieved something therapeutic that goes far beyond the removal of a symptom or a conflict.

Can a program of special education that operates in a group setting meet the highly individualized and unique needs of severely disturbed children, each of whom comes to our school with his set of symptoms, problems and pathology?

There are children admitted to the School whose behavior and intellectual functioning are so infantile, aimless and disorganized that they need an intensive training program on an exclusively one-to-one-basis before they can begin to function meaningfully within a group. They are the very withdrawn and lethargic and the extremely restless and hyperactive children, many of whom need to be trained to sit in a chair, to make eye contact, to look, listen and attend to a simple detail or respond to a simple directive.

Their perception of the world is disoriented, vague and confused. Most of them reveal a totally inadequate comprehension of space, size, shape and sequence and are unable to cope successfully with the symbols and concepts of language and learning.

In this individualized training program the teacher will discover whether the child is ready or has the capacity for learning anything more complex than a conditioned response. Some of these children seem unable to understand or follow anything beyond the most obvious and concrete.

The teacher's communications must be free of all excess verbiage so that the child can grasp essential clues. All directives and questions must be given simply, slowly and clearly. Major emphasis may have to be on simple tasks and activities that will help bring the child's behavior under some control.

Getting a helpless child to work at the daily tasks of self-care: learning to put on and take off his clothes, tie his shoelace, wash his hands, toilet himself, use a spoon, etc.—has many educational and therapeutic implications beyond helping him to take care of basic needs and become self-managing. By involving a child in some of the essential demands and realities of daily living we are taking him out of his own preoccupation with self. We are helping him develop manipulative skills that may facilitate other more advanced skills and activities. The child's mastery of any of these simple tasks will often increase his feelings of adequacy and self-control.

Through well-planned daily programming and procedures with consistency of purpose and direction many of these children begin to have some understanding of what is expected of them. Increased demands and expectations are made upon each child as he progresses. Gradually most of them are able to acquire all the self-managing skills and to perform other tasks and activities that bring their behavior under some stimulus control by the teacher.

Once a child begins to recognize and accept some teacher control, we believe he can benefit more from a group than from an individual setting. With so many of these isolated and withdrawn children a one-to-one relationship serves only to feed their very pathology and need to cling to a dependency figure that each child wants all to himself.

When they first come into a group setting most of our children are isolates who seem to be totally indifferent or oblivious to the presence and activities of other children. Their inability to communicate, as well as their failure to understand social stimuli and to pick up adequate clues for understanding social procedures and group situations make it much too confusing or too threatening for them to participate in group activities—even if they wanted to. The few who try to initiate contact with others don't seem to know how or where to begin.

The individual and group learning experiences of the child and his relationships with his teacher are the basic instruments of our program. To be effective, such programming and relationships require one teacher for every three children. Often a child may need one teacher all to himself for intervals during the day. We are not suggesting that three children to one teacher is the magic or maximum ratio. So much will depend on the severity of the pathology of the children and on the skills, resources and capacities of the teacher.

Much thoughtful planning goes into the process and criteria for grouping. We never forget that it is children and not numbers that we are grouping. A child's impact on the group and the impact of the group on that child must be carefully considered. We must therefore assess each child's specific needs, pathology, management problems and levels of intellectual and social functioning.

Although we have no scientific formula for effective grouping of deeply disturbed children we do try to avoid placing within the same group any two children whose problems and pathology might be intensified or contaminated by their mutual presence and interaction. In order to have effective group activities we try not to have too wide a spread in the intellectual and social functioning of the individual children within a group. At the same time, we try to avoid placement of children with similar management problems within the same group: a group of three non-toilet trained children with one teacher could create obvious management problems for that teacher; a group of *all* hyperactive, *all* withdrawn or *all* non-verbal children would not make for balanced group interaction.

So many of the major problems of severely disturbed children are problems in interpersonal relationships and group living. In teacher-planned and directed group activities and interaction, these children can and often do help each other develop the capacities to work and play and live together—something they must achieve if they are to remain and function within the community. This kind of learning can only take place in a group setting. Social relationships are lived—not taught.

While an educational program for disturbed children within a group setting will inevitably create problems (that can be avoided only by having each of these children living and learning in a vacuum of isolation) the group process and the group setting can be utilized by the teacher to reduce or correct inappropriate and unacceptable behavior. I have seen many omnipotent and domineering children gradually learn to accede to the wishes and needs of formerly submissive children who, in the give and take of living together, and with the support of their teacher, have become more self-assertive.

In the group setting at meal time, rest time, play time and work time, our children learn that certain procedures and regulations are not only fair but essential for group living; they learn to wait their turn, to ask for—and not grab, to share, to postpone, to comply as well as to assert. It is in the process of group living that many of our children begin to recognize and respect the presence, needs and rights of others as well as of themselves.

The classroom curriculum, atmosphere, grouping, scheduling, regulations and routines, and how they are handled by the teacher, all have implications and potentials for positive learning and socializing experiences that can induce change, adjustment and growth.

The educational and therapeutic value of the daily program will depend on how effectively the teacher employs individual tutoring and remediation based on an ongoing assessment of each child's learning and behavioral problems and deficits, and on how well she can integrate each child's individual skills, interests and needs into the programming and group processes of the classroom curriculum.

The curriculum consists of reality oriented, living-playing-learning experiences and activities that offer continuity, stability, security and a sense of achievement. Whenever possible it will utilize many of the educational techniques and material used with normal children in the preschool, kindergarten and elementary school classes. Where appropriate, many of the remediation techniques successfully used in classes for the retarded, visual and auditory handicapped, perceptually impaired and the aphasic are incorporated into the program.

Until we know more about the causes and the possible cures of childhood mental illness the most we can hope to do for these children is to correct, reduce or eliminate their learning disabilities, disorganized behavior and emotional disturbances.

While every effort is made to restore or correct the primary disability or disorder we realize that very often this is impossible. We are dealing with many elusive unknowns and with many knowns that we cannot correct. We must therefore select from the wide range of a child's deviant and disruptive behavior those symptoms and disabilities which we can identify, remedy or correct, partially or completely.

Our primary aim is to lessen the anxiety, withdrawal and confusion of the child and to stimulate maturation by helping him cope more effectively with inner needs and tensions and with life situations. This is done by presenting new learning situations and experiences aimed at correcting and gradually replacing inadequate habits and patterns of behavior with more appropriate and effective ones.

The teacher never attempts to uncover or interpret unconscious material in order to "make the unconscious conscious" but tries to build up socially acceptable defenses against those drives and impulses which are so threatening and disorganizing to the child. She tries to fill the gaps and discontinuities in a child's development which if left unfilled will impede future learning and social growth.

It has taken a long time for many child therapists and authorities in the field of early childhood education to discover that a child can derive pleasure not only by satisfying the primitive impulses of the id but by developing an ego that can control these impulses and that can function autonomously and effectively within the realm of reality. It is becoming quite evident that most disturbed children not only can find satisfaction by assuming responsibilities, following directives, completing difficult tasks and mastering new skills—but that they grow and thrive in the process.

Many of our children have never assimilated the pre-academic skills, experiences, and concepts that are essential for reading readiness, arithmetic and other academic work. As the child begins to feel more comfortable with his teacher and his surroundings he is encouraged to approach and explore more of the world. A wide variety of planned experiences, inside and outside the school may help to enrich, enliven and expand the interests and background of the child preparatory to academic work.

On the other hand there are those withdrawn children with meager and peripheral contact with the world who seem to be more comfortable with the symbols of words or numbers than with people or objects. In such cases, preoccupations with reading or with numbers as a means of escape from the world of people and things can often be used to initiate contact, encourage communication and expand interest in other spheres of activity.

All academic work must be highly personalized and timed to fit the interests, needs, preoccupations and life experiences of each child. The very pathology of a child can often be used very successfully as the basis for beginning an academic program.

The teaching process attempts to modify behavior and growth within an interpersonal relationship. In relating to a teacher, children are reacting not only to the teacher's methods but to her "manner"—her total personality. Much of the success of any teacher will depend on many intangibles such as sensitivity, spontaneity and empathic qualities which cannot be measured.

Each teacher brings into the classroom her own unique style of work as well as her own standards, values and needs. She, in turn, must try to understand the unique style and process by which each child learns. She must develop sufficient self-awareness to recognize if her own values, needs and style of work are furthering or interfering with the program and needs of her children.

A child who can identify with his teacher and gain satisfaction from this relationship is more likely to be motivated to learn, to change and to grow. The relationship however must offer more than the radiance of "love, understanding and acceptance." It must not be used to make the child dependent on his teacher but to help him become a less disorganized and more autonomous human being.

A professional relationship has little meaning unless it has professional purpose. In reacting to the educational and social needs of her children, the teacher's role is an active, directive, comprehensive and diversified one: she *relates* while she instructs, suggests, sustains, informs, corrects, clarifies, protects, modifies, calms, supports, limits, stimulates, reassures, intervenes, encourages and guides.

The teacher will be constantly challenged and, unfortunately, often frustrated by the many serious obstacles and handicapping factors which these children bring to the learning situation: low frustration tolerance, self-preoccupation, short attention span, impulsivity, perseveration, language handicaps, reading disabilities, disorganized thinking and a wide assortment of disruptive, disturbed and disturbing behavior.

The teacher must provide purposed structure and definition for every activity. At the same time, because of the lack of flexibility of most disturbed children, she must often bring increased flexibility to her classroom procedures and program. She must be sensitive and alert enough to stop an activity before it becomes bogged down by inattention, disinterest, frustration or failure. While she must live with the failure and frustration of many of her efforts, as well as her children's, she must, wherever possible, try to build some measure of success—no matter how small—into every individual and group activity.

We have found that in working with seriously disturbed children the differentiation often made between education and therapy becomes largely a semantic one. A teacher who fosters self-discipline, emotional growth and more effective functioning is doing something therapeutic. Any educational process that helps to correct or reduce a child's distorted perceptions, disturbed behavior and disordered thinking, and that results in greater mastery of self and one's surroundings is certainly a therapeutic process.

Whether we call it education, re-education, counseling, guidance, remediation, conditioning, rehabilitation—any process that helps a child lose some of his feelings of helplessness and that, to a greater or lesser extent, helps him attain greater mastery of self and life situations is therapy.

A disturbed child's self-image, like that of any other child, is enhanced by experiencing success and diminished by frequent failure. It is imperative therefore, therapeutically and educationally, that we organize a highly individualized program of teaching and a learning procedure and pace for each child to meet his own capacities and needs.

As yet there is very little solid evidence based on statistical studies or controlled research to measure the value of any special educational program.

Nearly everyone who works with children—psychiatrists, psychologists, social workers, teachers—finds it easy to attribute any improvement that takes place to something they did. I am sure that we—who have an intellectual and emotional investment in our children—suffer from some of this same professional vanity.

The truth is that we really aren't sure how much of the improvement any of our children make is the result of the philosophy or program of the League School, the impact of a gifted teacher, the tranquilizing magic of a drug, parental influences and life situations outside the classroom, or a child's own wish and will to be helped.

We do believe however that the discipline of special education can help reshape the chaotic world of a mentally ill child into something more sensible and less threatening. We believe, too, that the teacher who helps promote the highest potential and achievement of a child, does strengthen that child's feelings of adequacy, well-being and self-esteem. Can any other procedure or human effort be more therapeutic than this?

12. The Concept of a "Therapeutic Milieu"

FRITZ REDL

If you are not directly involved in running a psychiatric children's hospital or a residential treatment center of some sort, you may be tempted to skip the following pages, for isn't milieu therapy a rather specialized business, quite remote from the usual channels of child therapy, to say nothing of normal school and family life?

My suggestion: Please don't. For the issues of just what constitutes a supportive life experience for a child, of what we should look for in order to make a realistic assessment of what his "life space" holds, require exactly the types of thought and conceptualization that have been applied here to the residential-treatment milieu. With increasing emphasis on the need to help others help kids, to design school life and community experiences in such a way as to support "mental health," the

SOURCE: Fritz Redl, *When We Deal with Children* (New York: The Free Press, 1966), pp. 68–94. Reprinted with permission of The Macmillan Company.

adult's sensitivity to what constitutes powerful "environmental givens" in a child's life has increased in importance way beyond the specialized field.

Now, the issues used in this article in order to open up the concept of "therapeutic impact of milieu ingredients" have admittedly been taken from the experiential framework of psychiatric-treatment institutions. The implications of those issues, however, reach far beyond that. It might pay, as it has done in physical medicine, to learn from the problems that emerge in the treatment of the sick what needs to be known in order to plan the life of the healthy.

Speculations about the therapeutic value of the "milieu" in which our patients live are neither so new nor so revolutionary as the enthusiasts, as well as the detractors, of "milieu therapy" occasionally want them to appear. If I may risk shocking you so early in the game, the most extreme degree of "holy respect" for the tremendous impact that even the "little things" in an environment can have is represented in the original description of the conditions for a Freudian psychoanalytic hour. The ritual of interaction between patient and therapist is certainly sharply circumscribed. Even conditions like the horizontal body posture and geographical placement of the analyst's chair are considered important. Of course, the "basic rule" must be strictly adhered to; there should be no noises from the analyst's children coming through from the next room, and one should worry about whether or not patients might meet one another on the way out or in. The idea that months of solid work even by the greatest genius of transference manipulation might be endangered if doctor and patient should happen to meet at the Austrian equivalent of a cocktail party, instead of in the usual office terrain, is certainly impressive evidence of the great impact classical psychoanalysis has ascribed to factors like time, space, and other "external givens."

If you now want to argue with me by reminding me that all this is true only for the duration of the fifty-minute hour and that other "milieu" factors in the patient's wider circle of life have not been deemed so relevant, then I might concede that point. But even so, I should like to remind you that we have always had a holy respect for two sets of "milieu" factors, at least in child analysis: We have always lived in the terror that the parents or teachers of our child patients might do things to them that would be so traumatic that we could, of course, not analyze them while it was all going on; and we have insisted that we cannot touch a case unless we can get the child out of the terrain of parental sex life and into a bed of his own or unless the parents stop some of the more extreme forms of punitive suppression at once. These are only a few of the illustrations we could think of. You will find a much more impressive list of "milieu variables" that certainly need to be influenced by the therapist in Anna Freud's classic *Introduction to the Technique of Child Analysis,* though not under that heading, of course.

The other case in point of my argument that even classical psychoanalysis has not neglected concern with "milieu" influences as much as it is supposed to have relates to our evaluation of failure and success. At least in our informal appraisals, I have time and again observed how easily we ascribe the breakdown of a child analysis to the "negative factors in the youngster's environment," and I have found in myself an inclination to do the same with the other fellow's successes. If my colleague seems to have presented an unusual therapeutic "breakthrough," I find the temptation strong to look for the good luck he had with all the supportive factors that were present in his case and that, to my narcissism, seem to explain his success much better than the technical argument he has put forth.

Now, seriously, if we secretly allow "milieu particles" to weigh so strongly that they can make and break even the most skillfully developed emotional therapy bridges between patient and doctor, hadn't we better look into this question some more?

The fortunate fact that the answer to this question has, historically, been an enthusiastic "yes," however, has started us off in another problem direction. As more and more of us become impressed by more and more "factors" that in some way or other can be subsumed under the term "milieu," the word has assumed such a variety of connotations that scientific communication has been overstimulated and at the same time blocked in its development toward precision.

Because avoiding the traps of early concept confusion is an important prelude to a more rigid examination of meanings and their appropriate scope, we might allow ourselves the luxury of at least a short list of "dangers we ought to watch out for from now on," provided we keep it in telegram style, so as not to take too much attention from the major theme. As space for argument is dear, I shall be presumptuous enough to confront you simply with my personal conclusions and to offer them as warning posts, without further apology.

Traps for the Milieu Concept

First, the cry for *the* therapeutic milieu as a general slogan is futile, and in this wide formulation the term doesn't mean a thing. No milieu is "good" or "bad" in itself—it all depends. And it depends on more factors than I want to list, though some of them will turn up as we go along.

Second, it won't do to use our own philosophical, ethical, or political convictions or our taste buds, in order to find out what really has or has not "therapeutic effects." Even the most respectable clinical discussions around this theme drift all too easily into A's trying to convince B that his setup is too "autocratic" or that what he called "democratic" group management isn't really good for those youngsters. Whether or not a ward should have rules, how many, and which must not lead to an argument between those who like rules and those who don't; I have seen many a scientific discussion end up in the same personal taste-bud battle that one otherwise finds acceptable only when people talk about religions or brands of cars.

Third, even a concept of "total milieu therapy" does not imply that all aspects of a given milieu are equally relevant in all moments in clinical life. Every game, for instance, has some kind of "social structure" and, as part of it, some kind of "pecking order," which determines the power positions of the players for the duration of the game. Whether or not the specific pecking order of the game I let them play today had anything to do with the fact that it blew up in my face after five minutes is a question that can be answered only in empirical terms. I know of cases in which the pecking order was clearly it; I had to look no further. I know of others in which it was of no clinical relevance at the time. The boys blew up because they got too scared playing hide-and-seek with flashlights in the dark. In short, the scientific establishment of a given milieu aspect as a theoretically valid and important one does not substitute for the need for diagnosis on the spot. Such diagnosis alone can differentiate between potential milieu impacts and actual ones in each case.

Fourth, the idea of the "modern" and therefore social-science-conscious psychiatrist that he has to sell out to the sociologist if he wants to have his "ward milieu" studied properly is the bunk. Of course, any thoughtful appraisal of a hospital milieu contains many variables that the mother discipline of a given psychiatrist may never have dreamed of. On the other hand, the thing that counts is not only the description of a variable but also the assessment of the potential impact on the treatment process of a given group of patients. That is basically a clinical matter, and it remains the clinician's task. The discipline that merges social science with clinical criteria in a balanced way still has to be invented. There is no short cut to it either by psychiatry's stealing particles of social-science concepts or by selling out its own domain to the social scientists.

Fifth, the frequently voiced expectation that the discovery of what "milieu" one needs would automatically make it easy to produce that style of milieu in a given place is downright naïve. An instrumentology for the creation of "ward atmosphere," of "clinically correct policies of behavioral intervention," and so forth has yet to be created, and it will cost blood and sweat to get it. The idea that all it takes to have a "good treatment milieu" is for a milieu-convinced ward boss to make his nurses feel comfortable with him and to hold a few gripe sessions between patients and staff is a daydream, the simplicity of which we can no longer afford.

"Therapeutic"—In What Respect?

The worst trap that explorers of the milieu idea are sometimes goaded into is the ubiquitous use of the term "therapeutic," coupled as an adjective with the noun "milieu." I have described the seven most common meanings squeezed into this word in scientific writings and scientific discussions elsewhere,[1] but I must at least point out this possible confusion before we go on. Whenever people demand that a really good "therapeutic milieu" have this or that quality, they may be referring to any one—or any combination—of the following issues:

"THERAPEUTIC," MEANING DON'T PUT POISON IN THEIR SOUP Not only is the adjective "therapeutic" often used in such a wide way to cover anything that is "good for a patient"; it is also made to serve as an umbrella for all demands that "damaging influences" be excluded.

Example

Any "therapeutic milieu" in which children are supposed to be treated would certainly pride itself on an absence of stupid punishments and of cruel and thoughtless handling by disinterested or poorly trained employees; it would have to guarantee protection against exposure to too many "traumatic experiences" either from staff or from the other children. In fact, often enough we find this negative request upon a milieu sufficient to distinguish one setting proudly as a "residential-treatment home" from another, which is then relegated to the lowly connotation of "just a children's institution."

In short, on this level, the term "therapeutic" usually is confined to the request made upon the people who design a milieu not to do to their patients what they wouldn't do to people anyway—any people—and to keep injurious substances out of their diets.

The questions, of course, of just what is or is not "good for people" and of how we know whether the specific impacts of living arrangements, atmosphere, patient handling by staff, and so forth are "thera-

[1] Fritz Redl, "The Meaning of 'Therapeutic Milieu,'" in Walter Reed Army Institute of Research, *Symposium on Preventive and Social Psychiatry* (Washington, D.C.: U.S. Government Printing Office, 1958), pp. 15–17.

peutic" or not in a given case provide a story in their own right and go far beyond the scope of this discussion. May I be allowed to add at least the demand that we become more specific about this point and stop confusing our own recreational taste buds, philosophical convictions, and habits of social interaction with objective assessments of what is or is not useful in the treatment of a given patient at a given time?

"THERAPEUTIC," MEANING YOU STILL HAVE TO FEED THEM Widening this heading to the concept of "basic-need coverage," we can easily remember that patients in a hospital—or children in any institution—are a "captive audience." They have come there not only with the special pathological conditions on which the institution's therapy hopes to focus and for the sake of which they were referred to begin with. They also bring with them all the other "basic human needs" of a given person in a given developmental phase with a given cultural background, regardless of whether or not such basic needs are closely related to the problems for which they were sent or even have anything to do with them. Once we declare a given need "basic," it must be well taken care of, or else some serious damage is done to the patient, no matter how well the specific therapy for which he was referred may look for the time being.

It is this fact that speakers often have in mind when they raise the question of the "therapeutic value" of special features in their institutional settings or their ward programs. In short, when we use the term this way, we refer to the conviction that it is important not only "not to put poison in their soup" but also to see that their psychological nourishment contains all the vitamins individuals of a given age need—beside the medication administrated for specific subgoals. Just what, in a hospital setting for instance, should be considered a "basic need" is, of course, dependent on the nature of pathology, age, previous life habits, developmental phase, and many other factors related to the specific patient in question.

By the way, the form in which such "basic needs" must be taken care of is as important as the content and varies greatly, especially in terms of developmental phase, pathology, and social background. What might be called "good basic-need coverage" in terms of an occupational-therapy program for a group of young adult neurotics may have little relevance to the activity program that has to be developed for a group of hyperaggressive twelve-year-olds of the borderline variety, and both programs may be downright unrecognizable as such by anybody who is used to catering to the art needs and activity tastes of a normal population in a given neighborhood. It seems to me that this issue especially is frequently neglected in the planning of milieu designs. The expectation, in all this, is not that "basic need coverage" in itself will bring about the desired therapeutic change. It is, rather, that, without its guaranteed provision, the intended therapy will be counteracted or that damage in other areas of the patient's life will be produced while we are busy blindly treating the one for which he was admitted.

Examples

Even with six hours of intensive individual therapy guaranteed each child per week, one would not consider a milieu "therapeutic" in which the children are expected to sit on benches waiting for their therapy hours, living in large groups with staff not trained to discover damaging influences of one patient upon another, bereaved of the basic ingredients of activities, and thrown into a group atmosphere heavy with hatred, fear, boredom, lethargy, and social strain.

Looking at the activity program of our six boys at the Bethesda project—youngsters selected for their "borderline, acting-out type of behavior disorders"—during the first few months after their admission, one would hardly have recognized much similarity between it and what is customarily considered a "good youth program" in the open community or on the school playground. Yet it was, at that time, most important to administer to those children the basic recreational vitamins that they needed in forms that, in spite of their illnesses, could make them "go down and stay down." For instance, organized athletic-team competition had, for a long time, to be carefully excluded, as it would only have produced a new chain of disruptive hostility. The essential experience of "participation in group living" had to be smuggled in through all sorts of deviously planned games with special care for proper dosage of all ingredients all the way through.

"THERAPEUTIC," MEANING DEVELOPMENTAL-PHASE APPROPRIATENESS AND CULTURAL-BACKGROUND AWARENESS This item is, of course, especially urgent in work with children. The very style of adult-child relationships that is normally expected to convey the impression of "caredforness" and warmth is quite different for a five-year-old than, for instance, for an adolescent. Squeezed into a group of adolescents, three five-year-olds might find themselves entirely out of focus in this important aspect. Their play-therapy hours might be as frequent as those of the older group and as well planned, but they would still find the "milieu" in which they lived very puzzling and strange. To limit myself to one issue picked from a hundred possibilities: The very adult behavior that the five-year-old might consider most reassuring would produce spasms of hostile rebellion in the adolescent, who could never tolerate such a gush of infantilizing motherly care. On the other hand, the more matter-of-fact "palsy" style of the young adult with the young-group client, well suited for the older group, would badly scare the little ones: They would be traumatized by the panic produced in them by watching the "loose" give and take between the adult and the adolescent group.

Obviously, subcultural and other differences would complicate the issue even further.

Example

It would not be "therapeutic" to keep adolescents in an infantilizing "little boy and little girl" atmosphere. A "fine lady" fussing over a little boy's hair grooming might convey "warmth" to a neglected middle-class child but would simply be viewed as a hostile pest by a young toughie from the other side of the railroad track.

Just what "developmental-phase appropriateness" means in different "socioeconomic, subcultural, racial, and national strata" is, of course, in itself an issue in need of much more elaborate and specific exploration.

"THERAPEUTIC," MEANING CLINICALLY ELASTIC Not only what facilities or program provisions a potential milieu contains, but also how adaptable it is to the whims of clinical movement and therapeutic exigencies, makes one setting more "therapeutic" than another. I mean by "clinical elasticity" the ability of a given milieu aspect or ingredient to yield to specific therapeutic demands, without the over-all structure getting entirely lost in the shuffle.

In so many discussions, I have noticed people swept away by "flexibility demands" to the point at which it is not even clear any more just what there is to be "flexible" about anyway. Such terminological preference may, however, be based on my chance experiences only and may not be of real importance, as long as we remain aware in our demands for either elasticity or flexibility that they are not values in their own right and that there has to be some clear-cut issue of structure, or else there is nothing left on which to base these adjectives to begin with. More specifically, the following demands by clinicians seem to me to fall into this category.

First, there is the ability of all milieu features to allow a wide leeway for "exceptions" for the partial toleration of downright "regression" even at high prices in other milieu features, whenever it is indicated.

Second, there is the ability of milieu features to absorb the surplus of pathological behavior that a given treatment technique may require or that a given treatment policy may demand and to provide safe handling of such surplus pathological behavior by the respective milieu areas outside their own domains (school, O.T., ward program, and so forth).

Examples

The teachers of the children on our closed ward, during the earlier phases of their stay with us, had to be able to hold back their ambitions to exploit learning potentials they might have discovered, if over-all clinical policy on a given child demanded such restraint. The same teachers also had to know what to expect and what it meant when, on certain days, a child came in to their classrooms straight from an exciting therapy session and hit them with "transference spillover" far beyond what they had learned to consider customary. They also had to be able to deal "hygienically," but clearly, with some of this surplus wild behavior in their classrooms, even though it came from different areas of the therapeutic space. In the same vein, the therapist, even while going through a phase when unleashing of the child's aggression was his basic main line, had to retain enough sense of proportion to slow down the rate at which he worked, so as not to destroy other ego-supportive life experiences for the child in school and elsewhere by unleashing more action-geared destruction than the rest of the outfit could cope with at the time or more than was compatible with the ward's concept of "group-psychological hygiene."

"THERAPEUTIC," MEANING ENCOMPASSING FRINGE-AREA TREATMENT GOALS Beyond the outspoken "auxiliary" aspects of a milieu design, many speakers and writers also ascribe to certain parts of the milieu a much more direct impact on treatment in a much more sharply focused use of the term. That puts it somewhere between "real therapy" and "important, but not really therapy-focused, basic-need coverage." We frequently find the idea expressed that, although the main part of the more basic pathology of the patient was to be tackled by the psychiatrist in his own individual or group-therapy sessions, many other things that are also "wrong" with this same patient should be corrected somewhere else, at some other time, by some other people in the institution. In short, those other areas of the patient's problem are also viewed as part of his "sickness," and what these "auxiliary" people are expected to do is also a "repair job" in its own right. But it should not be confused with the therapy done as the major clinical task. In this way, the recreational and social parts of the design of a milieu are often emphasized way beyond their function just for "basic-need coverage" and are elevated to regular jobs of "therapy." Or it may be considered a well-established treatment task to open up for a patient expressional channels like art and music, thus affording him access to an enriched life, just as soon as the psychiatrist is through unlocking the major door. On this level, we expect the psychiatrist to be busy with a frontal attack on the most "deeply rooted" phases of a patient's illness, but we also find him quite frankly relegating the other and also therapeutic jobs to other people on the team, to other phases of residential life, to other props and ingredients than those of the individual or discussion-group therapy room. In short, when we examine a milieu for its "therapeutic" properties on this level, we raise the question: "Who else treats other parts of the patient's disease, and how far do the setting and the over-all design of the place allow such work??

Examples

Johnny is here for treatment of his kleptomania, and his therapist works hard on that in individual therapy. Johnny also has a severe deficiency in school learning and is clumsy in his play life with his contemporaries. Even though the therapist is not yet in a position to pull any of these factors in, some other aspects of the milieu to which Johnny is exposed must give him corrective experiences in this direction, or else the place to which we sent him is not considered "therapeutic enough."

A therapist works hard at removing the unconscious hurdles in a child's ability to read during his work with him in his play-therapy hours. There are cases in which something else is needed beside. For some of our children it is important that somebody else, not his therapists, be loaded with the task of remedial work on the youngsters' reading problems. Beyond this, the production of an atmosphere indulgent to curiosity, even during the moments of a child's life on the ward, may be of equal importance.

"THERAPEUTIC," MEANING THE MILIEU AND I Some lecturers and authors go beyond this concept of "supportive milieu therapy as a fringe task, a relevant but not focal repair job to be done," as outlined under the previous section. They ascertain that there are ingredients in a good therapeutic milieu that could accomplish a specific therapeutic task directly—either all by themselves or at least as indispensable and equal partners in the major therapeutic task. These claims range all the way from repair jobs that a good therapeutic milieu alone is able to perform through tasks for the performance of which the "milieu" as such is claimed to be superior to other more specialized and long-term efforts to the more modest demands for a partnership arrangement of some sort.

In all those cases, however, whatever dynamic forces emanate from the milieu aspects mentioned are forces in their own right, well suited to be brought to bear on a "treatment" task of major proportions, and no more fooling about that! Enough of the pussy-footing about "auxiliary values." We are not discussing the issue of right or wrong here; we are merely outlining the conceptual content of a term. Though the verbiage used on the various levels previously listed may be misleading, it is quite clear that this one cannot be reduced to any of the other five—it is a claim in its own right.

Example

Among the kinds of therapeutic help the children on our ward are badly in need of is that of at least partial "superego repair." No matter what else ails them, something went wrong in the building and development of the type of value sensitivity or conscience children normally develop over the years. It is our impression that the more serious cases of superego damage can never be tackled by any kind of individual therapy alone; it must also be accompanied by an all-out total life-space engulfing approach, well attuned to this job, with plenty of "clinical resilience" built in, in order to guarantee a long-range focus on this major task.

Beyond what the individual therapist can do for such a child, it is our impression that we must provide living space for that child in which he can afford to let go of distorted defenses and allow himself the necessary emotional ties that have to precede any primary value identification whatever. It also seems clear to us that all experiences of daily life have to be geared to avoid guilt-flooding panic and more paranoid interpretations of daily life events than are compatible with an already heightened sibling rivalry—and that the roles of adult figures around whom value sensitivities are supposed to accrue or to be rearranged are protected from overlapping and from confusion that would make a mess of the clinical scene. In addition, for some children, there is a need for something like the tie to a "depersonalized group code," which alone can open the path to value incorporation, all previous personalized channels of that sort being hopelessly contaminated for a long time to come. In those cases, the "milieu" and what it begins to mean for the individual patient becomes as strong a force in therapy as the "therapist's relation with the patient" is customarily assumed to be.

"THERAPEUTIC," MEANING IN TERMS OF RE-EDUCATION FOR LIFE Even though all the previous criteria for a "therapeutic milieu" are checked out and found proper, we may want to give the term yet another twist. On this level, we are not satisfied with the appropriateness of the milieu for the present repair job to be done. We also want it to contain enough of the ingredients that the later, normal, open life situation will contain and to which the patient will have to adjust after his release.

In short, we measure our milieu in terms of its resemblance to "life for real." We find "nontherapeutic," on this basis, a milieu that contains no challenge to the patient to grow away from his disease and from the place in which it is meant to be cured. We consider a milieu "therapeutic" if it only aspires to "outlive itself" and if it builds into the hospital as many life experiences as the patient will have to meet later, hopeful that their taste may whet his appetite for more normal living rather than be obliterated by the smell of psychological detergents so importantly surrounding him now.

It seems to me that this use of the term "therapeutic" constitutes one of the most important problems in our usual debates. In fact, aren't we somehow drifting into a paradox? Isn't this demand to contain the "normal situations and experiences of life" really contradictory to the very idea of using a "special" milieu at all? For how is one and the same milieu supposed to provide maximum leeway for regression and at the same time to offer the patient all the challenges of life in the open community, with its rich rewards but even more frightening punishments? How are we to provide for Johnny a classroom experience with only two other children present and a highly trained teacher who also has time and skill to sit out five tantrums in a school hour without becoming punitive or disillusioned and at the same time to provide for the youngster the fascinating experience of watching more well-adjusted children happily at work, cheerfully succeeding, and smilingly accepting criticism if they fail, and at the same time taking all the aggression and disturbance he is liable to put out? It seems to me that, on this level, the term "therapeutic" requires the most careful examination of all, for the custom of making demands out of both sides of our salvation-greedy mouths, requesting opposites that cannot be delivered in one package at one time and place, is all too widespread already.

However, short of such abuse of our desire to have our clinical cake and to eat it with the normal life sauce too, the demand that a really therapeutic milieu contain enough ingredients to be supportive of growth and change beyond the present level of pathology-geared design is of great importance indeed. In fact, if we look at most of what comes close to the model for hospitals or "communities" emphasizing the therapeutic milieu, we may easily find that it ranges all the way from demanding protection and dependence as prime requisites to insistence on the patients' leading a nearly normal communal existence "even though they are all schizophrenics." Fortunately, things get that bad only when we leave the facts of daily life too far behind us. For in reality the issues are rarely that extreme. Rather, for any group of patients or any special therapeutic task, we can well define just which aspects of a given milieu should be emphasized for the immediate clinical job and which should be guaranteed and maintained out of the awareness that ingredients of later life must be inserted along the way. A community that would not create special milieu conditions for the therapy of the very sick could hardly be called a therapeutic community anymore, and a hospital that found no place at all to retain and build in essential ingredients of later open life in which patients will need and use such elements would lose its claim to doing "treatment." Sometimes the answer is that there is a limit to what one milieu design can possibly encompass and that the patients would be better off if they could move from one to the other, thus achieving consistency but at different locations or even under different staffs.

Example

In our children's ward at the Clinical Center, it was obvious from the start that we would have to anticipate problems of this nature. Although the "closed" section constituted an advantage at the beginning of therapy, especially as it was, of course, endowed with a rich and appropriate program design and with ample staff, it was to be expected that the children would outgrow the advantages of our milieu as soon as their ego functions were repaired to a certain point. Whereas protection in terms of the first six levels we have discussed constituted a great asset from the start, it would, at a certain point in the children's clinical advances, become important to substitute a design allowing much more opportunity for moving away from the highly supervised dependence we first had to lure them into. We would then have to insert the opportunity for a much more community- and real-life-related style of existence for them.

With this point in mind, the construction of an "open cottage" in a sort of "half-way house" style was begun and became available as a next step in their therapy. It becomes important for such children to move into a milieu that exposes them to a much higher degree of independent choice in conflict situations—though exploitation of such experiences by trained staff interviews and continuation of many of their other therapies still have to be provided.

Enough of this dissection of an adjective. I hope I am understood correctly: Any one of these meanings of the term "therapeutic" is justified in its own right. Any one of them may, in a given case, assume priority or may fade out in relevance to the zero point. All I am trying to convey is the importance of remembering who is talking about what—and about which patients—when we use the term in a scientific "free-for-all." So far I haven't been too impressed with our ability to do so.

By the way, even in all seven cases, the term "therapeutic" may still be used in a double frame of reference: Was it therapeutic for a given patient—if so, how do you know? Is it expected to be potentially "therapeutic"—meaning beneficial for the treatment goal—from what I know about the basic nature of the issue under debate? These two frames of reference should be kept asunder too.

A Milieu—What's in It?

Obviously I am not going to use the term in the nearly global meaning that its original theft from the French language implies. For practical reasons, I am going to talk here only of one sort of milieu concept, of a "milieu" artificially created for the purpose of treating a group of youngsters. Within this confine you can make it somewhat wider if you want, and you can think of the "children's psychiatric unit" on the fourth, eighth, or ninth floor of a large hospital, or you may hold before your eyes a small residential-treatment home for children that is not part of a large unit. Of course, I know that the similarity of what I am talking about to other types of setups may be great, but I can't cover them all. Therefore anything else you have in mind you keep strictly at your own risk.

So, here we are on the doorstep of that treatment home or at the keyhole of that hospital ward. And now you ask me: If you could plan things the way you wanted to, which are the most important "items" in your milieu that will sooner or later become terribly relevant for better or for worse? The choice is hard, and only such a tough proposition gets me over the guilt feeling for oversimplifying and listing items out of context.

THE SOCIAL STRUCTURE This is some term, and I have yet to see the psychiatrist who isn't stunned for a moment at its momentum—many would run and hire a sociologist on the spot. Being short of space, I have no choice, but let me hurry and add: This term in itself is as extendable and collapsible as a balloon. It doesn't mean much without specifications. So let me list a few of the things I have in mind.

First, a hospital ward is more like a harem society than a family, no matter how motherly or fatherly the particular nurses and doctors may feel toward their youngsters. The place I run at the moment is purposely shaped as much as possible after the model of an American camp, which is the only pattern I could find in which children would be familiar with a lot of adults walking through their lives in older-brother and parental roles without pretending to an equivalent of family life.

Second, the role distribution among the adult figures can be terrifically important for the amount of clarity with which children perceive what it is all about. Outspokenly or not, sooner or later they must become clear about just who can or cannot be expected to decide what; otherwise, how would one know when one is getting the run-around?

Third, the pecking order of any outfit does not long remain a secret to an open-door, neighborhood-wise toughie, no matter how dumb he may be otherwise. He also smells the "pecking order" among the adults who take care of him, no matter how carefully disguised it may be under professional role titles or civil-service classification codes.

Fourth, the communication network of any given institution is an integral part of its social structure. Just who can be approached about listening to what is quite a task to learn; and to figure out the real communication lines that are open and those that are secretly clogged in the adult communication network is usually an impossible task except for the suspicious outside researcher.

I mentioned only four illustrations of all the things I wanted included under "social structure." There are many more, and I have no quarrel with the rich inventory many social scientists have invented for it. The quarrel I have is against oversimplification, and if you tell me that social structure is only what goes into a power-line drawing or a sociogram or that social structure is the only important variable in "milieu" that psychiatrists have neglected in the past, then you have me in a mood to fight. By the way, if I list "social structure" as one of the important milieu variables, I'd better add in a hurry: A mere listing or description of the social structure extant on a given ward is of no interest to me at all if it doesn't go further than that. From a clinical angle, the excitement begins *after* the sociologist tells me what social structure I have before me. Then I really want to know: What does it do to my therapeutic goals? What does it imply for my choice of techniques? In which phase of the therapy of my children is it an asset, and in which other phase does it turn into a serious block? To use just one example of the clinical question to be added to the social scientist's answer: The kind of ward I have run—harem-society style—makes individual attachments of child to worker difficult to achieve; on the other hand, it pleasantly dilutes too-excited libidinous-attachment needs into more harmless distribution over a larger number of live props. Question: Is that good or bad and for whom during what phase of the treatment?

THE VALUE SYSTEM THAT OOZES OUT OF OUR PORES Some people subsume this point under "social structure." I think I have reasons to want a separate place for it here, but let's not waste time on the question why. The fact is that the youngsters not only respond to what we say or put in mimeographed writing; they also smell our value feelings even when we don't notice our own body odor any more. I am not sure how, and I can't wait until I find out. But I do have to find out which value items are there to smell. Does the arrangement of my furniture call me a liar while I make a speech about how much at home I want them to feel, or does that gleam in a counselor's eye tell the child: "You are still wanted," even though he means it when he says he won't let him cut up the tablecloth? By the way, in some value studies I have missed one angle many times: the clinical convictions of what is professionally correct handling, which sometimes even questionnaire-clumsy workers on a low salary level may develop and which themselves become motivating sources for their behavior, beside their own personal moral convictions or their power drives.

ROUTINES, RITUALS, AND BEHAVIORAL REGULATIONS The sequence of events and the conditions under which people experience certain repetitive maneuvers in their life space can have strong impacts on whether or not they can keep themselves under control or whether or not their impulse-control balance breaks down. Since Bruno Bettelheim's classic description of the events inside a child while he seems engaged in the process of getting up or getting himself to sleep, no more words should have to be said on this point. Yet many "therapeutic milieu" discussions still waste time on arguments between those who like regularity and those who think the existence of a rule makes life unimaginative drudgery. All groups also have certain "rituals" by which members get back into the graces of the group if they have sinned and others that the group has to go through when an individual has deviated. Which of those ceremonial rites are going on among my boys, thinly disguised behind squabbles and fights, and which of them do adult staff people indulge in, under the even thinner disguise of discussions on punishment and on the setting of limits? Again, the mere discovery of phenomena fitting into this category is not what I am after. We are still far from having good research data on the clinical relevance of whatever specific practice may be in vogue in a specific place.

THE IMPACT OF THE GROUP PROCESS We had better pause after pronouncing this weighty phrase—it is about as heavy and full of dodges as the phrase "social structure," previously pointed out. And as this one milieu aspect might well keep us here for a week, let me sink as low as simple word listing at this point. Items that I think should go somewhere under this name: over-all group atmosphere, scapegoating, mascot cultivation, subclique formation, group-psychological role suction, exposure to group-psychological intoxication, dependency on contagion clusters, leadership tensions, and so forth. Whatever you have learned from social psychology, group psychology, and group dynamics had better be written in right here. The point of all this discussion is: These phenomena are not simply interesting things that happen among patients or staff, to be viewed with a clinical grin, a sociological hurrah, or the curious stares of an anthropological slumming party. These processes are forces to which my child patient is exposed, as real as the Oedipus complex of his therapist, the food he eats, and the toys he plays with. The forces producing such impacts may be hard to see or even to make visible through X-ray tricks. But they are there and as much part of his "surroundings" as the unbreakable room in which he screams off his tantrum.

THE TRAIT CLUSTERS OTHER PEOPLE WHIRL AROUND WITHIN A FIVE-YARD STRETCH I first wanted to call this item "the other people as persons," but I know this would only call forth a long harangue about feelings and attitudes—isn't it people anyway who make up a group?—and so forth. From bitter experience, I am trying to duck these questions by this somewhat off-beat phrase. What I have in mind is this: My youngsters live as part of a group, true enough. But they are also individuals. And Bobby, who shares a room with John, is within striking distance of whatever personal peculiarities John may happen to throw at others. In short, we expect some children to show "shock" at certain colors on a Rorschach card. We expect children to be lured into excited creativity at the mere vision of some fascinating project outline or plane model seductively placed before their eyes. Well, the boy with whom Bobby shares his room is worse than a Rorschach or a plane model. His presence and the observation of his personality do something to Bobby, for John not only has character traits and neurotic syndromes; he also swings them around his body like a wet bathing towel, and they are going to hit whoever gets in their path, innocent or not. In short, personality traits remain psychological entities for the psychologist who watches them in the youngsters. They are real things that hit and scratch if you get in their way, for the roommate and all the other people on the ward.

We have learned to respect the impact of certain extremes in pathologies upon one another, but we are still far from inspecting our milieus carefully enough for what they contain in "trait clusters" that children swing around their heads within a five-yard range. Let me add: Not all traits and syndromes are "swung"; some stay put and can only be seen or smelled, so they become visible or nuisances only to the one who shares the same room. Also we are far from knowing what this all amounts to clinically. For the question of just what "milieu ingredients" my ward contains, in terms of existent trait clusters of the people who live in it, is still far removed from the question of just which ones *should* coexist with one another and which others should be carefully kept asunder.

THE STAFF, ITS ATTITUDES AND FEELINGS—BUT PLEASE LET'S NOT CALL IT ALL "TRANSFERENCE" This one I can be short about, for clinicians all know about it; sociologists will grant it to you, though they may question how heavily it counts. In fact, the attitudes and feelings of staff have been drummed up for so long now as "the" most important aspect of a milieu, often even as the only important one, that I am not afraid this item will be forgotten. No argument is needed; it is self-evident. Only two issues I should like to battle over: First, although attitudes and feelings are very important indeed, they are not always all that counts, and sometimes other milieu items may obliterate their impact. Second, attitudes and feelings of staff are manifold and spring from many different sources. Let's limit the term "transference" to those phenomena for which it was originally invented. If nurse's aid A gets too hostile to Bob because he bit him too hard, let's not throw all of that into the same terminological pot. By the way, when I grant "attitudes and feelings of staff" a place on my list of "powerful milieu ingredients," I mean the attitudes and feelings that really fill the place, that are lived—not those that are only mentioned in research interviews and on questionnaires.

BEHAVIOR RECEIVED I tried many other terms, but they won't work. There just isn't one that fits. In a sentence I would say: What people really *do* to one another counts as much as how they feel. This statement would then force me into a two-hour argument in which I would have to justify why it isn't "unpsychiatric" to say such a thing. For isn't it the underlying feelings that "really" count? That depends on which side of the fence your "really" is. The very fact that you use such a term already means you know there is another side to it; but you don't want to take it as seriously as yours. In short, there are situations in which the "underlying feelings" with which adults punish children count so much that the rather silly forms of punishment that were chosen are negligible. But I could quote you hundreds of other examples in which this is not the case. No matter what your wonderful motive, if you expose child A to isolation with more panic in it than he can stand, the effect will be obvious. Your excuse that you "meant well and love the boy" may be as futile as that of the mother who gives the child an overdose of arsenic not knowing its effect.

This item of behaviors received in a day's time by each child should make a really interesting line to assess. We would have to look about at "behaviors received" from other boys, as well as from staff, and see what the implications of those behaviors are, even after deducting from them the mitigating influences of "attitudes that really were aiming at the opposite." The same point, by the way, should also be taken into consideration in hiring staff. I have run into people who really love "crazy youngsters" and are quite willing to sacrifice a lot. Only they simply cannot stand more than half a pound of spittle in their faces a day, professional attitude or no.

In order to make such an assessment, the clinician would of course be interested especially in the *forms* that are being used by staff for intervention (limit-setting), expression of acceptance and love, and so forth. The prevalence of certain forms of "behavior received" is not a negligible characteristic of the milieu in which a child patient has to live.

ACTIVITY STRUCTURE AND THE NATURE OF CONSTITUENT PERFORMANCES Part of the impact a hospital or treatment home has on a child lies in the things he is allowed or requested to do. Any given activity that is halfway influential enough to be described has a certain amount of structure to it—some games, for instance, have bodies of rules, demand splitting into two opposing sides or staying in circles, and have certain assessments of roles for the players at least for the duration. At the same time, they make youngsters "do certain things" while the games last. Paul Gump introduced the term "constituent performances" into our Detroit Game Study and referred by this term to the performances required as basic within the course of a game. Thus running and tagging are constituent performances of a tag game, guessing word meanings is a constituent performance in many a charade, and so forth. We have plenty of evidence by now that—other things being equal—the very exposure of children to a given game, with its structure and demands for certain constituent performances, may have terrific clinical impact on the events at least of that day. Whenever we miscalculate the overwhelming effects that the seductive aspects of certain games may have (flashlight hide-and-seek in the dark just before bedtime), we may ask for trouble, whereas many a seemingly risky game can safely be played if enough ego-supportive controls are built into it (the safety zone to which one can withdraw without having to admit he is tired or scared and so forth). In short, although I hardly limit the job of total treatment of severely disturbed children in a mental hospital ward to that factor alone, I certainly do want to figure on it as seriously as I calculate the mental-hygiene aspects of other factors more traditionally envisioned as of clinical concern. What I say here about games goes for many other activities patients engage in—arts and crafts, woodwork, outings, overnight trips, cookouts, discussion groups, musical evenings, and so forth. Which of these things takes place, where, with which feeling tones, and with what structural and activity ingredients is as characteristic of a given "milieu" as is the staff that is hired.

SPACE, EQUIPMENT, TIME, AND PROPS What an assortment of names. But I know as yet of no collective noun that would cover them all equally well. As I have made such a fuss about this point for years, I may try to be shorter about it than seems reasonable. Remember what a bunch of boys do when running through a viaduct with an echo effect? Remember what may happen to a small group that is supposed to discuss plans for its next Scout meeting and is required to hold this discussion unexpectedly in a huge gym with lots of stuff around, instead of in its usual clubroom? Remember what will happen to a baseball that is put on the table prematurely while the children are still supposed to sit quietly and listen, and remember what happens to many a well-intended moral lecture to a group of sloppy campers if you have timed it so badly that the swimming bell starts ringing before you have finished? Do I still have to prove why I think that what an outfit does with arrangements of time expectations and time distribution, what prop exposure the youngsters are expected to stand or avoid, what space arrangements are like, and what equipment does to the goals you have set for yourself should be listed along with the important "properties" of a place where clinical work with children takes place? So far I have found that in hospitals this item tends to be left out of milieu discussions by psychiatrists and sociologists alike; only the nurses and attendants have learned from bitter experience that it may pay to lend an ear to it.

SEEPAGE FROM THE WORLD OUTSIDE One of the hardest "milieu aspects" to assess in a short visit to any institution is the amount of "impact from the larger universe and the surrounding world" that actually seeps through its walls and finds its way into the lives of the patients. No outfit is airtight, no matter how many keys and taboos are in use. In our own little children's-ward world, for instance, there were the following "seepage ingredients from the world outside" that were as much a part of our "milieu," as it hit the boys, as anything else: adult visitors and the "case history" flavor they left behind; child visitors and the "sociological body odor" of the old or new neighborhoods that they exuded, excursions that we arranged; old haunts from prehospital days that we happened to drive through unintentionally on our way to our destination; plenty of purposely pulled-in outside-world movies, television, pictures, and stories we may have told them. And, of course, school was a full-view window hopefully opened wide for many vistas to be seen through—if we only could get our children to look.

There was the "hospital impact" of the large building that hit them whenever they left the ward floor in transit and the physically sick patients they met on the elevator who stirred the question up again in their minds: "Why am I here?" There were the stories other boys and staff told, the secrets we were believed to be hiding from them whenever we seemed eager to divert attention to something else. As soon as the children moved into the open cottage, the word "seepage" wasn't quite so correct any more. Suffice it to say: The type and amount of "outside world" particles that are allowed or even eagerly pulled in constitute a most important part of the lives of the captive population in an institutional setting and should be given attention in an appraisal of just what a given "milieu" holds.

THE SYSTEM OF UMPIRING SERVICES AND TRAFFIC REGULATIONS BETWEEN ENVIRONMENT AND CHILD Those among you who have sharp noses for methodological speculations may want to object and insist that I am jumping category dimensions in tagging on this item and the next one on my list. In some ways they still belong, for whether or not there are any umpiring services built into an institution and what they are like are certainly important "milieu properties" in my estimation. What I have in mind here has been described in more detail in a previous paper. In short, it runs somewhat like this: Some "milieu impacts" hit the children directly; nobody needs to interpret or translate. Others hit the children all right but to make sure the proper impact is achieved someone has to do some explaining. It makes a great difference whether or not a child who is running away unhappy after a cruel razzing received from a thoughtless group is left to deal with the problem all by himself, or whether or not the institution provides interpretational or first-aid services for his muddled feelings. Some of our children, for instance, might translate such an experience, which was not intended by the institution, into additional resentment against the world. With sympathy in the predicament offered by a friendly adult who tagged along and comforted, this same experience might well be decontaminated or even turned into the opposite. A similar item is the one I had in mind in using the phrase "traffic regulations." Much give and take can follow naturally among the inhabitants of a given place. Depending on the amounts of their disturbances, though, some social interactions that normal life leaves to the children's own resources require traffic supervision by an adult. I should like to know whether or not a given milieu has foreseen this problem and can guarantee the provision of some help in the bartering among the youngsters and whether or not a new youngster will be mercilessly exposed to the wildest blackmail, with no help from anyone, the moment he enters the doors to my ward. In short, it is like asking what medical first-aid facilities are available in a town before one moves into it. Whether this problem belongs to the concept of what makes up a "town" or should be listed under a separate heading I leave for a later exploration. All I want to point out now is that the nature and existence or nonexistence of umpiring services and social-traffic regulations are as "real" properties of a setup as are its walls, kitchen equipment, and clinical beliefs.

THE THERMOSTAT REGULATING CLINICAL RESILIENCE If it is cold in an old cabin somewhere in the midst of "primitive nature," the trouble is obvious: Either there isn't any fire going, or something is wrong with the stove and the whole heating system, so they don't give off enough heat. If I freeze in a building artificially equipped with all the modern conveniences, such a conclusion might be off the beam. The trouble may simply be that the thermostat isn't working right. This, like the previous item, is a property of a given milieu rather than a "milieu ingredient" in the strict sense of the word. However, it is of such utmost clinical relevance that it has to go in here somewhere. In fact, I have hardly ever participated in a discussion on the milieu concept without having this item come up somehow or other. The term under which it is more often referred to is actually "flexibility," which most milieu-therapy enthusiasts praise as "good," whereas the bad men in the picture are the ones who think "rigidity" is a virtue. I have more reasons to be tired of this either-or issue than I can list in the remaining time. It seems to me that the "resilience" concept fits better what most of us have so long tried to shoot at with the "flexibility" label. A milieu certainly has to be sensitive to the changing needs of the patients during different phases of the treatment process. It has to "tighten up"—lower the behavioral ceiling—when impulse panic looms on the horizon, and it may have to lift the ceiling when self-imposed internal pressures mount. Also it has to limit spontaneity and autonomy of the individual patient in early phases of intensive disorder and rampant pathology; it has to insert challenges to autonomy and even the risking of mistakes when the patient goes through the later phases of recovery. Especially when severely disturbed children are going through an intensive phase of "improvement," the resilience of a milieu to make way for its implications is as important as its ability to "shrink back" during a regressive phase.

Just How Does the Milieu Do It?

Listing these twelve variables of important milieu aspects that can be differentiated as explorable issues in their own right is only part of the story. I hold no brief for this list, and I am well aware of its methodological complications and deficiencies. The major value of listing them at all lies in the insistence that there are so many of them and that they can be separately studied and explored. This point should at least help us to secure ourselves against falling in love with any one of them to the exclusion of the others and of forcing any discipline that wants to tackle the job, whether it be psychiatry, sociology, or what not, to look beyond its traditional scope and directly into the face of uncompromisingly multifaceted facts.

As the major sense in all this milieu noise is primarily the impact of these variables on the treatment process of the children we are trying to cure, the question of clinical assessment of the relevance of each of these items is next on the docket of urgent jobs. This one we shall have to skip, but we may point to the other question leading into the most important core of the problem: If we assume that any one of these milieu ingredients, or whatever you want to call them, may have positive or negative impacts on our therapeutic work—how does it do it? Just what goes on when we claim that any one of those milieu givens "did something to our youngsters"? This question gets us into one of the most noteworthy gaps in our whole theory of personality, and frankly I don't think even our most up-to-date models are quite up to it. True enough, we have learned a few things about how pathology is influenced in the process of a specific form of psychiatric interview, and we know a little about the influence of human over human, here or there. We are not so well off when we come to the impact of more abstract-sounding entities like "group structure." We have even more trouble figuring out just how space, time, and props are supposed to do their jobs, whenever we claim that they have the power to throw an otherwise well-planned therapeutic experience out of gear. One phase of this problem sounds familiar—when psychiatry first began to take the impact of "culture" seriously, we were confronted with a similar puzzler: Just where, within the individual, is what going on at the moment when we say a "cultural" factor had some influence on a given behavior of a person?

This problem is far from solved. I think it might help, though, to introduce a thought that might lead to greater specificity in observation and ultimately to more "usable" forms of data collection. Frankly, I have never seen the "milieu" at work. My children are never hit by the "milieu" as such. It always hits them in a specific form and at a given time and place. I think the researchers who play with the concept of "setting" have a technical advantage over us in this field. Of course, the setting alone doesn't interest me either. For what it all hinges on is just what experience a given setting produces or makes possible within my child patient and what this child patient does with it.

Rather than studying the "milieu" per se and then the "reactions of the children," how about making a four-step plan? Let's keep the "milieu" as the over-all concept on the fringe; its basic ingredients come close to my youngsters only insofar as they are contained in a given setting. For example, my children on the ward can be found engaged in getting up and eating meals or snacks. They can be found roaming around the playroom or in a station wagon, with all their overnight gear, on the way to their camping site. They can be found in their arts-and-crafts room or schoolroom engaged in very specific activities. Enough of illustrations. The point is in all those settings the whole assortment of milieu aspects hits them in very specific forms: There is an outspoken behavioral expectation floating through the arts-and-crafts room at any time. There are spatial characteristics, tools, and props.

There is the potential reaction of the other child or adult, the feeling tone of the group toward the whole situation as such; there is the impact of people's goal values and attitudes, as well as that of the behavior of a child's neighbor who clobbers him right now with his newly made Viking sword. In short, I may be able to isolate observations of milieu ingredients as they "hit" the child in a specific setting during a specific activity. On such a narrowed-down level of observation, I may also be able to trace the actual experience that such a concrete situation in a given setting produced in the child; and if I know what the child did with the experience, it may make sense, for I have both ends of the line before me: the youngster's reaction to his experience and the nature of the ingredients of the "setting" on both ends of the line, plus plenty of good hunches on the child's experience while exposed to its impact.

It seems to me that much more work has to be done with the concept of "setting" to make it clinically more meaningful and that sharper observational techniques, capable of catching "implied milieu impact," as well as "child's coping with" the experience produced by the setting, have to be developed.

One more word. It is time that we take Erik Erikson's warning more seriously than we have done so far—and I mention him because he represents a point of view that many of us have been increasingly impressed by. If I may try to say what I think he would warn us about after all this discussion of "milieu impacts" on therapy of children, it would run something like this: Why are we still talking most of the time as though "milieu" or "environment" were some sort of rigid structure and the individuals were good for nothing but to "react" to it? How does some of that "environment" we talk about come into being, after all? Couldn't we reverse the story just as well and ask: "What do your child patients do to their milieu?"—not only "What does the milieu do to them?" Mine, by the way, are doing plenty to it, and I have little doubt that many of the items we describe as though they were fixtures on the environmental scene are actually products of the attitudes and actions of the very people who, after they have produced them, are also exposed to their impact in turn.

I, for one, want to exclaim loudly what I didn't dare whisper at the beginning of this paper, as I would have scared you off too soon. I should like to find out, not only what milieu is and how it operates, but also how we can describe it, how we influence it, and by what actions of all involved it is, in turn, created or molded. At the moment I am convinced of only one thing for sure—we all have quite a way to go to achieve either of these tasks.

13. Psychiatric Clinic → Clinical Educator ← Public School*

MELVYN L. REICH

Special education programs for emotionally handicapped children can be observed in a variety of forms which pertain to a continuum of intensities of educational and behavioral symptomatology. "Special education programs," however, are not merely "special classes" but are defined to include any one or a combination of services necessary to restore or instill in an emotionally handicapped kid those academic traits, distinctions, and behavioral characteristics which no longer cause him to be perceived as nuts by peers, parents, and other appendages of his milieu. When such a handicapping condition in a kid creates a problem or problems in the school and/or community but somehow does not seem severe enough to fit him into the mode of special-class placement, he is customarily referred for therapy to one of the psychiatrically oriented professionals: psychiatrist, psychologist, or psychiatric social worker. The school then feels that such a special education program is in effect and that therapy of the psychological variety is so personal as to preclude the school's intervention into the private nature of the psychotherapeutic relationship.

Most educators are downright afraid of any problem that smacks of psychological disorder and it has been traditional (at least in the New England area) to refer such disorders *en masse* to psychiatric clinics. The underlying rationale has been, at least in the minds of the educators, that if people professionally trained to understand and treat the emo-

* This selection is published for the first time in this volume. The author wishes to extend his deep appreciation to Dr. A. J. Pappanikou for providing the questions and experiences leading up to the development of the ideas contained herein. Dr. Elias J. Marsh and Dr. Beatrice (Wolfson) Struzenski played major parts in that they allowed this approach to the treatment of behavior disordered children to invade their separate professional domains without overt insistence upon its departure.

tional disorders of children (the aforementioned mental-health trio) could not successfully work through the difficulties manifested by the child, then certainly the teacher, with less specific training in the technology of creating and fostering positive mental-health patterns, could have aided the child even less adequately. In other words, referral to a psychiatric facility or clinic for treatment is many times a declaration by the school that it does not know what to do and it is a request, a plea for someone to tell it what to do. The school does expect, at first, some magic formula from the clinic, either in the form of different trials of medication, a mystical explanation of Freudian dynamics, and/or a prescription typical of the following: "Don't put too much pressure on him." (When the kid is raising hell in school, however, this psychiatric prescription is read and utilized to advantage by the kid while the teacher feels guilty for all those impulses to really let the kid have a few limits.) As a sign of its pseudo-trust in the school, the clinic is usually gracious enough to bestow upon the child the precious gift of a fuzzy, educationally meaningless diagnosis (e.g., adjustment reaction of childhood) followed or preceded by some code numbers which are just as useless.

It is necessary to understand the school's motives in both referral for psychiatric treatment and attempts to continue programming recommended by traditional psychiatrically oriented mental-health professionals. The school is attempting to relieve itself of its sense of guilt over (a) its feelings of failure; (b) its desire to get rid of the oddball it has referred; (c) its inability to get involved or make progress in the treatment of the problem; (d) its subliminal contribution to the smoldering emotional fire of antisocial reaction in the kid. The fact of the matter is that for some reason, this kid does not fit into the structure or organization demanded by the school. Likewise, the school is usually afraid or unwilling to make *realistic* changes in its rather inflexible structures in order to accommodate individual needs.

In any event, the kid has been referred for some sort of clinic service. The school really does not expect much help (after several months of hoping that some miracle will occur), and as a matter of fact, not very much is received. There is, however, the ever-fading belief somewhere in the minds of all concerned with the kid that he will somehow be straightened out to the degree that he can take doses of education and its structure, no matter how small the amounts might be.

Keeping to the tradition of "tell the educators as little as possible but thank them for their insight and referral," the psychiatric clinic spends a while gathering background information from parents and school authorities. Usually, a school conference takes place once or twice a year. It is during this conference that psychiatric attitudes are firmly impressed on the teacher:

1. In a rather condescending manner, clinic staff attempt to reduce the guilt feelings of the educators. As a result of these rather poorly veiled efforts, the school personnel usually leave such a conference feeling more guilty, more confused, and shamefully hostile.
2. If the kid is not improving, various generalities are suggested by the mental-health professionals in the traditional nondirective manner: "Why doesn't the teacher do this or that?" This only implies that the teacher is a very definite impediment to the wonderful therapy provided by the clinic.
3. When the teacher requests information from the clinic staff regarding motivation or predisposition to certain aggressive or withdrawing behavior on the part of the kid, it is often the policy to reply by either changing the subject or by wondering why an educator shows such undue interest in this particular sphere. Though implied, but never said directly, the clinic conveys its apprehension that perhaps the school will get involved in the mental-health business.
4. The school may very well request information on the family's part in contributing to the problems currently exhibited by the kid. In this vein, the school also seeks to ascertain whether family dynamics can be utilized to help alleviate some of the present difficulties. The clinic personnel, after shuddering slightly, continue to refuse positive help by making a bland comment such as "The family may be ready to offer assistance, because it is possible that they have the ability to show some interest." This is just enough to let the school know that as far as the kid's family is concerned, (a) "The clinic won't tell you anything," and (b) "Don't meddle with the family!"
5. The location of this grand conference is usually in a conference room at the clinic, perhaps even an inner sanctum office, resplendent with unusual knickknacks, pictures of bearded men, and loads of toys. The working time of the clinic staff is quite valuable, so riding back and forth to a school would only be a tremendous waste of time. Besides, it is easier for the clinic to maintain the upper hand in its own environment, as opposed to walking into the unknown (maybe even dangerous) environment of the public school. It's a matter of insecurities and defenses, but the psychiatric team is usually the institution to which the educators travel to do homage.

The conference concludes with some fuzzy goals outlined in behalf of the kid and some even hazier principles for handling the kid left marginally delineated. This sequence, when repeated often enough on the same kid or by the same two groups of professionals, eventually becomes just so much nonsense to all concerned. The result is usually more confusion, with each side becoming more suspicious of the other.

The foregoing is intended to briefly enumerate the dynamics of the two institutions commonly involved in the referral and treatment processes for children evidencing peculiar behaviors labeled emotional disorders. These two institutions often are neither aware of the motivations and aspirations of the other involved party, nor does each one evidence much concern for the other. What slowly evolves, rather, is the realization in the minds of both parties that the other interested faction does not really know what it is doing; furthermore, each faction has contributed little, if anything, in the way of a partial (much less a complete) solution to the problems of the kid as well as the problems posed by him to the two involved institutions.

It is to avoid the difficulties inherent in the historical nature of these two agencies, the seeming conflict of egos between both institutions, that a professional liaison is necessary between them. Logically, such an individual should possess the credentials of both institutions, having received training and experience both in educative procedures as well as the clinical assessment and treatment function. It is also probably more advisable that this liaison be employed by the clinic, thereby giving education an "in" (entry into the mental-health team) while still allowing the basic thrust to be met with much less resistance on the school's part. Thus, the two rather realistically antithetic agencies can unite under the banner of this liaison in a most effective way, because the position will be endowed with "equality" in stature on both sides of the "fence."

Reflecting the attempts at unity of the institutions of school and clinic, the duties of this liaison person (for lack of a better term, he will be designated as the clinical educator) may read somewhat like the following:

1. Assist in the diagnostic assessment and treatment of children with problems of adjustment, paying particular attention to those children who present behavior problems in the school and/or problems in adequate academic achievement;
2. Consultation with fellow clinic team members on the educational problems of child clients in relation to the goals of their respective schools through participation and equal voice in all clinic team and staff meetings;
3. Interpret the problems of the emotionally disturbed child and the

treatment goals of the clinic staff to community agencies, specifically the schools;

4. Provide clinic liaison when necessary with educators at all levels;
5. Assist in the development of methods derived from learning theory for application to the treatment of children with behavior patterns differing to some degree from the norm;
6. Devise techniques of developmental instruction for application in the management and treatment of adjustment and personality reactions and disorders of childhood and adolescence;
7. Determine appropriate remedial intervention and planning in consultation with the clinic team and the school;
8. Serve as a consultant to the schools, on loan from the clinic, concerning problems of classroom management, discipline, suspension, and the drop-out;
9. Assist classroom teachers and pupil-services personnel in understanding and dealing with aspects of psychopathology as it is directly related to the educative process;
10. Develop continual assessment and follow-up procedures and studies on children having clinic contact in an effort to determine the effectiveness of the combined school and clinic course of intervention.

That this position can exist and provide for the amelioration of disagreement and hostility between the prongs of the clinic's force and the school's force on the emotionally handicapped child has been demonstrated successfully, through this author's experience, on a limited basis. The following anecdotes and excerpts from some case materials may help to explain and clarify the operations of the position of clinical educator.

Leo A. is a nine-year-old boy, born out of wedlock to a Negro mother and Puerto Rican father. His family includes an older brother (also born out of wedlock but to a different father) and several younger brothers and sisters born of his mother's first marriage. Several years ago Mrs. A. married for a second time. Her husband was chronically unemployed, drank heavily, and could not get along well with Leo to the degree that he gave Mrs. A. a choice of putting Leo out of the house or Mr. A. would not return.

Mrs. A. contacted the state welfare agency for placement of Leo in a foster home. The caseworker's investigation revealed a rather long history of inconsistent handling of Leo, rejection by both parent figures, Leo's inability to handle discipline, and numerous accounts of aggression, destruction, and petty theft. In school, Leo was extremely difficult to discipline, achieved three years below the level expected for his chronological age, and was described as extremely aggressive and hyperactive, someone who could not follow the rules of games and a bully to other children. Individual IQ testing was accomplished with a modicum of difficulty, the result being in the borderline retarded range (IQ=78), according to school records.

The child-welfare caseworker placed Leo in a Negro foster home in a middle-class semirural community. Leo's behavior at home and in school was a source of great consternation to all who were acquainted with him. Behavioral complaints came continuously to the foster parents, both from school and the neighborhood. While some difficulty in following his new routine was verbalized by the foster parents, they also expressed the wish to keep Leo in their home. The caseworker referred Leo to the clinic for psychiatric help, as the result of the school pressuring for some assistance in handling Leo's acting out as well as seeking some sort of therapeutic aid for him.

Leo was assigned to a clinical psychology intern for individual psychotherapy. Leo related easily on a one-to-one basis, his almost every whim being satisfied during the therapeutic hour. The clinic felt that Leo was emotionally deprived, "an empty pit which could never be filled with all the love available to him." The school, meanwhile, attempted to remain calm, overlooking much in the hope that psychotherapy would help.

At the end of approximately ten months, the intern rotated to another agency and the clinic staff indicated that group therapy with a male would be more beneficial in developing the social strength Leo needed. Because few male therapists were available and because the school was so much concerned with the disturbing influence Leo presented, the case was assigned to the clinical educator.

Leo was seen in a group situation for one and one-half hours per week for approximately forty-five weeks. In the group, structures were set for the privilege of group participation. Leo attempted to demolish these structures week after week. In the one-to-one setting he was most pleasant, almost angelic, but in the group he participated only in those discussions he could control, those games he could win, and those fights in which he was sure of victory. The rules were accepted very slowly, with much regression and continual testing in the group situation. It was also noted that Leo could follow structure imposed by the group significantly easier than that imposed by the adult figure.

A conference was held at the school's request five weeks after Leo's assignment to the clinical educator. The school wanted the child placed in an institution for retarded children. With the clinical educator as group leader, several clinic team members traveled to the school for the conference with the following results obtained:

1. Leo would receive one hour of classroom instruction per day in addition to one hour of home tutoring (he would thus attend school after other children had arrived and remain for one hour).
2. Leo could request permanent additions of fifteen-minute intervals to his daily schedule from the principal. Teacher, principal, and Leo sat down together to discuss the requests. The clinical educator was forced to veto the additional time requests in several instances because the school wanted him back too quickly. The emphasis was for Leo to "earn" additional time.

3. The clinic would continue to provide group experiences of a therapeutic nature.
4. An individual IQ test would again be administered by the clinic at the school's request.

The following is the clinical educator's report to the school:

Mr. Andrew Jones, Principal
Elm Grove School
Mapleroot, Massachusetts

Re: Leo A.

At a recent school conference (October 23, 1967) held at Elm Grove School, you requested that Leo A. be given an IQ test. Leo was seen here on November 9, 1967, by Mrs. Natalie Smith, staff psychologist, and was administered the Wechsler Intelligence Scale for Children. Some of Mrs. Smith's observations are important to note. For example, she stated, "Leo was cooperative and seemed to respond very well on a one-to-one basis throughout the testing period. He was encouraged to walk around and stretch between some of the tests in order that he not become overtired or lose interest. This he did and seemed to enjoy the situation quite a bit."

The results of the intelligence testing indicate that Leo's verbal, performance, and full-scale intelligence quotients at present all fall within the average range. When these scores are compared to previous intelligence testing, it is easily seen that going from an IQ in the high seventies last year to the mid-nineties (after a year in your school) indicates a good deal of growth. The sub-tests on which Leo performed poorly seem to be generally culturally based; that is, when asked what was celebrated on the Fourth of July, he replied, "Thanksgiving." Thus, any gaps in the testing seem to be due to a lack of experiential learning usually occurring in early childhood. In other instances Leo A. displayed a real concentrated attempt at working on several manipulative tasks.

The evidence from this testing situation, then, points out that Leo A. has made tremendous gains while having been in your school. To quote Mrs. Smith again, "There are tremendous gaps in his learning. One wonders how much of this is culturally induced, and how much could be attributed to emotional turmoil." This should indicate that Leo's education will be more difficult than with most other children, because these gaps must be narrowed while allowing him successful peer experiences.

The results of this testing should be as pleasing to you as they are to us. The increase in Leo's tested intelligence is a tribute to the extended efforts made by you and your staff. The fact that Leo A. is being more negative in school and generally more acting out is also a positive sign in that he is now seeking limits to be placed upon him. He would not even bother to do this if he did not have some sense of trust in the atmosphere you at Elm Grove School have created.

Continued individual tutoring as well as current highly structured educational programming are indicated. Helping Leo A. bridge the information gap, while at the same time providing a secure atmosphere for him in school, should aid him considerably in the problems of adjustment life may offer in the future.

The fact that tenuous situations continued to crop up during these periods is certainly to be mentioned. Things did not happen overnight, but the compounding of positive incidents may have caused the necessary motivation to make an attempt at living with the structure. In these instances, the social caseworker, school principal, clinical educator, and foster parents were in continuous contact. The fundamental role of truth was ingrained in these people so that Leo could never "catch" anyone in a lie. Furthermore, everyone knew about his behavior because of the continual contact so that Leo could no longer manipulate the environment through a juggling of truth.

The clinical educator's function was also to provide consultation to the classroom teacher, in this instance, and the types of techniques offered were utilized and kept or discarded as the teacher evaluated them. The effort was not to tell the teacher what to do, or to ask why she didn't do certain things; the effort was to suggest possibilities for action, a procedure most nonthreatening to the educational personnel.

The notes below summarize Leo's educational progress:

REPORT CARD

(1st Quarter) "Leo is very inconsistent in his work habits, behavior, and attitude. This, of course, affects his progress in school. He still has a great deal of difficulty adjusting to the routine of a regular classroom."

(3rd Quarter) "Leo has recently seemed to be trying harder both in his behavior and his work. He is doing much better in spelling."

PROGRESS NOTE FROM TUTOR

(3rd Quarter) "Leo is more cooperative than he was earlier in the school year. He continues to become discouraged easily and to underestimate his ability to understand new material.

"Although he is not up to grade level in math, he is doing well in multiplication and division. He is very weak in simple addition and subtraction facts, but the drill method you have set down is beginning to bear fruit. With success, Leo seems to seek more success."

"Recently, Leo started reading in a new book. He enjoys it very much and shows enthusiasm in reading for the first time. He is beginning to use reading skills he has learned to figure out words for himself. Never before has he put this much of himself into anything in the way of academic materials.

"I am encouraged with Leo's progress this marking period."

Summarizing these results, the prospects currently envisioned for a kid like Leo would not have been imaginable had not the various factors in his environment been manipulated:

1. warm considerate foster family;
2. concerned yet sincere school environment;
3. therapeutic support given to Leo by the clinic;
4. consistent and coordinated approach to the whole problem;
5. the strengths already possessed by Leo.

Such a program could not have been initiated by the school. The school, in moments of severe frustration and anxiety, was ready to institutionalize the kid. The clinic staff, on one occasion, was ready to "throw in the towel." The clinic, acting alone, could not have provided the intensive work with the kid, because kids are not customarily seen five hours a day for five days a week for some forty weeks per year. Likewise, the clinic underestimated the factors that could be provided in school to ensure the probability of a successful outcome. The clinical educator, however, through his dual training and experience, coordinated these two agencies as well as their adjunctive personnel into a successful educational and treatment modality. There is no doubt that "empty" Leo would be institutionalized today had not these particular efforts been focused in his behalf.

A. Day Classes in Regular Schools

14. Special Classes for Emotionally Disturbed Children

JAY L. BISGYER, CARL L. KAHN, AND VERNON F. FRAZEE

We believe that public schools have an obligation to provide educational facilities for handicapped children, including those who are

SOURCE: *American Journal of Orthopsychiatry,* XXXIV (July, 1964), 696–704.

emotionally handicapped. A few years ago this conviction was implemented in the form of a pilot program of special classes for emotionally disturbed children, a joint effort of the Department of Special Education of the School City of Gary, Indiana, and the Lake County Mental Health Clinic, a tax-supported agency. Our purpose was to provide a therapeutic experience for certain emotionally disturbed children with the goal of their relatively prompt return to regular classrooms.

Children are selected for the special classes because they are too disturbed to profit from a regular school placement, or because their behavior, as a result of their emotional disturbance, has been so disruptive that they could not be maintained in regular classrooms. The adaptation of these students after they have been returned to regular classes (usually within one to two years) serves as a major index of the efficacy of the program.

Most emotionally disturbed children can be helped to achieve a much higher level of integration, including the capacity for academic and social achievement. This can be accomplished by a dynamic teaching process, including the development and maintenance of a strong, positive relationship between teacher and student, which precedes and makes possible later instructional activities. Students whose previous school experience has been one of frustration, humiliation and rejection first need to become reoriented to the school setting. (The extent of this reorientation is soon apparent to a visitor. Children who formerly hated school and were often truant are observed running eagerly to the classroom. They dislike holidays, weekends, summer vacation and time off for teachers' meetings.) Although teacher and curriculum must be palpably "different" from what the students have previously known, the setting remains a classroom, the teacher a teacher, and the goal educational. The recognition that the conventional goals of educators can be achieved for disturbed children only through an unconventional, flexible approach makes these classes unlike others. While not all, or even most, emotionally disturbed children should be segregated in special classes, for certain children such classes can provide a reconstructive experience particularly suited to their needs. For this reason the selection of students is the primary responsibility of an orthopsychiatric team expanded to include the supervisor of special education.

The idea of our present special classes evolved from many discussions between schools and clinic in 1957 and 1958. Since the school administration wanted to begin the program at once, we elected to proceed with a pilot project, sacrificing the advantages of controls and a more elaborate research design. The first class was formed in October, 1958, a second added in February, 1959, and a third in September, 1959.

The clinic contributed its full diagnostic facilities, the services of its director as psychiatric consultant, and the time of a social worker to coordinate the program. The schools assigned the Supervisor of Special Education to establish, develop and oversee the project.

The State Commission on General Education gave temporary approval to this program and, since February, 1960, has reimbursed the local school system for 80 per cent of the excess cost of instruction.

The maximum enrollment in each class is seven, but the group is usually smaller, the size depending on the degree of disturbance of individual children and the readiness of the group and the teacher to accept a new student. The children have ranged in age from six to 12 years, and they all have at least average intellectual potential. The classes are located in regular elementary school buildings wherever possible. Each class is responsible to the administration of the school in which it is located, and each is integrated with the general activities of the school to the extent that it is able to participate.

Avenues of communication between school and clinic and within the structure of each must be open and free. Such crucial mechanical details as procedures for referral and for interpretation of the program to the parents must be clearly delineated and interpreted to all concerned.[1]

A detailed diagnostic study of all children considered for the program is performed within the clinic, with the clinic participants in the special class program serving on the diagnostic team.

Weekly meetings of the parents' discussion group, led by the social worker who acts as program coordinator, produce information about events at home, help parents acquire constructive attitudes toward the classes and provide guidance toward better ways of dealing with their children. The social worker consults weekly with each of the teachers to offer support, interpretations and suggestions. Periodic group meetings of teachers led by the coordinator provide mutual support and opportunities for helpful exchange of experiences.

In regular rotation, weekly conferences are held at the schools in which the special classes are located. These conferences examine and discuss the problems and progress of the class as a whole and of individual students. They are informal, and over the course of time the participants have become sufficiently secure in their roles and with each other to discuss frankly many difficult problems, including their own interaction when problematic.

One of us had become particularly aware of the effect of subtle disagreements and tensions among therapeutic personnel and administration in his study of the development of a therapeutic environment

[1] A mimeographed report, "A Supplementary Report on Operational Details of the Program," is available from the authors.

within a psychiatric unit of a general hospital. These same phenomena were also observed in the special class program. A principal had been very resistant to the assignment of a special class to her school. Although she regularly attended the meetings, since they were held in her office, her attention was usually directed out the window. The special class teacher and her students felt isolated in this school, and were even subjected to derogatory remarks, not only from other students but also from at least one other teacher. This was a principal of the older educational tradition and her anxiety about this experimental program was understandable. After many months she signaled her acceptance of the program by volunteering to help the teacher meet a technical academic problem. By contrast, another principal welcomed the special class as both a stimulating challenge and a unique opportunity to obtain assistance with children who were presenting problems to his teachers. In this setting the special class flourishes, the children take part in many school activities and the teacher feels that she is an accepted member of the faculty.

The school social worker is particularly important in dealing with families whose active participation is minimal. She visits the home, offers casework help and obtains information that would not otherwise be available.

The teachers are the most important individuals in the program. Their selection requires the greatest possible care. Our teachers have had varied backgrounds, one having come from the ranks of homebound tutors, another from art education, a third from a position as supervisor of counselors in a residential treatment center. Because of the flexibility required and the necessity for patiently reorienting the children toward school, it is our bias that regular classroom teachers of long experience would probably find it difficult to adapt themselves to this type of work.

The Supervisor of Special Education recruits the candidates and then each is interviewed psychiatrically by the clinic Director. Our experience has taught us that this evaluation must be thorough, and that one must guard against setting aside one's misgivings and accepting a teacher in response to the pressure of the needs of the program. Where this has been done we have regretted it. Unless a suitable teacher can be found, it would be far better to postpone the establishment of a special class.

The teacher must possess genuine warmth and interest in children, together with the capacity for instituting firm controls without guilt. She needs to be patient, capable of orienting herself toward future goals and able to accept the many frustrations inherent in working for six hours a day with disturbed children. She must also have the capacity for introspection and the ability to use the assistance offered by the other participants in the program. Her past experience must be carefully evaluated, including wherever possible her typical responses to difficult classroom situations and her relations with the school administration. (One quickly discovers that teachers having unresolved problems of rebellion against authority augment these tendencies in the students.) It is necessary to evaluate carefully the motivation of the applicant for this position, especially if guilt feelings toward a child or sibling are prominent.

The teacher is not a psychotherapist but she does exert a powerful therapeutic effect. Through psychiatric consultation she is helped to understand the interactions and communications of the children in their creative play and to meet individual needs while still remaining oriented to the group. Although the teacher maintains the goals of academic achievement, she accepts the reality that much activity which differs from academic work is necessary before her students are ready to learn.

The principal motivation for learning for these emotionally disturbed children is the relationship with the teacher. How the teacher feels about the child is of the utmost importance to him. The consistency with which she accepts him and applies limits without anger creates a dependable, secure milieu in which the pupil finds it rewarding to control himself and to achieve.

A second powerful supportive force is the group of children in each class. The rivalries, the making of scapegoats and the ostracizing that develop can be dealt with by the teacher. The group usually becomes tolerant of the problems of each member and tends to lend its support to those children whose ego integration is precarious.

Virtually all candidates for enrollment in these classes have experienced much parental pressure to learn. Academic study is made available to these children but never forced upon them. Whenever a child shows a disposition to advance academically or to spend more time at study, he is encouraged to do so. The teacher is careful to present tasks within the child's range of abilities. Thus pleasure through mastery begins to replace frustration due to failure.

Play is part of the curriculum, the only part in which many children will participate initially. Its observation provides useful information, for it is used not only to express resistance to learning but also to master emotional conflicts. As the child learns to play with others he acquires suitable social behavior. Directed, sedentary play sets the stage for later academic study.

The class day must have structure, but it must also be flexible and attuned to the group's current needs. The teacher instructs the class as a group wherever possible, but a great deal of individual attention is always necessary. Since the children are not of the same age or similar school experiences, they study at widely different levels ranging from reading readiness to sixth grade. The regular elementary courses of study are followed, but with many modifications. Classroom equipment and supplies include creative play materials, toys conducive to the expression of feelings, a puppet stage, record player and tape recorder.

Whenever possible, the special classes participate in their respective schools with other classes in physical education, music and art activities. The children also eat in the school cafeteria unless the class is in a particularly disturbed state. When the class as a whole has made sufficient progress, we encourage the teacher to eat separately in order to permit her some relief and to give the children an opportunity to conform to a social situation without the support of the teacher. These arrangements vary from time to time and from class to class. Teacher and children utilize a hot plate in their room to prepare special treats, which they eat together.

The usual number of pupils in each class has been five. With one exception, the students have been boys. The average age of the children in class A is eight years, three months; class B, eight years, seven months and class C, twelve years, three months. Three former students are now in regular classes and doing well, one is attending regular classes in another community because the parents moved, and one child was transferred to a residential treatment center.[2]

Diagnoses have ranged from adjustment reaction of childhood (the most common) to borderline psychosis. We have attempted to test the limits of the program's effectiveness by including children who were more seriously disturbed. An important criterion for selection is our expectation that the child can benefit from placement in the special class. The classes may not be used simply as repositories for difficult children. Children are selected whose intellectual potential is within the average range or higher, and preference is given to younger students. We have attempted to restrict admission to those children whose home environments appear to be within satisfactory limits or modifiable. Diagnosis

[2] Since this was written eight more have left the classes. Of these, three have changed so greatly that their success in regular classes seems assured. Two others have improved considerably but will need much support. Both are in treatment at the clinic and will continue. Another child has made a much better social adjustment but has not advanced academically enough to warrant expectation of success in a regular class. Placement in a special residential school has been recommended. An impulse-ridden, character-disordered older boy and a younger child who is psychotic and brain-damaged have made an improved social adaptation but both are still too disturbed for regular classes. Institutionalization will probably be necessary for both.

and recommendation by the Lake County Mental Health Clinic are prerequisites for admission, and approval must be granted by the Supervisor of the Special Service Division of the schools.

Common symptoms encountered were hyperactivity, poor academic achievement, daydreaming, social withdrawal, infantile speech, extreme immaturity, destructiveness, temper tantrums, fighting, stealing, distractibility and fearfulness. Three major pupil groups observed were: children who clung to infantile modes of behavior and were fearful of learning and of growing up; aggressive, defiant children; and severely disturbed children too preoccupied in fantasy to participate effectively in school situations. We have found that children in this last group often require individual treatment as well as placement in a special class.

Our experience is not yet sufficiently extensive for us to predict precisely which children benefit most from the special class approach. This appraisal is difficult because *all* the children have benefited substantially, and the degree of improvement has often been related more closely to the length of time in the special class than to the diagnostic category. We do not exclude the one child who was sent to a residential treatment center. Our original recommendation had been hospitalization; since it was not available we decided to place him in one of the classes. Although at first very frightened and somewhat bizarre in his reactions, he made considerable progress, and, when an opening became available for him in a residential treatment center, our decision to send him there was based more upon the disruptive situation in his family than on any other factor.

In another case, the parents could not accept our recommendation for residential treatment, but when they demonstrated willingness to participate actively in a treatment program for themselves, the child, Roger, was placed in a special class and is now showing remarkable improvement.

Roger, six, was so severely impulse-ridden that his placement in a special class was made with many misgivings. After several months the teacher became discouraged, feeling she could not help this boy to progress. During a review conference at the school, the psychiatric consultant, by using the teacher's own cataloging of Roger's achievements, was able to demonstrate that his improvement had been considerable. The teacher was helped to realize that her more spectacular accomplishments with another child would be more the exception than the rule. With her aims altered, she could accept Roger as he was and help him by painstaking, ego-building techniques to develop at his own rate. Now in his second year in the class, Roger is quite a different child, much more mature and beginning to show a real interest in academic learning. The teacher's experience with Roger prepared her for a new boy, not unlike

Roger, who began to show progress within a month of enrollment.

Jack, 11 years old, had been able to manipulate a previous teacher through his aggressive behavior and his leadership of the other boys. This teacher had unconsciously fostered his rebellion out of her own needs. In his therapy with a male social worker, one was impressed with his wish to please a man. His disruptive behavior was manifested only in the classroom. He was clearly imitating his extremely domineering truck-driver father's relationship with Jack's meek, masochistic and depreciated mother. The special class teacher had been carefully prepared for this boy's almost certain attempt to control the class. She was able to hold firm without anger or punitiveness until he recognized that he was in fact the pupil and she the teacher. He then dramatically regressed to such childish behavior as smearing his face with food and mildly accepted the leadership of others. The other class members were visibly relieved. They began to assert themselves as individuals, free from his intimidation. Jack gradually resumed his former leadership of the class but only occasionally vied with the teacher for control. His academic work improved as more of his energy was channeled into his studies. He became eager to return to a regular classroom in order to prove himself, and, since the fall of 1960, he has been adjusting satisfactorily in the same school from which he had formerly been excluded.

Another special class child was Raymond, who had literally given up reading in the second grade. His high-pitched speaking voice, nightly enuresis and preference for younger companions were a few of the signs of his immaturity. He was unable to grow up because this would have meant the loss of his mother's love: She had clearly indicated during the diagnostic process that she liked her children best when they were babies. After a year and six months of complete rejection of academic work, this boy one day picked up a book and started to read. This was the first in a series of steps toward maturity. The enuresis stopped. Raymond began to speak in a lower register. He made new friends of his own age. His hostile nagging and bickering subsided, to reappear transiently when his mother suffered an accidental injury. She had previously been in individual treatment without much improvement, but she seemed to thrive in the setting of the parents' discussion group. She attended regularly and became much more accepting of her son's desire to grow up.

Approximately one-fourth of the children also receive direct treatment at the clinic. It is difficult to determine the extent to which the special class program has helped children who have been concurrently in therapy. Seven of the 19 children have received psychotherapy, five of them during the time they were enrolled in the class. In two instances therapy had been terminated prior to the special class experience, and the improvement can be largely attributed to the latter.

It is our impression that individual therapy and the special class program are synergistic, especially when good communication exists between the therapist and those involved in the special class program. In one instance there was much evidence that most of the child's improvement was directly related to the working through of significant and specific neurotic conflicts in individual treatment.

Our conservatism led us to recommend psychotherapy for two children who were much improved through their special class placement and who were about to be returned to regular classes. Their parents no longer saw any need for special assistance, and we have been gratified to learn that these children have done well in the regular class without individual treatment.

We do not yet have sufficient data to determine the extent to which the special class program may be able to modify internalized problems. Our follow-up studies do not yet include a sufficient number of children nor do they extend over a long enough period of time. Encouraging symptomatic changes have occurred, including the acceleration of maturation and the amelioration of such symptoms as speech defect, enuresis, soiling, poor coordination (on a functional basis), hostile aggressive behavior of various types and learning disturbances.

The special class experience has been most therapeutic for children who exhibit a fear of growing up and more infantile modes of behavior than can be tolerated in a regular class. School represents a reality demand that they are not ready to meet. The process of learning, which as a concomitant of normal maturation should fall within the "conflict-free-ego-sphere" as described by Hartmann, has instead become involved in conflict. The reorientation and ego-building opportunities provided by the special class operate through the new relationship with the teacher, who, unlike the mother, permits and encourages the normal maturational processes without ambivalence. Identification with the teacher and unconscious acceptance of her ideals help to remove the activities of school and academic learning from the area of conflict, and, if the parents have learned not to interfere, the child's own maturational thrust should carry him forward. Children who begin to achieve academically usually show other improvements also, suggesting that symptoms in several areas are related to the same central conflict and that some alteration of the equilibrium of the ego-adaptive mechanisms has taken place.

The program has given some indication that improvement can be brought about in children who seem clinically to be amenable only to residential treatment, provided that significant changes can be accomplished simultaneously in the home. We have learned that a special class program can bring about significant changes in less disturbed children even when the home is not modifiable. The home problems continue to act as a limitation, however.

The undertaking of a special class program faces certain obstacles. Parents and educators are slow to understand the needs of emotionally disturbed children. Suitable teachers are scarce. Few colleges offer training for this work. State licensure requirements may block the hiring of desirable applicants. Overcrowded schools may resist giving up a room to such a small class of five to seven children. The heavy demands the program makes upon the time of the supervisor of special education tends to limit the number of classes. The clinic, too, must invest much time, especially that of the coordinator. Parental participation is often minimal.

On the basis of our experience, we make the following recommendations for those who are considering the establishment of special classes for emotionally disturbed children in public schools:

1. The participating members of the clinic staff and the school staff must enter into a collaborative effort in which they form a new group with loyalty to "the program," while retaining their individual professional identities.
2. The administrative heads of both the clinic and the schools should lend their support to such a program, especially since some criticism will be inevitable.
3. The special classes should be housed in regular elementary schools whose principals accept the program and favorably influence the attitudes of teachers and student body toward the teacher and pupils of the special class.
4. Exclusion from regular classes should not become the selective factor: The special classes are not custodial facilities.
5. Our experience suggests that younger children respond more rapidly to the special class experience and undergo greater change than older pupils. We believe that early identification of children with emotional problems could lead to selection of suitable students *before* they have suffered the frustration and humiliation of school failure. We believe that children can be selected at the end of kindergarten or during the first grade and that, within one or two years, sufficient change can usually be brought about to enable these children to return to regular classes with the ability to perform academically at the level of their contemporaries.
6. In spite of the shortage of teachers, selection should be rigorous. Of course, some abstract ideal of mental health cannot be demanded, but the personality and life history of the prospective teacher must be carefully evaluated. The characteristic adaptive mechanisms of the teacher-candidate must be considered, for these will become an im-

portant part of the transactional process involving teacher and class. Sufficient support for the teacher must be built into the program.

Summary

Since 1958, a special class program for emotionally disturbed children has been operated by a public school system and a public psychiatric clinic on the premise that education must be provided for all children including the emotionally handicapped. These special classes are not repositories for difficult children but facilities for clinically selected children too disturbed to profit from regular education or too disturbing to remain in the regular classroom, or both, yet capable of responding positively to the therapeutic experience of a relationship with teachers selected for their capacity to accept children warmly and limit them consistently. The classes aim to effect changes in the children's response to the school situation and to learning opportunities, so that in a year or two they may be returned to regular classes. The careful selection of teachers is crucial. Younger children profit most rapidly and most completely from the special class experience. Clinic and school have found a way to work co-operatively in the pursuit of their common objective—to help children grow.

15. Toward a Broader Concept of the Role of the Special Class for Emotionally Disturbed Children

Peter Knoblock and Ralph A. Garcea

This report describes recent attempts by a group of professional workers affiliated with a special class program to broaden the scope of their ef-

SOURCE: *Exceptional Children*, XXXI (March, 1965), 329–36. Reprinted by permission.

forts. This included the influencing of educational practices as applied to disturbed children in regular classrooms by directing efforts to professional workers responsible for the education of these children.

It is believed that the uniqueness of the proposal described in this paper lies in the utilization of specific special class program personnel for the express purpose of disseminating their skills and experiences to others in the school who were facing the same problems of educating disturbed children, but on a larger scale. In essence, the approach used was a form of mental health consultation directed toward the needs of the participating schools and their personnel.

After three years of experimentation in the developing of a special class program for emotionally disturbed children, the Syracuse Scholastic Rehabilitation Program, hereafter referred to as the SSRP, reached the following conclusions: First, that the program personnel had acquired through trial and error, experimentation, and testing of hypotheses, a number of techniques and theories which needed further testing in order to validate their efficacy for larger groups of disturbed children in educational programs. Second, that there are certain kinds of children and problems that could be dealt with in the regular classroom, provided some program modification is made. Third, that as the program became known and accepted by the community and public school personnel the number of children referred for admission into the special program far outweighed available openings.

It would not be accurate to conceptualize the need for a broader concept of intervention only from the standpoint of the needs of the children involved. It is patently clear to those professional workers who deal with disturbed children that the interaction process is such that strong needs and feelings on the part of the adult are aroused. These feelings may operate to impede or hasten the development and maintenance of a relationship (Katz, 1963). The SSRP personnel in their contacts with teachers and administrators began to focus on the needs of other school personnel in relation to programing for emotionally disturbed children. For example, it became clear that many teachers and administrators were simply in need of factual information. Closely related was the inability of many professional workers in the schools to effectively utilize the information in their possession. More importantly, many others desired ways in which they could conceptualize the educational needs of such children. Along with supplying of factual information, it became apparent that once such efforts were made to change or modify attitudes it was necessary to offer support to the school personnel involved. In still other instances, the nature of the school population in certain areas of the city was changing so rapidly that the public school personnel involved were under considerable pressure to effect certain changes in curriculum and management for great numbers of children, including those children with emotional handicaps.

Related Literature

The proposal and ideas presented in this article reflect the influence of two sources. The first is found in the substantial writings of Caplan (1959) and his colleagues who have attempted to employ public health concepts in an effort to design preventive approaches to mental health. In the conceptualization of their program they have advocated mental health consultation as one method to achieve their goal. Kazanjian, Stein, and Weinberg (1962) quote Caplan's definition of mental health consultation as follows:

> Mental health consultation may be defined as an interaction process taking place between two professional workers, the consultant and the consultee. In the interaction an attempt is made to help the consultee solve the mental health problem of his client or clients within the framework of his usual professional functioning. The process is designed so that while help is being given to the consultee in dealing with the presenting problem, he is also being educated in order that he will be able in the future to handle similar problems in an effective manner (p. 1).

The second source influencing our approach is the technical assistance to public school personnel described by Newman, Redl, and Kitchener (1962). Similar to our concerns, they began by focusing on the problems of effectively dealing with disturbed children in the public schools. Their sensitivity to this need developed in the residential treatment of disturbed boys when it became apparent that the teachers needed definite skills and understandings in order to maximize their functioning as professional workers. In their monograph they described the expansion of their efforts to the public schools once they had begun to systematize their supervising and interstaff communication methods in the residential center. Thus we see in their approach a much closer rapprochement between the consultant and the public school, with the original plan stemming from the practical problems arising in the management and education of disturbed children in a residential center.

Cutler and McNeil (1960) viewed with skepticism the utilization of specialists employed by the school as seen in the following statement:

> To some degree the teacher attempted to turn to the mental health specialists in her school for the solution of these practical problems. But here, she met obstacles in the short supply of specialists, and the limited clinical orientation

which had been transplanted in the schools and which flourished in the hearts of the specialists themselves. Further, the specialists, as employees of the school system, were placed in a difficult position when it came to "training" colleagues who, in theory at least, were responsible professionals in their own right (p. 19).

Again, it is felt that the approach outlined in this article negates several of the concerns discussed in the quotation. First, personnel directly involved with disturbed children are deployed for consultation purposes, thus drawing from a ready source of specialists, who were also dynamically oriented. Second, the training approach utilized by the consultants was essentially one of enabling school personnel to capitalize on their existing skills along with aiding them to mobilize their school and staff to program for disturbed children. It is felt that by the implementation of such an approach, the high degree of resistance referred to by Cutler and McNeil is considerably reduced.

Planning Phase

The plan involved an attempt to influence administrative and teaching personnel in elementary schools so that their perceptions and attitudes of disturbed children could be positively modified. The authors firmly believe that such changes in attitude can lead to more adequate educational programing for these children and further that much of this programing can be accomplished within a regular classroom setting.

Two clinical psychologists and one psychiatric social worker who were working regularly with the SSRP attempted to offer consultative services in regard to these problem children who were not in the special program. It was felt that the authors' identification with the SSRP would offer certain advantages. It was presumed that they would be perceived by the school personnel as having particular training and interest as well as concurrent experience which would qualify them to discuss problems meaningfully and appropriately.

The initial focus was the large number of children referred to the special class program who could not be accepted, usually because of the small size of the special program. Based on the authors' growing conviction that much of their experience in a special class program would possibly have wide applicability, they decided to employ a form of mental health consultation. Such an approach was designed to focus on school personnel who were responsible for programing for disturbed children in general, and did not deal only with those children on the waiting list.

With this in mind, the authors faced their next strategic question;

that is, which schools should be approached with these ideas. The plan was given no advance publicity and therefore no one was in a position to request this aid. There were three factors taken into consideration in this selection: (a) a school which showed a high density of emotionally disturbed children; (b) a visiting teacher assigned to that school who showed better than average ability to profit from the experience so that she could perpetuate and refine the procedures developed; and (c) a building principal who had shown an interest in dealing with this kind of problem. With this combination of factors in mind, three schools were selected as possible sites, one for each consultant.

With this rationale, the director of special projects was approached and the plan was presented to him. He felt the magnitude of the problem of programing for disturbed children called for a special effort and that this plan was feasible. He agreed to meet with the three principals involved along with the chairman of the special class program who would eventually serve as a consultant. The purpose of the meeting was to give as much administrative encouragement as possible to the implementation of the plan.

There was mutual agreement that all planning would begin with the building principal. The authors believe, as do Newman, Redl, and Kitchener (1962), that no plan can be effective without this key person's endorsement and support. During these conferences, the principals raised reasonable questions as to how an attempt would be made to deal with these children, for all agreed that they were a problem in school. In reply, it was noted that the help given would be in terms of the services of one consultant, one-half day per week for the remainder of the school year. Also, that this consultant's activities would depend on what was mutually agreed upon by both the principal and the consultant. It was made clear that any ensuing plan would be based on the principal's estimation of where the emphasis should be placed. In short, the initial step was to design a plan with the principal using the services of the consultant which would help to meet the needs of the staff and of the emotionally disturbed children in that elementary school.

On this basis each of the three principals agreed to become involved in the project. A consultant was then assigned to each school. He, in turn, contacted the principal and together each of the three teams began its planning.

The initial stages were very difficult for everyone. One question which had to be faced by all was: What could one person working one-half day per week accomplish? The needs were so many and so great yet the means offered toward their accomplishment seemed so insufficient. With this recognition more traditional services, such as individual therapy with children, counseling with problem families, more psychological testing service, and group counseling with children, were discarded. An awareness grew that something else which would have a broader impact on the problem needed to be developed.

The Consultation Process in One School

Initially, the consultant found that the school had made certain manipulations in class grouping which enabled the staff to better handle a certain percentage of the problems. It was felt by the principal that such procedures were effective where tried, but that attempts were limited. The limitations came from faculty members who had strong reservations about such planning. It was felt that these reservations often resulted from lack of both information and personal involvement in further planning. This, in turn, resulted in insufficient interest which prevented school personnel from experimenting with these difficult problems. Many of the school personnel including the principal felt the need for new information and understanding which would involve the faculty in a meaningful manner. By joint agreement of the consultant and principal it was decided to focus initial efforts on the teachers of younger children.

The plan involved a meeting of the consultants with all of the first and second grade teachers. The purpose of the meetings was to discuss the effective handling of emotionally disturbed children by the classroom teacher. It was decided that such meetings would be offered to the teachers on a voluntary basis and that they would take place on a once a week basis, during the teacher's lunch hour. It was further decided that the principal would not attend such meetings, since it was felt that the teachers should feel as free as possible to express any feelings in regard to school routine or practices which affected programing for children. It was made clear to the participating teachers that the meetings would in no way be used to evaluate teacher performance and further, that no individual teacher would be discussed by the consultant and the principal.

A procedure was worked out so that the consultant would visit one classroom each week, usually for one or two hours. During this time he would observe the group at large and focus particularly on the disturbed children who were earlier identified by the teacher. During the lunch period, which followed the classroom observation, the consultant and the teacher would share their morning observations with others.

The focus of the group was directed by the consultant into two main areas. First, by using classroom observation, what could the teacher learn about disturbed children. Second, once the behavior was understood what intervention techniques were available to classroom teachers. The discussions revealed, among other things, that all of the teachers demonstrated a sincere interest in more effectively coping with these children. Also, that many had more ability to understand the meaning of behavior than they believed themselves capable although symptomatic behavior was frequently accepted without an appreciation of underlying dynamics. The group as a whole seemed to feel that they could deal with the behavior, but they felt generally pessimistic about the ultimate effects of their intervention on the status of the child. This feeling was somewhat modified as the group consciously dealt with one little girl who was recognized by all as a problem. The change in the girl's behavior as a result of teacher understanding and altered techniques was both exciting and rewarding to them. All such problems were discussed by the group of teachers with the consultant's role being that of resource person. He also served the purpose of keeping the discussion centered on two main areas as agreed upon by the group.

The teachers' evaluation of the project indicated that they, as a group, became more interested and involved in the problem solving process as it related to planning for emotionally disturbed children. This was indicated in their general acceptance of the meetings and in their critical appraisal of their own practices. They did feel, however, that they could benefit further from more group sessions, and that the consultant should have more direct contact with the children with whom they were concerned. They also felt that more of the traditional mental health services should be made available for the schools.

Discussion

It is hoped that the approach described in this article will be replicated and improved upon by other school systems facing the same educational planning problems related to emotionally disturbed children. It is with this purpose in mind that several facets of the approach have been spelled out in considerable detail. As a case in point, what transpired during the planning phase, and even prior, had a great bearing on the form and content of the plan which evolved in a school. To illustrate this point a description of the planning phase in a second school is described in detail.

In the following discussion of the consultation procedures at the second school, it should be pointed out that the consultant had, on prior occasions, spent several very brief periods of time in the school. The consultant felt that this previous contact made the initial phases of the consultation process smoother.

Several meetings were held during the early stage of the consultation process. It was mutually agreed upon by the principal and consultant that perhaps the school social worker should be involved in this early planning phase. The initial question was one of determining how and in what ways the consultant would be of service to the school. The initial suggestion was one of allocating time for the evaluation of individual children who presented the greatest management and planning problems. It is of interest to note that the earlier contact with the school had followed the procedure of evaluating individual children. The principal spent a considerable portion of time discussing such children, and this proved to be of great benefit in regard to the initial question of where to focus time and energy. By discussing individual children, the consultant was provided with an opportunity to familiarize himself with the kind of child with whom the school was concerned and to gain a clearer picture of the operating philosophy of the school as it was directed to the management of difficult children. In contrast to procedures adopted at the first school, it was agreed that in this instance it would be of benefit to have the principal participate in the group meeting. Those familiar with the scheduling problems confronting the public schools will acknowledge the difficulty experienced in finding a meeting time that was mutually convenient for the teachers, principal, visiting teacher, school psychologist and consultant. The principal informed each of the kindergarten and first grade teachers of the proposed plan and gained some expression of their interest in participating and in accepting a meeting during their lunch hour.

It is of interest now to chart the differences between what occurred in the first school described in the previous section, and in the second school just discussed. In the second school, much less emphasis was placed on discussing individual children but rather the group focused on the development of a comprehensive school plan. This plan was drawn up by the group and included curriculum and school programing modifications which were finally put in written form and submitted to administrative officials in the school system.

Needless to say, it is difficult to pinpoint the precise reasons for the variation in process and outcome between the two schools. Careful analysis revealed, however, that several factors differed from school to school: (a) the principal, school social worker, and school psychologist were present at the second school's group meeting; (b) that unlike the situation faced in the first school, the consultant did not come into a school which had done any appreciable preplanning; and (c) the orientation of the teachers involved seemed to focus directly on the need for long-range plans. Closely related to this was their strong belief in the therapeutic advantages which could be realized by the curriculum and administrative changes in the schools.

From the very outset, the consultants pondered what the effect would be of going into the schools without, so to speak, being invited. It was felt, at least initially, that this factor had a great deal to do with the structuring of the relationship between the consultants and the school principals. Support of this perception is seen in Caplan's (1964) statement: "In many cases where contact is initiated from higher levels of administration, as by a directive of the superintendent of schools, the consultant is asked by the school principal to consult with the newest and least experienced teacher on the staff" (p. 234). At least in one of the schools the consultant was asked to deal with teachers in the early grades not primarily because of any firm belief in prevention, but rather because the personnel was experiencing a great amount of difficulty coping with the behavior. Caplan goes on to say: "From experience we have learned that, although initial entry into an institution may be a result of an invitation by a peripheral member of the system, it is essential to understand the authority pattern and quickly contact all key figures" (p. 234). It has already been described as to how much valence was initially placed on the evaluation of individual children. Once relationships and ground rules were worked out, the consultant was drawn into larger problems and came in contact with more key school personnel.

What looked like fortuitous circumstances at the time eventually turned out to greatly enhance the relationship and process of consultation. For example, early in the consultation process both consultants offered support, suggestions, and techniques to the groups in terms of dealing with specific problem children. Much to everyone's delight the children improved, seemingly in ways directly related to the new intervention techniques employed. Such incidents gave credence to the group's sometimes wavering belief that changes could be effected. The adage "Nothing succeeds like success" seemed to apply in these instances.

It is the authors' belief that this modest and relatively short term experiment has justified itself on the basis of the following outcomes:

1. A small number of mental health specialists were able in a short period of time to effect changes in the attitudes, techniques, and programing approaches of public school personnel in three separate schools.
2. Others in leadership positions in the schools, including the teachers themselves, were afforded an opportunity to consolidate their skills and to continue such school planning on an all school basis or in their individual classrooms.
3. A form of advance screening of youngsters in need of special class placement was accomplished. By spending time in these schools the

consultants became familiar, either directly or indirectly, with many such children. No attempt has been made to suggest that this particular approach is a panacea for the problems confronting schools in planning for disturbed children. Rather, it should be considered as just one of many potential plans which judiciously uses existing school personnel.

As with any intervention technique, it will be necessary for those interested in continuing or refining such an approach to conceptualize in clear terms what their role as consultants will resemble. For example, Caplan (1964) points out that the consultant's role may take many forms such as inspection, supervision, manipulation, collaboration, psychotherapy, liaison, to name just a few. He stated: "I believe that we will attain a higher level of professional functioning when the specialist is able to differentiate these various activities and employ each of them consistently in relation to his assignment, his professional goals, and his understanding of the demands of each situation" (p. 213). In conjunction with being able to differentiate the procedures of mental health consultation, it is equally important to focus on the stages or progression through which such procedures pass.

References

CAPLAN, G. *Concepts of Mental Health and Consultation.* U.S. Department of Health, Education, and Welfare, Office of Education, Publication No. 373. Washington, D.C.: Government Printing Office, 1959.

CAPLAN, G. *Principles of Preventive Psychiatry.* New York: Basic Books, 1964.

CUTLER, R. L., and MC NEIL, E. B. *Mental Health Consultation in Schools: A Research Analysis.* Ann Arbor: University of Michigan, 1963.

KATZ, R. L. *Empathy: Its Nature and Uses.* Glencoe, Illinois: Free Press, 1963.

KAZANJIAN, V., STEIN, S., and WEINBERG, W. L. *An Introduction to Mental Health Consultation.* U.S. Department of Health, Education, and Welfare, Public Health Service Monograph No. 69. Washington, D.C.: Government Printing Office, 1962.

NEWMAN, RUTH G., REDL, F., and KITCHENER, H. *Technical Assistance in a Public School System.* Washington, D.C.: Washington School of Psychiatry, School Research Program, 1962.

16. Resource Programing for Emotionally Disturbed Teenagers

EILEEN M. CONNOR AND
JOHN F. MULDOON

One of the seriously puzzling problems in contemporary education is that of involving the emotionally disturbed person in the formal learning process. Home tutoring or special class teaching, the usual public school provision for those with learning disabilities, can be offered to the student whose aggression, withdrawal, or disorientation precludes the satisfactory classroom management needed to implement his learning. However, these solutions have built-in limitations, because they can restrict where the child needs freedom to correct his own errors; they can protect where he needs to assume responsibility for the task at hand, his education. Neither tutoring nor the special class use the social aspect of the total community, the community within which the child can meet, recognize, and be involved in natural interactions at all levels, and in the process of these interactions master the developmental steps necessary for involvement in the learning process.

If learning—both process and product—is to be considered a valid goal for the disturbed teenager, then a comprehensive approach to the problem is indicated, an approach that would retain the strengths of both regular and special handling, and program around their inadequacies. Resource programing is an exploratory step in this direction.

History

Technoma Workshop moved into resource programing in February, 1965, in an effort to meet the developmental needs of its clients. It is an

SOURCE: *Exceptional Children*, XXXIV (December, 1967), 261–65. Reprinted by permission.

agency that was established in August, 1961, to provide a day care program for severely disturbed teenagers who for practical purposes had been dropped from the regular therapeutic and education programs in the community. These young people had been too openly aggressive or withdrawn to be maintained in public schools or were "too unmotivated" or "too impulsive" to be offered regular agency services.

The basic agency goal for these young people, adequate functioning in the community, required provision of extensive educational and vocational services. As these teenagers improved in their ability to learn and in their ability to meet the educational and social demands of the agency's classroom, the day care staff faced the need to return them to regular public school classes. This move gave the staff a way to maintain the child's educational level and provided the child with a halfway step for resuming community living. (Technoma also recognized the needs of the marginally functioning student in the public schools whose disorganization could lead to a break with his education unless extensive supportive measures were readily available. It was felt that such a break with accepted peer group goals unnecessarily compounded the student's basic problems.)

To implement this plan, Technoma sought the help of the Pittsburgh Public Schools. There, the agency director obtained permission from the superintendent of schools to explore means of educating disturbed teenagers in a joint agency-public school program. Technoma's educators worked out the procedures with the department of pupil services and the principal of the high school involved. A plan was agreed upon whereby the high school would accept the agency's students at their grade or achievement levels on a full or part time basis, and it would consider the agency's offer of special help for the troubled teenagers already enrolled in the school if some provision could be made for offering support to the school, teacher, and student, in both general educational planning and in the event of crisis.

The day care center agreed to provide a qualified teacher to develop and staff this public school based program for disturbed teenagers and to give the teacher continued support in the form of consultation and supervision. The school, Schenley High School, provided classroom space, gave the agency teacher the freedom to operate as a regular staff member in the school, and offered administrative guidance and protection for the program. The board of education offered appropriate consultation through the available services in administration, school social work, psychology, and psychiatry. The teacher and representatives of these services formed a committee dedicated to making the program work at all levels. Meeting weekly, the committee became a resource to the disturbed teenager, the classroom teacher, and the school, both for crisis situations and for ongoing programing.

In the first two years of its exploratory existence, resource programing has shown two positive results: (a) adolescents use the program, and (b) school administrations accept it. The extent to which this programing serves modification of the learning difficulties of disorganized teenagers is yet to be determined, but it has shown demonstrable success as a method for helping the adolescent to maintain himself in the physical space and emotional climate where learning can take place.

Problem

Involving the student in the learning process through the use of public education is a multilevel problem requiring consideration of the following needs.

WHY THE STUDENT NEEDS TO BE INVOLVED The disorganization of the disturbed adolescent is reflected in obscure and unrealistic goals, in an inability to see the continuous relationship between goal and steady effort, and in resistance to assuming responsibility for determining goals or maintaining purposeful action. Learning provides the goal of education, which leads toward a primary life goal of work. This educational goal is rational, oriented to a teenager's peers. The goal is also personal enough to motivate, yet general and impersonal enough for the student to "hide in." The disturbed student needs goals that "fit." The student's task of seeing and assuming responsibility for cause and effect—the continuous effort that results in education—requires a degree of organization and self-control not readily at his command. Outside controls, which can be supplied by public education, are required to aid him in developing learning skills and gathering content.

HOW THE NEEDS OF ADMINISTRATOR, TEACHER, AND STUDENT CONFLICT The solution to this problem is more complex. First, the administrator must keep the contagion of disorder to a minimum in the total school and protect the teachers from excessively disruptive or demanding children.

Secondly, the teacher must maintain a balance between educating a group of students and using evaluation and remediation to meet the specific needs of the individual student whose previous emotional stresses prevented him from learning subject content. The teacher must personally offer to motivate this student, to keep him coming to school, and to help him in class when his anxiety spills over into the acting out or withdrawn behavior that commands the adult's total attention.

Third, the disturbed teenager himself must be able to use the supportive measures which are offered. He is not consistent; his needs are in a state of flux. The burden of meeting and allowing for these needs falls on both teacher and administrator, who must operate within a well defined educational structure. The difference between the extremely wide range of the student's needs and the limited range of active responses allowed to personnel by the structure of school sometimes leaves a gap, a gray area, through which the teenager cannot grope and into which the school cannot reach. The adolescent who does not have the inner controls with which to work through his own problems or wait out such periods is often forced to break with his educational goal because he lacks the capacity to use the educational vehicle, the public school classroom.

Education in a public school setting is a practical goal for many disturbed adolescents. When the paradoxical quality of their needs is recognized, public school education is also a possibility. The task of the resource programer and program is to meet these excessive, inconsistent, and uncontrolled needs in such a way that the disturbed adolescent can achieve the necessary balance to make progress toward education and the mental health goals in education.

Description

The best way to describe resource programing is to study the resource person and the tools he has at his command. This person is both one and many individuals. The "one" is a teacher, because he can use education, the natural product of the school system, as the entree to solving the multiple problems of the disturbed teenager. This teacher's goal is to involve the student in learning within the structure of the regular class, to help the student to maintain himself within this structure, and to enable the student to profit from it. The resource teacher's methods are as varied as the changing needs of the child, the capacity of the regular class teachers, and the resourcefulness of the administration. The "many" are the people within the school who symbolize the reality of school functioning and who in any way touch the lives of these students, from friend to counselor, from janitor to principal.

The resource teacher meets the disturbed teenager as a teacher counselor. The adolescent comes to the resource teacher for help by way of the school social worker's office for being truant; by way of the vice principal's office for being a hall walker; by way of the counselor's office as an underachiever; and by way of the regular class as a noncommunicating daydreamer. And sometimes he comes by himself. He comes in search of "something" to which he cannot assign realistic dimensions. He comes because his behavior impresses school personnel who come in contact with him as disoriented, as expressing need.

He is received at the level of the help he seeks. He comes to explain that he cuts class due to a home problem; his father is angry with him and therefore he cannot do school work. He wants to talk; he is listened to. He comes blaming academic failure for his inability to read; he begins a diagnostic reading evaluation. He comes saying nothing is wrong, he just didn't have any place to go; he looks out the window. Initially the student asks for and is given this personal support. He may never ask for, or be able to accept, anything more, but a student coming to the resource person is usually in need of extensive care if his goal, participation in public education, is to be realized.

The tools the resource teacher has at his command are evaluation procedures, educational techniques, personal counseling, the resource space itself, and programing.

Evaluation can be both behavioral and academic. A behavioral reading is gained from the combined personal observations of regular school staff and resource teacher, plus, where indicated, an optional psychiatric interview and psychological testing. (A child may receive full benefits of resource programing without psychiatric evaluation, if it is felt that such inquiry might create unnecessary anxiety in child or parent.) To predict and help prevent the self-destructive behavior that can result in separation from school, the following questions are asked: At what level might the student see normal school group pressure as a personal attack? How does this student defend himself? What type of caring response will he accept from the adult? Academic evaluation, both informal (teachers' records and resource teacher observations) and formal (achievement and diagnostic records), provides the base for the diagnosis of skill and content deficits and for the remedial help fundamental to the student's capacity in acquiring new content and skills.

Education is directed toward helping the adolescent acquire the learning essential to survival in the classroom. The resource teacher does not replace the regular class teacher, but cooperates with him. He assists students whose emotional problems are manifested in learning difficulties by modifying these difficulties. He may reteach subject content which the student has missed or which the student has been unable to absorb. For the student whose anxiety severely limits his attention span in a particular class, the teacher may help him to structure study time so that subject continuity is not lost. The teacher may also use specific techniques, such as self-teaching devices, to implement the learning of a student whose negative reactions prevent him from accepting direct help when tutoring is indicated. The unmotivated student may be encouraged to attend to the assignments of the regular teacher by being involved in learning through the use of creative projects in which he feels interest and sees value.

The purpose of counseling is to assist the adolescent in meeting the demands of responsible interaction with adults and peers who are encountered in daily school life. How can a student go back into a class he has walked out of? How can he ask a teacher for a makeup test? How can he go to lunch, when there is no one to sit with? How can he walk down a hall when everybody is looking at him? The caring—burden sharing—aspect of group discussions carries many; others need a personal listener. The aim of personal counseling is to provide the tools, in this case the social tools, needed to relate to the school group in such a way that spending the day in their company is a possible and often gainful experience.

The resource space is a classroom complete with chalkboards, texts, and desks, readily accessible, located in the mainstream of student traffic away from the school discipline and counseling areas to reinforce its identification with education. It is orthodox in appearance and essentially mobile. The student uses this physical space supportively, sometimes at the request of and in cooperation with the resource teacher and sometimes in lieu of personal contact. A young person whose anger threatens to overwhelm him in the classroom can escape to the room, pace, and slam his books on the floor. The frightened person can push chairs into a corner and hide; the hurt one can stare out of a window; the anxious one in need of activity can rearrange the furniture in the room. The student who has mentally played truant from an emotionally stressful class can study, use self-teaching devices, or be tutored without interference; the student who temporarily cannot tolerate the physical presence of another person while writing an assignment can pull a screen around a desk and isolate himself. The student who cannot respond to peers in open halls and classrooms can put out tentative smiles and conversation feelers or can get angry within the protection of a familiar space and in the presence of friends. And the student who cannot or should not use this space is met in his own "space"—the halls, cafeteria, or locker area, where he is offered the degree of supportive care he can accept.

The student is taught to take responsibility for using this room and its teacher as a support, a crutch, that can be deliberately used and set aside when the needs that precipitated use of this crutch can be met in the regular school setting. The student is asked to commit himself to staying in school and make the effort to do so.

Programing is both a tool and minor goal. The adolescent who uses the skills of the resource teacher and the space provided for him in the resource room finds the arrangement comfortable. An ongoing, goal-directed procedure is to gradually transfer the young person to full participation in the regular school program and to plan for meaningful experiences with other skilled adults, peer groups, and other areas of space, thus giving support at a reality level. The resource teacher becomes a programer: he sells the quality of a student, his skills, deficiencies, and needs, to the teacher and administrator most competent to handle him. He counsels the student on approaching these adults regarding the kind of support to be expected, how to ask for it, and how to use it. He supports both adolescent and adult in their initial attempts to relate to one another. He teaches the student to use the space provided within the school—that the library is a quiet room, that the cafeteria line is a place to try a conversation, and that the gymnasium is an area in which it is possible to work off anger. He asks that the student be held responsible to the administration for his actions, and supports both child and administration in the task of carrying out disciplinary controls.

In the process of taking the care, control, and responsibility of transferring the disturbed teenager into the regular school programs, the resource teacher comes in contact with school personnel and becomes a source of help to them in handling other problem adolescents who have not been considered for programing. This concern for mental health and the general mental health climate is greatly extended and results in more thoughtful handling of troubled students. The possibility of preventing crises becomes appreciably greater, and so do the child's chances of profiting from his school experiences.

17. A School-Based Therapeutic Environment for Emotionally Disturbed Children

E. LAKIN PHILLIPS, SALAH EL-BATRAWI, AND ROLAND H. TANCK

In this paper we are concerned with a rationale of behavior change, and with some methods available in the school for implementing change.

SOURCE: *High School Journal,* XLIX (March, 1966), 254–58. Reprinted by permission of The University of North Carolina Press.

The standards by which behavior change is evaluated constitute a different problem and will not be dealt with in this paper.

Emotional disturbance is usually defined in some formal diagnostic terms which appear to us to have little usefulness when we wish to implement a behavior change program. Terms like ". . . meeting the emotional needs of . . ." or ". . . understanding the disturbed child . . ." offer popular appeal, but do not give us specific grounds on which to effect behavior change.

In view of the lack of agreement upon definitions of "mental health" (Scott, 1958), we consider it important to enter the problem of defining and dealing with disturbed behavior in the school in terms of *specific behaviors* which we want to modify. In final analysis, and in relation to specific change objectives, we are always talking about particular behavior in a given child (or group of children) under an observable set of circumstances.

We will not be led into a fruitless and endless quest for listings of undesirable, disturbed or unwanted behavior. Undesirable or unwanted behavior patterns must be classified according to the circumstances under which they occur. These circumstances may vary considerably from an elementary to a secondary classroom setting, from school to employment situations, and so forth. We are thinking of circumstances defined by educational objectives and by conduct (or behavioral) objectives, the exact nature of which is left up to the reader to supply to his own circumstances.

The following set of principles will indicate a non-exhaustive list of considerations specific to behavior change objectives; the implications of the principles will be elucidated in the final section of this paper.

Principles:

1. Undesirable or disturbed behavior is not different in kind from any other behavior. It has been learned as has any other behavior and is under the same control as any other behavior. Often undesirable or disturbed behavior is very loosely defined, subject to momentary evaluations or even biases by an observer or evaluator. Unless the circumstances of any behavior can be adequately defined, it is not a suitable topic for serious study. This lack of accurately defining the circumstances relating to the disturbed behavior often leads us to ask "What is wrong with the child?" "What makes him act that way?" Rather, we should learn to ask a different question: "What are the circumstances under which the undesirable behavior occurs, and what conditions appear to maintain the undesirable behavior?"
2. Behavior is elicited and maintained by variables which are open to investigation and manipulation (or control). In line with this principle, disturbed behavior may be inadvertently maintained by the

parent, the teacher, the classroom environment, by other factors, or by combinations of them. Variables in the environment may "allow" the disturbed behavior to occur, and other variables may reinforce or maintain the disturbed behavior, once initiated.

3. The same principles of learning or behavior modification apply to changing from undesirable to desirable (or from disturbed to non-disturbed) behavior as they apply to learning a skill, a subject-matter area, or social behavior. Emotional disturbance is a set of more or less complex learned responses inadequate to, or undesirable for, some defined context(s). Disturbed behavior, therefore, is not a "symptom" of something "more basic," but is simply another aspect of behavior, important in its own right, and has its own eliciting and maintaining variables. We make this point explicit because a "medical model" is often used to explain or describe disturbed behavior. This model assumes the task of therapy to be "discovering" the origin and analyzing the dynamics of the disturbed behavior. We see the task quite differently. We wish to identify and describe the undesirable or disturbed behavior, and the circumstances under which its occurrence is maintained. Once this is accomplished, behavior modification can be initiated through environmental changes (Ullman & Krasner, 1965; Krasner & Ullman, 1965; Phillips & Batrawi, 1964).
4. Although feelings and subjective states are often useful in the early identification of a problem, they should not be regarded as the primary objects of behavior change. Instead of being causal factors, these subjective states are known to accompany or result from behavioral inadequacies. Batrawi (1964) has found that the student who fails to apply himself at the appropriate times "feels inadequate" after he has failed an exam or after he has shown himself to be unreliable in some social interaction. Feelings may be linked to some behavior data and may represent reaction to a "balance sheet" which shows behavioral deficit when compared with a standard acceptable to the individual and to the environmental demands.
5. The conditions under which the disturbed or undesirable behavior occurs afford many opportunities for change. These opportunities deal with two broad categories of effort: skills in a generic sense, and environmental demands. One may attempt behavior change through:

   A) Increasing the *skills* of the individual(s) through such specific procedures as: a) daily assignments that are well-scheduled and/or programed; b) exploring new skills to meet environmental demands; c) using existing skills to initiate and promote the development of new skills.

B) Identifying and altering the *demands* made by the environment. These demands, for example in the classroom, may be: a) increased; b) decreased; c) systematized or ordered in some improved way; d) programed and refined more gradually over an extended period of time.

6. As with all complex learning situations, a great deal of *control* must be maintained over the individual and his environment. The word "control" here need not conjure up authoritarian implications to the reader. We refer more precisely to managing and optimizing the *conditions* leading to behavior change in the desired direction, and to minimizing the variables associated with the elicitation and maintenance of undesirable behavior. These conditions are in fact variables characterizing the individual and his environment in some important ways and are thereby open to some degree of control and manipulation. The emphasis on control applies not only to the classroom environment but also to other related circumstances such as the playground, and commuting between home and school, and especially the home. It has been shown in studies of emotionally disturbed children (Haring & Phillips, 1960) that the controlling of classroom conditions could profitably be extended to the home through parental cooperation. If this extension into the home is not accomplished, the home environment may actually counteract the constructive control offered in the classroom. The school environment should provide control over the variables which prepare the student to acquire the behavior in question (whether academic or social). The elements of control should *order* the sequences of behavioral acts and their conditions, *offer correction* when errors reach a specified level, and *reinforce* and augment desired behavior. The controls should also provide for repetition of success under a variety of conditions. When control is maintained by these procedures, it assumes a meaning different from that found in a mere authoritarian enforcement of rules.

When the above principles are applied to the classroom for disturbed children, the following practices are strongly recommended.

1. Smaller classes which would afford near optimal conditions for achieving the appropriate measures of control cited.
2. Placing classes in a context that is generally well-structured. In this way, the overall school and home environment will complement and support rather than contradict the behavior change purposes of the classroom.

3. Emphasizing the vital role of the teacher working with parents, school administration, and others in the behavior change program. The teacher gives and receives advice and support in ways that foster the behavior change enterprise. This includes such teaching objectives as: setting definite goals, providing stepwise progress toward goals, handling correction and reinforcement objectively, and generally keeping the structure of educational tasks and social requirements uppermost. The teacher can identify and control many variables that move the disturbed student toward agreed upon objectives of behavior change.

Programs of the type outlined briefly here offer good prospects for developing the technology of behavior change in the school and in the classroom. Recently, great strides have been made in behavior change technology in which the school system provides situations with many interesting potential applications and opportunities.

References

BATRAWI, SALAH A. "Comparative Effects of Two Therapeutic Techniques on Adolescent Behavior." Unpublished Ph.D. Dissertation, The George Washington University, 1964.

HARING, NORRIS G. & PHILLIPS, E. LAKIN. *Educating Emotionally Disturbed Children.* New York: McGraw-Hill, 1960.

KRASNER, LEONARD & ULLMAN, LEONARD P. *Research in Behavior Modification.* New York: Holt, Rinehart & Winston, Inc., 1965.

PHILLIPS, E. LAKIN & BATRAWI, SALAH A. "Learning Theory and Psychotherapy Re-visited: With Notes on Illustrative Cases," *Psychotherapy: Theory, Research and Practice,* 1964, *1,* 145–150.

SCOTT, W. A. "Research Definitions of Mental Health and Mental Illness," *Psychol. Bulletin,* 1958, *55,* 29–45.

ULLMAN, LEONARD P. & KRASNER, LEONARD. *Case Studies in Behavior Modification.* New York: Holt, Rinehart & Winston, 1965.

18. Remediation of the Conduct Problem Child in the Special Class Setting

HERBERT C. QUAY, JOHN S. WERRY,
MARJORIE MCQUEEN, AND ROBERT SPRAGUE

A special class program within the public school system for children with behavior problems should have two basic guidelines. First, direction should be obtained from knowledge of the nature of behavior disorders in children and the methods whereby such disorders can best be remediated. Second, the program should be guided by knowledge of the nature of the public schools as a setting for such remediational attempts. The experimental class described in this paper is a cooperative effort of the Urbana public schools and the University of Illinois Children's Research Center.

Nature of Children's Behavior Disorders

On the basis of present evidence, it appears that children's behavior disorders can be viewed most profitably, both in diagnosis and remediation, in terms of the problem behavior itself, rather than in terms of deviant personality types or disease entities. It is further assumed that it is most useful to attempt to conceive of problem behavior in terms of external observable events, rather than internalized hypothetical constructs like the unconscious, the ego, and so on, even though such concepts may serve heuristic functions. The goal in treatment is the elimination of the problem behaviors, and when this is achieved, the child is viewed as no longer exhibiting any disorder. Thus, the authors' philosophy can be described as pragmatic and practical.

SOURCE: *Exceptional Children,* XXXII (April, 1966), 509–15. Reprinted by permission.

As regards etiology, the problem behavior is seen to be the end product of an interaction between environmental experiences and predispositional factors, such as heredity and status of the central nervous system. This interactional process is called learning, and it is this process which is of primary concern to the authors. Predispositional factors are seen as limiting the ultimate complexity of possible behaviors, increasing the probability of emission of certain classes of behavior, and influencing the rate at which learning may occur. The environment, through discriminative stimuli and through response-reinforcement contingencies, is seen as the major influence determining the precise behavior repertoire of an individual child. Thus the child with a cerebral dysfunction might be prone to the excessive emission of motor responses (hyperactivity), but it would be the environment which, through patterns of reinforcement, would determine the precise nature of the behaviors observed in the child and would serve to increase or decrease their frequency in various situations.

Even though the primary focus of attention is on discrete, observable problem behaviors of the individual child or is, in short, ideographic, the nomothetic approach is nevertheless assumed to be of definite, though limited, value. A wide range of discrete problem behaviors has been shown by factor analytic techniques (Peterson, 1961; Quay and Quay, 1965; Quay, Morse, and Cutler, 1966) to represent four underlying dimensions of behavior along which all children will vary. The child who comes to be known clinically as emotionally disturbed is one whose behavior has come to be extreme on one or more of the dimensions. Certain specific problem behaviors cluster along the different dimensions and have thus given rise to descriptive labels for each dimension. Though different studies have used different terminology in labeling the dimensions, the constituent specific behaviors are essentially similar.

One such dimensional cluster of behaviors is called unsocialized aggression, psychopathy, or conduct disorder and is composed of such behaviors as aggression, overactivity, defiance, irresponsibility, and other such disrupting behaviors. The neurotic or affective dimension includes such behaviors as self-consciousness, chronic fearfulness, shyness, and sadness. The immaturity-inadequacy dimension contains such behaviors as daydreaming, lethargy, suggestibility, and laziness. The dimension called socialized delinquency is made up of behaviors most closely associated with the young delinquent of the urban, deteriorated area where deviant, rather than deficient, socialization is characteristic.

Dimensional assessment, as opposed to individual problem or target symptom assessment, has two main functions. First, because there is some normative data for a variety of populations (Peterson, 1961; Quay,

1964; Quay and Quay, 1965), it is possible to quantify the degree to which an individual child departs from various population means on the dimensions and thus to estimate the degree of maladjustment. This information is, of course, helpful in arriving at decisions as to whether or not a child should be placed in a special class. Second, the dimensional profile of a given child has some general predictive value for response to particular treatment approaches and for prognosis which, though rather limited at the moment, is likely to increase with further validation studies.

Though theoretically the number of individual dimensional profiles is practically unlimited, it is convenient to delineate certain typologies of children who have extreme loadings on one or another of the dimensions. Thus, one may speak of the aggressive, the neurotic, and the immature-inadequate child and the socialized delinquent. Such specifications, however, do not preclude children of mixed categories, nor do they carry any implications of etiological specificity.

While there is no denying the importance of programs for the neurotic, immature, and socialized delinquent child, the special class described in this paper is comprised of children who manifest behavior mainly associated with high loadings on the unsocialized aggressive dimension. This is partly through choice, but also partly because this is the type of child who is most obviously troublesome in the usual public school setting and therefore most likely to be referred to a special class. This is also the child who seems most predisposed to an entire life of maladaptive behavior (Robins and O'Neal, 1958; O'Neal and Robins, 1958; Morris, Escoll, and Wexler, 1956) and who is thus particularly deserving of energetic, secondary, preventive efforts.

General Concepts of Remediation

Since the proper focus of attention in remediation is considered to be on the maladaptive behaviors which, as discussed above, are seen as learned responses, it follows that the key to remediation is seen in the application of both the basic principles of learning theory and the interaction of selected techniques with the behavioral characteristics of the child (Quay, 1963; Quay, 1966). The aim is to bring about the elimination (extinction) of inappropriate behaviors, or the substitution of incompatible but adaptive alternative behaviors (counter conditioning), or the acquisition of personally and socially productive responses where none presently obtains (conditioning).

There is now considerable evidence from both laboratory studies (Bandura and Walters, 1963) and from field experiments (Zimmerman and Zimmerman, 1962; Azrin and Lindsley, 1956; Patterson, Jones, Whittier, and Wright, 1965) that maladaptive behavior can be modified in a variety of situations by the direct manipulation of response-reinforcement contingencies (that is, the *immediate* consequences of the behavior in terms of reward or punishment).

It is important that the nature of reinforcement be clearly understood. Positive reinforcement is any definable environmental event consequent upon or coincident with the termination of a response which can be *demonstrated* to increase the probability of that particular behavior. In general, reinforcement is according to the pleasure principle—the obtaining of reward and the avoiding or termination of pain. Punishment which has two forms (the application of a noxious or aversive stimulus and the withdrawal of reward or pleasure) also has powerful effects upon responses which immediately precede it—in general, the opposite to that of reinforcement.

There are two important principles in the use of reward and punishment in behavior modification. The first is that the reinforcement must follow immediately upon the behavior under study. This principle of immediate contingency is probably one of the most crucial factors in behavior modification and yet probably one of the least appreciated among those working with children. The second important principle is that in the complex human organism, reward and punishment may be at times quite idiosyncratic, and it may require considerable clinical skill to devise therapeutic programs which are meaningful to the child concerned.

In dealing with the aggressive outbursts so characteristic of conduct problem children who make up the experimental class under discussion here, it is the aim of all concerned to see that the environmental responses to these outbursts are not reinforcing or rewarding to the child. This does not mean that the child must be necessarily punished for his aggressiveness, but rather that a conscientious search must be made for less obvious forms of reinforcement which may be maintaining his aggressive behavior in order that they may be eliminated. Very often this hidden reinforcement will prove to be attention (even though the content of the attention is disapproving) from adults or peers. All too frequently, programs which are designed to remediate maladaptive behavior in children can be seen in practice to be rewarding that very behavior, particularly where the emphasis is on discussions relative to the "meaning" and the antecedent history of the problem behavior, rather than its here and now characteristics.

With the aggressive child, there is usually little difficulty in getting him to emit this maladaptive behavior. As Bandura and Walters (1963) have pointed out, it is more efficient to attempt to counter condition maladaptive behavior or replace it simultaneously with incompatible, adaptive alternatives than attempt merely to extinguish it without replacement. It is therefore important to find methods of facilitating the emission in the child of these adaptive alternatives which can then be promptly rewarded and thus rendered more probable.

The most obvious approach to this problem is to cue the child in through verbal instruction. The second technique is the use of modeling or imitation in which the child can observe appropriate models emitting the desired behaviors and preferably being subsequently rewarded for his efforts. The third principle is that of successive approximation whereby one rewards types of behavior which, while well below the desired standard, nevertheless are within easy reach of the child under treatment. When these initial adaptive behaviors have been well learned, the goal is then raised until the socially acceptable norm is achieved.

Special Characteristics of the Conduct Disorder Child

In addition to the general remediational principles, there are certain characteristics of the unsocialized aggressive child which carry special implications for retraining in the special class setting. Aggressive behavior, using the term in its broadest sense, is obvious and therefore carries a high potential for modeling. Thus, it seems important as a practical point to increase the size of the class slowly to insure that the teacher can maintain control of the group situation. In this way, examples of acceptable behaviors are available for modeling by the incoming child as well as the maladaptive aggressive behaviors.

There is also research (Johns and Quay, 1962; Levin and Simmons, 1962) to suggest that social reinforcers, such as praise and other verbalizations, are relatively weaker in effect in individuals with conduct disorders. It therefore appears that in the early stages of retraining the aggressive, unsocialized child, it may be necessary to utilize reinforcers of a fairly concrete nature, such as candy, trinkets, and toys. However, the dispensing of more primary rewards ought to be paired deliberately with social reinforcers, such as praise and approving gestures, to facilitate the development of responsivity to more usual reinforcers. In short, then, the use of concrete reinforcers is not seen as an attempt to subvert the moral fiber of the American child, but rather as the first halting step on a long and difficult path of rehabilitating a child who is both rejecting of and rejected by normal society.

Another problem particularly characteristic of the conduct disorder child is the high probability that behavioral maladjustment is accompanied by significant academic retardation. This is not surprising since these children have histories of poor school attendance, frequent ejection from class, and rejection by their teachers; and they very often exhibit hyperactivity, distractibility, short attention span, and specific cognitive deficits (Clements and Peters, 1962).

This academic retardation suggests that, at least in the initial stages, it is probably necessary and desirable to tailor the academic program individually to the requirements of each child (Haring and Phillips, 1962). Further, though it may seem somewhat heretical to so state, there seems no good reason that the learning of academic skills should be qualitatively different from the learning of socially acceptable behavior. Hence, the principles of remediation outlined above—principally maximizing the probability of successful behavior and the immediate reinforcement of desired or successful behavior utilizing primary or concrete reinforcers—should be applied, if necessary, to improving academic skills.

The authors have been impressed in their own class by the very poor attention and hyperactivity of the pupils as a serious impediment not only behaviorally, but also academically. Before they can be taught anything, whether it be social or academic, it is necessary to obtain their attention. In general, this problem can be minimized through individual tuition and individually programed courses of instruction. If, however, the ultimate goal of the special class—namely, to rehabilitate the child into the normal classroom (vide infra)—is kept in view, there is merit in attempting systematically to train the children in attending to the teacher in group instructional situations.

Examples of Empirical Attempts to Deal with Specific Problems

TRAINING VISUAL ORIENTATION TO TEACHER IN GROUP SETTING In an attempt to increase the attending behavior of the pupils in the experimental class, the authors devised a situation in which reinforcement could be silently and unobtrusively delivered to an individual child if he had kept his eyes, as instructed, on the teacher during that period. Each child was observed serially for a ten second interval for a total of fifteen such intervals (total for the class of five pupils=75). Observation was carried out at the same time each day and during the same activity (listening to a story). Prior to the instituting of reinforcement, observation was carried out over a period of 12 days to obtain a baseline. This showed that between and within subject variation was large and that the mean for the group was low at 6.18 of a possible total of 15 (41 percent success).

After the baseline period, a box containing a light which could be flashed on by the experimenter was placed on each child's desk. The children were told that if they were paying attention to the teacher, their light would go on from time to time and they would receive one piece of candy for each light flash at the end of the story. From a technical point of view, the reinforcement of the orienting behavior is on a fixed ratio schedule of 1:5. This would be predicted to result in greater resistance of the behavior to extinction after acquisition, but to require a much larger number of learning trials for acquisition. It is to be hoped that the advantage of the experimenters' being able to condition five (or more) children at once would outweigh the disadvantage of more trials resulting from the intermittent reinforcement schedule. Results accruing from 52 days' reinforcement suggest that this method is, indeed, having some effect. The group mean for the entire reinforcement period is 9.09; for the last 20 days of reinforcement, it is 11.43.

INDIVIDUALIZED REMEDIATION OF RETARDATION IN BASIC ACADEMIC SKILLS The fact that most special classes for the emotionally disturbed necessarily contain children at various levels of academic achievement presents serious problems in group instruction. One way of mitigating this problem somewhat is to provide some individual instruction for those children so deficient in basic academic skills as to limit their participation in various phases of the group instruction. This has been done primarily with reading, using programed instructional methods coupled with immediate concrete reinforcement.

In one instance, a six year old child of average ability acquired the alphabet in approximately 12 ten minute sessions spread over about two weeks. In the course of this procedure, it was also possible to shift from primary reinforcers (candy), delivered immediately and on a continuous or 1:1 basis, to a symbolic reward (poker chips) to be traded for a concrete reward (candy) at a later time (lunch hour) on a ratio of 4 correct reponses for 1 reward. Thus, at the same time that reading was being taught, the child was also being taught (a) to work for symbolic rewards, (b) to delay gratification, and (c) to work on an intermittent reinforcement schedule—three characteristics which must be developed if the emotionally disturbed child is to participate ultimately in a regular school program.

TEACHING SOCIAL SKILLS Rejection by the peer group, so common of the child in the special class, seems in some instances due to the failure of the emotionally disturbed child to acquire the basic social skills necessary for successful peer interaction. It is hard to see how such a rejected child can acquire these skills on his own or from the rejecting peer group, and it seems that some kind of active instruction must be inaugurated. Such a process of education presupposes some knowledge of the technology of peer interaction, such as acceptable verbalizations and recreational activities, and of the learning process.

To this end, a recreational specialist has been working with one child, teaching him how to approach the children, how to greet them, and how to initiate and engage in acceptable activity. The adult model first demonstrates the behavior which the child then imitates. If the subject does so successfully, he is then reinforced with a token which he may subsequently exchange for candy. In the next stage of instruction, the adult plays the role of a second child and, when in this simulated interaction the subject emits socially appropriate behavior, he is reinforced or corrected as necessary.

In the third stage another child participates in the practice sessions who is not in the special class and who has been selected for his high probability of reinforcing, rather than rejecting, the subject's overtures. This still takes place under the surveillance and reinforcement of the experimenter. The fourth stage involves the subject's finding himself a playmate on the playground while he is still under adult supervision, which lasts until he has acquired sufficient skill to ensure some minimal acceptance by the peer group. Hopefully then, peer group reinforcement will serve to maintain and improve the socially adaptive behaviors, permitting the withdrawal of the experimenter.

Remediation of Behavior Disorders in Public School Setting

GROUP VERSUS INDIVIDUAL TECHNIQUES The economics of public schools obviously require the development of techniques that will allow children to be handled in a group situation by as few adults as possible. Most of the techniques of behavioral remediation have been developed for use on an individual basis and it seems crucial at this stage to attempt to extend these techniques to group situations. This is a problem to which the authors are most seriously addressing themselves, since even if the techniques of behavior remediation should prove to be very highly effective when applied on an individual basis, they are nevertheless likely to remain economically unfeasible, unless they can be adapted for use in a group setting such as the classroom.

ROLE OF THE MENTAL HEALTH PROFESSIONAL It seems clear that because of their scarcity and their high costs, mental health professionals such as psychiatrists, psychologists, and social workers should give careful attention to defining their roles so as to maximize their usefulness in special class settings. Obviously, they will have to continue to make the behavioral diagnoses that are so vital for the initial placement and the planning of therapeutic programs. However, it seems essential that such therapeutic recommendations be couched in such terms that they can be readily implemented by the teacher and be of demonstrable effectiveness.

The authors consider that the present effort by clinicians to help teachers understand their pupils is less likely to be successful than the problem oriented approach in which attention is focused on overt problem behavior as exhibited in the classroom, rather than on its remote historical antecedents. Clinicians should provide the teacher with information on how to elicit adaptive behaviors, which reinforcers are most likely to promote these adaptive behaviors and extinguish the problem behaviors, how to schedule these reinforcers in terms of immediacy and consistency during the course of remediation, and how to plot a course of priorities or to program the acquisition of social and academic skills for a given child.

TREATMENT OUTSIDE THE CLASSROOM If one were to arrange a hierarchy of treatments for children according to their social acceptance in the present thinking of many mental health professionals, it is likely that individual psychotherapy would head the list and the special class would be found near the bottom. Such an attitude, of course, weights professional training much more highly than the length of time to which the child is exposed to the particular treatment. It fails to take into account the unique possibilities of the special class, and it could be argued that a more realistic view, especially in light of the scarcity and expense of mental health professionals, would be a complete reversal of the therapeutic hierarchy.

The child has three quantitatively major learning situations: the family, the peer group, and the school. It is obvious, therefore, that the ideal therapeutic program would attempt to operate in these three areas, but this is something which will be only rarely attained. Although some kind of parental counseling aimed at generalizing the adaptive behavior outside the classroom situation is highly desirable, it seems nevertheless apparent that society would be derelict if it neglected these unique opportunities to remediate problem behavior in children, even where parental counseling is either impracticable because of a shortage in professionals or is rejected by the parents.

Hence, concurrent individual psychotherapy or parental counseling should not be prerequisite for placement in the special class setting unless the number of candidates greatly exceeds the facilities available. Even in this latter case, it is possible to argue that the children who cannot obtain other kinds of therapy should actually receive priority for placement in the special class.

GOAL OF THE SPECIAL CLASS While it is probably unrealistic in the case of every child, the goal of the special class should be to rehabilitate its pupils into the regular class system. Partly as a result of legal restrictions, special classes tend to be better staffed and often better equipped than regular classes. This can easily lead to the development of what can be called "hot house" techniques and standards of behavior. This is probably both necessary and useful initially in shaping the child's behavior to approximate the norm; but real life procedures such as group, rather than individual, instruction and less tolerance for deviant behavior must ultimately be instituted, preferably by successive approximation. This is the principle of instituting rather than assuming generalization of behavior.

ROLE OF THE TECHNIQUES OF THE SPECIAL CLASS IN THE REGULAR CLASS A final but certainly no less important point is that techniques developed in the special class setting should ideally have some general applicability in the regular classroom. In the last analysis, the aim should be that of prevention, rather than that of remediation—of preventing children from becoming discordant enough in their behavior to warrant special class placement, rather than simply attempting to modify disturbing behavior once the situation has become intolerable. The special class should see itself not only as a treatment setting, but also as a laboratory in which techniques for teaching adaptive behavior in a group setting can be developed and then communicated to teachers in the regular class system, possibly through behavior remediation specialists drawn from the teaching profession itself or from special education officers.

References

AZRIN, N. H., and LINDSLEY, O. R. "The Reinforcement of Cooperation Between Children." *Journal of Abnormal and Social Psychology*, 1956, *52*, 100–102.

BANDURA, A., and WALTERS, R. L. *Social Learning and Personality Development.* New York: Holt, 1963.

Clements, S. D., and Peters, J. E. "Minimal Brain Dysfunctions in the School Age Child." *Archives of General Psychiatry,* 1962, *6,* 185–197.

Haring, N. G., and Phillips, E. L. *Educating Emotionally Disturbed Children.* New York: McGraw-Hill, 1962.

Johns, J. H., and Quay, H. C. "The Effect of Social Reward on Verbal Conditioning in Psychopathic and Neurotic Military Offenders." *Journal of Consulting Psychology,* 1962, *26,* 217–220.

Levin, G. R., and Simmons, J. J. "Response to Food and Praise by Emotionally Disturbed Boys." *Psychological Reports,* 1962, *11,* 539–546.

Morris, H. H., Escoll, P. J., and Wexler, R. "Aggressive Behavior Disorders of Childhood: A Follow-up Study." *American Journal of Psychiatry,* 1956, *112,* 991–997.

O'Neal, Patricia, and Robins, L. N. "The Relation of Childhood Behavior Problems to Adult Psychiatric Status: A 30 Year Follow-up Study of 150 Subjects." *American Journal of Psychiatry,* 1958, *114,* 961–969.

Patterson, G. R., Jones, R., Whittier, J., and Wright, Mary A. "A Behavior Modification Technique for the Hyperactive Child." *Behavior Research and Therapy,* 1965, *2,* 217–226.

Peterson, D. R. "Behavior Problems of Middle Childhood." *Journal of Consulting Psychology,* 1961, *25,* 205–209.

Quay, H. C. "Some Basic Considerations in the Education of Emotionally Disturbed Children." *Exceptional Children,* 1963, *30,* 27–31.

Quay, H. C. "Personality Dimensions in Delinquent Males as Inferred from the Factor Analysis of Behavior Ratings." *Journal of Research in Crime and Delinquency,* 1964, *1,* 33–37.

Quay, H. C. "Dimensions of Problem Behavior in Children and Their Interactions with Approaches to Behavior Modification." *Kansas Studies in Education,* 1966, *16,* 6–13.

Quay, H. C., Morse, W. C., and Cutler, R. L. "Personality Patterns of Pupils in Special Classes for the Emotionally Disturbed." *Exceptional Children,* 1966, *32,* 297–301.

Quay, H. C., and Quay, Lorene C. "Behavior Problems in Early Adolescence." *Child Development,* 1965, *36,* 215–220.

Robins, L. N., and O'Neal, Patricia. "Mortality, Mobility and Crime: Problem Children 30 Years Later." *American Sociological Review,* 1958, *23,* 162–171.

Zimmerman, Elaine H., and Zimmerman, J. "The Alteration of Behavior in a Special Classroom Situation." *Journal of the Experimental Analysis of Behavior,* 1962, *5,* 59–60.

19. Therapy with "Latchkey" Children

JOSEPH ROSNER

"Latchkey" children are those who come from homes where parents work all day. After school the boys and girls let themselves into empty homes with keys provided them by parents who will not see them until the day's labor is done. From the end of the school day at three o'clock until the parents return home, these children are on their own. The adults are generally employed in a factory in unskilled or semiskilled work. Homes are usually overcrowded and small; economic want exists in a tangible fashion. The emotional deprivation is just as obvious to the interested observer. This paper is an attempt to describe a program available in the community for treating some of these children who present rather severe behavior disorders without recourse to institutionalization. Specific interview techniques will also be described as part of the total treatment plan. The problems to be discussed are not limited to "latchkey" children, however. Hence the material in this paper may find wider applicability in a field where children of similar background are known to need help.

In recent years the problem of "reaching the unreached" has been discussed in the literature. The New York City Youth Board has described the problems that the usual child guidance clinic faces with resistive children and parents. This agency has devised new casework and group work techniques to meet the challenge.

It is thus recognized by those close to these situations which present severe social pathology that traditional child guidance clinic treatment methods, with the emphasis on psychotherapy with child and parent, need to be studied and probably revised. It has been suggested that more intensive work by school social workers and school psychologists right in

SOURCE: *American Journal of Orthopsychiatry*, XXVII, No. 2 (April, 1957), 411–19.

the schools, using psychiatrists as consultants, may offer more help to these children, who are the victims of very disturbed social conditions. In the areas where these conditions exist, schools tend to refer those children who constitute a source of disturbance to the teacher, in other words, children who have failed to respond to remedial efforts made by the school. This does not always mean that the parent is also distressed. She may not even care. In cases in which the mother is disturbed by the child's behavior, she often desires placement.

To treat such children in the community presents formidable problems. In view of the severe pathology present in the total environment, the question arises as to the effectiveness of weekly or even semiweekly interviews in child guidance agencies. Yet these children may present serious problems to their families and communities alike. Placement in institutions is one solution. However, in New York City at any rate, the resources do not nearly meet the need for such facilities. If treatment is to be undertaken in the city, something more than the isolated contact of a child guidance agency, located away from the central area of infection, is needed. A place where children can be reached in the midst of their hostile aggressions is essential. Such a place does exist. While the setting described in the following paragraphs concerns itself with Puerto Rican children, it should be noted that the symptoms presented are prevalent among many other groups of disturbed children.

The treatment of these children took place in an elementary school setting. In this environment neither the children nor their parents came for help with their problems. The school authority referred the child to the school social worker, who had the facilities to carry on treatment directly in the school setting. A private room with a telephone was available in which to see children and parents. The population of the school referred to in this paper is approximately 98 per cent Puerto Rican. Since children can be seen in the school, they are available for treatment during periods of resistance, when they might otherwise avoid agency contact. School hours from 7:45 A.M. to 5:00 P.M. make it possible to see children as needed rather than on a rigid weekly schedule, as must be done in the usual child guidance clinic. Because of the great deprivations present in this area, it has been designated by the New York City Board of Education as one of the six All Day Neighborhood Schools in the city. In addition to the 45 regular teachers for 1500 children, there are 6 ADNS teachers and a coordinator. The latter arrive at the school at 10:45 A.M. and leave at 5:00 P.M. During the regular school day, their duties include special programming with the various classroom teachers. They take an active part in helping to blend the Puerto Rican culture of the children with the American culture that the school represents. At 3 o'clock these 6 specially trained teachers take charge of 6 afternoon clubs, each of which is limited to 25 children. The children are involved in a diversified program of sports, arts, crafts, and music. Food is an integral part of the program, and the children in each club have a supervised daily snack, consisting of a sandwich, milk and fruit. The club leaders become acquainted with each child's behavior in the classrooms as well as the club rooms. The child's adjustment at home and in the community is also often known by the teachers in the ADNS program. Approximately 10 per cent of the total school population is thus served. The ADNS program represents an effective and critically important attempt to meet the group needs of these children.

The children in individual treatment, referred by teachers from regular classes, are often members of the afore-mentioned clubs. They are referred to the social worker, who is placed in the school on practically a full-time basis by the Bureau of Child Guidance of the New York City Board of Education. Psychological services and psychiatric consultation are available one day each week. In addition, certain mandatory services are carried out by the social worker, psychologist and psychiatrist working as a team. In this setting, beset by numerous social problems, the social worker acts as the coordinator for the other members of the team, who are not at the school full time. The psychologist tests children in the school one day each week, and the psychiatrist is available in the Bureau's unit office located in the area. The psychiatrist in this setting is the person responsible for any treatment carried out in the school, and is kept informed of the treatment process through regular weekly treatment conferences.

In order to treat the children referred to in the above setting, it would be of importance to involve parents in the treatment process. However, here one of the realities of working in such a setting becomes obvious. In this area few parents are available during the day for treatment. Almost every parent who is not receiving aid from the Department of Welfare works. The difficulties of living under severe economic hardships often make any psychological relationship insufficient for these people and ineffective in meeting their total life needs. This is especially true when parents and relatives do not see the needs as their own, but rather as related to a child who is a problem to them. While the maximum constructive objective might be reached in working with adults associated with children referred, this is not often possible. Since this is a demonstrable fact, it has been necessary to evolve substitute plans that will be effective in helping a child adjust realistically and in a personally satisfying manner.

There are some children who have such violent outbursts in the classroom or playground that they sometimes seriously injure other children. Cases of skull lacerations are by no means rare; fist fights are common.

These are the children who need help for themselves, but from whom others need immediate protection. It should be stressed that while many children with diverse problems are referred for treatment, the type of child of greatest concern to the teachers of this socially and economically deprived area is the one displaying overt physical aggression as one of his symptoms.

Children emerging from such total deprivation react quite differently from children who come from less disturbed and deprived backgrounds. The severe physical aggression to be noted in such children is not wholly determined by "unconscious chaos." It is not just symptom behavior, but is a way of life. The aggressive behavior of these children is not always the result of repressed hostility; they suffer instead from imperfections of ego development. The more primitive types of experiences available to them have not afforded these children an opportunity to integrate more socially acceptable forms of behavior. Their entire social cultural milieu has thwarted their efforts at psychological growth.

The setting, in which the children are in school from eight to nine hours a day, sets the tone for the general framework of treatment. All services offered by the school are considered from the guidance point of view for each child. Cooperation exists with the Spanish Auxiliary Teacher, who is in the school three days a week. His firsthand knowledge of the language and culture of Puerto Rico is a valuable contribution to the school's efforts to understand and integrate Puerto Rican children and their parents. The classroom teacher and the ADNS leader, as well as the principal, custodian (a crucial person), lunchroom attendants, nurse, speech teacher and teachers of special classes, such as health improvement, all work cooperatively with individual children. Planned conferences are held with the afore-mentioned personnel as necessary. The social worker is available for this purpose three work hours a week. This is in addition to regular lunch hours used by the social worker to see the classroom teachers. Community resources (i.e., clubs, camps) are utilized in the attempt to help each child.

The careful thought given to the use of every resource available is important in the treatment plan of each child. It is necessary to help the child obtain basic satisfactions from as many areas as possible. The case records adequately point out the glaring inconsistencies and unmet needs in the lives of these children.

The program as thus far outlined is predicated on the basis that with full use of agency, school and other community resources, severely disturbed children can be kept at home without recourse to institutionalization. This means, however, that the children need to obtain further support through community-sponsored opportunities, in order to obtain personally satisfying experiences. When this is a planned and constructive action, it results in solidifying home relationships, insofar as possible. Such a program eases strains and tensions when the child is in the home, and shows community planning at its best.

The question of the age at which it is best to begin this type of intensive treatment with children in the community deserves full study. It appears that very young children (five through eight), who are still physically dependent on their parents, benefit less from such a total program than children above this age group. Young children can often be kept in the school as long as the older children, but cannot go to clubs in the evening. They are less able to mobilize (or may not have) ego strengths against the destructive onslaughts of hostile, emotionally destructive parents or parental substitutes, who are themselves deprived. This appears to be a direct result of the fact that parents are not available for individual or group treatment.

Children of nine or ten usually appear able to accept the rather long period away from the home which is necessitated by home conditions, and seem to benefit from the facilities made available to them. Even without discussion on the part of the caseworker, they appear to understand the need for outside programming and cooperate in this action. They often express positive feelings about staying in school all day and express satisfaction with the school lunch program.

In individual therapy another time factor becomes obvious. These children relate slowly in treatment. It takes from 6 to 9 months and sometimes much longer for a child to accept and trust the caseworker. This is very similar to establishing a relationship in an institutional setting. Unlike the institution that cares for the child on a 24-hour-a-day basis, this is not possible in our setting, since children still live in the larger community. The lack of trust sometimes prevents children from benefiting from positive experiences, as the following example will make clear.

D was referred for aggressively attacking a number of girls. He had blackened the eyes and lacerated the skulls of at least three girls. His suspicion of the worker was obvious. He feared being sent away by the worker and was unable to accept an opportunity to go to camp when it was first offered to him. This offer was made after D had been in treatment approximately two months. He gave no explanation for his refusal although the worker attempted to explore his fears in this area. Six weeks later, D spontaneously requested that the worker arrange for a camp vacation for him. The worker pointed out the delay and questioned whether camp was available at this late date. D explained that he had previously refused camp out of fear of being sent away from home. He had changed his mind when some of his friends had told him that camp was "on the level."

The problem with such children is further complicated because of their antisocial behavior and the need for the application of limits long before a relationship is established. Here the caseworker's role as a permissive person is jeopardized. It conflicts with the realistic need to impose limits on destructive and aggressive children. Yet the children so limited are not lost to treatment. They continue to return and are usually relieved that the caseworker exists as a limiting person who will restrain their antisocial impulses. They have failed, and are comforted that someone else is available to help them control themselves. The ego support given by the worker makes him an ally of the positive and healthy aspects of the child's personality. The necessity of discussing the negative aspects of the child's behavior, long before a relationship has been established, is a reality that cannot be ignored in treatment. Further it is important, it seems to me, that the worker state his position clearly to the child. This places the worker in an authoritative role, but nevertheless must be risked in order to clarify where the worker stands. It is not done punitively, but rather as a matter of fact. No threat is involved, nor is guilt emphasized, but the realistic attitude of the worker is made known to the child. This is quite different from the punishment of a hostile adult who basically rejects the child. It should be emphasized that the worker's opinion should be made known to the child only where a definite need exists. Actually the child is also being helped to see the consequences of his action. The two examples cited below will perhaps help clarify where the worker must make his opinions known to the child, and where the realistic consequences of a child's actions will lead him within the larger framework of the school's authority.

D, referred to above, displayed such severe outbursts of aggression toward other children that the worker had to discuss them with him quite early, and could not wait until D brought the episodes to his attention. Instead the worker had to use the teacher as source material. When D became hostile and wanted to know why the teacher was "squealing" on him, the worker pointed out that what D did was common knowledge and not a private matter. The worker insisted that this was unacceptable behavior and would have to be modified.

W was referred by the attendance officer for truancy. His truancy had lasted almost his entire school career. He was referred because it was felt that he came from a stable family unit and would respond to therapy. Careful exploration of this boy's activities by the caseworker disclosed that his family relationships were tenuous and that he was not a "lone wolf" in his truanting from school. He was a member of a club that was open during school hours. It was not possible to see this boy in the school setting. When the principal was informed that it might take six months to bring this boy back into school, he decided to transfer him to one of the special schools for maladjusted children in the area. This matter was discussed with the boy as a reality facing him. It was not done in a punitive fashion, but the caseworker pointed out the realistic limits of his own ability to continue seeing this boy in his present school setting.

The above examples not only show the need to set limits early, but also that there is a limitation of activity on a worker's part in every existing setting. Helping the child see the realities facing the worker also helps him accept limitations applied to him.

It is also necessary to identify for these children common meeting grounds with the worker treating them. While consistency between word and action is the principle involved here, it is not the specific. The child has to understand the worker's consistency in terms of his own experience. A promise must be kept, but this is not enough. In order for the child to identify himself with the worker on a fundamental level, the worker must understand the child and meet him on that level. In this instance the fact that there are subcultural values and value identifications is important. The worker must be alert to cultural similarities and differences in the total treatment process. The example below is an illustration of the above principle. It helped accelerate rapport between caseworker and child, and recognized the child's reality on a level understandable to him.

M was referred because of a wide range of symptoms. He was extremely suspicious of adults and aggressive toward other children. He displayed sexual preoccupation in the classroom. Later, severe sibling rivalry toward his younger brother came to the fore. While playing catch with the worker in the room one day, he asked why the worker did not remove his jacket. Before an answer could be given he answered his own question, saying that the worker did not really like playing with him. The worker said that he couldn't afford a fresh shirt every day, and was trying to keep his shirt clean for the next day. The boy laughed and said that was what his mother made him do.

In the treatment of children in a school setting, the changing of symptomological patterns may be a preliminary step in helping a child. Adjustment to the school setting is one of the purposes for which a child is usually referred to the school social worker. This factor must be given consideration in accepting a child for treatment. This is true of the aggressive child who is not manageable in the classroom, and of the truant who does not attend school. In both cases a change of symptom is necessary if the child is to remain in a school setting.

C was referred by his aunt and his grandmother for truancy. The social worker's contact with him was made when the boy was brought to school forcibly after a three-week period of truancy. When left alone with the worker, C gave him what the boy later described as "the silent treatment." It was finally agreed, after a great deal of effort on the part of the worker to reach this boy, that C would come in for his first real interview that afternoon after school. He left and truanted for the rest of the school day, but returned for the interview. He stopped his truancy that day.

For the past year and a half he has not truanted. A number of other symptoms of an aggressive and sexualized nature have come to the fore and are being handled. To emphasize the need of stopping the truancy, this boy recently told the worker that during school hours he had gone to a club. He was on his way to becoming an habitual truant.

It is necessary to emphasize again and again the role played by aggressive behavior in the lives of these children. Quite often the child referred for help with aggressive behavior has no knowledge of other social defenses. He simply does not know how to handle legitimate aggressions that more mature children take in their stride. Without attempting to give a detailed history concerning the need for aggressive or assertive actions, it should still be emphasized that some aggression in and of itself is necessary. As new satisfactions replace old frustrations, however, the need arises to help children handle legitimate aggressions in everyday life. This is especially true of children between nine and twelve years of age, who are dealt with in this paper. With the increase in relationship strength, there is increased ability to verbalize about the sensitive areas of life, as they concern the individual child. At this point the ego is open to new realities and new defenses. Verbal communication is the channel of expression for these children. They begin to differentiate between an authoritarian personality and inherent authority. They can then use this ability constructively whereas before they saw only direct aggression as the way of meeting life situations.

For the most part, the children referred for treatment come from rejecting families of low economic level; hence it is important to consider the approach in treatment that will lead to desired results. Not only are the children rejected and not trusting of adults, in the beginning, but the rejection is often overt, without the niceties usually associated with the rejection of middle-class children. A word is quickly followed by a blow in many cases, and there is not the suspense of trapping the adult into displaying the rejection, which is so often found in the case histories of middle-class children. This has implications for the worker involved in establishing a relationship with these children in treatment. Most adults are openly authoritarian figures to these children. The risk is therefore not too great if the worker does not try to disturb this conception at the beginning. In fact since it is usually the only type of relationship known to these children, it is the only one they will form. The reality and limits faced in treatment are support for a weakened ego. It appears to be a comfort to the children to know that the caseworker is not too different from the other adults they meet in everyday life. This extends to the language used by the caseworker. The change occurs slowly as the child recognizes the accepting nature of the caseworker and forms an attachment to him. The worker is not the authoritarian person the child expected to find in the beginning. By this time it is almost too late for him to withdraw from treatment. The child has become trusting and dependent on the worker. It is at this point that the caseworker can afford to become very permissive and emphasize the type of relationship that he might have wished to express earlier. To have done so when treatment was beginning, however, would probably have lost the child for therapy. He would not have trusted the worker's professions of interest, and any emphasis on the voluntary nature of the relationship would have given him permission to break off the contact.

The following two examples illustrate the relationship between worker and child during the early phases of treatment.

F was referred for constant fighting in the classroom and refusal to do work. While quite ready to discuss his fighting, he was quick to point out that it was the "other kid's fault." Questioning was not always successful in bringing out his provocative behavior. At times the worker repeated his story exactly as he told it, and F was quite content with the repeated version until the worker would ask if F thought the worker was a "sucker." F would ask what the worker meant and would invariably fill in slight details that clarified his role in the many fights in which he became involved. Eventually the fighting stopped and he was able to gain some insight into his own behavior and establish some control over his own aggressive impulses.

A was referred for truancy and inability to adjust to the school routine. During the interviews, he delighted in telling the worker stories about the gangs that roamed the area. When the worker was able to identify some of the gangs, and expressed a thorough knowledge of the neighborhood, A was visibly impressed. The worker's knowledge of the slang used and of the very houses used in the exploits helped A express himself more easily, and eventually brought about his acceptance of the worker in the role of a giving, understanding person.

Whatever the example, the important point with the children described is to foster a dependency relationship in the early phase of treatment so that growth, integration and independence can occur in the end. This paper has been an attempt to present the problems and show possible designs for action that will be oriented to meet the specific problems presented by the children described. Much more work has to be done with these children before new treatment techniques can clearly be established. All too often it is contended that the usual mental hygiene clinic was not established to cope with such aggressive children. It is nevertheless these severely aggressive children who fill our institutions, and who must be treated in the community wherever possible, if institutions for disturbed children are not to be extremely overburdened.

References

1. AICHHORN, AUGUST. *Wayward Youth.* Viking Press, New York, 1935.
2. GARRETT, ANNETTE. *Interviewing: Its Principles and Methods.* Family Welfare Assoc. of America, New York, 1942.
3. GLUECK, SHELDON and ELEANOR. *Delinquents in the Making: Paths to Prevention.* Harper, New York, 1952.
4. NEW YORK CITY BOARD OF EDUCATION. *Extended School Services Through the All-Day Neighborhood School Program.* Curriculum Bulletin, 1947–48, Series No. 2.
5. NEW YORK CITY YOUTH BOARD. *Reaching the Unreached: Fundamental Aspects of the New York City Youth Board.* N.Y.C.Y.B., 1952.
6. PECK, HARRIS B., and VIRGINIA BELLSMITH. *Treatment of the Delinquent Adolescent: Group and Individual Therapy with Parent and Child.* Family Service Assoc. of America, New York, 1954.
7. REDL, FRITZ, and DAVID WINEMAN. *Children Who Hate.* Free Press, Glencoe, Ill., 1951.
8. ———. *Controls from Within.* Free Press, Glencoe, Ill., 1952.

20. A New School Channel for Helping the Troubled Child

LOUIS HAY

The prospects of referral of most troubled children for therapy are slight. There is little reason to believe that in the foreseeable future the

SOURCE: *American Journal of Orthopsychiatry,* XXIII, No. 4 (October, 1953), 676–83.

gap between need and help will be bridged adequately. The question, therefore, might well be raised, whether closer cooperation between clinicians and better trained school personnel might not tap new resources for helping these children.

The community must recognize that teachers are the only trained social representatives who are in a position to contribute toward the better adjustment of the greater number of disturbed children. The school is the child's first and most sustained contact with a social institution, other than the family. Can early detection and more appropriate management, within the school setting, aid in the reduction of the number of troubled children? Clinical knowledge has a contribution to make in determining the answer.

Despite the multiplicity of the symptoms of maladjustment, troubled children might be nurtured to more adequate functioning in guidance classes designed to meet their needs. This is the underlying thesis of the present proposal.

The pioneer work of Dr. Lawson G. Lowrey and the recent work of Rogers, Bettelheim, Redl, Slavson and Betts are representative of rich resources available for new applications. For example, the reading readiness idea, stressed by many experts, lends itself to an easy transition to the learning readiness concept. The emphasis here is upon maturation, successful individual and group experiences, and respect for individual histories and tempos. Likewise, the impulse of individuals to strive for health; the release opportunities of expressive materials; the salient significance of possibilities of relating to an interested adult and of group associations and activities; the related teacher's growing awareness of the dynamics of child behavior as well as the close involvement of clinicians in all important educational areas are all major components of the present perspective.

The everyday classroom relationships and functioning and the concomitant emotional tones offer a new and somewhat unexplored resource for constructive efforts. These would include speech, carriage, coordination, peer and adult relationships, as well as academic achievement, etc. These aspects of living are usually routine and incidental to the adult, but to the child they are crucial and among the major determinants and indicators of his well-being. Therefore, the school setting itself seemingly can offer most appropriately a fertile field for children to work out their conflicts.

What is proposed here is not offered as a substitute for individual therapy, when available and acceptable. Most educationally oriented mental health projects are conceived for normal populations. Their program is usually limited to special periods of verbal content. On the other hand, the stress in the guidance classes is on all of the content and all of the relationships, of the entire day, within the school, for a select population. There are, of course, extremely well considered plans and efforts to help certain types of troubled children. Several of the best known are well represented by members of this panel. These are usually on a custodial basis or in institutions divorced from public school systems. They are concerned with the delinquent or with those of more profound psychopathology. Agencies that work with children similar to those in the guidance classes have long waiting lists and their cooperation with the schools is peripheral. We are also concerned with adjustment problems not as yet necessarily personality-rooted nor thought worthy of intensive consideration; if these are detected and worked through during the early grades the establishment of patterns of maladjustment may frequently be prevented.

The New York City school system has been experimenting with several projects in a school setting. In one such program, poorly adjusted children are selected by the teachers of the kindergarten, first and second grades. Each child is studied by a clinic team. The parent is interviewed by the social worker. In groups of four or five the children spend two hours a week in a playroom with the group teacher. The planning for the child then becomes a group responsibility that involves a group teacher, the class teacher, the principal and the clinic team. The results have been most fruitful in pointing up new ways of helping school personnel to help children in need.

In September 1950, we initiated a guidance class program in a Brooklyn school (kindergarten–sixth grade) of approximately 1600 children. The school's socioeconomic composition, although widely diversified, is largely lower middle class. We started with a third-grade group and added two classes a year later. Today the three original groups are in the third, fourth and fifth grades with a total of 60 children.

The early plans envisaged one class for each of the six grades. Thus about one hundred of the most poorly adjusted children would make up the population of the guidance channel. By following the regular grade sequence they would be kept with their age mates and there would be minimal interference with the attitudes of the community, the parents and the school. The withdrawal of these children from the regular grades should be recognized as a major contribution to all the children because disturbed youngsters frequently control a disproportionate focus of class and teacher.

The children selected included those who were withdrawn, submissive, of low vitality, hyperactive, or aggressive; those with school phobias or with marked speech defects; those with notable physical disabilities such as asthma and epilepsy; and the academically retarded. The candidates often revealed clusters of symptoms. All of the original third-grade group manifested a reading disability as well as marked personality difficulties. The reading disability prerequisite was modified for the later groups.

Teacher referrals, record cards, health histories, standardized tests and conferences with teachers, past and present, as well as with some of the parents, and in some cases the psychologist's classroom observations were the primary sources of selection. The problem of grouping was recognized from the outset as most crucial. An attempt was made to avoid overweighting these classes with the overtly aggressive and the hyperactive children. All of the children were of average or better intelligence.

There has been an annual re-evaluation to determine whether the child shall continue in the guidance channel or return to the regular grades. Gains for some children have been sufficiently marked to permit their return to the regular grade after one year. Many need a longer stay. There are others who will need a supportive environment beyond the sixth grade. We feel, however, that when they leave the guidance channel they will be stronger in many respects.

The involvement of the teachers is both selective and voluntary. They serve by invitation, with the understanding that they may leave the project at the close of the school year. Teachers are considered in the light of the following criteria: an ability to relate well to children; a maturity evidenced by a capacity to work as a constructive team member; professional interest and flexibility that evince a respect for learning; and skills in the arts and crafts.

We have been fortunate in finding teachers within the school who enjoy experimenting and learning. Their association with the project has fostered a greater interest in the dynamics of child development. They have read more, have attended conferences, and have taken related courses. The teachers, the assistant principal, who is expert in educational techniques, and the Bureau of Child Guidance workers (social worker and the psychologist, who also acts as coordinator) are the basic members of the team. For specific purposes we are joined by other specialists. Channels of communication are kept readily available through weekly meetings of the team and individual teacher conferences. All of us know only too well that these children generate emergencies routinely, and additional meetings to cope with such emergencies are not infrequent. The teachers have retrospectively evaluated their initial contacts with these children as among their most harrowing experiences. As one who has spent many years in the classroom, it is especially pleasant to report that they have survived—scarred but unbent. To date, no teacher has asked to leave the channel.

The curriculum for the child guidance classes is determined by the needs of the children and the special abilities of the teacher. The teachers have shown a keen consciousness of emotional readiness in approaching all activities. They try to avoid pressing an individual child in any area before there is acceptance on his part.

Nonacademic units are stressed to help the child who is not succeeding in formal schoolwork to develop self-confidence. With each new group much of the school day is devoted to music, painting, ceramics, carpentry, block-building, housekeeping, playing store and similar activities.

Academic work is not overlooked. The reading program is an outgrowth of experiential and language arts activities. These include well-motivated projects as well as other selected social experiences that are particularly meaningful in nurturing reading readiness. The experience chart is the basic tool. Into this the teacher tries to weave the vocabulary of the reading text. The reader itself is not used until the vocabulary has been mastered and successful reading is assured. The new developmental mathematics program is most helpful in these classes. Again the work is adapted to the individual students. There are as many as three or four groups in each class arranged according to current levels of academic achievement.

Small registers are considered essential. There is now a maximum of 20 to a class. Next year we hope to set the limit at 18, with 15 as the eventual goal. In order not to disturb established relationships there are very few pupil changes during the year. We believe that the children are building significant bonds that are worthy of more intensive study. For related reasons the teacher has remained with the same class for more than one year.

The largest classrooms in the building are assigned to these classes. They are about as large as a good modern kindergarten room. There are sizable corners for housekeeping and carpentry, space for rhythms and dancing, and room to move about and engage in varied activities. Art materials, lumber, tools, and other daily educational needs are abundantly supplied. There is a piano in each room, one of them a contribution from the parents' association. The cooperation of this organization has been sought from the beginning. As a consequence their support, financial as well as sympathetic, gives the channel substantial backing in the community.

The role of the school administration has been very important. The principal has participated in the over-all planning and in all crucial matters of policy. The assistant principal has been involved in the day-by-day planning and application, and has been available for conference to any member of the team. Unless the administration shows a real understanding of mental hygiene goals and practices such a project must founder.

Because of its interest in exploring new ways of extending mental health knowledge to the schools, the Bureau of Child Guidance has assigned a social worker and a psychologist to the project on a part-time basis, in spite of serious personnel shortages.

The New York City school system has curriculum specialists in art, music, reading, mathematics, etc. These specialists were invited to help us. Time spent with the guidance classes varied from a day to a week, and in one case an educational counselor came once a week for a term. Frequent consultations with the school nurse are an integral aspect of the project.

We know that parents of troubled children are by and large seriously troubled, often defensive, and with little insight into their children's problems. In this area of parent-school relationship we encountered the most difficulty. The parents resisted a special school grouping which they felt to be a reflection upon them as parents, and a threat to their child's and their own status. As the gains of the children became more apparent, the parents began to feel less threatened. We discovered, pleasantly enough, that the early resistance, almost violent at times, receded gradually and the parents became increasingly cooperative.

We all know that disturbed parents, who can afford private therapy or who have access to agencies, may resist therapy for their children. I feel, however, that through their contacts with a setup like the guidance channel they may be helped to accept referrals to agencies and psychiatrists and working with school clinicians. The social worker of the staff has also helped to reduce parental pressure. The principal in a recent report stated: "Many parents of these children have become more active in the parents' association. They spark many stimulating questions at parent meetings. It has been interesting to see the shift in the direction of their questions from those dealing previously with school situations to those involving the home. This change indicates a degree of confidence in the school which was just a faint hope when the Child Guidance Project was launched."

Among the gaps we regret most is the lack of a control group. What follows in the way of an over-all summary is in some respects more "impressionistic" than we would have liked. In January of this year, we made a study of teacher personality ratings of our 60 youngsters throughout their school career. The New York City rating cards list 15 personality areas. Improvement is noted here only when the child had a consistently unsatisfactory record in the particular trait prior to his entering the guidance classes, and when the progress was subsequently maintained.

The greatest improvement was listed under the heading "Self-Confidence." Of the 60 children studied, 24 changed from "Lack of Confidence" or "Needs Frequent Encouragement" to "Usually Works with Confidence." The second greatest improvement was in "Aggressiveness." Here 21 children changed from either "Does Not Assert Himself" or "Overaggressive, Fights Frequently" to "Moderately Aggressive." There were many who shifted from "Shy" to "Overaggressive." In the next position we find "Responsibility" with 18 cases of improvement noted; "Leadership" with 17; and "Social Adjustment" and "Work Habits" with 16 each.

Academic progress was evaluated by means of standardized tests and teacher judgments based on the reading texts used by each youngster. Reading was not given any special emphasis. Current techniques familiar to all alert teachers were used. These children, although of at least average intelligence, were, with a few exceptions, retarded one or more years when they entered the guidance classes. Most of the youngsters were below the reading readiness level at the end of the first grade. By the middle of the third grade, almost all achieved reading readiness. By the middle of the fourth grade there is a wide range of achievement: 5 are doing third-grade work; 5, second-grade work; 6, first-grade work; and 3 are at a reading readiness level. In the fifth grade the wide range continues but there is steady and appreciable progress, with one exception in whom we suspect some organic involvement. In the fifth grade, 3 are reading at fifth-grade level; 4 at fourth; 10 at third; and 2 at first-grade level. Academic progress can be considered another indicator of better adjustment.

The following are brief excerpts on several children chosen at random:

David, nine, is now in the fourth grade. When he entered the third-grade guidance class in September 1951, he manifested real panic with spells of weeping and the clutching of his mother's arm. Now, his independence and vitality are quickly apparent. He comes to school alone, makes friends readily, and appears happy most of the time.

Roberta was so withdrawn and fearful that she had to be escorted into the classroom. She would sit isolated in a corner. When she walked, she hugged the walls. She is still shy but mixes with groups and will approach adults in whom she has confidence.

Ellen is Roberta's classmate and equally frightened. Recently she remarked to the psychologist, "Roberta told me not to be afraid of the dentist. Before, I was. My mother told me to stay with Roberta. She teaches me stuff and I'm not afraid so much. She always keeps telling me, 'Don't be afraid.' "

Joseph, eight, was withdrawn, did not participate in class activities and did not speak. He became involved in fights but could not hold his own. Now, he talks, but in a functional way, to meet specific purposes. He is more relaxed and is getting along better. At home, he runs errands without a written note.

Donald has a long history of asthma. His work is poor and he, too, is withdrawn. The family background is seriously disturbed. Asthmatic attacks are rarer and he has begun to fight back and hold his own with other boys.

Martha has a history of shyness and poor academic work. One day, she surprised her mother and the Sunday School teacher by volunteering to sing "Onward Christian Soldiers" as a solo in the church auditorium. At the end of the school year, Martha returned to the regular classes.

Henry was unusually aggressive and destructive from the beginning of his school career. After a year and a half in the guidance classes he has become more socialized and able to participate in group activities. There is less evidence of chronic hyperactivity. He is particularly proud of his ability to handle a primer.

What the warmth and security of the guidance classes mean to these children is best demonstrated by the words of one of the youngsters. In an interview with the psychologist Thomas said, "First I'm scared of school and then I got used to it. When I was in the second grade I was scared of reading. Then in the third grade with Miss O, I wasn't scared. I didn't feel like reading when I was scared. When I got used to reading, I said, 'Why can't I have more reading?' and she said, 'No, it would be too much.' So, I went to the desk and read by myself. I used to be scared to read to children. I'm still bashful to get up and tell the children what I did yesterday and other days [show and tell period]. I'm not scared to play now. I talk to other kids. I read out loud. Many times I know the right answer, but sometimes I'm scared to say it. It's true I'm scared I'm wrong and I don't want to say the answer and get into trouble. I'm not so sure I'm right. I am scared again and then I get happy again. When I was in the third grade I became happy all the time. I had another book and I felt scared. Then I got happy and I wasn't scared of the book. Then I went to Mrs. K's class and I'm still happy."

Every child in this group offers a dramatic story of unique combinations of inadequate homes, physical disabilities, arrested ego development, destructive compensatory mechanisms, and varying degrees of resilience and promise of more desirable adjustment.

Two questions that have been raised repeatedly deserve consideration. There is some fear that such a channel has segregative features. Segregation is usually viewed as a coerced deprivation of valuable opportunities in contrast to those of a more favored group. Deprivation is intensified when there is little or no mobility in the relationships. As this project has been envisaged from its inception there has been a keen awareness of this aspect. We feel, however, that since none of the elements usually associated with segregation is intrinsic here, the term does not apply. There is no coercion; neither child nor parent who is resistive need be included. Periodic reassessment allows for optional continuation. We have discovered that the reservoir of such children is so large as to allow for the inclusion of only those who are accepting. Furthermore the opportunities for these children are richer than usual. Hence there is neither coercion nor deprivation.

There is, however, a type of segregation that is extensively current and is seriously traumatic, namely, the functional segregation that is the lot of many of these unhappy children. The child who is not functioning well, academically or socially, stands out frequently as the proverbial sore thumb. Such an arrangement is much more segregative than the one in which an attempt is made by specialists to assess the child's needs and provide a healthful climate. At present the guidance classes are integrated into the school in such manner as to preclude stigmatization. In practice this has not been a serious problem.

The question is also asked whether the proposed plan is not simply good education. "Should not all children have the benefit of moderately sized classes, teachers who are aware of their emotional needs and a program that provides for activity, crafts, arts, etc., in addition to the three R's? In short what is the difference between this and a good private school?" We must remember that even the best of schools have disturbed children whose needs cannot be met by educators alone. The salient difference then is the intimate identification of clinicians with the educative process. This means close teamwork with the school and the teacher and supplemental clinical help for children and parents when necessary. Clinical case histories for each child are developed, the dynamic movement of the classroom is studied, conferences with teachers analyze the daily impact upon the child and the group, and various types of treatment are planned both individually and for groups of children and parents. The programs and pace that have a therapeutic rationale in a guidance class cannot be permitted in a regular class. The tolerance and limits of the one are not to be expected in the other. Since this is essentially a clinically oriented project the over-all direction and the individual patterns are invested with perspectives derived from psychiatrists, social workers and psychologists.

We hope that this report will be seen as that of an exploratory project that is working with limited resources. We are keenly aware of the limitations but we feel that what we are doing opens the door for more careful research into new ways of helping the troubled child. We believe that what is learned from these children can be of help to all children.

21. Intervention for Disadvantaged Girls: Insight for School Faculties

DONALD T. SCHAEFFER AND
ROBERT VON NESSEN

Although there have been conflicting reports in the literature about the efficacy of group counseling in the school setting, (1, 2) the authors felt that intervention techniques, such as the provision of easy access to accepting adults, short-term group counseling which utilized role-playing, and the replaying of tape-recorded significant incidents to help acting-out adolescent girls in a school setting, offered some promise for changing behavior where such change was a necessary condition.

The intervention processes noted in this paper were begun because of one girl, but the processes were found quite useful for the other girls who were involved in the intervention. These girls were first involved as participants in group sessions primarily to help Sally, the first girl of concern. But these girls, too, gained measurably from the experiences and in turn provided the authors with information and insight into the worlds within which these adolescent Negro girls were living.

The intervention began because of an emergency: Sally, a 14-year-old eighth-grade girl was facing expulsion from school because of her most recent fight. She had a history since kindergarten of fighting in school, impertinence toward adults, and general disruptive behavior. She was once more in trouble for fighting with another eighth-grade girl and for

SOURCE: *American Journal of Orthopsychiatry*, XXXVIII, No. 4 (July, 1968), 666–71.

being impertinent toward the teachers who had tried to intervene. Direct action was called for if the girl was to remain in school.

Sally was first interviewed by the school psychologist, who found that she was interested in school and in achievement there in spite of her history and her latest situation. The girl seemed to have some insight into the conditions which would lead her into trouble, but she appeared unwilling or unable to modify her behavior to keep from getting into such predicaments.

After preliminary assessment, the authors (a psychologist and the girl's counselor) met in conference and decided that, since there would have to be an immediate termination of Sally's aggressive behavior and since this could be accomplished most immediately by substituting behaviors which would be less likely to get Sally into trouble, a way would have to be found in which such substitutions could be brought about. Further, in order to initiate and maintain the changed behavior, Sally would need help in gaining a different view of herself, a view in which she could see herself as an important person who had strength and realizable goals. Finally, a way would have to be found to change Sally's view of the school, so that she could see it as a place where the adults around her regarded her as an important human being and as a place which could act as a facilitating agent to help her achieve some of the goals she had for herself.

It was agreed that in this process Sally had to know that we saw her feelings as being legitimate but her actions as not. In order to accomplish this, we had to provide some kind of safety-valve situation in which she could express her feelings when they got the better of her. This was done by encouraging Sally, and the other girls who were later in the group counseling sessions, to use the counselor on any occasion where they felt the pressures around them had become too difficult to handle without the possibility of trouble arising. The girls were to go to him at any time; if he were not available at that moment, he would make every effort to see them as soon as possible.

We soon found that one of the first things we had to do was change the girls' view of the counselor. His office was the only other office in a suite with the school principal, who had acted as the disciplinarian on previous occasions. Thus, the counselor was seen to be part of the administration. A change in this concept of him did gradually come about, as revealed by the number of times the different girls contacted him just after they had narrowly averted an explosion, had gotten into trouble (which was rare after this project was begun), or were concerned about some of their friends who were having the same difficulties they had previously experienced. Such seeking-out by these particular girls had not occurred prior to the initiation of the intervention program.

In order to change Sally's view of the school, and in part the school's view of Sally, the counselor met with each of her teachers to discuss briefly what we had in mind. The assistance of Sally's English teacher was elicited because Sally had indicated in an interview that English was one of her favorite subjects. This woman became Sally's "faculty sponsor" and a person who took a special interest in the girl, a person with whom Sally could realize some of her potential and with whom she could identify. The authors and this teacher worked out some techniques by which the teacher could be supportive of and could capitalize on the girl's strengths. One of these techniques was the use of Sally as a tutor for a less able girl classmate. Though not an outstanding student, Sally was able to help the other girl with her grammar and found some satisfaction in doing so.

Another step in the intervention process was the use of group counseling sessions, with an attempt to modify behavior through role-playing. We felt that here also was an opportunity to gain acceptance from the girls more quickly and to reduce the role distance between us—two white, middle-class, adult males from the authority-world of the school—and the girls, who were first of all adolescents, were in a minority in the school because of race, economic level, and social acceptance, and were at odds with the rest of the adult world. Riessman's (3) comments on the use of role-playing in such a situation were helpful to us. He indicates, ". . . it allows the practitioner (social worker, psychiatrist, educator) to reduce, in an honest fashion, the role distance between himself and the disadvantaged individual, who is frequently alienated from him. It also permits the practitioner to learn more about the culture of the low-income person from the 'inside' (through playing the latter's role in role reversal, for example)."

The counselor identified several girls who represented various problems and were old acquaintances of Sally. From this group we chose three girls who appeared to offer a balance for group work. One was a fairly capable girl seeming to have a high level of insight into the behavior of her peers, fairly verbal but having some nondisabling adjustment problems of her own. Another was a girl who came from a seriously disadvantaged family. She was having difficulty maintaining a "D" average and had been in minor difficulty for acting-out behavior. She also was the most cheerful and outgoing member of the group throughout the sessions. Another was a quiet, withdrawn girl with an indifferent school record who was a cousin and lifelong friend of Sally.

We felt that it was important to structure the first meeting carefully. The sessions began with an introductory explanation as to the purposes of the meetings: to help Sally stay in school and to help us gain some insight as to why some girls get into fights and other trouble. This second aspect served to make the girls partners in the school processes while at the same time assigning them the role of "expert."

The group met in the home economics laboratory, a model front-room/dining-room suite where we could sit in lounge-like comfort. This room provided a prestigious setting for the group, for it was used at times by visiting dignitaries for informal coffee meetings.

The voluntary nature of the work, the confidentiality of the meetings, and the use of the tape recorder were discussed. It was explained to the group that although they had been summoned for this first meeting, continued participation would be entirely voluntary. However, if any did wish to continue, they would be expected to attend all the monthly meetings.

A few basic role-playing situations were thought through and outlined by the authors prior to each meeting. During the session there would be a fairly free flow of discussion and the planned situations would be worked in where appropriate. Situations which would come up from the discussion would be used if they served as well. After each situation was played through, there would be analysis by the girls, part of the tape would be replayed to verify or reconsider some points, new situations would be enacted, or the role-playing itself would be used as a springboard for further group discussion. An attempt would be made at the close of each session to review the progress made to date. In conference after each session the authors would again replay significant portions of the tape, analyze the progress, and outline new situations.

One of the first role-playing situations reenacted was a situation where Sally had gotten into trouble. As the girls re-created it, Sally was accosted by another girl in the cafeteria because of reports that Sally had been making derogatory comments about her. Apparently this girl was encouraged by boys and other girls in the cafeteria to "do something about it to Sally."

On the first reenactment, Sally played herself, two girls took the roles of the accosting girl and the agitator, and the counselor took the role of the teacher. The remaining girl was assigned the task of observing the process and interpreting what she saw to the group. On subsequent reenactment, roles were changed and a new role was added, that of a mediator (played first by Sally) who tried to dissuade the others from fighting and to avert the explosion which took place when the teacher came to break up the group.

From these and similar incidents, it became evident that the girls had some insight as to why they got into such trouble, but that they had few skills with which to keep from getting embroiled in fights or with which to keep others from them.

We then set up role-playing situations through which the girls could explore ways they could develop techniques to turn aside aggression without withdrawing from the field. The girls placed a high value on not appearing to be "chicken" in the eyes of their peers. It was noted that at times when a girl was assigned the role of "turning aside aggression," she would not be able to go through with it but instead would become angry at her role-opponent, entering into the hostilities in contradiction to her assigned role. (It should be noted here that during most of the role-playing sessions, the girls responded with intense feelings and actually displayed and felt many of the emotions called for; each meeting, therefore, had to have a "decompression" time or experience built into it.)

When the tapes from these situations were replayed, the girls began to develop some insight into what upset them when they were actually trying to be mediators or were trying to turn aside aggression. They were able to pick out some key words, such as "dumb" or "stupid," which when used made them react directly and forget the role they were attempting to play. In addition, they were able to identify reasons why other girls or boys would try to challenge them or to lead them into fights. They also identified reasons within themselves why they tended to challenge others.

The effects of these insights were noted when, for the first time, these girls came to the counselor's office to use him for emotional release because they had just been challenged by other girls and had effectively turned aside the aggression, but not without some cost to their emotions. On other occasions they came to see him to get reassurance after they had narrowly avoided responding explosively to a teacher whom they felt had misused them.

The changes brought about by the girls were dramatic and positive. Except for two occasions immediately prior to the second session, no girl again was in trouble for the rest of the year. In addition, the grades of all of the girls improved; the lowest achiever (a perennial "D" student) made the honor roll for the first time in her school career. Sally tried out for the school cheerleaders group and got as far as the semifinals, the second Negro girl to do so in the school. When she was not elected she handled her defeat gracefully.

Since the authors had contact with but a small portion of the lives of these girls, it is difficult to assess the variables which most affected their behavior. We do feel that part of the change can be ascribed to the fact that after the four group sessions and a few individual counseling contacts, the girls did develop the skill and ability to turn aggression aside rather than meet aggression with aggression. In addition, we felt that part of the change came about because the girls' view of the school changed. They no longer saw it as a rather uncaring hostile environment but as one in which people cared and in which each girl could be helped to realize some goals for herself.

With this change came a change in the ways the girls began to see themselves and others around them. They could see those other girls who tried to get them into trouble through aggression as being people very much like themselves; instead of meeting such aggression with more aggression, as they had in the past, they were trying to meet it with a sense of understanding. A parallel here could be drawn in the way the girls saw the school. The school had been meeting aggression on the part of the girls with more aggression (suspension and threats of expulsion) and now the school was meeting aggression with attempts at understanding (the group work, the help of the counselor, and the support of the faculty sponsor).

Another clue to the change in the girls' views of themselves and of the school came as we replayed taped portions of the group discussions after role-playing. We compared the language used in the beginning sessions with the language used in the final session. In the early sessions the language used was often quite crude and grammatically immature; in the final session the girls' discussion of their role in the school was quite mature and in vernacular appropriate to most eighth-grade students. We wondered if this change in language usage had to do with the fact that we were meeting with the girls because at least one of them had been in trouble, because the rest were closely identified with her, and because we were adults representing the white middle-class world who disapproved of their behavior. By the final meeting the girls had become comfortable in our presence and saw us as adults who respected them and who had helped them find other adults ready to be allies. As they chose goals more closely in line with the goals of the school, they began to use language which was more appropriate to the situation—"school language." [1]

The final phase of this work with the girls came with the authors' meeting with the faculty during the opening of the following school year. Half of the faculty were new to the school that year and one-quarter of the staff were beginning their first year of teaching. Few had worked with disadvantaged children and fewer still with Negro children. Portions of the tapes of the group sessions were played back for these teachers. We had discussed such a use of the tapes with the girls and had received their permission to do so. The tape was edited so that the identity of the girls would not be revealed.

[1] These results are in agreement with findings of Baehr (4), who, although his findings did not hold for girls, found that boys with high nAch scores showed less use of Southern dialect than boys with low nAch in situations which called for achievement-oriented speaking.

The girls' views of teachers were presented as they had role-played them or as they had discussed them in the time prior to and after the role-playing. The girls indicated with sharp insight that they saw some teachers as being afraid of some of the students, especially of some boys, and that they saw teachers as being unfair, prejudgmental, and as "playing favorites." On the other hand they made it quite clear that they saw some of the teachers as being very important people; people whose opinion of them they valued. Their comments indicated that in general they tried to relate to the teachers but that their skills at doing so were limited. (One girl, commenting on being sorry she had caused a teacher some trouble, said that she wanted to tell her so but did not know how to do it. Therefore, during class she went up and stood next to her for awhile, just smiling, then walked away.)

These concepts were brought to the faculty, not in abstract terms, but through the direct recordings of the statements made by the girls. Follow-up with the teachers during the subsequent school year has indicated that the insights obtained in this meeting have been extremely useful to the staff, especially to the newer teachers, who have had to deal with other acting-out students.[2]

This attempt at intervention has proved to be successful. The girls have continued their adjustment and achievement into the succeeding year. The counselor has continued to have a different kind of rapport with these girls than was previously obtained through the usual processes (some of the girls are bringing their friends to him because they feel that these girls too "ought to talk with Mr. X about their problems"). And the faculty has additional information and insight for dealing with girls like Sally.

References

1. Carlson, N., and G. Weinberger. 1964. "Experimental Group Therapy in a Senior High School." *J. Soc. Psychol.* 64:241–247.
2. Meyer, H., E. Borgatta, and W. Jones. 1965. *Girls at Vocational High.* Russell Sage Foundation, New York.
3. Riessman, F. 1964. "Role-playing and the Lower Socioeconomic Group." *Group Psychother.* 17(1):36–48.
4. Baehr, R. 1965. "Need Achievement and Dialect in Lower-Class Ado-

[2] From such a beginning, the faculty have recently sought funds under Title I, ESEA, to engage a cultural anthropologist and a child psychiatrist who would spend time observing the entire school and the interaction of the teachers and students, with the view that the results of such observations would be used as the basis for further in-service work.

lescent Negroes." *Proceedings of the 73rd Annual Convention of the American Psychological Association:* 313–14.

B. *The Special School*

22. A Psychiatric Day Treatment Center and School for Young Children and Their Parents

RUTH L. LAVIETES, WILFRED C. HULSE, AND ABRAM BLAU

Despite the varied facilities in New York City, none is available for the child whose emotional difficulties necessitate his exclusion from school and who is not suitable for residential placement. Would a combination of special schooling, psychotherapy and treatment of parents be effective? Could these children continue at home and in the community if special services were available? While residential treatment is undoubtedly necessary for certain children, questions arise about the wisdom of removing young children from their families, for in the final analysis, children must adjust to a home and the social community. Perhaps in a special school many advantages and fewer of the disadvantages of resi-

SOURCE: *American Journal of Orthopsychiatry*, XXX No. 3 (July, 1960), 468–82.

dential placement could be achieved, and additionally, the cost would be lower.

In September 1956, we initiated a new psychiatric service, a Day Treatment Center and School which combined psychiatric treatment of child and parents with a therapeutic school. It was planned for the youngest school-age child as a pilot project to ascertain if it had more to offer such children than either a clinic or a residential program. In this paper, we describe this facility as it evolved in the first two years of operation, with clinical examples of its special function, and assess tentatively its value for the 27 cases admitted and for the 17 who were treated for one year or more.

The Godmothers' League Day Treatment Center and School was initiated following a survey and recommendation made by the Federation of Jewish Philanthropies of New York City. The private philanthropic Godmothers' League previously operated a nonsectarian shelter for infants, a function now better served by foster homes. For medical and psychiatric responsibility, a clinical affiliation was arranged with the Mount Sinai Hospital. A pilot program for 20 children and families was planned. It was also to be a training resource for child psychiatry fellows, social workers and teachers, with an opportunity for research in child psychiatry and special education.

The premises are a four-story modern elevator building in a residential and business area of Manhattan. The building includes four classrooms, two play therapy rooms, a gymnasium, and a roof outdoor play area. Three classrooms have bathrooms attached, and one play therapy room and one classroom have a one-way viewing mirror and one-way sound for outside observations. In addition, there are eleven offices, a waiting room, a large auditorium, and kitchen facilities.

The responsibility for the clinical program and staff rests with the Child Psychiatry Division of Mount Sinai Hospital and its Psychiatrist-in-Charge (A.B.). The program is organized as one of the units of the Child Psychiatry Division and is in direct charge of the Clinical Director (R.L.L.), who is also on the staff of the Mount Sinai Hospital. The Associate Attending Psychiatrist (W.C.H.) gives direct clinical supervision bimonthly. The staff attends the regular weekly conferences of the Child Psychiatry Division, and senior child psychiatry fellows have part of their training at the Center. The Board of Education of the City of New York joined the program a year after its inception and assigns three of the five teachers in the program.

The budget totals approximately $100,000 a year, contributed mostly by private funds raised by the Godmothers' League. The Board of Education pays three teachers and the half-time education supervisor and provides classroom supplies. State funds ($20,000) are received from the

New York State Department of Mental Hygiene, and a contribution ($4,000) comes from the Greater New York Fund. Fees from patients, based on a sliding scale according to income, contribute a small part ($5,000).

The staff consists of 22 full-time and part-time professional members, 4 secretaries, a cook, and a housekeeping couple. The full-time Executive Director, a social worker, is in charge of administrative functions regarding personnel, building and grounds, relations with the Godmothers' League Board of Directors and the community, and their liaison with the clinical program. The Clinical Director (half-time), a psychoanalytically trained child psychiatrist, is responsible for intake, psychotherapy, and the clinical therapeutic aspects of the school program. She supervises the staff individually and as a group, and coordinates the total program. Four part-time child psychiatrists give a total of 26 hours a week for individual psychotherapy, either of parents or children. Three second-year child psychiatry fellows in training each spend one afternoon a week at the Center. The social service department consists of a casework supervisor, one part-time and two full-time workers, and a student from the New York School of Social Work. One psychologist (half-time) tests and observes children and parents. There are five full-time teachers and one half-time education supervisor. A part-time pediatrician gives about two hours per week, examining children and supervising public health aspects.

Integration and supervision are maintained by the constant informal communication of a staff located in one building, by conferences, and by complete recording. In addition to meetings of each discipline and direct supervision of all professional personnel by the Clinical Director, there are various interdisciplinary meetings. There is a monthly team conference of all persons (psychiatrist, psychologist, social worker, teacher) involved with one particular family. Three weekly conferences are attended by the whole staff. At general staff meetings once a month, case or didactic material is presented regarding the current caseload. Approximately two to three times a year, in rotation with other units of the Child Psychiatry Division, case material is presented over three to four sessions at the weekly conferences of the Child Psychiatry Division at Mount Sinai Hospital, chaired by the Psychiatrist-in-Charge. Integration between the Board of Education and the Center is maintained by meetings between the Clinical Director and the supervisor from the Board of Education, and by conferences with the teachers.

Intake and Diagnostic Study

Youngest school-age children (5 years 8 months to 8 years) residing in any borough of New York City are eligible. The Center is nonsectarian, and the sliding fee scale is from $50 to $5,000 a year. Children with severe school difficulties, excluded from school or with exclusion threatened, are accepted. The family situation must be relatively intact and the child must be able to fit into a group of five or six children. Children are selected whose treatability (and whose parents' treatability) holds promise of their being able to return to a regular school within three years of their admission to the program. Subsequently, outpatient follow-up care is continued. The psychiatric diagnosis as such does not determine admission, although children with epilepsy, primary mental retardation, manifest organic brain damage and severely autistic children are excluded. Intake statistics for the first two years of operation are presented in Table 1, and intake diagnoses are given in Table 2.

TABLE 1

INTAKE STATISTICS

Number of inquiries	232
Number of applications sent out on basis of possible suitability	87
Number returned	71 (82%)
Of applications returned	27 (38%)
Accepted	4 (6%)
Withdrew	40 (56%)
Rejected	

TABLE 2

DIAGNOSIS OF ACCEPTED CHILDREN

Personality disorder (with immaturity, behavior disorder, anxiety, learning retardation, etc.)	16
Psychosis (childhood schizophrenia)	11

Detailed diagnostic studies are done to establish suitability. After initial screening of the parents by the Chief Social Worker, and of the child by the Clinical Director, they are seen individually in psychiatric interviews for evaluation as individuals and as a family group. Simultaneously, a social worker sees both parents for a casework history. The child's group reactions are observed for a month in the classroom in which a suitable opening exists; the daily period is brief at first and is increased gradually to a full day. The psychologist tests each parent and the child, and the pediatrician evaluates the child. Thus, for about a month, the parents and child are studied intensively by the team of psychiatrist, social worker, psychologist, teacher and pediatrician, and an initial diagnosis and intake decision is made at a team intake conference. The familial dynamics are discussed, and treatment assignments are made to teacher, psychiatrist and social worker according to their needs while planning psychotherapy, teaching or casework.

The extended diagnostic period exposes the parents to the demands regarding time and cooperation. Some parents seek merely school placement and are surprised by the participation required. The emphasis during the diagnostic period on mother and father as well as child introduces our special approach and thinking, even before formal therapy begins. Consequently, some parents withdraw during the diagnostic period because of unwillingness or inability to become involved. Those who remain are strongly motivated, though not always for the healthiest reasons.

Treatment Program

The comprehensive family treatment program by the team has a dynamic psychoanalytic orientation and consists of individual psychiatric and group treatment of all members as well as special schooling. Each case represents three patients, the child and both parents. Though it is accepted that most psychopathology in children is the outgrowth of disturbed interrelationships between the parents themselves and the child, one is not always able to formulate treatment accordingly. In our Center, we attempt to understand the psychopathology within the family setting and to treat each member so as to bring about an alteration both in individual personality structures and family interrelationships. The intensive quality of the therapeutic program depends not only on the number of hours of treatment, but on the spirit of the Center. Because of the small number of families, the physical setting, the great deal of time that fathers, mothers, children and often other siblings spend on the premises, and the consequent interrelationships, the program becomes very important to each member of the family. The positive community of the Center temporarily replaces the larger outside community from which they have been rejected, and the therapeutic and school programs become a significant part of their lives.

Each parent is in individual treatment, either psychiatric or casework, a minimum of one session per week. Each child is seen individually either by a psychiatrist or a caseworker from one to three times weekly, except for a few not yet ready for individual sessions. One case is being treated by a psychologist. In addition, all mothers are in counseling groups of five or six with a social worker. Moreover, milieu therapy exists in the atmosphere generated by the intimacy and the high ratio of professional personnel to patients.

The treatment program is continued on an outpatient follow-up level after discharge to the community school. Many children are able to return to school before they or their parents are able to stop treatment. The following are examples of different levels of therapy.

Individual psychotherapy of a child. C.E. (Case 6), aged seven, was withdrawn, depressed, and suicidal. He was preoccupied with abstract inventions, speculations about space, and had temper tantrums at minor frustrations. Mr. E. was obsessive and competitive toward his son, using all their contacts together to prove that he was smarter and therefore more deserving of dependency care from Mrs. E. Mrs. E.'s manner promised warmth and pleasure, but actually she was detached and almost completely incapable of either emotional or intellectual communication with others. In psychiatric therapy, the boy, preoccupied with distances and mechanical contrivances, attempted to turn his world into a big machine to avoid painful emotional relationships. By a positive relationship and interpretations of the machine concepts as a defense, the psychiatrist was able gradually to bring him to accept the human quality of the world around him, and to a greater readiness to deal with it rather than to defend himself against it. (A psychiatrist was selected for this child to focus especially on his internalized problem and to bring unconscious conflicts to his awareness.)

Casework treatment of a father. Six-year-old E.N. (Case 1) was phobic, depressed, and had severe separation anxiety. Both Mr. N. and the child were terrified of the mother, an infantile, narcissistic woman who had severe tantrums when she did not get the excessive maternal care she demanded from her husband and child. Mr. N. was fearful, impotent, stuttering, and guilty. In casework treatment, his strengths, such as his understanding, insight, capacity for action, and flexibility, were brought to his attention. By reducing his conscious guilt, he began to see his wife as she was, and to feel more justified in his criticism of her. He learned to stop using his daughter to appease his wife, and rather to ally himself with the child to withstand the onslaughts of Mrs. N. Both father and daughter grew in their individual strengths and ability to handle the mother, and she in turn received comfort and support from their strengths in place of the demonstration of weakness which she had previously extracted from them. (Casework was selected for Mr. N. because it was felt that his position in the family and his ability to help his daughter might be strengthened through conscious understanding of himself and his relations within the family, without exposing the unconscious roots of his difficulty. Even so, his sexual impotence cleared up during casework therapy, although it was not dealt with directly.)

Group counseling for mothers. Mrs. W. (Case 14) buried hostility and aggression beneath an overfriendly verbose exterior. Her son, aged seven, was aggressive, impulsive, and uncontrollable. In individual sessions Mrs. W. presented herself as a charming friendly person who had no idea why she should have such a difficult child. She constantly interposed her successful conventional life as evidence of her being unrelated to any of her son's difficulties.

However, in group sessions with peers, her antagonism was harder to hide. Other mothers became angry at her and her child, whom they saw as similar in their aggressiveness; they pointed up this similarity as well as their observations in the building and elsewhere that she encouraged her child's defiant behavior. Although she was extremely resistant at first, improvement occurred as the process of confrontation progressed, and she was forced to face in the positive supportive group setting the fact that she was using her son as an instrument of her own aggression.

Therapeutic Education Program

In this setting of the school as an integral part of the treatment program, the teacher is an important member of the team. Cognizant of the psychopathological dynamics, he can connect it with the child's behavior within the classroom. His work with the child is guided both by his skill as an educator, and the knowledge of the child derived in part from the other disciplines. Since each teacher has no more than five children, there is a better opportunity to observe and investigate the intellectual, social and interpersonal problems of the child, and also to work out individual methods of teaching and handling.

Children attend classes from 9:30 A.M. to 2:30 P.M., or less if necessary. The lunch hour is considered part of the therapeutic day, and the teacher eats with the children. Sometimes there are two teachers to a class of eight or nine children. The groups have thus far been arranged according to levels of ego function, in an attempt to have as homogeneous a group as possible (whether this is the most desirable grouping is still under study).

About a year after the start, the Board of Education entered the program. It is customary in New York City for the Board of Education to provide special independent schooling in institutions (such as psychiatric hospitals or residential treatment centers). However, the relationship in our Day Treatment School needs special consideration. The teachers have full academic responsibility, but there are therapeutic aspects in the classroom situation which have to be considered a clinical function. Two of the five teachers were additionally employed to increase the ratio of teachers beyond the Board of Education standards because this was considered necessary for our program. This new way of functioning, together with the fact that we were attempting an experimental combination of educational and clinical disciplines, led to some difficulties on which we are still working. The personality characteristics necessary in the special teachers, the group process versus the individual process, and the primacy of emotional growth versus academic learning are controversial issues. Such issues, while creating some problems, provide interesting differences of opinion with which to work. The Board of Education represents the usual community approach to a child, sick or healthy. A psychiatrically oriented group therefore would have to differ on some basic issues and would bring up the question of which attitudes should have preference in dealing with disturbed children.

In this kind of educational program, each child receives a special curriculum and individual attention, with greater tolerance for his deviant behavior, and the classroom plays a multiphasic role in that it is integrated in a psychiatric setting. The following are examples of how dynamic understandings enter into the teaching program.

M.P. (Case 13). Mrs. P. identified the child with the hated maternal grandmother from birth. She fought with the child constantly, vacillating between violent rages and guilty appeasement. Her technique of giving and feeding was to jam food into the child's mouth. The girl at seven years was an almost complete nonlearner. All learning, indeed all personal contact with others, was seen as forced feeding to which she reacted with skillfully developed techniques of avoidance, rage and efforts to frustrate the adult. For a year and a half, the child lived through a sort of demand feeding schedule with the teacher before she was ready to respond to organized academic teaching. Innumerable varieties of defensive resistances against receiving were displayed and were worked through in the classroom and in individual psychotherapy, before she could begin to separate the "bad" mother and "bad" food from the teacher and learning.

J.L. (Case 8). Mr. L., a seemingly well-functioning man, channeled his aggression into somatic symptoms. Mrs. L., charming, efficient, and active in community affairs, was in reality aloof and detached as a defense against hostility toward her own mother. The boy, aged six, was withdrawn and would freeze into immobility at any aggression occurring in his presence. His learning was impaired by his detachment and intolerance of the ordinary give-and-take in a group of children. In the group, the teacher helped him to discover that another's hostility, and later his own, was not necessarily destructive. He had heretofore been exposed only to people who made a great point of controlling their own angry feelings, considering it extremely dangerous to express them. The teacher encouraged his exposure to group emotions and even to her own, and at the same time gave him a great deal of physical and emotional contact of which he had been deprived. By her lack of anxiety about anger, she helped him to decrease his apprehension. His intellectual capacity improved gradually as he was able to accept emotional interaction.

E.H. (Case 10). The parents of this six-year-old girl were engaged in a sexual battle which they acted out primitively, Mr. H. being pressuring and violent, and Mrs. H. frightened and avoiding. Each of them manipulated the child in and out of bed and bedroom to further their own ends. The child was a nontalker and a nonlearner; her only words were garbled versions of sexual or excretory terms. Attempts to communicate with her were met by seductive posturing, giggling, and pretended innocence. She denied knowing anything to avoid admitting what she really knew. The teacher disregarded her seductive activities, gradually insisted on verbal communication while refusing to accept the child's pretence at ignorance (which had been highly satisfactory to the mother), and encouraged attention to the real skills of rote learning. In time, considerable learning of concrete subjects, such as reading, writing, spelling and arithmetic, took place. She gradually became verbally communicative and had a vocabulary of several hundred words.

Training and Research

Without goals of training and research, this expensive project could not be justified. While we have made only a beginning in the initial two-year period, considerable promise is apparent and it is felt that there will be major development.

Child psychiatry fellows in training in the Child Psychiatry Division of the hospital have been spending three hours weekly at the Center. Certain features not found in other parts of the hospital program are available here. These include observation of the school as a part of the milieu of a disturbed child, the opportunity to work with a group of highly motivated fathers and mothers, intensive teamwork, and participation in long-term intensive work with children. Because of the small number of families, and the Clinical Director's familiarity with all cases, supervision takes place on a more direct level than is possible in many other supervisory situations.

The social workers have an opportunity to study and treat family problems in a setting with many variables controlled and focused on the special problems of the psychiatrically sick young child. The long-term teamwork also brings them into intimate collaboration with teachers and school problems in addition to members of the usual other disciplines.

The psychologist has a unique opportunity to study psychologically all family members and to correlate various elements. This also adds dimensions to the individual psychological pictures, and periodic follow-up psychological tests of parents and children further enhance the study. It may be possible in the future to afford psychology externs some opportunity to participate in this program.

Few programs embrace teachers in a team as does this one. Considerable difficulty in recruiting suitable teachers had increased our awareness of the lack of organized specialized training for teachers of disturbed children. Teachers have an opportunity at the Center to understand as completely as is possible how the child's development and family interrelationships are reflected by the behavior of the child in the classroom. The teacher then can gear his teaching techniques to the individual needs of the child, rather than following fixed procedures. Another feature is the opportunity, rarely afforded teachers, to study their own emotional reactions to children and how these affect the teaching process. Because of the small setting and the teacher's intimate relation with the pupil, emotional interactions are set up which can benefit both teacher and child. Our teachers have the satisfaction of working closely with clinical disciplines in which there is a mutual interchange allowing better understanding and growth.

The stimulation of our own development through work with these special problems and research are also definite goals. We are learning in many areas—for instance, how concepts formulated at intake have to be changed later. The relation of the parents' psychopathology to that of the child shows a variety of aspects, as the less sick children often have the sickest parents and vice versa. The tentative prognosis established at intake does not follow through in many cases because seemingly sicker children may do better in treatment than others. Indeed, we are now experimenting by taking children with more severe symptomatology than originally. The differentiation of two groups—one less sick than the other—seems to offer a special opportunity for a research design in that a comparative study can be set up with one group as a sort of control of the other. These and other factors are being studied and will be reported.

Discussion

To assess a new community service, one must consider how that type of patient would have been handled previously. Our cases can be separated into two groups, moderately and severely sick children, both with difficulties in school adaptation. The first group might have gone to an outpatient clinic where treatment might or might not resolve the emotional problem with eventual return to school. These cases include the school phobias, various learning difficulties, and the child with infantile or aggressive behavior. The disadvantage of treatment in a clinic for these cases is that their education is delayed and that secondary complications develop due to prolonged school absence. Few clinics can integrate teaching with therapy, and later, education occurs largely without benefit of psychiatric guidance.

The second group, the severely sick children, could have been referred to a residential treatment center, because they tax the community's facilities or the family disturbance demands separation. A residential center seems advisable for many such children, but disadvantages are the artificiality of separation from parents, the lack of parallel growth of child and parents under treatment, and the removal of the child from the community to which he must return. Other drawbacks are the high cost of care and the reluctance of some parents to accept separation.

Among our special problems are the development of special classroom techniques and the integration of the clinical and educational services. Many questions remain and the answers will probably take considerable time and research. Should the primary orientation within a group of disturbed children be the group or the individual? A classroom is traditionally a place for group activities. How much group emphasis is practicable for a disturbed child? Should the teacher move from one child to another in order to attend to individual needs, or are the children expected to be helped through the group? What is the valid role for the teacher in a group of disturbed children? Traditionally the teacher has encouraged a respectful distance so that the children see him as an authoritarian on both educational and disciplinary levels. Is this traditional approach best for disturbed children, or should the teacher be able to feel free to use more tolerance or mothering rather than strict emphasis on formal learning? Does the mothering role conflict with the pedagogical one? How fine a line should be drawn between the functions of a teacher and that of a special therapist? While obviously the teacher cannot be expected to "treat" like a psychiatrist, there are widely overlapping areas in which a teacher's role resembles that of a therapist in endeavoring to strengthen ego functions. How much knowledge of therapeutic and dynamic concepts should a teacher acquire to be able to serve in this setting, and does such knowledge interfere with his ability as a teacher?

How much regression should be permitted? If a teacher exerts pressure on children to function at the highest level of which they are capable, they are often able to respond for limited periods, even though inner tensions may mount. Is it desirable for the emotionally ill child to experience severe tension to achieve certain goals in formal learning, or group activity, or should the teacher wait until the child's ego develops sufficiently to function at higher levels without undue pressure? Questions arise regarding the degree of structure in routine activities and time allotments during the school day. Do these children need more or less structuring than the healthy child?

The proper grouping of the children for maximum teaching effectiveness from the viewpoints of both the individual child and the teacher is a challenging problem. Homogeneous groups work out well for children who have fairly good ego controls. However, a homogeneous group of children with weak egos is not only extremely difficult to handle, but often has a destructive effect on the child who is easily panicked and disorganized by the group. It is therapeutically advantageous to organize classes of different levels of achievement and progress so that children who improve can be advanced.

The question arises whether a small group with one teacher or a larger group with two teachers functions better. The presence of two adults who can support each other and the child during stress periods, the opportunity for a child to have two personalities between which to choose, and the doubling of teacher skills for each class are advantages of one approach. A larger group is also preferable for certain activities. Disadvantages include differences in teachers' personalities which result in confusions to some children and sometimes in tensions between the teachers. A larger group also seems to acquire a tendency, despite the presence of two adults, for a greater degree of disorganization and anxiety than smaller groups with only one teacher. About five children to a teacher seems to be the maximum load in our setting; if sicker children are taken, the proportion of teachers to children will have to be increased.

Since a goodly number of the individual psychotherapeutic sessions are held during the school day, a conflict often arises within the child about where he would prefer to be. A desire to participate in what is currently going on in the classroom, or concern that other children will get something that he will miss, causes occasional problems in individual psychotherapy; the reverse also occurs.

Frequently, destructive relationships among the various parents develop because they are often disturbed people who are thrown into much informal contact with each other. Friendships and feuds develop both on and off the premises and these often exert a harmful effect on the therapeutic process. Efforts have been made to diminish informal groupings of parents, but this is difficult to achieve.

While there has been no dearth of applications, there is a shortage at times of the type of applicants whom we feel best able to help. Most referrals are severely autistic children whose needs seem beyond the capacity of our program. However, as our experience has increased, we have had some success with a few children who originally were considered too withdrawn for our setting. This has led us now to accept, on an experimental basis, a few more withdrawn children.

While it was felt originally that 20 children and their parents were the maximum number that could be treated in our facility, increasing experience and skill of the staff have made it possible to plan to serve 25 children and families. Furthermore, we now prefer to take children nearer the age of six, rather than those close to eight. This applies therapy at an earlier age, before certain fixations have taken place, and also reduces the total age span of the patient population. Flexibility in the use of staff has increased over the two-year period. Whereas in the beginning we tended to have psychiatrists treat the children, and social workers the parents, this has changed; we evaluate more selectively which discipline is most skilled for each use.

Finally, it should be emphasized that our program is primarily a medical one, and under direct psychiatric supervision. This is determined by the affiliation with a hospital, and by the position of the Clinical Director, who is charged with direct supervision of all diagnostic and therapeutic procedures. We have very sick children, many of whom would otherwise be hospitalized. The use of medication when indicated, and of hospital and laboratory facilities, as well as the high incidence in the parents of psychoses that often decompensate, necessitates responsibility by a psychiatrist trained to deal with such matters.

Conclusions

After only two years, we have no conclusive answers as to the place of the Day Treatment School in the community and in the therapeutic facilities for severely disturbed children and their parents. Certain impressions have been derived from the 27 families admitted and the 17 who have been with us for at least one year (Table 3). Eight cases (Nos. 1, 2, 3, 5, 6, 7, 11 and 13), approximately half, would have ordinarily been referred to a child psychiatry clinic; 3 of these had been or were with a clinic at the time of referral, but the referring clinic felt that the children and families needed a different resource because of insufficient progress. The results have been best in this group; 4 have returned to public school (Cases 1, 2, 3, and 11); 2 (Cases 5 and 6) have made good progress and will return to school in a few months; one (Case 13), while having made considerable progress, retains a severe learning problem so that special schooling may have to go on for several years. Case 7, it is felt, should continue at the Center for another year to obtain maximum benefit. However, the simple criterion of the return to regular school does not convey adequately the progress which has actually occurred with these families. They had severe emotional problems (six parents are psychotic) and previously made only marginal adaptations; with two exceptions (Cases 6 and 11), this situation was reversed so that these families now see themselves as independent and goal directed; they have acquired greater resources to meet stress.

Seven children (Cases 4, 9, 10, 14, 15, 16 and 17) would have been or were referred to residential centers previously; their prognosis is

TABLE 3

CLINICAL MATERIAL *

Case Age Sex	Diagnosis	Symptoms	Siblings Sex	Siblings Age † + or —	Father Age	Father Symptoms	Mother Age	Mother Symptoms	Treatment and time	Progress
1. E.N. 6–3 Girl	Personality disorder, anxiety neurosis	Phobic, depressed, separation anxiety	Girl	—4	41	Passive, stuttering, guilty, intimidated by wife, sacrificed child to appease wife	34	Infantile, narcissistic, demanding, hostile outbursts, periodic depression	C: S.W. F: S.W. M: Psych. 1½ yrs.	C: Symptomatic improvement, return to school. F: Increased self-esteem, strength and ability to handle wife and support child. M: Unchanged, referred for private psychotherapy
2. A.G. 5–3 Girl	Personality disorder, oral-aggressive	Infantile, omnipotent, acting-out		0	53	Rigid, passive-aggressive, used child to frustrate wife	45	Guilty, ineffectual, appeasing, acts as slave to child, feels hostile and misused	C: Psych. F: S.W. M: S.W. 1½ yrs.	C: Behavioral improvement, return to school. F: Unchanged except for gross behavior to child. M: Growth in self-understanding, strength, goals and attitude to child
3. M.S. 7–0 Girl	Personality disorder, oral-aggressive, impulsive	Sullen, demanding, coercive, manipulative, feeling deprived	Boy	—3	39	Rigid, latent homosexual, distant, intellectualized, avoids family	37	Withdrawn, latent homosexual, schizophrenic, distant from children	C: Psych. F: S.W. M: S.W. 1½ yrs.	C: Moderate character change with sublimation of impulses. Considerable behavioral and symptomatic improvement. Return to school. F: Better understanding of child. Little change in self. M: Intellectually motivated change in behavior. Essentially unchanged. All referred for private psychotherapy
4. M.M. 7–0 Boy	Personality disorder, paranoid, depressed	Suspicious, depressed, severe tantrums	Girl	—2	49	Passive, withdrawn, schizophrenic, avoids family, hostile when forced	42	Volatile, impulsive, schizophrenic, seductively guilty or angry with children	C: Psych. F: S.W. M: S.W. 1½ yrs.	C: Symptomatic and behavioral improvement. Decrease in depressive and paranoid behavior. F: Moderate improvement in behavior. M: Considerable calming of anxiety and some behavioral improvement
5. G.C. 7–5 Girl	Personality disorder, obsessive	Acting-out, inhibited, obsessive, fearful	Girl	—5	57	Dependent, passive-aggressive, irresponsible, seductive	39	Infantile, competitive, somatic complaints, rivalry with child	C: S.W. F: S.W. M: S.W. 1 yr.	C: Improvement of symptoms, freeing of rigid behavior. F: Moderate change in behavior, not in character. M: Improvement in symptoms and behavior to child
6. C.E. 7–6 Boy	Personality disorder, depressive, paranoid	Withdrawn, depressed, suicidal, food idiosyncracies		0	53	Hostile, competitive, obsessive, rivals child for maternal care	44	Distant, seductive, confused, inadequate, illogical thinking, promises much, delivers little to child	C: Psych. F: S.W. M: S.W. 1½ yrs.	C: Behavioral and symptomatic improvement; underlying character remains. F: Improvement in attitude to child. M: Unchanged
7. I.K. 7–3 Boy	Childhood schizophrenia	Withdrawn, infantile, frequently autistic	Girl	—5	41	Passive, dependent, inhibited. Performs duties with child at wife's insistence	39	Intelligent, assertive, dominating, depreciating, pressures husband and patient	C: S.W. F: S.W. M: S.W. 1½ yrs.	C: Social and intellectual improvement. No withdrawn behavior. F: Strengthening of self-esteem and ability to be assertive. M: Increased understanding of role
8. J.L. 6–7 Boy	Childhood schizophrenia	Withdrawn, bizarre, preoccupied, aggressive fantasies, panic at aggression	Boy Girl	+8 +4	43	Repressed, dependent, aggressive, hysterical and somatic defenses	41	Detached, repressed hostility. Handles child mechanically	C: Psych. F: Psych. M: S.W. 1½ yrs.	C: Passive-aggressive defenses. Social and intellectual change. F: Awareness of role in family, not of personal difficulties. M: Increased closeness, fear of emotions

9.	N.M. 6–3 Boy	Childhood schizophrenia	Infantile, withdrawn, fearful, autistic at times		0	43	Irresponsible, antisocial, deserted when child 2 yrs.	42	Depressed, fearful, inhibited, clings to child, fearful of emotional contact, depressive episodes	C: Psych. F: — M: S.W. 2 yrs.	C: Social and intellectual improvement. No infantile and autistic behavior. M: Less depressed, more effective and emotionally closer to child
10.	E.H. 6–4 Girl	Childhood schizophrenia, symbiotic	Bizarre, silly, intellectually retarded. No communicative speech	Girl	+9	49	Irresponsible, antisocial, borderline intelligence	47	Infantile, ingratiating, controlling, sexual fears, uses child to avoid husband, needs child to be "stupid"	C: S.W. F: S.W. M: S.W. 2 yrs.	C: Intellectual growth including speech. Social improvement. F: Greater self-control. M: Increased ability to let child mature and separate
11.	D.R. 5–7 Boy	Personality disorder, anxiety neurosis	Anxious, phobic, infantile, separation anxiety	Girl	+7	50	Childish, dependent, irresponsible, manic-depressive episodes	41	Helpless, clinging, schizophrenic, needs child infantile and close. Psychotic episode to child's growing independence	C: Psych. F: Psych. M: S.W. 1½ yrs.	C: Improvement in self-esteem and desire to mature. Return to school. F: Unchanged. M: Unchanged. Unable to tolerate separation
12.	A.D. 7–3 Boy	Personality disorder, paranoid features	Anxious, suspicious, aggressive, nonconforming		0		Deceased when child infant, irresponsible, exploitative	48	Childish, dependent, fearful, seductive, inconsistent, poor judgment	C: Psych. F: — M: S.W. 1½ yrs.	C: Decrease in fear, suspiciousness, aggressiveness. M: Behavioral improvement. Character unchanged
13.	M.P. 7–4 Girl	Personality disorder, infantile, oral-aggressive	Angry, infantile, temper outbursts, complete nonlearner	Boy	−3	48	Passive, aggressive, dependent, competitive with child	44	Fiercely hostile, controlling, competitive, violent, coercive	C: Psyl. F: S.W. M: Psych.	C: Social improvement. Learning difficulty persists. F: Behavioral improvement. M: Greater control of anger and tolerance for child
14.	D.W. 7–5 Boy	Personality disorder, infantile	Omnipotent, tyrannical, acting-out		0	42	Obsessive-compulsive, repressed hostility	39	Hysterical, aggressive, encourages child to defiance and rebellion	C: Psych. F: S.W. M: S.W. 2 yrs. for F and M; a few months for C	C: Behavior improvement. Essentially unchanged. Return to school. F: Better with child. M: Unchanged, controls behavior better
15.	J.E. 7–7 Boy	Childhood schizophrenia	Fearful, confused, fantasies not separated from reality	Girl	+6	47	Passive, helpless, overwhelmed by wife	45	Mother died when child 3. Stepmother when child 5; dominating, obsessive, harsh	C: S.W. F: S.W. StepM: S.W. 2 yrs.	C: Social and intellectual improvement. Better reality testing. Immature. F: Better understanding and protection of child. StepM: Unchanged
16.	B.S. 6–11 Boy	Childhood schizophrenia	Hyperactive, destructive, preoccupied, bizarre fantasies	Girl	−3	37	Hostile, dependent, passive, schizophrenic. Denies child's illness, avoids family	30	Immature, narcissistic, hostile, and regards husband and patient as burdens	C: Psych. F: Psych. M: S.W. 2 yrs.	C: Improved behavior. F: Less hostile, more realistic with child. M: Better understanding in dealing with child
17.	N.B. 7–1 Boy	Childhood schizophrenia	Hyperactive, tense, obsessive, anxious		0	49	Obsessive-compulsive, timid, restricted	47	Obsessive-compulsive, dominating, depreciating, cold, rigid standards	C: Psych. F: S.W. M: S.W. 1½ yrs.	C: Decrease in anxiety. F: Better understanding and attitude to child. M: Improvement with child

* Key to abbreviations: C, child; F, father; M, mother; S.W., social worker; Psych., psychiatrist; Psyl., psychologist.
† The plus and minus signs indicate whether the sibling is older or younger than the patient, and by how many years.

guarded, though 2 (Cases 16 and 17) have improved. In the other 5, progress has been sufficient to assure them a place in the community without the continuous threat of removal; one (Case 14) has returned to school; 3 (Cases 9, 10 and 15) will be returning within a few months. Two children (Cases 8 and 12) have done well enough to remain permanently out of residential centers. In our judgment, neither would have profited from the usual child psychiatry clinic because of the amount of therapy, special education, and family casework which they required.

In judging the progress which an individual child or family has made, the starting point must be taken into account. Some who have made considerable improvement are not yet functioning as well as others who have made less improvement. Long-range follow-up studies are planned and these will determine whether the present tentative conclusions are warranted. Evaluations have been based on the judgment of the staff, on the opinions of parents, on repeated psychological examinations, and on the ability of parents and children to handle adequately situations in which they had hitherto been unsuccessful.

Summary

A Day Treatment Center and School is described as a new type of community resource for young psychiatrically disturbed school-age children and their families, and impressions regarding its first two years of operation are given. Twenty-seven children were admitted; the results in 17 children who had a minimum of one year's service are tentatively evaluated. Our preliminary study suggests that for certain types of children there was substantially greater benefit than could be expected from other community resources. The conclusion is that this type of facility provides a necessary and often preferable service to certain disturbed children. It also has value as a training center for child psychiatrists, social workers, and teachers, as well as a resource for research in child psychiatry and special education.

23. Therapeutic Education and Day Treatment: A New Professional Liaison

ROSALYN S. COHEN

Therapeutic education may be defined as the incorporation into educational practice of the clinical understanding of the dynamics and treatment of emotional disorders of childhood. It involves the application of clinical principles to the education of the emotionally disturbed child. The program of the Children's Day Treatment Center and School of New York City is based on this concept of therapeutic education (La Vietes, Cohen, Reens, and Ronall, 1965).

The School's Beginning

With the goal of rehabilitation through combined psychiatric treatment and education, the Children's Day Treatment Center and School (formerly Godmothers' League) was founded in September, 1956. Six year old children whose severe psychiatric illness made their attendance in public school impossible were admitted to this new program. Treatment of parents was an integral part of this effort of total psychotherapeutic intervention (La Vietes, Hulse, and Blau, 1960).

The children in the program suffered from a variety of degrees and symptoms of psychiatric disorders which were dramatically demonstrable in the classroom. They were disoriented, frightened, bewildered or wildly destructive, oppositional, and unmanageable. They hid in corners, played all day with one toy, ran around in circles, escaped from the classroom or building, attacked each other and the teacher, threw over furniture, and killed pets.

SOURCE: *Exceptional Children,* XXXII (September, 1965), 23–28. Reprinted by permission.

Whether overaggressive or noncommunicative and withdrawn, all of these children suffered from tremendous anxiety in school. This anxiety often took the form of resistance to learning and deviant behavior which made group life difficult. Confronted with the monumental task of the reeducation and readaptation of these very sick children, the staff was faced at the outset with the following questions:

1. What kind of atmosphere and school structure would best serve to undo pathological behavior and serve the goal of rehabilitation?
2. What combinations of children should be grouped together into classes?
3. What types of people would be best qualified to teach these children?
4. In what ways could the teacher effectively help and be helped by the other members of the orthopsychiatric team?
5. How could the staff determine an appropriate individual treatment plan for each child which could be carried out in the classroom, which by definition is a group situation?
6. By what special methods of control, group management, communication, and reduction of anxiety could the teacher best educate children whose illnesses at the age of six had already made it impossible for them to adapt to the classroom?
7. How might the staff best use this experience to develop a body of knowledge applicable to other community agencies serving the emotionally disturbed child?

The School's Development

Beginning with a small group of five children and one teacher, the school gradually expanded over the past seven years to a population of 24 children. These children are grouped into four classes with six children to a class. There are four classroom teachers and two auxiliary teachers. The latter serve a dual function—they provide relief periods for the four classroom teachers and work with children whose special needs cannot be met within the group.

The impact that children have on each other was kept in mind and much thought and planning on the part of the clinical staff went into finding the appropriate combinations of children for each classroom group. Efforts were made to group those children together who might affect each other constructively, for, in the manner of "David and Lisa," children can sometimes "cure" each other. Or conversely, in the dismal spirit of "Lord of the Flies," children can have a diabolical effect on each other, leading to their own destruction. For the sheer survival of teachers and children, efforts were made to group children to achieve a workable balance between aggressive and nonaggressive children. Factors involving level of functioning, depth of pathology, maturity, and accessibility of the child were carefully weighed by the team before determining group placement.

In placing a child it was also necessary to consider the personality of the teacher, her anxiety level, her ability to handle certain types of children, her method of organizing and structuring a group, as well as her specific preferences and anxieties.

Present Structure and Grouping

The school is roughly divided into a beginning, middle, and graduating class broadly resembling the primary grade system (first three grades) of the public schools. Over the course of a three year stay, children hopefully pass from one group to the next; of course, there are exceptions.

Children who enter the program at six years of age are placed in a first year group broadly resembling the kindergarten or first year of the public schools. Since many of these children are functioning on a nursery level in certain areas, the first year class is initially geared to this level. The major function of this introductory class is to create an emotional climate—a relaxed and accepting atmosphere—which will reduce anxiety and stress in these children. There is an abundance of food and sweets, toys, play materials, and interesting projects. There is ample opportunity for exploration in terms of relationship and materials, as well as for mobility through the provision of a large, spacious classroom with free entry to an outside porch.

There is a very gradual introduction of challenge alternated with more restful or nonchallenging activities. While the child's day is structured in terms of blocks of time (work time, pasting time, juice time, table game time, coloring time, etc.), there is no pressure to participate in the group activity of the moment. Each activity has an equal value and no greater stress is placed on academic periods as being more important or of greater value than games, toys, lunch, or juice. Individual expressions of feeling or communication of thoughts and experiences are accepted, responded to, and when necessary, translated by the teacher to the other children. Each child's relationship to the teacher is used as an instrument to help him communicate more acceptably to other children. Introduction to academic work is timed in accordance with the teacher's appraisal of each child's readiness, development, and progress.

There are two middle groups based on level of functioning. The focus here is to introduce the children to more formal group academic efforts. Greater controls in the direction of group conformity are gradually introduced to enable the children to raise their academic grade levels. Teaching routines are introduced to the child. Social standards of right and wrong and fairness are introduced in accordance with the child's development. The small size of the group enables the teacher to help work out problems of social relationship which would ordinarily have to be ignored or suppressed in the larger classes of the public schools.

The third year graduating group has as its focus the preparation of the children for adaptation to the greater demands for routine and conformity in the public schools. In this group, desks are separated facing the blackboard and the teacher's desk. The largest portion of the day is spent in the pursuit of academic tool subjects. Also, children are encouraged to minimize symptoms and distinguish between appropriate and inappropriate school behavior. The values and rewards of conformity for greater group goals are presented and stressed. Problems of the children with their parents and upsetting feelings experienced in the classroom are referred to the therapist for resolution and discussion. This group is conducted by an experienced public school teacher who is highly skilled in conventional teaching procedures.

Factors in Teacher Selection

The organization of a class of children with disorganized, unpredictable, and bizarre behavior presented an unusual challenge for the teacher. Applicants for this job were carefully selected in terms of personality rather than specific courses completed or degree earned (although a master's degree is required). Some of the most successful teachers have been inexperienced teachers with a natural gift for working with these children. This is not to say that the knowledge of techniques acquired through experience is unimportant, but the ability to develop and use such techniques is more contingent upon the teacher's disposition and personality rather than specific courses or previous experience.

Since emotionally disturbed children suffer from interpersonal difficulties and failure in human relationships, the pupil-teacher relationship assumes greater significance in the reeducative process of these children. It is the tool used in undoing feelings and attitudes which have hindered the child in his school adaptation. In addition, the special sensitivities of emotionally disturbed children made the impact of human personality and communication greater, both as a destructive or potentially therapeutic tool. Regardless of the specific symptomatology of emotional disorder, all of the children seemed to suffer from inordinate anxiety. This high anxiety level made it imperative that the teacher did not further irritate or contribute to the child's already heavy load of inner anxiety.

For these reasons a deliberate attempt was made to obtain teacher applicants with a low level of personal anxiety, a relaxed and giving manner, as well as personal integrity and strength, devotion, warmth, flexibility, and imagination. To serve as a model for these children, the teacher had to be a strong, dependable, fair, consistent, and benign person who was able to tolerate anxiety and hostility and to freely use herself to help the child in a variety of ways. It was necessary to eliminate applicants with overtense, compulsive, moralistic, humorless, narcissistic, overbearing, hostile, aggressive, or dominating personalities. Applicants with particularly pathological motives for seeking this type of work were screened out through a series of interviews and classroom observations by a clinician. Applicants were selected for their personal warmth with children, relaxed manner, and ability to respond to and evoke effective response from children.

Team Spirit and Collaboration

Members of all disciplines—social work, psychology, psychiatry, and administration—are available at all times to assist the teacher through the many daily emergencies that arise. The staff spirit of, "I am my brother's keeper," provides the unified support and cooperation needed by the teacher in handling classroom crises. It has also served to prevent the turnover of teachers and consequent lack of a permanent and competent teaching staff. In early days, this spirit helped to obtain and maintain a stable and qualified teaching staff, the lack of which led to the early downfall of similar programs. It gave each member of the staff the responsibility for knowing each child and his "therapeutic prescription." There was also an opportunity to participate in handling daily life situations in a therapeutic manner as opposed to the frequently artificial device of avoiding a crisis with a child by postponing action or proposing that he "discuss this with the therapist." Fritz Redl (1963) described this method of instant therapy and called it the "life space interview." The presence of the clinical staff on the premises made them immediately available to handle an upset child, consult with the teacher, observe behavior, etc.

With certain children, a special private teacher was necessary to help the child in his group adaptation. Children whose special needs could not be fulfilled in a group of five or six children were assigned to an auxiliary teacher for one period during the day. Children who needed a particular type of child-teacher relationship, which was best carried out on an individual basis, were assigned to an auxiliary teacher. This procedure was used to tide the child over difficult periods of group life or to aid in the pursuit of specific learning goals which could not be met within the group. The children remained basically in the group. These two teachers, in turn, worked with the classroom teacher as well as other members of the team connected with this child and family.

Description of Treatment Plan

To evolve and carry out an appropriate therapeutic prescription for each child, a four way cooperative effort among teacher, psychiatrist, parents, social worker(s), and psychologist was organized.

In certain emotional disorders the child suffers from malignant forces in the family environment which, hopefully, can be altered by the treatment of the parents. In these cases the team might recommend a specific classroom climate and/or teacher-child relationship which would help to undo or mitigate these detrimental environmental influences on the child. Severe pathology was not always present in the parents of the most seriously ill children. However, regardless of the genesis of the child's illness, a specific type of classroom environment was recommended to provide maximum therapeutic benefit for his particular symptomatology.

Certain children were assigned to psychiatrists or other clinical staff for psychotherapy and were taken during school hours to the play room on the school premises and then returned to the classroom. Close contact between the therapist and teacher was maintained during interim periods between treatment sessions. Psychiatric recommendations for the classroom were translated into practical everyday living by the teacher. For example: if the psychiatrist recommended expression or suppression of certain fantasies, the teacher was in a position to carry out this therapeutic policy. If a psychiatrist prescribed drugs for the child, the teacher carefully observed the effects of the drug on the child's functioning and thus aided the psychiatrist in evaluating the effects of medication. Also, the teacher was able to recommend appropriate changes in prescription or dosage.

Regular contact with the social worker was maintained by the teacher to discuss problems related to school life and adaptation which carried over to the home and vice versa. Teachers met with parents at intervals in an interview, the contents of which were jointly planned with the social worker. Discussions of the psychological test results were held with the psychologist to help the teacher work out remedial methods and special handling of behavior. For example, the psychologist might recommend that a particular schizophrenic child responded to the sound of a word rather than to its meaning. The use of phonics would then be contraindicated as a technique for teaching reading, because it would further perpetuate such a symptom.

As part of the teacher's function of serving as a liaison between the field of education and clinical knowledge, the teacher was responsible for the collection and meaningful synthesis of information about the behavior of the child in his everyday life in the classroom. This information was provided to the other members of the team at periodic case conferences, and through formal written and oral reports on the child's appearance, behavior, perception of reality, emotions, relationships, as well as intellectual and social progress.

The pooling of this information, together with information about therapy sessions and home life, provided a well rounded picture of the child's difficulties and progress in the course of his three year stay in the treatment program. It helped the staff to evaluate new developments or revise proposals for treatment and management.

Carrying Out Treatment Plan in the Classroom

Since each emotionally disturbed child differed in genesis, dynamics, and symptomatology of illness, the therapeutic prescription worked out by the psychiatric team, of necessity, had to be individually tailored. However, in terms of daily classroom life it was found that practically all children, to one degree or another, evidenced certain common behavioral manifestations. Basic to almost all children were the following: (a) a very high level of anxiety in the classroom; (b) great oral hunger; (c) low level of frustration tolerance; (d) some degree of acting out, deviant, nonconforming behavior and anti-adult attitudes; (e) some resistance to learning; and (f) some disturbance of self-image and sense of identity.

To provide relief from anxiety many special techniques for creating a relaxed but structured classroom environment were devised. An abundant supply of food, sweets, toys, cooking activities, and an attractive classroom were found to reduce tension and scrambling for provisions by orally hungry children. To counteract the low level of frustration tolerance, frustrations were minimized in the classroom and later on given only in small doses. Challenge was alternated with restful activities. Motor release was provided by abundant physical activity. Demands and challenges were reduced and easy success was given to the children by careful selection of activities and curriculum.

Acting out and nonconforming behavior as well as anti-adult attitudes in the classroom were counteracted by efforts to gradually transform feelings and attitudes toward adults through the use of the teacher-pupil relationship. Power struggles were avoided.

Short lived and self-limited rebellious behavior was ignored. Deviant behavior that was symptomatic and not dangerous was accepted. Dangerous aggression was halted instantly through use of minimal necessary interference. Children were protected from others' aggressions as well as their own loss of control by the teacher's strength in coping with behavior. Consistent, clear, and predictable limits were set and removal for a calming down period was used when necessary. One of the most effective methods of controlling aggressive behavior of children was through prevention of volatile situations. Lethal or overstimulating materials were removed from the classroom. Live pets were avoided for these tended to arouse the children's sadistic impulses. Administrative controls often invisible (by scheduling and careful planning) led to a knowledge of the location of the children at all times. A special receptionist with ability to handle children was posted at the entrance of the school building to lead children to their classrooms and to prevent runaways. Classroom doors were kept closed to reduce distractions and avoid temptations or invitations to escape. Emergency telephones were installed in classrooms to enable teachers to call for help when necessary. Methods of discipline and control were individualized in accordance with a treatment plan evolved by the team for the child. For example, one child might need very strict outer controls while another might need a relaxation of these.

A variety of techniques was developed to lessen resistance to learning, to aid disoriented and withdrawn children, and to improve the sense of identity in children with impaired self-concept and body image (Cohen, 1964). A variety of sensory modalities and methods was used. All teaching was individualized in accordance with the child's abilities. Daily orientation periods accompanied by simple repetitive routines were used.

Summary

Seven years of experience in the combined treatment and schooling of emotionally disturbed children has yielded a considerable body of knowledge of the treatment, education, and management of emotionally disturbed children. The inclusion of the teacher in the treatment team and the four way cooperation among the disciplines of psychiatry, teaching, social work, and psychology have led to a higher quality of day treatment.

An effort has been made in this presentation to suggest some of the ways in which the liaison between teacher and clinician has borne fruit in the operation of a day treatment center and school. Some special methods of handling deviant and aggressive classroom behavior have been suggested. An interest has developed in formulating principles of clinical selection of curriculum for these children (Cohen and La Vietes, 1965). The effect of teacher personality and the variations in teacher communication on a variety of emotional disorders have been investigated (Cohen, La Vietes, Reens, Rindsberg, 1964). The findings in each of these areas of investigation will be presented and published later in a series of separate articles. In the meantime, some directions and approaches to the implementation of a program of therapeutic education for young children have been suggested.

References

COHEN, ROSALYN S. "Some Childhood Identity Disturbances: Educational Implementation of a Psychiatric Treatment Plan." *Journal of the American Academy of Child Psychiatry,* 1964, *3,* 488–499.

COHEN, ROSALYN S., and LAVIETES, RUTH. "Clinical Principles of Curriculum Selection." Paper read at CEC 43rd Annual Convention, Portland, Oregon, April, 1965.

COHEN, ROSALYN S., LAVIETES, RUTH, REENS, RENEE, and RINDSBERG, BIANCA. "An Inquiry into Variations of Teacher-Child Communication: Implications for Treatment of Emotionally Ill Children." In P. Knoblock (Editor), *Educational Programming for Emotionally Disturbed Children: The Decade Ahead.* Syracuse, New York: Syracuse University, Division of Special Education and Rehabilitation, 1964, 71–101.

LAVIETES, RUTH. "The Teacher's Role in the Education of the Emotionally Disturbed Child." *American Journal of Orthopsychiatry,* 1962, *32,* 854–862.

LA VIETES, RUTH, COHEN, ROSALYN S., REENS, RENEE, AND RONALL, RUTH. "Day Treatment Center and School: Seven Years' Experience." *American Journal of Orthopsychiatry,* 1965, *35,* 160–169.

LAVIETES, RUTH, HULSE, W., and BLAU, A. "A Psychiatric Day Treatment Center and School for Young Children and Their Parents." *American Journal of Orthopsychiatry,* 1960, *30,* 368–382.

REDL, F. "The Life Space Interview in the School Setting, Workshop 1961." *American Journal of Orthopsychiatry,* 1963, *33,* 717–733.

24. A Community Educational Program for the Emotionally Disturbed Child

SOL NICHTERN, GEORGE T. DONAHUE, JOAN O'SHEA, MARY MARANS, MARGARET CURTIS, AND CHARLES BRODY

Seriously emotionally disturbed children frequently present extensive problems in training and education. Their intrinsic distortions in personality often serve to interfere with the normal learning process so that many of them develop severe educational disabilities. This disruption makes their education in the normal setting extremely difficult and may lead to their exclusion from the established educational facilities within the community. Thus, the natural difficulties of these children in integrating into their social milieu and peer group are compounded by their segregation and isolation. At the same time, providing the necessary specialized facility and services for their education and training becomes costly. The expense of such a program is usually so great that many of these children are denied the opportunity of obtaining an education based on their capacities and needs because neither the community nor the family is able to provide the appropriate service.

Accumulating experience with these severely disturbed children suggests that the therapeutic milieu can be of great importance to their achievement of some degree of maturity. Many present such serious problems in personality integration that the elements of relationship loom large in making possible the learning process. If this learning process can be influenced successfully, then the relationship of the disturbed child to himself and others improves. This cycle compounds itself and

SOURCE: *American Journal of Orthopsychiatry*, XXXIV, No. 4 (July, 1964), 705–13. Copyright, The American Orthopsychiatric Association, Inc. Reprinted by permission.

frequently plays a critical rôle in the ultimate level of intellectual, emotional and social development achieved by the child.

Recognizing these factors and faced with the problem of an ever present group of seriously disturbed children who could not be adequately handled in the regular classroom, the Elmont, New York, Elementary School District set about to create a specialized program within the established educational framework of the community. The general objectives were to provide each of these seriously disturbed children with an individual education and training program based on identifiable needs.

These children are the little people described in the *Saturday Evening Post* as "attic" children.[1] They are childhood schizophrenics, in some instances giving evidence of "organicity" or brain damage. They range in age from five to nine. They display the extremes in behavioral patterning. They run the gamut from withdrawal with autistic overtones to the exceedingly aggressive, hostile, disruptive child. They are atypical to a high degree. In most, there are poor biological patterning and serious maturational lags. In some cases there is evidence of diffuse damage to the central nervous system with visuomotor deficits. Most have either fine or gross motor coordination difficulties. Some have both. They are hyperactive and clinging. All have problems of impulse control. Time and spatial orientation are poor. They view the world as frightening and overwhelming. Their environmental awareness varies markedly. Some are hypersensitive to auditory or visual stimuli. All have some distortions in basic life concepts. There appears to be insular development of skills and achievements. All have some degree of distractibility, unpredictability, rigidity, perseveration, anxiety, disorganization and resistance to authority.

On a social level, most experience poor peer relationships. They are unaware of social standards, have isolationist tendencies and display disruptive and destructive attitudes toward others.

It is apparent that the intelligence testing completed with these youngsters cannot be reliable because of the variables involved. However, it would appear that with one exception these children fall within a normal to superior range.

The literature is scanty concerning the "how" of dealing with these children. In fact, some of it is discouraging in the sense that it includes little description of what has succeeded educationally with them. Certainly not enough has been achieved for these youngsters by public education around the country. As a consequence, this group represents an appalling waste of human resources, the need for the conservation of

[1] Congdon, T. B., Jr. 1960. The "attic children" go to school. *The Saturday Evening Post*. October 1:38.

which is today receiving national attention. If it is believed, as it is in Elmont, that public education has a responsibility to educate all the educable children of all the people, then these children must cease to be excluded from school. But how to work with them?

They have been characterized as distractible. Then any program must be structured to reduce distractibility to a minimum. This meant to Elmont no more than two children to a classroom. Some of them are hyperactive. This meant increasing the amount of adult supervision. This, coupled with the fact that these children are laden with anxiety, poorly oriented in space and time, suffering from intrinsic personality distortions, complicated oftentimes by segregation and isolation and sometimes by parental lack of understanding, strongly indicates the need for a one-to-one relationship with a teacher. Not just any one-to-one relationship—but a relationship of great warmth, acceptance and understanding—of love. This kind of teacher, in addition, must be able to help these children operate within identifiable and acceptable limits and to enforce such limits without destroying the basic relationship in the process. Teaching materials need to include more tactile devices than for other children. Teaching methods must be completely flexible with only one criterion—if it works, use it; if not, discard it and try some alternate approach. Finally, some group activities must be included.

To structure a program that would include all of these elements was a staggering administrative problem, the more so, because Elmont is not an economically favored community. The task then became one of finding five classrooms, teachers for nine children on a one-to-one basis, educational supplies of an unusual nature, professional direction and a sponsoring organization. Why a sponsoring organization? Because the State of New York, like most states, has been slow in providing the communities with the financial support and leadership needed to work intelligently with the seriously emotionally disturbed child of school age.

The ultimate goal of the educational program was individualized training through optimum relationship and final reintroduction of the child to the regular classroom setting without ever totally separating the child from the family or community structure. By providing the necessary specialized program within the context of a one-to-one relationship and preventing the child's exclusion from the community, it was felt that the educational program itself could become therapeutic to the child. A basic premise of this approach is that proper education and training can be a therapeutic process. If accomplished within the established framework of the family and community, the disruptive effects of separation anxiety can be eliminated. And, if successful, perhaps these children can the sooner be returned to regular classrooms, able to function in a group and not handicapped by educational deficits serious enough to constitute a barrier to their adjustment in the normal educational setting.

In casting about for a possible solution, it seemed that all the resources needed were at hand in the community but were either unorganized or under jurisdictions apart from the Board of Education. Since space could not be provided in the schools—there are 6,000 children in buildings with a rated capacity of 4,800—space would have to be provided, and free of charge. As in almost all communities, there were areas not normally used during school hours, for example, church halls and basements, fire department meeting halls, an American Legion dugout and the like. A neighbor, the Elmont Jewish Center, was just completing a building with eight or ten classrooms, an arts and crafts room, kitchen, playground and even an outdoor swimming pool. This seemed ideal. Permission was asked and received to use six classrooms during the mornings and any of the other facilities the program needed. The Rabbi was understanding enough to suggest that, if the children caused some damage, his Board would understand.

The Board of Education agreed to supply transportation for the children and was understanding about a number of other matters.

The Elmont Kiwanis Club agreed to sponsor the project and provide financial support. For instance, the Club paid the premiums to insure the Temple and the staff from suits, should a youngster be injured and his parents sue. The Club has provided about $600 for special equipment needed such as the two-sided easels and flannel boards used for each child, electric answer boards, large locked steel cabinets in which to store and secure gear and equipment and the milk and cookies provided for each child daily during snack time.

This provided an almost ideal place and financial and sponsoring support. What about staff?

Obviously, the school psychologists and the head school physician would help—they were employees of the School District and dedicated people. The psychiatric director was associated with the West Nassau Mental Health Center. When approached, he undertook to convince his Board of Directors that he should be allowed a reasonable flexibility in his schedule, so as to assist with the professional direction of the enterprise, and at no charge to the program. He knew the children because the Mental Health Center was providing guidance for most of them, or their parents, or both.

The most difficult problem, however, was how to procure a teaching staff sufficient to accommodate a one-to-one relationship. Few school districts, least of all Elmont, can afford one teacher to one pupil. Furthermore, the kind of people needed—warm, empathic, mature, emotionally stable and dedicated—are difficult enough to find, even when salary is available. There were in Elmont, as in most communities, women of this kind who have done a good job with their own children and who were in a position to contribute some of their time to community activities. From among such women came the volunteer teachers. No broadcast appeal was made for these volunteers, which eliminated the necessity for refusing the help of people not suited to working with these children. By personal contact, a number of mothers were invited to contribute two mornings each week to working with a child—the work to be done under the supervision of the professional educational staff and the psychiatric director. These mothers were interviewed by the educational administrator and the psychologists. Every effort was made to discourage them by painting a black picture of what they were about to get into. These interviews also provided a good opportunity for the professionals to get some insights with regard to each of the volunteers. It was felt that if two mothers were teamed and assigned to a particular child two mornings a week, this would come close to resolving the problem of a one-to-one relationship. There was no trouble in securing the original 12 volunteer teachers to start with six children—now expanded to 18 working with nine children.

The teams were thoroughly briefed by the professional staff concerning the child with whom each would be working. They were given educational materials appropriate for their child and a sketchy introduction to teaching methodology, and the enterprise was under way. An early elementary teacher was detailed to the project to assist the volunteers as needed, to supervise, and to coordinate the details of supply, transportation and the like. The School District's psychologists, head school physician, and psychiatric consultant worked closely with the volunteers as they began to feel their way in assisting these children toward personality integration and educational development.

This individual teaching had to be merged with a group activity program. At the outset, group activities consisted of morning exercises, including salute to the flag, Regent's prayer, and a "show and tell" period. In addition, one other group activity of about 20 minutes was provided toward the middle of the morning; this included arts and crafts, music, physical education and story time. The other group experiences included a daily snack of milk and cookies and the children's experience in riding together in the School District's station wagon bus to and from school. Every child's birthday was celebrated by a simple party during snack time. The volunteer teachers supervised these group activities on a rotating basis, usually two or three to an activity. Increasing use is being made of the playground facilities for free play and it seems to work reasonably well.

Another facet of instruction is worthy of note. Music lessons for some of the children seem to be worth-while. One organic schizophrenic eight-year-old boy, for instance, who constantly fiddled with anything he could get his hands on, has been found to have perfect pitch and is progressing quite nicely on the piano.

The key to progress appears to be the one-to-one relationship, and the physical contact provided thereby. The volunteer teachers soothe the children with their hands, shelter them with their arms and mollify them by holding them on their laps when necessary. This physical contact has proved to be the strongest teaching aid used. Not solely because of the physical contact, but because the volunteers are the kind of people who, in this manner, communicate a genuine warmth and affection to children not always lovable. In the process, they absorb the children's anxiety. Important is the fact that, because of this one-to-one relationship, the need of the child can be fulfilled at once, with no delay. Therefore, it is unusual to see any of these children in the tantrums characteristic of such children.

Another successful technique, not unique but uniquely used through the one-to-one ratio, was to call upon the visual, auditory and tactile senses simultaneously for learning. When a child can't learn a word or letter by just seeing it, he hears it, and, using block letters and the individual flannel board easels, can feel it and trace it with his fingers. This seemed to facilitate considerable educational progress with the children.

What are the outcomes of this program after a year and six months of operation? First, for the children, three of the original six children are now in school in regular programs on a half-day basis. They are:

D.C., male, 7 years, 5 months. His diagnosis was schizophrenic reaction of childhood. His situation was complicated by considerable pathology in the total family situation. His mother has been hospitalized for mental illness and his father was also disturbed. The child developed much better controls, a longer attention span, real enthusiasm for the work and learning situation and a positive relationship to his volunteer teachers and some of the other children. His hyperactivity was greatly reduced and coordination showed marked improvement. He is now functioning in a regular first grade of 30 children.

B.T., female, 7 years, 7 months. Her diagnosis was mild cerebral palsy and mental retardation, with poor coordination, short attention span, little interest in other children, poor hand-eye coordination, distractibility and hyperactivity. She progressed so that she could handle a pencil and produce basic forms. Her attention span increased. Her interests broadened. She acquired some impulse control, completed the readiness program, learned to identify and write her name, developed arithmetical concepts of most-least, first-last, sequence, bigger-smaller and so on, and left-to-right progression. She is now successfully functioning in one of the District's classes for the educable, mentally retarded.

J.A., male, 8 years, 8 months. His diagnosis was schizophrenic reaction of childhood with the severe regressive symptom of soiling. He was hyperactive, harmful to others and disruptive so that he could not be contained in the regular classroom. There was considerable family pathology. His parents would not co-operate with the therapeutic proposals offered by the local mental health center. When placed in the educational-therapeutic milieu, this child progressed rapidly, academically and socially. His soiling ceased. His relationships at home improved. He began to relate well to the other children in the program. He is functioning at present in regular third grade on a half-time program.

Three more children are in the process of being weaned away from the special program and reabsorbed into the regular classroom. They are:

C.M., female, 8 years, 1 month—an aphasic child with organic involvement and extensive emotional problems. This child was known to many clinics in New York City as well as some local mental health facilities, who advised that she was completely hopeless and should be totally exempted from school. She was a completely withdrawn child. She now enjoys physical contact. She has improved impulse control, and in appearance is a happy, normal, attractive little girl who plays with others and occasionally assumes leadership. She is reading at the second grade level, is anxious to learn and writes and spells adequately for an eight-year-old. Most important of all, she speaks—in fact, at times, is a chatterbox—not always easy to understand, but has a sizable vocabulary and is anxious to communicate. She is doing nicely in second grade and is in the middle group in reading in her class.

R.L., male, 8 years, 1 month—a schizophrenic child with bizarre behavior, violent at times, who hurt other children, did not participate with group, did not respond to reasoning and was egocentric, autisticlike, immature, demanding and given to extreme temper tantrums and sulking. He was physically large and poorly coordinated. He now has positive relationships with his peers, particularly with adults. His coordination is improving. He has lost much of his impoliteness and is receptive to suggestions and authority. He tries to play successfully with other children and sometimes shares willingly and voluntarily. He has a high degree of academic ability, particularly in mathematics and science. In mathematics he can solve problems mentally that most of us need pencil and paper to figure. His resistance to reading has been overcome and he is reading on grade level. He is performing well in fourth grade.

C.C., male, 8 years, 9 months—a schizophrenic child who seemed superficially to be a severe behavior problem. He demonstrated gross distortions in conceptualization, visuomotor perceptualization and extreme unevenness of performance. His deficits inhibited his adjustment in all areas. When entered in the special program, it was found necessary to start his academic program at the beginning. He needed much repetition and variety of approach. He advanced again to the second grade level and is now functioning with competence in a regular second grade; this despite a family with much pathology, including severe marital discord and extreme inconsistencies in the handling of the child.

It is believed that all the other children, in time, will progress to the point where they, too, will be able to function within acceptable limits in regular classrooms.

As to the impact of the program on the volunteer teachers, they have persisted. During the second year of operation only three of the original 18 had to be replaced—one for reasons of pregnancy, one with a complicated family situation and one who just did not want to continue but agreed to act as a substitute when needed. It is thought they are deriving a good deal of personal satisfaction from the contribution they are making directly to the children. In addition, they have achieved a certain status in the community because of their generosity, which has been recognized by testimonial dinners and some publicity. Perhaps the socializing with the other women, too, has helped reduce the separation rate. They have been treated by the professionals working in connection with these children as professionals, and undoubtedly have profited in terms of developing keener insights into some of their own problems, and in understanding their own children better. Although they were untrained when they started, they have, over the months, acquired a good deal of training in an unorganized way, which, when coupled with their own intrinsic characteristics, has greatly increased their stature.

It has taken its toll, however. A transference mechanism has resulted at times in the volunteers' identifying with their pupil too closely. Progress with these children has been slow and long-term. Sometimes the volunteers were discouraged and unable to see the gains being made. Accordingly, the professionals had to be alert to this and, through group discussions and individual consultations with the volunteers, absorb some of their anxieties and avoid having the impact of their experience influence their own families and personal lives in an undesirable way.

At times the volunteer teachers have become somewhat competitive in their zeal to make academic progress with their pupils. This is both desirable and undesirable. It is important that the volunteers be cognizant of the children's need for academic progress and, concomitantly, their need for more adequate integrative personality processes. Here the psychologists were useful in their constant supervision of the individual programs.

The program has had a catalytic impact on the community, both within and beyond the school. A greater awareness has developed on the part of principals and some teachers that adaptations to the individual needs of children are profitable and satisfying investments of imagination, time and effort. There has been a great expansion of their efforts in grouping children so that this or that child is placed with the teacher who, by personality, will provide the optimal conditions for the child's total growth. Some children with problems are now being accommodated by part-time programs weighted with more art, or music or physical education. Some are being given a good deal more individual instruction. In general, the resources of the School District are being mobilized and adapted for accommodating to children's individual needs. Teachers are developing not only an awareness but also some skill in identifying children who are in need of specialized help—and at an earlier age. Most important of all, the professional educators are undergoing a subtle improvement of attitude, brought about perhaps by greater knowledge, which has led to understanding of children, acceptance of them as they are and, as a result, adaptation to their needs.

The school children themselves, while not familiar with the project for emotionally disturbed children, are nonetheless developing the same kind of awareness in connection with mental health as with cerebral palsy, the heart fund, Red Cross, Boy Scouts, Girl Scouts and the like. They included a $400 donation to the local mental health center in their children's community chest last year and again this year.

The community itself is developing a similar awareness and understanding. This is an important step forward in its education in connection with the whole mental health problem. It feels some pride too, and comfortable, now that all of its exceptional children, not just the physically handicapped, are in organized programs of education. This, in turn, is the finest kind of public relations for the school system and could be helpful at budget time when citizens are asked to vote on school expenditures.

The impact of the program on the parents of these children and their families is difficult to estimate. The psychologists, of course, keep in touch with the parents by telephone and home visits. It seems apparent to them that in some instances the children's progress has had a salutary and stabilizing influence on the total home situation. In some others, there seems to be neither awareness nor understanding of what is operative with the child and what the community is contributing. With several, the only preoccupation is that of when the child will be in regular school. No attempt has been made to develop any relationship between the volunteer teachers and the parents. In fact, the children's parents have been discouraged from making contact with the volunteers, to prevent exposing the volunteers to these parents, who, because they are often somewhat disturbed, should be handled only by professionally trained people. One group meeting of the parents was attempted some time ago for the purpose of exploring the establishment of regular meetings, on the theory that they might gain some support and some insights from regular association with parents of children like their own. This meeting produced absolutely nothing constructive, and no further attempt has been made to bring the parents together.

This whole enterprise, of course, is informative and simultaneously raises some questions. It suggests first, that one of the primary requisites for success in handling the seriously emotionally disturbed child is a one-to-one relationship with a particular kind of teacher. The needs of these children are so diverse and can change so from day to day, hour to hour, and even moment to moment, that individualized supervision and teaching is a *sine qua non* for successful treatment and educational development, at least during the years of their greatest disorganization. It suggests too, that the educative process is in itself therapeutic and, when conducted in an atmosphere impregnated with therapeutic principles, can become the vehicle for great progress with these children.

It further suggests that the resources for working successfully with the seriously disturbed child are at hand in most communities and need only to be mobilized and channeled. Without minimizing a bit the need for state and federal support for programs for such children, it demonstrates that great strides can be taken by determined communities without relying on government for solutions, or the public for fund drives. It seems to imply, too, that untrained personnel of the right kind can make enormous contributions to the well-being of such children when carefully selected, oriented and guided. This perhaps is most important because, even if all the funds needed were made available, it would not be possible to train personnel in adequate numbers in the immediate future. Then too, some professionals might not achieve the success of the volunteer teachers, since to them it would be a career and in some instances not the labor of love it is to the volunteers.

The questions it raises are many, but the two most important are, first, that of identification procedures and, second, that of whose responsibility these children are, the educator's or the mental health department's. Sometimes it was found that diagnoses conflicted even in terminology, let alone work-up procedures. Perhaps the question is best resolved by asking another: "Is this the kind of child who needs this kind of program and can profit from it?" If the answer is yes, maybe this is the only criterion that needs to be applied until there is more agreement among the professionals concerning diagnostic procedures and terminology.

Educators and mental health people have been debating for years over whose responsibility these children are. Meanwhile, not enough of a constructive nature is being done for these children and their bewildered parents. Perhaps a part of the answer lies in what Elmont has demonstrated in a small but significant way—a decent joining of forces by the two, so that each contributes from its own discipline. When this is done, it should make an unbeatable combination professionally, and in the meantime society can get on with the job of rehabilitating these unfortunate children.

25. A Day School for Schizophrenic Children

CARL FENICHEL, ALFRED M. FREEDMAN, AND ZELDA KLAPPER

The role of a day school must be considered within the framework of other services available to children who are diagnosed as schizophrenic. Considering the wide variety and range of itensity of clinical syndromes, it is obvious that no single facility or program can meet the needs of all such children.

On the one hand, there is the less seriously disturbed child who lives at home and manages to function in a public or private school; on the other, the severely disturbed child who is confined within an institution. Until recently there has been no facility for the child who does not belong to one of these two groups.

While a residential center is a necessity for certain children, it has many disadvantages: 1) Separation from the home is often traumatizing for some children and parents. 2) The child removed from his home loses the positive aspects of family life. 3) The child becomes accustomed to institutional life and this may create difficulties when he is ready to return to community living. 4) While the child is away, the family may become so reorganized that it can no longer accept the schizophrenic child back in the household. 5) Residential centers are often some dis-

SOURCE: *American Journal of Orthopsychiatry,* XXX, No. 1 (January, 1960), 130–43.

tance from the home, thus making it difficult to work closely with the parents.

In an effort to overcome these objections and to explore new ways of working with seriously disturbed children within a community setting, the League School was founded in 1953. We are presenting our experiences at the School to demonstrate that the needs of many seriously disturbed children and their families can be met by a day school within the community.

The League School grew out of the desperate need of schizophrenic children and their parents. Psychiatrists who had seen these children had stressed that it was desirable for most of them to remain at home while in treatment.

Although most parents wanted to keep their mentally ill child within the family, the many overwhelming and exhausting problems they had to face each day, with little or no relief, made this almost impossible. Public and private schools had excluded these children as "uneducable." Nor was there any available day care program to relieve parents even for a few hours so that they could regain their energy and handle their child more positively.

Few of these children were getting any kind of professional help or therapy. Clinics rejected them as untreatable. Private psychiatric treatment was too expensive for most families. Even when parents could afford such treatment, it was the opinion of many psychiatrists that treatment without the support of a planned day care and school program failed to get results.

The League School started with the working hypothesis that many children diagnosed as schizophrenic can live at home and be helped in an adequate day care or day hospital setting. Such a setting required a school program in a therapeutic environment which could treat and educate these children under psychiatric and educational guidance.

The School opened in February 1953 with 2 children, a director, a teacher, a psychiatric consultant and a part-time social worker. Additional children were screened and admitted one at a time. An additional teacher was appointed for every two children. Within a year the capacity enrollment of 12 children was reached.

The purchase of a larger building in 1955 made possible much needed expansion of treatment and research facilities, including the organization in 1956 of a nursery group. The League School, with 38 children and a professional, administrative and house staff of 28, now occupies a three-story building which formerly housed a private elementary school. The professional staff includes a director, a psychiatric director, 2 clinical and research psychologists, a psychiatric social worker, a dance therapist, a music therapist and 14 teachers.

School Population

Only children who have been diagnosed "childhood schizophrenia" by an outside psychiatrist or agency are considered for admission to the School. Children who have been diagnosed as primarily organic or retarded are not accepted. However, among the children with the label "childhood schizophrenia" numerous clinical pictures are seen. We therefore look for certain general features that we feel are essential in the diagnosis of all schizophrenic children (1), whatever their manifest behavior.

First we look to their history for evidence of disorders of development—that is, regression, or precocity and retardation existing simultaneously. Then we look for the presence of the three fundamental psychological problems in the schizophrenic child: 1) anxiety and the variety of defenses for handling the anxiety; 2) problems in relationships and identification, including impaired communication with others; 3) the presence of body-image problems, including confusion of body boundaries and uncertainty of orientation in time and space.

On the basis of manifest behavior or secondary symptoms, we can describe several categories of children at the School (2).

1. THE AUTISTIC CHILD A large group of our children are autistic (3), with their primary source of stimulation derived from their own body. They have little or no speech, rarely display any affective awareness of people, and maintain a level of activity which has the barest relation to objects or events in the real world. We distinguish two subgroups:

a) Those who have been retarded in maturation from birth. The differential diagnosis of "childhood schizophrenia" from mental deficiency is often a difficult one. The differential is based upon the presence of the primary symptoms.

George is an attractive, bright-eyed eight-year-old with no speech, little toilet training, and few interests. His developmental history contains no evidence of normal development at any period. He is always in motion, displaying extraordinary physical agility and coordination with exquisite judgment of his own body position in space. If he is not interfered with, he comfortably occupies himself with the sensations derived from his own motility. His interest in the outside world is more likely to take the form of a pursuit of small glittering objects, such as beads, than involvement with a child or adult. He makes no apparent distinction among people and relates to no one. He asks for little from the outside world and gives little.

b) The child who has a history of regression. These may be children with allegedly normal early development who began regressing seriously at some time. A few of the children in this group remind one of the "symbiotic" child described by Mahler (4). According to Mahler, early maturation in such children can be considered normal up to the point of preliminary ego differentiation, at which point the threatening effects of such growth or the actual experience of separation from the mother panics the child and precipitates regression.

Bruce is an extremely thin, frail nine-year-old boy with a normal speech pattern, enormous charm and pitiful vulnerability. In his developmental history there are two periods of regression noted before the age of five. Each of these periods of regression followed enforced separation from the mother.

Bruce walks on his toes as if chronically on the brink of disaster. He is usually observed moving around slowly in a detached preoccupied manner, rolling a rubber band or a bit of clay in his hand, and droning a song to himself. His separation from the outside world is quite definite, even to the point of his refusing to eat. He eats almost nothing. All he asks of the outside world is the impossible: that it never change, and that it make no demands upon him. His reactions to change and to pressure are devastatingly extreme. He maintains a peripheral awareness of people, objects and events, and with gentle stimulation from very familiar and trusted sources, can occasionally enter into a give-and-take relationship with the outside world. During these brief interludes, he displays warmth, intelligence and even humor, and appears to be accumulating pleasant experiences from these skirmishes with the real world, meager as they may be.

2. THE ORGANIC TYPE OF SCHIZOPHRENIC CHILD While these children present no clear-cut history of cerebral damage or dysfunction, they manifest certain of the symptoms associated with organic children, for example, distractibility, short attention span and motor drivenness.

Grace, a pretty, well-built, five-year-old girl, is in perpetual motion. She speaks well and constantly. Her contact with the outside world is an intense and overreactive one. She cannot shut out or screen impulses from the environment. As she frantically washes her dolly in the tub, her head is turned to the right to watch the little boy hammering there, and at the same time she is announcing to the little boy on her left that the teacher is calling him from the back of the room. An atmosphere of bustle and excitement is created in any room in which Grace is present. Not only is there a drivenness to respond to all stimulating aspects of the external environment, but there is also the continual impact of internal pressures on this small child. Her confusion about herself, her vagueness about the order of her universe, and her chronic anxiety affect her total person, casting her relationships with people into an impersonal mold, and constantly interfering with the development of her capabilities.

3. A NEUROTIC VARIETY OF SCHIZOPHRENIA This category is similar to the pseudoneurotic schizophrenic described by Lauretta Bender (5). Some of these children have at one time been autistic. However, the clinical picture is marked by anxieties and anxiety defenses such as phobias, obsessive compulsive symptoms and bodily preoccupations.

Shelly is a methodical 11-year-old boy who has successfully developed structured anxiety defenses and thereby achieved a measure of self-sufficiency and independence. Every movement and every word is measured and deliberate for Shelly. When he walks down the stairs, his slow-footed, cautious gait gives him steady assurance that each step is where it is supposed to be and he will not fall. Before he puts on his jacket he wards off danger by placing the jacket on the table in a certain position, raising it, and then lowering it again four times before putting it on. In place of the wildly assaultive, disorganized, autistic child he was in earlier years at the School, he is beginning to present the picture of a well-groomed, pedantic, ritualized young man who is able to participate in academic work.

4. AN ASOCIAL AGGRESSIVE TYPE These are generally somewhat older children who are poorly related, aggressive, difficult to manage, often somewhat paranoiac. This group corresponds to those described by Lauretta Bender as pseudopsychopathic (5).

Sandy is a very bright, tall, owlish-looking 12-year-old. As he strides through the School with an air of enormous self-assurance, eager to describe his most recent Superman achievements, he never once loses hold of the small straw horse he carries in his hand. Although he can find his way through closets up to the school roof, can easily climb the highest tree, and complete a complex scientific experiment, he sleeps in a bed filled with the tiny stuffed animals he places in it before retiring. He lies and steals on a petty level, and leads some of the older boys in planned escapades which invariably include the basis for detection. His relationships with people are superficial and he never asks anything of them except that they give him ample opportunity to exhibit his physical and mental omnipotence.

5. THE SCHIZOPHRENIC CHILD IN TRANSITION These are children who have a meager relatedness but are distinguished from the remaining children by their maintenance of continual contact with their environment, however meager this contact may be. Although anxiety-ridden, they have not yet developed any structured defenses. It is likely that these children will move in the direction of the neurotic variety of schizophrenia.

William is a small, slim, bright five-year-old with a freckled, elfish face and no conversational speech. Although he has some language, he depends upon pantomime and squeals to get what he wants. William appears to be aware of everything that is going on and seems to manipulate people and objects in a goal-directed way. He seems more in contact with the outside world than most of the other children in the School. Although constricted, anxious, and hostile, he is cooperative to an extent which makes it possible for him to work in an organized manner for short periods of time. Thwarting or failure has a disorganizing effect upon him, however. He tries to maintain his distance from people and does not permit more than a limited intrusion on his own privacy. He has still to develop safety mechanisms for some form of protection against the overwhelming effect of anxiety.

Thus, despite a common diagnosis, the children reveal great diversity and marked contrast in their levels and patterns of functioning. For those who function on a very primitive and infantile level, the School is more of a day hospital. On the other hand, there are two classrooms in each of which one teacher and three children work in a structured academic program. Many of the children show normal or superior intelligence but this is usually scattered and fragmented. There may be precocity in mathematics, science, art or music, and retardation in other areas.

Fourteen of our children do not talk at all. Some talk only to themselves, or just repeat unrelated phrases. Others talk incessantly but what they say is often inappropriate or confused.

A few of the children are completely withdrawn. Some just stare into space; others cover their eyes or ears with their hands to shut out the world. Many whirl around or rock back and forth in perpetual motion. Some laugh for no appropriate reason or make crying noises that seem to result from inner tension rather than from outside cause.

Many are not toilet trained; others are completely self-managing. Some show extremely tight and awkward motility; others have amazing dexterity in the use of big and small muscles. Some are hypersensitive to sound; others seem to ignore it.

Many ignore toys; others pervert their use by incorporating them into their mouths or limit their interest to minute parts of the toy. Play is usually isolated or parallel. For most of the children social play is meager or nonexistent.

Program

A tentative plan for the study and treatment of each child is established at the time of his admission to the School. Continual revisions of the plan evolve from the joint thinking of the clinical and teaching staff at weekly staff conferences and teacher-director conferences. The assignment of the child to a specific group is based on the child's needs, levels of functioning, the potential impact of the group on him, and his impact on the group. In the assignment of a child to a teacher, consideration is given to the teacher's skills, abilities, interest and suitability in working with this particular child and group.

The daily six-hour program is one of living-playing-learning experiences and activities that offer continuity, stability and security. It is a program of remedial or therapeutic education utilizing as many of the activities and techniques of preschool and elementary school as possible. Some techniques of play therapy, relationship therapy, group therapy, and music and dance therapy are applied.

The program is divided into two phases: a preliminary or preparatory phase, to make the child as comfortable as possible by removing stress situations and relieving anxiety; and a re-educational or rehabilitation phase, to stimulate maturation by helping the child to cope with inner needs and tensions, and with the outside world.

In such a program, the teacher-child relationship is basic. To be effective, such a relationship demands one teacher for every two or three children. Often a child needs the exclusive attention of one teacher for many weeks or even months. Therapy at the School is, to a great degree, the cumulative impact of the feelings, attitudes and behavior of the teacher with whom the child has contact six hours a day, five days a week, in the significant functions and activities of eating, playing, dressing, toileting, washing, resting, dancing, singing, painting, and, wherever possible, the more traditional academic activities.

Teacher-child relationships are initiated on whatever level the child is functioning. Often this is on a most primitive, nonverbal level with the teacher acting as an accepting, comforting, mother figure who holds, fondles, cuddles, rocks and feeds her child. Teachers have to be alert to any signs of response from a child. Contact with the outside world is often begun by body contact with the teacher.

A teacher may have to use her body as part of the child's to produce different types of motility until the child can do it on his own. Teachers need to know when to encourage a child to approach, explore, and try a new experience or activity. Care must be taken to avoid pressing a child beyond his fragile hold on reality. A new stimulus or experience may be too threatening and be met by withdrawal or increased resistance to outside contact.

New play experiences and academic activities provide a basis for reality testing. Every satisfying experience or mastery of a new routine or activity makes for decreased anxiety and increased self-awareness and confidence.

A disturbed child needs help, too, in experiencing and coping with the give-and-take of human feelings. A teacher must be able to recognize and identify with a child's feelings of anger, fear, confusion, frustration and aggression. Freedom to express and work through these feelings has often led to a lessening of anxiety and greater relatedness and response to the environment.

Teachers must know when to stimulate and permit such expression and how to deflect, dilute or control it before it becomes too overwhelming. The gradual imposition of limits upon a child's impulsive outbursts can be reassuring if applied in a nonpunitive manner. Limits and controls can also help in ego development and in differentiating the self and the outside world.

It is difficult to separate the teacher-child relationship at the School from the specific program and activities prescribed for the child. The conscious and unconscious influences and impact of the teacher and child upon each other are much too difficult to measure. Efforts are being made to develop sufficiently sensitive and accurate tools of observation to determine the relative contributions of specific play, educational and treatment techniques in a child's improvement and growth.

Much of the work of the League School centers around efforts at play activities. To the seriously disturbed child whose verbal communication is limited or distorted, and whose world is most confusing and threatening, play is vitally important for growth. By manipulating, organizing and reorganizing the small world of blocks, water, clay, dolls and puppets, the disturbed child may learn more effective ways to handle his inner needs and impulses and the complex world around him.

As we observe the play of these children we are struck by its impoverished quality, in marked contrast to the richness, spontaneity and creativity that characterize normal play. The very term "play" has to be used cautiously with our children, since a given activity which suggests play may, in reality, be obsessional in character. The play of these children is usually stereotyped in selection of activities and in patterning. There is a tendency to respond to the same few objects in the same way, day in and day out. For example, one child who is accustomed to arrange his blocks daily in a linear pattern reacted with anxiety when the teacher added a curved block to the building, and he compulsively returned the block to the shelf every time it was introduced.

In evaluating play interests in our nursery, we find that the children tend to favor material like water, balloons, balls, rocking boats and musical instruments. The majority of the materials favored fall loosely into three categories: those with mobility, those having a granulated texture like sand and those connected with sound. Of these, mobile toys are especially popular. Even the most autistic child is likely to show some response to a spinning top, a rolling tire or a bubble floating in air. As a matter of fact, the nursery children often convert almost any object in the classroom into a mobile one by throwing it.

By applying limits and pressing a child at the opportune moment, we can often help the child to change a particular play pattern. Slowly, cautiously, with proper dosage and timing, new materials and routines become part of the familiar, lose their threat and are accepted.

Because of their withdrawal from or limited response to the world, their desperate need for sameness, and their inadequate relationships with people, most of the children at the School lack the background and experiences that are essential for reading readiness and other academic work. As a child begins to feel comfortable with his teacher and his surroundings, he is encouraged to approach, meet and explore more of the world. A rich variety of experiences is presented: trips to neighborhood stores, playgrounds, parks, the firehouse, museums and subway and ferry rides to other places of interest. These experiences help to enrich, enliven and expand the interests and background of a child preparatory to any academic work.

All academic work must be highly individualized and timed to fit the personal interests and needs, special preoccupations and the life experiences of each child.

Leonard is compulsively preoccupied with lights, switches, strings and fans. When these stimuli are near he manifests intense hyperactivity and disorganized behavior patterns. For several months he refused to participate in any activity for more than a few minutes at a time. Whole days were punctuated with uncontrollable outbursts of aggression and subsequent anxiety.

When he was not disabled by his obsessions, Leonard revealed a highly intelligent personality and good learning potential. Since he was quite verbal and keenly aware of his environment, it was felt that he was ready to learn to read. Like most of our children, he was tremendously threatened by any new learning situation.

Instead of waiting for his conflict to be worked through, it was decided to utilize Leonard's pathology in the learning situation. Leonard started learning words through picture associations—but only words that had special meaning for him: light, string, fan, parachute, etc. After these words became part of his working vocabulary, he accepted the idea of learning enough to be able to make a sentence. Slowly, neutral words like "cup," "ball," "house," "street," etc., were introduced. Former anxiety was mobilized for a short time every morning into excitement over mastering a new skill. Compulsivity was directed into printing a list of words every day. Leonard now has a definite reading period every morning which gives new structure to his day and to which he reacts with great enthusiasm and interest.

Karen for a long time resisted all efforts at academic work. She wanted to be a baby, she said, and preferred to spend much of her day with the very young children. She loved to eat and went down to the kitchen every morning to ask: "What's for lunch?" This interest in food was exploited and Karen was soon eager to help make and print the day's menu. Playing around with the words in menus and recipes was the beginning of reading readiness. Within a year she was reading at the fourth grade level.

Karen's interest in scissors, paste and crayons and her love of color were used to get her interested in arithmetic. One day while her teacher and another pupil were making multiplication flash cards, Karen asked if she could make some with her scissors, crayons and colored paper. Interest in multiplication began. Flash cards in addition, subtraction and multiplication followed. Arithmetic is now part of Karen's program, and each day she brings in homework done artistically in a variety of colors.

Shelly clings to his teacher for protection and support whenever he is faced with an unfamiliar or threatening situation. He is extremely fearful of any new academic experience, convinced that it will be too difficult for him. Trial-and-error learning is rejected by Shelly because he cannot accept the frightening possibility of failure.

Shelly's daily ritual of academic work and homework must have sufficient sameness in it to make him comfortable. He must always sit in the same chair, to the left of his teacher, and with his ever-present shoelace that he jiggles in his hand. His previous day's homework must always be checked before his lessons can start. "I don't enjoy this," "I'm bothered," and other distress signals and reactions follow the introduction of anything new. Slowly, cautiously, gradually, with proper dosage and timing, new materials and routines become part of the familiar, lose their threat and are accepted.

Other Therapies

While every aspect of the School's environment and program has a therapeutic potential, there are some children at the School who are ready for and could benefit from more intensive individual psychotherapy. Since the School does not at present have the personnel or facilities to provide this service, six of our children are receiving individual psychotherapy, either privately or at outside agencies. Efforts are being made to obtain psychotherapy for four more children who are now ready for it. Unfortunately, child guidance facilities have long waiting lists, and the fact that there is a diagnosis of "schizophrenia" is apparently an additional deterrent to accepting referrals from the School.

The administration of drugs to some of our children is considered an integral part of the therapeutic program at the School. Ten of our children are receiving tranquilizers so that they can profit better from the total school program. Stimulant drugs are administered to six children who are severely withdrawn and regressed.

Teacher Selection

Since there is as yet no well-defined or organized teacher-training program in our colleges to help teachers acquire skills, techniques and competencies for work with seriously disturbed children, it is no surprise that our teachers have a varied professional background. Some of our staff have been trained as nursery school teachers. We have found that nursery school training, with its emphasis on early childhood development, is ideal for working with most of our children, no matter what their age. Seriously disturbed children are children who have failed to grow up. To help a child move and grow, a teacher must have a clear idea of the level on which a child is currently functioning and what her specific developmental goals for that child should be. Others on our teaching staff have had elementary school training and experience, supplemented by courses in special education, remedial techniques and play therapy. A few have been trained in psychology rather than in education.

Far more difficult than evaluating the academic training and background needed for our teaching staff is the still unanswered question of personality criteria for selection of our teachers. We know that working with our children demands a combination of skill and art, and much of it is still an art rather than a science. Such essential qualities as imagination, intuition, spontaneity and sensitivity are not easy to detect or measure at the time a teacher is interviewed or selected for the job.

While we have had a few teachers who were equally at home with normal or disturbed children, we do not believe that a teacher who is effective with normal children can necessarily work well with seriously disturbed children. Conversely, not every teacher at the League School is suited for work with normal children.

Our teachers must feel at home with dirt, destruction, hostility and all kinds of deviant and bizarre behavior. A child at the School may eat his mucus, smear food all over himself, or play with his urine. If a teacher reacts with disgust to such behavior, it can damage any relationship which she may have established with a child. In panic, a child may smash windows or throw things. Such behavior can be quite threatening to a teacher who interprets it as defiance or rejection of herself personally.

A teacher may understand intellectually that for a child's emotional growth he should be permitted to play with dirt, and yet the teacher's real feelings about cleanliness may get in the way. The child will sense that while he is being permitted to play with dirt, there is something in the teacher's own feelings that doesn't quite accept the activity. Often a teacher's unconscious needs and standards are imposed on a child. This may make the teacher more comfortable, but it isn't necessarily helping the child.

Our teachers need sufficient ego strength to absorb large quantities of provocation, hostility, aggression and negativism without feeling threatened or rejected. They must have adequate personal and professional maturity and insight to examine and constantly reappraise their own feelings and reactions to the children with whom they are working. While they must have genuine feelings of warmth, acceptance and kindness, teachers must not become overprotective, oversolicitous or "smothering" as a reaction to the strong dependency needs of the children.

Teachers at the School do not have the support of syllabuses, courses of study or lesson plans with clearly defined academic objectives. Blueprints and answers are not readily accessible in our work. We have had a number of highly skilled and experienced teachers who have found this lack of sufficient structure most threatening. There is compensation for our teachers, however, in the feelings of creative spontaneity, autonomy and self-direction which such an uncharted situation encourages and demands.

Our teachers must believe deeply and sincerely in the possibility for growth and improvement in the children they work with. A hopeless or negative attitude toward a child's growth potential would make the teacher's role ineffectual and untenable. However, because of their strong belief that they can help a schizophrenic child, our teachers must be on constant guard against seeing improvement where none has taken place; they must have the capacity for objective observations. These children change slowly. Satisfaction for the teacher comes in tiny doses, and when it comes there is always the possibility that regression may follow. The teacher's investment in time, skill, physical and emotional energy makes lack of progress or regression hard to accept. The frustration that may follow must not be allowed to be turned into feelings of failure or inadequacy toward oneself, or hostility and blame toward parents or supervisors.

Parents

Space does not permit a presentation of the School's work with parents, i.e., the counseling and guidance services of our psychiatric social worker, the referral of some parents to community agencies or to psychiatrists for individual therapy. Mention must be made of the initiation at the School of weekly group therapy sessions for parents which have proven helpful to the parents and the children. At first, parents come to these sessions to find out more about their child's illness and to get blueprints for managing the child.

An intellectual probing of the origin of the illness, the prognosis, and methods of treatment dominates the early sessions. Information and discussion on mental illness provide an intellectual basis for relieving some of the parents' feelings of personal responsibility for their child's illness. Later, various expressions of shame, anxiety, inadequacy, isolation and resentment are aired, explored and often worked through, with group interaction becoming more prominent.

Direct guidance in the daily management of the child emerges from the interchange among parents. Some insight into the parents' feelings about themselves and their own conflicts contributes to increased personal comfort.

Psychological Evaluation of Progress

The specific features of the School's program can only be evaluated in terms of their effect upon the individual child. It has been possible to maintain a record containing psychiatric, educational and psychological data for each of the children in the School. Of the 38 children, 16 can be tested by the use of standard tests of intelligence and of personality, applied in the prescribed manner. With flexible handling of instructions and test material, it is possible to use some parts of these standard test materials with 7 additional children. The remaining children cannot be tested by using any standardized test material. Instead, "controlled observations" have been used. These children are observed in the classroom, playground and dining room for the purpose of recording the child's state-of-being in these various situations. His relations to objects, children, adults; his patterns of behavior during music therapy, or in transitions from inside to outside the School, are examples of the types of notations made periodically. Ten-minute periods of exposure to a standard playroom structure provide additional sources of observational data.

The psychological observations are integrated with data from other staff members for final analysis. Other sources include the teacher's daily observations, reports and anecdotal records, the staff conferences on the individual child, the psychiatrist's observations and the parents' accounts of the child's pattern of functioning at home as outlined in a "Parent's Journal" submitted by each mother and father at the beginning and end of the school year. This journal records the child's behavior from the beginning to the end of a typical day at home.

Follow-up Study

Since its opening five years ago, the League School has admitted 50 children. Thirty-eight are presently enrolled; 10 have been discharged; 2 were withdrawn because of transportation difficulties.

Four children were discharged after they had passed the 12-year age limit at the School. The parents of these four children would have preferred to keep them at home and have them attend a day school for adolescents. However, no such day school existed. One of these children had to be placed directly in a state institution since no other facility would accept him. The other three were accepted at a residential center where two of these boys are doing very well in their relationships with children and adults, and are progressing in academic work and in other areas. The third boy could not adjust to the residential center and was subsequently placed in a state institution.

Three other children at the School were so disrupting to their families, particularly to their siblings, that the School recommended institutionalization. Another child was institutionalized because improper care and lack of cooperation by the parents negated all that the School was trying to do for the child.

Two other boys had made sufficient progress so that they no longer needed such a special environment; they are living at home and attending regular private schools. Both have made excellent social and academic adjustment; one of them has just received an award for achievement from his school.

Conclusion

In reviewing the first five years of the League School, one is struck by the unusually rapid growth of the institution. The pressure for further expansion, as evidenced by the ever-increasing number of applications, is an indication of the need for such a service within the community mental health program.

The School has been able to maintain 50 children within the community for varying periods of time. These children were so seriously disturbed that no private or public school would admit or retain them. A great many of these children would have had to be institutionalized had it not been for the existence of the School. The establishment of the League School made it possible for such children to remain at home, participating in family life, and attending a therapeutically oriented school.

The children's experiences in the School have been varied. For a few, the School has been essentially custodial; for most, it has been therapeutic.

Many of our children have achieved self-management for the first time in their lives. Children with poor motor coordination have learned to play ball, swim, roller-skate, ice-skate, ride a bicycle and manipulate woodworking tools. Children with overwhelming fears and aggressions have learned to control impulses and tolerate change and frustration. Children who were afraid to cross streets, go into stores or playgrounds, ride a subway and meet people have overcome these specific fears and taken first steps toward socialization. Children who were considered "uneducable" have learned to read, write, do arithmetic and other academic work.

Up to now, emphasis at the School has been chiefly on services and treatment. We are in the initial stages of our research program. We have developed systematic methods for the observing and recording of data by the clinical and teaching staff. The children are being studied in an effort to see if clinical categories are truly differentiating in regard to natural history, behavior patterns and prognosis.

Basic to the projected research plans at the League School is the intensive study of these data. Our method of observing and measuring must be validated over longer periods of time. It is only through development of such methods here and elsewhere that the effectiveness of the variety of therapies and management programs can be evaluated.

Another area of research is the intensive psychological and sociological study of the parents of children at the School. Such a study can help us to evaluate the extent to which impaired child-parent relationships derive from disturbances in the parents or from the schizophrenic disturbance in the child. Further, there is need for collaborative studies comparing parents of schizophrenic children at day schools with parents whose children are at residential centers and state hospitals.

In summary, we have presented some of our experiences at the League School: its origin, purpose, program, growth and research plans. We believe that our project has demonstrated that such a day school serves as a successful therapeutic setting for schizophrenic children and fills an important role in the total community mental health program.

References

1. BENDER, LAURETTA, and ALFRED M. FREEDMAN. "A Study of the First Three Years in the Maturation of Schizophrenic Children." *Quart. J. Child Behav.*, 4:245–272, 1952.

2. Freedman, Alfred M. "Childhood Schizophrenia: Nosological Considerations." Unpublished manuscript.
3. Kanner, Leo. "Early Infantile Autism." *J. Pediat.*, 25:211–217, 1944.
4. Mahler, Margaret S. "On Child Psychosis and Schizophrenia: Autistic and Symbiotic Infantile Psychoses," in *The Psychoanalytic Study of the Child,* Vol. VII, 286–305. New York: Internat. Univ. Press, 1952.
5. Bender, Lauretta. "Treatment of Juvenile Schizophrenia." *Proc. Ass. Res. Nerv. Ment. Dis.,* 34:462–465, 1954.

26. The Acting-Out Boy

Ruth G. Newman

In November of 1953, the children's branch of the National Institute of Mental Health, under the direction of Dr. Fritz Redl, took on its first group of patients.[1] They were six hyperactive boys of 9 to 13 years of age with behavior disorders of a kind both troublesome to society and destructive to people and property; in a loosely descriptive word, "delinquent."

Since that time there have been two other patient groups. The second group included boys from 10 to 12 years, while the age range of the boys in treatment currently is 8 to 11 years. It was planned that the first two groups be studied for dynamic diagnosis—a term intended to include in addition to the usual battery of psychological, educational, and physiological tests, an electroencephalogram, sample observations of the child in school, on the ward, in therapy, in groups, and individually, by participant observers and non-participant observers, the study of notes and records through conferences, case studies, discussions, and progress reports at regular intervals by all those concerned with the care of the child (therapists, group workers, teachers, case-workers with parents and

[1] These observations were made on the learning difficulties of boys with severe behavior disorders as they are exhibited in a special school at the children's research branch of the National Institute of Mental Health, Bethesda, Md.

SOURCE: *Exceptional Children,* XXIII (February, 1956), 186–250. Reprinted by permission.

foster parents, child care workers, research workers) so that all might share in bringing to light as much significant data as possible concerning the patterns of behavior and fantasy material operating in the child.

The boys in the present group will be maintained here until they have been cured or as long as residential treatment is useful to them and to our research needs.

All of the boys who have been admitted to the children's branch have shared a common pathology to which the phrase "acting-out" has been assigned. By this is meant a type of behavior where an impulse or fantasy, conscious or unconscious, is immediately acted upon whether or not it be an appropriate or realistic response. The inner controls which serve to inhibit most people from such behavior are undeveloped in these boys. They lack the ability to postpone, regulate, or foresee consequences. Such behavior appears as involuntary as the flare up of a firecracker once it is ignited. The child seems no more able to muster up controls, to stop or to alter his act, than the firecracker can stop itself from exploding.

More specifically, the kind of boy included at the children's branch for treatment and study is physically and verbally assaultive. He has frequently run into difficulties with authorities—be they school, police, or juvenile court—and he has frequently been brought to the attention of various social agencies. He may have established a reputation as thief, vandal, fire-setter, bully, bed-wetter, and sometimes a combination of these. His rages seem to come from nowhere and are expressed with the violence and variety of a three-year-old. No matter how old he is or how tough he tries to be, he appears infantile and, like an infant, he demands that his needs (often contradictory) be met instantly and absolutely. He has more likely, though not necessarily, come from a less privileged socioeconomic level. Through his history has run an inescapable line of affectional deprivation, which is more often than not embellished by tragedy and a series of traumatic and rejecting experiences.[2]

The basic research at the children's branch of NIMH is planned to cover three areas of these children's lives: (a) to study the acting-out boy in a total living situation; (b) to study him in individual therapy; and (c) to study his learning difficulties as they exhibit themselves in school. It is only with the third area that this paper is concerned. It should be made clear that this study is at the observation gathering stage and few scientifically measurable statements can yet be made. At the present time, even the tentative observations that have been gathered must be

[2] The boys who have been admitted to NIMH have been committed to us through the courts, through welfare agencies, or by the parents' temporary release to the welfare agency, for the purpose of committing the child to us.

confined to the life on our ward in this particular residential setting, situated in a large clinical-research hospital.

In order to understand the school program and its problems, it is necessary to have a brief picture of the way in which these boys live at the National Institutes of Health. Life for the boys is not only distinct from non-institutional life in a home setting where a child attends a regular school or even a special class, and perhaps goes for therapy hours to a clinic; it is also distinct from a residential treatment home which is built specifically to house children, whose facilities are child centered, and whose prime concern is clinical rather than a combined goal of research and treatment that is attempted at NIMH.

The group is housed on part of the fourth floor of a gigantic new clinical center. In order to have any sports and games, or just outdoor play, the children, with adequate adult escort, must leave their locked ward, go through halls and elevators where they encounter patients from the other divisions of the clinical center, various employees of the Institutes, as well as expensive and enticing research and clinical equipment. A normal child would find such a setting a difficult one in which to adjust comfortably, and these children, not as aware of the needs of external reality, are nonetheless affected by the form of life in such a place. Therefore the environmental factor must be considered in any generalizations that are made.

Nevertheless, taking into consideration this special setting, observations have led to certain hypotheses concerning the learning difficulties of the "acting-out" boy, the creation of a school program to fit his learning needs, and the problems a teacher will have in working with him individually, or in a group.

Since the difficulties that surround learning are of major clinical and research importance in working with the acting-out boy, a school program was planned whose goals were to attempt to overcome these difficulties and to study their source, manifestations, and cure. In order to offer these children an opportunity to learn, according to their abilities and interest, teachers needed to be equipped to handle the emotional and educational needs of these particular children in such a way as to help them learn how to relate to other children, as well as to the adult, in a flexibly structured environment, as well as to help the children develop assets and increase their frustration-tolerance level in learning and structured situations. Obviously the selection, training, and supervision of such teachers are a prime concern in launching a school program.

Past School Background and Experience

In order to create a suitable school program, it was necessary to understand what "school" and "teachers" had come to mean to these boys. Their past school experience had to be evaluated in order to determine sensitive areas, special resistances, as well as any positive experiences.

The concept "school" for every child carries with it the values, aspirations, and motivations he has brought from his home, his culture, and his neighborhood. School may be a place to avoid home scrutiny, a place to fail, or a place to strive; a way to make friends, a battlefield for bitter competition, or withdrawal; a way to feel more competent by learning, or to be shamed by ignorance. Adults will be thought of as kind, indulgent, easy to manipulate, unfair, strict, or mean. Other children will be sought out as rivals, buddies, followers, or leaders, or will be avoided. How school comes to mean what it does for each child will be something more than the total of his home and school experiences and will depend on his ability to deal with the reality that confronts him.

The pathologically acting-out boy has little ability to deal with reality without severely distorting it. His concepts of school, teachers, and peers have developed from the damaging experiences he has lived through and from his distortions of additional experiences which have, in turn, led him into more damaging experiences. Therefore, his perception of "school," "teachers," and "learning" has been weighed down by the same anger, resentment, defeat, and refusal that he has taken from, and brought to, his other living experiences.

In every case, the children at the children's research branch have experienced serious difficulties in school. Only two out of the total 16 have had no severe academic problems (these two were operating at grade level according to standard school achievement tests) but notwithstanding, even these two had been in trouble because of behavior: inability to conform to regulations, or routine, to follow directions, or to relate to other children and adults. The other 14, in addition to the above behavior problems, had been unable to learn academic subjects. Reading, that tremendous hurdle for so many emotionally disturbed children, had been impossible for many of them. Arithmetic, with its demand for concentration, logic, and accuracy, was frequently a hopeless task. Some boys could not write, most could not spell. None of the boys had been able to comply with directions, to organize material, to complete a task, or to sustain an effort.

In some cases no standard tests could be administered, in others the tests had to be administered in unusual ways. Where possible Standard Metropolitan

Achievement Tests, Stanford Achievement Tests, Gale Oral Reading Tests, Munroe Silent Reading Tests, were given.

16 Boys	*Expected Grade Level*	*Actual Grade Level*
(1) 13 yr old	8th grade	8th grade
(1) 11 yr old	6th grade	6th grade
(1) 12 yr old	7th grade	5th grade
(1) 11 yr old	6th grade	4th grade
(1) 10 yr old	5th grade	3rd grade
(1) 10 yr old	5th grade	4th grade
(2) 11 yr old	5th grade	3rd grade
(2) 9 yr old	4th grade	1st grade
(1) 8 yr old	3rd grade	kindergarten
(2) 10 yr old	5th grade	3rd grade
(2) 9 yr old	4th grade	2nd grade
(1) 12 yr old	7th grade	3rd grade

For a classroom teacher, who brings to the classroom her own expectations, cultural values, and emotional investment, to have a child in her schoolroom such as the ones described above is a strain, indeed. In all probability, it will be this child who disrupts class activities, destroys property, hurts himself and other children, is unable to remain quiet, refuses to be involved in group work, and who gives up on any set task. To complicate matters the teacher may well be puzzled by the fact that the child's behavior has little to do with his intelligence quotient. This child may be quick or slow, able to grasp a difficult idea, and remain blank at a simple one, or he may assimilate nothing the teacher says. Even when the boy is permitted to initiate his own task he probably will not be able to complete it, and may at any time, for no reason at all, or no apparent reason, play havoc with the lesson-plan for the day. Any failure may bring him to fury and success reassures him, if at all, for no more than a minute. The teacher's reaction to the child has little to do with personal attractiveness. The boy may look like an angel; speak, at times, with courtesy, and be capable of disarming charm; he may be unattractive, gross, sloppy in apparel, or he may have speech defects, tics, or unpleasant physical habits.

Regardless of his mental endowments or personal appearance, he takes more of the teacher's time and energy than any other child in the room. He is the child who is first sent to the principal's office, often with such regularity that the principal sees him as much as his classroom teacher.[3] He is the child over whom many hours of consultation and test-

[3] One of the NIMH boys reported that he liked third grade because he spent every day in the principal's office and never had to do any work.

ing are spent. His parents, or foster parents, or the agency responsible for his care are frequently called and invited for conferences.

The school may be aware of other types of emotional disturbance, but it is the hyperactive, aggressive, behavior problem for whom drastic measures are taken. The course of action usually taken is suspension and the inauguration of a visiting teacher program, or he may be put in a special class. Few school systems have special classes for the "emotionally disturbed." More often he is put in classes for the brain-injured, the physically handicapped, or the retarded, where it is hoped that he will cease to be a torment for anyone but the special teacher to whom he is assigned, and that, incidentally, he may be able to learn.

All of the boys at the children's branch have lived through most of the above school experiences. Each experience has solidified their concept that they live in a hostile, rejecting world, peopled by adults who can be defeated by their behavior. In their knowledge of the adult's helplessness and anxiety, they become convinced that they are unable to be helped, that they are unlovable, unreachable, and hopeless. They cannot afford to be aware that they have participated in creating their own rejection—to do so would be to give up the defense they have been able to maintain at such great cost—if I am unlovable, I will hate and punish you; if you will not give me what I want and need, I will not take what you want to give me. In school, this means a strike against learning, a strike against those who teach and against those children who succeed in complying. By virtue of these children's distortions and experiences, school has become a hostile, rejecting, need-denying place where *not* to learn is a natural response and where to learn evokes defiance, rage, and failure.

The Special Class, The Special Teacher

Sometimes, during this school history, the acting-out boy may be placed in a special class for the emotionally disturbed. Where such classes exist, they contain a large proportion of the type boy included in this study. In such a class, or in a school like the one at NIMH, the acting-out boy will encounter the special teacher.

When a teacher departs from ordinary classroom teaching and undertakes to teach the emotionally disturbed child, his expectations for himself are distinctly different from those he would have in teaching an average class. Aside from a probable determination to succeed where others have failed, to turn his pupils' past failure into success, change attitudes, inoculate the child with learning as painlessly as possible, he may have decided to teach emotionally disturbed children because of his own personal motivations. He may have had painful school experiences of his own, or may be unhappy with large groups, and comfortable only in small ones. His own need to be specially treated, to be non-conformist, to "fix people up," to help, or to change them, may have had a determining role in his vocational choice.

The acting-out boy has as great a skill as the proverbial schizophrenic for feeling out anxious areas in others and in discovering those goals that the teacher desires for himself. Since the child is a past master at the art of defeating others as well as himself, unless the teacher becomes aware of his motivations and expectations, he may well be made so anxious that he ends by being unable to teach, thus confirming the child's conviction that no one can, or will, help him. Thus, the teacher will need to evaluate how realistic his expectations of himself and the children are in the light of their actual performance and his own limitations. In the experiences with the three groups of boys at NIMH many occasions have arisen where it is this kind of interaction between child and teacher that has temporarily brought learning to a standstill.

Notwithstanding what inner drives the special teacher brings to the group, he has usually had extra training in the use of techniques and materials and will be called upon to use all these and many others he has never learned. He requires the ability to plan ahead and then to scrap all plans and develop others on the spot. He needs a variety of approaches and techniques from which to draw.

Limit-Setting

If the school is situated in a residential-treatment setting, such as exists at the children's branch, where the exhibition of the acting-out pathology is part of the treatment, in contrast to a day public school setting where an overload of acting-out behavior cannot be tolerated, and on occasion encouraged, the boys will frequently behave in a most disorganized fashion, and the teacher may fear that like the creator of a Frankenstein monster he has let loose more than he can handle, or more than is beneficial to the child. He may be concerned that he has participated in destroying rather than building up controls. He will have to wend his way through a morass of behavior and his consequent feelings in order to establish what limits are essential for the welfare of the boys. For with these boys, even with a permissive atmosphere that seeks to examine rather than repress pathological behavior, the establishment of appropriate limits is an essential part of setting the stage for learning.

To discover the limits that are appropriate for each child at any given moment presupposes the living through of many anxious periods and many failures. It becomes necessary to distinguish what behavior is acceptable as an expression of present disorder, what must be tolerated as a necessary evil for the time being, and what must be stopped immediately. Such decisions are delicate and open to human error at best. Since timing is a major factor the task requires skill, knowledge, experience, intuition, and self-respect. One second too late is plain too late and one minute too early, while preferable, may be equally ineffective. To help the acting-out boy build his ego controls and increase his ability to avoid the disintegrating experiences of his past, appropriate and well-timed limits must be established even to the point of physically removing the child from the classroom.

Closeness

It has been learned that closeness is a serious problem to acting-out boys. In all of his school experience, the acting-out boy has demanded the teacher's complete and absolute attention. He has insisted on being the first, having the most. Because of his demands, derived from affectional deprivation in his past, he both craves a one-to-one relationship and fears it. Thus, an essential part of his learning is to afford him the chance of an unshared one-to-one relationship and to help him feel safe in using it.

Proceeding on the premise that a child must learn how to relate in a one-to-one relationship before he is able to relate and learn in a group, periods each week have been set aside for each child at NIMH for individual tutoring. The need for such a program is the more important when it is recognized that no matter how small the total group, each of these children's levels of attainment, methods of learning, interests, and motivation vary to such a degree that only by some strictly individual help can they assimilate any of the academic skills. (The range of grade level ability in reading alone in the current group runs from ninth grade to first grade.)

The goals of the tutoring sessions are many: to give the child the individual attention he has been demanding; to indicate to him that adults are not necessarily enemies but may be the instruments by which he can feel and become more adequate; to give him, by materials and techniques, specific remedies for his particular educational deficiencies and make it possible for him to learn according to his own perceptual pattern; to give him enough quick successes without the need to compare himself with others so that he will increase his toleration for frustration and build up sufficient controls in learning to be able to complete a task, lengthen his attention span, and broaden his motivating interest.

In carrying out the individual tutoring program it has been repeatedly noticed to what an extent this coveted one-to-one relation becomes threatening at the very moment it becomes meaningful. Closeness is often met by the very child who has demanded it the most vociferously, with panic and resistance.[4]

A teacher may feel bewildered when a child who has clamored for individual attention pushes him away, rejects the offer, screams insults, and runs in panic. Rejection is never easy to take, and to be assimilated, the dynamics behind the child's behavior must be understood.

Closeness implies the establishment of a relationship, an experience which to all these children has been impossible or devastating. To attempt it and fail is far too frightening, and to be made vulnerable by becoming dependent is insupportable, so that at the very moment the relation begins to have significance, the child will push the teacher away or take to flight himself. The child needs to go through long periods of testing out, and of living with non-damaging adults before he will be able to perceive them as friends rather than enemies. To give up his battle before he is ready would be more than his shaky organization could sustain.

If the dynamics are understood by the teacher, it will help him to forestall too close situations and to foresee times when techniques, position, or methods should be altered. The importance of the teacher's awareness of these dynamics cannot be minimized for if the problem of closeness is doubly loaded by carrying the weight of the teacher's problems as well as the child's, it may well prove a trap wherein the child relearns the damaging lesson, learned too well already, that is, that he can defeat all adults and therefore, no one remains to help him.

[4] One child in the first group after having established a good one-to-one relationship with his tutor, became frightened of the very closeness he sought. He refused to come for his tutoring period unless a male counselor was with him and when, unavoidably, he was left alone with her he flew into a tantrum, threw books and crayons, ran from the room, fled down the hall screaming that the teacher was trying to kiss him. It took three months of cautious, non-pressing proffering of the relationship, before the child could feel safe enough with this teacher to ask for the help that had always been offered. Then, careful to combine distance with closeness, the teacher could proceed with the tutoring and the child was able to begin to learn how to learn.

A boy in the current group began his tutoring sessions by making clay models and then dictating stories about these creatures which he was able to read back. He liked this creative method of making his own reading text and he proceeded with poems and stories. He was momentarily proud both to have written them and to be able to read them. As the stories became more personal and meaningful to him, he grew panicky and threw over the whole method that he had been able to use so well. He refused tutoring sessions and lashed out at the teacher. He only felt safe when he was offered the most routine drills and exercises that he had hitherto rejected with violence.

Recapitulation of Educational Evolution

The greater part of the school day at the children's branch involves group activities which center around a series of projects. The goals of these projects are: to offer the child an opportunity to relate to a limited number of other children; to form a group wherever this is possible; to relate in a group to a teacher; to provide skills in manipulating a variety of materials; to motivate interest in learning; and to indicate different methods and approaches in handling a given task. The kind of a project that is planned, how it is carried out, and how long it lasts depends on the children's interest and what they are able to do with it at any given time.

In looking over the groups, current as well as past, that have participated in the projects at the children's unit, a pattern of behavior seems to emerge which, if it is indeed a consistent pattern, has many implications.

It has been noticed that when new boys appear at the children's branch there is an inevitable "honeymoon" period. The boy behaves in a rigidly controlled best-school manner. He is reasonably courteous, unenthusiastically compliant, and tries to conceal his academic weaknesses.

When it becomes clear, by means of the other children's behavior, the physical set-up of the school, the attitudes and behavior of the teacher, that this is a different type of school from that which he was used to, the child is, for a while, a bit dazed. He may drop his "Sir" and "Ma'am," he may refuse to work on material he had thought any self-respecting school insisted on, and yet be afraid to participate in the program, language, or attitudes he sees the other children using. He acts lost and restless, and is frequently frightened by his isolation or his blow-ups. He may complain that this is no real school, and that he is getting worse every day; or he may express enthusiasm for its difference. Either way he feels unable to share in it.

As he becomes acclimated, he loosens up, or "defrosts." He has an increasing number of blow-ups and shows of violence, frequently on the issue of being "first," or being "best," or being "left out." These blow-ups may be between him and the teachers, or more usually, between him and one or another of the children. His academic level, no matter how high or low it was when he came, falls off. If he reads at fourth grade level, he no longer reads at all, or he tries only encyclopedia material where he is bound to fail. If he reads at second grade level he becomes illiterate so far as use of past knowledge is concerned. If he came to the school as a painter, he stops painting. If he came with skill in arithmetic, he no longer uses it. The period is a disorganized, searching one and he seeks out a level where he can feel comfortable.

Invariably, the teacher offers him a series of projects and materials and, in an effort to reach him at the level where he is, feels frantic as the level changes from day to day, moment to moment. It would be of some comfort for such a teacher to know (if such be the fact in all cases, as it has been with the limited sample of boys at the children's branch) that it is not necessarily the teacher's lack of resourcefulness or insight in reaching these children, but that children with this pathology seem to pass through this stage in reconstructing for themselves a new perception of school.

Furthermore, it has been observed that these children, in descending the educational scale, break their fall downward at a nursery-school level. Though the range of the boys observed has been from 13 to 8, during this phase they use nursery school and kindergarten materials; their inter-action with the other children is of a parallel-play type typical of nursery school children, who can be interested in an activity next to, but not with, another child. They need large doses of complete and unshared adult attention, much as a nursery school child seeks out his teacher to substitute for his missing parents. They use blocks, dramatic play, water, boxes to climb in, or hide in, objects that move, nursery school storybooks, pacifying and passive activities, and simply directed tasks in the manner of a nursery school child.

Since children learn by various forms of play, it is possible, though perhaps fanciful, that if a child has been deprived (because of his life history) of the ability to learn through play, he cannot begin to learn academically until he has lived through the experience of playing with, and manipulating materials that three- and four-year-old children find fascinating and involving, and from which they learn so much.

The teacher may feel confused and inadequate when these boys fall from what appeared to be a higher academic level to such an immature use of materials and projects. If he is aware that this descent to nursery-school learning through play is an expected development, he can plan for it, and can be less anxious when it occurs. If he is not prepared, he is likely (because of his own panic) to try to stop or alter it too soon, and by so doing may prevent the child from getting what may be an essential background for later learning. Thus, the acceptance of the acting-out child's infantile needs by creatively using them may become a basic part of establishing a relationship with him which in turn may lead to further learning.

This period does end. Its duration varies with the child. He moves up to a first grade level where he still needs to manipulate some of the same materials that he has been using, but he does so in a different way. He sometimes can work in conjunction with another child or children. Occasionally, at this stage, he is able to follow directions and to complete a short task without destroying the product. Although he is wary of academic learning and group participation, if a proper diagnosis of his particular method of learning has been made, he can make a beginning at reacquiring academic skills on a more secure basis. His attention span will be short, but what he takes in he will be able to assimilate, retain, and use. A series of quick successes may help him to partially erase the failures of the past.

At this point, some recognizable structure and materials reappear; however it is a structure that grows out of the acting-out boy's demands and needs and it is often quite different in method, and materials, from those that are useful in ordinary school classes. Within the boundaries of this simplified and flexible school structure, he begins to be able to function more comfortably. Although he still has blow-ups and times of withdrawal as well as periods when he has to be removed from the classroom, they are less frequent. Many times, in this period, his disintegration can be related to real frustrations in the classroom, to some interpersonal friction between the boy and his peers, or between himself and an adult, to a home visit, or a visit from home, or to an anxious period in his therapy, instead of seeming to come from nowhere as it did hitherto.

Summary

The past two years in planning and executing a school program at the children's research branch of NIMH have yielded the generalizations described above. The observations are not yet precise nor are the implications or applications clear. However, certain tentative hypotheses have emerged that may prove useful in expanding and deepening our knowledge concerning the learning problems of the acting-out boy, the problems of creating a school program appropriate for him; and the problems of the teacher in successfully dealing with him.

1. In order to understand the acting-out boy's perception of "school," "teacher," and "learning," it is necessary to become well acquainted with his life history before entering a residential setting. Only in this way can an appropriate school program be established.
2. The particular means an individual boy can learn, the way he perceives, his motivations, interests, and use of materials, need to be examined closely in order to create a program in which the acting-out boy can eventually succeed in learning.
3. It is necessary to have specially trained teachers who can understand

and accept the pathology of the acting-out boy and utilize his assets. It is of primary importance that this teacher be aware of his own motivations, expectations, and areas of anxiety so that he will be able to avoid the pitfall of allowing the acting-out boy to defeat him and thus defeat himself.

4. The acting-out boy needs limits set for his behavior in order that he may avoid disorganizing experiences and may eventually build inner controls. The timing of the limit-setting process is a delicate and important factor in its effectiveness. The distinguishing between the times when it is necessary to set a limit and those where it is necessary to permit the acting-out behavior is equally difficult and important.
5. The acting-out boy demands a close one-to-one relation with the teacher in order to learn, yet, when it is offered he frequently finds it threatening and rejects it. The psycho-dynamics of this paradoxical behavior needs to be understood and planned for so that the essential relationship of teacher and child does not disintegrate.
6. The acting-out boy needs opportunity to use a variety of materials in a group. When he is given a permissive atmosphere he demonstrates his need to play and to manipulate materials at a three- to four-year-old development level before he can proceed up the educational scale to group activity and academic learning.
7. Once having been accepted at his operating level, and having established the beginnings of a relationship with the adult, the acting-out boy can begin to learn skills and subject matter. He can sustain some frustrations, can complete some short and simple tasks individually and with a group.
8. Setbacks are frequent, but the quality of blow-ups and tantrums begin to change in the school settings. Instead of arising for no perceivable cause, they are more often related to traceable factors in the child's current life.

Further study and research of a more detailed and measurable nature need to be carried on in order to determine the validity and implications of the points made above. Nonetheless, the study of the acting-out boy in a special school program within a residential-research-clinical setting provides an excellent opportunity to better understand the problems of the teacher in working with acting-out boys and the problems these boys have in learning and in relating.

C. Residential Centers

27. Establishing a School in a Psychiatric Hospital

FRANK M. HEWETT

When educable, emotionally disturbed, school-age children leave the community and become inpatient residents of a psychiatric hospital, continuation of their formal education is of concern to parents, public school educators, and hospital staff members. Schooling is not viewed as an expendable activity of childhood, but as indispensable to a normal and healthy adjustment. Therefore, some provision is usually made to continue the child's education while he undergoes treatment in the hospital setting. This may be on an extramural basis, with the child attending a public school in the vicinity of the hospital, or intramural, with public school teachers working within the hospital. A third arrangement, the one that is the subject of this paper, is provision of a separate psychiatric hospital staffed by institutional teachers.

Despite the general acceptance of the desirability of including an educational program for children and adolescents in a psychiatric hospital (1–6), a number of problems arise in the establishment and operation of an inpatient school. A dramatic example of the disastrous results of such a school's operating in isolation from the rest of the hospital program has been given by Falstein (7). A rigid, academically oriented institutional teacher who pressured students for achievement and conformity, without understanding the broader treatment goals of other members of the hospital staff, contributed to a violent outbreak of

SOURCE: *Mental Hygiene,* L (April, 1967), 275–83. Reprinted by permission of The National Association of Mental Health, Inc. and the author.

vandalism, which had far-reaching effects in the institution. The term "contributed" is used advisedly, for the teacher's rigidity and lack of understanding were fostered by an equally undesirable rigidity and lack of understanding of the role of the school on the part of the other staff members. The crisis that resulted was not without its beneficial aspects, as it led to a thoughtful reassessment of interdisciplinary role definitions and communication problems that proved useful in correcting the outbreak and preventing such occurrences in the future.

It is the expressed goal of this paper to delineate some of the central problems in establishing a school in a psychiatric hospital and maintaining it as an effective adjunct to the total treatment program. The material to be presented has been gathered over the past five years at the Neuropsychiatric Institute, built on the campus of the University of California, Los Angeles, by the California Department of Mental Hygiene to facilitate training and research in mental illness of childhood, adolescence, and adulthood. A psychiatric residency program is also an integral part of the Neuropsychiatric Institute.

The Neuropsychiatric Institute (NPI) School was provided for in the initial planning and assigned the responsibility for conducting an inpatient educational program for the 42 children and adolescents to be housed in the children's service of the hospital. A principal and five teachers, all employees of the Department of Mental Hygiene, were to staff the school.

The school now maintains an efficient, well-integrated educational program for patients and provides teacher training and research in conjunction with the university. Its "growing pains" can be subsumed under three major problem areas: initial planning, role definition of teacher and school, and lack of effective interdisciplinary communication.

Initial Planning

In planning a medical facility, the special needs of non-medical programs associated with treatment may be minimized or even overlooked. The psychiatrist, psychiatric social worker, psychiatric nurse, and rehabilitation therapist operate within a frame of reference based on the psychotherapeutic treatment of mentally ill patients. They readily communicate with one another, and a planned hospital facility is more likely to accommodate their special interests because of this common orientation. Even when educational consultants participate in the planning of a psychiatric hospital that will have a school, the compromises in space and facilities inevitable in the final stages are often made at the expense of the school unit. This is not so much a result of disciplinary bias as it is an example of disciplinary distance, which is evident even before the hospital is off the drawing board.

Failure to recognize this distance and to narrow it not only causes problems in initial planning, but also handicaps the operation of the school and its participation in the total treatment program from the day the hospital doors open. When space allocation was made for the NPI School, two classrooms designed for elementary-school-age children and a principal's office were planned for the 42-student population, which would range from pre-school through high school level. It was inconceivable that a program covering children 2 through 15 years of age could operate within such a limited space and with the equipment and facilities provided, regardless of double scheduling of rooms. In addition, the rooms were limited in size (approximately 500 square feet), which made accommodation difficult for the ten-student grouping that proved necessary.

It is only fair to point out that part of the planning difficulty resulted from lack of determination of whether extramural schooling in the public school would be provided for some patients. Had this been settled before the building was constructed, a more adequate school unit would no doubt have been developed.

In the case of the NPI School, the problem was slowly corrected by allocation of additional space for two more classrooms and a school office. This was disruptive to the space needs of the hospital; but, fortunately, what was missing in foresight was corrected through hindsight and the genuine desire of the medical staff to co-operate, support the teachers, and develop an efficient school unit. Mention of these difficulties is made here because more adequate planning for the school and more consideration of the scope and nature of the program it would be assigned could have prevented many later space and program problems.

During the initial planning stages, the following questions should have been asked and answered, with the help of experienced school personnel:

1. What is the rationale for placing the school in a particular area? Does this best meet the needs of the total hospital staff? Are transportation or supervision problems likely to arise?
2. What purpose is the school to fulfill in the hospital? Is it to cover a major portion of the patient's day?
3. What age groupings will students fall in? How many patients will be eligible to attend the hospital school? Will any patients attend public school?

4. What are the State Education Code requirements covering space allocation and size of class groupings for exceptional children within these age groups? How many classrooms will be needed? What provision should be made for outdoor playground space?
5. Are observation facilities going to be required in the school? If so, where will they be placed, and of what will they consist (e.g., one-way mirrors, closed circuit televison)?
6. What will be the responsibilities of the rehabilitation therapy program? Will these overlap, integrate with, or parallel the school's program in arts, crafts, music, home living, vocational training, or recreation?
7. Is built-in storage space more desirable than portable storage? What special counters, sink facilities, books and material storage, study booths, and the like will be required in each classroom? How can these be planned to fit each age group's needs?
8. For older children, what type of worktables or desks will be used? How can the size and arrangement of the classroom be planned to accommodate these desks best?
9. Will drinking fountains and toilet facilities be available for each classroom, or in an outside location? What arrangement seems best suited to the needs of the school?
10. Is general office, preparation, meeting, and storage space adequate for the entire school?

Definition of the Teacher's Role

As was mentioned earlier, the importance of school in the lives of all children is generally recognized, but the actual contribution a school can make to the total treatment program of hospitalized emotionally disturbed children may not be clearly understood. In the early development of the NPI School, it soon became apparent that some hospital staff saw the school's primary function as one of custodial care and considered the school's program a success if children were never returned to the ward as a result of misbehavior during class hours. There was little interest in the educational functioning of the children or in the school's specific program for them. Containment and removal from ward areas during specified hours of the day were the main concern. Some psychiatric residents were inconsistent in their communication to patients regarding the importance of school. As a result, they sometimes unintentionally contributed to a given child's resistance to attending school.

The teacher, as a non-medical participant in the hospital milieu, often must strive to keep from being isolated, theoretically and physically, from members of the treatment team whose training and experience are centered in a medical model (e.g., psychiatry, psychiatric social work, psychiatric nursing, rehabilitation therapy, and, to some extent, clinical psychology). Nothing is more devaluating or discouraging to an institutional teacher than the realization that the school is considered primarily a custodial service; and, after a while, some teachers acquiesce to providing just that—daily baby-sitting. It should be stated, however, that this may represent the path of least resistance for teachers who are not motivated to re-define their role.

Isolation of the school from the total treatment program and dismissal of its function as a baby-sitter service represent a tragic oversight and a disservice to the emotionally disturbed child. When such a child arrives at the hospital, he finds himself in a strange new world, run in different ways by different sorts of people than he has known before. He is, however, greeted by the two people who have direct counterparts in his life in the community—the doctor and the teacher. All children have had experiences with the doctor who cares for them when they are ill, and most have had contact with a teacher, who is in charge of a major portion of their time each day and who helps them learn the things they must know. Many hospitalized children find a great deal of satisfaction in being in school, because it represents a setting with which they are familiar in a generally unfamiliar environment; but there are those whose emotional problems and previous school experiences have caused them to view the school and teacher with mistrust and fear.

Because of the unique relationship the teacher has almost immediately with the hospitalized child, the school should be central to the implementation of treatment goals established by other hospital staff members. In this setting, the child has the opportunity to engage in reality testing, to learn to handle limits, to deal with peer and adult authority relationships, and to acquire essential skills and information that will aid him in his future adjustment. Since most emotionally disturbed children will eventually leave the hospital and go back to their homes and communities and attend public school, their experiences in the hospital school can be extremely important in preparing them for a successful return. Toward this end, sending a child back to the ward when his behavior is wholly inappropriate in school is not for the convenience of the teacher, but may be an essential learning experience for the child.

Another problem encountered in the early development of the NPI School was in direct contrast to the one just discussed. Some hospital personnel viewed the teacher's role as being in therapeutic competition with that of other hospital staff. Was the teacher operating as a psychotherapist in building a close relationship with the child, discussing his emotional problems, and vying for his trust and loyalty? This concern was voiced by some psychiatric residents, who felt at a disadvantage in treating patients for a limited time each week when the child spent many more hours in school with the teacher. Some nursing staff members who became attached to particular children also felt they were competing with the teacher for the "good parent" role with the children. This seemingly absurd overattachment was not the problem of the nursing staff alone: some teachers allowed themselves to become subjectively involved and overly invested in particular patients.

This problem must be brought out into the open and dealt with directly if it is to be kept from undermining the over-all effectiveness of the interdisciplinary treatment team. The teacher is neither a psychotherapist nor the "good parent" for the child while he is in the hospital any more than is the teacher in public school. That problems dealt with by the child's therapist and connected with the parent-child relationship will crop up in school is inevitable, but they do not become the primary concern of the teacher.

Teachers are socializing agents with specific educational roles. Their contribution to the treatment program of the child centers around specific educational tasks undertaken in the classroom. They do not discuss the child's dreams, interpret his problems, or offer counseling. They create a learning environment in which the child can successfully acquire skill and knowledge related to a more adaptive adjustment; and they operate as educators, not as psychotherapists or parent surrogates.

Some educational activities of the school overlap with other disciplines, such as occupational and recreational therapy. In many hospitals, music, physical education, arts and crafts, and shop work may be offered by both the school and the rehabilitation therapy program. The same materials and, in many cases, the same experiences are provided for the child in both settings.

This has a parallel in the community, where the child may participate in group art, music, and recreational activities in school and also undertake them in Cub Scout, YMCA, church, school playground, and community recreation center programs. On a more individual basis he may take music or art lessons, have individual coaching in the development of physical skills, or engage in these activities as part of a hobby at home. In school, art, music, and recreation serve both social and curriculum functions, but are often not individualized to meet the needs of the child. This individualization is more likely to occur outside the school.

So it is in the psychiatric hospital, where the teacher finds these activities invaluable in augmenting the total class program but may not be trained or oriented to use them in the individual and therapeutic manner of the occupational and recreational therapist. This parallel between the larger community from which the child comes and the hospital community in which he is placed may be an oversimplification because of the specialized treatment goals of the multidisciplinary staff. But, in the case of a teacher and a rehabilitation therapist, there would seem to be no basic conflict of roles, and their common interests and activities should engage them in a close working relationship. Unfortunately, such a relationship does not always materialize, and this may present one of the early problems that must be resolved in establishing a school in a psychiatric hospital.

Lack of Effective Interdisciplinary Communication

Just as ineffective interdisciplinary communication as described by Falstein led to an unfortunate breakdown of the total institutional treatment program, so communication difficulties between the educational and the other disciplines created numerous problems in the establishment of the NPI School. These will be considered first on a theoretical, and later on a practical, level.

Psychodynamic personality theory, which dominates the treatment approach used in most psychiatric hospital programs for emotionally disturbed children, is seldom understood by teachers. Its focus on the total adjustment of the child and its use of specialized concepts and terminology often cause difficulty in translation to the practical, day-to-day reality of the classroom.

On the other hand, the pragmatic program of the school, with its emphasis on achievement and detailed curriculum standards, may seem, to other members of the hospital staff, mundane and remote from the treatment program for the emotionally disturbed child. The teacher who "communicates" only academic standing, school attendance, citizenship records, and grades obtained by the child may not be recognized as a vital or integral member of the treatment team. Therefore, a need exists for the development of a meaningful frame of reference for the teacher and other staff members.

This communication problem was apparent to the teaching staff of the NPI School shortly after the school began operation, and a two-year period was devoted to establishing a frame of reference that would convey the total role of the educational program in the treatment plans for individual children. There was a need for a total child-oriented school philosophy and a practical means for communicating the school's daily experience with the child to other staff members. The philosophical problem took the greatest amount of time and school effort.

Although education of the emotionally disturbed child has been greatly influenced by psychoanalytic tenets, the gap between psychiatric theory and classroom practice has not been narrowed to a suitable degree in the literature. Therefore, a unique educational strategy, encompassing the goals of the psychiatrist and other members of the treatment team, was necessary. Such a strategy was systematically developed through examination of the psychodynamic, motivational, and developmental theories of Freud, Erikson, Maslow, Havighurst, and Skinner.

This strategy was conceived as a hierarchy of educational tasks that reflects normal socialization stages through which all children pass and which often represent critical deficits in the learning and development of emotionally disturbed children. A truly therapeutic school experience for such children while they are in a psychiatric hospital must surely involve other than academic and intellectual dimensions. These other dimensions are unquestionably a vital part of every hospital school program but, unfortunately, are frequently underplayed and overlooked in the communication process between the teacher and other staff members.

The NPI School staff set out to define these additional dimensions in its program and arrived at seven basic levels that actually constitute the major goals of special education with all exceptional children (8). The hierarchy of educational tasks views the teacher and the child undertaking a series of mutually significant assignments, starting on the *attention* level, where getting the child to pay attention is paramount; moving through a *response* level, where getting the child involved in learning is basic; through the *order* level, where the child is assisted in engaging in routines with defined starting points, systematic follow-through, and scorable conclusions; through an *exploratory* level, where reality-oriented, multisensory exploration of the environment is emphasized; through a *social* level focused on standards of social appropriateness; and, finally, to *mastery* and *achievement* levels, where intellectual and academic achievements receive attention.

It has been found that, by referring to this hierarchy in contacts with hospital staff, the teacher can simply and directly communicate within a frame of reference similar to those used by the psychiatrist, psychologist, social worker, and other members of the staff.

Regardless of the good intentions of the teacher, the communication problem can be resolved only when the school achieves a consistently visible relationship with the rest of the psychiatric hospital. The NPI School realized the importance of teacher visibility early in the establishment of the program and planned teacher schedules so that a representative of the educational program could be present at every hospital milieu, administrative, or case conference meeting. The teachers were encouraged to be vociferous, enthusiastic contributors to discussions involving all patients and to bring up constantly the provisions of the school for assisting children to accomplish the educational tasks enumerated in the hierarchy described above.

Active participation in hospital staff meetings was augmented by a written weekly report submitted to the doctor by the teacher and placed in the child's ward chart, where all staff members would have access to it. This weekly report, although time-consuming for the teacher, proved to be one of the most worthwhile contributions of the school. It not only specified the attendance record of the child, but also rated him on several continua related to his behavioral, intellectual, and social functioning in school. These reports constituted weekly report cards, not in terms of letter grades, but of meaningful evaluations of the child's total school experience. The weekly report form used by the NPI School staff is shown on the facing page.

The child's doctor and other hospital staff members were encouraged to seek out the teacher and discuss any aspect of the report that was of interest or concern to them. In addition, conferences were set up between the teacher and other staff members whenever problems arose regarding patients who refused to come to school, ran away from school, or carried complaints of teachers and school back to the ward and doctors. In this way many major communication breakdowns were short-circuited. Emotionally disturbed children are often skilled in manipulating adults, pitting them one against another and creating misunderstandings among them. It is only when accusations, complaints, and problems between patients and staff are directly dealt with by all parties concerned that they can be placed in proper perspective and resolved.

One of the early problems relating to the school, which became of major concern to all staff, was the resistance of some children and adolescents to attending school. "I am in a hospital; school is not important," "This isn't a real school anyway, so why should I have to go?" "The teacher has it in for me and picks on me all the time," and "I don't feel like going to school (angrily)—make me!"—were but a few of the reasons given by patients for not going to school. When the ward staff or doctor tacitly or explicitly took the child's side without contacting the teacher, a serious disservice was done to both the school and the child, and resumption of the child's education was most difficult to accomplish. This was essentially a one-way problem because complaints about doctors and other hospital personnel brought to the teacher by the child were quickly dismissed as not being appropriate for discussion in school.

In an effort to resolve this early resistance to attending school, the NPI School staff used three approaches. The first has already been dis-

NPI School Weekly Report

Dr.———— Student ————
Teacher ———— Week of ————

I. *School Functioning*

A. Academic performance (based on student's own norm)	Underachieves	1——2——3——4——5	Exceeds expectations
B. Ability to concentrate on and finish assigned tasks	Extremely limited	1——2——3——4——5	Concentrates and works well
C. Attitude toward school and learning	Negative	1——2——3——4——5	Positive
D. Classroom behavior	Consistently non-conforming	1——2——3——4——5	Appropriate at all times
E. Teacher relationship	Rejects teacher	1——2——3——4——5	Readily accepts teacher
F. Peer relationships	Isolated and withdrawn	1——2——3——4——5	Approaches others readily
	Rejected by peers	1——2——3——4——5	Well liked

II. *Attendance*

	Mon.	Tue.	Wed.	Thu.	Fri.
Present					
Absent					
Tardy					

III. *Comments:*

cussed—careful and complete communication with other hospital staff on all problems and the issuance of weekly reports covering each child's school status.

The second approach centered around establishing a "student role," which all children who came to school were expected to fulfill. The message here was "Schooling for everyone—but school *only* for students." Only those children who could fulfill the minimum standards of the student role—respect for the working rights of others, reasonable tolerance for the limits of time, space, and activity—would be allowed to attend school. Those who could not would receive their schooling on a one-to-one tutoring basis on the ward. The establishment of this student role was discussed with the total hospital staff, and the importance of every staff member's supporting it was stressed.

Once this role was understood and accepted, children sent back to the ward for non-student behavior were not supported overtly or covertly, and the resentment felt by the ward staff at having a child who had been scheduled to go to school returned for ward care was lessened. (These unscheduled returns understandably constitute inconvenience for nursing personnel, but their willingness to support the school at these moments of crisis has largely eliminated the problem at the present time in the NPI School.) The children soon realized that attendance at school and maintenance of appropriate behavior in the classroom were not isolated school expectations, but part of total hospital standards. Passes for off-ward trips and activities were also restricted for those children unable to function as "students."

It is important to stress that being a student carried no academic or intellectual demands with it. Once in school the teacher carefully assessed the child's needs and assigned tasks appropriate for him without concern for grades, competition with peers, or curriculum standards for his age. The student role mainly carried with it minimum responsibility for the conformity and control essential for learning.

The third approach used by the school to reach children and adolescents in the NPI hospital was to make the school "the place to go." This was accomplished through building an enthusiastic and creative teaching staff that constantly sought to provide stimulation and success for the students and to form positive relationships with other hospital staff. Science, art, and music activities were especially useful in establishing an appealing classroom program. In addition, a complete array of remedial teaching materials was assembled; and, where these materials were not adequate, the staff developed its own programs accordingly. One such program in the area of reading has made it possible to teach many severely disturbed, neurologically impaired, and mentally retarded children, who are often considered non-educable (9).

The NPI School has developed into an integral department within the institute, and its teachers have assumed full-fledged positions on the psychiatric treatment team. The fact that much of this development has occurred through trial and error has pointed up the lack of established guidelines for integrating an intramural educational program into a hospital, for defining the role of the teacher in such a school, and for resolving interdisciplinary communication problems. It is hoped that this paper has provided some such guidelines.

The school is as indispensable to the psychiatric hospital community as it is to the larger community. It can, and should, maintain a program for child and adolescent patients, not in isolation, but in wholehearted collaboration with the disciplines of psychiatry, clinical psychology, social work, nursing, and rehabilitation.

References

1. COLVIN, R. W.: *American Journal of Orthopsychiatry,* 31:591, 1961.
2. DOUGLAS, K.: *Exceptional Children,* 27:246, 1961.
3. GRAVE, C.: *The Nervous Child,* 3:236, 1944.
4. RABINOW, B.: *American Journal of Orthopsychiatry,* 25:685, 1955.
5. RUBIN, E. Z.: *Exceptional Children,* 29:184, 1962.
6. SCHOENBOHM, V.: *Exceptional Children,* 22:219, 1956.
7. FALSTEIN, E. I., *et al.:* "Group Dynamics: Inpatient Adolescents Engaged in an Outbreak of Vandalism." Paper presented at the 39th Annual Meeting of the American Orthopsychiatric Association, Los Angeles, Calif., 1962.
8. HEWETT, F. M.: *Exceptional Children,* 31:207, 1964.
9. HEWETT, F. M., MAYHEW, D. L., and RABB, E.: *American Journal of Orthopsychiatry,* 37:35, 1967.

28. The Role of Education in a Residential Treatment Center for Children

POVL W. TOUSSIENG

As more child guidance clinics and other psychiatric outpatient facilities are becoming available throughout the nation, residential treatment centers are dealing more and more with only those children who cannot be treated on an outpatient basis.

The reason why a child cannot be helped at home may be that he and/or his family no longer are able to cope with or to control his intense emotional conflicts or overwhelming impulses. In other cases the child is so deviant, so bizarre or has such poor judgment that he cannot live in the community. The community may have refused outright to put up with him and his behavior, or perhaps all community resources have been tried and exhausted.

In all these cases, admission to the residential treatment center is made to meet the child's need for an around-the-clock environment which continuously can be adapted to the fluctuating levels of functioning so characteristic of severely disturbed children, and which at all times can provide support, control and protection. Such an environment usually cannot be created out in the community, especially not in a family home, but it is a prerequisite before these children can be helped through psychotherapy and other forms of treatment and often before they can benefit from education.

Many residential treatment centers have their own academic schools. These schools are set up within the residential setting because they have to serve a dual purpose:

SOURCE: *Mental Hygiene,* XLV (April, 1961), 543–51. Reprinted by permission.

1. They have to support the total residential treatment program, by helping to create the emotional climate needed by the child at any given time, and
2. They have to teach the child or to help him in such a way that he can resume learning.

It is the aim of this paper to describe and discuss this dual role, a role which has a surprising number of applications to what goes on in classrooms in the community—where disturbed children also are not rare.

Most residential treatment centers will attempt as soon as possible to get newly admitted children to the point where they can attend school full time. Once this has been accomplished, the teachers spend a substantial number of hours with the children, and it becomes crucial from the standpoint of the over-all treatment effort that the experiences the children have in school are consistent with the experiences they have in the group living area, in their extracurricular activities and in formal psychotherapy, if they are receiving such treatment.

Just as the school is an integral part of the total treatment setting, the teachers are not just teachers in the school but are also members of so-called "therapeutic teams" consisting of all the people who work directly or indirectly with an individual child in the treatment setting. Corresponding to the number of children in his class, the teacher is a member of a number of teams, and he must be in close communication with the rest of the teams. In his teaching efforts he is asked primarily to identify himself with the therapeutic efforts made with a child, as well as with the therapeutic goals. We may say that the teacher is asked to be therapeutic before he tries to teach.

At a superficial glance, this places the teacher in a role for which he has no professional preparation, and which seems to make it impossible or at least very hard for him to get around to his other obligation: to provide the child with educational experiences.

In actual experience these two roles are not at all incompatible because successful education in itself can be particularly therapeutic for a disturbed child. As the child learns and finds himself learning, he acquires more tools to assess and understand the world around him. His awareness of his environment and of reality becomes sharpened; he gets help in thinking gradually on a more abstract level; he acquires more tools with which to communicate and to receive communication. Misinformation which may have threatened the child is dispelled by new knowledge.

Last, but by no means least, the educational progress in the classroom provides the disturbed child with tangible, measurable evidence of his ability to achieve, to grow, to progress, and this in itself can be an unbelievably great boost, as these children frequently have become discouraged about themselves and their abilities.

Most children who are admitted to a residential treatment center are at least one to two years retarded educationally, sometimes considerably more, even though they are of average or even very superior intellectual ability. Many of these children have been promoted socially year after year, while the gap between their performance level and that of their classmates gets wider and wider.

Even defiant, seemingly callous and poker-faced teen-agers or very disturbed psychotic youngsters with a tenuous hold on reality are on some level painfully aware of their inability to keep up with other children, although perhaps they would rather die than admit it, or although they are unable to verbalize this awareness. Feelings of failure, of worthlessness and of extreme frustration are the result. These feelings may become even more pronounced if friendly, interested teachers make valiant and desperate efforts to teach or tutor these children and fail because the learning blocks in these children cannot be removed by educational efforts alone. Very often both at home and in the school, discipline has been tried to make the child study and learn; this leads to further blows to the child's self-respect and feelings about education as well as to many painful clashes.

By the time a child comes to a residential treatment center, schools and classrooms therefore often have become associated with painful experiences, with failure, defeat, frustration, anger and despair. As he enters the classroom in the residential treatment center, the child automatically assumes that he will have experiences similar to those he had in previous classrooms, and he will project some or all of his experiences with previous teachers onto the new teacher.

If the child, in spite of all this, is helped towards a different outcome, if he finds himself learning and able to learn, this in itself will represent a crucial corrective emotional experience, which in turn may make him more available for such other kinds of help as psychotherapy or planned group living experiences with the other children in residence.

Before the teacher can map his strategy and before he can accomplish this goal, he will have to have a thorough understanding of the factors which are preventing an individual child from making use of education and educational experiences. Such factors are always present.

Even retarded children can be expected to learn, although they learn at a slower pace and cannot progress as far as other children. If they are not learning or if they have stopped learning, there must be reasons beyond retardation which are causing this, and these reasons need to be understood. Intensive and extensive diagnostic studies need to be done as soon as possible on each child who is not learning, preferably before he is admitted to the residential setting.

These studies should include a psychiatric examination, psychological tests, a comprehensive neurological and physical work-up, often supplemented by X-rays, laboratory studies, hearing and vision examinations, brain wave tests and so forth, but they must also establish the child's history and background, his home environment, the nature of his relationships with his parents, with siblings, with other important people in his life, with peers, with school and so on. From these studies, from further observations and from therapeutic work with the child following admission, a deepening understanding of the child's difficulties will gradually emerge within the therapeutic team, so that more rational, comprehensive and effective plans can be made for further therapeutic intervention.

The teacher in a residential treatment center contributes many crucial observations to this diagnostic process, but he in turn must lean heavily on the observations made by the rest of the team. Sometimes the teacher has a crucial role with the child from the very start; at other times the teacher must bide his time, as it were, until the rest of the therapeutic program has helped the child improve enough that he becomes available for the teacher's efforts.

Teachers are not accustomed to working in this way and they have not been prepared for it in their training. At present, therefore, residential treatment centers have to provide on-the-job and inservice training for teachers. Other teachers obtain preliminary training by working as child care workers in a residential treatment setting before they assume teaching roles in the academic residential school.

Even with this kind of preparation, the teacher has a difficult task, primarily because of a curious paradox. On the one hand, the teacher must show tremendous flexibility in order to meet the children's needs, and must not ask more of them than they can manage because their levels of functioning fluctuate from day to day or from moment to moment.

On the other hand, the teacher must avoid further confusing these children, who usually already are terribly confused, and he has to define the classroom setting as well as his own role as teacher very crisply, clearly and above all, consistently. The classroom setting must be kept simple, quiet, without too much commotion. Disturbed children crumble when they have to deal with too many stimuli, particularly because so frequently they are still unable to assess and interpret adequately these stimuli.

The academic school in a residential treatment center setting is therefore the antithesis of what used to be called "a progressive school." The children do not have the initiative; the classroom structure and the dignity of the classroom are rigidly upheld. The teacher very clearly maintains his role as a mature adult and as an educator. He is ready at all times to respect the child but, on the other hand, he expects that the child will respect him and the classroom structure. As can easily be surmised, just to be able to hold himself together and not to disturb the classroom atmosphere frequently is the first and only possible goal a disturbed child has in school.

The teacher will do his utmost to bring out the child's own strengths and controls, and if these fail or prove inefficient the teacher will attempt to lend his own strength to the child. Initially, the children sometimes are unable to use the teacher's support, however, and if the child cannot hold himself together enough and if he begins to show unacceptable behavior, he will be temporarily removed from the classroom, with the very explicit understanding that this is not punishment and that he is welcome back in the classroom as soon as he thinks he can tolerate it again.

A number of children, particularly psychotic children, at times become overwhelmed by too much closeness or by their own wish for affection and closeness—which at the same time they dread. In removing a child from the classroom, the teacher respects the child's temporary need for greater distance but he will try—for example, by looking through the window, or by going outside once in awhile—to convey his continued interest in the child as well as his understanding of what is causing the child's upset just then.

The child soon will calm down and will be able to return to the classroom later the same hour or later the same day. If the child has enough strength to do so, the teacher will talk with the child about the episode and will try to understand more specifically what caused the child's upset and subsequently make plans as to how further upsets can be prevented or at least channeled.

Within this rather rigid structure the teacher also has to be tremendously flexible in order to be able at all times to adapt himself to the child's changing levels of psychological integration, as well as to his ability to stay in contact with the environment and to perform within it. It must be understood that this in no way implies permissiveness.

It is not helpful to the child—nor "therapeutic"—passively to endure his inappropriate behavior or his episodic disorganization, mainly because it keeps the child from realizing that his behavior is inappropriate, but also because it becomes impossible to perform the tasks which both the teacher and the child expect to work on during the school hours.

If the classroom is allowed to become chaotic, this will increase a child's panic and internal chaos and will only make matters worse. On the other hand, the teacher must be able to simplify or temporarily abandon the educational tasks whenever a child is on a more infantile level or becomes totally disorganized, without feeling that he, the teacher, and/or the child failed, and without resentment. If the teacher does feel disappointment—even though he tries not to show it—the uncannily sensitive psychotic or very disturbed child will invariably know it and he will become even more discouraged about his own abilities.

It is not easy for a teacher to get used to this, nor is it always easy to understand that the child's—particularly a teen-ager's—behavior does not represent naughtiness, manipulation or any other willful act, but a temporary breakdown in personality organization. The teacher is helped in this task by the fact that emotionally disturbed children, when given the support and protection of a residential setting, almost invariably show a strong wish to make use of education, even though they do not yet have the strength to act continuously on the basis of this wish.

In dealing immediately with the inappropriate behavior, the teacher allies himself with this wish and he appeals to the remaining strengths in the child. In essence, when he removes the child from the classroom, the teacher implicitly or even explicitly says to the child that he knows that the child has strength, and that he trusts that the child sooner or later will be able again to use this strength and to control himself enough to take his place in the classroom again. When this happens both the child and the teacher see it as an accomplishment, as a small but important victory, as another evidence of the child's growing strength.

As these and similar considerations stand out in the teacher's task, it will be understood more easily why giving the children tools and helping them acquire knowledge are equally important goals to teachers in residential treatment centers. The primary emphasis is on removing the blocks which are preventing the children from learning, as well as on opening up avenues along which the children can learn if they are unable to learn through conventional methods. This amounts to preparation for later learning.

The gratifying fact is that the great majority of children eventually can be helped to learn. Not at all infrequently they then catch up with themselves and make up for the time they got behind in school, as well as for the time it took to help them to become able to learn again. This preparation for later learning is accomplished by giving the children strictly educational tasks and not by trying to play with them in hidden or more overt ways.

Reading, writing and arithmetic are the usual tasks given. These assignments, of course, have to be adapted to the child's level of functioning. The teaching method used takes into consideration the child's abilities, the rate at which he is able to learn, his degree of distractibility, the length of his attention span, his difficulties in perception, his possible need for motoric outlets, etc.

In this respect an adequate initial diagnostic work-up will be of crucial importance to the teacher, as it helps define exactly what a child's strengths and handicaps are and what it will take to help him to get to the point where he can resume learning. It does make a difference whether a child has extreme difficulties in keeping his thoughts organized, whether he is constantly fighting off confusion, or whether he, for example, is suffering from some degree of aphasia, which makes it impossible for him to learn by conventional methods.

Sometimes several difficulties are present simultaneously; it then needs to be established which difficulties are most prominent just then, and the educational tasks have to be presented accordingly. One ten-year-old girl came into a residential treatment center with a severe psychotic adjustment, even though it also was suspected that she was retarded and brain-damaged. Previous painful school experiences made it necessary first to give the child a corrective experience with the teacher.

Much work involving rote memory was used to help her organize her thoughts and herself, while the same problem also was being dealt with in psychotherapy. Even so, the child continued to have great difficulty with her educational tasks. As she gradually improved and gained more psychological strength, it stood out that she still could not learn to read and could not be helped to retain word pictures. Some aphasic difficulty was suspected, particularly because of her extreme difficulty in abstract thinking.

Intensive tutoring was started, using a kinesthetic method for the analysis of words. The child responded dramatically to this and made remarkable strides in her academic achievement. While she had struggled slowly and laboriously through the third and fourth grades, she whisked through the fifth and sixth in 10 months.

Her newly acquired ability to read, to accomplish something academically, has been a tremendous boost to this child's morale and has helped her gain strength in other areas, particularly in the area of interpersonal relationships where before she had overwhelming difficulties. In the book *The Brain Injured Child* [1] Strauss and Lehtinen describe similar dramatic effects of remedial tutoring.

[1] Strauss, A. A., and L. E. Lehtinen, *The Brain Injured Child* (New York: Grune & Stratton, Inc., 1947).

Many aphasic children can be helped by these methods to return to regular classrooms for some subjects, maybe even full time. It must be stressed, however, that even a sensitive method of tutoring is useless until a corrective emotional experience has mobilized a disturbed child's strength and makes it possible for him to do what he could not do before, or at least to try.

The following excerpt from the latest educational report on the ten-year-old girl mentioned above—who is now fourteen—will illustrate this in more detail:

Mary is much more comfortable and exhibits less tension than before in working at her school assignments. She seems not so fearful of the exposure of her inadequacies and does not feel the inevitability of failure. This is particularly true of her reading performance and has resulted in more efficient work as well as changes in her voice and expression.

It is the teacher's opinion that the fact that she has made gains in reading, and that she has profited from the reading technique employed, has been a major factor in the progress seen in all of her school work. The experience of success and the gaining of confidence has carried over into the rest of the learning areas, giving impetus to her performance in all subjects. She seems to feel gratification from her progress and to be seeking less for the "magic way" of learning and overcoming deficiencies—which she showed when she came to the school.

She still is often preoccupied with "catching up," obsessed with problems of how much there is to do and how long it will take her to catch up to her chronological age level in school; although there is evidence of feelings of depression and futility around this, she more and more is evidencing a realistic view of her limitations and levels without the need to feel that there is a "formula" to overcome these.

It may be noted that Mary displays a great need for "sameness" and consistency in the environment. She becomes confused and disturbed when things and events are not in their "place." She usually is unable to tolerate changes in the physical environment or in routine without "worrying" about them, or until they become more familiar to her. She is often preoccupied and disturbed with details in the environment or with what she feels to be discrepancies or contradictions. It is felt that she displays an excessive reliance on organization from the "outside" as a result of her limitations in achieving an internal organization and an understanding of environmental relationships.

With the reading technique being utilized—an auditory-visual-kinesthetic approach which uses rules and drill to overcome limitations of perceptual and conceptual organization—she has made measurable gains. She displays good retention of the "base" words of consonants and vowels and has mastered the sounds presented. She is able to read much faster and is better able to "sound out" words.

She can go through the whole pack of drill cards with few mistakes and usually will read in phrases instead of reading a word at a time as she had previously done. Reversals of letters have largely disappeared in both reading and writing. She has done well on the syllable division rules and on the spelling rules presented, although these have not yet been committed to memory.

She is very low in spelling and much repetitive drill seems indicated. It is characteristic for her to spend long, hard effort on all the tasks given her and it is felt that the concrete approach of this technique makes it a helpful and profitable one for her.

Another example is provided by Max, age fifteen, who was admitted to the Kansas Industrial School for Boys because of his stealing and other delinquent activities.

The patient obtained a median of 8.8 on a Stanford Achievement Test given on admission. The schools he had attended had been unable to cope with him. He frequently fought in school and played truant. The initial intensive work-up, done on all boys recently admitted to the Industrial School, revealed that Max was seriously emotionally disturbed and that his hold on reality was inconsistent and tenuous.

Intense efforts were made in the group living situation, but also through group psychotherapy, to gradually help Max get himself under better control. During this period he was unable to do any work in the academic school, and the teachers at first merely concentrated on making it possible for him to stay in the classroom without having to be sent back to the cottage for defiant behavior.

As Max's anxiety gradually diminished, and as he gained greater control over himself, he began to be able to respond to direct educational efforts. When he was paroled from the Industrial School, after a stay of 15 months, he achieved a median of 12.7 on the Stanford Achievement Test. At home he entered the eleventh grade and did extremely well in high school.

Still another example is the case of a ten-year-old adopted boy who has intense conflicts about the meaning of growing up. As so often happens, his parents had several natural children after the adoption of this child. The boy has had a very strong emotional reaction to this, fearing that any evidence of growing independence on his part will give the parents an excuse to send him away forever.

These struggles and fears were carried over into the school, gradually resulting in more and more destructive classroom behavior and in the development of a complete learning block. The situation at home as well as in the school gradually became so impossible that the parents had to admit him to a residential treatment center.

Here it was found that he still could not read and that he had picked up very little of the elementary school subjects, in spite of the fact that he was of high-average or possibly even bright-normal intelligence. There is some evidence in the tests that organic brain functioning may be mildly impaired. The work which the teachers have done with this boy so far is described in the following educational report:

During the second half of the school year, John has made advances in school which suggest significant shifts in his adjustment and his capacity to perform in a learning situation. This has not been in the accomplishment of learning tasks or in the attaining of direct academic goals, but it has been in the beginning of a different concept of school and in a new adjustment which is essential to the establishment of an educational process.

Work with John has been aimed at what might be termed pre-educational goals. He is not as yet ready to profit in a major way from the educational tasks and guidance which are offered to others of John's age level because the difficulties of adjustment and performance—both psychological and organic—which resulted in his original failures in school have become intertwined with his reaction to the long history of inadequacy, rejection and guilt regarding his past failures in school.

He views school as a frightening, hostile, anxiety-provoking situation, where he can only have his inadequacies exposed and be subjected to humiliation, rejection and retaliation. The emphasis of the school work with John has been on the formation of a comfortable teacher-pupil relationship, which may be utilized to alter his adjustment and to permit education to be accomplished. It is in the area of the formation of such a relationship that the greatest advances may be reported, although it must be stressed that this still is in the beginning and tenuous phase. As the relationship with various teachers is being established, inroads have been made through these relationships into his feelings of inadequacy, worthlessness and unacceptability. As this has occurred, it has been possible for the teachers to place increasingly more demands on him for work, for his participation in tasks, and to gain his involvement in this.

Particularly firm stress has been placed on the expectation that he will pay attention, with satisfactory results as his ability to make use of instruction increases. He still relies excessively on the structure which the teacher poses, having little capacity to organize his tasks and his time, and he functions best when the teacher is near to him or touches him. In almost all his school work, he and his teacher perform tasks together.

It must be noted that he is still limited in the amount of time he can spend at his work, or even in the amount of time he can pay attention and involve himself with the teacher. His work and attention span is often no longer than 10 minutes, and he frequently does not appear to be directly attentive to the teacher, regardless of what they are doing together. It seems that he is able to mobilize the strength and energy to accomplish school work only in order to please the teacher and to avoid the punishment he seems to feel would follow if he did not make an attempt.

John has begun work with phonics and has completed the beginning workbook in this subject. He has shown some gains in identifying the beginning sounds of words, but he is unable consistently to connect sounds with letters. Although he can look at words and identify each letter, he is unable to associate the sound with the letter, even in his own name. However, he has shown a surprising ability to connect words with objects in multiple-choice exercises with enough consistency to warrant the speculation that he has begun to develop in reading and that reading-readiness tasks are profitable at this time. In arithmetic he has continued in tasks which give him experiences with concrete objects in order to allow him to arrive at his own abstractions and memorize combinations at his own pace.

In preparing plans for John for the next year, it is necessary to continue to view the main objectives of the school as pre-educational, with the estimate that it may be some time before he will be able to learn with normal skill and ease. Although the teacher's goal will be to explore, assess and prepare him to make greater use of learning experiences, his work will center around actual educational tasks as a necessary and expedient way to form the correct teacher-pupil relationship, to provide a therapeutic school situation which may mend his earlier concepts and conflicts, and to begin an educational process.

He will continue to have individual sessions with the reading teacher to strengthen and capitalize on the relationship he has formed with her, and because of this probability, based on the symptomatic picture, he will need specialized help in this area.

The conclusion offering itself from this discussion is that the teacher's role in a residential treatment center is surprisingly similar to the role of a teacher in a community classroom, even though there also are significant differences.

It is evident that the teacher's contribution in a residential treatment setting can be very therapeutic for a child but that the teacher, isolated from the total treatment setting, cannot be therapeutic. In order to be of help to the child, the teacher must maintain his role and identity as an educator and he therefore cannot and must not try to become the child's therapist.

While upholding the dignity and importance of the classroom, the teacher continuously can draw upon the deepening and extensive understanding of the child's difficulties, which gradually emerges as the teacher and all the other staff members working with the child pool their observations and experiences in a continued diagnostic process. On the basis of this understanding and on the building of the child's other therapeutic experiences in the residential treatment setting, the teacher can employ strictly educational tasks to first prepare the child for learning and later to help him to learn—up to the limits of his native endowment.

The therapeutic value of this well-defined educational approach may well have implications for how far teachers in the community should allow themselves—in the most literal sense—to be deflected from their teaching role.

29. Education of Adolescents in a Psychiatric Hospital

FRANZ E. HUBER

Education of disturbed adolescents in a psychiatric hospital setting has certain basic similarities to education of adolescents anywhere. Unless unusual circumstances are in effect for individual cases the disturbed adolescents or patients, as they are called in the psychiatric hospital, are expected to attend classes, take prescribed content courses, meet daily and term requirements, govern their behavior in accordance with classroom protocol and respond appropriately to peers and the authority-figure role of the special educator. For the most part these goals can be attained with disturbed adolescents as is done with their less deviant counterparts under what could be called maximum utilization of a therapeutic milieu and educational design.

The educational design is an integral part of the overall milieu therapy program of the psychiatric hospital as much as individual and group psychotherapy or the adolescent's life space on the psychiatric ward. The special educators' role within the milieu broadens or contracts depending on the prevailing philosophy of integrating or non-integrating occupational therapy and recreational therapy within the realm of the educational program. While largely operating outside the "milieu," psychiatric social workers and clinical psychologists provide necessary functions in their work with parents and evaluative testing. Completing the milieu therapy "team" are the psychiatric nurses who have administrative and program responsibilities of the wards and the ward attendants whose interaction with patients assumes a wide variety of interpersonal relationships. In order for the milieu therapy program to function effectively the multi-discipline team members must, by design, work closely together. Factors tending to disunify the multi-discipline team approach are many. Inter-rivalry between disciplines

SOURCE: *The High School Journal,* XLIX (March, 1966), 287–91. Reprinted by permission of The University of North Carolina Press.

striving for status in the loosely formed hierarchy must be minimized. Divergent philosophical treatment orientations need to be explored in order to develop a cohesive milieu therapy program. A thorough understanding and appreciation of how each discipline functions in relation to the patient; its assets, its handicaps and its inherent characteristic problems can lead toward complementary inter-disciplinary interaction. Personality idiosyncrasies leading toward conflict between staff members prevent the formation of an "esprit de corps" so essential for continual reinvestment in the primary task. Extremes of authoritarian or "laissez faire" leadership emanating from the service directors present problems characteristic to each type of management organization. The resultant complexities, unless continually resolved, can result in a fragmentation of the patient into a number of discrete entities allowing the individual psychopathology to thrive through manipulation, secondary gain reinforcement and control of the so called therapeutic environment.

Milieu therapy in the context of a psychiatric hospital offers disturbed adolescents a 24 hour "milieu" in the case of in-patient treatment or a part-time "milieu" on a day care basis. In either case the essential concepts of milieu therapy need to be present. Basic to other considerations is the formulation of an individual treatment plan for each patient with implementation of this treatment design within the framework of the various disciplines. Formulation of the treatment design evolves from a thorough understanding of the individual case history, dynamic considerations and etiological factors. Leadership in this endeavor is supplied by the psychiatric personnel. Implementation is accomplished through consolidated efforts of the team. Necessary revisions of the treatment plan are mutually discussed and a consensus is established before proceeding. Without a basic treatment program delineated for each individual patient the ideal of milieu therapy is likely to develop cross-purpose treatment patterns, with the resultant confusion in the ranks.

Operating within and as part of the treatment plan are other necessary ingredients of milieu therapy. The milieu team members must be available for the establishment of relationships which each individual patient is capable of assuming; be they based on transference, identification or other psycho-social processes. The evolvement and resolution of conflicts engendered in these relationships forms the therapeutic model for future interpersonal contact. The relationship process is furthered through "on the spot" staff intervention in conflict or "crises" situations involving either one patient or groups of patients. While staff intervention in "crises" arising in the milieu produces temporary disruption for all concerned and, at times, occupies what seems an exorbitant amount of time, the insight and understanding gained through the process of mediation and resolution of these conflicts produces the raw materials on which milieu therapy thrives. Communication between staff regarding the "crisis" and its resolution enable other staff members to give reinforcement to positive values inherent in each situation. The psychotherapist has virtually unlimited choice of incidents to pursue or not to pursue during the course of therapy. The reliving of emotional conflicts can occur during daily encounters in the milieu or in the confines of the psychotherapist's office.

The development and furthering of ego skills becomes a function of the total staff through the planned activities provided in the milieu. Continued growth in skill acquisition, performance capabilities, creative endeavors, self-assurance and the mastery of tasks hitherto felt inaccessible are positive and influential aspects in the milieu therapy of disturbed adolescents.

The special educator incorporates his therapeutic educational design within the confines of the milieu therapy treatment plan. Emphasis is placed on a differential educational design for each patient based on the presenting psychopathology, attitude toward authority figures, present learning performance as well as future potential and past educational history. Other aspects of milieu therapy mentioned previously, the development of teacher-student relationships, "on the spot" therapeutic intervention in crises situations occurring in school, reliving of emotional experiences, ego skill development and providing for the growth of self-concept are major avenues for the special educator to reach the disturbed adolescent. For this to become feasible, the educational setting as well as the total milieu setting has to sanction the philosophy of behavioral control as an initial prerequisite for effective milieu therapy. A total "set" for complying with verbal controls needs to be established throughout the milieu and becomes even more prominent in the educational sphere. Since verbal controls will not always suffice, provision must be made in such event. Temporary and brief exclusion from the classroom scene followed by examination and clarification of the precipitating and related events between the special educator and the patient are generally sufficient to set the stage for readmission to the class. The reclarification of acceptable and non-acceptable classroom behavior re-establishes "a clean bill of health" with a reduction of the need for further testing.

Educational planning for the adolescent is more subject matter and course oriented than for a similar elementary-aged youngster. Since the eventual goal is a return to the normal junior high or high school setting the adolescent's previous program of courses and grade requirements needs to be scrutinized. Early and continued communication with the home school enables the special educator to tailor an educational program that "meshes" and facilitates return procedures. Course content needs to be geared along individualized lines with considerable emphasis on stimulating, creative and thought-provoking teaching. Initial educational diagnosis and assessment identify the considerable number who are in need of special individual or group remedial help. The educational program will of necessity have to be tailored to the type of clientele selected through the hospital's intake procedures; psychiatric hospitals admitting only intellectually superior youths or specializing in specific psychopathologies will govern the type of educational program to be developed.

School is often fraught with severe conflicts for the disturbed adolescent. For the chronically aggressive, anti-social and rebellious youth school becomes an arena for the power struggle. The special educator epitomizes the authority figures inoperative in past circumstances and the resentment, by word and deed, flows in a continuous stream. Firm, consistent reality oriented controls administered in a benign, non-threatening manner eventually break the past recurring cycle of aggression-punishment—counter hostility—aggression, etc. The anxiety-ridden adolescent preoccupied with inner conflicts and self-deprecation needs continual reassurance that he can compete, can fulfill requirements and that he is a worthy individual. Identification with a teacher who has less exacting "self" standards for the patient than the patient's own rigid system facilitates the treatment process. The adolescent who suffers from an incapacitating psychosomatic condition needs the provocation provided by the non-concerned, non-retaliatory special educator on which to vent some long-stored aggressive reactions. Ego support and verbal clarification of external reality aid the adolescent with temporary ego disintegration to maintain some sense of reality contact through the highly structured school tasks.

The special educator possesses the training, the knowledge, and the self-insight to respond differentially to the varied educational and personality problems presented by adolescents such as these. Complicating and somewhat limiting the extent of differential response available to the special educator is the process of group instruction. The wide character of individual one-to-one responses is of necessity curtailed when dealing with groups of individuals. Latitude in verbal and behavioral expression is always more circumscribed for the group than for the individual. As team members, psychotherapists especially must have understanding of this phenomena.

Techniques of individualized and group instruction as well as subject matter need to be well in hand in order to leave the special educator free to circumvent group disruptive situations before they culminate in chaos. Perceptivity, flexibility and ingenuity enable the special educator to understand, motivate and manipulate both individual and group toward desired goals. An essential requirement for this task is a goodly supply of psychic and physical energy contained within a substantially stable personality. The special educator in the psychiatric hospital works as a member of the milieu team, sharing and receiving information essential for the adolescent's continued readjustment. The education and reeducation the adolescent receives within the educational design is a crucial part of the milieu therapy treatment process.

Bibliography

1. Aichhorn, August, *Wayward Youth,* New York, Viking Press, 1935.
2. Hendrickson, W. J., Holmes, D. J., and Waggoner, R. W., "Psychotherapy with Hospitalized Adolescents," *American Journal of Psychiatry,* Vol. 116,6, December 1959.
3. Hendrickson, W. J. and Holmes, D. J., "Control of Behavior as a Crucial Factor in Intensive Psychiatric Treatment in All Adolescent Wards," *American Journal of Psychiatry,* 115: No. 11, May 1959.
4. Huber, Franz, "Contributions of an Educational Program in a Psychiatric Hospital," *Selected Convention Papers, 40th Annual C.E.C. Convention,* 1962.
5. Morse, W. C. and Small, E. R., "Group Life Space Interviewing in a Therapeutic Camp," *American Journal of Ortho.,* Vol. 29,1, January 1959.
6. Polsky, H. W., *Cottage Six—The Social System of Delinquent Boys in Residential Treatment,* Russell Sage Foundation, N. Y., 1962.
7. Redl, F., "Strategy and Techniques of the Life Space Interview," *American Journal of Ortho.,* Vol. 29,1, January 1959.
8. Scofield, J. B., "Adolescent Treatment in an Adult Hospital," *American Journal of Ortho.,* Vol. 32,4, July 1962, pp. 660–667.
9. Hirschberg, C., "The Role of Education in the Treatment of Emotionally Disturbed Children Through Planned Ego Development," *American Journal of Ortho.,* 23: October 1953, 684–690.

30. The Academic-Activity Program at Hawthorne: A Specially Designed Educational Program for the Troubled Adolescent

HERBERT COHEN

For many years, the antisocial, nonacademic child has been a problem to himself, his peers, and adults. He has presented a picture to the world about him of a sneering, hostile, defiant youngster who swaggers around wearing the proverbial chip on his shoulder. School has always been a succession of failures for him and he has resisted violently the traditional type of classroom education.

Every institution for disturbed or delinquent children has its share of such children. Lonely, feeling worthless, retarded in basic school subjects, these students have posed severe program problems to educators in institutional settings. For many years, this was also true at Hawthorne Cedar Knolls School.

We struggled with a group of such boys who had little or no interest in academic subjects and who wandered from one program to another. They ranged in age from 13 through 16 and functioned three to six years below their normal achievement level. These boys usually would be assigned to the dining hall, the truck, the farm, the kitchen, and other service jobs at Hawthorne. Even in this limited type of program they soon became bored and frustrated and after a short period would ask for another program change.

SOURCE: *Exceptional Children,* XXX (October, 1963), 74–79. Reprinted by permission.

Some of the pupils had as many as fifteen program changes in a six-month period. They resisted any type of remedial help and insisted that they wanted no more of school. Even our shop program did not hold any challenge and motivation for these boys. They were the problem children of Hawthorne.

After much soul searching and discussion, we decided to set up a modified form of an academic program within an industrial arts setting. We felt that a shop teacher—a man who worked with his hands and mind and who dignified work—would represent to these boys a different picture from that of school teachers whom they had known in the past.

The class setting was to be an industrial arts general shop. We outfitted this shop with a classroom section which contained tables and chairs, maps, globes, and other facilities of an academic classroom. The first class we chose consisted of ten boys ranging in age from 13 to 15, who functioned from the second to the fifth grade level in reading and from the second to the sixth grade level in mathematics. These ten pupils had had a total of 64 different program changes in the past four months.

This class was to be assigned on an all-morning basis to an industrial arts teacher. The first period in the morning, from 9:20 to 10:25, was scheduled for academic subjects, and the second period, following a short recess, ran from 10:35 to 11:45 and was to be a shop period. The academic work was to be as follows:

Monday—Current Events and Social Studies
Tuesday—Mathematics
Wednesday—Science
Thursday—English
Friday—Job Information

The class would have approximately 35 hours per subject during the year and as a result, all minor details would have to be left out and most attention given to the major areas in that particular subject field. As far as possible, all of the academic subjects were to be integrated with industrial arts. Within the shop environment, it is possible to use actual shop problems to teach all of the subject areas. Although it is much easier to relate mathematics and science to industrial arts, we found many ingenious ways to use English and social studies in these classes.

One of the most important elements in this program was the immense task of preparing the special material that was needed in the classroom. Over 150 work sheets were produced during the first year, and many of them were revised after testing them in a class situation. We found it necessary to prepare much of our own materials after thoroughly searching the field and finding very little material that could be purchased which would meet the needs of these pupils. All commercial material that was used had to be carefully screened to make sure that it did not contain pictures of very small boys and girls, which would prove to our adolescents that they were functioning on a childlike level. We are now engaged in the third year of this type of program, and we have several academic-activity classes on various levels. In addition, a whole new approach toward teaching the various academic subjects with an industrial arts emphasis needed to be developed, and the problem of retraining an industrial arts teacher to teach academic subjects was a formidable one.

We found that all of the boys had huge voids in their backgrounds. Most of them did not know how to read a map and had no idea, in most cases, of the location of the Atlantic Ocean, Pacific Ocean, Europe, Asia, etc. Since most of them never took the opportunity to read a newspaper, they really did not know what was going on in our world. This, too, was a major area that had to be explored. Although many of the boys realized that some day they would have to work for a living, they had no idea of job opportunities, salary, unions, social security, income tax, and what would be expected of them in a job. Their interest and motivation were extremely low and most of them were wandering in an effortless way.

Social Studies

In working out the social studies curriculum, it was decided that the first 12 weeks, or 12 actual periods, would be devoted to basic geography. Geography was emphasized primarily in terms of location of minerals and other materials used in the shop situation. They studied the broad areas of the world, the continents and hemispheres, as related to sources of our raw materials. This included the study of transportation across oceans and the work necessary to obtain these materials. We found that we had materials from 17 nations in the shop. The boys learned how to read a map and to locate the important features of the earth. Visual displays of many of the materials used in the shop were labeled by country of origin as an important part of this unit.

The next 14 weeks of the social studies curriculum concerned itself with the study of New York City and New York State. Again, the stress was primarily on the materials of industry, where they were to be found and how they were transported to the various manufacturing centers of the state. After studying New York City for several sessions, the class was taken on a bus tour of the city, which culminated in a visit to a clothing manufacturing plant. This was the forerunner of many such trips. A discussion preceded each trip and a follow-up was completed by the group at the end of it. This was written or was tape recorded by members of the group who did not yet possess enough ability to put their thoughts in writing.

The last 15 weeks of social studies were devoted to the United States as a whole. The broad areas were discussed with the emphasis again on the differences in the various areas and what each provided to the manufacturing economy of our country. Films and filmstrips helped to give the boys a "trip" to the various parts of our country. Map and globe work was an important aspect of this part of the curriculum. In addition, many of our staff members who had visited various facilities in different parts of our country spoke to the group. Some boys made scrapbooks of various materials that came from different states.

Some of the pupils were interested enough to send letters to the various states requesting information. This was incorporated as part of the English curriculum. Throughout the social studies curriculum, the theme of crafts and materials was stressed. We found that the boys were able to relate to this area because the things they used and talked about were meaningful to them.

Each social studies session opened with a ten minute discussion on current events of the week. We found that the *New York Times* news supplement was our best source of information for this. The teacher would read a digest of the most interesting articles of the week to the class. After a slow start, many of the boys became interested enough to listen to news on the radio and read newspapers so that they would have something to contribute to this part of the session. In this way, we were able to acquaint the boys with some of the important world happenings.

The social studies outline, broken down into its various units and time sequences, follows:

1. Geographical orientation—twelve weeks
2. New York City and state—ten weeks
3. United Nations—three weeks
4. United States economic and manufacturing regions—ten weeks
5. Current events (weekly)—ten minutes

Mathematics

We found the area of mathematics an extremely easy area to integrate with the activity program. This subject is meaningful to the boys in many respects. The basic facts of addition, subtraction, multiplication, and division were all taught in relation to shop processes and projects. The entire problem of mensuration was given a high priority, and many basic skills were taught through the use of the ruler and calipers. We found it necessary to divide the class into two groups for this subject and used a work text for the basic course of study. As the class progressed, we used simple geometry represented by flat, round, and square shapes in both wood and metal working. Fractions were discussed in terms of cutting correct pieces of material according to plan and figuring out how many pieces were needed for a project. Each boy was expected to figure out the cost of each project that he was working on during the shop period, and this, too, became a meaningful thing to the class. It soon became apparent to many of the boys that if they were to gain skill in any particular medium, mathematics was a vital subject. It was in this area that the pupils first started asking for extra assignments. This was the beginning of homework for this particular class. Although each boy had only 35 hours of actual class time in mathematics, most of them did at least the same amount in homework and extra assignments. Many of the extra assignments in class were manipulative in nature. As part of the curriculum, pupils used the ruler and calipers to measure various materials and then were able to use these instruments to create a project of their own choosing. It was necessary to develop many separate information sheets for this subject area. We found that most of our pupils were retarded in basic skills in mathematics and, as a result, could not measure accurately any of the work done in the shop. Therefore, the curriculum outline for mathematics consisted primarily of basic skills as applied to practical mensuration and daily use.

Science

The area of science was also found to be easily integrated with industrial arts. This course of study included the study of simple and complex machines, magnetism and electricity, our solar system, and air pressure. All of these areas were given meaning and usefulness when it was shown that everyday living contains working examples of them. Most of the time the equipment of the shop was used to demonstrate the theories and principles used in these areas. The machines and tools were used to show practical uses of scientific knowledge. The race for space proved to be very interesting when the group studied the solar system and its implications for daily life. In many of the sessions, the class was divided into three groups of four boys each, which carried out various experiments to illustrate scientific principles. When the class studied electricity and magnetism, electrical answer games were made using the principles that were being studied at the present time. Telegraph sets were built as part of the shop curriculum and four of the boys became interested enough to learn Morse Code and later demonstrated this to the class by hooking up sending and receiving sets across the classroom area. Here, too, visual aids were extremely important in illustrating many scientific principles. This was the second area in which members of the class asked for extra assignments. In addition, we brought in many simple texts, films, and filmstrips which had been carefully screened so that they did not contain pictures or illustrations of small children doing science experiments. This was extremely important because it was necessary for these boys to feel that they were doing work commensurate with their age and not, as in many cases, with their reading ability.

The following books were included in the science bibliography: *The World About You,* by Ware and Hoffsten, Austin, Texas: Steck Publishing Co.; *This Earth of Ours,* by Ware and Hoffsten, Steck Publishing Co.; *Elementary Science Charts,* by Milton O. Pella, Chicago, Illinois: J. Nystrom and Company; *Fun with Science,* by Mae and Ira Freeman, New York: Random House; *First Book of Science Experiments,* by Wyler, New York: Franklin Watts. It wasn't long before the boys asked to borrow these books so that they could read them in the cottage. In the 35 sessions given to this subject area, many worthwhile principles were learned and many pupils attempted to go beyond the scope of the curriculum on their own.

The science area, which was divided into six basic units, is outlined below:

1. Sound—six weeks
2. Magnetism and electricity—six weeks
3. Weather—six weeks
4. The changing earth—six weeks
5. Simple and complex machines—six weeks
6. Living things—five weeks

English

The subject of English, which we felt would be least related to industrial arts, proved to be a pleasant surprise to us. We found, for instance, that letter writing became a rewarding project when a reply was received. Each boy, in the process of learning how to write a letter, wrote to various trade and industrial concerns, all of which replied. Many of them, in addition, sent samples of their materials and other literature relating to phases of industry. In this way, many of the students read articles on industry and products, and for many boys this was the only literature they had read for a long time. It was again necessary to develop our own work sheets in order to teach the simple rules of grammar, which very few of the pupils knew. All of the language was slanted in the direction of industrial arts. An example of this approach would be one of the questions that was on a simple work sheet, "We placed the work (into, in) the lathe." We found that there was very little resistance to this type of methodology, and that boys who would ordinarily resist doing English exercises actually clamored for more when the work was placed in this type of setting. The boys were taught how to make a simple report on such topics as the story of inventions, discoveries, or basic industrial processes. After visits to industrial plants, the boys learned how to make simple oral and written reports.

When dictionary work was introduced, it was surprising to discover how many boys had never used a dictionary before. We went on from this to a telephone directory and finally an encyclopedia. Simple articles in *Popular Science, Popular Mechanics,* and similar publications were read, and many of the boys made reports on articles which interested them. The teacher carefully screened the material that each boy would read to make sure that each would have a successful experience with the article he had chosen. In some cases it was necessary to let a boy fail to reinforce the teacher's contention that he was not quite ready for this level of work. Although only 35 hours of class time were involved in the English curriculum, many of the boys went far beyond this in their homework. Having a series of work sheets prepared in advance proved to be the key to teaching this subject. Each boy was able to move at his own pace. The initial fear that English would present a difficult situation for this class was dissipated.

The course outline for the English curriculum follows:

1. Basic language skills—fifteen weeks
2. Study and reference skills—five weeks
3. Reports, letter writing, composition work and literature—fifteen weeks

Spelling was given every week for the first 15 minutes of each English lesson. The spelling word list consisted of the technical terms used in everyday shop practice plus the words most commonly misspelled in daily use. The New York State spelling word-lists for the fourth, fifth, and sixth grades were used for the latter.

Job Information

The area of job information intrigued our boys from the very start. This represented to them an approach to the adult world and the realization that they were being prepared to do a man's job. Various films were used to illustrate the different processes of industry and the skills required to obtain jobs in the various fields. Guest lecturers representing the areas in which our boys could work were invited to speak to the class. During the first year, the personnel manager of a supermarket, the owner of a gas station, a representative of the United States Employment Service, a representative of the carpenter's union, and a representative of the U. S. Armed Forces spoke to the group. In addition, the boys learned to fill out a job application form and write a short resume, and we play-acted several employment interviews. The boys were attuned to the realistic requirements for jobs that they could hope to get when they first started out to work. Our trips to various plants helped in this respect as many of the boys saw jobs that they could fill when they were ready to work. At the same time, it soon became apparent that there are many processes that require a greater degree of education and skill than our pupils possessed. This had the dual function of urging some of the boys to work harder and causing others to revise some of their goals. Taxes, social security, unions, and other topics were explained simply and many interesting questions were raised and discussed. In many cases, we used simple literature that was obtained from many sources including those of the U. S. Armed Forces. Each member of the group was given a battery of aptitude and inventory tests. This, too, helped to sharpen the boys' focus of where they would fit in the working world.

The job information area was broken down into the various aspects listed below:

1. Job opportunities—ten weeks
2. Field trips—seven weeks
3. Taxes, social security, unionization—five weeks
4. Industrial processes—eight weeks
5. Job interviews, guest lecturers, films—five weeks

Academic Achievement

Each pupil in this group had been tested prior to admission, at midyear, and finally at the end of the school year. They averaged a 2.7 increase in reading and a 2.3 increase in mathematics for the year. Of the original group of twelve boys, only one had dropped out because of lack of interest and two others had been added during the year. Seven of the group had requested remedial reading or remedial mathematics some time during the school year. Emphasis in the remedial reading program was in the field of industrial arts. The rest of the daily program consisted of industrial arts shops, where it soon became apparent that the boys' interest remained high, as opposed to previous years in which they had become easily frustrated and bored. It was interesting to note that as the year progressed, many of these pupils were able to relate in a more positive fashion to their peers and to adults. They did not possess the same sense of worthlessness that had characterized their previous apathetic and belligerent behavior. No longer did these boys feel that they were at the bottom of the school ladder when it came to achievement. For the first time in their lives, these boys proudly carried books to school and actually looked forward to doing homework in the evening. Until this type of education became available to them, they were the ones who used the evenings in the cottage to watch television or wander aimlessly around bothering those other boys who were engaged in doing homework. Now they, too, took their place at the study table and had something worthwhile to contribute to the cottage life.

31. Helping Disturbed Children: Psychological and Ecological Strategies

NICHOLAS HOBBS

I wish to present a case study in institution building, an account of a planful effort at social invention to meet an acute national problem, the problem of emotional disturbance in children.[1]

[1] The work here reported was made possible by Grant No. MH 929 of the United States Public Health Service, and by funds provided by Peabody College, the State of

SOURCE: *American Psychologist,* XXI (December, 1966), 1105–15.

I should like to cast this account in large context as an example of the kind of responsibility psychologists must assume in order to respond to a major challenge of our time: to help increase the goodness of fit between social institutions and the people they serve. This commitment demands that we invent new social arrangements designed to improve the quality of human life, and, in doing so, to adhere to the exacting traditions of psychological science: that is, to be explicit about what we are doing, to assess outcomes as meticulously as possible, to relate practice and theory to the benefit of both, and to lay our work open to public and professional scrutiny.

Let me acknowledge here that the work I report is the product of a cooperative effort to which a number of psychologists have contributed, notably Lloyd M. Dunn, Wilbert W. Lewis, William C. Rhodes, Matthew J. Trippe, and Laura Weinstein. National Institute of Mental Health officials, mental health commissioners, consultants, and especially the teacher-counselors have invented the social institution I shall describe. If on occasion I seem unduly enthusiastic, it springs from an admiration of the work of others.

The Problem

"Project Re-ED" stands for "A project for the reeducation of emotionally disturbed children." Re-ED was developed explicitly as a new way to meet a social need for which current institutional arrangements are conspicuously inadequate. It is estimated that there are some 1½ million emotionally disturbed children in the United States today, children of average or superior intelligence whose behavior is such that they cannot be sustained with normal family, school, and community arrangements. There is one generally endorsed institutional plan for the care of such children: the psychiatric treatment unit of a hospital. But this is not a feasible solution to the problem; the costs are too great, averaging $60 a day, and there are not enough psychiatrists, psychologists, social workers, and psychiatric nurses to staff needed facilities, even if the solution were a good one, an assumption open to question. There is a real possibility that hospitals make children sick. The antiseptic atmosphere, the crepe sole and white coat, the tension, the expectancy of illness may confirm a child's worst fears about himself, firmly setting his aberrant behavior.

Tennessee, and the State of North Carolina. We are grateful for the support and wise counsel of Commissioner Joseph J. Baker and Commissioner Nat T. Winston, Jr., of Tennessee, Commissioner Eugene A. Hargrove and Sam O. Cornwell of North Carolina, Leonard J. Duhl and Raymond J. Balester of NIMH, and Paul W. Penningroth and Harold L. McPheeters of the Southern Regional Education Board.

But worse things can happen to children, and do. They may be sent to a state hospital to be confined on wards with psychotic adults. They may be put in a jail, euphemistically called a detention home, or committed to an institution for delinquents or for the mentally retarded; or they may be kept at home, hidden away, receiving no help at all, aggravating and being aggravated by what can become an impossible situation.

The problem is further complicated by the professional advocacy of psychotherapy as the only means of effecting changes in behavior and by the pervasive and seldom questioned assumption that it takes at least 2 years to give any substantial help to a disturbed child. Finally, the availability of locks and drugs makes children containable, and the lack of evaluative research effectively denies feedback on the adequacy of approved methods. We became convinced 8 years ago that the problem of the emotionally disturbed child cannot be solved by existing institutional arrangements. The Re-ED program was developed as one alternative, surely not the only one or even the most satisfactory one, but as a feasible alternative that deserved a test.

The Re-Ed Schools

The National Institute of Mental Health made a test possible by a demonstration grant in 1961 to Peabody College to develop residential schools for disturbed children in which concepts of reeducation could be formulated and tried out. The States of Tennessee and North Carolina, represented by their departments of mental health, joined with Peabody College to translate a general idea into an operational reality. The grant further provided for a training program to prepare a new kind of mental health worker, called a teacher-counselor, and for a research program to evaluate the effectiveness of the schools to be established.

Cumberland House Elementary School in Nashville received its first students in November of 1962, and Wright School of Durham in January of 1963. The schools are located in residential areas not far from the universities (Vanderbilt and Peabody, Duke and North Carolina) that provide personnel and consultation. They are pleasant places, open, friendly, homelike, where children can climb trees and play dodge ball, go to school, and, at night, have a good meal, and a relaxed, amiable evening.

Both schools have nearby camps that are used in the summer and on occasion throughout the year. The camps are simple, even primitive, with children erecting their own shelters, preparing their own meals, making their own schedules. For staff and children alike there is a contagious serenity about the experience. Cooking is a marvelously instructive enterprise; motivation is high, cooperation is necessary, and rewards are immediate. Children for whom failure has become an established expectation, at school and at home, can learn to do things successfully. Nature study is a source of unthreatening instruction. And there is nothing quite like a campfire, or a dark trail and a single flashlight, to promote a sense of community. In this simpler setting, where avoidant responses are few or weakly established, the child can take the first risky steps toward being a more adequate person.

At capacity each school will have 40 children, ages 6 to 12, grouped in five groups of 8 children each. Each group is the responsibility of a team of two teacher-counselors, carefully selected young people, most of whom are graduates of a 9-month training program at Peabody. The two teacher-counselors, assisted by college students and by instructors in arts and crafts and physical education, are responsible for the children around the clock. Each school has a principal and an assistant principal, both educators, a liaison department staffed by social workers and liaison teachers, and a secretarial and housekeeping staff, who are full partners in the reeducation effort. The principal of a Re-ED school has an exacting job of management, training, interpretation, and public relations. The two schools have developed under the leaderships of four able men: John R. Ball and Neal C. Buchanan at Wright School and James W. Cleary and Charles W. McDonald at Cumberland House.[2]

Of course, the teacher-counselors are the heart of Re-ED. They are young people, representing a large manpower pool, who have had experience in elementary school teaching, camping, or other work that demonstrates a long-standing commitment to children. After careful screening, in which self-selection plays an important part, they are given 9 months of training in a graduate program leading to the Master of Arts degree. The program includes instruction in the characteristics of disturbed children, in specialized methods of teaching, including evaluation and remediation of deficits in reading, arithmetic, and other school subjects, in the use of consultants from mental health and educational fields, and in arts and crafts and games and other skills useful on the playing field, on a canoe trip, in the living units after dinner at night. They get a thorough introduction to child-serving agencies in the community and to the operation of a Re-ED school through an extensive practicum. Finally they are challenged with the task of helping invent what Re-ED will become.

But most of all a teacher-counselor is a decent adult; educated, well

[2] So many people have worked to make Re-ED a reality it is impossible even to record their names. They will have received recompense from seeing children flourish in their care. Yet Alma B. McLain and Letha B. Rowley deserve special recognition for long service and uncommon skill and grace in managing many problems.

trained; able to give and receive affection, to live relaxed, and to be firm; a person with private resources for the nourishment and refreshment of his own life; not an itinerant worker but a professional through and through; a person with a sense of the significance of time, of the usefulness of today and the promise of tomorrow; a person of hope, quiet confidence, and joy; one who has committed himself to children and to the proposition that children who are emotionally disturbed can be helped by the process of reeducation.

The total school staff, and especially the teacher-counselors who work directly with the children, are backed by a group of consultants from psychiatry, pediatrics, social work, psychology, and education, an arrangement that makes available to the schools the best professional talent in the community and that has the further attractive feature of multiplying the effectiveness of scarce and expensive mental health and educational personnel.[3]

The Children

What kind of children do the teacher-counselors work with? It can be said, in general, that diagnostic classification has not been differentially related to a successful outcome; that the children are normal or superior in intelligence but are in serious trouble in school, often retarded 2 or 3 years in academic development; that they do not need continuing medical or nursing care, and that they can be managed in small groups in an open setting. Re-ED is not a substitute for a hospital. There are children too disturbed, too out of touch, too aggressive, too self-destructive to be worked with successfully in small groups in an open setting. However, Re-ED schools do take many children who would otherwise have to be hospitalized.

Susan was 11, with a diagnosis of childhood schizophrenia. She had attended school 1 day, the first day of the first grade, and had been in play therapy for 4 years. She was a pupil at Cumberland House for a year, staying longer than most children. She has been in a regular classroom for 3 years now, an odd child still but no longer a prospect for lifelong institutionalization. Ron was a cruelly aggressive child, partly an expression of inner turmoil and partly an expression of class values and

[3] The consultants have meant much more to Project Re-ED than can be recorded in this brief account. We here inadequately recognize the invaluable contribution of our colleagues: Jenny L. Adams, MSW, Gus K. Bell, PhD, Lloyd J. Borstelmann, PhD, Eric M. Chazen, MD, Julius H. Corpening, BD, Jane Ann Eppinger, MSW, John A. Fowler, MD, Ihla H. Gehman, EdD, W. Scott Gehman, PhD, Maurice Hyman, MD, J. David Jones, MD, and Bailey Webb, MD.

habits; he is much less destructive now, and is back in school. Danny was simply very immature, so that school was too much for him; his problem could be called school phobia if that would help. Dick was extremely effeminate, wearing mascara and painting his nails. Both boys responded to masculine activities guided by a trusted male counselor. Billy was a gasoline sniffer and an ingenious hypochondriac; he returned to a reunion recently much more mature though still having trouble with school work. Larry, age 12, was quite bright yet unable to read; nor were we able to teach him to read. So we failed with him. It is such children as these that we aspire to help. To call them all "emotionally disturbed" is clearly to use language to obscure rather than to clarify. Nonetheless, they are all children who are in serious trouble, for whom the Re-ED idea was developed.

During the past summer, under the direction of William and Dianne Bricker and Charles McDonald, we have been working at Cumberland House with six of the most severely disturbed children we could find, mostly custodial cases from state institutions. Regular Re-ED activities are supplemented by a 24-hour schedule of planned behaviors and contingent rewards, the staff being augmented to make such individualized programming possible, but still using inexpensive and available personnel, such as college students. While it is too early to assess the effectiveness of this effort, we are pleased with the progress that most of the children are making, and we are certain we are giving them more of a chance than they had when their principal challenge was to learn how to live in an institution.

Ecological Concepts

Let us turn now to an examination of the theoretical assumptions and operational procedures involved in the process of reeducation. We do not, of course, make use of the principles involved in traditional psychotherapy; transference, regression, the promotion of insight through an exploration of inner dynamics and their origins are not a part of the picture. The teacher-counselor is not a psychotherapist, nor does he aspire to be one.

We have become increasingly convinced that a major barrier to effective national planning for emotionally disturbed children is the professional's enchantment with psychotherapy. Everything in most model institutions revolves around getting the child to his therapist 1, 2, or maybe 3 hours a week. A few superb treatment centers combine psychotherapy with a program of daily activities conducive to personal growth and integration. But these are rare indeed. It is not uncommon to find children locked 15 stories high in steel and glass, with a caged roof to play on, drugged to keep them from doing too much damage to the light fixtures and air conditioning, while they await their precious hour, guarded by attendants who think disturbed children must scream, fight, climb walls, cower in a corner. Most frequently, of course, therapy is not available; most hospitals hold children hoping somehow they will get better.

An overcommitment to individual psychotherapy seems to us to stem from an uncritical acceptance of "cure" as the goal in working with a child, a consequence of defining the problem initially as one of "illness." That some disturbed children are "ill" in the usual sense may be accepted, but to define them all as such leads, we think, to a host of unvalidated and unquestioned assumptions; to a preoccupation with the intrapsychic life of the child, with what goes on inside his skull; to an easy use of drugs without knowledge of their long-term effects on character development; to the extended isolation of children from their families, the presumed source of contagion; to a limitation of professional roles; to the neglect of schools and of schooling; and so on. The preemptive character of a definition and the semantic sets that ensue are major barriers to innovation in working with disturbed children.

Of course we have our own ways of talking about the problem, and our metaphors are no less preemptive, making it all the more important for us to be explicit about definitions. We prefer to say that the children we work with have learned bad habits. They have acquired nonadaptive ways of relating to adults and to other children. They have learned to perceive themselves in limiting or destructive terms and to construe the world as an uncertain, rejecting, and hurtful place. We also recognize that the child lives in a real world that often falls short in giving him the affection, support, and guidance he needs. So we deal directly with social realities as well as with private perceptions.

This kind of thinking has led us gradually to a different way of defining our task, a definition of considerable heuristic merit (see Figure 1). For want of a more felicitous phrase, we have been calling it a systems approach to the problem of working with a disturbed child. We assume that the child is an inseparable part of a small social system, of an ecological unit made up of the child, his family, his school, his neighborhood and community. A social agency is often a part of the picture when a child has been designated emotionally disturbed, and other people—a physician, a clergyman—may be brought in as needed. The system may become "go" as a result of marked improvement in any component (the father stops drinking and goes back to work, a superb teacher becomes available, the child improves dramatically), or it may work as a result of modest improvement in all components. The effort is to get each component of the system above threshold with respect to the requirements of the other components. The Re-ED school becomes a part of the ecological unit for as brief a period of time as possible, withdrawing when the probability that the system will function appears to exceed the probability that it will not. We used to speak of putting the child back into the system but we have come to recognize the erroneous assumptions involved; the child defines the system and all we can do is withdraw from it at a propitious moment.

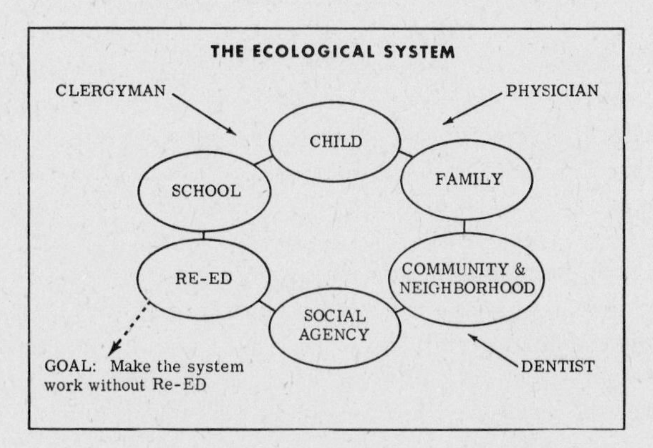

FIGURE 1. Chart of ecological system, the smallest unit in a systems approach to working with a disturbed child.

Once we abandoned cure as a goal and defined our problem as doing what we can to make a small social system work in a reasonably satisfactory manner, there ensued a number of operational patterns that contrast sharply with the practices of existing residential treatment centers for children.

For one thing, parents are no longer viewed as sources of contagion but as responsible collaborators in making the system work. Parents are involved in discussion groups and are helped to get assistance from mental health centers. They actively participate in the ongoing program of the school. They organize an annual reunion, publish a parent's manual, sew for the children, and in many ways assume responsibility for reestablishing the child as quickly as possible in his own home, school, and community.

The children go home on weekends to keep families and children belonging to each other, to avoid the estrangement that can come from prolonged separation, and to give the child and his parents and brothers and sisters an opportunity to learn new and more effective ways of living together. Visitors ask "Aren't your Mondays awful?" They are, indeed, but we cherish their chaos as a source of new instruction; we try to keep in mind that our goal is not to run a tranquil school but to return the child as quickly as possible to his own home and regular school.

The ecological model requires new strategies to involve home, neighborhood, school, agency, and community in a contract with us to help a child. It requires new patterns for the deployment of personnel, and it has led to the development of a new kind of mental health worker: the liaison teacher. The liaison teacher is responsible for maintaining communication with the child's regular school, again to prevent alienation and to arrange optimum conditions for the child's early return to a regular classroom. For example a liaison teacher may personally accompany a child to a new school to which he has been transferred in order to increase the probability that that component of the ecological system will function effectively.

The social worker in Re-ED honors an early heritage of his profession, before the lamentable sit-behind-the-desk-and-do-psychotherapy era got established. He reaches out to the family, to community agencies, and to individuals—to any reasonable source of help for a child in trouble. Again, the goal is to make the system work, not simply to adjust something inside the head of the child.

The Process of Reeducation

Now, let us turn to the child himself, to our relationships with him, and to what is meant operationally by the process of reeducation. Here are an even dozen underlying concepts that have come to seem important to us as we try to talk about what goes on in a Re-ED school.

ITEM 1: LIFE IS TO BE LIVED, NOW We start with the assumption that each day, that every hour in every day, is of great importance to a child, and that when an hour is neglected, allowed to pass without reason and intent, teaching and learning go on nonetheless and the child may be the loser. In Re-ED, no one waits for a special hour. We try, as best we can, to make all hours special. We strive for immediate and sustained involvement in purposive and consequential living. We constantly test the optimistic hypothesis that if children are challenged to live constructively, that if they are given an opportunity for a constructive encounter with other children and with decent adults, they will come off well—and they do, most of the time. They learn, here and now, that life can be lived on terms satisfactory to society and satisfying to themselves. Our task is to contrive each day so that the probability of success in this encounter clearly outweighs the probability of failure. I paraphrase Jessie

Taft when I say, in the mastery of this day the child learns, in principle, the mastery of all days.

ITEM 2: TIME IS AN ALLY We became convinced, in the early stages of planning the project, that children are kept too long in most traditional treatment programs. The reasons for this are many. The abstract goal of cure through psychotherapy leads to expectations of extensive personality reorganization, of the achievement of adequacy in a wide array of possible life roles. It thus takes a long time either to succeed in this ambitious endeavor or to become aware that one has failed. Staff and children become fond of each other, making separation difficult. The widespread practice of removing the child from his home for extended periods of time causes a sometimes irreparable estrangement; the family closes ranks against the absent member. While everyone recognizes the importance of school in the life of the child, mental health programs have neither operational concepts nor specialized personnel necessary to effect an easy transition for the child from the institution back to his own school. Furthermore, the expectation of a prolonged stay in a treatment center becomes a self-validating hypothesis. A newly admitted child asks "How long do kids stay here?" He is told "about 2 years," and he settles down to do what is expected of him, with full support of staff and parents who also "know" that it takes 2 years to help a disturbed child. Myriad other constraints get established; for example, the treatment center hires just enough secretaries to move children in and out of a 2-year cycle, and it is not possible to speed the process without hiring more secretaries, a restraint on therapeutic progress that is seldom identified. So before we admitted the first child, we set 6 months as the expected, average period of stay, a goal we have now achieved.

Time is an issue of importance in the process of reeducation in yet another way. We work with children during years when life has a tremendous forward thrust. Several studies suggest that therapeutic intervention is not demonstrably superior to the passage of time without treatment in the subsequent adjustment of children diagnosed as emotionally disturbed (Lewis, 1965). Treatment may simply speed up a process that would occur in an unknown percentage of children anyway. There is a real possibility that a long stay in a treatment center may actually slow down this process. Furthermore, in ecological perspective, it is clear that children tend to get ejected from families at low points in family organization and integrity. Most families get better after such periods; there is only one direction for them to go and that is up. The systems concept may entail simply observing when the family has regained sufficient stability to sustain a previously ejected child. The great tragedy is that children can get caught up in institutional arrangements that must inexorably run their course. In Re-ED we claim time is an ally and try to avoid getting in the way of the normal restorative processes of life.

ITEM 3: TRUST IS ESSENTIAL The development of trust is the first step in reeducation of the emotionally disturbed child. The disturbed child is conspicuously impaired in his ability to learn from adults. The mediation process is blocked or distorted by the child's experience-based hypothesis that adults are deceptive, that they are an unpredictable source of hurt and help. He faces each adult with a predominant anticipation of punishment, rejection, derision, or withdrawal of love. He is acutely impaired in the very process by which more mature ways of living may be acquired. A first step, then, in the reeducation process, is the development of trust. Trust, coupled with understanding, is the beginning point of a new learning experience, an experience that helps a child know that he can use an adult to learn many things: how to read, how to be affectionate, how to be oneself without fear or guilt.

We are intrigued by the possibility, indeed are almost sure the thesis is true, that no amount of professional training can make an adult worthy of the trust of a child or capable of generating it. This ability is prior to technique, to theory, to technical knowledge. After seeing the difference that teacher-counselors in our two schools have made in the lives of children I am confident of the soundness of the idea that some adults know, without knowing how they know, the way to inspire trust in children and to teach them to begin to use adults as mediators of new learning.

ITEM 4: COMPETENCE MAKES A DIFFERENCE The ability to do something well gives a child confidence and self-respect and gains for him acceptance by other children, by teachers, and, unnecessary as it might seem, even by his parents. In a society as achievement oriented as ours, a person's worth is established in substantial measure by his ability to produce or perform. Acceptance without productivity is a beginning point in the process of reeducation, but an early goal and a continuing challenge is to help the child get good at something.

What, then, in the process of reeducation, does the acquisition of competence mean? It means first and foremost the gaining of competence in school skills, in reading and arithmetic most frequently, and occasionally in other subjects as well. If a child feels that he is inadequate in school, inadequacy can become a pervasive theme in his life, leading to a consistent pattern of failure to work up to his level of ability. Underachievement in school is the single most common characteristic of emotionally disturbed children. We regard it as sound strategy to attack directly the problem of adequacy in school, for its intrinsic value as well as for its indirect effect on the child's perception of his worth and his acceptance by people who are important in his world. A direct attack on the problem of school skills does not mean a gross assault in some area of deficiency. On the contrary, it requires utmost skill and finesse on the part of the teacher-counselor to help a disturbed child move into an area where he has so often known defeat, where failure is a well-rooted expectancy, where a printed page can evoke flight or protest or crippling anxiety. The teacher-counselor need make no apologies to the psychotherapist with reference to the level of skill required to help a disturbed child learn.

So, in Re-ED, school keeps. It is not regarded, as it is in many mental health programs, as something that can wait until the child gets better, as though he were recovering from measles or a broken leg. School is the very stuff of a child's problems, and consequently, a primary source of instruction in living. Special therapy rooms are not needed; the classroom is a natural setting for a constructive relationship between a disturbed child and a competent, concerned adult.

Much of the teaching, incidentally, is through the unit or enterprise method. For example, a group of boys at Cumberland House was invited to go camping with some Cherokee Indian children on their reservation. The trip provided a unifying theme for 3 months' instruction in American History, geography, arithmetic, writing, and arts and crafts. At Wright School, rocketry has provided high motivation and an entrée to mathematics, aerodynamics, and politics. The groups are small enough to make individualized instruction possible, even to the point of preparing special programmed materials for an individual child, a method that has been remarkably effective with children with seemingly intractable learning disorders. The residential character of the Re-ED school means that the acquisition of competence does not have to be limited to increased skill in school subjects. It may mean learning to swim, to draw, to sing; it may mean learning to cook on a Dakota Hole, to lash together a table, to handle a canoe, to build a shelter in the woods; it may mean learning to talk at council ring, to assert one's rights, to give of one's possessions, to risk friendship, to see parents as people and teachers as friends.

ITEM 5: SYMPTOMS CAN AND SHOULD BE CONTROLLED It is standard doctrine in psychotherapeutic practice that symptoms should not be treated, that the one symptom removed will simply be replaced by another, and that the task of the therapist is to uncover underlying conflicts against which the symptom is a defense, thus eliminating the need for any symptom at all. In Re-ED we contend, on the other hand, that symptoms are important in their own right and deserve direct attention. We are impressed that some symptoms are better to have than other symptoms. The bad symptoms are those that alienate the child from other children or from the adults he needs as a source of security or a source of learning. There is much to be gained then from identifying symptoms that are standing in the way of normal development and working out specific plans for removing or altering the symptoms if possible. The problem is to help the child make effective contact with normal sources of affection, support, instruction, and discipline. We also work on a principle of parsimony that instructs us to give first preference to explanations involving the assumption of minimum pathology, as contrasted to professional preference for deep explanations and the derogation of all else as superficial.

ITEM 6: COGNITIVE CONTROL CAN BE TAUGHT Though little emphasis is placed on the acquisition of insight as a source of therapeutic gain, there is a lot of talking in Re-ED about personal problems and how they can be managed better. The teacher-counselor relies primarily on immediate experience, on the day-by-day, hour-by-hour, moment-by-moment relationship between himself and the child; he relies on specific events that can be discussed to increase the child's ability to manage his own life. The emotionally disturbed child has fewer degrees of freedom in behavior than the normal child, yet he is not without the ability to shape his own behavior by self-administered verbal instruction. He can signal to himself if he can learn what the useful signals are. The teacher-counselor works constantly to help a child learn the right signals. The focus of this effort is on today and tomorrow, not on the past or the future, and on ways for the child to signal to himself to make each day a source of instruction for the living of the next. At the council ring at night, at a place set apart from the business of living, children in a group are helped to consider what was good about the day just past, what went wrong that might be handled better tomorrow, and what was learned, especially in successes and failures in relationships among themselves. Possibly more important than the solving of particular problems is the acquisition of the habit of talking things over for the purpose of getting better control over events, a habit that can frequently be carried over into the child's home and become a new source of strength for his family.

ITEM 7: FEELINGS SHOULD BE NURTURED We are very interested in the nurturance and expression of feelings, to help a child own all of himself without guilt. Children have a way of showing up with animals and we are glad for this. A child who has known the rejection of adults may find it safest, at first, to express affection to a dog. And a pet can be a source of pride and of sense of responsibility. Anger, resentment, hostility are commonplace, of course, and their expression is used in various ways: to help some children learn to control their violent impulses and to help others give vent to feelings too long repressed. In Re-Ed schools one finds the familiar ratio of four or five boys to one girl, a consequence in part, we believe, of a lack of masculine challenge in school and community today. Thus we contrive situations of controlled danger in which children can test themselves, can know fear and become the master of it. The simple joy of companionship is encouraged. We are impressed by the meaningfulness of friendships and how long they endure. The annual homecoming is anticipated by many youngsters as an opportunity to walk arm-in-arm with an old friend associated with a period of special significance in their lives. And we respect the need to be alone, to work things through without intrusion, and to have a private purpose. Feelings also get expressed through many kinds of creative activities that are woven into the fabric of life in a Re-ED school. Throwing clay on a potter's wheel gives a child a first sense of his potential for shaping his world. A puppet show written by the children may permit freer expression than is ordinarily tolerable. Drawing and painting can be fun for a whole group. And an object to mold gives something to do to make it safe for an adult and child to be close together.

ITEM 8: THE GROUP IS IMPORTANT TO CHILDREN Children are organized in groups of eight, with two teacher-counselors in charge. The group is kept intact for nearly all activities and becomes an important source of motivation, instruction, and control. When a group is functioning well, it is extremely difficult for an individual child to behave in a disturbed way. Even when the group is functioning poorly, the frictions and the failures can be used constructively. The council ring, or powwow, involving discussion of difficulties or planning of activities can be a most maturing experience. And the sharing of adventure, of vicissitudes, and of victories, provides an experience in human relatedness to which most of our children have been alien.

ITEM 9: CEREMONY AND RITUAL GIVE ORDER, STABILITY, AND CONFIDENCE Many Re-ED children have lived chaotic lives, even in their brief compass. They may come from homes where interpersonal disarray is endemic. We have stumbled upon and been impressed by the beneficence of ceremony, ritual, and metaphor for children and have come to plan for their inclusion in the program. The nightly backrub is an established institution with the Whippoorwills, a time of important confidences. Being a Bobcat brings a special sense of camaraderie and has its own metaphorical obligations. And a Christmas pageant can effect angelic transformation of boys whose ordinary conduct is far from seraphic.

ITEM 10: THE BODY IS THE ARMATURE OF THE SELF We are intrigued by the idea that the physical self is the armature around which the psychological self is constructed and that a clearer experiencing of the potential and the boundaries of the body should lead to a clearer definition of the self, and thus to greater psychological fitness and more effective functioning. The Outward Bound schools in England developed as an experience for young men to overcome the anomie that is the product of an industrial civilization, are built around the concept. Austin Des Lauriers' ideas about treatment of schizophrenia in children emphasize differentiating the body from the rest of the world. Programmatically, in Re-ED, the idea has been realized in such activities as swimming, climbing, dancing, tumbling, clay modeling, canoeing, building a tree house, and walking a monkey bridge.

ITEM 11: COMMUNITIES ARE IMPORTANT The systems concept in Re-ED leads to an examination of the relationship of the child to his home community. Many children who are referred to our schools come from families that are alienated or detached from community life or that are not sufficiently well organized or purposeful to help the child develop a sense of identity with his neighborhood, his town or city. He has little opportunity to discover that communities exist for people and, while the goodness of fit between the two may often leave much to be desired, an important part of a child's education is to learn that community agencies and institutions exist for his welfare and that he has an obligation as a citizen to contribute to their effective functioning. This is especially true for many of the boys referred to Re-ED, whose energy, aggressiveness, lack of control, and resentment of authority will predispose them to delinquent behavior when they are a few years older and gain in independence and mobility. This idea has a number of implications for program planning. Field trips to the fire, police, and health departments are useful. Memberships in the YMCA, a children's museum, a playground group, or a community center may be worked out for a child. Church attendance may be encouraged and a clergyman persuaded to take special interest in a family, and a library card can be a proud possession and a tangible community tie.

ITEM 12: FINALLY, A CHILD SHOULD KNOW JOY We have often speculated about our lack of a psychology of well-being. There is an extensive literature on anxiety, guilt, and dread, but little that is well developed on joy. Most psychological experiments rely for motivation on avoidance of pain or hunger or some other aversive stimuli; positive motivations are limited to the pleasure that comes from minute, discrete rewards. This poverty with respect to the most richly human of motivations leads to anemic programming for children. We thus go beyond contemporary psychology to touch one of the most vital areas of human experiencing. We try to develop skill in developing joy in children. We believe that it is immensely important, that it is immediately therapeutic if further justification is required, for a child to know some joy in each day and to look forward with eagerness to at least some joy-giving event that is planned for tomorrow.

Costs and Effectiveness

Now, let us turn to the practical questions of cost and of effectiveness.

A Re-ED school costs about $20 to $25 per child per day to operate. Thus the per-day cost is about one-third the cost of the most widely accepted model and perhaps four times the cost of custodial care. Cost per day, however, is not the best index to use, for the purpose of a mental health program is not to keep children cheaply but to restore them to home, school, and community as economically as possible. In terms of cost per child served, the cost of a Re-ED program is equivalent to or less than the cost of custodial care. The cost per child served is approximately $4,000. If Re-ED can prevent longer periods of institutionalization, this is a modest investment indeed.

Appropriate to the systems analysis of the problem, most of our studies of effectiveness of Re-ED schools have employed ratings by concerned observers: mother, father, teacher, our own staff, and agency staffs, all important persons in the ecological space of the child. However, Laura Weinstein (1965) has been interested in the way normal and disturbed children construct interpersonal space, as illustrated by the accompanying representations of felt board figures. She used two techniques. In the first (the replacement technique), each of two figure pairs —a pair of human figures and a pair of rectangles—is present on a different board and equally far apart (Figures 2 and 3). The child is asked to replace the felt figures "exactly as far apart as they are now." Normal and disturbed children make systematic errors, but in opposite directions: normal children replace human figures closer together while Re-ED children replace human figures farther apart (Figure 4). In the second technique (the free placement technique), human figures are used, representing mothers, fathers, and children. The children are asked to place the figures on the board "any way you like." Again systematic differences occur. Normal children place the child very close to the mother. Re-ED children place greater distance between the mother and

FIGURE 2. Geometric felt figures used in replacement technique (after Weinstein, 1965).

FIGURE 3. Human felt figures used in replacement technique (after Weinstein, 1965).

the child than between any other human pair (Figure 5). The mother-child relationship is clearly crucial in the life space of the 6- to 12-year-old children with whom we work. It is gratifying to report that children after the Re-ED experience put the child figure closer to the mother than they did before; that is, they structure interpersonal space as normal children do.

The basic design for evaluating the effectiveness of the Re-ED schools involves observations taken at time of enrollment and repeated 6 months after discharge. Preliminary results present an encouraging picture. A composite rating of improvement, based on follow-up information on 93 graduates provided by all evaluators, gives a success rate of approximately 80%. We are in process of obtaining comparison data from

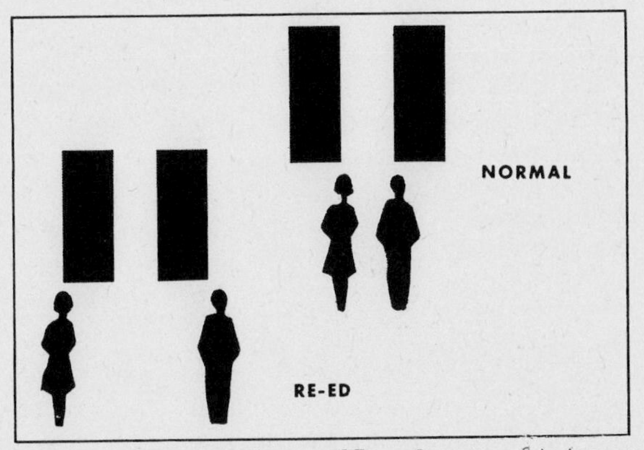

FIGURE 4. Placement of geometric and human felt figures by normal and disturbed children (after Weinstein, 1965).

control groups to determine the extent to which the reeducation effort is superior to changes that occur with the passage of time.

Detailed analyses show that mothers and fathers independently report a decrease in symptoms such as bedwetting, tantrums, nightmares, and school fears, and an increase in social maturity on a Vineland type check list. School adjustment as rated by teachers shows the same favorable trends. On a semantic differential measure of discrepancy between how the child is seen and parental standards for him, there is an interesting and dynamically significant difference between fathers and mothers. Both see the child as having improved. For fathers the perceived improvement results in lower discrepancy scores between the child as seen and a standard held for him. For some mothers, however, improvement

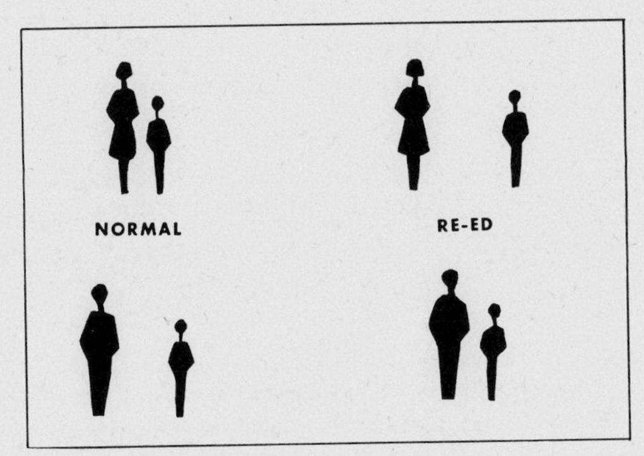

FIGURE 5. Mother, father, and child felt figures as placed by normal and disturbed children (after Weinstein, 1965).

results in a raising of standards so that discrepancy scores frequently remain high. This is not true of all mothers but it is more frequently true of mothers than of fathers.

But *T* tests seldom determine the fate of institutions; public and professional acceptance is crucial.

To obtain an informed and mature professional appraisal of Re-ED, we have established a panel of visitors composed of men whose judgment is held in high esteem: Eli M. Bower, psychologist; Reginald S. Lourie, psychiatrist; Charles R. Strother, psychologist; and Robert L. Sutherland, sociologist. Members of the panel have been visiting the schools regularly since their inception and will make public their final appraisal at the end of the project period. It is enough to say now that they are all strong supporters of the Re-ED idea.

A test of public support of the Re-ED idea was adventitiously obtained when the Legislature of the State of North Carolina last June terminated state funds for the support of Wright School after July 1, 1966. Protest from all over the state was immediate and strong; in less than 3 years of operation the school had won impressive public support. Funds have been raised to continue Wright School in operation until the Legislature convenes again.[4] The Governor has assured the mental health officials of North Carolina that he will support legislative measures to restore state funds for the operation of Wright School. Fortunately the Tennessee school has not been put to such public test but professional and political endorsement is evident in the decision to build two new schools, one in Memphis and one in Chattanooga, that will be operated as reeducation centers. Finally, it is encouraging that several other states have committees working to establish Re-ED schools.

Our aspiration and our growing confidence are that the Re-ED model will be replicated in many states, that it will have its influence on the character of more traditional treatment programs, and that the beneficiaries will be the disturbed children of America.

We further think of Re-ED as an institution that exemplifies, in its development, the contemporary challenge to psychologists to concern themselves with the invention of social arrangements that put psychological knowledge to use to improve the quality of human life.

[4] Among the major contributors are the Wright Refuge Board, the Sarah Graham Kenan Fund, the Mary Duke Biddle Foundation, the Hillsdale Fund, and the Stanley County Mental Health Association. Many gifts have come from churches, mental health associations, civic organizations, and individuals. We gratefully acknowledge their help in keeping Wright School in operation.

References

HOBBS, N. "Mental Health's Third Revolution." *American Journal of Orthopsychiatry,* 1964, *34,* 822–833.

LEWIS, W. W. "Continuity and Intervention in Emotional Disturbance: A Review." *Exceptional Children,* 1965, *31* (9), 465–475.

WEINSTEIN, L. "Social Schemata of Emotionally Disturbed Boys." *Journal of Abnormal Psychology,* 1965, *70,* 457–461.

32. Special Education in a Psychiatric Hospital

ELI Z. RUBIN

The majority of young emotionally disturbed children who come into residential settings for treatment have shown a history of maladjustment in school. These children have demonstrated their inability to adjust behaviorally or to learn under the usual circumstances of the public school. The majority are educationally retarded. They have failed to benefit from the ordinary methods of instruction and show either specific or general deficiencies in one or more significant areas of learning. This finding is even more startling when one considers that these children are generally of average or better than average intelligence. More often than not their achievement is uneven. Some children may show adequate progress in arithmetic, with an ability to handle simpler number combinations and concepts, but show an inability to read beyond the primary level. Others may show specific deficits, such as inability to grasp concepts for number work and similar difficulty in gaining meaning from their reading work or in understanding fundamental concepts involved in language skills.

SOURCE: *Exceptional Children,* XXIX (December, 1962), 184–90. Reprinted by permission.

There are other children whose academic achievement is consistent with their age expectancy, but who have failed to adjust to the social situation of the school setting. These are the children with behavior problems, who manifest poor attentiveness, short spans of concentration, excessive motor restlessness, daydreaming, withdrawal, fear, impulsive aggressive behavior, temper outbursts, or other forms of immature reactions. These youngsters, because of their behavior disturbance, eventually become disturbed in their learning progress. In addition, they are often considered detrimental to the other youngsters in the classroom and there is the desire on the part of teachers and administrators to exclude or segregate them. While segregation is often beneficial to the other members of the class, it does not contribute to social improvement or learning progress of the disturbed child without the addition of some special program.

Efforts to understand and help these children are constantly attempted by many school systems. Psychologists are employed to investigate the students' intellectual and personality resources and school social workers delve into family situations to explain the distorted adjustment. Individual psychotherapy at child guidance clinics is sought for some, and although it is successful for many, it is ineffective for others. In spite of these attempts, there has been a considerable lag within educational systems in the development of new or altered approaches to the education of those children for whom special facilities are obviously indicated (Bower, 1959 a, b).

A residential treatment setting incorporating a special school program within its own institution has much to contribute toward the formulation of rationale and guidelines in the establishment of educational programs that may prove beneficial to emotionally disturbed children. The interrelationship between the emotional problem and learning difficulties indicates the need for modifications of the school situation and the approach to learning if educational progress is to be furthered. The experience of many of these centers, including the Lafayette Clinic school department, suggests that even with little time for school per day, children with previous histories of educational failure alter their attitudes toward school and can make considerable progress. This is often achieved by children having one or two hours of academic schooling per day. There is a need to demonstrate this observed occurrence through careful measurement. However, it is equally important to formulate a rationale to account for these clinically observed results. By making explicit a rationale for the operation of a school department within a clinical setting and observing the progress of children in this department, we may develop a clearer understanding of the dynamics of school failure and the relation of schooling to treatment of emotional disturbances in children. It is hoped that this will lead to the development of special education classes for the emotionally disturbed child based on assumptions and principles which stem from an understanding of his problems (Haring and Phillips, 1962).

Problems of Educational Planning

Impairment of ego functioning by overwhelming anxiety is a consistent finding in severely disturbed children who require hospitalization. These children are unable to sustain attention on tasks for any appreciable length of time. They are easily distracted by ideas, fantasies, or feelings from within. They are quick to respond to stimulating events or unusual happenings around them. They are quick to anticipate failure, and through their fantasies and fears tend to misinterpret the attitudes of teachers and others, expecting undue pressure or rejection for not achieving at some expected level. Motivation to learn and interest in school are markedly low. Those children whose anxiety has been kept at a high level have chronically failed to develop and practice cognitive functions important in perceptual discrimination, thus creating reading problems and interference with comprehension of meaningful material. In some children, motor control is impaired, showing up in poor handwriting, writing reversals, or in impulsive and restless motor movements. In some cases there is a fundamental lack of basic skills in academic areas, making adequate adjustment or progress in a regular class exceedingly difficult. Detailed analysis of the child's functional assets and limitations must be undertaken early for proper educational planning. Any assessment of value must point to an appropriate remedial program. Clinical psychiatric diagnoses do not provide sufficient precision to allow for adequate school planning (Haring and Phillips, 1962; Rubin and Simson, 1960). Investigations are being undertaken to provide a classification that will be more meaningful for educational planning.

One of the first goals of the institutional setting is to provide an atmosphere that is supportive to the child's impaired ego functioning, weakened by excessive stress placed upon him by frustrations within his prior environment. Reduction of overstimulating situations by removal from home and community is the initial step in this direction. The child is then provided substitute parental figures who are more neutral and objective in their response to his behavior, reducing the reinforcement of maladaptive patterns of response. Another ego-supportive technique within the total milieu is the provision of planned daily routines which are consistently followed and predictable. The child can begin to rely upon certain events and happenings from one day to the next which are unaltered by his own behavior and allow him to form a relationship to the unit, thus providing the first step toward relating to individual members of the staff. Opportunities for pleasure through tension release in games and play contribute to the security the child feels within the institution. Careful planning of peer group interactions further protects the child from being overwhelmed by those superior to him in size, strength, or ability, and from opportunities to lose control over his aggressive feelings directed at those less strong or capable than he. Finally, when the child is given an opportunity to learn whatever basic skills he lacks, and to practice at whatever level he happens to be, he can begin to alter his self-picture of unacceptability to others or feeling of helplessness at being unable to master frustrations of everyday life. The development of those skills which are necessary in participating with other children in play and school achievement is a significant contribution to increased emotional stability (Llorens and Rubin, 1961; Rabinow, 1955).

A child's inability to adjust to the public school environment is often a major factor determining the need for hospitalization. In many instances the school failure is symptomatic of the child's impaired ability to cope with reality situations in an open environment demanding independent functioning. In some instances failure at school can be seen as leading to further ego decline, resulting in secondary symptoms that tend to fix the disturbance and preclude improvement, even with treatment on an outpatient basis.

For other children the regular school situation with its social complexities and achievement requirements overtaxes the intellectual, conceptual or discriminative abilities to such a degree as to constitute an overwhelming stress situation. The child cannot find satisfactions for basic needs for acceptance, status, reward, or identity through school achievement and so may take on those methods of achieving his ends which are available to his characterological makeup. For some children, the situation is completely overwhelming and they can only avoid the stress through daydreaming, inattentiveness, withdrawal, or even autistic behavior. Others may attempt to seek their satisfactions through attention-getting devices, such as clowning, teasing, or provocative behavior. For others, the only solution lies in avoiding the demand for more independent behavior and retreating to immature methods of response, including negativism, stubbornness, clinging, or temper outbursts.

The Lafayette Clinic School

The Lafayette Clinic is a 146-bed psychiatric hospital, the research and training unit of the State Department of Mental Health affiliated with Wayne State University. It provides diagnostic and short-term intensive inpatient treatment services for children, adolescents, and adults who show a wide variety of psychiatric conditions. Outpatient diagnostic and treatment services are also provided. One of the primary aims of this unit is to conduct research in the field of mental health that will contribute to the understanding of mental illness and to attempt to develop more effective methods of treatment. Through its service to patients, the clinic provides training for students in a variety of disciplines, including adult and child psychiatry, clinical psychology, psychiatric social work, special education, nursing, occupational therapy, and vocational rehabilitation.

The school department is under the Division of Rehabilitation and provides separate but coordinated educational programs for adolescents and for children of elementary school age. Schooling is considered one aspect of the total treatment plan. Special education programs are devised in order to (a) prevent the child from losing ground in his schoolwork; (b) provide those skills that will enhance the opportunity for progress in learning by involving the child in successful academic accomplishment and gratification; (c) contribute to a total therapeutic milieu that is supportive to the individual treatment of the child by supplying satisfactions of the normal emotional and social needs, including the need for achievement and success, for structure, stable relationships and healthy identification; (d) effect a beneficial school placement following discharge through a follow-up program involving close liaison with the staff of the school to which the child returns.

This school department within the clinical setting recognizes and accepts the need for education goals upon which to establish its programs. The Lafayette Clinic school program is designed, in general, to provide an atmosphere that will reduce those conditions which put the child under undue stress and which further contribute to the maintenance of his anxiety at a high level. While in the hospital, the child undergoes many other experiences that help to reduce the effects of externally induced anxiety, such as removal from home, dilution of parental authority, and provision of a planned day.

The school's contribution to the total treatment of the youngster is to provide an atmosphere which is adapted to the capacities and needs of the disturbed child so that he may show progress in learning and gain satisfaction from his progress. In contrast to those goals of the clinical approach, which are aimed at the resolution of the emotional conflict, the educational team orients its techniques and attitudes toward promoting improved attitudes toward school and achievement in learning. Techniques and attitudes applied to each child are planned and directed in accordance with an understanding of his current efficiency level of ego functioning. The teaching staff learns about the child's functioning in a classroom situation as well as from contributions from educational, psychological, and psychiatric examinations.

They recognize that this child comes to the school situation with poor motivation for learning and an accumulation of negative attitudes toward school and school personnel. They are ready to recognize the role of anxiety in disturbing the individual's capacity to take advantage of learning opportunities which, although consistent for his age and intellectual level, may be beyond his capacity to integrate and incorporate. Thus, a school program for each child is planned to provide basic skills where indicated or to give opportunity for successful practice of acquired skills. There is a major emphasis on school conditioning experience for all the children. In graduated steps, the child is exposed to classroom conditions, attitudes, and procedures that will allow him to increase his tolerance for the demands made on him by a school situation.

Our children's unit is a short-term intensive treatment unit, providing inpatient clinical services for 22 youngsters between the ages of six and 12. The school department is a major component of the milieu therapy program and is closely coordinated in its planning with the occupational therapy and recreational therapy departments, all of which are within the division of rehabilitation.

Tables 1, 2, 3, and 4 provide some basic descriptive data on 97 young-

TABLE 1

97 Patients Discharged from Lafayette Clinic 1956–60

				Average	Average Age		
Year	*Number*	*Female*	*Male*	*LOS* (Months)*	*at Admission*	*Average IQ*	*IQ Range*
1956	10	3	7	4.2	10.3	93.3	62–109
1957	26	5	21	7.6	9.1	89.0	68–117
1958	26	10	16	8.0	9.2	88.9	56–115
1959	20	3	17	7.3	9.2	94.0	55–125
1960	15	6	9	10.5	9.2	97.3	56–125
Totals	97	27	70	7.5	9.4	92.5	55–125

* Length of stay

TABLE 2

School Adjustment Prior to Admission Number=97

Behavior Disturbance	28
Behavior Disturbance and Academic Difficulty	45
Academic Difficulty	11
No School Problem	13
Excluded from School	20

TABLE 3

Distribution of Psychiatric Diagnoses

Adjustment Reaction of Childhood with Behavior Disorder	15
Adjustment Reaction of Childhood with Neurotic Traits	3
Psychoneurotic Conditions	16
Personality Disorder	21
Chronic Brain Syndrome with Psychosis	15
Chronic Brain Syndrome with Behavior Disorder	15
Schizophrenic Reaction	7
Psychotic Reaction	5
	97

TABLE 4

Disposition upon Discharge Number=97

	1956	*1957*	*1958*	*1959*	*1960*	*Total*
Home	6	22 *	14	11	10	63 *
Foster Home	2	1	1	1	0	5
Group Placement	1	0	2	3	4	10
Institutional Care	1	3	9	5	1	19
Totals	10	26	26	20	15	97

* 3 to await placement at Institution
1 to await Group Placement

sters who have been in our school program and have been discharged since the opening of this unit in 1956. These tables reveal that an overwhelming majority (87 percent) of our patients had experienced serious difficulties in school. Twenty-one percent (20 children) had been excluded from school. These results support the concept that rehabilitation must include schooling experience. Table 3 indicates that a wide variety of clinical types are provided treatment. Differences in diagnosis do not appear to preclude grouping together.

Our experiences with those children who have participated in the school department over the past five years have led to the formulations reported here. Educational experience has always played a significant role in the treatment program for the children. The specific programs offered have varied, depending upon the population on hand. However, the current program has evolved over the years. The pattern of groups is determined primarily by the level of educational achievement or readiness for school functioning. Every effort is made to put youngsters together in groups so that (a) the size of the class allows for individualized attention; (b) the grade achievement span is narrow; (c) children's readiness for school is essentially similar; and (d) the group composition will tend to reduce symptomatic behavioral difficulties. This means that children are not grouped by age or psychiatric diagnosis, but rather according to their readiness for school and classroom conditions.

Thus, at the present time the school department offers the following classes which provide educational experience for all but two of our 21 patients:

1. SCHOOL ADJUSTMENT GROUP This is designed as a small group. Children needing help in getting adjusted or readjusted to the routines of going to school are placed in this group. Educational diagnosis is carried out and each child is continually reviewed for reassignment to other groups. This class also serves as a temporary placement for a youngster whose adjustment in one of the other groups is showing deterioration.
2. PRE-PRIMARY GROUP This is also designed as a small group. The children placed here are those who are beginning first grade work and are ready to learn fundamental skills in reading, numbers, etc. Individualized instruction is provided.
3. PRIMARY GROUP This is a structured class situation for children with academic skills above the first grade level, but within the primary grades. These are children who are able to read and who show a capacity to adjust to this kind of school situation. There is a concentration on basic school subjects, although considerable attention is paid to helping the child adjust to the classroom conditions. This group currently has six members, but probably could contain up to 10.
4. ELEMENTARY GROUP This is essentially the same as the Primary Group, but is geared to those youngsters whose academic skills are at the fourth grade level or above. The setting is structured like regular school and more opportunity for independent functioning is afforded. This group, too, can accommodate a larger number, and at one time did serve 10 youngsters with a variety of psychiatric disturbances.

The results of our total program are promising. A majority (67 percent) of these seriously disturbed and disorganized children have been returned to the community to live in a family-type setting, either in their own home or in a foster home. These results are in general agreement with figures reported by other similar hospital units as well as by long term residential treatment centers. The ultimate criterion is, of course, the subsequent adjustment of these children over several years. As yet, the long range results of our school program have not been carefully ascertained. Such a study through follow-up evaluation of post-discharge school adjustment is in progress. Through this we hope to gain considerable knowledge about the impact of our total treatment program upon subsequent school adjustment.

References

Bower, E. M. "The Emotionally Handicapped Child and the School." *Except. Child.*, 1959, *26*, 6–11. (a)

Bower, E. M. "The Emotionally Handicapped Child and the School: An Analysis of Program and Trends." *Except. Child.*, 1959, *26*, 182–188. (b)

Llorens, Lela A. & Rubin, E. Z. "Occupational Therapy Is Therapeutic: A Research Study with Emotionally Disturbed Children." *Proc. Annual Meeting, Amer. Occupational Therapy Assoc.*, 1961.

Haring, N. G. & Phillips, E. L. *Educating Emotionally Disturbed Children.* New York: McGraw-Hill, 1962.

Rabinow, B. "The Role of the School in Residential Treatment." *Amer. J. Orthopsychiat.*, 1955, *25*, 685–691.

Rubin, E. Z. & Simson, C. B. "A Special Class Program for the Emotionally Disturbed Child in School: A Proposal." *Amer. J. Orthopsychiat.*, 1960, *30*, 144–153.

III

Classroom Problems of the Emotionally Disturbed

In this Part the articles are concerned with two areas of the educational process: curriculum and techniques. In terms of the curriculum needed for emotionally disturbed children, *Morse* (33) suggests the curriculum should follow the modern program but with a strong remedial flavor because the pupils are academically retarded. When disturbed children are on the road to improvement in their behavior they ask for a school like "school." We must discard the notion that because these children are disturbed they aren't ready for an educational program—this notion is too reminiscent of the sick-well medical model. Morse also stresses some basic principles for teaching the disturbed, such as pupil motivation, individualization of the curriculum, structuring the content, play and creative expression, and group life in the classroom. *Rhodes* (34) describes a set of twelve guides for the teacher to keep in mind while preparing lessons for emotionally disturbed children and then discusses five forms these preparations may take: basic lesson plan, behavior training, skill training, discussion sessions, and group interaction.

In the area of techniques, *Leton* (35) reviews six general concepts in teaching for mental health and presents a rationale for each as well as specific arguments against their use with particular types of emotionally disturbed children. His dissatisfaction with past attempts in mental-health teaching is with the approach in which general principles are established and then applied to all children through the curriculum. To correct this situation the author proposes an inductive approach to teaching emotionally disturbed children and illustrates this differential approach in teaching these children. *Newman* (36) examines some basic assumptions of any school program for the emotionally disturbed and then directs attention to some basic principles for those who are engaged in the education and treatment of these children. In the article by *Minuchin* and his associates (37) an experimental program to explore the learning style of the disturbed delinquent is described and an overview of socialization processes in the disorganized, low socioeconomic family is presented. Basic assumptions about the influence of these processes on the learning style of the children are noted and then the intervention curriculum and teaching methodology employed are described. The results of this experimental "game" curriculum proved to be quite promising in changing the learning behavior during the length of the project. Teachers will welcome *Emery's* (38) article which demonstrates how the standard materials and activities of the preschool program can be used to further the ego development of children classified as childhood schizophrenics. Music and rhythm, clay, pegs, finger paints, blocks, and paper are the tools for this very interesting discussion. In the next short article, *Miller* (39) describes a motivational summer reading program conducted by the Day Care Service at Children's Psychiatric Hospital at the University of Michigan Medical Center. The motivational event for each unit was a field trip; a sample weekly program of reading activities is presented. Teachers will no doubt find ways to make use of this program within the normal academic year.

By this time, the reader will have noticed that the readings in this book emphasize the need for individualization of the instructional procedures in working with emotionally disturbed children. In the next article *Brendtro* and *Stern* (40) feel that some form of sequential tutoring will be used in the future as in the past, but with a difference. As an alternative to the adult-initiated program, the authors present a child-initiated sequential tutoring system which would seem to produce a therapeutic atmosphere more conducive to the educative process. In the last article, *Lansing* (41) reports on a craft program that has been used with a group of severely disturbed children. Success, structure, and safety are shown to be of paramount importance when choosing a craft material; teachers will find much help in the wise counsel of this dedicated worker.

A. Curriculum

33. Educational Designs

William C. Morse

Curriculum and Methods for Educating the Emotionally Disturbed

Teachers in a school for the emotionally disturbed were asked what it was they taught. After a pause they replied that they taught everything, and they added that they taught by just about every known method. The relaxed tone and the sometimes amorphous form of the work in a special school should not be misunderstood. Behind this lies teaching with thought-out goals and planned content. Relating the goals and content to the children's capacities is a most complex task.

Unfortunately, when one examines actual practice, the mundane crowds out the creative, and the main difference between special and regular teaching is a consequence of the small size of the special class. Initially more emphasis is put upon control and management, motivation efforts, and individual remediation. The over-all orientation is educational rather than therapeutic. The vast majority of the time is spent on academics with art, music, and gym playing minor roles and formal discussions related to behavior even less. This points up the fact that the goal is schooling, although conditions force attention to the deeper control and motivation complex. The task of special education is to work out a more dynamic classroom experience for the children than

SOURCE: William C. Morse, "The Education of Socially Maladjusted and Emotionally Disturbed Children," in William M. Cruickshank and G. Orville Johnson, eds., *Education of Exceptional Children and Youth,* 2d ed. (Englewood Cliffs, N.J.: Prentice-Hall, Inc., 1967), pp. 598–608.

is now generally taking place. Creative teachers show that it can be done.

In over-all perspective, the curriculum for the disturbed child should follow a modern, well-planned regular program, but usually with a strong remedial flavor because so many of the pupils are academically retarded. Skill in reading, language, numbers, social relationships, and self-control are all important. The arts, social studies, and science studies are major concerns. More separation of content takes place throughout the junior high school level where material may be organized around the unified studies—English and social studies on the one hand, and science and mathematics on the other. Manual activities may be incorporated directly as a school experience or appear in related activities such as crafts or occupational therapy. Usually homemaking activities and practical arts are introduced here. With adolescents, some content dealing with social manners should be included. With older adolescents vocational preparation assumes major importance. Again, following the philosophy of modern education for normal children, a broad range of play activities, physical education, and extracurricular programs round out the picture.

In short, the educational birthright of the normal certainly belongs to the special pupil as well. The old idea that since they are different, one must wait until they are in good mental health before they can be taught has been disregarded. Some of the fear of their actions which used to make schoolrooms more like prisons has also been lost. If what is being done in modern education is useful, interesting, and supporting to normal children, it certainly has a place with the disturbed. It is interesting how well most children grasp the significance of school as a reality factor. When they begin to improve, one of the first signs is often the request for a school like "school." They ask for homework and are eager for evaluation. This suggests that the schoolroom is neither recreational therapy nor group therapy, although it contains traces of both. The therapeutic educator's implicit concern for the child and warm acceptance of him make this reality palatable for these upset children.

It is instructive that most theories of the past about organizing the special classroom have been successfully disregarded by certain master teachers. For example, formal textbooks and workbooks have been the backbone of some classes. This was held to be necessary in order to provide the pattern and security which disturbed pupils needed. However, other teachers use a problem-solving or simulation format with no piecework or rigidly defined tasks. Such wide variation in method may be possible because the total classroom impact under a perceptive, energetic, and enthusiastic teacher overrides the choice of a specific methodology. The nature of the teacher may be a more potent force than the method selected.

The Educational Tone of the Special Classroom

The classroom is a social and learning milieu where tone and balance are crucial. Group interaction is utilized to encourage the child's socialization. Fortunately, educators have passed through the period when permissiveness was considered the *sine qua non* of hygienic atmosphere. It is now recognized that a pattern with implicit limits is necessary for the security of normal children, and even more so for disturbed children. With the disturbed child, pattern is not expected to mean the elimination of classroom problems. But the problems should be those which stem from the child's pathology rather than from equivocal conditions perpetrated by the teacher. It is equally important for the teacher not to resort to rigid form. The teacher establishes and maintains the reality focus of school as a place for learning. At the same time the teacher's empathic recognition of pupils' feelings allows for flexibility within the broad pattern. Periods of regression, outbursts of frustrations, and short attention spans are all accepted as normal. The teacher is sensitive to over-all moods, such as those occurring at holidays when the school is enveloped in seasonal excitement. Daily routines, which were established to give security, go by the board to capture the emotion of the moment. Fun is as much a subject in the curriculum as is arithmetic. Nevertheless, the teacher remains the manager rather than the managed, fostering pupil initiative and resourcefulness, yet limiting energy here and channeling it there.

The teacher must have the permission and personal ability to enforce necessary limits even to the point of temporary exclusion of a pupil when he cannot make use of the classroom. The removal is talked through with the pupil without hostility in the hope that he will come to understand why.

Whether the teacher is more controlling or more permissive not only changes from time to time, but changes in relationship to the clientele. As has been seen, a group of asocial children requires different handling than a class of anxious, withdrawn children. Usually they are both found in the same class, meaning differential treatment is required within the same group. If this sounds as if special schooling runs along like regular schooling, nothing could be further from actuality. The child who is immersed in his own preoccupation or the child who is fighting society is unlikely to be ready to sit down at a desk and work gayly at his tasks. The necessary energy is at the service of other involvements. Such children are often far behind academically and frequently have blocks to learning. There are wide variations. Some never accomplish too much academically, while others concentrate on this avenue holding on tenaciously to this "normal" experience or even overcompensating through schoolwork.

Good teaching methodology which exerts a sustaining and directing force on normal children may have no effect at all on these children. To plan the reading therapy for a twelve-year-old who cannot recognize words or sounds, who never has gotten along with teachers or peers, while he is moving into a significant therapeutic relationship requires circumspection of the highest order. Perhaps one pupil can only fill out a workbook exercise after first testing his answer through the teacher; another storms into a classroom announcing she and her friends have as of now seceded from school. A boy carries on his antiauthority tirade at the teacher, arguing first that he was not told he had to do a given lesson, then that it is a crazy assignment anyway, and finally that he just won't do it. Yet these pupils can be taught and are being taught successfully. A few specific programs are described in the literature, and the reader will be referred to them in a later section. The material which follows immediately is organized around basic principles of this type of special education, regardless of the setting. They constitute the educational psychology for teaching the socially and emotionally disturbed. While this stratum is being examined separately, it should not be forgotten that it cannot be thought of apart from the role of the teacher or the grouping designs discussed elsewhere.

Special Teacher's Concern with Pupil Motivation

The teacher is far more consciously involved in motivational problems when working with disturbed children than would be necessary with normal children. After the problem of control, the next most pressing problem reported by teachers is motivation. Frequently, though by no means always, disturbed children have a history of poor school adjustment. Their attitudes toward teachers may be negative, and any sense of self-accomplishment through formal learning is lacking. Consequently a primary goal is to develop pupil-teacher rapport and to restore the sense of pleasure in learning. These attitudinal changes are also necessary preparation for return to regular schooling.

One author has delineated levels of readiness keyed to the psychosocial development. Hewett suggests that the key to motivation is to assess the real developmental level of the pupil. Some pupils are as yet so immature that a "concrete" gratification such as food is all that counts; others may be advanced to the stage where they can do things "for the teacher"; still others find gratification in the learning experience in and of itself. While most pupils operate on different levels, depending upon what the task is, there is no doubt that teachers often do expect the child to respond on a higher level than fits his capability.

There is, then, no magic method of motivation. Motivation is in fact part of everything the teacher does. Problems of motivation underlie all educational effort. To be effective, the school must come to be a place of pleasure and satisfaction. Sometimes and to some children the experiences provide intrinsic satisfaction and are sufficient. But the regular school implicitly utilizes an important but little recognized capacity of normal children. Stress on "democratic procedures," "pupil initiative," and "self-planning" sometimes obscures the fact that most of the teacher's purpose is really accomplished through a kind of motivational contagion. The expressed and tacit enthusiasms and purposes of the adult are responded to by the pupils. Sometimes the response may come through another pupil rather than through the teacher directly.

The disturbed child's dependent status predicates this contagion. While the normal child may object to being told directly, he does seek the comfort he gets by doing what pleases the adult. At adolescence, when the peer group has more power to induce goals than adults, the normal child is often caught between the two forces and school motivation becomes more complex. At times this wish to please the teacher is itself a problem, as in the case of the overdependent child who is upset when he has to be on his own and is afraid to displease. In the normal process of maturing, pupils incorporate and reflect adult values until they end up feeling self-satisfaction when they do the task. This is the psychological substratum of school motivation, for it is known that many necessary school experiences do not have inherent appeal. In fact, it is a source of never ceasing wonderment how many educational tasks pupils assume which have little intrinsic satisfaction. Between the task and the child is the teacher and the group.

With emotionally and socially disturbed children the development of this capacity is aberrant. Often they are immune to catching work-minded attitudes from either teachers or peers. The psychopath cannot identify; the partially socialized sees the teacher's goals as alien; the neurotic is frequently in conflict with authority and his peer group siblings; the psychotic is not in communication. Since most of them are having a very difficult time handling their impulsivity, they are much more likely to be influenced by negative examples. For example, one child starts a diversion from the educational tasks, and the next thing the teacher knows, they are all getting wild. For these reasons the teacher must go far more than half way if the problems of motivation are to be solved. Somehow the pupil must become involved. Endless patience and careful use of situations over an extended period of time are required to create the proper pupil-teacher rapport. Meanwhile, the child always tests the relationship, sometimes with quiet persistence and sometimes with desperate frenzy. Newman suggests that the uneven course toward accepting school and the teacher is preceded by a period of regression. At any rate, the actions suggested under the role of the special teacher are intended to give substance to what the teacher does to establish a useful relationship with pupils. The point to bear in mind is that this relationship is valuable not only as an interpersonal feeling, but as a mode of helping the pupil overcome his motivational defects.

Individualization of the Curriculum

There is one point universally agreed upon by special teachers: the program must be individualized. Each child is a school unto himself. The work of that school is dictated by the abilities and limitations of that pupil. There are particular things which the educational staff needs to know in planning the individualized school experience.

To begin with, there is the over-all learning ability which the psychologist assesses by adding his insight to the results on the performance and verbal scales. When appropriate, achievement tests indicate the base line for skill and content lessons. Teachers are just beginning to recognize the importance of special psychological factors in individualizing school work. It is just as vital to select procedures fitting to the individual as it is to select material at his level. For example, he may think well in concrete terms but fail with abstract concepts. Perhaps he has idiosyncratic ways of problem solving or perception. The learning diagnosis discussed elsewhere in this book is germane here. These studies may condition the approach to arithmetic or reading. A good many of these factors can be worked out by the teacher observing and the psychologist analyzing classroom work as well as by special tests and scales. This type of diagnostic teaching is especially needed in cases of stubborn failure to make progress under accepted teaching methods; it puts a new cast on the term individualization. As an illustration, some children need not only visual cues but also auditory cues and kinesthetic cues to learn to read. The special teacher cannot simply rely on applying methods of proven worth. The application must be specific. Pupils often provide evidence for the teacher. When a child wants to go back to easy material, or lingers long at a particular level before being willing to move on, the special teacher sees this as the need for security in the face of fears of failure. When gentle support and encouragement do not free the pupil, the teacher waits and lets the pupil know that he understands. Terms like laziness do not apply. Allowing one child to regress would be in sharp contrast with the program for a child who needs pressure at the proper time—the psychopath or the child retreating from reality. Without such diagnostic data, teaching is blind.

There are other aspects of individualization. While there are many group projects for a whole class, subjects are frequently studied at the same time by several pupils; but each studies on his own level, like the parallel play of young children. Individualization may go much further with ten distinct lessons going on simultaneously for ten students. This resembles the one-room school rather than the typical elementary or high school class where it is common for all pupils to be doing the same exercise in the same book at the same time.

Since so many emotionally and socially disturbed pupils are academically retarded, the material must be more than just cut to the performance level. While the difficulty level is reduced, the material must still be stimulating to the pupil, at his interest and sophistication level. A fourteen-year-old non-reader may be destined for work at the preprimer level, but not the preprimer for six-year-olds. Reading material designed for older pupils with very restricted backgrounds, paperbacks, magazines for English courses in a vocational school, and primers written around the evolution of an adequate self-concept are examples.

Many times the only answer lies in material designed for the particular pupil by his teacher. Time spent with children is effective only if there is time provided to prepare material for them. Haring makes a special point of the teacher's need to have preparation time and a sequence packet of short assignments for each pupil every day. The pupil is rewarded for each completed task.

There are other facets to individualizing the program. Attention spans differ. The periods of school may be short and interspersed with play, crafts, or free time for one child. Another has the sustained integration to keep at the task longer and can use more schooling. Many have times when they cannot stand the group situation in a classroom at all. Individualization may mean the exclusive one-to-one relationship with a teacher. Here school fears, fears of exposure to failure in a group situation, or need for psychological support can be provided for through a more intimate situation. Sometimes, as with a psychotic child, it may take the complete energies of a teacher to bring about any of the communication which must precede teaching proper. Understandably, this one-to-one tutoring often takes on a more therapeutic coloring, although it still focuses on school learning difficulties rather than emotional problems *per se*.

At least in the initial stages, the frequent cases of reading failure need this individual therapeutic tutoring. Here, more than elsewhere, the stigma of failure is apparent. It cannot be hidden, and it represents such a handicap that the child's defenses are most difficult to break through. Every educational program for the maladjusted must make special provision for reading therapy. More than a few disturbed children have reading failure as the core problem, and when this is true, reading offers the key to therapy. Other types of disturbed children may be approached through reading.

The history of the child's reading problem is most important. It may stem from a primary maturational lag or perceptual idiosyncrasies which make learning to read very difficult. Perhaps failure is due to secondary factors, such as poor teaching or emotional blocks. Both primary and secondary factors may be involved. Whatever the first cause, after years of failure there is bound to be an emotional component, hence the need for reading therapy. In most instances multisensory approaches are used so that visual associations may be combined with auditory and kinesthetic cues.

Claims for success in remedial reading are made for highly directive methods and for nondirective techniques as well. Close inspection would probably reveal that there are failures, too, when one uses only one method. Some programs rely heavily on the reading games and special devices, while others think in terms of interrelationship. To overcome the defeatist attitudes of the child, a good deal of emphasis is placed on infusing the teaching situation with new hope. Once aroused, hope will die unless the child achieves, even though it be minor growth. Generic to success is a comfortable, nonthreatening atmosphere; without this the techniques and devices, whatever they are, will be rote mechanical exercises, forgotten even as they are done. After a time in a nonthreatening atmosphere, new progress will show up in the regular school class, and there will be the courageous demonstration to his teacher of the breakthrough. Then the teacher can supplement the tutoring which may be needed for a long time before the child has anything like the level of confidence and achievement he needs to be on his own in reading. Even though reading failure may have been the starting point of emotional difficulty, one does not expect the improvement in reading to offset the inadequacy which has accumulated. New feelings about the self have to be learned too.

Structuring the Content

One of the characteristics of special schooling is the unsystematic way content comes to be presented. The actual nature of the teaching units depends upon two factors: the general maturity of the pupils and the degree of integration which these pupils possess.

In the elementary work, considerable time is given over to units, frequently on a contemporary topic of some general concern, or a particular interest evidenced by one of the pupils. Since they tend to tire of a theme quickly, no long period is devoted to one unit. The work seldom goes smoothly. When projects are included, the operations are often wasteful and destructive. The children may ruin their own product or someone else's. Tools and materials are dropped when they cease to be needed, but a blow-up is likely to ensue if they cannot locate what they want immediately. The teacher becomes a master at innovation and substitution, keeping a watchful eye to see that supplies are available for the more or less spontaneous ideas which develop. Within all of the confusion, the unit concept provides a start and a finish to an educational experience. From this the children get the much needed sense of accomplishment. It also provides a focus for the class group while allowing for contributing subgroups and individual work. Since topics are broad and boundaries are flexible, the unit organization permits different members to work at different levels and emphasize different aspects and yet be a part of the group. Manual skills, dramatics, visual aids, and excursions can be easily included. Reading and composition skills are practiced functionally.

It is important to include group related activities as a balance for the necessary individualization which absorbs much of the time. Multiple level units have been worked out where there is something all pupils can do together though one gets little further than tracing a map while another writes a special paper to expand an issue and reports back to the group. Simulation learning which uses a group role-playing interactive method is still another way to employ the group learning format.

But incidental learning alone is not enough to teach most of the basic skills. Brief but frequent sessions are needed on spelling, reading, arithmetic, and so on. For older children, who are adequately integrated, the content may be divided into various subjects taught in separate periods. But too much shuffling from one teacher to another is contraindicated for children who are very disturbed. A few teachers who have relationships with them can net more by handling various subjects than can several teachers, experts in their fields, only casually related to the pupils. Relating to one teacher may be all that a child is able to do at first. Consequently the design is adjusted to his needs.

The school program must be compatible for the levels of the pupils' integration rather than their age. For example, older children who are functioning at the nursery level of behavior, while they cannot be grouped with the preschoolers, may need a nursery school-like situation, where formal learning requirements are not imposed. On the other extreme, a child may have much disturbed behavior but still be able to follow a train of curiosity in science, or learn to type. Regardless of the organizational difficulties, these interests should be fostered. Significant gains are often made quite out of the context of the teacher's intended program. One boy who fell apart in the classroom during a crucial stage in his therapy was most purposeful and controlled in a self-chosen art project of major proportions. Here he was no problem. He worked on his own and the recognition and satisfaction he obtained through the effort far outweighed the hours of class missed during this period. He was ready to return to the regular school program at the conclusion.

While the individual child may deviate, and plans are shelved time and again, the teacher must organize the accomplishment expected for the semester. Otherwise it becomes a chaotic hodge-podge. The plans may not be realized in the sequence or way intended, but the teacher has even more obligation to set goals than the regular teacher who can depend more on curriculum guides and books to provide much of the format. When time permits, the special teacher keeps an individual educational log on his pupils so that there are adequate guidelines. Periodic assessments of progress may be in order. There will be wide variance in accomplishment, but work tailored to the particular needs of the pupil can be expected to produce gains. Since many bright pupils are far behind, there are cases which make astonishing catch-up gains. Security in test-taking sometimes accounts for change. On the average these pupils have been found to make somewhat under the gains made by normal children. Huber has shown that the compulsive and psychosomatic child is likely to be doing well in school while the psychopath will tend to be low in achievement.

Play and Creative Expression in the Special School

There is a vast difference between "recess" and "play" as used in special education. Many of the children do not know how to enjoy play, and literally have to be taught wholesome play. The function of play is not intermittent freedom from the discipline of tasks, but a therapeutic and creative effort in itself.

Play has powerful potentials. In nurseries for schizophrenic children, for example, the play of a few normal "control" children may start the cycle of recovery. Through play the child experiments with self-control, with control of his environment, with phantasy, and with legitimate disregard of reality. Play therapy is based upon the reconstructive nature of play. The motor components are useful channels of tension release. Play and games, free and structured, offer many opportunities for self and social learning. Some children are particularly responsive to games with music.

Craft work is an extension of play. The special school makes much use of creative crafts with various media: paper, clay, wood, and metal. Exhibits enable the child to drain the last possible ounce of recognition from his work. Puppets and dramas offer expressive play opportunities. Like any child, these boys and girls enjoy dressing up and will work diligently on a paper bag costume. The meaning of expressive productions in painting, drawing, and clay work are not interpreted to the child in school. In the children's psychiatric hospital and other institutional settings it is common to separate occupational and recreational therapy from the school proper. The special teacher cannot help but use these at times anyway, even though there is ample opportunity for the child to experience them elsewhere. Aggression through hammering and sawing or athletics is far better than pounding a desk. Play activity blends into educational activity in another way. With girls, playing house and making candy moves into homemaking skills and eventually life experience preparation. With boys, the making of models may give way to shop activities which may in turn move into vocational preparation. It is not possible to divide play and school in the perception of the child or the mind of the modern teacher.

Because these children always strain the educational program, they are frequently cheated out of the extracurricular fun of a regular school. This is in reverse to the order of their need for such experiences. Clubs, special interest groups, and hobbies on a self-chosen basis are very useful to them. Sometimes the special teacher disregards the curricular-extracurricular difference: photography becomes the way to teach science and the school newspaper becomes the class in English. The program needs to include the elements which the regular schools find exciting to the pupils: organized sports, music, art, clubs, assemblies, and parties.

As in everything else, it is the subtle skill of the teacher which spells success or failure. One teacher conducts a self-choice reading club for poor readers; another has taught guitar to teenagers and organized a chorus in which it is an especial honor to gain membership. Dance offers both an art form and practice at body control. Under the umbrella of sportsmanship, a team will accept criticism and rules they flout otherwise —but always so much depends upon the "coach." Fiascos are to be expected at times even under the best leadership. It is well to remember that disturbed youngsters, because of their behavior, have come with a history of reduced participation in activities. They lack recognition of a desirable sort from such experiences. When the conduct of activities serves legitimate ego needs of children the effect is therapeutic.

The Classroom as a Group

Each class embodies a group life regardless of the teacher's conscious intent or plan. With disturbed youngsters a disturbed group life is to be anticipated. Members act out their unsatisfactory social roles. It is uncanny how rapidly each finds his relationship to the other, some sadistic and some passive. The irritating child needles his fellows. The undercover agitator actually stirs up trouble while seeming to be only an innocent observer. The unsophisticated gets caught. Together they tend to catalyze each other's difficulties. As a team they can easily create chaos or a bickering feud which wears down the adult. This is the reason there has been a tendency to avoid group activities and suppress group behavior. But this doesn't work because many of the pupils have, as a major component of their problem, group interactive failures.

Thus the special teacher is also a group worker. As a student of groups, the teacher studies roles and interactions. Such behavior is discussed with the group and with particular individuals when relevant.

But more than this, the teacher works to build positive group identification, which in turn provides the motive power for members, giving up negative influence as they find gratifications in membership. Basically the teacher uses three devices. One is the leadership role of the teacher around which, at the start, the positive aspects cling. This is our class, *viz:* "Mr. So-and-So's class"; this is the way *we* do things. Fairness within the pattern is emphasized. Any positive friendships or satisfying interrelationships are encouraged and pointed out, even though they may be brief. Finally, "fun together" is built into the program. There should be chances to go places and have experiences of such high gratification that the negative aspects are submerged for the time being. Thus, the class takes on a desirable image. It is a long hard pull but a condition some teachers meet intuitively while other teachers avoid it in fear. Group life is a curricular experience and should be so considered.

34. Curriculum and Disordered Behavior

WILLIAM C. RHODES

Education can add an important dimension to the existing approaches to emotionally and socially maladjusted children. Its basic human concerns and major human goals differ quite radically from those of the clinically oriented professions. It is not concerned with cure or eradication of pathology and disease. It has no pills, no chemicals, no tranquilizers to be administered to sick organisms. Its methods all address themselves to positive drives—drives toward knowing, learning, discovering, exploring. It is concerned with liberating and catalyzing positive energies, potentials and capacities within the human being.

Education implies a ready to be born capacity in man which can be addressed or stimulated from the outside. It is a process which mediates between nature and nurture, exciting the interaction of one upon the other to bring forth new ways of being and reacting. It is a way of reconciling and transcending the claims of the individual and the claims of the culture.

Jacques Maritain has said that, "To liberate the good energies is the best way of repressing the bad ones. . . ." and in this statement suggests the way in which education can provide a different dimension to approaches traditionally used with the socially, educationally and emotionally maladjusted child. The real art of education, he says, "is to make the child heedful of his own resources and potentialities for the beauty of well-being."

To repress bad energies by liberating good ones, to make the child heedful of his own resources and potentialities has nothing to do with the art of positive thinking. The teacher expects to encounter resistance in the emotionally disturbed or socially maladjusted child. There is tension and resistance in all teaching-learning transactions. Learning de-

SOURCE: *Exceptional Children,* XXX (October, 1963), 61–68. Reprinted by permission.

mands change and the human organism resists change. Part of the teaching function involves resolution and transformation of resistance to change.

Despite the reality of strong resistance within the emotionally or socially maladjusted child, we can make the same assumption about him that we do for the average child. There are forces for growth, for exploration, for discovery within him. These motivations are every bit as real as basic tissue drives associated with thirst, hunger, sex, etc. We must prepare the lessons we direct toward this child in such a way that we engage such motivation. We must handle our human encounter with the child in such a way that avoidance behavior gives way to approach behavior and the child reaches out for the lesson presented him.

What are the lessons that the teacher offers the emotionally and socially maladjusted child? A lesson is a preparation for a particular kind of experience which the child needs in order to make him aware of and use his own resources and potentialities; an experience which releases positive energies and behaviors to replace destructive or discordant energies and behaviors. The lessons concern themselves with all aspects of behavior needed for living—particularly those behaviors crucial to living in the home, the school, the group, the community. We know that there are substantive skill deficits in the school behavior of the socially and emotionally maladjusted child. However, these are not the only areas in which he is in need of lessons. We must capture him in subject matter, but we must also transform relationships with authority, communication with other people, concepts of self, into constructive and positive new experiences for him.

We must concentrate upon existing disjunctions between the child and culturally cherished social organizations such as home, school and community play units. We must locate, specify and re-create the site and conditions of his disjunction with the culture of these social organizations. The child is part of a social microcosm, with various acculturation media constantly harmonizing his demands with the demands of the culture. Within the organizational independence of each of these media are myriad opportunities for disjunctions between the demands of the child and those of the culture. If the particular disjunction occurs between the child and subculture of more than one of these organizations, we usually speak of emotional maladjustment. If it occurs outstandingly in the school, we usually speak of educational deficiency or educational maladjustment; and, if it is localized more particularly in the community, we talk about social maladjustment or juvenile delinquency.

The preparations for experiences at the site of the child's disjunctions form the crucial nucleus for the educational approach to the problems of emotional disturbance and juvenile delinquency. We should be guided by all we know about ways to prepare vital new experiences and ways to stabilize these in behavior. The form in which we plan the preparation and the patterning of the forms can be called the curriculum. The crux of the educational approach to emotional disturbance and juvenile delinquency, then, is contained in the preparations we make for the child to have constructive new experiences which will make him aware of and use his own resources, capacities and potentialities and which liberate positive motivations and behaviors within him. It is the experience—something actually happening to the child, within the child, in an important life episode—that is the heart of the educational task. In order to accomplish this task we must develop preparations which provide as ideal a medium as possible for the experience. We should have a set of guides or criteria against which to measure our preparation. These can be distilled, derived or evolved from the composite of educational principles and crucial "learning" experimentation of great educational theorists and psychological theorists concerned with educational problems. A series of these developed and tried by the author are offered below as a tentative statement of guidance. Concrete examples and brilliant application of one guide or the other were found in Froebel (1909), Itard (1962), Montessori (1912), Seguin (1907), James (1939), Wolpe (1958), Eysenck (1960), and Jones (1958).

The author's current position holds that in order for the preparation to have maximum power and efficiency in insuring the intended experience, all of the guides are important for a single preparation or a series of preparations.

Guides to Preparation for Experiences

1. We should prepare surroundings, circumstances, situations and events so that they excite new experiences in the child in relationship to old problems. We cannot act as though the child has had such an experience. We must conduct our preparations in ways that insure the experience. His responses will provide the cues to the quality and intensity of the experience and will provide suggestions to the teacher for additional preparation.
2. The preparations must continue to surround the child with opportunities for new experiences which would strongly engage such excitatory motives as adventure, conquest, achievement, exploration and discovery. The preparations might also associate the experience with positive satisfaction of tissue drives such as hunger, thirst and sex.
3. New experiences and newly developed abilities should ultimately be

imbedded in events and settings very similar to those in which the child's responses have previously been a problem to himself and to others. The teacher can gauge the extent of success in approximating problem settings by the extent of transfer of qualitatively new behaviors to old problem situations.

4. If the child strongly rejects or avoids an approximate replica of the site and conditions of his disjunction, the teacher should decrease the similarity of the replica to the life setting until the child begins to respond positively to the replica. The aspects of the replica can then be prepared gradually to simulate the problem setting. The rate of approximation can be adjusted to the reactions of the child. As long as there is approach and intensity in the child's responses, the degree of similarity can be increased. When there is avoidance or when there is rejection by the child, the degree of similarity should be decreased until avoidance and rejection disappear.
5. Learning should be an active process in which the child has to do something with materials, conditions and surroundings. The more activity and manipulation required, the better the opportunity for a meaningful experience.
6. To increase the probability of excitation of new experiences in the child, the preparation should involve the engagement of as many sensory channels as possible. As long as the child is responding favorably, the teacher may assume that the more sensory channels which can be engaged, the better the conditions for learning.
7. Learning requires repetition of experiences until new abilities and positive behaviors begin to stabilize. The repetitions should be pleasurable to the child and should involve constant new discovery. Preparation for repetition should be guided by the child's reactions. Rejection or rebellion would be a signal for caution. Continued rejection or avoidance would signal the need for change or termination. Approach and eagerness from the child would be a signal for the teacher to continue.
8. Preparations should include the child's control over those parts of the surroundings, circumstances or events which concern him most, or which he most wants to control. This control should be reduced only gradually as the child seems willing to relinquish it.
9. Preparations for experiences and development of new abilities should be channeled toward goals which the child cherishes and which can be culturally tolerated; and should always include elements which the child prizes.
10. The preparation for experiences should include natural and immediate consequences for the child's activity. The consequences should

grow out of the lesson and should occur as soon as possible after the child performs in the lesson. It is very important that consequences early in the learning sequence should be satisfying and stimulating to the child. The child's behavior will inform the teacher of the quality of the consequences.

11. The preparations should require only performances which are in line with the child's present level of ability and accomplishment. In stimulating new experiences in the child, the teacher should nudge the child slowly up the gradient of achievement as increased mastery and challenge is apparent in the child's functioning.
12. It is important that the preparation for an experience should attempt to stimulate the child's awareness of the experience as it relates to his resources and abilities. The teacher should find ways to help the child reflect back upon the experience and its meaning for him so that it is bound as a permanent record within him. The teacher must test this out in many ways to be sure that there has been cognitive assimilation of the experience.

Lesson Forms

There are many forms which the above preparations might take, and many patternings for the forms selected. I will discuss five forms which I have experimented with in curricula for socially, emotionally and/or educationally maladjusted children.

THE UNIT The unit is a special form of preparation to induce specific experiences in a child. The unit is built around a theme which has dramatic appeal to a boy or girl in a particular age range. It should be a theme which has endless possibility for exciting positive motivations such as adventure, conquest, achievement, mastery or exploration. It should be a theme broad enough to incorporate many methods, activities, situations, etc. It should also be able to touch intimately upon the problem area of each individual. The theme can either be a substantive one such as "The Pioneers," or a psychological one, such as "Fantasy." In either case we should weave together both substantive areas and psychological areas. Psychological areas would embrace hostility, family interactions, sex, love, triumph, etc.

The important orientation to keep in mind is that we are attempting to produce experiences in the child which will release and develop positive energies in place of negative ones and make him aware of and use his own resources and abilities in his future behavior. We are particularly interested in producing new positive experiences at the very site of his disjunctions with the culture. All of the preparations which have been discussed should go into the unit. You will remember that these include simulating circumstances in which the child has had difficulty, leading step by step, making the child very active, engaging many senses, repetition, giving the child a measure of control, utilizing goals and elements cherished by the child, providing for natural consequences, and beginning where the child is at the particular moment of the lesson. The purpose of the theme of the unit is to provide coherence, organization and intrinsic relationship of experiences for the child.

BEHAVIOR TRAINING This is a very old form which can best be exemplified in the methods used by Itard (1962) to retrain the wild boy of Aveyron to wear clothes, to eat "properly," to show affection for his guardian, to distinguish sounds and to sense temperature differences.

This form can be much more effective if it will make use of experimental findings in psychology. This approach to behavior problems is not new, but it fell into disrepute during the period of extensive development of psychotherapy as the only way to deal with disjunctions between the child and his settings. It is beginning to emerge again as a useful method for modification of behavior.

An old example of this form is the conditioning procedure used by M. C. Jones (1924). She worked with a child who feared a white rabbit and had generalized this fear to all white, furry objects. The fear was "unconditioned" by presenting the rabbit in the corner of the room while the child was eating, and slowly, over a period of days, moving the rabbit closer and closer. The child was gradually desensitized and the pleasure of eating seemed to have been associated with the rabbit.

A new example is the method used by Wolpe (1958). He evokes a response antagonistic to anxiety in a situation which is disturbing for a particular individual. The person is placed in the problem situation and Wolpe adds elements which produce anxiety-inhibiting responses such as anger, sexual excitement, relaxation, competing motor activity, and pleasure.

The method of behavioral retraining requires a careful specification of the problem setting or situation, the particular disjunctive behaviors involved and the behaviors which would be more successful for the individual in that setting or situation. One then re-creates crucial elements of the setting or situation; and establishes procedures which will extinguish disjunctive behaviors, substitute new behaviors in their place or accomplish both behavioral goals at the same time.

In this form, the teacher is concerned with behaviors of crucial importance to the child's functioning in important life settings such as home, school and community. The preparation must be thought through carefully, structured economically, focused clearly and aimed toward more specific goals than any other form. More detailed examples of this form are briefly reviewed in Rhodes (1962).

SKILL TRAINING Another form, and one which teachers know very well, is skill training. It concentrates on basic subject matter skills, play skills and skills in human interaction which we call "manners." All of the preparations for experiences are important in the skill areas. The only emphasis that is crucial here is that there be special effort to appeal to the excitatory motives such as adventure, discovery, exploration, achievement, etc.

DISCUSSION SESSIONS Discussion is a supplement to experience and a cognitive replica of experience. It can be accomplished in a group situation or a person-to-person situation. Discussion is experience-dependent and age related. The child needs to have reached a certain developmental level and accumulated sufficient experience before the discussion can be useful to him. Therefore, it appears to be more effective for children over nine or ten years of age than for younger children. It provides a stimulus to reflection and rumination which binds the experience within the child and makes it available to future behaviors.

Discussion cannot substitute for experience, but it can add new interpretations and reflections. It can provide a form for release of motivations toward knowing, learning, discovery and exploring. It can help make the child "heedful of his own resources and potentialities for the beauty of well-being."

GROUP INTERACTION This involves teacher utilization of the flexible dynamics of functioning groups. Such group interaction cuts across all settings of the child's life. It offers a natural laboratory within which the child is constantly having to respond and interact, and in which he receives constant and immediate feedback on his behavior. The group presents ideal conditions for new experiences and new learnings. All the excitation, cues, responses and rewards which he needs for new learnings are recurrently present. The sensitive problem areas in his functioning are constantly being stirred.

In the group the teacher has a succession of conditions and surroundings which require little structuring effort and a series of concrete behaviors which might be reflected back to the child. Having analyzed the necessary areas for release of the child's positive motivations and for creating an awareness of his own resources and abilities, the teacher can utilize the natural flow of events in the group to provide the appropriate lessons.

Now that I have talked about one kind of curriculum for socially, emotionally and educationally maladjusted children, let me raise an important issue for educators to consider.

The Issue of the Setting

While I believe that education has a unique contribution to make in this area, the contribution should not be bound to the stereotyped pattern of classroom or school. Teaching can and should occur in many settings. The more flexible the teacher is in being able to use many settings, the more influential the proposed curriculum could be. For instance, a truly effective teacher should be able to capture the junior gang member on the streets and offer needed lessons on street corners, in community centers, settlement houses, camps or parks. Teaching should be able, when necessary, to environ lessons with real life circumstances and should be able to make use of any setting or situation which would most likely engage and liberate positive motivations, potentials and capacities within the child at the very site of his disjunctions with the culture.

The only important criteria for the setting are: (a) how close is it to that in which the performance of the child will be crucial in the future; and (b) how effective is it in providing the right kind of nurture to catalyze the nature and resources of the child?

The Issue of Special Training

It is not possible, in a single article, to deal with all the problems of the emerging area of educational approaches to disjunctive behavior. There are differing points of view about special teacher preparation which may have been raised by this article. However, all of the major ideas contained here can be found in a good history of educational theory and concepts. The only exception might be newer concepts and methods of behavior training. This does not call for radically new training programs.

Historically, such great theorists as Herbart, Kant, Seguin, Montessori and James have left a permanent imprint upon the theory and method of education and psychology. Education and psychology already provide a substantive background for regular teacher training. It would seem, therefore, that the most parsimonious approach to teacher training in this special area would be a simple matter of making more effective use of this substantive background.

Summary

The central theme of this curriculum discussion is the contribution which education can make to the problems of social and emotional maladjustment. The suggested educational approach was based upon two statements of Jacques Maritain: (a) the best way to repress bad energies is to liberate good ones; and (b) the art of education "is to make the child heedful of his own resources and potentialities for the beauty of well-being."

It was suggested that these two concepts be incorporated into lessons needed by the individual delinquent or emotionally disturbed child. The lesson was defined as a preparation for intense, positive experience within situations, circumstances and conditions very similar to those in which the child has previously had trouble. The curriculum was presented as the form and pattern of forms which such preparations can assume. Several experimental forms were suggested. There are endless varieties and patterns of forms which could and should be tried. The ingenuity of the teacher will be one of the most crucial factors in their effectiveness.

References

Eysenck, H. J. (Ed.) *Behavior Therapy and the Neuroses.* New York, Oxford, London, Paris: Pergamon Press, 1960.

Froebel, F. *The Education of Man.* (Translated by W. N. Hailman.) New York: D. Appleton & Co., 1909.

Itard, J. M. G. *The Wild Boy of Aveyron.* New York: Appleton-Century-Crofts, Meredith Publishing Co., 1962.

James, W. *Talks to Teachers on Psychology.* New York: Henry Holt & Co., 1939.

Jones, H. G. "Neurosis and Experimental Psychology." *Journal of Mental Science,* 1958, *104,* 55–62.

Jones, M. C. "A Laboratory Study of Fear. The Case of Peter." *Pedagogical Seminary (Journal of Genetic Psychology),* 1924, *31,* 308–315.

Maritain, J. *Education at the Crossroads.* New Haven: Yale University Press, 1943.

Montessori, Maria. *The Montessori Method.* (Translated by Anne E. George.) London: William Heinemann, 1912.

Rhodes, W. C. "Psychological Techniques and Theory Applied to Behavior Modifications." *Exceptional Children,* 1962, *28,* 333–338.

SEGUIN, E. *Idiocy and Its Treatment.* New York: Columbia University, Teachers College Foundational Reprint, 1907.

WOLPE, J. *Psychotherapy by Reciprocal Inhibition.* Stanford, Cal.: Stanford University Press, 1958.

B. Techniques

35. Differential Teaching Techniques for Emotionally Disturbed Children

DONALD A. LETON

It is generally recognized that the school is an important agency in the field of mental health. However, there are divergent opinions on the specific role schools should assume.

Many educators hold that the responsibilities for mental health reside in the home and in community medical and social agencies, and not in the school. Such a view is likely to lead to policies of suspending or excluding pupils who are emotionally ill; this view may also lead to ignoring, not recognizing, and not identifying those who are emotionally disturbed. On the other hand there are educators who feel that the school should assume an active role in mental health through the regular curriculum, through special classes and special services, through identification procedures, and by co-operating in child guidance treatment.

Actually, all schools deal with emotionally disturbed and neurotic children in some manner. The children's clinics and voluntary agencies

SOURCE: *Mental Hygiene,* XLVIII (April, 1964), 209–16. Reprinted by permission.

have not been able to meet the needs for treatment and guidance services. The school is the only agency with compulsory obligations and responsibilities to serve the entire population of children. On the basis of the incidence of social and emotional maladjustment it can be anticipated that neurotic and disturbed children will be present in any given classroom.

The classroom experiences of these children will either be aggravating or ameliorative. The problems these children present to the classroom teachers are very complex, and there are no courses or practice teaching experiences in the teacher-education programs to prepare the teacher for this responsibility. This article will focus on this situation.

Review of the Literature

The lack of experimental research on the education of children with emotional illness stands in sharp contrast to the extensive interest in mental health. A number of institutional (3, 9, 13, 16) and public school programs (1, 10, 15) for emotionally disturbed children are described in the literature. A few studies (8, 12, 14) in which public school programs are subjected to research are reported. There are no experimental studies on hospital instruction for children with neuropsychiatric illness reported in the literature.

The most extensive programs of mental health in education are those of Bullis (1) and Ojemann (11). The human relations courses by Bullis and associates (2) have been used increasingly in regular classrooms throughout the country. The evaluation of these materials in supplementing the usual curricula, however, has been based largely on the users' opinions rather than on measures of the mental health of the students. Ojemann's approach (11) differs from that of Bullis in that the dynamics of human behavior are integrated into the curriculum. Basic teaching materials which illustrate this approach have been mimeographed and used in evaluative research.

One of the few experimental studies in the teaching of emotionally disturbed children in the elementary grades is that of Phillips and Haring (12). The effects of orderly, structured and control methods used in the experimental classrooms were compared to the effects of "usual" or permissive methods for other emotionally disturbed children who served as control subjects. Teachers' nominations were requested to identify the hyperactive, distractible, and withdrawn pupils. Since the nominations were based on behavioral characteristics, the identification procedures led to a heterogeneous group of emotionally disturbed. The criteria of effectiveness were teacher ratings of pre- and post-adjustment of the children.

A comprehensive evaluation of four approaches to mental hygiene was conducted by this writer (8). In an experiment utilizing eight experimental and eight control groups the following four approaches were evaluated: (A) Bullis's human relations classes (1); (B) Slavson's activity method (16); (C) sociodrama; and (D) mental hygiene films.

The subjects for the experiment were screened from the ninth grade classes of four high schools on the basis of adjustment scores. The selection procedure led to heterogeneity in the types of maladjustment represented in the experimental groups. The criteria for evaluation, which included school grades, attendance, and pre- and post-test scores on adjustment and personality inventories, failed to disclose any significant improvement in mental health. The experimental subjects did, however, regard the classes with favorable opinions, and also showed improvements in social distance scores. Measures on these latter criteria were not available for the control subjects.

Another study which utilized an experimental design was conducted by Rosenthal (14). A variety of mental health techniques were employed with an experimental class of 26 Negro students. A control class was matched for social and intellectual characteristics. The experimental class achieved significant gains in personality and social distance scores.

Most of the public school systems in the major cities in the country offer various classroom programs for the mental health of normal as well as emotionally disturbed children. Although there is a general lack of validating research, these programs reflect the widespread and genuine interest of educators. Hertzman (7), who served as a consulting psychiatrist in the Cincinnati, Ohio, schools, described the high school courses in human relations. Goldsmith, *et al.* (6) reported attempts in the educational treatment of delinquents for the New York City schools. The Los Angeles city schools have had "adjustment classes" for the educational management of socially and academically maladjusted students. References to programs in other cities also appear in the literature.

One of the major objectives of the Forest Hills Village Project (15) was to render mental health services through the schools and its associations. Even though this was a community project the schools were utilized as the major vehicle for conveying mental health education and services to parents and children.

Ferster and DeMeyer (5) carried out comprehensive analyses of the performance of autistic children and postulated experiential bases for behavior deficits. Ferster (4) then experimented with reinforcement procedures toward establishing meaningful behavioral responses in autistic children. He was successful in developing systematized complex responses using candy, music, and coins as reinforcers.

Although the autistic behavior was not generally extinguished, the fact that it was amenable to change through operant conditioning holds important significance for education. First, the theoretical origin of this approach is identified. Secondly, it is based on a functional analysis of behavior rather than on traditional psychiatric classifications. Finally, it leads to experimental procedures which can be evaluated in research.

The failure of these procedures to effect a general reduction of autistic behavior tends to invalidate the concept of reinforcement history and the socio-interactional aspects of this theory. The fact, however, that certain behavior of autistic children could be experimentally controlled may eventually have more significance for educational method than for personality theory.

Differential Teaching Methods

There is no agreement or common view among educators and psychiatrists that special teaching techniques or special educational treatments for emotionally disturbed children are valuable or necessary.

It is apparent that an emotional handicap tends to reduce the educability of the child but its precise effect on achievement and pupils' behavior is not very well-known or understood. Such symptoms as fear, withdrawal, anxiety, daydreaming, fantasy, emotional regression, and defensive lying may not be sufficiently apparent for the teacher's recognition and consideration. Also, the emotional needs of some disturbed children are satisfied through achievement performance, and the teacher may then overlook or fail to recognize this as a symptom.

The management of acting-out behavior, however, is undoubtedly the most difficult problem in teaching children with emotional disturbance. This behavior is usually boisterous, disruptive, and idiosyncratic. It is symptomatic in nature and may be observed in the majority of these children. To encourage or discourage this behavior in the classroom situation may actually serve to reinforce it. The child's expression of acting-out behavior may not have much therapeutic value, and it may actually serve further to alienate the child from his peers and from adults. Since this behavior is symptomatic it should probably not receive differential treatment in either educational or social groups. Specific educational treatments might provide negative or positive reinforcements toward its continuance.

In the course of the past four decades, there have evolved from the field of mental hygiene some concepts that are now commonly held in education and psychiatry. These would include such views as: (1) the creative expression of children should be encouraged; (2) children's interests and self-directed activities have educational value; (3) frustration and anxiety should be avoided because of their detrimental effect on personality; (4) drill and practice have a negative effect on motivation; (5) teaching should be directed toward the whole child; and (6) activity is healthy.

These are just a few such concepts which prevail. They have their origins in both theory and research, and, in general, they seem to represent sound principles for the education of normal children. Educational practices have, to a large extent, been based on and justified by these concepts. In the teaching of emotionally disturbed children, however, they may actually be ineffective and also detrimental to the mental health of the particular child.

The following chart lists some of these general views and their sources. It also presents the specific arguments against their use for particular types of emotionally disturbed children.

GENERAL CONCEPTS IN TEACHING FOR MENTAL HEALTH

General view	*Rationale or source*	*Argument against*
Creative expression of the child should be encouraged.	Psychoanalytic theory, projection of emotional problems and conflict.	An emotionally insecure child may be made more insecure. An insecure child would lack initiative and spontaneity for creative expression. Imitative expression may serve better to fulfill dependency needs.
Children's interests and self-directed activities have educational value.	Progressive education and pragmatic philosophy.	The self-directed activities of a compulsive child are neither educational nor therapeutic. The interests of a child who is emotionally preoccupied would be too restricted to guide a child's educational experiences.

GENERAL CONCEPTS IN TEACHING FOR MENTAL HEALTH (*cont.*)

General view	*Rationale or source*	*Argument against*
Frustration and anxiety should be avoided because of detrimental effect on personality.	Clinical evidence and animal experimentation on conditioning and neuroses.	The constitutional psychopath would show shallow anxiety and intolerance to frustration. Efforts might be directed to heighten anxiety and improve tolerance to frustration.
Drill and practice have a negative effect on motivation.	Experiments in school learning.	A child with neurological impairment affecting kinesthetic or perceptual abilities may enjoy and profit from specific drill or practice. Repetition may improve neurochemical and metabolic efficiency.
Teaching should be directed toward the "whole child."	Organismic theory and evidence on the interrelatedness of physical systems.	A child with a segmental disability resulting from neural lesions or dysfunction is not a "whole child" in the usual sense of this term. Educational and psychiatric treatment may be directed toward development of assets rather than total function.
Activity is healthy.	Child development: maturation is based on nurture and *activity*.	A hyperactive child, for whom behavior is emotionally or organically driven, may need medical or environmental constraint over activity. Organity may require "containment" and physical support for physical security.

It can be seen in the above chart that the general principles relating to mental hygiene in the schools have come from a variety of sources and that they are now represented in a variety of curriculum practices. For specific cases, however, these general principles would not hold for children who are emotionally disturbed. The historical tendency has been to establish these general principles or concepts in mental health education and then to apply them to all children through the curriculum. For purposes of this discussion this might be defined as a deductive approach to mental health teaching.

In contrast, this paper proposes an inductive approach. This assumes that there are individual and group differences in the educational needs of children which are based on psychological and constitutional factors. The varying influences of these factors should require the development of different objectives and different techniques.

An attempt to illustrate the differential inductive approach to teaching emotionally disturbed children is shown in the chart.

The above chart does not detail the specific kind of teaching behavior or curriculum activity which should effect the intended objectives. Before proceeding with the curriculum application, perhaps the theoretical validity of the recommendations should be considered.

There are two obvious deficiencies to this kind of "cookbook" approach to mental health. The first criticism is that personality classifications of emotionally disturbed children are not sufficiently valid or distinct to serve as a basis for curriculum objectives. The classification of children on the basis of psychiatric categories is of questionable value for educational purposes. The problem, however, is that differential treatments should be based on differential diagnoses of some kind. Discrimination in the choice of therapeutic or educational methods is possible only with a distinct qualitative classification for the child.

A second criticism relates to the separation of functions, or the partition of the individual according to aspects of his development. It is recognized that intellectual, social, and emotional development are not discrete and independent processes. To account for the interrelationships of functions, however—through pairing or conjoining of several related functions—would require more distinctions than are currently listed.

A third criticism would be that this approach does not recognize differences in the dynamics of emotional development. The question arises as to whether certain groups of children could be classified on the basis of similarity in emotional history, or in the dynamics of their adjustments to emotional experience. Still others might question the validity of this model in that it does not give direct consideration to ego and superego processes and libidinal needs.

Areas of function	Classifications	
	Organic CNS impairment	*Obsessive compulsive*
Intellectual	Help direct and maintain attention. Reinforce through repetition. Emphasize overlearning of simpler essential concepts.	Expand attention from preoccupation. Expand concept. Introduce new learning. Adaptive learning.
Emotional	Help form a stable identification. Deepen or intensify feelings. Help child to a cognizant awareness of feeling. Help child to moderate extreme expressions of emotion.	Desensitize or recondition fear or anxiety responses. Identify and reflect feelings, needs, expression. Widen emotional security.
Social	Limit social interactions to those the child can contain. Teach respect for few; to generalize to more.	Create new social patterns through different peer relationships.
Speech and language	If dysphasic, promote oral and written vocabulary.	Limit verbal expression of compulsive patterns. Diminish repetitive responses.
Perceptual	Employ kinesthetic cues. Intensify sensory stimuli where there is associational loss.	Broaden perceptual field. Indicate emotional influences which alter fear and compulsive patterns.
Kinesthetic	Determine scope of movement skills. Reinforce physical skills. Develop patterns for new skill; e.g., learn by tracing. Work from gross toward finer physical movements. Physically supportive contacts.	Encourage gestural expression. Promote physical participation in games, dance, etc.

of Personality

Autistic	*Depressive withdrawal*	*Negativistic*
Arouse attention for learning stimuli. Teach problem-solving. Reinforce infantile expression at level of development.	Externalize attention to develop interests. Introduce new learning materials.	Allow independent discovery and learning. Indirect guidance through material. Teach critical thinking.
Encourage overt expression of feeling. Help child obtain real satisfaction through vicarious means—reading, writing, magic, etc. Bring out symbolic expression of fantasies.	Uncover conflicts. Overt expression of anger. Expressive release.	Avoid feeling expressions. Focus negative reaction at socially acceptable targets.
Establish firm dependency relationship to adult. Transfer to other adults and children.	Attempt single and sincere association. After relationship is formed, encompass several other friendships and activities.	Extend social skills. Reflect behavior which leads to social acceptance or rejection.
Increase vocal expression—laughing, mimicry, and vocal communication.	If speech is slow and language stilted, tempo increase.	Help child to verbalize feelings—negativism in oral expression.
Have child relate to material environment.	Extend perceptual field.	Objectify perceptual field.
Gesture and postural expression. Contact through holding hands, walking, pat on shoulder.	Supportive approval of movement and posture. Work from fine physical movements to gross participation; reaching to climbing—stepping to hopping.	Move from aggressive physical actions to constructive—example: cutting, papier-mâché, etc.

Perhaps the best way to evolve an acceptable model before proceeding to its testing would be to have a number of authorities propose differential treatments or objectives, using other dimensions. The relationships or agreements among objectives indicated in the cells could then be analyzed for common factors.

If mental health authorities and educators could arrive at a mutually acceptable model, the educator would still be faced with the task of determining what teaching actions and curriculum activities would best effect the objectives.

There are two contradictory viewpoints in regard to translating objectives into methods: The first of these holds that after the teacher learns the appropriate objective for the child's emotional growth—and perhaps also knows the principle or theoretical basis from which it was evolved—she will be able to select the appropriate curriculum activity and act in such a manner that the objectives can be realized.

The other viewpoint is that even though the teacher may know the objective and its theoretical source, she would still be at a loss to determine the subsequent teaching and curriculum actions. To illustrate this problem further, it is probable that any given instructional activity would result in a different curriculum experience for different pupils, because of the manner in which the teacher presented it and also because of the particular perceptions and interpretations of the pupil.

If differential education can be employed on an experimental basis, it is possible that a functional classification of emotionally disturbed children on the basis of their educational characteristics may eventually be established.

References

1. Bullis, H. Edmund, "An Educational Program for the Development of the 'Normal' Personality," *American Journal of Psychiatry,* 109 (November, 1952), 375–77.
2. Bullis, H. Edmund, *Human Relations in the Classrooms, Courses I, II, III* (Wilmington, Del.: State Society for Mental Hygiene, 1947).
3. Devereux, George, *Therapeutic Education* (New York: Harper & Bros., 1956).
4. Ferster, C. S., "Positive Reinforcements and Behavioral Deficits of Autistic Children," *Child Development,* 32 (September, 1961), 437–56.
5. Ferster, C. S. and M. K. DeMeyer, "A Method for the Experimental Analysis of the Behavior of Autistic Children," *American Journal of Orthopsychiatry,* 32 (January, 1962), 89–98.

6. GOLDSMITH, JEROME M., *et al.*, "Changing the Delinquent's Concept of School," *American Journal of Orthopsychiatry,* 29 (April, 1959), 249–65.
7. HERTZMAN, JACK, "Human Relations in the Classroom," *American Journal of Orthopsychiatry,* 26 (July, 1956), 635–42.
8. LETON, DONALD A., "An Evaluation of Group Methods in Mental Hygiene," *Mental Hygiene,* 41 (October, 1957), 525–33.
9. MORENO, J. LAND and ZERKA TOEMAN, "The Group Approach in Psychodrama," *Sociometry,* 5 (May, 1942), 191–95.
10. OJEMANN, RALPH H., "School-Community Programs," *Review of Educational Research,* 26 (December, 1956), 479–501.
11. OJEMANN, RALPH H., *et al.,* "The Effects of a 'Causal' Teacher-Training Program on Certain Curricular Changes on Grade-School Children," *Journal of Experimental Education,* 24 (December, 1955), 95–114.
12. PHILLIPS, E. L. and N. G. HARING, "Results from Special Techniques for Teaching Emotionally Disturbed Children," *Exceptional Children,* 24 (October, 1959), 64–67.
13. REDL, FRITZ and DAVID WINEMAN, *The Aggressive Child* (Glencoe, Ill.: Free Press, 1957).
14. ROSENTHAL, SHELDON, "A Fifth-Grade Classroom Experiment in Fostering Mental Health," *Journal of Child Psychiatry, 2,* (1952), 302–29.
15. SEELEY, JOHN R., "The Forest Hills Village Project," *Understanding the Child,* 23 (October, 1954), 104–10.
16. SLAVSON, S. R., *An Introduction to Group Therapy* (New York: Commonwealth Fund, 1943).
17. SLAVSON, S. R., *The Practice of Group Therapy* (New York: International Universities Press, 1947).

36. Conveying Essential Messages to the Emotionally Disturbed Child at School

Ruth G. Newman

The phrase—the emotionally disturbed child—is used to cover a multitude of miseries: the child who sits and stares off in space; the bully who makes other children miserable and who cannot stand the least bit of criticism or attack himself; the child with the 140 IQ who never gets his work done and who can't learn to read; the child who crouches by the wall on the playground, so shy, he does not even dare look longingly at the group playing kickball for fear the teacher will urge him to play; the child who gets the weeps every time an adult speaks to her; the child who flies into a tantrum when someone else is first in line; the child who, having done something wrong, flees down the school hall and out the door in panic; the child who does well academically, but gets so nauseated every morning at eight thirty that she cannot get to school; and, of course, the child who so discumbobulates the class and the teacher by clowning or breaking, fighting or tearing apart, that both he and the school feel that hours spent in the classroom are an utter horror and complete failure.

A Portmanteau Term

Granted that "emotionally disturbed" is a portmanteau term, ranging from severe crippling to the minor "slings and arrows of outrageous fortune," it nonetheless is a term that eliminates many other kinds of disabilities. For instance, although an emotionally disturbed child may,

SOURCE: *Exceptional Children,* XXVIII (December, 1961), 199–204. Reprinted by permission.

and often does, test at a minuscule level, he possesses a basic intelligence, potentially capable of learning at his own age level. Thus, though his behavior may sometimes parallel that of the mentally defective, especially since the mentally defective have as great a range of behavior patterns as anyone else, his problems are not the same as those of the retarded. The term does not, in itself, include the physically handicapped or organically damaged, though these children, too, may and frequently do suffer severe emotional disturbances.

Both the defective and the physically handicapped may benefit from the therapeutic teaching methods devised from the understanding of the emotionally disturbed. Likewise, the emotionally disturbed may profit from the application of methods found useful with the retarded or the brain damaged. It is not necessary to exclude areas of overlap, for those are areas where the findings in one aspect of a disabled child are helpful in working with a child whose disability is different. Yet because of the history of the work done with the disturbed child, the mingling and mixing of techniques and groupings, theories and approaches have often befogged the primary issues and thus failed to get at the source of the problem and to treat it. Although an antihistamine may relieve symptoms of the flu, it doesn't cure it.

It has been our custom for practical reasons, and until recently for reasons of ignorance, to lump all disabilities in the same "special class" in a school. And sometimes the emotionally disturbed child does seem better. He has been removed from the pressures of a large, normal group. Some of the new methods and approaches may attract or fit him. The specialness of the situation, itself, may fill a basic need. The structure of the special class setting may quiet much of his symptomatic misbehavior. Moreover (and let's face it, this fact is as operative as any other), he has been taken out of the hair of some teacher who has been trying to teach a class and has been prevented from doing so because of his presence. In the special class where odd behavior is a premise, the teacher feels called upon to try to handle him, if only custodially.

But all this is not actually dealing with the emotionally disturbed child's basic difficulties in the classroom. Symptoms, not causes, are being handled, and the apparent improvement may be illusory or temporary, in which case the illness may break out later in a form more difficult to reach. Sedation is fine, but if the headache comes back to hamper and haunt when the aspirin is gone, we had best look to the cause.

Many School Settings Available

Once he has been properly diagnosed, there are many school settings in which the emotionally disturbed child can be therapeutically handled, if his ills and his total life climate are adequately appraised. A certain kind of emotionally disturbed child can work best in a regular school class under a skilled teacher who has adequate supervision and support from the principal and from trained consultants. This is especially true where the child, while attending school, is being given individual treatment by a professional, connected with the school or outside, but one who is able to work closely with the teacher and the child's parents. Another child cannot do well in an ordinary public school but needs the protection of a small and especially programmed private school, be it a day school or a boarding school. And then there is the child who cannot function at any kind of regular school, no matter how well programmed, even with the additional help of psychiatrist, psychologist, or social worker. Such a child may require a special class or, when the case is extreme, a residential treatment center—of which there are all too few.[1]

In appraising the entire range of school settings which includes emotionally disturbed children, from a regular class to an intensive, total-treatment residential center with a school program, certain basic principles become clear. Without an awareness of these principles and without grappling with their implications, though children may be maintained in a school setting and may even make some progress, their basic disturbance and potential for health and growth is only being met accidentally, and its success cannot be duplicated for the use of other children.

Then, let us assume that the aim of a school program for the emotionally disturbed is to do its appropriate part in treating the child along with other forms of treatment, such as individual therapy, group work, program planning, and work with the child's parents (very intensive work if the child lives at home). Let us assume—and it would be the golden age of work with the emotionally disturbed if this assumption

[1] Because an intensive scrutiny of the extreme case of human behavior and dynamics often leads to a clearer understanding of the entire range of difficulties, the six-year study of the severely disturbed, hyperactive boys between the ages of nine and fourteen in total residential treatment at the National Institute of Mental Health provided many insights into the learning and school adjustment difficulties of emotional disturbance. The Child Research Branch, which operated from 1954 to 1960, was under the direction of Dr. Fritz Redl. It devoted itself to the study of the total life of the hyperactive child; i.e., his daily program, his internal and external difficulties, and forms of treatment, as well as his learning and school problems. The children selected for a long-term treatment program, which was one of three programs developed, had been, along with their other ills, completely and utterly unable to make a go of any school program whatsoever. For three years they attended a specially planned school on the hospital ward. For two years thereafter, they were introduced to carefully selected schools in the community. The clinical staff worked closely with the teachers and principals of these schools and gave the children and the teachers sufficient support so that these boys could both learn and, for the most part, maintain themselves in school without damage to themselves, their classmates or teachers.

were in fact realized in the majority of cases—that communication is good among all aspects of the child's treatment life, all the varied disciplines and people involved. Let us assume that there are united goals, no matter how different the approaches and the language used to express these goals by the various disciplines represented.

Moreover, let us assume that these overall goals maintain the hope that the child will change in the direction of increasing success in living, increasing awareness of his worth, increasing ability to realize his assets and accept his limitations, increasing ability to independently function and at the same time ask for, and use, help from adults and peers. We can further hope that he will ultimately become aware of the fact that he has something to give and something to receive and that though frustrations come, gratifications come also, and future rewards can be more satisfying than immediate gratification.

Basic Principles

If these are the goals, there are some basic principles of which all people concerned in the treatment of the emotionally disturbed child will be aware. The school people particularly, administrator, teacher, tutor, and supervisor, will have to work daily with these principles and focus upon them in the long, hard, discouraging, one-step-backward, two-steps-forward course from illness to health.

THE EMOTIONALLY DISTURBED CHILD CAN LEARN The emotionally disturbed child has already learned. He has already learned many unfortunate and unhappy things that have interfered with what we, society, would like him to learn. What we would like him to learn cannot be learned without the presence of a complex of factors; factors involving such things as the mental health of his parents, or at least one parent, of his and his parents' physiological health, their economic and physical situations, their conflicts and concerns, their needs and deprivations, their manner of handling life and the manner in which life has handled them, their constitutional make-up, and their economic and cultural opportunities. In any event, these children have not had the climate to teach them what we would like them to learn. Look deeply into any case history of a severely emotionally disturbed child, and you will be surprised that the child survived at all. In accordance with the human organism's adaptive ability, these children have learned what life has taught them about people, objects, danger, helplessness, terror, and survival.

EXTINCTION OF OLD PATTERNS Extinction of old patterns, even in the simpler instances of lower animals, is never as simple as that comfortable *tabula rasa* on which one prints precisely what one wants to print. The old learnings of these children have come out of bitter experiences with the world and the people in it—experiences not so readily ignored. For indeed the behavior patterns that these children have developed for themselves, be it intense withdrawal into a world of their own making or hostile attack, or diffuse, ill-coordinated stabs at the environment, have been the only way they have had to deal with the problems that beset them. To relinquish these tools for survival, regardless of how uneconomical, how unhappy, how inappropriate and self-defeating they may be, simply because we ask them to do so, is an absurd simplification of human processes. To any self-respecting emotionally disturbed child relinquishing these tools seems stupid, blind and consequently enraging or ridiculous just as if we were to ask a man to jump from a plane using a parachute with a broken shroud.

DEMONSTRATION OF NEW PATTERNS We in the school program need to demonstrate to the emotionally disturbed child over and over again that his old learnings are no longer valid, his situation is different, the adults in it are different, and the old patterns are not workable, useful, or necessary. We need to demonstrate that the world is not totally hostile, that adults are not necessarily ungratifying and untrustworthy, that he, the child, is not hopeless, or unacceptable no matter what he does and that hope exists in the world without ultimate disappointment. We need to convince him that a realistic evaluation of who he is and what he can and cannot do, while pretty terrifying to contemplate, has its gains and its rewards and that adults can help him with skills he wants so that with these skills he can feel less helpless and can elicit respect and love.

REINFORCEMENT OF NEW LEARNING Until such a constant demonstration of a benign world gets through to him, saturates him, and is reinforced day after day, there is no reason to expect that unlearning will take place and that we can extinguish the perception of the world as malevolent. Until we succeed in this task he will revert to his natural mode of reacting as surely as a Pavlov dog salivates at the ring of a bell until the effect of the bell ring has been extinguished by removing its reward and transferring it to some other stimulus. Until that time, there is not much hope that the new methods of handling anything that life offers will be available to him. He will not even give them an honest try. This does not mean we don't keep indicating by demonstration, not talk, alternate modes of behavior. It merely means they will not click until the kaleidoscope of his life has been shaken up and he sees the world with new colors and pieces.

How do we convey the message that school is a benign place to a child who thinks the whole world is a dreadful place and school the ultimate in dreadfulness? School is the place where all your faults shine through, where you are challenged and exposed, where you have to wait when you can't wait, sit still when you must move, keep quiet when you must scream, or let someone go ahead of you when you must be first. Further, you must share the teacher when you can't share so much as a chocolate bar, do something over and over when you can't even do it the first time, follow a direction when you don't hear a direction, do things the way people say when you are too angry to do what anybody says, love your neighbor when you can't even love yourself, think when your mind wanders, listen to an adult droning on about something you're not interested in when your thoughts are creating fantasies of power, violence, or escape.

SCHOOL IS A PLACE WHERE GRATIFICATIONS EXIST Somehow, day after day, regardless of the subject matter being used—blocks, paints, books, wood, arithmetic, writing, clay or songs—each small part of the whole daily school design must convey the information that gratifications exist. At first the gratifications must come immediately in the wake of the task. Later the interval between the problem and its fulfillment can lengthen out. At first the task must bring with it success, no matter how easy the job. Later the success can be postponed. Some errors can be encompassed on the way to success, some snags met and handled. Part of the reward of tolerating frustration need not be verbalized; it just happens that the subject matter becomes more interesting and involving as more frustration can be tolerated. The timing on this problem is tricky, for if one waits too long the child properly feels belittled and contemptuous of the teacher as well as of himself.

SCHOOL IS A PLACE WITH A PREDICTABLE ENVIRONMENT The school must convey the message that it is a place the child can handle, because it is a place that can handle the child. This means that a structure exists, no matter at what level or what the personal design of the teacher, in relation to the child's needs. This structure is maintained and the teacher indicates clearly, and without guilt, that certain things can go in school, certain things cannot, and that school is a place of safety and learning. In other words, the structure relays the message that what is appropriate at school at a given period, despite the effort for the child, is less boring in school than out of school.

SCHOOL AS A PLACE WHERE HELP IS AVAILABLE School becomes a place where personal interests can be explored and developed. It is a place where help is available to get something going that a child wants to get going, and to get it completed once started. There is help not to mess up, tear up, destroy relationships, work, or sense of adequacy. The amount of help needed may be enormous—to make a boat out of two pieces of wood may take 90 percent of the teacher's effort and 10 percent of the child's. If the task is important to the child, and if it is important that the child see a completed task in one school period at this time, then it is of no concern that the boat is more the teacher's creation than the child's. Later, more and more of the job will be left to the child. Later, more tasks can be begun one day and completed in two, three, or even more days. The importance of the task lies in the message that the teacher conveys to the child about adults, school, work, effort, and about his own abilities to come through.

TIMING IN REFERENCE TO PROPS There is a time for extra supports and a time for no supports. This whole complicated message cannot be conveyed at once. There are times for definitions to be marked according to the child's ability to receive the definitions. A child badly frightened of the very thought of a school room or teacher may well have to spend the first few weeks carrying with him the comic books that later will not be permitted in school as inappropriate. The child whose identity is tied up with an object at a given period of time may well have to bring the water pistol to school just to hold even if he misuses it and, as a result, is bounced from school. He may need the match sticks or the marbles for whatever magical, protective, or enhancing meanings they have to him. In a while, when the reality has come through that school is not necessarily a terrifying place but instead a place to learn with a teacher who will help, all these props will be excluded along with other inappropriate and no longer necessary behavior.

TIMING IN REFERENCE TO SELF-IMAGE There is a time to tell a child about the self-image he conveys. For a while it may be necessary to allow the child to come to school ill-clothed, shirt unbuttoned, belt unfastened, shoes off, socks not matching and not too clean in order to put across the message that the child himself, no matter how unattractive he thinks himself to be and no matter how unattractive he makes himself is acceptable. To let this go on too long, however, is to convey a poor message, one that says, I don't care how you look, or, anything's good enough for me, or, this doesn't matter. Therefore, when the initial message has been imprinted, the teacher will not allow unfastened belts, unbuttoned shirts, unmatching socks, or unshod feet.

For a while, when the child may be struggling to give up some of his violent physical aggression, he may replace it with language that even the teacher has never before heard. He has to be told this won't do, when the words are said so loudly or so hostilely they can't be ignored. But unless the dirty language itself upsets or excites the child and the class, he may be allowed to stay in class. Later, he will most certainly be removed, because language has its appropriate places, and this language doesn't go in school any more than hitting or kicking go in school. Group reaction, group contagion, specific offensiveness to a particular teacher will determine the timing, when things are no longer tolerated, just as much as the child's own personal needs. It is not useful to the child any more than it is to the rest of the group for him to feel he can powerfully destroy the purposes and meaning of school. At that point, the message that the child can handle school, because the school can handle him, breaks down. Letting too much go by is as poor a communication in his unlearning of old perceptions as is deprivation.

EXPECTED BACK-SLIDING Finally it grows clear that the message, that school is not what the child thought it was when he came, gets through. He is upset by this new perception and doesn't know what to do with it. He tries all his old tricks, out of habit, yes, but also to defend himself against the need to create new ways of responding. Behavior may appear much the same, but the tone of the behavior has changed sufficiently so that the teacher and clinical staff are aware that a difference exists.

ENTER—REALITY ABOUT SELF At this time new learning messages take place. The school, with its defined structure, now is used to define the child for himself, to point out his assets, and also his limitations. He is not superman, not all-powerful; his grandiose ideas for undertaking a project can't work but if he can shave them down to reality-size they can be put into action. A fantasy is fine, but to translate a fantasy into reality requires making the fantasy life-size. One cannot take a tour of the United States looking for turtles simply because one identifies with turtles but one can read about turtles, make maps of the places they live, and find out about these places from books and films. To do even this, skills are needed—one must learn how to read at a certain level, how to look at and use maps, and learn new words. This takes work. It doesn't just come; it comes with help and work. With this work and help, one can grow more able, stronger, less helpless, and more realistically knowledgeable. It may be that a child is terrible at spelling but possesses a genuine skill at manipulating figures and such work goes fast and seems easy and satisfying. Children are in school to explore their own abilities and to increase themselves.

ENTER—REALITY ABOUT THE TEACHER The teacher is there not to shame or expose but to help where it is needed because he wishes the child to be adequate and he feels he can be, no matter how many mess-ups and mistakes are made en route. He seems not to take the mistakes as seriously as the child. Mistakes are necessary in learning something new and not simply an indication that a child is stupid, worthless, and hopeless. Therefore, when a child has messed up beyond belief on Monday by using bad language, destroying the lesson plan, or getting into a fight with a classmate, he can still start fresh on Tuesday without dirty looks, warning fingers, or resentful reminders. After repetitive demonstrations of all the above amazing phenomena about school and the teacher, it is hardly worthwhile to keep "messing up." He may try (frightening though it may be at first) to respond to encouragement with faith instead of despair, to stick five minutes longer with the work that always seems too hard, to listen to the directions that are given.

The hand on the shoulder that so scared the child for months may not mean the teacher is going to trap him, pull him close only to turn against him, or demand a closeness which the child can't tolerate. The hand may just be there to give reassurance, encouragement, or a silent warning that the child's behavior is going off bounds. It may be a support, not a trap. The hand may, in time, feel good, and the child will be able to answer with a smile instead of a scowl, curse, or punch.

THE CONVALESCENT EMOTIONALLY DISTURBED CHILD When these messages are conveyed to the emotionally disturbed child and when, given time, patience, and opportunities for back-sliding, he has developed his own new patterns of feeling and responding, he will learn at school as other children learn. That is to say, he will have his good days and his bad, his easy subjects and his hard ones, his personal dislikes of teachers and peers, and his personal loves.

Often when a child is over the major hump of disease, we tend not to allow him the margin for error and regression that we give any ordinary youngster. We grow wary of any lapse. To be watchful and supportive is a good thing. To be wary and distrustful is another. Our very wariness and anxiety may become an unuseful message to convey. The convalescent emotionally disturbed child has a right to the same mistakes the rest of us make, to the same time lag between a new fact and its assimilation. With a reasonable amount of faith, watchfulness, support, and continued interest, once he has stabilized his new perceptions, he not only can, but should, be handled in the same way as other children, without an overdose of specialness.

Summary

It is true that the treated emotionally disturbed child lives with scar tissue. It is true that damages leave their mark. But who does not grow up with damages of some sort? It is true that life may again present him with conditions which may throw him back into his old perceptions temporarily or permanently. But we cannot guarantee that life will not throw the healthiest of us, nor can we know for certain our saturation point.

On the one hand, it may be that he will break again under too much pressure. On the other, it may be that emotional scar tissue is stronger than new tissue and that, just because of his past experiences and his new insights and ability to suffer through storms, he may have greater strength than most. It is the initial communication center that sends the clearest messages, and if, by our demonstration, we have made extinct the original messages, have made them untrue for the child, unuseful and inappropriate, and if we have given reinforcement to more useful patterns and perceptions, the child will choose the patterns most useful to him in living his life.

37. A Project to Teach Learning Skills to Disturbed, Delinquent Children

SALVADOR MINUCHIN, PAMELA CHAMBERLAIN, AND PAUL GRAUBARD

This paper will describe a pilot project conducted at the Floyd Patterson House, a community residential treatment center for juvenile delin-

SOURCE: *American Journal of Orthopsychiatry,* XXXVII, No. 3 (April, 1967), 558–67. Copyright, the American Orthopsychiatric Association, Inc. Reprinted by permission.

quents. The project was designed to explore certain hunches and experiences of the authors after extensive work with multiproblem lower-class families.

It has been our experience that the psychological disturbance of the children in such families almost always is accompanied by lack of achievement in school and academic subjects, despite individual intelligence tests showing that some children are of normal or superior intelligence. It was felt that an exploration of the learning style of the disturbed delinquent not only would help us discover ways of teaching the disturbed child, but also might bring to light evidence about ways of teaching his psychologically healthier but equally nonachieving siblings and peers.

The authors of this paper also were interested in exploring the feasibility of a model of interdisciplinary collaboration between clinician and educator. In this project the clinician, whose background and orientation included work in social psychiatry and family therapy, developed a profile of the cognitive-affective style of the children of disorganized low socioeconomic families. This profile was developed in such a way that it helped the educators in the project develop an intervention or repairing curriculum which made it feasible to teach these children.[1] This paper will, therefore, be organized in two sections. The first section will present an overview of (1) socialization processes in the disorganized low socioeconomic family as gathered through the psychiatrist's tools and (2) some of the assumptions about the influence of these processes on the learning style of the child and his encounters with school. The second part will describe the intervention curriculum and the pilot project which was developed to explore ways of enabling these children to learn.

Socialization Processes in the Disorganized Low Socioeconomic Family [2]

We will (1) summarize certain family interactions that contribute to disturbances in focal attention of the child and (2) delineate characteristics of the communication patterns in the child.

1. Parents' responses to children's behavior are global and erratic

[1] For a review of the literature, see the December, 1965 issue of the *Review of Educational Research*, Vol. 35, 5.

[2] This section has been elaborated further in a paper entitled *Psychoanalytic Therapies and the Low Socio-Economic Population*, by S. Minuchin, M.D.

and, therefore, deficient in conveying rules which can be internalized. The parental emphasis is on the control and inhibition of behavior rather than on guiding and developing responses. The unpredictability of parental controlling signals handicaps the child's development of rules. Since the child cannot determine what part of his behavior is inappropriate, he learns to search out the limits of permissible behavior through inspection of the parents' mood responses. He learns that the rules of behavior are directly related to the power or pain of an authoritarian figure.

Lacking norms to regulate behavior, and caught in experiences which hinge on immediate interpersonal control, the children need continuous parental participation to organize interpersonal transactions. Because of the undifferentiated qualities of the parent-child style of contact, these transactions are generally ineffective and perpetuate a situation in which an overtaxed mother responds erratically to a confused child. The child then behaves in ways which will reorganize his "known" environment: controlling contact by the mother. Thus, the child learns to search the immediate reaction of others for clues to the solution of conflict situations, and remains relatively unexercised in the use of focal attention for observing himself as causal in a situation, or in learning how to differentiate the specific characteristics of a situation.

2. In the disorganized low socioeconomic family there is a deficit of communication of information through words and the attendant rules which regulate the communicational flow. In the overcrowded and overburdened living conditions of these large families the adults pay little attention to the requests and needs of individual children. The children in turn accept the fact that their words by themselves will not be heard. In the development of the necessary techniques for making their needs known, the children discover that intensity of action or sound is more effective than the power or cogency of an argument.

Transactions involving power operations occupy a large part of family interaction, and the ranking of each other can occur around an infinite variety of subjects. The attempt is made to resolve conflict by a series of escalated threats and counterthreats. The conflict itself is unresolved and will appear and reappear in other contexts.

Diffuse affect is communicated through kinetic modifiers such as pitch and intensity of voice tone, grimaces, and body movements. In the resolution of conflict it often seems that it is unnecessary to hear the content of what is being transacted. Specific subject matter rarely is carried to a conclusion. It is unusual for more than two family members to participate in an interaction around a specific point. A topic usually is interrupted by a disconnected intervention of another family member. Since interactions usually revolve around issues of interpersonal accommodation, the "subject matter" can shift abruptly without changing the nature of the interpersonal conflict that is being negotiated.

The end result is a style of communication in which people do not expect to be heard and, therefore, assert themselves by yelling. There is a lack of training in elaboration of questions to gather information or garner the nuances of degree. There is also lack of training in developing themes to their logical conclusion, and there is no closure on conflicts. This communication style can be entirely adequate for the transactions of gross power and nurturing relationships, but it is insufficient to deal with chronic and subtle conflicts requiring the search for, ordering of, and sharing of different or new information.

There is an interaction effect (1) between the style of control exercised by the parents, which consists primarily of immediate but erratic reactions and, (2) the characteristics of the communication process in the family. Consequently, the child is trained to pay attention to the person with whom he is dealing rather than to the verbal content of the message (*1*). Because the child is trained to focus on the hierarchical organization of the social relationships in the family, he is less free to take in the more autonomous aspects of the transaction or the specific content. Numerous observations of both classroom and clinical sessions bear out this conclusion: in this population it is the prevailing practice to allow the constant defining of interrelatedness of people to outweigh the meaning of the content of all but the most dramatic content messages.

Being trained in this communication and control system prepares the child to clash with the demands of the school because the style violates certain school-held assumptions about the characteristics of learners. School emphasis is on the recruitment of focal attention to the service of abstract content and on the use of this content for symbolic exploration of the world.[3] These expectations violate the child's orientation and methodology of processing data. The child copes with the cognitive anxiety aroused by school demands by eliciting from the teacher that which is most familiar to the child in relating to people—proximal control. Thus, much of the "acting out" or disruptive behavior in the classroom is an attempt to repair relations with an important figure, and recreate a "familiar environment." The teacher usually perceives such behavior as an aggressive act and responds with removal of the child from the school.

We suggest, therefore, that the child's difficulty in school behavior

[3] Dr. Alan B. Wilson, during the discussion of this paper, reminded us that public schools in general do not encourage and reward attention to abstract content, and the exploration, ordering, and conceptualization of the world, but on the contrary, many schools with culturally deprived children encourage "mechanical reasoning" and docility.

and learning is related to: (1) difficulty in focusing attention; (2) a communications style that handicaps the child in the enlistment and ordering of new information, and (3) the child's search for a solution to conflicts in interaction with the teacher.

Within this context an intervention curriculum was designed to initiate children into the methods of learning in schools. The goal was to instruct them in the communications system used in school and to train them in observation of others as well as in self-observation.

Subjects

The subjects were six children in residential treatment at the Floyd Patterson House, a unit of the Wiltwyck School for Boys. All of the children had been remanded to the treatment center for aggressive and dissocial behavior. They belonged to the lowest social class, as defined by Warner (2), and it had been impossible to contain them either at home, at school, or in the community. All but one had been in residential treatment for at least a year. The children comprised one full special class for emotionally disturbed children which was run by the Board of Education and housed in a regular public school. The children carried various psychiatric diagnoses, but no child was diagnosed as psychotic or organically impaired.

Procedure

Class sessions were conducted at the residential center during school hours by a remedial educator. The children were told that they were going to receive remedial lessons at the center during school time and that they were required to attend. The goals of the program were made explicit. In fact, the keynote of the entire project was explicitness, and every step of the curriculum process was spelled out.

The children were told that they were going to be taught a curriculum which would help them do well in school even if the teacher did not like them.[4]

The children also were told that if they could master the communications curriculum, they could probably leave the special education class and begin learning in regular public school classes because of what they would bring to the situation.

[4] Teachers' liking them, or not liking them, was the primary way that children saw things happen in school. They got a good mark on a spelling test because the teacher liked them, or they were suspended because the teacher did not like them.

A room with a one-way mirror and an observation booth with sound equipment were used. A procedure was initiated in which the children assumed alternate roles as participants and observers. Two children rotated in the role of observers behind the one-way mirror. The family therapist and educational director trained the children in the process of rating the other children's ability to respond to the teaching, and in specifically enumerating behaviors which enhanced or interfered with learning.

The emphasis in judging was on performance in relation to learning, rather than on conforming or being well behaved. At the end of each session, the "judges" would tell the children their rating and the specific reasons for each point lost or earned. A small monetary reward was given for each point by the educational director. The "judges" were also rated and given points and a monetary reward by the educational director and therapist.

Curriculum

The 10 sessions focused specifically on communication and unraveling the process and mysteries of the classroom to the children. Lessons were sequentially built around the following skills: listening, the implications of noise, staying on a topic, taking turns and sharing in communication, telling a simple story, building up a longer story, asking relative and cogent questions, categorizing and classifying information, and role playing.

Each session was structured in the form of games.[5] It was felt that the use of games where the processes could be labeled by the teacher was the most efficacious way of teaching skills. The selection of games was made from activities designed for teaching listening skills to kindergarten or primary-age children; the teacher felt that the children functioned at approximately a five-year developmental level in terms of communication skill—even though their chronological age averaged 10 and their mental age was only slightly lower.

The teacher relied on her knowledge of the daily life of the children in school and the treatment center to introduce familiar elements in the stories and games. It seemed much simpler to involve them in focusing

[5] Many of the games were adapted from or suggested by *Listening Aids Through the Grades* by David and Mary Russell, and *The Preliminary Perceptual Training Handbook,* published by the Union Free School District in the Town of Hempstead, Uniondale, New York. The teacher kept as her own reference point the section on *Education of the Senses* in *The Montessori Method* by Maria Montessori.

attention on a story in which the names were familiar, for example, than on a story about a fictional character.

The first topic introduced was *listening*, and the first game played was Simon Says, a game the children already enjoyed and felt safe with. It was spelled out that winners in this game were people who knew how to listen and pay attention.

In the game that followed, the children listened to messages read over the telephone and then attempted to repeat them exactly. The difference between guessing and careful listening then was made explicit, and the results were contrasted.

The strength of the children in reading faces and expressions was discussed. It was explained that in the games played in these sessions it would be more useful to listen to the words than to try to feel out the speaker, since winning would depend on skill at the former exercise.

Number games also were played. The children had to listen to a series of digits and report a certain one. There was discussion around what it is like to wait to respond, to hold directions in mind, to concentrate, and other experiences common to classroom learning.

Since the children were making too much noise at the outset of these sessions, *noise* was a natural topic for the next lesson. A game was designed in which a child would tell a story and the others would begin, one at a time, to make such sounds as knee-thumping, seat-tapping, key-jangling, and the sorts of extraneous noises the children introduced during classroom discussions. One of the children increased the volume of his voice until he silenced the noisemakers and could finish his story, although at considerable expense to his vocal cords. Another child helplessly repeated the same words until he felt himself defeated, and joined in the noisemaking. Dialogue was developed on the effect on the speaker and the listener when such noise was going on, and this was related to its implications for classroom learning.

Since children had difficulty starting one at a time to make their noises and stopping them on cue, the next topic which evolved in the group was *taking turns*. Simple, well-known nursery rhymes were divided up, with each child taking his part in turn. Discussion centered on the difficulties of listening for one's own part, talking in turn, waiting for the other person to speak. Again, it was seen that the familiarity of the material was reassuring to the children and disposed them to thinking they could win the games.

In a later session, an unfamiliar story, made up by the teacher, was told and all the children participated. They had to listen for their own parts, decide when to come in, and let the others know when they were finished speaking.

At this point, it was possible to initiate discussion of the *logic in stories and then in conversations.* In a later session, the children cued each other in on "getting off the topic."

After the first five sessions, the mechanics began to become incorporated and the sessions turned to conceptual skills. Moreover, as the children began to experience hearing and being heard, *judging and being judged in positive terms,* and winning money and praise for explicit achievements, they seemed to join the teacher in wanting to understand the games and to win them.

This response was noticeable in the reduction of noise level in the room, in the questions about process from the children, and in their beginning attempts to regulate their own behavior in the direction of school expectations. At the same time, the children began to anticipate verbally what they would win or how they had lost. Outside the classroom they talked about what they would do with their winnings.

In the sixth and seventh sessions, the teacher engaged the children in games which involved skills such as *categorizing.* From a start with I Spy, involving objects in the room, the children were able to move to variations of 20 Questions. The latter involved asking questions so they could order their universe.

The children became actively involved in problems about which questions helped another person to guess the answer, and why some questions were irrelevant. They displayed growth in framing especially good questions and recognizing what made them useful. Excitement in the group was high as success grew.

After the children had had some experience in concentration on formal aspects of communication, the teacher turned to *role playing* to help them discover how attention to these skills could assist them in the classroom. She and the children took turns playing out situations in which a child "won" in an interaction with a teacher because of attention to the words being said, by asking good questions instead of blowing up, or by waiting his turn, etc.

Although they were later able to analyze what they had done, the children in the heat of role playing would be so overcome with indignation that they could not prevent themselves from flaring up and attacking the speaker.

They took the roles they felt they played with adults and authority figures. Although playing those parts involved much farce, there was also empathy by now with what the adult was experiencing. A child playing the part of a guidance counselor said to another child, "I'm willing to listen to you, and I expect you to let me finish."

It was obvious that the role playing brought the usefulness of the tools they were learning to a level where children could reach out and label their own actions accurately. In the final summarizing session, the adults and the children played roles in situations demanding various skills which had been the focus of the project, with children alternating in back of the mirror as judges.

Both the "judges" and the children in the group were quick to pick up and label "mistakes" purposefully incurred by the adults as getting off the topic or "asking irrelevant questions." More impressive, children within the group displayed an ability to help each other in these areas. Their increased self-awareness and their pleasure in their mastery of new skills caused the project to end on a note where adults and children were engaged in mutual pleasurable recall of the learning that had occurred.

Observation

Beyond the one-way mirror, the two rotating "judges" were trained in the process of rating the performances of their peers. The rating was done on a continuum from 0 to 5. At first, children seemed only to feel that they were being judges when they were giving out zeros, an interesting commentary on their previous experience of being judged. After the lesson, the "judges" came into the classroom and reported the rating of each child in the group. They needed to describe the reason for each evaluation. In this way the "judges" were being trained for differentiated observation and reporting. After the first lessons, the children accepted the peer evaluation with very little questioning.

From early notions of, "Give me all five, or I'll mess you up afterward," or "I'm going to give both of them 0's because I lost last week," the children moved to statements such as, "Really, you don't give points because you like somebody, but for good listening."

As they began to get the idea of judging performance rather than behavior, they also began to differentiate in their ratings between 0 and 5, giving a 3 for a response that was "good, but not so good," or a 4 for a point that was "almost right, but not quite." At the same time, they began to say, "When you were cursing (banging your seat down on the floor, etc.) you weren't listening to the teacher," instead of, "I gave you a 0 because you messed up."

The alternating in the "judging" functions seemed to have significant effects on the behavior and in the process of self-observation in the children. They were conscious of being observed and therefore observed their own behavior. A child stopped himself in the beginning of a fight, looked at the mirror, and put his hands in his pockets; children would apologize to the one-way mirror, etc.[6]

[6] We have elaborated elsewhere that we consider this process of self-observation and self-control due to increased awareness of an observing other as an intermediate step in the development of introspection in the acting-out child.

The Teacher

In this project the teacher and the children were working within an explicit mutuality of goals. The children were trying to move to a regular classroom and to learn how to learn; the teachers were attempting to teach the children a program that would facilitate their own goals.

The teacher introduced familiar topics, was explicit in her expectation, geared the introduction of new themes to the children's level of readiness, shifted from abstract to concrete demands depending on their level of cognitive anxiety, focused continuously on the learning task, and de-emphasized her role as a controller, or as a provider or rewarder. The rewards given were for performance, and the teacher reminded the children that the "judges" were their peers and, by implication, themselves. In general, the teacher's self-expectation was to present herself to the children as a benign and highly differentiated adult related to them through the complementation of their task.

In the beginning the program focused on children's attention on discrete elements of communication—listening, taking turns, labeling, etc. But to the extent that the mechanical aspect of communication was mastered, the teacher introduced the idea of the *relationship* of the discrete pieces of information. She taught "how to ask questions that will give you the best information for the solution to your problem." In role playing the relationship between personal behavior and interpersonal outcome was underscored.

Results and Discussion

The results of this pilot project are based on clinical observations of the children's behavior in and out of the sessions, and verbal reports by the counselors. We decided to rely on observations of the process to gather information for a more systematic study. We are well aware that the conclusions of this paper are quite limited, but we hope to extend our research in an area that appears quite promising. Within this scope, we shall discuss our observations.

ATTENTION There was a marked increase in the children's ability to maintain focal attention for increased lengths of time. In the beginning, children were disruptive and unable to pay attention. From the fifth session on, however, the disruptive behavior and the noise diminished, and the concentration on achievement became central. The increased ability for differentiated attention was clearly seen in the behavior of the "judges." From initial emphasis on rating only "all or nothing" patterns (5 or 0), they were later focusing on gradients of behavior and after the session were able to remember the why's of their rating, organize their data, and report on the behavior of their peers and also of the teacher.

In the sessions the division line between attention and disruptive behavior was very frequently crisscrossed by the children. When the teacher made an assumption that the children had greater ability than they had, or she moved too quickly for them, the structure they had been able to maintain broke down and their old maladaptive functioning reappeared.

Hyperactivity and diffuse disorganized behavior seemed to accompany lack of explicitness in the teacher's expectation about goals and the means of attaining them. We think that the children coped with situations of cognitive anxiety by an adaptation that has been proved successful at home: search for the controlling interpersonal contact with the teacher.

STYLE OF COMMUNICATION AND COGNITION From initial reliance on speed of response and intensity of sound and activity, the children moved to increased use of verbal responses within the context of "the rules of the game." They listened, took turns, and searched for the best questions. In their search for the right words, they slowed their tempo considerably.[7]

In the last sessions, when children were playing 20 Questions and later role playing, their language was not only improved in the "mechanics" of dialogue, but they were using a more differentiated and conceptual style. This was very evident in the 20 Questions game in which the child needs to organize and shrink the universe to find the correct answer. Their ability to improve very rapidly in this game in one session from "random and very concrete questions" to categories and system "questions" would seem to indicate the *availability* in these children of a more conceptual style of thinking and reporting that is generally not used in the classroom or in their daily life. This untapped capacity is *available* under certain conditions and not in others. As a matter of fact, at the end of each period when the rules were over and the "judges" became peers, the children's self-monitoring evaporated and their diffuse hyperactive "bumping" on things and each other reappeared. The seesawing from a "restricted" to an "elaborated" cognitive-communicational style according to the conditions of the field raises interesting theoretical considerations. It suggests (1) that between the ages of 10 and

[7] This self-editing process seems similar to Bernstein's description of the "hesitation phenomena" in middle-class children.

12 the cognitive-communicational style of these children could be reversible, (2) that educational remedial intervention with this population could be carried successfully with children much older than four years, and (3) that we should study changes over a period of time before assuming that they are integrated in the child's new way of learning.

Children's learning in the project was manifested in their life at the institution and in the classroom. For example, one child observing two adults talking at the dining-room table said to them: "I like to see the way you are talking." This same child in a family therapy session "rated" the members of his own family for performance in the therapeutic task and told them the reasons for his rating.

A rather withdrawn and silent boy told his remedial teacher, "I could tell you the names of the things on this table and we could play a game with them." He then invited her to play a 20 Questions game.

Children were heard by the counselors *planning* strategies of how to win the money in the session and what they would do with it. In informal talks with peers and in group therapy children would monitor each other: "You are talking out of the subject," "Do not interrupt, he is talking," etc. They would even correct the counselor for "not hearing" or "talking out of turn."

THE GENERAL CONSIDERATION The intervention curriculum and teaching methodology appeared to be quite effective in changing the learning behavior of the children during the length of the project. This change was achieved by focusing not on behavior, but on cognitive growth. We think that with these children, as in the general field of learning disabilities, the underlying correlates of the disability must be remediated before successful teaching of the skill *per se* can be accomplished.

In our population, but also perhaps in the group of disadvantaged children, they must master a curriculum which develops an ability to (1) focus attention and (2) use communication rules in ways that facilitate gathering and ordering of information. These tasks must be learned before they can master meaningful academic skill.

While the teacher emphasized in the beginning discrete skill in listening and simple learning, labeling, the children moved very quickly (10 lessons) to complex and formal operations: categorizing and role playing. The proper balance of concrete and abstract ingredients seem necessary in the curriculum for development of the capacity to move ahead in learning. It was surprising to the authors that so much change in the children could be achieved in such a short time. We attribute this phenomenon to the favorable effect on this program of the therapeutic milieu in Patterson House.

It seemed natural that most of the children regressed to previous patterns of contact and communication when the conditions of the field changed. We couldn't expect internalization of new behavior patterns in five weeks. But we finished the project with an optimistic sense that the road is worthwhile.

References

1. BERNSTEIN, B. 1961. "Social Structure, Language and Learning." *Educational Research. 3* (June).

2. WARNER, L., *et al.* 1960. *Social Class in America.* Harper Torchbooks, New York.

38. Use of Standard Materials with Young Disturbed Children

LOUISE E. EMERY

In the past decade, impetus has been given to the development of day school programs for seriously disturbed children. This discussion centers around the program of one such school, the Forum School in Ridgewood, New Jersey, which was established in 1954. It is now state supported and offers services to children excluded from public schools.

The children in this study range in age from five to ten years and have a diagnosis of childhood schizophrenia. Symptoms include autistic, symbiotic, aggressive, or hyperactive behavior. The illness is differentiated from conditions of organic brain damage or mental deficiency, although present diagnostic measurements are not infallible. Implicit in the diagnosis is the possibility that the child is potentially accessible.

The basic aim of the school program is to further the ego development of the child. The essential element in this development is the teacher-

SOURCE: *Exceptional Children,* XXXIII (December, 1966), 265–68. Reprinted by permission.

child relationship. The tools are many of the standard materials and activities used in preschool programs. These materials can be adapted to the functioning level and the individual needs of the child.

Music and Rhythm

Using the song circle as the first activity tends to give structure to the whole school day. Through music, initial contacts can be made with the withdrawn child. Materials are chosen for this period to fulfill goals of self-identification (action songs), development of readiness skills (learning songs), and encouragement of speech (sound songs).

To develop or strengthen self-identification, the first song is one of individual greeting. To the tune of "Happy Birthday," each child is greeted with "Good morning to you, good morning to you, good morning, dear (child's name), we're glad to see you." Along with self-awareness, the names of other children are learned. An action song is used to develop awareness of the parts of the body. To the words "Oh, look, see what I can do" children touch their heads; shake their hands; swing their arms; stamp their feet; or touch their noses, ears, or chins. Each child takes his turn in performing some action, and the group imitates his gestures. The part of the body brought into action is named.

"Looby-Loo" and "Hokey-Pokey" are additional songs used to teach body parts. For some children the teacher must use his own body as an extension of the child's in performance of the motions. Many are resistant to involvement, but progress in self-awareness can be noted in actions initiated by the child and his independent participation in the activity. An identification song which intrigues the children is the nursery song "I see you, I see you." As the song is sung by the teacher, he points to the child on "you" and to himself on "me." The correct use of pronouns has followed many repetitions of this song.

The ABC song, "Today Is (day of the week)," seasonal songs which call attention to weather, nature changes, or holidays provide pleasure in a learning situation. Self-care and articles of clothing are introduced to the tune of "Mulberry Bush," with "This is the way we wash our hands" or "This is the way we put on our coats." "John Brown Had a Little Indian," "Five Little Chick-a-dees," and "One-Two-Buckle My Shoe" serve as introductions to numbers. A clock song, a train song, and "Old MacDonald's Farm" have been avenues of experimentation for nonverbal children. Group singing does not demand individual verbalization. One nonverbal child with a strong response to music was frustrated into speech by unfinished lines of his favorite songs. His teacher sang these songs but stopped before the last word of each line. The child had to hear the line completed and supplied the omitted word himself.

Music seems to have unique value as teaching material. Through song the child is helped to recognize himself as a person, taught acceptable play contacts with other children, introduced to academic readiness which he rejects in the classroom setting, provided with speech training under pleasing conditions, and given the opportunity to contribute to a group activity at the level of his capability.

The rhythm period which follows the circle is a welcome change of pace. In the physical activities of marching, tiptoeing, skipping, and skating, excessive energy finds release, muscle coordination is strengthened, and interpersonal relationships are encouraged. Few beginners perform independently. Guidance and support from the teacher are necessary through the period. Some children need a close physical contact as they participate. Others need to be encouraged to join the activity. Some, because of their distractibility or inability to relate, need the reassuring handclasp of the teacher to keep them in the group. Progress may be estimated by the child's increased ability to perform independently.

Clay

Some autistic children are repelled by the feel of clay. If it is to serve as a satisfying manipulative tool, clay must be introduced slowly and carefully. A soft consistency is preferred, for if it is too stiff the child becomes frustrated and refuses to work with it. One successful introduction was a watered down mixture with the consistency a little thicker than fingerpaint. This very thin substance was presented, because the teacher was aware of the child's need to mess; his only self-initiated activity was water play. Gradually, less water was added until the child accepted clay in its natural form and began to use it to pound and cut. Another teacher rolled out the clay and gave a child a cookie cutter. The child was then able to cut the forms and place them on a tin.

Other children have responded to rhythmically intoned directions from the teacher: "Roll, roll, roll the clay and pound, pound, pound." As proficiency increases, the children are encouraged to form objects such as balls, baskets, small animals, etc. The teacher verbalizes what is being done. Baskets are filled with clay eggs, and balls are rolled from teacher to child or from child to child. An activity to develop small muscle control is rolling the clay into snake form and twisting it into a mat form (as a braided rug). One child learned to use scissors by cutting the snakelike form into small pieces. Clay is a medium easily handled and, for most children, enjoyable and gratifying. For variety, a flour dough mixture presents a different tactual experience. Adding food coloring to the mixture extends the variation and strengthens color identification.

Pegs

For the ingenious teacher, the pegboard becomes a versatile tool in teaching disturbed children. Through pegs, color recognition can be taught; small muscle control, developed; attention span, increased; form perception, improved; number concept, strengthened; and lateral dominance, practiced. Pegs may be used by a child for quiet play on a one to one basis with the teacher or in a small group where taking turns in placement of the pegs is an aid in the socialization process.

To introduce pegs the teacher places the empty pegboard in front of the child and a small pile of pegs beside the board. Picking up a peg he verbalizes the action: "I'm going to put a blue peg in this hole. Now, it is your turn, Tom. Put a blue peg next to the one I put in." The teacher may have to assist the child on the first few tries. As color recognition increases, the child is able to select the color called and place it on the board.

Simple forms of squares, triangles, and circles may be taught through pegs. A paper pattern placed on the board and outlined with pegs serves as an introduction. After the pegs have been placed around the pattern, the paper form is lifted and the child sees the form shaped by the pegs. He is then encouraged to make the forms without the patterns, starting with a straight line at the bottom of the board and building the vertical lines from this base. When the teacher desires an intimate rapport, he works individually with the child. When socialization is the goal, a pegboard may be shared by three or four children.

Finger Paint

Finger paint is to smear! The seriously disturbed child in this age range seldom uses this medium as a means of communicating feelings or for creative art. The children who need to mess (the ones who find the mud puddles on the playground) revel in finger paint to their elbows and happily cover the large sheets of paper, which are used to encourage breadth of movement. For reasons of economy, the base of the finger paint is liquid starch. This colorless liquid is an easy introduction for the child who becomes upset by dirty hands. After the child becomes accustomed to the feel of the starch and familiar with the sweeping motions, color in the form of powdered paint is added gradually; and the child is able to accept the medium. A pail of water nearby to clean hands often was the reassurance needed for one child's beginning. For some children, the teacher spread the paint before they experimented by making designs with a rigid index finger. For other children the teacher's grasp on the wrist to propel the child's hands was enough incentive to learn to enjoy the activity.

Finger paint can be used as a transition from compulsive waterplay to a more constructive activity. It is one avenue by which to bring the child into group activity. It may be used to teach color. As the paint is distributed, the teacher asks the child to identify the color given him. Experimentation in blending colors is a delight to the more aware children. Finger painting gives the child another experience in developing muscle control, whereby the child learns to use both hands simultaneously, attention span is lengthened, and relief from tensions is provided. There is never a demand for design or a finished product. The child's enjoyment and self-satisfaction are the ultimate goals.

Blocks

Of the forty-nine children who have been enrolled in the program over the past eleven years, only two showed any interest in or were able to build with the wooden blocks usually found in every kindergarten. In each instance the structure of the blocks appeared to be related to obsessive phases of their problems. The majority of the children lack the dexterity, the attention, or the awareness necessary for intricate building. Some place one block atop another and delight in knocking them over, but seldom attempt constructive building.

The types of blocks used most satisfactorily in the program are the large, reenforced cardboard blocks (block busters) and the small varicolored, varishaped blocks (parquetry). Highly recommended for durability and easy handling, the block busters have been many things, from protective walls to stepping stones. As stepping stones they are used as a substitute for the walking board to teach balance and control. On initial attempts, few of the children can make this journey without the steadying hand of the teacher. Some put one foot on a block and bring the other foot up to meet it, using the same footwork pattern with which they negotiate the stairway.

Most of the children respond to the challenge of the bright colors and geometric shapes of the parquetry blocks, but some are confused by too much color and too many blocks. Using simplified patterns painted on squares of white show card paper, with two colors instead of the six included in the set, is an easy introduction. These simple designs assure a quick success without too much frustration. As the child becomes adept in matching simplified designs, he moves to the more intricate ones where the six colors are used. These blocks have been used for identification of color; to initiate experimentation in design; to lengthen attention span; and, when two or more children work together, to provide the setting for peer rapport.

Paper

Newsprint, construction paper, wallpaper sample books, and magazines are paper products constantly used in the learning situations. On large sheets of newsprint, children learn to make horizontal and vertical lines and circles with crayons. Often the teacher must begin this activity by placing the crayon in the child's hand and moving his hand to make the lines and circles. The lessening of tension in the child's arm indicates a decreasing resistance to the new activity. Eventually, the child's arm moves freely with the teacher's motions. The child is then encouraged to perform independently. From this beginning of lines and circles, numbers and letters are taught. Lines and circles also form stick figures from which body parts are identified.

Construction paper cut in triangles, squares, circles, and long narrow strips to be pasted on newsprint in a variety of designs appeals to most of the children. As ability to handle paste and the precut forms increases, random designs can form pictures. Circles become wheels, flowers, balloons, or faces; the squares may be houses, boxes, or bodies of cars or wagons.

Wallpaper sample books (discarded patterns from paint stores) provide an excellent practice area to learn how to use scissors, and the weight of the paper is good for beginners. Straight lines in patterns serve as guidelines as children learn to "open and close." Diversity of color and pattern challenges interest. For the more advanced child, the decorative uses of wallpaper are unlimited.

Advertisements in the housekeeping magazines related to items of everyday living are an excellent means for increasing awareness and identification. Through pictures of food, clothing, furniture, people, and family living, children learn to identify objects; increase vocabulary; and recognize colors, letters, and words. From magazine clippings, individual children or groups can make posters or wall murals depicting self-care, family pets, foods, clothing, or homes. An advantage of using magazines, as opposed to workbooks, lies in their availability in the home, so that what has been learned in the classroom can become a satisfying activity for after school hours.

39. Out of the Classroom: A Motivational Reading Program for Disturbed Children

NANDEEN L. MILLER

The Day Care Service at Children's Psychiatric Hospital, University of Michigan Medical Center, assumes a unique role in the treatment and education of disturbed children. Since the children require psychotherapy, one aspect of their treatment is similar to that of inpatients, and must be continuous throughout the year. But these children live in their own homes, participate in the more normal aspects of community life, and have siblings and peers who attend public schools. In this aspect, Day Care must at least be aware of the family and the school custom of a long summer vacation and make some allowances for it.

With these divergent needs in mind, the staff designed a summer reading program based on motivational experiences. The regular schedule of individual reading instruction was discontinued in favor of all-school unit projects. The staff, including reading therapists, classroom teachers, occupational and recreational therapists, all contributed to an integrated curriculum.

Reading therapists planned and wrote unit materials. These included reading, per se, at three group levels; beginning and prereading; elementary (second and third grades); and intermediate (fourth grade and above). Supplementary reading activities included phonetic and vocabulary games.

The motivational event for each unit was a field trip. Most of the trips required several hours, so that picnic lunches were needed. Occupational therapy staff arranged this part of the day's schedule.

One might approach such a project in two ways: (a) to investigate field trip resource possibilities requiring the cooperation of business concerns, governmental agencies, etc., and then to write corresponding

SOURCE: *Exceptional Children,* XXXI (October, 1964), 91–92. Reprinted by permission.

units of study; (b) to write units of study with age group interest and tolerance in mind, and then to locate points of interest which would climax the unit study. We decided on the first approach. Field trips and their suggested subjects were:

Detroit Zoo	Animal Unit
Grosse Ile Naval Station	Weather Unit
River Rouge Plant	Automotive Unit
Greenfield Village	History of Transportation Unit
Bolgos Dairy	Dairy Products Unit
Visit to a Farm	Farm Unit
Detroit Tiger Baseball Game	Baseball Unit

Each child made a scrapbook in occupational therapy at the beginning of the program. This scrapbook served as a thread of continuity throughout the summer; it contained all of the written assignments from each unit, plus souvenirs and other items collected on the trips. An element of competition was introduced when scrapbooks were judged and awards presented at a party on the final day of the summer program.

While this program was used in the Day Care Service during the summer, we see possibilities for its application within the curriculum of the normal school year. The integration of study units throughout the entire service (occupational therapy, education, recreational therapy), and the cooperative efforts of all staff members toward a central theme has been a motivational experience for both students and teachers.

READING ACTIVITIES
Sample Weekly Program

Monday

1. Introduction of field trip subject.
2. Class activities.
   a. Develop vocabulary list related to subject.
   b. Display pictures, books, bulletin board.
3. Movie or listening (appropriate content story).

Tuesday

1. Vocabulary review through games, crossword puzzles.
2. Language arts activities (activities prepared Monday afternoon or previously by reading staff using vocabulary suggested by group).

3. Listening comprehension—related stories from S R A, Reader's Digest Skill Builders, using comprehension checks.

Wednesday

Field Trip

Thursday

1. Discussion of trip—things seen, behavior problems.
2. Vocabulary review—through word study—variations.
3. Experience story—told by class, written by teacher, read by class.
4. Word Book, dictionary, word card files.
5. Art activities suggested by trip.

Friday

1. Vocabulary check test for charts or graph.
2. Scrapbook activity—to retain reading worksheets, souvenirs, and other collections.

40. A Modification in the Sequential Tutoring of Emotionally Disturbed Children

L. K. Brendtro and Phyllis Rash Stern

In their study of public school classes for the emotionally disturbed, Morse, Cutler, and Fink (1964) found that the primary intervention technique by special teachers was the provision of a great deal of individual attention, with the teacher rotating from student to student. This

SOURCE: *Exceptional Children,* XXXIII (April, 1967), 517–21. Reprinted by permission.

"taking turns process tended to become a continual, nagging, competitive focus. The sight of children receiving the teacher's response while others were denied it, except for a periodic turn, upset many youngsters in this feast or famine arrangement" (p. 76). In a subsequent article, Morse (1965) has labeled this intervention technique "sequential tutoring" and argues convincingly that "in the individualization . . . there must be a counterbalance, since we are involved in teaching groups" (p. 31). Morse then suggests several nontutorial interventions which might serve to minimize the necessity for excessive use of sequential tutoring.

The widely acknowledged heterogeneity in the educational functioning of almost any group of emotionally disturbed children continues to present an irrefutable case for individualization. The only question is how this individualization process should be structured. Some argue that teaching machines provide the most effective means of meeting individual needs (Quay, 1963) or that self-sustaining programs (Haring, 1964) or multilevel group projects (Morse, 1958; Rhodes, 1963) would best serve this end. While each of these approaches has much to offer, it is likely that some form of sequential tutoring will continue to be necessary in classes for the emotionally disturbed. The purpose of this paper is to (a) examine the rationale for and limitations of sequential tutoring as typically structured in classes for the disturbed, and (b) suggest an alternate way of structuring sequential tutoring designed to minimize these problems. Each section of the discussion will begin with an observer's recording of the classroom interaction characteristic of the particular approach to sequential tutoring.

Typical Interactions in Sequential Tutoring: Classroom A

Each of the eight students in this class for the emotionally disturbed is seated at his desk with a workbook or worksheet before him. The teacher is leaning over the desk of one child, helping him with a particular question. She then walks from one child to the other, observing each child's progress, occasionally interrupting a working child to point out an error. As she is tutoring one individual, the hands of other children are raised; for several minutes she "gets behind" so that there are always at least two or three children waving their hands to get her attention. Two boys, seemingly tired of waiting their turn, begin to throw pieces of an eraser at one another. The teacher moves in their direction. . . .

The observation cited above is so typical that most teachers will question the purpose of its inclusion. Although sequential tutoring of emotionally disturbed children presents certain problems, are not these some of the unavoidable by-products of assembling a group of such youngsters in one classroom? Since it cannot be disputed that disturbed children need much individualization, would not the logical role of the teacher be to go from child to child giving the needed assistance?

There seem to be several reasons why this style of sequential tutoring is so widely practiced. It allows the teacher to exert the central role in the classroom, as she assumes a dominant position by standing over the children or moving among them. She is in the best possible position for surveillance activities; she can note behavior problems in the early stages and is in a better position to deal with them. She can readily employ the important control technique of proximity (Redl, 1952), since simply moving in the direction of trouble often eliminates the disturbance.

Less obviously, such an approach may give the teacher the feeling that she is exerting maximum energy to benefit the child; were she to sit at her desk in the corner, she would feel that she was withdrawing from the group and perhaps even cheating the children of the benefit of her central presence. Furthermore, the very activity of moving about the room may serve to reduce anxiety in the teacher. In certain cultures, adults carry around a string of beads which serves the purpose of keeping their hands busy in potential anxiety arousing situations; in any culture, cigarette smokers have a readily available technique for motoric discharge at times of tension. Likewise, many teachers of the disturbed have developed ways of "being busy" when classroom interactions become tense; this enables them to conceal their anxiety beneath a veneer of calmness.

In contrast to the foregoing, there are several rather serious problems which emerge in this practice of sequential tutoring. The first and most obvious is that the teacher may provide distracting and disruptive stimuli to the individual child who is trying to attend to a learning task. The advocates of stimulus reduction theories (Strauss and Lehtinen, 1947; Cruickshank, Bentzen, Ratzeburg, and Tannhauser, 1961) have suggested that bright clothing or even the jewelry of the teacher may distract many hyperactive children; if this is true, then most certainly a mobile, five foot tall, noise-making stimuli complex (*viz.*, a special education teacher) would interrupt the attention of such children. In our universities we often provide graduate students with private carrels located in the silent recesses of the library, yet we expect distractible children to function with a teacher wandering in and out of the rows, pausing frequently here and there for a spell of all too audible conversation with a particular child. The teacher's almost continual movement and verbal communication provide a readily available program of stimuli which is often much more novel and interesting to the child than the task at hand.

As Morse (1965) stated, "one could hardly imagine conducting a series of individual interviews in a social setting, yet we assume we can teach this way" (p. 31). Usual procedures in sequential tutoring force the child to reveal his inadequacies to the peers who surround him. No matter how much effort is made to individualize each child's program, the tendency of children to assess their progress according to the achievements of their classmates cannot be totally eliminated. Thus, a common problem in sequential tutoring is that a neighboring child will interrupt with a comment such as "I know that—that's simple!" or he may even blurt out the answer, compelling the teacher to remind him to attend to his own business.

Certain disturbed children do not respond well to being watched and the intensity of surveillance inherent in sequential tutoring may have a detrimental effect upon their classroom learning or performance. Furthermore, the teacher often finds herself in the role of imposing assistance upon a highly reluctant client, with the result that further negativism and resistance are encountered.

Analyzing the behavior in the sequential tutoring situation from the viewpoint of operant conditioning, it would appear that the children are frequently engaged in attention seeking behavior. At its best this behavior is ostensibly appropriate, as when the child raises his hand to obtain socially reinforcing interaction with the teacher; on the other hand, much behavior is inappropriate and maladaptive, as the child engages in various troublemaking efforts, which then secure for him the attention of the teacher. Those children who do not know the answer to a problem are sure to receive potentially reinforcing social attention from the teacher. In contrast, the more diligent students who complete their work quickly and correctly may get very little of the teacher's attention. Thus, social reinforcement, a most efficient and significant reward for many disturbed children, may frequently serve to maintain undesirable behavior.

Modifying the Interaction in Sequential Tutoring: Classroom B

The students are seated at trapezoidal tables arranged in a circular pattern. The teacher's desk is situated in a corner of the room designated as the "helping corner." During periods of individual work, each child brings his paper to the helping corner as he completes a specific assignment. The teacher and the child then go over the work and the child is assigned either remedial work or is given another task. The teacher sometimes uses this time to give instruction in a particular skill or to explain a new task to the child. The interaction of teacher and child is relatively private, and the teacher often engages in a brief moment of pleasant or supportive conversation with the child prior to his resuming individual work.

It is readily apparent that the teacher child interactions in Classroom B are quite unlike those in Classroom A. The two styles of sequential tutoring can be differentiated on the basis of (a) the initiator of the interaction, (b) the locus of the interaction, and (c) the focus of the interaction. These comparisons are summarized in Table 1.

TABLE 1

A COMPARISON OF STYLES OF TEACHER CHILD INTERACTION IN TWO CLASSES OF EMOTIONALLY DISTURBED CHILDREN

	Classroom A	*Classroom B*
Initiator of Interaction	Teacher	Child
Locus of Interaction	At child's desk in the group	At teacher's desk marginal to group
Focus of Interaction	Teacher engaging in surveillance of child	Child engaging in evaluation with teacher

In Classroom A, the teacher generally initiates the interaction, which takes place at the child's desk, central to the activity of the group; the basic focus of the interaction might be conceptualized as surveillance, and the child may or may not be requesting teacher assistance. On the other hand, in Classroom B the child generally initiates the interaction by coming to the teacher's desk, usually to show a completed piece of work and then to receive his next task.

What are the advantages of child initiated sequential tutoring structured in the manner of Classroom B as contrasted with the teacher initiated style in Classroom A? There seem to be at least eight distinct advantages to the former approach.

1. Assuming that the group is under control, the children's work area is relatively quiet and is not disturbed by the wanderings of the teacher.
2. The privacy of the tutorial exchange is much greater; it is almost impossible for peers to monitor the conversation since it is carried out on the margin of the group. This gives the teacher and child more freedom in what they choose to discuss.
3. When the child comes to the teacher rather than the teacher to the child, there is probably less resistance to receiving help. This expectation is compatible with the frequent observation of psychotherapists

that success is most likely when the client seeks help rather than having it imposed upon him.

4. The child is not forced to work under excessively close surveillance, but rather works somewhat independently in a manner more closely approximating the regular classroom.
5. The teacher can evaluate the performance of each child upon completion of a given task and provide the necessary corrective measures or appropriate subsequent task. Her location at her own desk, rather than in the middle of the room, provides ready access to the file of available materials.
6. Each child is provided with systematic feedback upon the completion of a logical unit of work.
7. The child is allowed a brief period of motor activity upon the completion of each task: he brings his work up to the teacher and then walks back to his seat with a new assignment. It is probable that this activity reinforces task completion behavior, according to Premack's (1959) principle. A response (*i.e.,* task completion) will be strengthened if followed by a response with a higher independent rate of occurrence (*i.e.,* motor activity).
8. Finally, and perhaps most important, social reinforcement becomes most readily obtainable, not by competition with peers for teacher attention, but by completion of an assigned task and bringing it to the teacher. By association with social reinforcement, the completed task itself should eventually acquire reinforcement value: in Classroom B this generally appears to be the case, since the children soon come to take great pride in the quality and quantity of their work.

Some Practical Concerns

The foregoing discussion has compared the styles of sequential tutoring used in two different classes for disturbed children. A number of reasons have been suggested as to why the child-initiated approach (Classroom B) might be more therapeutic and educationally sound than the adult-initiated approach (Classroom A). There still remain, however, several practical concerns about the implementation and operation of a child-initiated system of sequential tutoring; four of the most frequently raised questions are considered below.

HOW DOES ONE ASSIGN TASKS TO THE CHILDREN? The teacher must prepare in advance a series of appropriate tasks (worksheets, pages from workbooks, etc.) for each child, usually having a tentative collection of materials sufficient to keep each child involved for one school day. Each child has his own in-out box where he receives new tasks and deposits completed and checked tasks. Exactly how the teacher decides on appropriate tasks depends to some extent upon the child's stage in the program: (a) initially, the teacher may have to rely primarily upon tests and previous teachers' reports of achievement; she should determine his apparent level of functioning, and then develop tasks below this level to insure initial success; (b) subsequently, the child's performance on the daily tasks will determine where he needs more work, what areas he might be able to skip over, what specific remedial tasks or tutoring he might require; (c) finally, academic materials used in the regular class to which he will presumably be transferred will serve as the basis for task determination.

WHAT ABOUT THE CHILD WHO DEMANDS HELP, CLAIMING HE DOESN'T KNOW HOW TO DO HIS WORK? With exceptions of course, the response would probably be, "I think you are able to do that problem, please look at it again." This tends eventually to cut down the incidence of "educational malingering" and encourages the child to get into the habit of first using his own problem-solving skills before turning for help. On the other hand, it may very well be that the child is right: he doesn't know how to solve the problem or is not capable of facing the frustration which seems imminent in the task at hand. In this case, the plea of the child signals the teacher that she has made a tactical error in assigning this particular task to this child at this time, and she must modify the length or complexity of the task, or substitute a different task. Some children need frequent support from the teacher if they are to remain busy and satisfied. However, rather than constantly going by this child to keep him working, the teacher can select tasks which are much shorter; this gives the particular child legitimate access to the teacher upon completion of each short task. It is then possible to extend the length of the task gradually and decrease the amount of teacher attention required.

WHAT CAN ONE DO IF A CHILD REFUSES TO DO ANY WORK? Since the entire emphasis of this approach is upon the value of work, the most consistent response is to agree with the child, take away all of his work, and tell him that work is special, and if and when he is ready he may ask for it. If he becomes disruptive, he may be isolated from the mainstream of the group (without his work or other entertainment) and told that he may get his work when he can behave. Most children will usually ask for work after only a brief period of idleness. Furthermore, contrary to some teachers' expectations, it has not been found to be true that other children will also refuse work just to get out of it.

HOW DOES ONE KEEP SEVERAL CHILDREN FROM WANTING THEIR WORK CHECKED AT THE SAME TIME? This problem is really one of logistics. By a certain amount of preplanning, the teacher can gear the length of assignments so that she is usually able to handle all of the children. Yet, it is not possible to predict just when children will complete tasks, so one of two procedures may be employed when a pile up occurs. (a) The children are told that when the teacher is busy they may, if they desire, go to their boxes and get another sheet to begin working on. Since the teacher has preplanned, each child has several available work sheets which he is able to do independently. (b) Some teachers have found it helpful, particularly with adolescents who are less inclined to do extra work, to designate a waiting chair for the pupil who is next in line. This assures him that he will indeed get to see the teacher, and it removes him physically from the group (where he might create a disturbance) and the tutoring situation (where he might eavesdrop or interfere).

References

CRUICKSHANK, W. M., BENTZEN, F. A., RATZEBURG, F. H., and TANNHAUSER, M. T. *A Teaching Method for Brain-Injured and Hyperactive Children.* Syracuse, N.Y.: Syracuse University Press, 1961.

HARING, N. G. "Educational Research with Emotionally Disturbed Children." Paper presented at the University of Michigan Colloquium on Special Education, Ann Arbor, December, 1964.

MORSE, W. C. "Education of Maladjusted and Disturbed Children." In W. M. Cruickshank and G. O. Johnson (Eds.), *Education of Exceptional Children and Youth.* Englewood Cliffs, N.J.: Prentice-Hall, 1958. Pp. 507–608.

MORSE, W. C. "Intervention Techniques for the Classroom Teacher of the Emotionally Disturbed." In P. Knoblock (Ed.), *Educational Programming for Emotionally Disturbed Children: The Decade Ahead.* Syracuse, N.Y.: Syracuse University Press, 1965. Pp. 29–41.

MORSE, W. C., CUTLER, R. L., and FINK, A. H. *Public School Classes for the Emotionally Handicapped: A Research Analysis.* Washington, D.C.: The Council for Exceptional Children, 1964.

PREMACK, D. "Toward Empirical Behavior Laws: I. Positive Reinforcement." *Psychological Review,* 1959, *66,* 219–233.

QUAY, H. C. "Some Basic Considerations in the Education of Emotionally Disturbed Children." *Exceptional Children,* 1963, *30,* 27–31.

REDL, F., and WATTENBERG, W. W. *Mental Hygiene in Teaching.* New York: Harcourt, Brace and World, 1959.

RHODES, W. C. "Curriculum and Disordered Behavior." *Exceptional Children,* 1963, *30,* 61–66.

STRAUSS, A. A., and LEHTINEN, LAURA E. *Psychopathology and Education of the Brain-Injured Child.* New York: Grune and Stratton, 1947.

41. Crafts for Severely Disturbed Children

MARGARET D. LANSING

Every teacher who has had contact with emotionally disturbed children knows that their reaction to various materials is unexpected and often upsetting. It is this unexpected reaction to the materials, the product, or the structure of a craft activity that is so often upsetting to the teacher, disturbing to the group, and crippling to the child himself. Yet if the teacher can anticipate the trouble and understand its cause, she is then in a position to help the child handle his problem.

For the past two years, the writer has been teaching a craft program to a small group of severely disturbed children. This experience, combined with the ideas from the limited literature available, suggests the importance of the following considerations when choosing a craft material: (a) Success—Is the task easy enough? (b) Structure—Can the task be presented clearly? (c) Safety—Is the task safe, physically and emotionally, for the child to do? Every teacher who handles craft materials should be alert to these considerations. Not only may there be a disturbed child within the normal group, but also these considerations are appropriate to normal children to a lesser degree. The teacher who knows her children and is aware of the material's varied effects on them can modify her program to suit each group and each child.

Our group contains three boys and three girls, ranging in age from seven to nine. Most of these children began group therapy on an out-

SOURCE: *Exceptional Children,* XXXI (April, 1965), 421–25. Reprinted by permission.

patient basis more than four years ago. As they approached school age, an educational program was developed, and two half-hour craft periods a week are now part of their total treatment program. All of the children are currently in either a grade placement appropriate to their age or in a special education class. Their developmental achievements, for example, in communication and manual dexterity, range from three to nine years. No child is at a consistent level of development and there are obvious areas of functional retardation. Five of the six children have been diagnosed as psychotic, and several have severe speech problems. Our goal is to give them support in handling their school experiences, and to teach them ways of expressing themselves through speech, writing, painting, claywork, and gestural language. The following descriptions of some reaction patterns that were observed will introduce the reader to some of the children.

Success

The first consideration in planning an activity is success; this is not necessarily the completion of a project or curriculum, but rather it is the feeling of success in each child. For one child this may be merely the accomplishment of actually handling the materials; for another it may mean the completion of one step without adult help; or for another, success may be the achievement of making an independent choice of color. Each child in the group has his own needs for growth and achievement. By "success" is meant the accomplishment of one step toward these goals for each child.

The materials and procedures must be simple enough to offer the hope of this type of success to every child in the group. This is a prime consideration for every teacher, but with disturbed children the tolerance of failure is extremely low. They will guard against failure by never beginning if the activity appears difficult. Because the range of development in the group is so wide, each activity is planned to offer some degree of success for every level of ability. Verbal, eight year old Bob can read directions on a box, but he cannot cut a straight line. Walter, who is physically aggressive and a poor talker, can imitate complicated manual procedures, but cannot follow a verbal direction.

Success is most easily available to all levels of ability when an activity is presented as a series of steps. The first step must be simple enough to offer success at the lowest level of development; each succeeding step must offer continuing interest and success for higher levels. For example, one of our first projects was making baskets for holding crayons. The children were each given the basic shape cut from a Clorox bottle.

Step one was to wind yarn around the handle. Three of the children with poor coordination and short attention spans were able to finish or partially finish only step one. Yet they felt successful and took this product home at the end of the period. Step two was the crayon decoration of the bottle, and this offered wide variation in achievement, all of which were considered successful by child and adult alike.

Standards of self-satisfaction are extremely varying with disturbed children, not only varying from child to child, but fluctuating within each child depending on the mood of the day. The disturbed child is often very independent in his standards of success. He may be aware of teacher standards and group standards, and still be compelled to meet his own internal standards. In some cases these are negative ones; the work must not be finished, must not be perfect, must not be done when asked for. Bob, the group's oldest boy, is only hesitantly accepted by the other children. He shifts from the boys' social group to the girls', and seems unsure of where he belongs. He is bright, very verbal, and an excellent reader. His superiority to the other children in academic activities is considerable. Yet Bob is careful not to be the first one to complete a project, not to do a neat job, and to obtain mild teacher criticism especially in front of the other children. On the other hand, Mike's need for absolute perfection makes success an impossibility. For complicated psychological reasons, he has set inner standards that are almost unreachable. Whenever his production falls short of this standard, he destroys it completely.

Perhaps because the disturbed child's inner satisfaction is so fleeting and hard to perceive, it is easy to feel that he is getting nothing out of an activity. In our group, we often get delayed confirmation of the success of an activity. The mother may report that her child has been asking to continue a school activity at home. A girl who grudgingly did the barest minimum of work on a paper owl treasured it in her room at home, and months later, she referred to it in school. It is the author's feeling that when the materials used and procedures involved offer success in some degree to every child, then the activity will give satisfaction and learning will take place.

Structure

The second consideration in the choice of materials is one of structure: How easily can the teacher organize the presentation of these materials and the resulting procedures? Maintaining the structured classroom environment when working with creative materials is vital to the learning process and to the satisfaction derived from accomplishment.

When material and procedures can be introduced in both verbal and nonverbal ways, the activity will have a greater chance of success. For some of our children, a direct verbal instruction (e.g., "Draw a circle"), forces them into an old conditioned response, "You can't make me." However, the nonverbal demonstration ("Here is the shape we're making today") can often short circuit the negative response. Any teacher who has been maneuvered into "warfare" knows how much this can reduce her actual teaching time.

When presenting a new activity to the children, it is essential to show a finished example. If the product requires several steps to complete, as with hand puppets, it is helpful to show the product in an intermediate stage also. The disturbed child is uncomfortable in any situation of doubt. He needs to know three things: (a) what he is making, (b) how long it will take, and (c) how difficult it will be to make.

Our group is not composed of hospitalized schizophrenics, but of severely disturbed children who are able to manage a public school environment. They may be given a ball of clay with no specific instructions but within a structured situation. We say, "Here is some clay. You may make anything you like with it. You must stay in your chair and keep your clay on the board. You may not throw it, eat it, or put it on your body. Clay is to squeeze, pound, roll, and poke. You may make anything you like." The disturbed child has a very difficult time controlling his impulses. One can almost see a child's mind constantly nagging him, "Shall I tear it up, shall I throw it?" This is not a discipline problem; it is a running battle he has within himself.

When the structure of the activity reduces the temptations and when the limits are clearly defined, then the child can give full attention to the activity and express himself creatively. We have been alert to this question: Will a structured program discourage the child's creativity? We have seen no evidence that it will. Creativity relies heavily on these two factors: a knowledge of oneself and the skills to express this knowledge in some medium. A few of the children do not have skills adequate for self-expression. They do not speak; their gestural language is confused; they cannot control a pencil, crayon, or brush. Others do not have a clear enough concept of themselves as a separate entity to know what to say. Those children who do have both a degree of self-awareness and the skill to express it seem able to speak out creatively through many types of structured activities.

Along with the physical properties of the materials used and the work space available, one must also consider the fourth dimension—time. Nearly all the children in our group have a poorly developed sense of time. For some this lack of understanding is causing them constant anxiety. One verbal and academically advanced child is obsessed with time:

"How long will it take? What will we do next? When will the glue dry?" He needs a well-planned time structure. The activity should last the whole period but should not require rushing in order to finish. Another child will become so involved in the activity, especially painting and clay modeling, that he is totally unaware of time. For him there must be ample warning and preparation for the coming termination.

The adaptability of various materials to this type of carefully structured activity would depend on the group of children with whom one is working. Our restrictions are limited table space, a maximum of five minutes to clean up after class, no storage for wet or unfinished work, and several children whose skills are below the five year level. We have had the greatest success with clay, paints, paper construction, papier-mâché, sewing, and wood and glue activities. It is important for the teacher always to try an activity herself before planning how to structure the period around this activity. One small step, like the twisting of a piece of wire, can easily be overlooked if one merely thinks through an activity. Yet sometimes the child's inability to perform this one small step can disrupt the planned structure of the whole period.

Safety

Because of the individual limitations, phobias, and attitudes of disturbed children, we think more often of emotional safety than of physical safety. We naturally protect a child from physical harm, but we sometimes must protect the disturbed child from his own fears and fantasies.

All teachers consider physical safety routinely. Poisonous paints, glues, clay, etc., are avoided. We have to be especially careful as our children will ingest and chew objects not ordinarily considered chewable. Sharp tools, knives, scissors, pins, and nails all have to be used only when the structure of the period permits close supervision. Even a toy rubber hammer intended to be used in a peg-in-hole activity immediately suggested itself as a weapon to two boys with low impulse control.

These physical dangers are fairly easy to predict if one has had any experience with disturbed children. Planning to avoid emotional dangers and fears is far more difficult. This is such an individual thing that the best way to demonstrate these considerations is with a few examples from our group.

Walter, a hyperactive, extremely strong boy of eight, has been suffering from severe terrors following his grandfather's death and burial. These terrors arise every time he passes the elevator doors, which he equates with the descent into the grave. He has spent months drawing elevator doors and up and down buttons. Several weeks after this period had passed we were making a Christmas angel and the project was clearly causing special tension in Walter. Only later did we learn why: his grandfather had "gone to live with the angels." This object had reactivated his old fears. Because of such reactions we avoid fearful subject matter such as ghosts, dragons, giants, and other imaginary symbols.

Sometimes the mere fluidity of a medium will produce anxiety and suggest a fear-ridden subject to a child. Mike, a very intelligent boy of eight, has excellent small motor control and is capable of the most perfect work. He finds it impossible to let himself join the group, and will never follow directions or complete an assignment. For Mike to say, "Yes, I will," would be like saying, "I am no longer myself." Therefore it is only during a free nondirective period that he can enjoy his productions. He routinely makes the same object out of whatever medium is offered.

At the time of this writing, he was making a pinwheel. This object is emotionally safe for Mike and he uses it to communicate nonverbally with others. Last summer Mike watched his kitten die when his mother accidentally backed the car over it. A few weeks after this episode, we had a clay period. Clay is a fluid medium in that it can be rolled, poked, pounded, and squeezed. Mike began making his usual pinwheel, but the coil that represented the stick of the pinwheel curved so that it suggested a kitten's tail. Almost immediately Mike was facing the horror of his summer experience and needed immediate adult control. The fluidity of this medium was too suggestive, and he could not maintain his inner controls. When he can control the medium, Mike is very productive. But once the paint runs or drips, he loses control.

A fluid medium may suggest dangerous subjects to disturbed children. Once suggested, an idea can come painfully close to reality in their understanding. It is our feeling that these disturbed children should continue to have experiences with fluidity, and that only through such experiences can they learn to develop inner controls against the special threats that these movements have for them. However, it is vital for a teacher to consider the great threat of each medium in relation to its fluidity, and to guard against it by careful structuring. The adult must be prepared to assume control once it is clear that the child has lost the use of his own inner controls.

Summary

There are three general areas to consider when planning a craft or art program for disturbed children. The materials and procedures must be simple enough to offer the hope of success to every child in the group. Success means movement toward each individual's goals of growth and achievement. The activity must be one that can be structured so that a step by step development is easily understood by the child. A teacher should always perform the activity herself with her own group of children constantly in mind.

Disturbed children have such individual limitations that it would be impossible to perfect a program to fit all groups. These children often have a problem with dissociation. Because of their inability to see things as a whole, or gestalt, they cannot invent methods of procedure even when the goal is understandable and attainable. They must depend on adult directed structure. The activity must offer the child both physical and emotional safety. Tactile experiences offer great satisfaction as touch is often the disturbed child's strongest sensory modality. Yet, at the same time, these experiences can be the most dangerous to their emotional safety as they quickly awaken painful fantasies. Fluid mediums are a threat to the inner controls of these children. It is as important to know one's children as it is to know one's materials and procedures.

IV

Preparing to Teach the Emotionally Disturbed Child

Since the psycho-educational approach to working with emotionally disturbed children places so much emphasis upon the teacher, it would seem appropriate at this point in the book to consider some of the competencies needed if these persons are to function to the best interests of the child and themselves as well. Following the lead of Morse and others presented in this volume, it must be assumed that the teacher will need to rely heavily upon a number of disciplines to assist her with these children in the public schools. This means that the teacher herself must be able to work effectively with personnel in these allied disciplines as well as be conversant with the skills and orientations of the various disciplines. The first five articles in this section examine some of the personal and professional concerns of these teachers, while the last three articles discuss the kinds of teacher-training programs needed to give us the personnel to do the job.

The opening article by *Rothman* (42) suggests that if we are to deal effectively with emotionally disturbed children in an educational setting, then teaching must not be restricted to curriculum areas alone but must expand to include helping students develop adequate self-concepts and inter-personal relationships. Pointing out that an emotional display by a student is an attempt to communicate, Rothman emphasizes the need for the teacher to understand this attempt and to accept the emotions expressed while being critical of the behavior used to express them. Rothman advises that the successful teacher must be a specialist in human relations. What kind of person is best suited to teach emotionally disturbed children? Although the characteristics thought to be desirable are as numerous as the people writing on the subject, *Hewett* (43) compiles a hierarchy of teacher competencies—objectivity, flexibility, structure, resourcefulness; in addition, the teacher must be a social reinforcer, a curriculum expert, and an intellectual model. Hewett feels the list will be helpful to those engaged in recruiting and developing training programs for professionals in this field. Is the teacher to be an educator or a psychotherapist? To whom should he listen—the education supervisor or the clinician? *LaVietes* (44) sees the teacher as one who fulfills both roles and then compares the goals of the traditional teacher of normal children with the prerequisite goals of the teacher of emotionally disturbed children. Preparation for teaching both skills and subject matter is fundamental in training teachers to treat disturbed adolescents, says *Morse* (45). Also important is "the ability to cultivate tool skills." This often requires that the teacher provide "encouragement and support on the one hand and reasonable demands and pressure on the other." "Symptoms must be interpreted before they can become the basis for hygienic handling": to gain this kind of insight the teacher must have a firm grounding in the psychology of adolescence. Morse believes that the training of teachers of emotionally disturbed children requires a subject-matter skill-complex, an intensified study of normal and disturbed adolescent behavior, a high level of self-insight, and the ability to work with others. *Dorward* (46) reports on a study to determine the competencies needed by teachers who are planning to work with emotionally disturbed children. The study was unable to identify special competencies needed by teachers of disturbed children. Dorward is quite right in saying this study "raises questions concerning the content of special courses for teachers of disturbed children."

The *Knoblock* article (47) calls attention to such problems as teacher selection, breadth of training, field experience, and leadership training as important considerations in the development of good training programs. In *Balow's* article (48) the University of Minnesota program for training teachers of emotionally disturbed children is presented as a model of a teacher-training program designed for the experienced teacher and graduate student. In the last article *Johnson* (49) notes that undergraduate programs for training teachers of disturbed children are being phased out, leaving the field of training at the graduate level only. Johnson examines this trend and finds that while the evidence from the field does not indicate existing undergraduate programs are good, neither does the evidence suggest we should discontinue them. The author calls for a new kind of teacher-training program that would be more creative and less confined to traditional preparation programing. He cites the need for flexibility in programing and directs attention to volunteers in the Peace Corps, the young people who became members of the Mississippi volunteers in the summer of 1965, and the training given to combat soldiers to enable them to perform complex medical procedures under field conditions, as examples of the ability of young people to perform at high levels.

42. Needed: The Teacher as a Specialist in Human Relations

ESTHER P. ROTHMAN

The nation's concern is centered upon poverty. In addition to the many programs which are aimed at an adult population, we are engaged in federal, state, and community projects geared to helping groups of teenagers who often are categorized as the "school drop-out," the "socially disadvantaged," "culturally deprived," "educationally retarded," etc. Call these teenagers by whatever name for which there is a current penchant, the fact remains that struggling young persons *are* struggling young persons by whatever name they are called. The fact also remains that these same young people are rooted in their economic poverty often in the same rigid manner that they are rooted in emotional poverty—a paucity of inner resources—an inability to mobilize whatever resources they do possess in a meaningful direction.

It is rapidly becoming apparent, therefore, that in order to wipe out economic poverty, it is necessary to attack the problem on at least two distinct fronts: First, to provide the economic opportunity for upward mobility, and second, to help the individual take the opportunity that is offered. It is the latter aim which is most difficult to achieve; for while it is relatively easy to make opportunities available, it is extremely difficult to give people the inner strengths which enable them to grasp a chance, mobilize their energies, and utilize an experience. It is with helping children mobilize their inner resources that the school must be concerned. For assuredly, if we are dedicated to the concept that all high school students should remain until graduation and that all students who have dropped out of school and not found a place for themselves in the vocational community should return to school, then we must also admit that to a large extent, the schools have failed. How else can we explain the fact that large numbers of students drop out of school annually and that larger numbers of those students still attending school are

SOURCE: *The High School Journal,* LXIX (March, 1966), 266–70. Reprinted by permission of The University of North Carolina Press.

not succeeding and are only waiting for the time of legal departure?

A hard look at school policy and at school teachers seems to point toward a need to expand what is traditionally called teaching. No longer must teaching be concerned only with curriculum areas and methods and materials, but it must also center upon helping students develop an adequate concept of themselves and helping them make meaningful interpersonal relationships in a manner that is both personally gratifying to them as well as socially acceptable to society.

To accomplish these goals is no small feat. The teacher must be able to do two things. She must understand the student, which presupposes that she must understand herself. Sound simple? Yet, it is a highly complex science, skill, and art, all rolled into one. The teacher must understand these basic tenets: One, behavior is communication. A pupil is telling the teacher something when he hurls his book down and refuses to work. He is telling her something when he slouches in his seat. He is saying something when he curses, cries, slams the door, works compulsively, or cuts classes. The student is giving a statement of his feelings. He is angry or afraid or frustrated or unhappy or envious. He is feeling an emotion. Two, the teacher must accept the emotions the student expresses while she may be critical indeed of the behavior which is expressive of the emotions. She can let the pupil know that while no one has the right to quarrel with an emotion, the teacher and the group and society at large cannot have inflicted upon them the aggressive expressions of that emotion. A child has a right to feel, but he has no right to hurt anyone else because of his feelings. The teacher, then, must not only be capable of understanding what a pupil is saying, but she must also be able to let the child know that she understood. This is an extremely hard lesson a teacher must herself learn and an extremely difficult one to teach to students.

Ernest Hemingway wrote of people who "come deep into our lives" and while Hemingway was not writing of teachers, or parents for that matter, who, besides parents, comes deeper into the lives of other people than teachers? Much has been studied and written about the meaningfulness of parents. Less has been studied and written about the influence of teachers on children's lives. The truly great influence that teachers exert upon students has really not received the attention, study, or recognition it deserves. While the general community should share some of the blame for this sad nonrecognition of what should be considered a great profession in the true significance of the word "great," teachers themselves are more than equally responsible for their own lack of public regard for self-esteem. This lack of public acclaim is certainly related to the concept teachers have of themselves. And how do teachers see themselves? Perhaps the following situations are revealing:

1. There is a teacher shortage nationally. There is a national cry for better instruction, more teachers. What, in fact, do teachers ask for as a partial solution to their problems. Volunteers. A former superintendent of schools in New York City, in the face of an impending teachers' strike several years ago, called for volunteer teachers.
2. Teachers themselves, privately and through their professional organizations, call for volunteers for remedial reading, arithmetic, library, etc. They also ask that non-professional people supervise lunchrooms, study halls, and yards. Yet, every teacher knows that it is these very non-academic areas that usually present the greatest difficulties. In lunchroom supervision, real teaching can take place. The lunchroom, the yard, the auditorium, where large groups of children meet, can be the arena for the greatest teaching of all—the teaching of social skills and inner controls. Yet, teachers give up this teaching aspect of their profession because it is non-academic, and relegate it to people who are not skilled in dealing with the dynamic interactions of children and who often produce more difficulties than they control. Teachers do not recognize that the social milieu is the scene for teaching and keeping social order *is* teaching. Teachers, not non-professionals, belong in these areas of "supervision." These duties should be considered a part of the teaching program and should not be considered an addenda.

Take an analogous profession. When doctors went on strike two years or so ago in Canada, there was no discussion of calling for volunteer doctoring. At the other extreme, when gravediggers talked of striking in New York City several years ago, did anyone ask for volunteers? Can anyone imagine walking into a dentist's office and being turned over to a non-professional for an extraction—or going to a surgeon and being told, "See my non-professional assistant!"

And yet, without a doubt, the most delicate operation of all, the interpersonal relationships that are nurtured in a classroom and in the school are often turned over to non-professionals. Why? Because teachers essentially have little regard for the profession—little ego involvement in it—little ego status in what they themselves do. If all teachers were to be asked nationally, "What is teaching?" there would be as many different definitions as there are people. Yet, no one has any doubts about what astronomy is, or medicine, or politics. Unfortunately, not knowing what teaching is, the general consensus appears to be that anyone can teach. Not only does the general public accept this fallacy, but sadly, teachers too appear to accept this public judgment.

Teachers need ego. They need a belief in themselves. They need to know what teaching is and who they are. They need to ask themselves such questions as, "Why do I want to be a teacher?" "How do I feel about children?" Teachers in the course of their training must reach down into the layers of their personality and conflicts, and through a process of self-erosion and then self-reintegration, learn to understand themselves so that they in turn can understand a child.

I remember, in my first days of substitute teaching, slapping a child who refused to open his books. I slapped him out of anger, frustration, and self-defeat. I felt humiliated because the child had dared to defy me. I felt ridiculed because the other children might laugh at me. I felt angry because I did not have enough skill to make the child do as I wanted. I felt that I had fallen from the pedestal—a pedestal I had placed myself upon. I felt defeated. Now why? Why should my own self-esteem as a teacher hinge upon whether children laughed at me? It did not say much for my own ego strength. Yet, I daresay, thousands of teachers undergo a similar incident, and they scorn the child with some bit of inappropriate insult, or they slap him, or they send him to the principal, or they send for his parent. Just like a surgeon, I daresay, who when operating, throws his knife to the floor in rage, if some unforeseen physical reaction occurs—or plunges his knife deeper into the patient —out of anger. Is it possible that teachers come to their trade without emotional preparation for it?

To work with all children, but especially with those children who are troubled, teachers must be prepared in the intricate, highly complex skills of understanding not only behavior but emotions. This kind of understanding can only come out of self-understanding. The teacher must be able to differentiate between her feelings and the child's, and to distinguish between her values and the child's. With this kind of separation, the teacher becomes able to establish a meaningful dialogue between the pupil and herself. Upon this communication is a relationship established. The child who often has not felt that any teacher was "on his beam" begins to make an emotional investment. He begins to trust the teacher. With trust, he wants to please her, and so he begins to behave socially and academically in a way that will incur the teacher's pleasure and overt approval. Upon the receipt of this approval, the child, perhaps for the first time in his school life, begins to succeed. Success stimulates further success. He tries even harder. He incorporates the teacher's values. Her goals become his own goals. Teaching has been successful. Perhaps the child stays in school to graduate, or is able to set a goal for himself, or perhaps simply becomes happier. In any event, the teacher has taught, even if what she has taught has not been written in the content course of studies.

Teachers must be specialists in accepting the sensitivities and sensibilities of the pupils before them. They must be specialists in human relations. It is incumbent upon the teacher of the disturbed child to assume this role if she is to treat the child effectively.

43. A Hierarchy of Competencies for Teachers of Emotionally Handicapped Children

FRANK M. HEWETT

Tender without being sentimental, tough but not callous, sensitive but not irritable, possessed by conviction, profoundly aware without loss of spontaneity, trusting in the intuitive humane responsiveness of one's self and one's colleagues, and self-actualized. While this description may seem an excerpt from the canonization of a saint, in actuality it is a statement of desirable characteristics for teachers of emotionally handicapped children compiled from writings of Rabinow (1955); Mackie, Kvaraceus, and Williams (1957); and Haring (1962). The implication is that teachers must possess a personal giftedness and an educational artistry in the tradition of Maria Montessori, Grace Fernald, and August Aichhorn in order to be effective with disturbed children.

Elsewhere, Rabinow (1960) has stated that "the artistry of the teacher is more significant than the trainable competencies" (p. 293). Such a statement may be valid, but it is of questionable usefulness if recruitment and training of teachers are to keep pace with the growing demand for special classes for disturbed children.

Mackie et al. (1957) have attempted to be more specific and objective in delineating necessary qualities for teachers of the socially and emotionally maladjusted. They had teachers of such children rank 88 competencies in order of importance, from understanding of techniques adaptable to the classroom situation for relieving tensions and promoting good mental health (rated number 1) to knowledge of the cul-

SOURCE: *Exceptional Children*, XXXIII (September, 1966), 7–11. Reprinted by permission.

tural patterns of other societies (rated number 88). Although this is an impressive and ambitious undertaking, the reader may not feel well informed after completing the study, due to the large number of competencies ranked and the wide scope of educational skills covered.

In an effort to be more concise while retaining the operational flavor of Mackie's work and reflecting some of the dynamic personal qualities suggested by Rabinow and others, the staff of the Neuropsychiatric Institute (NPI) School at the University of California, Los Angeles, has developed a hierarchy of competencies for the teacher of the emotionally handicapped. These competencies were selected after four years of offering a one semester training course to public-school teachers in a psychiatric hospital school setting. Many of these competencies have been stated elsewhere (Mackie et al., 1957; Lord, 1950; and Stullken, 1950) as desirable for all teachers of exceptional children. The purpose of this paper is to emphasize their order of importance and to attempt to define them objectively.

The hierarchy of teacher competencies roughly parallels a hierarchy of educational tasks for children with learning disorders developed earlier in the NPI School (Hewett, 1964). The hierarchy presupposes that teachers entering the field of education of the emotionally handicapped will possess the dedication and vitality necessary for all individuals who become effective teachers of exceptional children. In order of importance (from most basic to highest level), the hierarchy emphasizes that the teacher of the emotionally handicapped child should be objective, flexible, structured, resourceful, a social reinforcer, a curriculum expert, and an intellectual model.

Objectivity

The most important single requirement for the effective teacher of the emotionally handicapped is to be objective. He must be knowledgeable in the field of normal and deviant psychosocial development and familiar with professional literature relating to special education, particularly with the emotionally handicapped. More important than familiarity with theory and experimental findings, however, is the development of an objective, questioning, educational attitude toward teaching. It is not enough to rely on the cafeteria approach to special education, using this technique because it seems appropriate or that material because of its previous success. The teacher should make an objective assessment of why particular approaches are successes or failures and communicate his findings to others, particularly the student teacher.

Educational artists often prefer to radiate inspiration and personal example, rather than to attempt to quantify successes and failures.

Also within the framework of an objective, educational approach is the need to relate professionally to other disciplines such as psychiatry, clinical psychology, and social work. The teacher must strive to define educational goals and practices so that they are understandable to members of these disciplines and relate to the broadest treatment plans for the child, whether in a hospital or day school setting.

Mackie et al. state that the teacher of the emotionally handicapped child must be emotionally stable and not "need to be loved by all, or given to achieving vicarious satisfaction through the antisocial feelings and behavior of others" (p. 17). Rabinow (1960) has described the "crackpots" who are drawn to the field and whose own needs are met through involvement with disturbed children. At the NPI School, some 10 percent of the teachers who enroll in the training course appear too unstable to work successfully with such children. A full discussion of this problem, including whether or not mildly neurotic teachers actually are more effective with disturbed students, is beyond the scope of this paper. Suffice it to say that the objective teacher has some recognition of his own emotional needs and attempts to separate these from the needs of his students.

Flexibility

Closely related to an objective approach to the education of the emotionally handicapped child is the need to be flexible. Perhaps in no other area of education is the teacher faced with such variability among students. What promotes a student's success today may result in a classroom catastrophe tomorrow, depending on the shifting needs and interests of the child. The flexible teacher is comfortable operating in such a state of flux. Continual assessment of students' available learning capacities and subsequent modification of educational goals are essential. As in all special education programs, success experience for the student is given primary focus. The flexible teacher communicates complete acceptance of all students as individuals, regardless of their manifest intellectual, perceptual motor, and social skills, or current emotional states.

Structure

While maintaining a flexible approach, the teacher of the emotionally handicapped child must be structured and must set consistent and reasonable behavioral and educational limits. If these two competencies seem incompatible, they are not. Some aspects of classroom routine and expectation will change on a day to day, minute to minute basis; but there must be a clearly defined substructure operating at all times. At the NPI School, allowance is made for the changing needs and interests of the children as long as they successfully fulfill the role of a student. This role is carefully defined for the child upon admission to class, and it assumes the ability to tolerate some restriction of space, noise level, and activity and to respect the working rights of others. When a child is too upset to function as a student, he is removed from the classroom immediately. Although school is taken away, schooling is not. The latter is provided on a one to one basis until the child can resume the student role.

In addition to maintaining predictable behavioral limits, the teacher must carefully structure student assignments. Units of work which are well defined and realistically attainable, rather than vague and open ended, are preferable. Immediate feedback is also an important adjunct to the structured approach. Assignments should be corrected at once and errors discussed. Daily behavioral rating scales have also been requested by several NPI School students as a means of providing feedback regarding their current class standing.

Resourcefulness

The objective, flexible, and structured teacher who is also resourceful is in an excellent position to teach the emotionally handicapped child. The resourceful teacher provides classroom experiences which emphasize maximum reality testing and multisensory stimulation. He also selects materials and activities that are meaningful and impactful and which draw the child into an exploratory relationship with his environment. Chronologically appropriate curriculum assignments are not utilized at the expense of student motivation and satisfaction. Not only must the teacher create entirely unique lessons for individual students, but he must be prepared to alter or replace these at a moment's notice. The resourceful teacher also assesses sensory and perceptual motor needs of the child and selects learning activities which provide development in these areas and promote readiness for more formal curriculum experience.

Social Reinforcement

In all contact with the emotionally handicapped child, the value of the teacher as a social reinforcer cannot be overemphasized. Most such children display seriously disturbed relationships with others, particularly with adults. At all times it is important to understand how the child perceives the teacher and what opportunities and limitations exist in the teacher-student relationship. Having assessed the child's capacity for relating to an adult authority figure, the teacher can use positive social reinforcement, such as praise and individual attention, in an appropriate manner to motivate and control the student. Negative reinforcements are also essential in maintaining a structured working relationship. For some children, a stern look, a shaking of the head, or a restraining touch may be meaningful and effective. For others, allowing inappropriate behavior to extinguish by ignoring it may be the most successful approach. Selecting successful reinforcement techniques and constantly evaluating their effectiveness are important tasks for the teacher who, as an adult model, can often aid in reshaping the child's social attitudes and behavior. At times, peer groupings may also be used to promote positive social experiences for the child.

Curriculum Expertise

Despite the fact that the competencies previously discussed tend to emphasize the teacher's clinical judgment and psychosocial awareness, skill as a curriculum expert cannot be overlooked. Regardless of the psychological sophistication of the teacher of the disturbed, his ultimate success will depend on a sound basic understanding of educational practices and techniques. As a result, in the selection of the best candidate for a teacher of the disturbed, the individual with an advanced psychology degree but no training in education is often less promising than the stable, flexible, and resourceful classroom teacher who is thoroughly knowledgeable in basic curriculum methods and materials. During the four years of teacher training experience in the NPI School, this has generally been the rule. There is a point in the special education program for most emotionally handicapped children when the primary contribution of the teacher is good teaching. The ability to set realistic academic goals in keeping with the student's intellectual and achievement levels and to institute appropriate developmental and remedial procedures in reading, arithmetic, and other basic skills is an essential competency.

Intellectual Model

Finally, the teacher must be competent in functioning as an intellectual model with those emotionally handicapped students whose problems do not interfere with intellectual functioning and who are often best helped by an educational program of enrichment. Development of good study habits, pursuit of academic work in considerable depth, frequent discussion with the teacher on issues of importance to the student, and involvement in special projects of research may be important aspects of such a program.

An effort has been made to rank seven basic areas of competencies for teachers of the emotionally handicapped. The concept of a hierarchy immediately raises the question of priority of one competency over another. Since objectivity and flexibility are given the most important places in the model, would a teacher possessing these qualities but who is poor as a social reinforcer and curriculum expert be a better teacher of the emotionally handicapped than one possessing social reinforcement and curriculum skills but who is more subjective and rigid in his approach? No definitive answer to this or the other numerous possible comparisons can be given. The competencies within the hierarchy must be viewed collectively. Each is important. Certain teachers adequately compensate for limitations at a particular level and certain emotionally handicapped children respond best to teachers who are more competent in one area than in another.

The value of the concept of the hierarchy is in placing emphasis on the most basic competencies. Objectivity, flexibility, and structure are requisites for the resourceful teacher who functions effectively as a social reinforcer, curriculum expert, and intellectual model. In addition, the hierarchy attempts to aid recruiters, trainers, and prospective teachers in the field of education of the emotionally handicapped by replacing the vague and mystical notion of the gifted artist with a more objective concept of the trainable teacher.

References

HARING, N., and PHILLIPS, E. *Educating Emotionally Disturbed Children.* New York: McGraw-Hill, 1962.

HEWETT, F. "A Hierarchy of Educational Tasks for Children with Learning Disorders." *Exceptional Children,* 1964, *31,* 207–214.

LORD, F., and KIRK, S. "The Education of Teachers of Special Classes." In *Forty-ninth Yearbook of the National Society for the Study of Education.* Chicago: University of Chicago Press, 1950. Pp. 103–116.

MACKIE, ROMAINE, KVARACEUS, W., and WILLIAMS, H. *Teachers of Children Who Are Socially and Emotionally Maladjusted.* Washington, D.C.: U.S. Department of Health, Education, and Welfare, 1957.

RABINOW, B. "Role of the School in Residential Treatment." *American Journal of Orthopsychiatry,* 1955, *25,* 685–691.

RABINOW, B. "A Proposal for a Training Program for Teachers of the Emotionally Disturbed and the Socially Maladjusted." *Exceptional Children,* 1960, *26,* 287–293.

STULLKEN, E. "Special Schools and Classes for the Socially Maladjusted." In *Forty-ninth Yearbook of the National Society for the Study of Education.* Chicago: University of Chicago Press, 1950. Pp. 281–301.

44. The Teacher's Role in the Education of the Emotionally Disturbed Child

RUTH LAVIETES

In recent years there has been an increasing awareness of the numbers of emotionally disturbed children in public, private, and special-teaching institutions. These children present difficulties both in learning and in conforming to behavioral standards that are sufficient to prevent their participation in the classroom. Various programs are being devised to deal with their problems, some of them marked by pragmatic trial-and-error efforts as the response to immediate crisis, and others carefully designed in relation to particular groups, goals, etc.

The teacher's role in any of these programs is considered vital, and there have been descriptions offered as to the qualities necessary in the teacher. Nevertheless, there has been a tendency to keep the teacher separate from the therapeutic team. Such an attitude as "The teacher's job is to teach and not to be a therapist," while having certain truth to it, reflects the idea that the teacher's role can be separated from that of a

SOURCE: *American Journal of Orthopsychiatry,* XXXII, No. 5 (October, 1962), 854–62.

therapist and indicates that there is a clear-cut difference between the pedagogical and therapeutic handling of certain situations. The teacher is the one professional person who has the largest amount of time with the child; as is well known in the education of disturbed children, a great part of this time is not spent with academic matters.

In the education of the emotionally disturbed child, what is the teacher's role to be? Should she harken to some education supervisors, and with kindliness, sympathy, tolerance, and imagination do the best she can to teach these children while accepting the impossibility of usual procedures? Or should she yield to a clinical viewpoint, that treatment must precede learning, and devote her efforts to the former? If she falls in between, will she be neither fish nor fowl, which is not only confusing to herself but to the children she undertakes to unconfuse?

This paper proposes the idea that the teacher of the emotionally disturbed child must function in a special role which integrates both the traditional role of the teacher and the clinical role of the psychotherapist if she is to enable these children to learn and if she is to help and not hinder their total development. Her understanding of her methods and goals and of the individual children in her care, through her joint supervision by an educator and a clinician, will clarify and integrate her function to the desired ends. It is proposed to demonstrate with the aid of certain conceptual formulations and clinical material how the role of the teacher of the emotionally disturbed differs to a large degree from that of the teacher of normal children. The teacher of emotionally disturbed children is faced by alternative attitudes and courses of action toward the children. One course would be dictated by current average use in the schools of the community, and the other dictated by the individual child's need. The resolution of this conflict necessitates her accepting the proposed special role if her goal is the greatest benefit to the child.

The observations for this paper were made largely at the Godmothers' League Day Treatment Center and School for Emotionally Disturbed Children. This institution, affiliated both with the Mount Sinai Hospital of New York [1] and the Board of Education of the City of New York,[2] has been operating since 1956 and in the first five years dealt with 48 children. The school is attended by children between six and nine, who have been excluded from public schools in the community because of difficulties in either learning or behavior. The difficulties must be of emotional origin, stemming from intrafamilial pathology. They must

[1] Abram Blau, M.D., Attending Psychiatrist-in-Charge, and Wilfred Hulse, M.D., Associate Attending Psychiatrist, Child Psychiatry Division, Department of Psychiatry, The Mount Sinai Hospital, New York, N.Y.

[2] Irving Boroff, Principal, P.S. 622, Board of Education, New York, N.Y.

offer a good enough prognosis so that, after up to three years of a special school, individual treatment, and treatment of the parents, the child will be able to return to the community school and to continue to improve. In each class there are from five to seven children. The diagnostic range is wide. Most of the children have severe conduct disorders or childhood schizophrenia of the nonautistic type. Twenty-three of the children dealt with in the period 1956–61 have already returned to community schools. There is a follow-up program of treatment for children and parents.

There is a theoretical and practical difference between the goals of the traditional teacher with normal children and the goals of a teacher of children who are emotionally disturbed. Briefly, goals with normal children are as follows:

1. Achievement of a specific organized body of useful knowledge.
2. Maintenance of group discipline to the degree necessary for other goals and not beyond the point where it interferes with other goals.
3. Stimulation of creativity, resources, and potentials.
4. Imparting of social and ethical standards on a larger scale than may take place in the home.
5. Making of learning a satisfying experience with pleasurable goals but at the same time increasing the child's ability to meet challenge and frustration.

We can assume that these goals are also present with disturbed children, but that they are not immediate goals and cannot be reached by the methods employed with normal children. Rather, they are long-range goals to be achieved after certain prerequisite goals have been attained. These prerequisite goals fall within the sphere of the teacher of emotionally disturbed children. They may briefly be described as follows:

1. Making the child feel adequate, hopeful, and unafraid in the group teaching experience through
   a) undoing distortions in interpersonal relationships by means of the teacher's behavior toward the child;
   b) reducing anxiety in the child through the reduction of inappropriate expectations from him;
   c) presenting benign social reality to a child who has experienced distortions in reality perceptions in the past or who has withdrawn from adapting to reality;

d) overcoming resistance to learning through stress on nonpainful, nondangerous, pleasurable, ego-building aspects of learning.

2. Substitution of mutual aid (cooperation, sharing, awareness of others' needs) for competition and suspicion of others.

These two sets of goals have certain technical implications. These are outlined in Table 1. It should not be thought that there is necessarily a higher value on the items in Column B than on those in Column A. Rather, the emphasis in Column B grows from the goals for the teaching of disturbed children. Those items in Column A which might be criticized, e.g., No. 8, do not necessarily exist in every class of normal children but certainly do exist in a great number of classes of them. Strong efforts must be made constantly to eliminate these methods from classes for disturbed children. It is the planned aspect of Column B which should be stressed.

It would be perhaps helpful to give some clinical examples of choice which a teacher of disturbed children has between a traditional, group-oriented means devised for an average child and an experimental, individualized means devised for a disturbed child. These examples were obtained from observations in several institutions where disturbed children are taught and from collecting data from the clinical team working with such children over a period of several years. While it is certainly true that "mistakes" provided many of the examples, these were not so much errors as they were the following of traditional methods by teachers either because they were inexperienced with disturbed children or had not previously adapted traditional methods to deviant groups. The fact that they were well-intentioned people emphasizes the fact that professional direction on a clinical basis is a necessary part of the teacher's equipment.

A. Customary procedures around the areas of homework, ceremonies, assemblies, salute to the flag, performances on the part of the children, the exercise of democracy by means of choice and vote, and group activities, such as parties or the eating of lunch together, can present difficulties to disturbed children both because anxiety is provoked and because the child can distort such procedures to satisfy his own sick needs.

Example 1. Johnny, a 9-year-old boy, repeatedly requested homework from his teacher. Since the child seemed to want it so much and certainly needed extra tutoring, the teacher gave him daily assignments to complete at home. Through Johnny's therapy it was discovered subsequently that the boy used the homework assignments to provoke his stepmother into harsh, punitive behavior in order to reduce the guilt he felt over his own mother's death. He would then feel freer to express anger toward his stepmother, for which she

TABLE 1

Col. A *Technical implications of goals for normal children*	Col. B *Technical implications of goals for disturbed children*
1. Larger classes	1. Smaller classes
2. Group process always dominant over individual process	2. Individual process dominant over group most of the time
3. Emphasis on content, curriculum, materials	3. Emphasis on child's feeling about self, group, teacher, and learning process
4. Expectation of verbal and motor control	4. Tolerance of verbal and motor discharge
5. Personality of teacher less significant to process	5. Personality of teacher strong influence in achievement of goals
6. Teaching techniques designed for average child	6. Teaching techniques devised on individual basis using knowledge of child
7. Expectations usually held higher than performance and geared to group	7. Expectations usually held to level of performance and variable with each child
8. Use of pressure, reproach, guilt, and competition in stimulating conformity. Goal of learning justifies means to it	8. Avoidance of such methods. Means of learning are a large part of the goal
9. Distance and formality of relationship between teacher and child	9. Closeness and informality of relationship; more physical closeness unless contraindicated
10. Displays of achievement by chronological age standards	10. Recognition of achievements suitable to capacities
11. Teacher's relationship to parent haphazard, mostly decided by individual teacher	11. Teacher's relationship to parent calculated for benefit of child, decided clinically
12. Thinking dominated by survival of the fittest with exclusion of the deviant	12. Survival of all is dominant. Tolerance of the deviant
13. Standard equipment, room design, furniture with displays, etc. designed for average children and augmented by individual teacher	13. Planned room size, furniture, displays, etc., with effect on child as basis for arrangements
14. Teacher has clerical responsibility during class	14. Teacher must be free of clerical responsibility when with children

would retaliate. He thus used homework in the service of an established sadomasochistic pattern. The teacher's alternative, i.e., understanding the implications of the homework, would be to refuse the child homework and to keep tutoring on a professional level, thus interrupting the sado-masochistic pattern.

Example 2. During the gym program with a group of seven 6-year-olds, the teacher called for a vote on what activity to do next. As a response to this invitation to exercise democratic choice, two of the children began to fight, one jumped up and down excitedly masturbating, two ran up to the teacher screaming and beat him with their fists to get their choice, one sat impassive, and one looked frightened. It is apparent that this group is not ready to exercise choice and that the teaching of democracy must be postponed or given in small, careful doses.

Example 3. During the group lunch period, Robert, an 8-year-old boy, would take certain items of food, go across the room with his back to the others, and eat by himself. There was a staff discussion as to whether Robert should be required to sit with the others or be allowed to follow this rather bizarre pattern. The latter was decided upon because, in therapy, it was known that Robert had such strong fears of being devoured that the sight of people chewing resulted in panic and disorganization. This choice was made because of clinical knowledge of the child rather than because of any adherence to conventional procedure.

B. The latitude of personal expression and behavior allowable to a teacher has generally been left to the judgment of the individual teacher. Some teachers are reticent about themselves while others share a good deal of their personal lives with their classes. It is a well-known principle that psychiatrists do not share their personal lives with patients as it is thought that this is not in the best interest of the patients and the development of the treatment process. In the teaching of disturbed children, the degree of personal expression permissible to the teacher must be decided by the effect upon each child rather than by the teacher's own inclinations.

Example 4. Mr. G. had a close relationship with a boy in his class who, fatherless, was torn between passive, dependent, feminine identification and strong, aggressive, masculine denial of this. One day, as had been his occasional custom as a teacher, Mr. G. brought his daughter to class. This casual behavior could have negative effects on the pupil.

Example 5. Mrs. L., a divorced teacher, upon being questioned by her children in the class told them she and her husband had not gotten along well together and that he had moved to a different city. Two of the children who came from homes where fighting was frequent and where they feared the marriage would break up became frightened at hearing this. This is a case in which it is not in the best interest of the children to learn that the teacher on whom they depend for stability can be identified with their unstable parents. It would have been better in this case for the teacher to have avoided giving the information by relating to the child's interest in her rather than to the content of his questions.

C. A curriculum which is designed for average or large groups often presents difficulties to disturbed children. Certain features of workbooks, reading books, visual art materials, etc., can be confusing or disturbing to certain children.

Example 6. A group of schizophrenic children, several of whom were showing clear difficulties in differentiating fantasy from reality, were being taught about American furniture. The lesson required them to look at a picture of a room in a museum which was in their workbook, and to answer stated questions. Despite frequent repetitions from the teacher several children appeared confused as to the meaning of the entire experience. This was evidenced by answers that indicated the children did not know where the room was or what it was supposed to portray. Even the questions in the text were confusing because they offered multiple-choice answers. For example, one of the questions asked was what a placard on the table of the room said, either "Please Do Not Handle" or "For Sale $1.00." For children who have difficulty in distinguishing reality, this picture was not an effective way to help them. A room with extremely unfamiliar furniture can only augment their confusion, and such questions as quoted throw more doubt on the entire matter. This kind of curriculum is obviously unsuited for the teaching of this kind of child.

Example 7. Mike, a 6-year-old boy who had been deserted by his father at a time when he felt quite ambivalent toward him, seemed unable to learn to read from the usual reading books. By accident, his teacher discovered, when she gave him a book from the library, that his seeming inability to read was his avoidance of the typical family situation which is portrayed in the beginning reading books. Given other contents this resistance to reading markedly decreased. This is an example of the adaptation of curriculum to an individual child dependent upon understanding the child's pathology.

D. Understanding the impact of the child's pathology needs to be developed in teachers of the emotionally disturbed child if they are not to go along with pathological wishes. If the staff is not alerted to what the child is trying to do and not supported in efforts to resist the repetition of events in the child's previous life, there is a great likelihood that the teachers will fall into the "trap" of the child and render themselves unable to help him.

Example 8. Anne, an 8-year-old girl who had experienced marked parental rejection since her birth, at first aroused much sympathy in her teacher which resulted in her receiving a great deal of support, attention, etc. However, instead of responding with gratitude and some demonstration that she was being gratified at last, Anne responded by increasing her demands and by performing acts against the teacher, destroying the contents of her desk, flooding the room, breaking windows, etc., which became intolerable. The teacher, and indeed most of the staff who had contact with the child, developed negative feelings so that they found themselves in the position of repeating the parental attitude toward Anne. Only by considerable discussion of the problem and comprehension of the child's intention in this regard was it possible to prevent the continuance of this undesirable attitude.

Example 9. Leo, a 7-year-old schizophrenic boy, used obsessive, intellectualized questioning as a means of avoiding what he considered was painful contact with others. Since these questions always began on a reasonable level appropriate to the schoolroom, the teacher responded to them. In a short time she would become embroiled in endless and meaningless abstractions. This resulted in her having to terminate the questions in a way that she felt was defeating both for the child and herself. It was only after understanding what both she and the child were doing that she was able to refuse to answer his questions and to relate to the fact that it was anxiety which was producing them.

E. The physical handling of the disturbed child is of great significance; it cannot be dealt with casually as it can with normal children. With the disturbed child it is often necessary to have either a greater or a lesser amount of physical contact between teacher and child than is considered desirable in public school.

Example 10. Ely, an 8-year-old schizophrenic boy, would have periodic breakthroughs into consciousness of aggressive, destructive impulses which had been imperfectly repressed. Efforts to help him control them were ineffective, except for extremely firm, physical containment. Strong external prohibition with punitive rather than accepting physical restraint helped the ego recognize and predict limits and so regain control. Most teachers avoid intensely restrictive physical contact, some, usually with a nursery-school background. bring to the restriction a great acceptance of the child. Neither of these alternatives was effective with this boy. He could relax only with a physical contact, which was difficult for most teachers to make.

F. The place of food in the classroom preoccupies teachers of emotionally disturbed children. Since so many of them have ungratified oral needs it would seem reasonable to fulfill them. Food is usually prohibited in classes for normal children, except at certain specified times. It could be felt that the gratification interferes with learning development of controls of normal habit patterns.

Example 11. Betty, a 7-year-old girl, who had been affectively deprived by a detached mother, was extremely irritable and had frequent and severe temper outbursts throughout the day. These could be abated by feeding her on a demand schedule. However, this interfered with class routine and appearance, the lunch hour, etc., and there was considerable discussion as to whether this was the most desirable method of helping the group and the child. The clinical opinion held that in this case the tantrums were anxiety attacks that could be helped only by the reassurance of food. Ultimate results substantiated this, and there were no noticeable ill effects on the child or the group.

G. Discipline of emotionally disturbed children has a place in their therapy but must be individually tailored for the particular child at the particular time, lest it not only fail to accomplish its purpose but be harmful.

Example 12. Ida, a 10-year-old schizophrenic girl who was attacking all the children in her class was sent to a neighboring class as a punishment. Here the teacher sat her on a chair in the middle of the room with nothing to occupy her. She immediately regressed into hallucinatory experiences, holding her fingers up in front of her and talking to them out loud. In this case the punishment did not suit the crime or, more exactly, the criminal. Although it might or might not have taught her how to behave, it induced a regressive experience which was harmful to her development.

H. The protection of a weak child from the aggression of others is a time-honored function of the teacher. Yet even this can be questioned in the case of some children.

Example 13. Richard, a 6-year-old phobic child, had a very depreciated self-image as the result of the extreme overprotectiveness of his mother. He seemed so helpless and appealed for help so charmingly that the teacher took over his defense against attacks from other children. This helped him to continue his passive, feminine identification and his repression of anxiety. It was very difficult for the teacher to expose this child to the aggression of other disturbed children. The teacher was also subjected to the mother's threats to withdraw the child unless he were protected. When left on his own, the child himself managed to work out a much more effective defense against the other children. This also enhanced his self-esteem.

I. The degree of emotional expression is usually limited in a school situation. School is not considered a proper sphere for strong displays of pleasure, fear, rage, etc. This concept needs to be altered when one is dealing with disturbed children.

Example 14. Jules, a 6-year-old boy who reacted to knowledge of his own aggressive feelings with a desire to withdraw from reality, had been encouraged in this by his parents. Both of them were very angry people with a strong, defensive system against their anger. Since in therapy Jules created little opportunity to display his rage, it was in the classroom, where he met with opposition and frustration from the group, that there was the greatest opportunity to observe this reaction and to help him with it. Rather than aiding him to suppress his anger, which would certainly have made for an easier classroom experience, the teacher was encouraged to promote angry displays, to accept them from the child, and to make them effective for him. While this made for a noisier classroom with displays which were, by usual standards, not acceptable, it helped Jules in his self-acceptance. In addition, because the other children understood what she was doing, the proceedings neither alarmed nor tempted them.

J. Sexual activity and preoccupation on the part of children, both normal and otherwise, has long been a problem for teachers. In classes for disturbed children there is more sexual pathology and a chance for more expression of this preoccupation on their part. This is a particular area where the teacher's own feelings about sexual questions affect her handling of them and therefore become a province into which the psychiatrist must enter. This is, of course, true in every area discussed, but the application appears most delicate and difficult in this area.

Example 15. Mrs. P, the teacher, reported constant use of sexual slang, masturbation, displays of genitals, and sexual activity among the children. Observation of Mrs. P in her classroom revealed the following incident. Two children, Ricky and Louise, were amusing themselves by Louise's pulling down her pants and displaying her genitals to Ricky. Mrs. P forbade them to do this and sent them to separate sides of the room. They continued to be extremely excited, and when the class was scheduled to go to another room, Mrs. P kept the two children behind with her. Then she busied herself cleaning the room, telling the children "to play house." She gave them a blanket under which the two of them lay and pretended to sleep. After a few minutes Louise called out to her: "Mommy, is it time to get up and go to school?" Mrs. P replied: "I'm the teacher, not your mommy. You will have to play mommy and daddy together." The children thereupon began to push and shove each other under the blanket to the accompaniment of excited shrieks. One is very familiar with parents who unconsciously encourage the very thing they complain of in their children. That this should also occur with teachers is not unexpected, and it is an area in which clinical help is essential.

K. Group teaching, whether it be in a large class for average children or in a small group for disturbed children, has been accepted as the *sine qua non* of school. But even this must be adapted on occasion to individual needs.

Example 16. Al was an 8-year-old boy who dreaded failure in competition with other males. Despite his adequacy in the academic area, he became clownish and aggressive at the beginning of each day during the more formal parts of the teaching. This interrupted the class to the point where he had to be removed. It was decided to avoid this defeat for him by having an individual tutoring session the first thing every morning. As a result, his behavior for the rest of the day was much better, and after a few months he sought on his own to return to the group. There he was able to display his privately acquired adequacy and begin a group learning program. Had Al, because of our knowledge of his adequacy, been forced to remain with the others he would have imagined himself defeated day after day. This could only have augmented the original difficulty.

Since the teacher plays a central role in the total therapy of the disturbed child, considerable attention must be paid to the selection and preparation of teachers for this work. Four areas of emphasis are the orientation of teachers, personality of teachers, knowledge of the children they reach, and techniques for teaching disturbed children.

The orientation of the teacher of emotionally disturbed children to her job should be twofold. She should see herself both as an educator and as a member of the orthopsychiatric team responsible for a segment of the total therapeutic program. Teachers trained in current schools of education often find it difficult to see themselves in the latter role both because they have received little or no training for it and because they have little acceptance of the idea. Educators must therefore emphasize the broader conception of the teacher's role. Directly or indirectly, the teacher working with disturbed children should be supervised both by an educator and by a clinician. Methods and goals adapted to this special group of children must be worked out in collaboration by educational and psychiatric specialists and offered to the teacher in a way which will bring clarity and direction to her work. Differences of opinion between the two disciplines can exist, and answers can be sought on an experimental level. However, lack of integration with regard to techniques and aims can only result in disorganization, immobilization, and nontherapeutic action of the teacher, with the expected consequences to the children. Teachers who are unprepared in their training for working with other disciplines are frequently fearful of exposure to the psychiatrist. Although the right kind of experience should alter this, the cooperation of the clinician and the education supervisor can make this aspect of supervision more acceptable.

In order to perform such a supervisory function with teachers the clinician must have had special experience with developmental psychodynamics, with normal and deviant children in classes, and with teaching techniques. He needs this kind of experience so as not simply to transpose psychiatric experience with individuals and groups to the classroom for disturbed children.

The importance of the personality of the teacher of emotionally disturbed children cannot be overemphasized. The academic training and passing of licensure examinations do not qualify a teacher in this field.

Teachers in it should be selected with regard to their interest, motivation, and personality. Such factors as the level of anxiety, tolerance to frustration, sensitivity to emotional motivation, identifications, types of defenses, and the ability to understand oneself should be considered in the selection of teachers. It is difficult to evaluate many of these factors except by observing the teacher and her group of children. The preoccupation and exaggerated behavior of disturbed children tend to bring out the teacher's character structure more sharply. Even the selection and use of techniques are affected by the teacher's likes and dislikes, tolerance for deviation, need for order or disorder, affinity for a certain subject matter, etc. When certain tendencies are observed by a clinician who is in a better position than an educator to understand manifestations of unconscious behavior, it must be possible for the teacher to gain understanding of herself and her attitude toward the children as part of her supervision. Emphasis should be placed on the personality of the teacher who works with disturbed children, just as it is on that of students of psychiatry, social work, and psychology while they are in training.

Knowledge of the individual children under care is essential to therapeutic education. The total handling of each child becomes more therapeutic if the teacher has a knowledge of his background (see Example 1 above), diagnosis (see Example 6 above), and level of functioning (see Example 9 above).

Methods and techniques of teaching and of interacting with disturbed children are a vital part of the equipment needed by teachers who work in this area. The adaptation of the usual curriculum and techniques for use with disturbed children and, further, for use with the disturbed child individually must be worked out in collaboration by the educator and the clinician. This cannot be left to chance (see Example 6 above).

Because of the large number of emotionally disturbed children in our population and the seriousness of the problem that they present, their education has become an area of increasing interest both to educators and to clinical people. To work out a comprehensive plan for dealing with these children, whether it starts in the guidance clinic or in the school, needs the collaboration of several disciplines of which one of the most important, if not the most important, is that of the teacher. To rely, as in the past, on traditionally trained and well-meaning teachers to do the job themselves is to lose the opportunity to give maximum help to these children. Areas of behavior and interaction occur in the classroom which a teacher, unaided by the rest of the team, cannot handle therapeutically. The contention is therefore made that a great deal more cooperative planning between the educators and the rest of the clinical team with regard to goals, methods and techniques, curriculum, and the selection and preparation of teachers is necessary to ensure optimum results in the education of emotionally disturbed children.

45. Preparing to Teach the Disturbed Adolescent

WILLIAM C. MORSE

All secondary teachers are teachers of disturbed adolescents. There may sometimes be a term with not one in a single class, but the greater likelihood is there will be several each and every term. Some of these adolescents will suffer only the exaggerated inflections common to their age. Others will show persistent deviancy of a more profound sort where the predictability of long term maladjustment is only too certain.

In the past, schools have rested their case for meeting the needs of disturbed students who were not excluded from school largely through guidance, psychological, and social work specialists on the staff. This is not to say there were never "special rooms for misfits." It is only to say the nature of these special classes usually fell far short of the quality which present knowledge indicates as minimal if anything beyond custodial is anticipated. Modern concepts of intervention include active planning of the total milieu and corrective influence through day by day school activities as well as by classical therapy. Thus schools have begun an about-face in their approach. At the lower levels special classrooms themselves have been seen as the core of school provision and treatment. Classes for the emotionally and socially maladjusted were usually started at the later elementary but their use spread to primary and secondary levels. While many children were restored to regular classrooms, it soon became clear that others, while not too disturbed to keep and help in school, were long time cases. In fact, there were those who would need continuous protection of one type or another even in post school society as well.

SOURCE: *The High School Journal,* LXIX (March, 1966), 259–65. Reprinted by permission of The University of North Carolina Press.

Some of the early secondary classes for the disturbed tended to imitate those for the elementary which depended largely on self-contained classes with a single teacher. The mistake here was to activate the resistance of the adolescent to being different, "one of the dumb ones," which were the only segregated pupils of this type they knew about. The more adequate design maximizes the similarity of this secondary program to other secondary school classes. Two subject matter area teachers work with the clientele in tandem, one teaching a science and math core, the other an English and social studies core for students who cannot find a possible class in any of the regular classes. The many opportunities for individual placement are tried when feasible. When one teacher works with the group which is left, his companion tutors, counsels, helps with homework, or visits the other teachers where the students take classes for liaison work.[1] Parenthetically, it is an interesting thing that girls are referred in a ratio of about one in five to boys. This must mean that, though they are less of a problem to the schools, many girls who are disturbed are not referred because we know that in adult life disturbance is not found in any such inequality.

The type of a teacher preparation needed for teaching the disturbed adolescent is predicated on one's assumptions about the purpose of the special school program. The two assumptions here are that the school has an obligation to maximize the pupil's knowledge and skills. Second, that disturbed youth will use interpersonal relationships in a more complicated manner which dictates the need for deeper knowledge and insight on the part of the teacher. This does not mean that "soft" handling is necessarily helpful as shall be evident in later paragraphs. Nor does it imply that any one design, class or otherwise, will be sufficient to help all disturbed adolescents.

As was indicated, the first need on the part of the teacher is for subject and skill teaching preparation. These pupils are not selected for intellectual limitations even though some may test low or function in highly idiosyncratic ways and present special learning and motivation problems. The essential point is that, with modern mass communication, even the school-stunted learner has many areas of information and the mental age to deal with more than elementary content. The fact that no teacher can have the renaissance man's breadth of knowledge means that teams will be necessary in the secondary school as was suggested. Perhaps for secondary school teachers subject matter preparation can be taken as axiomatic, but skill in therapeutic teaching cannot. Equal to subject matter is the ability to cultivate tool skills, often in the presence

[1] Branoff, Peter K. "A Public School Design for the Education of Disturbed Adolescents." Livonia Public Schools, Livonia, Michigan. 10 Pgs. Mimeographed.

of a learning handicap. That is to say, frequently learning does not come easily to these pupils because of emotional or perceptual blocks. The special teacher will know the difference between simple remediation and educational therapy. Educational therapy implies the recognition, through subtle technique, of both conscious and unconscious inhibitions and fears on the part of the student. It requires walking the tightrope between encouragement and support on one hand, and reasonable demand and pressure on the other, always employing tasks and using methods adapted to the pupils' present capacity. By the time a pupil is in secondary school most of his limitations will be only too evident and incapacities too glaring to him. It may be that part of the educational work can be accomplished only on a one-to-one tutorial basis; all of it will require handling with an awareness of nuances. The special teacher can never learn too much about the intricacies of learning.

Adolescence itself is such a complicated phenomenon that society blanches before it. We move from distant admiration of the open impulsiveness to fear driven punitiveness. The school, as the major socialization force for adolescents, follows suit. It becomes clear why the teacher of disturbed adolescents must have a far more firm grounding in the psychology of the age. Normal adolescence implies the vacillation of self-identity seeking with one's own nature, one's sexual attributes, and one's destiny, all in a state of flux. There is exploration of new patterns and an attempt to balance dependency-independency with peer and adult. As if this were not enough, for the special pupil there is also the matter of the overlay of maladjustment.

The major insight of the special teacher is the unique receptivity to motivations which underlie the presenting symptoms. This is the important matter of differential diagnosis. The clinical awareness enables the teacher to deal empathically with the underlying feelings and, most often, without any direct interpretation. Tolerance increases and knowledge of what to do increases apace as one really understands the dynamic nature of the individual adolescent's behavior.

In bold fact, it becomes first nature for the special teacher to operate on the knowledge that symptoms must be interpreted before they can become the basis for hygienic handling. One youngster's hostility may need to be listened to until it drains off, while another's may be his way of life and his very existence. Here an attempt to drain off the hostility would be as unproductive as would be adult counter hostility. It would be impossible to list all of the behavior patterns to which the school must respond in this knowledgeable manner, but three types of difficulties prevalent to the school community and specifically to the teacher will be noted in terms of school appearance rather than the usual diagnostic terms.

First, there is the school alienated youth, but it is necessary to separate the truly alienated from the pseudo-alienated. The truly antagonistic are those for whom any adjustment to the school, as it is now conceived, will have little meaning. They operate on a short time perspective and look for immediate return of a concrete gain. Their life experience, regardless of their socioeconomic class, has taught them to hope for little and obtain what you can at the moment. They are tuned into the money economy wave length. It is often not so much that these young people are intra-psychologically disturbed as that they are very disturbing to the school and for this reason they are often first referred for special classes. Watered down curricula, dispirited "third tracks," and resigned teachers are no answer. Their main goal is to participate in the economic economy (even work if they must) to purchase clothes, and with boys, a car. Some are not above taking what they want and they may openly reject the sexual morality the school tries to maintain. Easily provoked, the school provokes them more often than helps. The present bromide is "get them a job." The point is, to become a functioning member of any segment of society, they will have to learn to stick at a job, take orders at times, and develop a reasonable degree of dependency. This means that employment is not a simple end but only a means for helping the youth achieve whatever stability and place in society he can. It will require counseling, support, encouragement, and down to earth talk about material ends and means. Traditional educational experiences for these pupils will be at a most rudimentary and ancillary level. The teacher learns how to use this mode of education and work for therapeutic purposes but it is as difficult and frustrating as one might predict if one is frank.

But there are other pupils who appear alienated and accumulate the trappings without the essence. There is nothing many of the discouraged youth would like to do as much as join the succeeders. But they have given up. They feel too far behind. The pseudo-alienation is their cover-up. Wistfully defensive though they may be, the road to hope is long and arduous because they lack the intestinal fortitude to accompany the regeneration of hope from outside. They are prone to pleasure and low on the ego capacities of persistence and hard work. A youngster whose real nature is of this type will find ways to make any work therapy fail. The pathetic inability of these youngsters to come through with even simple intentions is well known to the experts. Thus again, a teacher must know more than symptoms or he will be easily discouraged.

Many of the students referred will have conflict within themselves which they will try to work out, at least partly, in the school arena. There are those neurotics where the whole of life success has become dependent upon over-achievement but they seldom are referred since they fit in school with their effort. More likely it is the underachievers, the school playboys and, to some extent, the shy and odd members of the school clientele who will be considered for special classes.

These symptoms are seen by the special teacher as having depth to be plumbed. School has become of late such a control of the open door to the future that it has at the same time become a Pandora's Box. Because so much depends upon school success, school behavior can be used as a way of striking out in many directions, frequently in ways having nothing to do with the issue at hand. A teacher cannot find an interesting subject or reasonable assignment because the disinterest or unreasonable aspect is not really of school itself. Both Lichter and Riessman [2] have discussed these reactions at length. The vital matter at present is again the recognition that behavior is seldom what it first seems. The special teacher learns to recognize sex used for mere pleasure in contrast to sex for buying relationship or a sense of power. Academic failure can become a weapon for unexpressed hostility to parents. Disinterest and inability to concentrate can blanket deep self-discouragement or guilt in areas hidden from view. Thus differential diagnosis of the meaning of symptoms precedes differential handling. Only as we come to appreciate what lies beneath the surface can this be done.

The third common category of young people referred are the few but potent very disturbed and even psychotic children. While one hopes that eventually they will have the benefit of complete treatment, there are severe limitations in placement. Then we know too that many very disturbed young people can maintain themselves to some degree in a public school under a special teacher. Here intensive individual treatment should be correlated with the school experience. In some instances, after schooling they will need a protected workshop for life. Incidentally, those model students who commit homicide to the astonishment of everyone are not of this type. They would seldom be referred for such classes unless there is careful scrutiny of the school population. They are basking in their all-over goodness.

Thus, the main skill of the special teacher of adolescents is a keen sensitivity which enables him to use his own personality in useful interpersonal relationships—which are not always the same as easy or pleasant ones. Since any relationship is only half produced by the pupil, it becomes part of the teacher's training to understand this self as well as the other self. Unfinished emotional business is all too easily activated by adolescent maladaptive behavior. It is both trying and exasperating

[2] Lichter, S. O.; Rapien, E. B.; Seibert, F. M. and Sklansky, M. A. *The Dropouts*, Free Press, 1962.

Riessman, F. *The Culturally Deprived Child*, Harper & Bros., 1962.

to respond without irritation for they are skilled at upsetting adults in one way or another. As is commonly said, they "get to me." This will be true unless one is aware of his own nature. This is common talk for the well-known fact of counter-transference. Counter-transference is the generation of feelings within the therapist about his own life by how the client reacts to him. Being in a power position, and "adult," what we do we can easily rationalize even if it is immature. We must be free to act as the pupil's nature dictates, rather than as our impulses might suggest. Self-understanding modulates the teacher's own cycle of behavior.

But it is not enough to be free to work with adolescents. We must have skills of a particular sort. One of these is the skill to work with colleagues who may not have seen what really is operating because of their less intensive relationship with the youngster. The teacher must be able to identify with these peers as well as with the pupils involved. The insights of the one teacher are of limited value unless they can be communicated to the others. Secondly, the special teacher will need to work comfortably with the other helping disciplines as mentioned above. For the more disturbed, one hopes also the psychiatrist will be available. These personnel are the sources of consultation and help if the teacher comprehends their particular functions. Since teachers are by and large "king of the hill within their room" operators, this team is a change. In many instances it will be necessary to work with many community agencies in the course of helping a youngster.

Underlying these competencies of the special teacher is the ability to communicate effectively with others, particularly distraught pupils. The skill here is interviewing of a new type which is dependent upon the events of the day, so to speak, but which at the same time cuts into the significant underlying structure of the behavior at hand. It is neither non-directive counseling nor traditional therapy. It is designed for the on-the-line worker to use in exploiting certain life events in order to help pupils with their adjustment. Like any skill, the special teacher will devote considerable time to mastering this interactive process. Without it, however good the intent it will fall short.

We are at the point of recognizing the unique training required for teaching disturbed adolescents. It is a blend which retains its educational flavor while at the same time adding a deeper dynamic component. The subject matter-skill-complex is, if anything, intensified. The study of normal and disturbed adolescent behavior is also far beyond that of the typical teacher. To this is added a high level of self-insight, ability to work with others, and high proficiency in interviewing of the type suited to the school teacher's role. It may occur to the reader that none of this training would be lost on the regular secondary teacher as well.

46. A Comparison of the Competencies for Regular Classroom Teachers and Teachers of Emotionally Disturbed Children

BARBARA DORWARD

In spite of the increase in special education programs for emotionally disturbed children and the concurrent rise in teacher preparation courses in this area of exceptionality, there has been little research conducted in this field. One of the first questions raised concerns the competencies needed by teachers of disturbed children. This study attempted to single out any special competencies needed by teachers of disturbed children over and above those needed by regular classroom teachers, and to investigate any differences in competencies needed by teachers of disturbed children in two different settings, residential schools and special day classes.

In 1957 the U. S. Office of Education produced a bulletin on the qualifications and preparation of teachers of socially and emotionally maladjusted children (Mackie, Kvaraceus, and Williams). The opinions of teachers of socially maladjusted children (delinquents) and teachers of emotionally disturbed children were pooled, but the list was not rated by a sample of regular classroom teachers to provide a frame of reference. A list of 88 competencies was rated on a four-point scale and ranked in order of importance. This study neither identified the specific competencies needed for teachers of emotionally disturbed children which dif-

SOURCE: *Exceptional Children,* XXX (October, 1963), 67–73. Reprinted by permission.

fered from those needed for a good teacher in a regular classroom, nor attempted to differentiate between the competencies needed by teachers of disturbed children in different educational settings. Indeed, at that time there were few, if any, special day classes for disturbed children. The present study was designed to take up where this one left off and forge another link in the chain of knowledge in this area.

Method

INSTRUMENT A competency list, built on the earlier one developed in the U. S. Office of Education (Mackie, Kvaraceus, and Williams, 1957), attempted to refine and expand the list to *only* those items specific to teaching emotionally disturbed children. The questionnaire, composed of 100 items, was divided into 11 categories. Respondents were asked to rate each item on a three point scale:

1. *Vital* indicated a competency which was absolutely necessary, without which an effective job of teaching could not be done.
2. *Good but not Essential* referred to skills and knowledges which would be beneficial to have, but without which the teacher could still do a good job.
3. *Unnecessary* items were those which were not specifically needed for this type of teaching.

RESPONDENTS Each state department of education was sent a letter requesting the names of successful teachers of special day classes for emotionally disturbed children and an equal number of names of classroom teachers in the elementary grades. Of the 35 states replying to the original letter, 12 submitted names of teachers.

The residential schools contacted for teachers to participate in the study were chosen because they dealt primarily with pre-adolescent children, did not include delinquents, and had an educational program within the residential setting itself (Sargent, 1958; Reid and Hagan, 1952; Robinson, 1957). Of the 58 residential schools contacted, 26 submitted names and 20 were represented in the final study.

Basic information on the respondents is found in Table 1. About 50 percent of the questionnaires sent out were completed and returned. Residential teachers had less total teaching experience than teachers in special classes but had taught disturbed children longer. The fact that teachers in residential schools had less training could be explained by the fact that they had been in the profession for a shorter period of time and were probably not required to meet state certification requirements.

TABLE 1

BASIC INFORMATION ON THE EIGHTY RESPONDING TEACHERS

Measure	*Residential School Teachers (RS)*	*Special Class Teachers (SC)*	*Regular Class Teachers (RC)*
Questionnaires mailed out	75	49	44
Questionnaires returned	33	25	22
Total years of teaching			
median	7	10	20.5
range	1–35	1–39	1–39
Years of teaching disturbed children			
median	4	3	—
range	1–17	1–19	—
Degrees			
None	5	0	—
AB	14	15	—
MA	14	10	—
Special courses			
None	4	1	—
1–3	9	6	—
4–6	8	4	—
More than 6	10	14	—
No information given	2	0	—
Major field			
Elementary education	13	10	—
Special education	4	3	—
Psychology	2	3	—
All others	14	9	—

ANALYSIS OF RESPONSES The responses to the questionnaire were tested with a χ^2 statistical technique using 3x3 cells and the .05 level of significance. Only 17 items were found to be significant. A 2x2 sub-analysis was made of each of the 17 significant items to determine the teacher groups between which there was a significant difference on that particular competency.

Results

On the basis of the combined responses of all three teacher groups, 61 items were rated as Vital, 39 as Good, and none as Unnecessary. Since a significant difference between groups was found for only 17 items, 83 items showed no significant differences in the ratings given by residential school, special class, or regular class teachers. The most important finding of this study was that only two items were found to be significantly more important for both groups of teachers of disturbed children than for regular classroom teachers. These were "the ability to accept pupils who are violent" and "experience on a clinical team with psychiatrists, psychologists, and social workers in studying disturbed pupils." Closely related to this was "knowledge of the competencies and roles expected of psychiatrists, clinical psychologists, and social workers," which was rated significantly more important for residential school teachers than for regular classroom teachers but not more important for special class teachers.

To compensate for the different number of respondents in each group of teachers, the raw scores were weighted as indicated in Table 2.

TABLE 2

RAW SCORE WEIGHTED VALUES

Group	*Number*	*Value of Vital*	*Value of Good*	*Value of Unnecessary*
Residential School (RS)	33	3	2	1
Special Class (SC)	25	3.96	2.64	1.32
Regular Class (RC)	22	4.5	3.0	1.5

A total weighted score was obtained for each item by combining the subtotal scores of the three groups. Competency items are listed in rank order by total weighted score in Table 3. For example, in the category Personal Qualifications of the Teacher, "Have the ability to be flexible and adaptable" received the highest total weighted score; "Have no need for emotional support from pupils" received the lowest total weighted score. The rank order given each item in a particular category by the three groups, Residential School teachers, Special Class teachers, and Regular Class teachers, is also recorded in Table 3. Significant differences in rankings are indicated.

Criteria for evaluating a competency as Vital, Good, or Unnecessary was as follows. The absolute total number of points if everyone rated an item as Vital would have been 297; Good, 198; Unnecessary, 99. The line of division between competencies rated Vital and those rated Good was arbitrarily placed halfway between absolute Vital and absolute Good, or at 247.5, and any competency with a total weighted score of 247.5 or above was rated as Vital. The critical line between competencies rated Good and those rated Unnecessary was arbitrarily placed halfway between absolute Good and absolute Unnecessary, or at 148.5, and any competency with a total weighted score of at least 148.5 but less than 247.5 was rated as Good. An item was rated Unnecessary if the total weighted score was less than 148.5.

TABLE 3

RANK RATINGS OF COMPETENCY ITEMS LISTED IN RANK ORDER BY TOTAL WEIGHTED SCALE

	RS	*SC*	*RC*
I. PERSONAL QUALIFICATIONS OF THE TEACHER			
Rated Vital			
Have the ability to be flexible and adaptable	3	3	1
Be able to remain stable in emergencies	5	3	3.5
Have the ability to live with the unpredictable nature of emotionally disturbed pupils	3	3	7
Have the ability to accept pupils who express dislike for you as a teacher	7	3	3.5
Be able to remain stable under prolonged stress	3	8.5	3.5
Be able to be satisfied with even slight improvement rather than perfection	7	8.5	3.5
Have a working and adjustive knowledge of one's own personality structure including one's idiosyncrasies	10	3	9
Have good physical health and endurance	7	11	7
Have an awareness of the amount of pressure you can stand	1	8.5	13.5
Have more than the average amount of patience	12.5	12.5	7
Have the ability to accept pupils who use obscenity and profanity	12.5	8.5	11.5

* Significant difference among groups

[a] Significant difference between residential school teachers (RS) and special class teachers (SC)

[b] Significant difference between residential school teachers (RS) and regular class Teachers (RC)

[c] Significant difference between special class teachers (SC) and regular class teachers (RC)

TABLE 3 (*cont.*)

	RS	*SC*	*RC*
Have the ability to display a sense of humor with acting-out children	10	14.5	11.5
Have the ability to differentiate between sympathy and empathy for emotionally disturbed pupils	14	12.5	10
Have the ability to accept pupils who expose you to physical violence *	10 [b]	6 [c]	17 [b, c]
Have the ability to display a sense of humor with withdrawn children	15	14.5	15
Have a wide range of interests, hobbies, and friends outside the field of education *	16 [b]	16	13.5 [b]
Rated Good			
Have the ability to express to pupils one's personal weaknesses and errors	17	17	16
Have no need for emotional support from pupils	18	18	18
II. PERSONALITY DYNAMICS			
Rated Vital			
Knowledge of the differences between normal and abnormal behavior at various age levels	1	1	1
Knowledge of defense mechanisms (rationalization, compensation, projection, sublimation, etc.)*	3 [b]	2	2 [b]
Have an understanding of the theory and principles of group dynamics	2	3.5	3.5
Knowledge of the characteristics and causes of the psychoses of childhood and of such neurotic behavior disorders as hysteria, phobias, obsessive compulsions, etc.	4	3.5	3.5
Rated Good			
Knowledge of the theories of and research in the causes of juvenile delinquency	6	5.5	5
Knowledge of the theories of the structure of personality including Freud, Jung, etc.	5	5.5	6

TABLE 3 (*cont.*)

	RS	*SC*	*RC*
III. CULTURAL AND SOCIAL			
Rated Vital			
Knowledge of the effects of socio-economic status, home and community conditions on the child	1	1	1
Understand the implication for adjustment of the female-based household and other patterns of child rearing	2	2	3
Knowledge of the special emotional problems of minority groups *	3 [b]	3	2 [b]
Rated Good			
Have the ability to avoid imposing middle class standards on children from lower class culture	4	4	4
Knowledge of the mores and modes of living of differerent social and cultural groups in the U.S.*	5 [a, b]	5 [a]	5 [b]
IV. COMMUNITY SERVICES			
Rated Good			
Knowledge of the types of cases seen by child guidance clinics and mental health centers, methods of referral, etc.*	2 [a, b]	1 [a]	1 [b]
Knowledge of the types of cases seen by family service and social welfare organizations, methods of referral, etc.*	4.5 [a, b]	2 [a]	2 [b]
Knowledge of the national professional organizations concerned with the education and/or welfare of emotionally disturbed pupils	1	4	4
Knowledge of the state and local laws, policies, and ruling regarding provisions for emotionally disturbed children	3	3	3
Knowledge of the responsibility of the state for the care and treatment of emotionally disturbed children	4.5	5	5.5
Knowledge of the services of Vocational Rehabilitation	6	6	5.5

TABLE 3 (*cont.*)

	RS	*SC*	*RC*
Knowledge of the local, state, and federal laws pertaining to juvenile delinquency, probation, etc.	7	7	7
V. MENTAL HEALTH TEAM			
Rated Vital			
Be willing to refer problems to other team members without a feeling of failure and guilt if one is unable to solve such problems	1	3	1
Knowledge of professional ethics in dealing with confidential information	3	1	2
Have the ability to interpret the disturbed pupil's educational needs to other professional workers	2	2	3
Have the ability to participate with mental health specialists in developing a comprehensive educational plan for a disturbed pupil	4.5	4	5
Have the ability to demonstrate and explain educational techniques to other disciplines	4.5	5	4
Rated Good			
Knowledge of the competencies and roles to be expected of psychiatrists, clinical psychologists, and social workers *	6.5 [b]	7	7 [b]
Knowledge of the language of psychiatry so as to converse with persons in this profession	8	8	6
Experience participating on a clinical team with psychiatrists, psychologists, and social workers in studying emotionally disturbed pupils *	6.5 [b]	6 [c]	8 [b, c]
VI. PUBLIC AND PARENT RELATIONS			
Rated Vital			
Have the ability to interpret the educational problems and needs of emotionally disturbed pupils to their parents *	1 [a]	1 [a]	1

TABLE 3 (*cont.*)

	RS	*SC*	*RC*
Rated Good			
Have the ability to interpret the emotional problems and needs of emotionally disturbed pupils to their parents *	4 [a, b]	2 [a]	2 [b]
Have the ability to talk to professional groups on the educational needs of emotionally disturbed pupils	3	3	3.5
Have the ability to talk to lay groups on the educational needs of emotionally disturbed pupils	2	4	3.5
VII. DIAGNOSTICS			
Rated Vital			
Have the ability to see lying and stealing as symptoms of a more serious adjustment problem	2	1	1.5
Have the ability to differentiate between educationally retarded and mentally retarded pupils	1	7	1.5
Knowledge of the behavioral characteristics of withdrawn and acting-out pupils	3.5	2.5	4.5
Have the ability to anticipate emotional crises which might endanger the pupil or society	3.5	4.5	4.5
Have the ability to arrive at the level of expectancy of school work in light of intelligence and degree of adjustment	5	2.5	7.5
Have the ability to use family background materials provided by social workers in educational planning for the disturbed pupils	7	4.5	4.5
Have the ability to infer causations of such behavior as temper tantrums, stealing, enuresis, and nail biting	7	7	4.5
Have the ability to make anecdotal records on the behavior of disturbed pupils, including an evaluation of this behavior	7	7	11
Have the ability to make educational interpretations from individual intelligence test results	10	9.5	9
Have the ability to administer and interpret achievement tests	9	12	7.5

TABLE 3 (*cont.*)

	RS	*SC*	*RC*
Have the ability to give and interpret diagnostic tests of reading and arithmetic difficulties	11	9.5	10
Rated Good			
Have the ability to interpret psychiatric and psychological reports.	12	11	14.5
Have the ability to make a comprehensive case study of family background of disturbed pupils in the event that a social worker is not available *	15 [b]	13	13 [b]
Have the ability to administer individual intelligence tests *	15 [b]	15 [c]	12 [b, c]
Have the ability to administer social maturity scales *	15 [b]	14 [c]	14.5 [b, c]
Have the ability to make educational tests from psychological and psychiatric reports	13	16	16
VIII. CLASSROOM ORGANIZATION AND MANAGEMENT			
Rated Vital			
Have the ability to reject behavior without rejecting the child	2	2.5	1.5
Have the ability to teach individually and in very small groups	1	2.5	3
Have the ability to give sincere verbal praise for honest effort and minute success	3.5	9	1.5
Have the ability to set different classroom limits for different children in terms of their psychological diagnosis and treatment plan for rehabilitation	3.5	2.5	5
Have the ability to form a warm two-way relationship with pupils who are extremely aggressive	5.5	6	5
Have the ability to form a warm two-way relationship with pupils who are extremely withdrawn	7.5	6	5
Have the ability to evaluate and modify classroom limits as indicated by pupils' emotional growth	5.5	2.5	11

TABLE 3 (*cont.*)

	RS	*SC*	*RC*
Have the ability to form a warm two-way relationship with pupils who are extremely excitable	7.5	6	8.5
Have the ability to establish a variety of flexible classroom limits from extreme permissiveness to extreme restrictiveness devised primarily to help emotionally disturbed pupils with personal adjustment	9	9	8.5
Have the ability to channel "disgusting" behavior into positive activities	10	9	8.5
Have the ability to design and tolerate a school program which de-emphasizes traditional academic objectives and substitutes as the chief objective the development of an adequate personality	12	12	12
Have the ability to establish, maintain, and live with classroom limits which allow emotionally disturbed pupils extreme deviations in behavior	11	11	13.5
Have the ability to give physical affection to emotionally disturbed pupils	13	13	8.5
Rated Good			
Have the ability to use art work in educational evaluations	14	14	13.5
Have the ability to talk the language of emotionally disturbed pupils (slang, colloquialisms, fads, etc.)	15	15	15

IX. TEACHING TECHNIQUES

	RS	*SC*	*RC*
Rated Vital			
Have the ability to devise concrete means for letting the emotionally disturbed child see progress and improvement	1	2	1
Have the ability to select and teach those arts and crafts with which disturbed pupils can succeed, express themselves and find a physical outlet for feelings	4	1	2.5
Have a broad acquaintance with many series			

TABLE 3 (*cont.*)

	RS	*SC*	*RC*
of textbooks and supplementary reading materials in the various academic areas	6	5	2.5
Have the ability to use nonverbal communication	2.5	3.5	5
Have the ability to devise special educational procedures for disturbed pupils based on psychiatric findings	2.5	3.5	5
Have the ability to avoid selecting those educational materials which will upset children (i.e., reading materials involving family)	6	6	7
Knowledge of the strengths and weaknesses of different types of programs for emotionally disturbed children, such as special classes, special schools, institution settings	6	7	8.5
Rated Good			
Have the ability to use art work in emotional evaluation	10	10	5
Knowledge of specific techniques for teaching remedial reading	8	8	10
Have the ability to select appropriate toys to use in play therapy	9	9	8.5
Understand Strauss-Lehtinen techniques for teaching brain injured children	11	11	11
X. THERAPEUTIC TECHNIQUES			
Rated Good			
Knowledge of the procedures used in personal counseling *	1 [a, b]	1 [a]	1 [b]
Knowledge of the procedures used in play therapy *	3 [a]	2 [a]	2
Knowledge of the procedures used in group psychotherapy	2	3	3
Have the ability to conduct play therapy	6.5	4.5	4
Knowledge of the procedures used in psychodrama	5	4.5	5
Have the ability to use psychodrama	8	6	6
Have the ability to conduct group psychotherapy	6.5	7.5	7

TABLE 3 (*cont.*)

	RS	*SC*	*RC*
Knowledge of the procedures used in psychoanalysis	4	7.5	9
Have the ability to conduct individual psychotherapy *	9 [a]	9 [a]	8
XI. TECHNICAL KNOWLEDGE			
Rated Vital			
Acquaintance with the publications, literature, and research in the field of education of emotionally disturbed pupils	1	1	1

Discussion

The seventeen significant items in Table 3 are easily explained in terms of the location in which the respondents were teaching the children with whom they worked, and their relation to other professional workers or to the community. The only finding which is contrary to expectation is that teachers in residential schools do not feel the need for interests and friends outside the field of education.

Regular classroom teachers would probably never be called upon to work with violent pupils or to participate on clinical teams, so these were abilities which they felt were relatively unimportant. However, it is important to them to make case studies, to administer social maturity scales and individual intelligence tests, and to have a knowledge of defense mechanisms.

The teachers in public schools, in regular or special classes, have less professional help, more contact with parents, and closer association with the community. Therefore, they feel that they need to know about different cultural and social groups, and about the needs of minority groups. They need to know the types of cases seen by various agencies and how to make referrals. In a residential school a social worker is probably responsible for most of the parent contacts, but in a public school the teachers must interpret both emotional and educational problems of their pupils to parents. The fact that teachers outside of residential schools attached more importance to counseling again points to the fact that there are no other team members available. Moreover, teachers in public schools may be interpreting the term "counseling" in a more general and less therapeutic sense. Feeling seemed to be strong from teachers in all three groups that knowledge of therapeutic techniques was good, but that use of them by the teacher was dangerous since such techniques might encourage the child to express something which the teacher was not able to handle. It was pointed out that a teacher should differentiate between treating and educating.

Two competencies found more important for teachers of disturbed children could be developed through college preparation: (a) experience on a clinical team with psychiatrists, psychologists, and social workers, and (b) knowledge of the competencies and roles expected of psychiatrists, clinical psychologists, and social workers. It is probable that "tolerating violence" is a personality characteristic which cannot be acquired through college courses and should be more appropriately sought in teacher selection. The content of specialized courses for teachers of emotionally disturbed children will be determined by further research in this area. It is probably more relevant to strengthen the program for all teachers in order to provide them with an understanding of the personality problems of all children, some of whom will need specialized treatment outside the regular classroom. If there are special competencies in this field of teaching, they were not identified by this study.

The conclusions of this study must be considered in the light of its weaknesses. The examiner-made instrument was weak. Although the competencies were assumed to be specific to this type of teaching, regular classroom teachers rated more items Vital than did residential school teachers. The conclusions were drawn from opinion data. The sample was not as great as it was hoped it would be at the beginning of the study. Several states known to have programs for disturbed children and a number of residential schools were not represented in the study.

The trend in further study of this topic must be away from opinion data and toward more refined techniques. Actual classroom observations of teachers rated poor and those rated effective by their supervisors might be valuable in determining the factors which were responsible for this difference. The ultimate measure of the teacher's effectiveness would be a measurement of the progress of the pupils themselves.

Summary

The purpose of this study was to develop a competency list for teachers of emotionally disturbed children and by its use in a questionnaire to determine which specific competencies are needed by such teachers in contrast to those needed by regular classroom teachers. The differences between the competencies needed for teachers of disturbed children in different educational settings were investigated.

On all but three of the 100 competencies, the regular classroom teachers rated the competency as being as important or more important than did the teachers of disturbed children. On only eight items was there a difference between the ratings of teachers of the disturbed in different educational settings, the teachers in special classes considering the competencies of greater importance.

This study was unable to identify special competencies needed by teachers of emotionally disturbed children. It raises questions concerning the content of special courses for teachers of disturbed children, and points to the needs of regular classroom teachers for preparation in this area.

References

MACKIE, ROMAINE P., KVARACEUS, W. C., and WILLIAMS, H. M. *Teachers of Children Who Are Emotionally Maladjusted.* Washington, D.C.: U.S. Government Printing Office, 1957.

REID, J. H., and HAGAN, HELEN R. *Residential Treatment of Emotionally Disturbed Children.* New York: Child Welfare League of America, 1952.

ROBINSON, J. F. (Ed.) *Psychiatric In-Patient Treatment of Children.* Washington: American Psychiatric Association, 1957.

SARGENT, F. P. *Directory for Exceptional Children.* Boston: Porter Sargent, 1958.

47. Critical Factors Influencing Educational Programming for Disturbed Children

PETER KNOBLOCK

Within the last five years there has been a perceptible increase in published articles of a professional and popular nature dealing with the

SOURCE: *Exceptional Children,* XXX (November, 1963), 124–29. Reprinted by permission.

education of emotionally disturbed children. That increasing attention is being directed toward this area is also apparent from a recent U. S. Office of Education study (Mackie and Robbins, 1961) which shows that between the years 1948 and 1958 special education enrollment of disturbed children in public schools approximately doubled. Professional workers in this area are finding a need to formalize their status and share common experiences by forming professional groups. The most recent attempt is the organization of the Council for Children with Behavioral Disorders, a division of The Council for Exceptional Children.

The formation of the Joint Commission on Mental Illness and Health under the Mental Health Study Act of 1955 is viewed as a positive measure. The scope of this project was perhaps indicative of society's willingness to allocate financial resources as well as technical and professional skills to include, as one aspect of the Commission's function, the study of the role of the public school as a therapeutic agent of society (Allinsmith and Goethals, 1962).

While there is some cause for optimism when considering the above trends, they are, to be sure, only trends. Professional workers involved in educational programs for these children are finding much to be concerned about in matters directly related to the development of their programs. At best, progress in terms of the adoption of state certification laws for teachers of disturbed children has been slow. A survey conducted by the U. S. Office of Education (Mackie and Dunn, 1954) indicated that nine states have special certification requirements for teachers of disturbed children. Actually, four of those states are certifying visiting counselors and not classroom teachers. This writer recently conducted a survey in an effort to bring such information up to date. Information obtained from forty-three state departments of education revealed that only nine of those states have such certification laws. Thus, between the years of 1954 and 1962 the list of states with such specific certification laws has grown at a minimal rate. It should be noted, however, that a dozen states are in the process of investigating the desirability of adopting such legislation.

The situation in the public schools also presents some cause for concern. In the opening paragraph of this article, figures from a recent U. S. Office of Education study (Mackie and Robbins, 1961) were cited to show that enrollment of disturbed children in special programs had doubled between the years 1948 and 1958. It is necessary to point out, however, that the base line for such enrollment in 1948 was very low in relation to the number of students now being serviced in special programs and that only 500 communities out of 5,000 sampled in 1958 had provisions for emotionally disturbed children. Also, the rate of growth in this area was comparatively lower than the development of special programs in other areas of exceptionality. In the 500 communities cited above, 28,500 emotionally disturbed children were being provided special education opportunities. The inadequacy of such provisions is highlighted rather dramatically in the findings of the first nationwide survey of seriously disturbed children conducted by The National Organization for Mentally Ill Children (1960). This study reported that there are at least 500,000 seriously disturbed children in this country. It seems reasonable to assume that this figure would more than double when one considers children who are not psychotic or borderline schizophrenic but who manifest signs of having emotional handicaps and who would also benefit from special provisions.

It is the writer's belief that before substantial progress can be made in this area in both educational and community spheres, we must attempt to delineate clearly those factors operating to impede progress in designing educational opportunities for these children.

Realness of Pathology

Basic to a discussion of possible factors accounting for delayed progress in the development of educational programs for emotionally disturbed children, as Redl and Wattenberg (1959) point out, is the tendency to gloss over the realness of pathology. Many of the problems with which children confront us in the school setting can be handled without the necessity of planning around the specific difficulty or disrupting the routine. With many disturbed children, however, such techniques and approaches are often only minimally effective.

The educator's task in accurately recognizing the scope and depth of emotional problems is complicated by the puzzling array of symptomatic behavior which disturbed children present (Berkowitz and Rothman, 1960). In addition to the fact that many problems may be subtle and covert, the classroom teacher is further confronted with the inconsistencies in behavior which many disturbed children exhibit. This inconsistency of behavior, which frequently takes the form of darting back and forth from acceptable to disturbed and disturbing behavior, not only complicates diagnostic evaluations by teachers and clinicians but may also account for the minimizing of problems in the identification and special programming for emotionally handicapped children.

In many situations we have been content to label the problem and ignore the child who has the problem. As Kvaraceus (1962) points out, the very process of labeling a youngster may in itself evoke unique reactions on his part. Also it would seem that, aside from the false sense of security which many workers gain from engaging in such a practice, there is also an element of resistance involved. By labeling a child or his problem, it may thus be possible, in part, to maintain distance both professionally and emotionally.

It is also quite possible that school personnel and others have been content to leave a problem at the labeling stage for lack of any clear operational frame of reference. There is some attempt on the part of states with certification laws (Michigan, Minnesota) and some school systems (Syracuse, New York) to define clearly the types of youngsters they consider emotionally disturbed and to devise programs to deal specifically with the defined groups. Many educators are employing a recent framework by Bower (1960) which spells out the types of youngsters and problems for which programs can be devised.

Role Confusion

The difficulties which center about the classroom role of the teacher are not unique to teachers of disturbed children (Morse, 1956). In the framework of present day education, the classroom teacher is being deluged by multifarious demands, not only in terms of her time and energy but also as these demands relate to the skills and approaches she uses with children.

Historically, the question of the proper role of the classroom teacher received extensive scrutiny with the publication of a study by Wickman (1928). This study was an attempt to compare the perceptions or attitudes of teachers and clinicians toward symptomatic behavior of children. The Wickman study stated rather directly that teachers were not attending to the important behaviors. The implication and interpretation was that teacher attitudes should be molded so as to approximate more closely those of clinicians.

The Wickman study dramatically highlighted the confusion, in this writer's opinion, which existed in the public's conception of just how the mental hygiene role of the classroom teacher and school should be defined (Kotinsky and Coleman, 1955). A recent critical evaluation of the Wickman study (Beilin, 1959) attempted to analyze the roles of teachers and mental hygiene workers in terms of role theory. It was Beilin's conclusion that the attitudinal hierarchies of teachers, as opposed to those of clinicians, dictated different orientations and concerns and that it is doubtful if teachers could or should be pressured or encouraged to depart to any great extent from their task-oriented approach.

The encouraging of such broad roles has not clarified the classroom teacher's role as far as the teachers themselves are concerned. A field study conducted under the auspices of the Joint Commission on Mental

Illness and Health (Wilson and Goethals, 1962) sampled a group of teachers, and the results clearly highlighted the confused values operating in the public schools.

It would seem reasonable to conclude that the problems of role definition are made even more complex when one considers a teacher of disturbed children (Long and Newman, 1961). A teacher of disturbed children quickly finds himself in the position of having to carefully plan and tailor the curriculum to cope with each particular youngster's needs and pathologies; at the same time he must fulfill his needs as a teacher, and this involves certain goal-directed behaviors on his part. A good example of the present concern in this area can be discerned from a U. S. Office of Education study (Mackie, Kvaraceus, and Williams, 1957) which dealt with an evaluation of a list of teaching competencies by teachers. The sample was composed of teachers of disturbed children who were asked to rate a list of competencies, both as to importance and as to their own proficiency in these particular competencies. One outstanding finding was that these teachers, as a group, felt most proficient in areas they considered of less importance. Specifically, they felt less proficient in areas requiring knowledge and application of definite skills and techniques for working with disturbed children.

Training of Teachers

It is important to approach the problem of developing adequate programs of teacher training both critically and with some degree of caution when interpreting the present situation. Until a few years ago, teacher training institutions were unable to find job placements for the few students they had trained to deal with the educational development of emotionally disturbed children. Also many institutions were, and still are, awaiting the findings of various demonstration and research projects which have recently been initiated to validate the efficacy of different educational approaches for disturbed children. With these two conditions as important factors, training institutions have been reluctant to develop specialized training programs for teachers of disturbed children.

It is hypothesized that a considerable upsurge of interest in this area could be effected by the greater involvement of institutions of higher learning. While many colleges offer one or two courses in the education of the disturbed child, the advantages of a complete and intensive training program are many. First, many of the educational problems and approaches encountered in dealing with the emotionally disturbed child are unique and often not manifested in the study of retarded, physically handicapped, or other specialized groups. Second, for the student-in-training, the availability of such coursework in his special field materially fosters an atmosphere of professionalism and identification with his teaching as a skill area. Third, research into educational problems, programs, and techniques will be promoted by having students-in-training focus their thinking and work onto this special group of children.

If we are to operate on the premise that intensive and organized training programs for prospective teachers of emotionally disturbed children are essential, then it is necessary to consider several problems directly related to the satisfactory development of such training programs.

TEACHER SELECTION With the current interest in five-year teacher training programs, the question of the feasibility of undergraduate versus graduate training in this area is no longer a burning issue. Of far more importance is the selection of candidates for this particular type of training program. While it is generally recognized that the demands made upon a teacher of disturbed children are enormous and that she must function with some sort of implied "saintliness" if she is to be effective, there has been virtually no attempt to isolate important variables related to selection of prospective teachers of disturbed children and their subsequent effectiveness. Admittedly, this is an extremely thorny problem to investigate (Barr, 1958), but the success of university training programs and ultimately the quality of educational programs depends most directly on the initial screening procedure. It has been this writer's experience that the choice of this particular teaching area is not, in a large number of cases, a capricious one. It is hoped that within the next few years investigators will direct their attention to selection studies grounded in theoretical frameworks and away from the unreliable methods which are generally employed, such as the clinical interview and obtaining of autobiographical information.

One pitfall, although there are many others, which has consistently plagued studies of teacher selection and effectiveness has been the largely unrewarding search for the "ideal" teacher. In a teaching area in which the syndromes of emotional disturbance are conceptually confusing entities, it is reasonable to assume that we are seeing many different types of teachers operating effectively with various groups of disturbed children.

BREADTH OF TRAINING A problem exists in recognizing the need to build into such a training program coursework and experiences in many different areas and university departments. It is unrealistic to assume that one specific focus or orientation will be sufficient in such training.

There are those who maintain that many of the courses in fields outside education to which we expose our trainees are basically anti-educational in content and philosophy. Implicit is the fear that such students will be diverted from their primary interests and concerns. On the other hand, a well-rounded training program should introduce the student to many diverse frames of reference and points of view in an effort to help him perceive the complexities involved. Another benefit which could possibly accrue from such a broad exposure to other areas and philosophies would be the opportunity for prospective teachers to gain a clearer realization of their role as compared to and contrasted with the approaches of other disciplines.

FIELD EXPERIENCE In this teaching area which is plagued by a multitude of philosophical and methodological problems, there is one aspect of training which receives consistent recognition. There is strong support for the inclusion of field experiences in the training programs for teachers of disturbed children (Kuenzli, 1958). The problem arises in our attempts to implement such experiences. The striking feature of this problem has to do with the dearth of facilities available. Coupled with this is the recognition that a field experience is only as good as the supervisory personnel available to the students (Rabinow, 1960). A recent evaluation of the mental health manpower shortage in the United States (Albee, 1959), when considered along with the sparsity of public school programs for disturbed children (Mackie and Robbins, 1961), points up the clear need to capitalize on existing quality programs and personnel. Although residential treatment centers handle considerably fewer disturbed children than the public schools, many of our treatment centers have carefully programmed educational opportunities into the life experience of the child in residence (Reid and Hagan, 1952). It is recommended that closer working relationships be established between university training programs and residential treatment centers which emphasize educational programs. While some will contend, with a degree of justification, that the approaches and skills required in a residential center differ from those needed in a public school program, the intensity and scope of training received in a total living situation, such as is simulated in residential centers, would serve as valuable training when combined with experiences in a public school program.

LEADERSHIP TRAINING Implicit in our concern for the development of adequate training programs is an emphasis upon preparing teachers to staff special classes. While the use of the special class as one organizational pattern has gained wide acceptance, it is by no means the most beneficial approach in many situations. The high incidence of disturbed children in the public schools alone argues against the feasibility of training sufficient numbers of teachers to fill positions in special classes if such an approach is to be used exclusively. It is hoped that training programs will in time turn some of their emphasis toward preparing supervisory teachers carefully trained to work in consultative capacities within the public schools (Newman, Redl, and Kitchener, 1962). Such individuals would be in a position, for example, to aid the regular classroom teacher and school administrator in planning for the educational growth of disturbed children who remain in the regular classroom or for whom some modifications are made, but which would not necessarily include special class placement (Mackie and Robbins, 1961).

An equally pressing need has to do with the desirability of developing doctoral programs which would channel highly qualified individuals into much neglected areas (Kirk, 1957; Gallagher, 1959). For example, if college programs are to develop, it will be necessary to staff them with competent special educators experienced in the educational needs of emotionally disturbed children. Such highly trained individuals could also be employed as coordinators of public school programs and be in positions to focus on important research needs and encourage creative program planning.

References

ALBEE, G. W. *Mental Health Manpower Trends.* New York: Basic Books, 1959.

ALLINSMITH, W., and GOETHALS, G. W. *The Role of Schools in Mental Health.* New York: Basic Books, 1962.

BARR, A. S. "Problems Associated with the Measurement and Prediction of Teacher Success." *Journal of Educational Research,* 1958, *51,* 695–699.

BEILIN, H. "Teachers' and Clinicians' Attitudes Toward the Behavior Problems of Children: A Reappraisal." *Child Development,* 1959, *30,* 9–25.

BERKOWITZ, PEARL H., and ROTHMAN, ESTHER P. *The Disturbed Child: Recognition and Psychoeducational Therapy in the Classroom.* New York: New York University Press, 1960.

BOWER, E. *Early Identification of Emotionally Handicapped Children in School.* Springfield, Illinois: Charles C Thomas, 1960.

GALLAGHER, J. J. "Advanced Graduate Training in Special Education." *Exceptional Children,* 1959, *26,* 104–109.

KIRK, S. A. "A Doctor's Degree Program in Special Education." *Exceptional Children,* 1957, *24,* 50–52.

KOTINSKY, RUTH, and COLEMAN, J. V. "Mental Health as an Educational Goal." *Teachers College Record,* 1955, *56,* 267.

KUENZLI, A. E. "A Field-Experience Program with Emotionally Disturbed Children." *Exceptional Children,* 1958, *25,* 158–161.

KVARACEUS, W. C. "Helping the Socially Inadapted Pupil in the Large City Schools." *Exceptional Children,* 1962, *28,* 399–408.

LONG, N. J., and NEWMAN, RUTH G. "The Teacher's Handling of Children in Conflict." *Bulletin of School of Education, Indiana University,* 1961, *37.*

MACKIE, ROMAINE P., and DUNN, L. M. *State Certification Requirements for Teachers of Exceptional Children.* U.S. Department of Health, Education, and Welfare, Office of Education, Bulletin 1954, No. 1. Washington, D.C.: Superintendent of Documents, Government Printing Office, 1954.

MACKIE, ROMAINE P., KVARACEUS, W. C., and WILLIAMS, H. M. *Teachers of Children Who are Socially and Emotionally Maladjusted.* U.S. Department of Health, Education, and Welfare, Office of Education, Bulletin 1957, No. 11. Washington, D.C.: Superintendent of Documents, Government Printing Office, 1957.

MACKIE, ROMAINE P., and ROBBINS, PATRICIA P. *Exceptional Children and Youth: Special Education Enrollments in Public Day Schools.* U.S. Department of Health, Education, and Welfare, Office of Education. Washington, D.C.: Superintendent of Documents, Government Printing Office, 1961.

MORSE, W. C. "Teacher or Therapist." *School of Education Bulletin, University of Michigan,* 1956, *27,* 117–120.

NATIONAL ORGANIZATION FOR MENTALLY ILL CHILDREN. *The Mentally Ill Child in America.* New York: National Organization for Mentally Ill Children, Inc., 1960.

NEWMAN, R., REDL, F., and KITCHENER, H. *Technical Assistance in a Public School System.* Washington, D.C.: Washington School of Psychiatry, School Research Program, P.H.S. Project OM-525, 1962.

RABINOW, B. "A Training Program for Teachers of the Emotionally Disturbed and the Socially Maladjusted." *Exceptional Children,* 1960, *26,* 287–293.

REDL, F., and WATTENBERG, W. W. *Mental Hygiene in Teaching.* (2nd ed.) New York: Harcourt, Brace, 1959.

REID, J. H., and HAGAN, HELEN R. *Residential Treatment of Emotionally Disturbed Children.* New York: Child Welfare League of America, 1952.

WICKMAN, E. K. *Children's Behavior and Teachers' Attitudes.* New York: Commonwealth Fund, 1928.

WILSON, W. C., and GOETHALS, G. W. "A Field Study: Sources of Potential Tension in the Public Educational System." In W. Allinsmith and G. W. Goethals, *The Role of Schools in Mental Health.* New York: Basic Books, 1962. Pp. 175–302.

48. A Program of Preparation for Teachers of Disturbed Children

BRUCE BALOW

"I don't think anybody knows, even now, just exactly what we are trained for. . . ." "This year has been the most valuable, exciting and interesting experience I have ever had. . . ." These are comments from two experienced teachers judging a program they had jointly shared—The University of Minnesota program of preparation for teachers of emotionally and socially maladjusted children.

The year in question had begun the previous September for these two teachers and ten fellow graduate students with a full schedule of formal coursework and seminars plus internship in treatment facilities for disturbed children. For three academic quarters and a summer they were immersed in practical work, theory, and research on emotionally and socially maladjusted children.

Practicum and Internship Experience

Observation and teaching in a psychiatric hospital schoolroom, in a residential treatment center for disturbed children, and in public school

SOURCE: *Exceptional Children,* XXXII (March, 1966), 455–64. Reprinted by permission.

classrooms for disturbed children provided a range of treatment experiences. Diagnostic case studies in a psychoeducational clinic and a reception center for delinquent youth helped produce practical diagnostic skills for later decisions in the classroom. These internship experiences were planned according to individual needs of the student, and each student was carefully supervised while on the job.

A typical sequence might begin with a two to three month placement in a psychiatric hospital schoolroom in order to learn something about hospitalized children and varied techniques of dealing with them, as well as the full range of resources of other professions for treating such children. Following his hospital experience, the student might be placed in a two month practicum in a psychoeducational clinic to receive carefully supervised diagnostic and remedial treatment practice with learning disabled children and their parents. The final practicum experience might consist of a series of one to four week placements in the state reception center for delinquent youth, public school special classes for disturbed children, and a juvenile detention center which includes some direct observation of the juvenile court system.

The experienced teacher who enters this graduate program has greater need for practical experiences in management of problem behavior and for communication with other professional personnel such as psychologist, social worker, physician, and probation officer than he has need for additional training in educational skills, such as lesson planning and selection of materials. Therefore, long term exposure to public school special classes is not a routine element of the Minnesota program.

Didactic Training

The teacher needs to be able to make professional decisions in the classroom and must be able to communicate with other professions offering services to disturbed children. Consequently, there exists a strong need for thorough backgrounding in theories and research in relevant areas. Psychology of learning, school learning difficulties, normal and abnormal personality, child development, and delinquency are given formal attention. Techniques of statistics and measurement, educational diagnosis, remedial and therapeutic teaching, behavior management, and counseling are treated in formal courses as well as practical situations throughout the year. A weekly seminar is a vehicle for the integration of theory and practice, for professional orientation, and for discussion of ethics and responsibilities. Possibly more important, it serves as a setting for direct and systematic efforts at developing greater self-understanding as well as sensitivity to others.

Self-Understanding

Formal coursework and internship experiences per se seldom make a recognizable change in the emotional responses of the graduate student. Unless a direct effort is made to place emotional responses under a greater degree of rational control, the students leave the program with essentially the same responses they brought to it. Therefore, in an attempt to develop increased control of emotional responses through understanding of self and of others, the weekly seminar focuses on a group process method of operation. This method forces the student to develop greater sensitivity to others and to the impact of his own behavior on others. In the process, he comes to evaluate facets of his personality which he had not previously been able to allow to come to the surface. Out of it all, responses in emotionally loaded situations become more thoughtful, more supportive to others, and less self-protective.

Evaluating the effect of the seminar, the staff believes that through it the students have, indeed, gained increased sensitivity to others, a better understanding of themselves and the influence of their behavior on others, greater awareness and understanding of nonverbal communication, and the ability to interpret voice tone and physical response as part of verbal behavior. The students evaluate the seminar on a semantic differential scale and have judged it to be "interesting, strong, difficult, mature, profound, practical, new, inspiring, and useful." In all evaluations of the program, the graduating students return again and again to this seminar. Some of the comments reflect great distaste for the seminar, some are redolent with praise; but there is never any doubt of the great impact on these experienced teachers of this attempt to work conjointly with emotions and intellect.

Program Development

This program came into being in 1961, following a period of rapid developments in the state of Minnesota for the education of exceptional children. In 1957 the state legislature passed mandatory legislation calling upon every school district to provide special instruction and services for handicapped children of school age. The legislature specifically included "every child who by reason of an emotional disturbance or a special behavior problem . . . who is educable, as determined by the standards of the State Board of Education . . ." (Section 120.03, Subdivision 3, Minnesota Statutes, 1957). The state department of education appointed a committee of people, broadly representative of the professions serving disturbed children, to define and articulate the roles of essential professions in a school program for disturbed children and to advise the department concerning rules and standards for implementation of the law.

The committee report calling for teacher certification based on an MA program was completed in October, 1960, and charged the university with establishing a program of preparation following the general outlines included in the report. A partial program was established at the university in 1961, but the full program came as a result of financial support from the National Institute of Mental Health (NIMH) in 1962. The NIMH provided additional staff, graduate student stipends, and the impetus for careful evaluation of the program. More recently, additional fellowships have been provided by the United States Office of Education under Public Law 88-164 for students wishing to prepare for classroom teaching or for more advanced leadership positions.

The program was designed to add special knowledge, skills, and competencies on top of the foundation represented by a normal four year degree in education. These special competencies were to be in therapeutically oriented behavior management, diagnosis and remediation of school skill weaknesses, and interprofession cooperation and parent consultation, all supported by special knowledge and techniques for implementing them.

Selection of Students

For entry into special areas, a selection process is necessary. Both academic and personal characteristics are relevant in selecting teachers of disturbed children. Because the Minnesota program is in the graduate school of a major university, candidates must have high academic promise as demonstrated by undergraduate record and aptitude tests. Equally important, the candidate must have or give promise of superior personal characteristics in such elements of maturity as emotional stability, flexibility, resourcefulness, tolerance, humor, and physical stamina. In general, candidates should represent the fullest meaning of emotional maturity; those who are themselves emotionally maladjusted are frequently attracted to professions dealing with disturbed children and should be carefully screened out.

Initial selection is based on tests of personality and ability, academic record, employment record, letters of recommendation, and a brief autobiography. Approximately three of every four applicants are rejected. Among those entered in the program, the attrition rate is low, but fallout does occur. Thus, a continuing process of selection is in operation; it consists of self-selection, wherein an occasional student decides that teaching disturbed children is the wrong activity for him despite auguries for the appropriateness of a career in this specialty, and of staff decision to counsel out of the program that rare student who does not live up to the preprogram predictions of emotional maturity or academic prowess.

Another essential element of the selection process reveals itself at the end of the training year. Because there is no single, definitive description of the role of the teacher of disturbed children, but rather a multiplicity of vaguely defined roles complicated by varied within role expectations of hiring agencies, and because there is no evidence that within broad limits a given type of teacher is more effective than another type, the placement decision becomes an integral part of the selection process. Indeed, placement decisions may be more important than selection decisions, assuming that gross misfits are not allowed into the program to begin with.

There is no reason to expect every teacher of disturbed children to be able to work effectively with the full range of disturbances. Successful teachers vary widely on nearly all characteristics which can be observed or measured, and one of the critical elements in the teaching-learning equation is the nature of the "teaching situation"—the milieu and the type of pupil. Emotionally and socially maladjusted children are not homogeneous in characteristics or needs. Probably the sole reason they are all thrown into one general category is that they are causing problems for adults. Consequently, the differences among pupils are frequently greater than their similarities.

Teachers who are quite different on a wide variety of personal and social characteristics presumably can be equally effective, but not always with the same pupils. In the absence of evidence to the contrary, it is conceivable that the teacher who is unsuccessful with one type of pupil in a given setting may be precisely what is needed with another type of disturbed child in a different placement. A given teacher who cannot work well with aggressive children may be ideal for a group of withdrawn youngsters.

In this matter, the responsibility and opportunity of the training program is to help teachers understand themselves well enough so that a wise placement can be made. Even with entry level screening based on relatively rigorous procedures, the state of the art is such that the selection decision is still somewhat akin to a widely scattered shotgun blast while the placement decision can be a relatively pinpointed rifle shot.

Outcome

At the end of the training year what has been accomplished? Do graduates accept positions consonant with their special training? Are their attitudes different from those brought into the program? Do they teach effectively? These and similar questions beg for answers. Such questions plague teacher training programs of all types because neither adequate criteria nor criterion measures are available. Most people agree on what a good teacher should be like when the discussion is couched in broad terms and vague generalities, but few agree when details are discussed. The good teacher can be defined by everyone and no one. If the definition were agreed upon, the problem of measuring the behavior explicated in the definition would still remain to be resolved. Despite these problems, certain gross indicators provide impressions of value.

In the most recent two years of experience with certificated graduates of the program described here, there are two college instructors continuing their graduate study on the education of disturbed children, one student continuing in full time advanced graduate study, two teachers in residential treatment units, six teachers in public school special classes for disturbed children, one teacher in a detention center for delinquents, three teachers of public school special classes for the retarded, one teacher of a special class for the gifted, one regular class teacher, and two graduates temporarily not teaching because of family considerations. Among those not teaching disturbed children, only two made a volitional choice rejecting the opportunity to work with the emotionally disturbed. The remainder are married women who were restricted to job opportunities in the locale of their husband's employment, where appropriate positions were not available. The preponderance of graduates has, indeed, filled positions for which they were trained.

A distant, but nonetheless related element is the outcome for those teachers who began but were unable to complete the full program. Insofar as the program is concerned, there is no problem; they were unable to meet the standards of the program and consequently were dropped. However, for the individuals it is a moot question whether they gained or lost by their partial exposure. While they gained a good bit of self-knowledge and a little academic knowledge, they were forced to inspect themselves; in the process they lost some illusions. As pointed out by a successful student, the program year was quite ego deflating; for a student forced out of the program at midyear, the price in wear and tear on the psyche may be too high. Such experience argues not only the careful application of selection standards, but the continuing application of evaluation and counseling as well.

A second matter concerns attitudes. Pre- and post-training program measurement has been done with the Minnesota Teacher Attitude Inventory and, while the sample is much too small to do more than generate hypotheses, the data suggest a decided shift in raw score to a more realistic view of pupils. Those teachers who entered the program reflecting a rigid and dominating approach in their teaching had at the end of the program shifted toward the more flexible and sympathetic, understanding side of the scale, while those teachers who entered with overly idealistic attitudes also shifted to a more realistic view of children.

At the completion of their training year, and again following their first year of experience as special teachers, the students were asked to make a written evaluation of the training program. In general, they report that the program has made them less rigid and more relaxed with pupils, has given them a better understanding of human behavior, particularly deviant behavior, and has improved their teaching skills. In the students' judgment, the seminar and internships provide the essence of the training year.The internships are valued for the practical skills that the students developed in them and for the reality situations they provided. The seminar is seen as personally upsetting and of particular value—a set of evaluations very likely causally related.

In general, the students express satisfaction with the program—a recognition of knowledges and teaching skills gained, as well as increased personal maturity. These students would eliminate nothing and would add more of everything. In particular they seem unable to learn enough about remedial education and routinely ask for additional instruction in remedial teaching methods and materials.

By design, the Minnesota program is not structured in the sense that students are shepherded through, nor is a single method of teaching disturbed children inculcated. In view of the evidence that teachers of emotionally disturbed children generally work independent of any ancillary help except possibly that of the building principal, an overweening involvement of staff in daily decisions of the students is counter to reality. Certainly it is antithetical to our goal of encouraging independence of thought, maturity of judgment, and reliance on one's own skills. To build dependence on the staff would repeat the error of institutional living, wherein all decisions are made by the staff or the environment; as preparation for self-sufficiency outside the institution, such preparation is bound to produce failures.

Opportunity to make error is an important element of the Minnesota program, as is the opportunity for each student to formulate a system of teaching which he accommodates to his own personal characteristics. Rarely has a student been unable to profit from this relative independence; these few students have needed more direction than the staff judged the program should provide and, in the absence of direction from the staff, they have tended to do much less well academically than they otherwise might have. However, this situation has simultaneously helped the staff to recognize a personal characteristic which is important for selection and placement decisions. Usually also, the student has obtained self-knowledge, if not the power to behave differently.

Despite occasional expressed wishes of the students for more guiding by the staff—sometimes a frank request for psychotherapy or personal counseling—the staff is not shaken in its judgment that great gain accrues to the student from a degree of "muddling through" on his own resources with the support of the student group. The staff gives emotional support and a sympathetic ear; they will help the student evaluate the problem but will not enter into a psychotherapeutic relationship and will not make decisions for the student. Frequently this procedure is painful for the staff as well as students but the staff is convinced, at this point at least, that relative independence is the optimal behavior to encourage.

A third question is whether the graduates are effective teachers. This question cannot be answered in simple fashion. A given teacher may well receive six different ratings of competency from six different observers. However, in a structured interview conducted by Frank Wood, Assistant Professor of Special Education at the University of Minnesota, with a small sample of the public school supervisors of graduates of the training program, the supervisors generally gave high marks to the work of program graduates, mentioning favorably the ability of the graduates to relate to very difficult children.

Realistic pressures seem to force public school programs into an academic, remedial instruction mold, even when teachers and supervisors feel that this detracts from the therapeutic value of the program. Such pressures are especially difficult to resist because the teachers generally must work with limited supportive service from special education directors, psychologists, and social workers. Such assistance as is available centers around the placement and discharge decisions. Day to day classroom management and part time integration into regular classes fall almost entirely on the special class teacher and the local building principal. Few children receive supplementary psychotherapy, and when psychotherapy is being received, it is rarely coordinated with the child's school program.

It appears that teachers functioning in such situations require a broad range of specialized training. The supervisors expressed a wish for more teachers and, while recognizing the limitations of a one year program, felt that the teachers could benefit from a heavy emphasis on remedial education techniques and counseling procedures since supplementary assistance in these areas is practically nonexistent. It is interesting that these observations parallel precisely those of the program graduates themselves, whether teaching in public school special classes or in residential programs.

In our judgment, the training institution is wise to respond to the practical needs of its consumers, but foolhardy to depend upon such immediate "realities" as the major criterion for program goals. Along with preparation for "what is," the training institution has the responsibility to prepare its graduates for leadership, so that they may help to bring current realities into accord with advancements in theory and research.

49. Teacher Preparation for Educating the Disturbed: Graduate, Undergraduate, or Functional?

JOHN L. JOHNSON

The future direction of college undergraduate programs in special education is bleak, if not seemingly marked for extinction. Commitment to programs of undergraduate education has become unfashionable, and an extreme positive value has been placed upon graduate preparation for the classroom teacher of exceptional children. Is such a position justifiable? Are the interests of the field, of the potential teacher of the exceptional child, and of the exceptional child himself served best when such a position is assumed?

These are issues which have profound implications upon the future direction of special education, particularly in light of the recognition being given by the general educational enterprise for special education's

SOURCE: *Exceptional Children,* XXXIV (January, 1968), 345–51. Reprinted by permission.

contribution to the understanding of such problems as learning difficulties and the maximization of individual differences, and in light of the increasing demand for effective teachers of the exceptional.

The Case in Point: Should Undergraduates Teach Disturbed Children?

The specific case in point is the teacher of emotionally disturbed children, for whom there is increasing demand and for whom programs and procedures which transmit the special knowledge, attitudes, and skills to the teacher remain in a stage of infancy, the major development being in graduate level programs to the exclusion of bachelor's level preparation.

Is there a place for continued undergraduate preparation for teachers of disturbed children and, in fact, for continued endeavor in other fields of our domain (i.e., blind, mentally retarded, and learning disorders)?

The growing trend toward graduate education or graduate training for teachers of emotionally disturbed children has come to our attention as more and more college and university programs have been established. New undergraduate programs have not been established and in some instances are being phased out. The major impetus to program development has been, of course, the provisions for grants in aid from Public Law 88-164 and its predecessors. In its first year of assistance (1964–1965), PL 88-164 offered college programs for teachers of the emotionally disturbed in the form of senior year traineeships, thereby providing direct stimulation to undergraduate programs. Under the unique conceptual system which operates in the field, approval (by a respectable authority) of the concept of undergraduate programs was thereby given. However, since that initial period, no further financial resources have been available for undergraduate endeavor, based upon the assumption that federal financial resources would be more wisely used in graduate programs. This assumption specifically affects programs on the emotionally disturbed. In contrast, continued aid and "approval" are given to undergraduate programs for teachers of the blind and mentally retarded, where there are also significant demands for well trained personnel. Thus, in reality, undergraduate programs are discouraged.

Cotter (1966) reported that 87 colleges and universities are currently engaged in preparation of teachers for disturbed children. She listed the names of 32 college and university programs which offer full and partial programs (sequences). Fourteen programs reported sequences at both the bachelor's and master's levels while eighteen reported sequences only at the master's level. From her reports, she drew the following conclusion of the existence of "Core courses, and generally student teaching" at the undergraduate level:

> It might be noted here that considering the high degree of maturity and professional skill needed for teaching disturbed children, it seems inadvisable to offer teacher education programs at this level, and that admission to graduate programs should be predicated on a reasonable period of successful teaching experience in regular classes [Cotter, 1966, p. 465].

Rabinow (1964) suggested that there are advantages and disadvantages which may accrue for the younger teacher and the experienced teacher working with emotionally disturbed children. In his essay, he utilized a dynamic orientation from which to expand the problem, and concluded that "training, supervision, or consultation" is useful in helping the younger teacher assume an effective professional role; he suggested that the experienced teacher may have difficulty changing patterns of "accustomed isolation with no consultation, supervision, or collaboration [pp. 19–20]." However, Rabinow suggested that recruitment of teachers come from two sources: (a) from "within the school system itself," and (b) from "graduate schools of education [p. 42]," thereby giving tacit acceptance of the "graduate-experienced" hypotheses, without so much as a discussion of the undergraduate resource pool nor of the feasibility of expanding the opportunity for training, supervision, and consultation for undergraduates, omitting discussion of the feasibility of bachelor's level personnel in the field. It is clear that Rabinow leans heavily in the direction of graduate preparation programs.

Balow (1965) has described the history and operation of one teacher training program which may come to serve as a prototype for future development in the field. There is no doubt that Balow's program accommodates only the experienced teacher and graduate students.

The implications to be drawn from these seemingly representative statements follow:

1. Undergraduate programs are not an "approved" means for producing classroom teachers for disturbed children.
2. Undergraduate education, by reason of the presumed lack of maturity and professional skill of the clientele, is undesirable.
3. Teaching experience, per se, is a necessary prerequisite for successful preparation to teach disturbed children.
4. Graduate education in special education is not predicated upon prerequisite knowledge and skill in special education at an undergradu-

ate level; i.e., the content of the field can be transmitted equally to any person who has completed an undergraduate program such as elementary education, secondary education, psychology, history, etc.

The issue, therefore, is the concern that undergraduate preparation for teachers of emotionally disturbed children has been deemphasized without a systematic appraisal of its feasibility and effectiveness. Given the fact that specific selection and recruitment procedures can be employed here, the issue becomes one of undergraduate versus graduate programs.

One can realistically submit that there is little demonstrated evidence to support the assumption that preparation programs for teachers of emotionally disturbed children should focus only upon "experienced graduate" sequences. Such an assumption, evidently based only upon opinion of experts, serves to limit special education in its striving for excellence. Such a self-imposed limitation is indicative of the "rigid and unimaginative" nature of teacher education (Cotter, 1966) and is conceptually self-defeating for the growing need for programatic research and experimentation.

Some discussion of this issue seems warranted. The focus of this paper is to highlight the issue and to make available factual evidence from one source: the proven experience which exists in a geographic segment of the field.

Evidence from the Field

The advisability or inadvisability of undergraduate preparation can be partially viewed from the status of the field itself. In this regard, the experience generated from Michigan, a state which has served as a forerunner in the field, might suffice. Six of Michigan's seven state universities and colleges offer preparation sequences for teaching of the disturbed child. Four offer both undergraduate and graduate programs while one offers only a graduate sequence and one offers only an undergraduate sequence. The results of an informal survey of the extent of undergraduate programs of five of the six schools are given in Table 1.

There are, as can be ascertained from the table, a significant number of undergraduate students already involved in training and seemingly committed to teaching disturbed children. We surmise that several faculties are similarly committed. In the current academic year, 81 graduates will enter the field, and the majority will assume teaching positions in various treatment centers and public school special classes. It is possible, therefore, that the field in its "graduate programs only"

TABLE 1

SURVEY OF THE EXTENT OF UNDERGRADUATE PREPARATION FOR TEACHERS OF DISTURBED CHILDREN IN MICHIGAN (SPRING, 1966)

University	*Total Enrollment in All Special Education Undergraduate Programs*	Enrollment-Education of Disturbed Children (EDC) Program: *Graduate*	Enrollment-Education of Disturbed Children (EDC) Program: *Undergraduate*	*Number of EDC Graduates 1965–1966*
A	120	44	60	20
B	420	36	105	20
C	168	20	25	12
D	700	32	130	21
E	241	0	30	8
TOTAL	1649	132	350	81

emphasis is overlooking an important source of potential teachers who enter preparation programs with no preconceived biases as to classroom teaching, no unfortunate teaching failures, and openness to change—change in themselves as forces for helping the disturbed child, and commitment to change in the children they teach.

The literature describing examples of our best efforts in educational practice for disturbed children is another source of evidence from the field. Smith (1964) has described three programs which have had marked success with disturbed children and have contributed significantly to educational theory. Each program is well known, and represents a particular treatment mode (residential, psychiatric, and day care); one innovative public school program is also discussed. In each program, education is emphasized and comprises a significant portion of the treatment of the child. The teachers who are involved are considered to be crucial to the total program, as acknowledged in Smith's description. What is not readily discerned is that significant numbers of bachelor's level teachers hold responsible positions in these exemplary treatment and educational settings. Seemingly, their maturity and professional skill are not greatly questioned and they are an important force in these cited programs for disturbed children. In addition, numerous public school and state hospital programs whose educational service has had like success with teachers who complete only undergraduate sequences can be found. More recently, the bachelor's level graduates of one university program have been successfully employed in New York, Ohio, Illinois, Minnesota, Colorado, and the District of Columbia. Reports of their effectiveness and maturity are quite encouraging.

In sum, undergraduates are being prepared in significant numbers and are assuming positions as teachers of disturbed children. Several universities have been and continue to be committed to undergraduate education in this field and, further, initial evidence is that undergraduates are employed in responsible positions in many parts of the country. Teaching experience does not seem to be a drawback in preparing undergraduates. Given the choice between teaching experience and openness to change (flexibility), potential for change should take precedence.

Implications

This cursory account of status evidence certainly does not provide the kind of hard data required to demonstrate that undergraduate training programs are any more feasible than graduate level training. This evidence simply demonstrates that undergraduate programs exist and that a significant number of students are involved and enter into professional work. In reality, we have no more evidence to suggest that bachelor's level programs are good and should be continued than we have to bury them, as we seem to be doing now.

Whatever the reasons for the phasing out of bachelor's programs and the approval of only master's level training, this status evidence seems to suggest that it may be necessary for professionals in the field to look closely within, before allowing the weight of expert opinion to burden them and to greatly influence decision making at a time when appraisal, empiricism, and open-mindedness are most required.

One can argue that acceptable teaching experience and advanced education are the only precursors to effective teaching of the disturbed. More critical issues might be the individual college selection process and the nature of training (Balow, 1966), quality of supervision (Berman and Usery, 1966), and the specificity of consultation (Seagull and Johnson, 1966) which are given to the young teacher who is preparing to teach disturbed children or is within the first year of professional work. University professors, in their effort to contribute new knowledge and in their unceasing search for truth, are the logical persons to begin exploration of this issue and to lead the resistance to the fallout of expert opinion.

A New Teacher Preparation

The need for scrutiny of the preparation for teachers of the disturbed and for continued supervision and consultation has been stated. The term "preparation" is being used to indicate the integration of the concepts and techniques of training and education, since both activity modes are necessary in effective programing for prospective teachers. The suggestion is now made that many teacher education programs are rigid and unimaginative in both process and content. More recently there has been a call for "creative teacher education" and a plea to refrain from the "adherence to tradition, fear of change, and to the maintenance of the status quo [Cruickshank, 1966, pp. 8–9]." To be sure, some of special education teacher preparation can be characterized by the prevalence of this traditional state. For instance, most preparation programs were grafted to elementary education (even after Conant's well known criticisms were published), to the exclusion of the needs of preschool and secondary school pupils. More specifically, the proposal to exclude undergraduate programs and to initiate only graduate programs can reasonably be construed as unnecessarily rigid and lacking in creativity. Several concerns are stated here, to emphasize that effective and innovative preparation programs must occupy our thought.

The first concern has to do with the rigidity of "graduate programs only." This cannot be allowed to become the dominant mode of preparation; in fact, we must strive for a system which is considerably more flexible. This is especially true in light of some of the preparation activities which are occurring all around us. Particular attention must be paid to special programs for preparing young people to carry out functions and to do jobs which require maturity and a high degree of skill.

Perhaps we can look at three examples, which, although not generally conceived to be within the educational domain, are nonetheless significant evidence of the ability of young people to exhibit effective and skilled performance, often under less than "normal" conditions. First, we must take a careful look at the intensive training which is now being given to Peace Corps volunteers who are being sent to live under oppressive conditions and who evidently effectively help groups of people in numerous ways, while working across language barriers. We might also want carefully to examine the training given to the numerous young people (many college undergraduates) who made up the group of Mississippi volunteers in the summer of 1965. They were engaged, to our knowledge, in relatively short periods of intensive training and anticipatory guidance which prepared them to work under very stressful conditions. Third, we might also want to look at the training now given to combat soldiers which enables them to conduct rather complex medical procedures under field conditions.

What is important about the citation of these three seemingly unrelated activities is that in each instance the selection procedure and preparation activities are firmly based upon the functions which the individual is expected to perform following his preparation. In short, the form of training must be related to the functions to be carried out

(Brown, 1964). In each of the three, clearly established functional criteria are seemingly set up, upon which selection and preparation can be based.

In the Peace Corps, the form of education used to teach volunteers about various cultures and the behavior of persons in these cultures and to teach the ability to bring about desirable behavioral change has been related to the functions involved in teaching and in interpersonal communication. Thus, specific selection, assessment, *and* training criteria have been established (Hunt, 1966). The example of the Mississippi volunteers is cited to give reference to the procedures of self-examination, motivational determination, and understanding of the psychological stages from which a strong individual and group commitment emanates (Coles and Brenner, 1965). The procedures for selection and training of the elite special forces soldier, who acquires many functional skills in intensive training, have also been described. These training and simulation activities in specific skill areas are very definitely related to the functions which the trainee is likely to be required to perform (Moore, 1965).

In each of the examples cited, there is no requirement for "a graduate program" or "a sequence of methods courses" to prepare any of these groups of individuals to carry out their functional assignments. What does occur is an *optimum period* of intensive and systematic preparation designed to impart to the trainee the knowledge, attitudes, and skills he will require to fulfill the role he will assume after preparation. It is possible to select well motivated students and to evolve effective preparation for specific behavioral outcomes. Can a similar preparation mode be undertaken with teachers of the disturbed?

What has been suggested is a far different system than our current concepts of graduate program, undergraduate program, or course sequence. Blatt (1966) has implied that a similar analysis is required within the structure of university programs. He asks that we answer questions pertaining to (a) what the university student is exposed to, (b) specifically how the program is structured, (c) who structures it, and (d) what the student does himself. These, seemingly, are important questions to answer; however, could it be that the model utilized by the university in preparation of teachers for the disturbed is no longer relevant, either in form or in function? University teacher education, with its emphasis on courses and lectures, with the presumption that independent study between lectures takes place, and with provision for concurrent work with children, ceases to be relevant when in fact what is actually found is that there are courses on "human behavior" with 250 students enrolled, that the student reads the book two nights before the exam and then sells the book, and that the practicum provides the prospective teacher with first hand experience of how wide the gap between theory and practice really is.

The second concern has to do with the implications of creative teacher education. It is fairly obvious that all around us a revolution in education and an apparent revitalization of purpose and methods of training in many of the service professions are occurring. The newly found community mental health movement (social psychiatry) and the entrance of noneducational establishments (Office of Economic Opportunity: Project Head Start and the Job Corps) into educational work are all part of the changing nature and purpose of our field. It is evident that while many professions are undergoing radical changes in their purpose and training programs, professional education and in particular special education seemingly choose, perhaps, to misperceive the problem. One can contend that special education has become more "hidebound" in its propensity to separate disability areas and that this has led us to believe that what we are doing serves a useful purpose in society. It is fashionable to speak out against "hardening of the categories," but our language verily betrays us. One has only to look at the confusion generated in the literature: we speak of "emotionally disturbed," "socially maladjusted," "juvenile delinquent," "culturally deprived," and "mentally handicapped." This situation becomes more complex when one is apprised that certain funds for programs are allotted by virtue of the legally determined status of certain groups (the juvenile delinquent versus the emotionally disturbed child) rather than by the need for an adjusted school program or by evidence of specific learning deficits. The effort expended in categorical preservation is far greater than the effort expended in evolving effective preparation programs for young people to work in a very difficult field. It is almost as if we would prefer to maintain categories and sanctimoniously preserve our professional integrity rather than help children! The increasing dichotomization of the major professional organization of this field constitutes additional evidence for this position. What is most disturbing is that one finds that categories are preserved exclusively upon the basis of criteria which are not educationally relevant, i.e., emotionally disturbed, juvenile delinquent, etc. It is almost as if we do not recognize the existence of the massive social and educational problems within our midst and, in fact, our denial of reality.

Further, we tend all the more to cling to our vested interests and hallowed traditions. Cain (1964) has cited one such hallowed tradition:

We often say that it is highly desirable that a teacher of handicapped children be a good teacher and have experience with normal children. While we may say this, we really have little experimental research that proves this point [p. 216].

Our attempt to arbitrarily exclude undergraduate programs when the evidence around us suggests otherwise is perhaps becoming another hallowed tradition. For instance, in relation to experiences necessary in teaching, there is some evidence to demonstrate that a formal internship program with undergraduate students can be an effective element in the preparation process (Corman and Olmstead, 1964). More recently, Beck (1966) has described such a formal internship which has been equally effective with both undergraduate and graduate students.

A new form of teacher preparation is required, one which is educative and functional, and allows greatest utilization of the manpower resources currently available and highly motivated toward service in a growing field. It is possible that teachers of the disturbed—or teachers of children with "special needs" (the latter term implying that a focus on significant aspects of learning is likely to involve a decategorization process)—might be more effectively prepared in a special study institute format, where a variety of learning experiences would be available and organized to fulfill the basic educational, attitudinal, and skill requirements necessary in teaching in the classroom. A well supervised internship (in the formal sense) would follow this experience.

An institute should have experienced teaching faculty, who could devote their full attention to the trainees, through classes, small group activity, and closely supervised but independent teaching of children. An integral part of such an institute would be the provision for simulation, immediate feedback of results, and, in general, the creation of a therapeutic milieu in which prospective teachers would learn how to learn, and become proficient in solving problems which arise in the course of teaching disturbed children. One could envision a regular work day with specified periods of activity, designed to enable the trainee to accomplish certain tasks, all divorced from traditional university credit hour and core course requirements. It is possible that two or three months of such intensive activity and study would be less wasteful of time and money than the year and a summer required to obtain a master's degree in teaching the disturbed. How much more effective would our teachers be then?

The answer to such a question lies, of course, in our involvement in creative teacher preparation and in the formulation of a functional assessment system to test the differences between respective methodologies. This form (breaking away from the university tradition), and testing the product of preparation, offer a poignant hope for preparation of teachers of handicapped children, no matter what the children's assessed special needs may be. What is even more evident is that there is a lack of experimental and empirical evidence to suggest that any method is effective!!

It is time for a revitalization in special education. This revitalization can, and in fact must, include young people, whether undergraduate or graduate, so that we can carry on with the major purpose in special education: that of the equalization of educational opportunity for handicapped children.

Summary

One can submit that the issue of undergraduate versus graduate education for teachers of emotionally disturbed children reflects a form of rigidity in our own behavior in the field and a lack of recognition of what truly are the underlying problems of effective preparation and need for qualified people in a critical area. To arbitrarily state that it is inadvisable to have undergraduate programs is to deny both the evidence which can be gathered and the experience of several universities. The evidence seems to show that undergraduates can and do have a role in teaching emotionally disturbed children. We might also want to look at the idea that longer training does not necessarily mean better training, and that, rather, the intensity and therefore the quality of preparation enable one to approximate the behavioral outcomes which may be desired as a result of any particular program.

There is little evidence to demonstrate the inadvisability of carrying on certain preparation programs. Currently, the prevailing opinion is expert, and this is conceptually limiting to the field. What is required is a new teacher preparation—a breaking away from the traditions of the university and a movement into functional, innovative preparation. The demand is highest in special education. One particular preparation mode, the intensive training institute, has been suggested. We cannot afford to wait—the time for revitalization is upon us.

References

BALOW, B. "A Program of Preparation for Teachers of Disturbed Children." *Exceptional Children,* 1966, *32,* 455–460.

BECK, GAYLE R. "Training of Teachers of Emotionally Disturbed." *Journal of Teacher Education,* 1966, *17,* 137–141.

BERMAN, LOUISE M., and USERY, MARY L. *Personalized Supervision: Sources and Insights.* Washington: Association for Supervision and Curriculum Development, 1966.

BLATT, B. "The Preparation of Special Education Personnel." *Review of Educational Research,* 1966, *36* (1), 151–161.

BROWN, M. "Form Follows Function—Psychologists in Broadening Role." *Comprehensive Psychiatry,* 1964, *6,* 274–281.

CAINE, L. F. "Special Education Moves Ahead: A Comment on the Education of Teachers." *Exceptional Children,* 1964, *30,* 211–217.

COLES, R., and BRENNER, J. "American Youth in a Social Struggle: The Mississippi Summer Project." *American Journal of Orthopsychiatry,* 1965, *34,* 909–926.

CORMAN, B., and OLMSTEAD, ANN G. *The Internship in the Preparation of Elementary School Teachers.* East Lansing, Michigan: College of Education, Michigan State University, 1964.

COTTER, KATHERINE C. "Emotionally Disturbed Children and Teacher Preparation." *The Catholic Educational Review,* 1966, *44,* 457–469.

CRUICKSHANK, W. C. *The Teacher of Brain-Injured Children.* Syracuse, New York: Syracuse University Press, 1966.

HUNT, D. E. "A Model for Analyzing the Training of Training Agents." *Merrill Palmer Quarterly,* 1966, *12,* 137–156.

MOORE, ROBIN. *The Green Berets.* New York: Avon Books, 1965.

RABINOW, B. *The Training and Supervision of Teachers for Emotionally Disturbed Children.* New York: The State Education Department, 1964.

SEAGULL, A. A., and JOHNSON, J. L. "Second State Intervention: Reality Based Consultation for Teachers of the Emotionally Disturbed." In Peter Knoblock (Editor), *Intervention Approaches in Educating Emotionally Disturbed Children.* Syracuse, New York: Syracuse University, Division of Special Education and Rehabilitation, 1966.

SMITH, B. K. *No Language But a Cry.* Boston: Beacon Press, 1964.